OF LIFE

Code of Jewish Law

KITZUR SHULHAN ARUKH

A COMPILATION OF JEWISH LAWS AND CUSTOMS

BY
RABBI SOLOMON GANZFRIED

TRANSLATED BY
HYMAN E. GOLDIN, LL.B.

ANNOTATED REVISED EDITION

Hebrew Publishing Company
NEW YORK
1998

HEBREW PUBLISHING COMPANY
P.O. BOX 222
SPENCERTOWN, NEW YORK 12165
TELEPHONE: (518)392-3322
FAX : (518)392-4280

Reprinted and bound October 1998
QP/K

MD
M

ISBN 0-88482-779-8 Paperbound

ISBN 0-88482-423-3 Clothbound

Printed and bound in the United States of America

L

CONTENTS

Volume 1

Contents

CONTENTS

Volume 2

CONTENTS

CONTENTS

Volume 3

Contents

CONTENTS

VOLUME 4

CONTENTS

VOLUME 1

Chapter 1

Rules of Conduct upon Rising in the Morning

1. "I have set the Lord always before me" (Psalms 16:8).

The aforesaid is a cardinal principle in the Torah and a fundamental rule of life among the pious. For the attitude and conversation of a man when he is in the presence of a king are not the same as when he is in his own home among his family and his intimates. In the presence of royalty a man takes special care that his speech and demeanor be refined and correct. How much more should a man be careful of his deeds and words, realizing that the Great King, the Holy One, blessed be He, whose glory fills the whole universe, is always standing by him and observing all his doings, as it is said in the Scriptures: "Can a man hide himself in secret places that I cannot see him?" says the Lord. "Do I not fill heaven and earth?" (Jeremiah 23:24). Bearing this in mind, he will acquire a feeling of reverence and humility and he will be ashamed and afraid to do anything wrong.

2. A man should be conscious of the presence of God even while still lying in bed; and as soon as he awakes he should acknowledge the loving-kindness of the Lord, blessed be He, inasmuch as the soul, which was committed to God faint and weary, was restored to him renewed and refreshed, thus enabling him to serve God devotedly all day. For this is the goal of every man; as it is said: "They are new every morning; great is Thy faithfulness." (Lamentations 3:23), which means, every morning man is like a new-born living being; and for this he must thank God with all his heart. While still in his bed he should say: "I thank Thee, O living and eternal King, Who hast mercifully restored my soul within me; Thy faithfulness is great." (One may say this prayer although one's hands are yet unwashed, since the name of God is not mentioned in it). When saying this prayer, one must pause briefly between the words *beḥemlah* (graciously) and *rabbah* (great).

3. "Judah, the son of Tema, said: 'Be bold as a leopard, light as an eagle, swift as a deer, and strong as a lion, to do the will of thy Father who is in heaven'" (Abot 5:23). "Bold as a leopard" means that a man should not be ashamed to worship God, blessed be He, in the presence of people who laugh at him. "Light as an eagle," refers to our sense of vision; that is, we must be swift to close our eyes so as not to look at evil; because sight is the initial act of sin; the eye sees, the heart covets, and the limbs, the instruments,

execute it. "Swift as a deer," refers to the legs; that is, our feet should always run swiftly to perform good deeds. "Strong as a lion" refers to the heart, because the zeal to worship the Creator, blessed be He, is in the heart. It is our duty to do our utmost to worship Him, and to prevail over the Evil Impulse just as the hero makes every effort to prevail over his enemy, until he subdues him

4. It is therefore every man's duty to make himself strong as a lion. Immediately upon awakening from sleep, he must rise quickly and be ready to worship our Creator, blessed be He, before the Evil Impulse is given an opportunity to dissuade him from rising. In the winter time, for instance, the Evil Impulse uses this subtle argument: "How can you rise so early in the morning when it is so cold?" In the summer time, he uses this crafty argument: "How can you rise now when you have not had enough sleep?" Or, he is using other similar arguments. For, the Evil Impulse possesses the art of ensnaring man in his trap, and dissuade him from rising. Therefore, every man who fears the word of God, must overcome the Evil Impulse and disobey him. Even when it is hard for us to rise because of fatigue or because of habitual indolence, we must make it as our aim to fulfill the will of the Supreme King of kings, the Holy One, blessed be He. A man must have in mind the following: If someone would call him to attend to a profitable business transaction, to collect a debt, or to save his property from being destroyed by a fire or by any other cause, then he would surely not be slothful, but would rise quickly. Or if he should be summoned to perform the king's service, then he would certainly not be dilatory, but would rise speedily, either because of fear of punishment or because he would be anxious to find favor in the king's sight. How much more so must one rise swiftly, when one is called upon to perform the service of the Supreme King of kings, the Holy One, blessed be He. He who accustoms himself to rise early, four or five times, will experience no difficulty after that; as the Sages say (Yoma 38b): "He who makes an effort to do good, is assisted (by Heaven)."

5. If one is able to rise at midnight and perform the midnight service, there is nothing more meritorious than this; as it is said (Lamentations 2:19): "Arise, cry out in the night, at the beginning of the watches;" just as the Holy One, blessed be He, laments at that moment, as it is written (Jeremiah 25:30): "The Lord will roar from on high, and from His holy habitation utter His voice; He will roar mightily because of His fold." And our Sages tell us (Beraḥot 3a) that the Almighty then says: "Woe to My children on account of whose iniquity I destroyed My house, burnt My Temple, and exiled them among the nations." But if one is unable to rise at midnight, let one at least make an effort to rise before dawn; as King David said (Psalms 57:9): "I will

awake the dawn," which means, I awake the dawn, but the dawn does not awake me. One may perform the midnight rite even past midnight, and then engage in the study of the Torah, according to one's knowledge. The study of the Mishnah is preferable to any other thing. But if one is not a scholar, one may read the Psalms, *Maamadoth*, or some book of ethics. A little with devotion is better than much without devotion. Rabbi Ḥiyya taught (Tamid 32b): "The Divine Presence is in the presence of him who studies the Torah at night; as it is said (Lamentations 2:19): "Arise, cry out in the night, at the beginning of the watches; pour out thy heart like water before the presence of the Lord;" which signifies that the Divine Presence is then before us. Our Rabbis, of blessed memory, said again: "He who engages in the study of the Torah at night, is called 'a servant of the Lord;' as it is said (Psalms 134:1): 'All ye servants of the Lord who stand by night in the house of the Lord." When the nights are short and it is impossible to rise so early, he should at least try to rise early enough to have sufficient time to prepare himself to go to the synagogue to pray together with the congregation.

6. Psalms and other portions of the Pentateuch, Prophets and Hagiographa which ordinarily people do not know by heart, must not be recited by heart even by one who is well versed in them. A blind man, however, may recite any portion of the Torah by heart.

7. We must enjoin those who read *Maamadoth*, to omit God's name from the concluding benediction; and is to read thus: "Blessed be Thou (*not*, "Thou, O Lord") who hearest prayers."

CHAPTER 2

Hand Washing in the Morning

1. Since every man upon rising from his sleep in the morning is like a newborn creature, insofar as the worship of the Creator is concerned, he should prepare himself for worship by washing his hands out of a vessel, just as the priests used to wash their hands daily out of the wash-basin before performing their service in the Temple. This hand-washing is based on the biblical verse; (Psalms 26:6-7): "I will wash my hands in innocency, and I will compass Thy altar, O Lord; that I may publish with a loud voice," etc. There is another reason given by the Kabbalists, (Zohar, quoted in Beth Joseph), for this morning hand-washing; when a man is asleep, the holy soul departs from his body, and an unclean spirit descends upon him. When rising from sleep, the unclean spirit departs from his entire body, except from his fingers, and does not depart until one spills water upon them three times alternately. One is not allowed to walk four cubits (six feet) without having one's hands washed, except in cases of extreme necessity.

2. The first garment which a male must put on, is the *tallit katan* (the small four-fringed garment, commonly known as the *arba kanfoth, four cornered*), for one is not allowed to walk even as much as four cubits without having a fringed garment on. But as his hands are still unwashed, he may not say the benediction on putting it on.

3. The ritual hand-washing in the morning is performed as follows: Take a cup of water with the right hand and put it in the left; pour some water upon the right hand. Take the cup back in the right hand and pour some water on the left. This performance is repeated three times. It is best to pour the water over the hands as far as the wrists, but in case of emergency it suffices if the water covers the hands up to the joints of the fingers. One must also wash his face in honor of the Creator, as it is said (Genesis 9:6): "For in the image of God He hath made the man." One must also rinse the mouth, because we must pronounce the Great Name in purity and cleanliness. Afterward the hands are dried. Special care must be taken to dry the face thoroughly.

4. The hands must be washed into a vessel only. The water thus used must not be utilized for any other purpose, because an evil spirit rests on it (contaminated, and injurious to health), and it must not be spilt in a place frequented by human beings.

5. Before the morning hand-washing, one should not touch either the mouth, the nose, the eyes, the ears, the lower orifice or any kind of food, or an open vein, because the evil spirit that rests upon the hands before washing them will cause injury to these things.

6. It is best to perform the morning ablution with water poured from a vessel by human effort, just as it must be done when washing the hands before meals. (See chapter 40, below). But in case of emergency, and one wishes to pray, one may wash his hands in any manner, even when the water is not poured by human effort, and one may pronounce the benediction: *Al netilat yadayim* (concerning the washing of the hands). If there is a river or snow at hand, one should dip the hand in it three times. If, however, there is no water in any form available, one may wipe one's hands with some material, and say the benediction: "Blessed art . . . for *cleansing* (not *washing*) the hands." Afterwards, upon finding water and the required vessel, one must wash the hands properly without pronouncing any benediction.

7. It is written (Psalms 103:1): "Bless the Lord, O my soul; and all that is within me, bless His holy name." Since it is a man's duty to bless the Holy Name with all that is in him, he is not allowed to begin worshiping God before he has cleaned himself of bodily impurities. As one ordinarily has to respond to the call of nature in the morning, therefore one shall not pronounce

the benediction over washing the hands in the morning, until one has eased one's self, then wash the hands again, pronounce the necessary benediction, and afterward proceed with the rest of the benedictions as given in the prayer-books.

8. If a person rises from his sleep while it is still night, and washes his hands as is required, and then stays awake until dawn; or if he falls asleep again while it is yet night; or if he sleeps sixty breaths (about one-half hour) in the daytime; or if he is awake the whole night—in all these cases it is doubtful whether or not hand-washing is necessary. He shall therefore, wash his hands alternately three times (as prescribed in paragraph 3), but without pronouncing the benediction.

9. Hands must be washed on the following occasions: On awakening from sleep, on leaving the lavatory or bath, after paring one's nails, after having one's hair cut, after taking off the shoes with bare hands, after having sexual intercourse, after touching a vermin or searching the clothes for vermin, after combing one's head, after touching parts of the body which are generally covered, after leaving a cemetery, after walking in a funeral procession or leaving a house where a corpse lay, and after blood-letting.

CHAPTER 3

On Dressing and Deportment

1. It is written (Micah 6:8): "And to walk humbly with thy God." Therefore it is the duty of every man to be modest in all his ways. When putting on or removing his shirt or any other undergarment, he should be careful not to expose his body unduly. He should put it on or remove it while still lying covered in bed. He should never say to himself: "Lo, I am all alone in my inner chamber and in the dark, who can see me?" For the glory of the Holy One, blessed be He, fills the universe, and darkness and light are alike to Him, blessed be His name; and modesty and a sense of shame indicate humility before Him, blessed be His name.

2. It is forbidden to follow the customs of the idolaters or to be like them either in the way they dress, cut their hair, or the like; as it is said (Leviticus 20:23): "And ye shall not walk in the customs of the nation;" and it is said again (Leviticus 18:3): "Neither shall ye walk in their statutes;" and again (Deuteronomy 12:30): "Take heed to thyself that thou be not ensnared to follow them." We must not wear the kind of garment worn by them for ostentation, a garment worn by princes. In the *Talmud* (Sanhedrin 74a) it is stated that a Jew is not allowed to resemble the idolaters even in regard to shoe laces; if they tie them in one way and Israelites in another way, or if it is their custom to have red shoe laces and Israelites have black ones (because the

color of black is indicative of humility and modesty) an Israelite is not allowed to change either the knot or the color in order to imitate them. From this *Talmudic* injunction, every man can learn how to act, depending upon the place and time. An Israelite must not wear a cloak revealing pride and immodesty, the kind worn by the heathens; the garments of an Israelite must be such as betoken humility and modesty. It is thus told in the *Sifri* (Deuteronomy 12:30): "You shall not say: 'Because they walk about dressed in purple, I, too, will walk about dressed in purple; because they walk about helmeted, I, too, will walk about helmeted.' For, these are the ways of the proud and the haughty, but not the lot of Jacob (Israel). Their mode of life is to be modest and humble and not to look up to the proud." An Israelite should not imitate any of their customs, even if there is but a slight suspicion of idolatrous intent connected with it. A Jew must not cut his hair or let it grow as they do, but he should differ from them in dress, manner of speech, and all other deeds, just as he differs from them in knowledge and opinions. And thus does the Scripture say (Leviticus 20:26): "I have set you apart from the peoples."

3. We should avoid wearing costly garments, for this is conducive to pride; nor should we wear clothes that are too cheap or soiled, in order that we may not be ridiculed by people; but we should wear moderate priced and clean clothes. The *Talmudic* sages say (Shabbat 129a): "A man should even sell the beams of his house in order to secure shoes for himself."

4. Since the Scripture has given importance to the right hand, choosing it to perform certain Divine Commands, such as, the sacrifices (when the priest dipped his finger in the blood, and sprinkled it seven times on the altar) (Leviticus 4:6; Zebaḥim 24a-b), on the thumb of the right hand and the great toe of the right foot of Aaron and his sons during the consecration of the Temple (Leviticus 8:23-24), and in the ceremony of *ḥalizah* (Deuteronomy 25:5-10; Yebamot 104a), therefore, when dressing ourselves, we must always give preference to the right hand or foot over the left; but when removing shoes and other articles of apparel, the left comes first. With regard to fastening a lace, the left should be given precedence, because the *tefillin* are fastened on the left hand. Any knot, therefore, should be made on the left side first. When our shoes have laces, we first put the shoe on the right foot without lacing it, then we put the one on the left and lace it, and afterward we lace the one on the right. This method of dressing also applies to all other articles of clothing.

5. Two garments should not be put on at one time, because it is harmful to the memory.

6. A male person must not walk even as much as four cubits (six feet), or utter a single holy word, while being bareheaded. Minor children, too, must be trained to cover their heads, so that they may be imbued with the

fear of God. As it is related in the *Talmud* of Rab Naḥman bar Isaac (Shabbat 156b): "The astrologers said to the mother of Rab Naḥman bar Isaac: 'Your son is destined to be a thief.' He would not let his mother cover his head. So she said to him: 'Cover your head, so that the fear of God may be upon you.'"

7. It is forbidden to walk haughtily erect, with neck fully outstretched; concerning this, it is said (Isaiah 3:16): "And they walk with outstretched necks." Nevertheless, a man should not walk with the head bent too low, so that he may see approaching people, and also to watch his step. From the manner a man walks, we can tell whether he is wise and intelligent, or a fool and a boor. Thus Solomon said wisely (Ecclesiastes 10:3): "Yea, also when a fool walketh by the way, his understanding fails him, and he saith to everyone that he is a fool."

8. A man should be careful not to pass between two women, two dogs, or two swine. Nor should two men permit a woman, a dog, or a swine to pass between them.

CHAPTER 4

Rules of Decency

1. A person should accustom himself to respond to the call of nature once in the evening and once in the morning; such a habit is conducive to alertness and cleanliness. If he is unable to ease himself, he should walk a distance of four cubits (six feet), repeating it several times if need be; or he should divert his attention from other matters. He who defers easing himself, is guilty of violating a biblical command (Leviticus 11:43): "Ye shall not make yourselves detestable;" and he who defers urination, is also guilty of violating the Divine Promise (Deuteronomy 7:14): "There shall not be male or female barren among you."

2. A man must exercise modesty when in the lavatory; he should not expose himself before he sits down, and should not expose his body more than is actually necessary. One should not ease oneself in the presence of other people; but one may urinate in the presence of other people even in the day-

time, because there is danger involved in this restraint. Nevertheless, even in the latter case, one should at least turn aside.

3. One should not ease himself while standing, nor should one overstrain oneself, lest one ruptures the glands of the rectum; nor should one leave the lavatory too soon before one is certain that one is no longer in need of it. When one urinates while standing, one should take care not to splash any urine on one's shoes or clothes, and one should be extremely careful not to hold the membrum.

4. While in the lavatory, it is forbidden to think of sacred matters; it is, therefore, best to concentrate there upon one's business affairs and accounts, so that one may not be led to think either of holy matters or, God forbid, indulge in sinful thoughts. On the Sabbath, when it is forbidden to think of business, one should think of some interesting things that one has either seen or heard, or something similar to that.

5. One should be careful to wipe oneself thoroughly, for should even a trace of feces cling to the body, one is not permitted to utter a holy word. One should not clean himself with the right hand, for with this hand one puts on the *tefillin*. A left-handed person should clean himself with his right hand, which is like everybody else's left hand.

6. After each defecation or urination, even of one drop, one must wash one's hands and say the benediction *Asher yatzar*. If one has forgotten to say the benediction, and after having responded to the call of nature again, one became aware of one's neglect, one need not say the benediction more than once. If one takes a laxative and knows that one will have to ease oneself several times, one should say the benediction only after surmising that this would be the last call.

CHAPTER 5

Cleanness of Places Used for Holy Purposes

1. It is written (Deuteronomy 23:14-15): "Thou shalt cover that which cometh from thee, for the Lord thy God walketh in the midst of thy camp . . . therefore shall thy camp be holy, that He see no unclean thing in thee." From this the Rabbis, of blessed memory, have deduced that whenever the Lord our God walks with us, that is, when we are engaged in a holy task, such as the reading of the *Shema*, a prayer, the study of the Torah, or the like, then the place must be holy, so that no uncovered excrement may be found there, and that nothing unseemly should be visible to any one who worships.

2. It is forbidden even to think of anything holy in a place where there is excrement or urine, or anything that produces a bad odor, unless it is covered, as it is said (Deuteronomy 23:14): "And thou shalt cover what cometh from thee." One may pour a quart of water into the fluid of one urination, and it is immaterial whether the urine was first in the vessel and the water is poured over it, or the water was in the vessel first. However, if the urine was contained in a pot specifically kept for urination, the pouring of water into it is of no avail (see section 13, below). For two urinations, two quarts of water are required, and so on. Even if the urine has become absorbed in the ground or in a garment, as long as there remains some moisture, water must be poured over it.

3. If there is excrement on any part of one's body, although it is covered with one's garments, one is not allowed to utter anything that is holy; for it is written (Psalms 35:10): "All my bones will say, Lord, who is like Thee;" therefore one's whole body must be clean. Some authorities are lenient regarding this matter, but it is proper to follow the stricter opinion. If there is but a small particle of excrement in the anal orifice, although it is covered, all agree that the covering is of no avail, because excrement in its original place is more loathsome.

4. Whenever there exists any doubt concerning the existence of unclean matter, we must not utter a holy word, before we examine the place. It is forbidden to pray in a house in which there is foul matter in the garret.

5. We must keep away, while praying, from the excrement and urine of an infant who is able to eat as much as the size of an olive, of any breadstuff, even when cooked, in the space of time that an adult can eat a slice. It is better, however, to stay away from the excrement of an infant eight days old.

6. When praying, we must keep at a distance from the excrement of a human being, even if it has no bad odor, and from the excrement of a cat, marten, and Idumean cock. We are not bound to remove from the excrement of any other animal or bird, because it ordinarily produces no bad odor, but we must remove from it, if it does. Likewise we must keep away from anything that is malodorous, due to decay, such as carrion, and the like. We must also keep away from a chicken coop, evil-smelling water, or water in which flax or hemp is soaked, and which ordinarily emits a bad odor. We must keep at a distance from the aforementioned things just as from excrement.

7. When excrement has become so dry that it crumbles when rolled, it is considered like earth, provided it no longer has a bad odor. But frozen excrement, since it will return to its former state in warm weather, still bears the original name. Snow, covering excrement, is considered a valid covering.

8. How far must we keep away from excrement (in order to be allowed to utter holy words)? If the excrement is in the rear, one must remove a distance of no less than four cubits from the spot where the bad odor ceases; even if one is unable to smell, one must keep away the same distance. However, if it does not have a foul odor, it suffices to remove a distance of four cubits from the place where it is found. If the unclean matter is in front of one, one must remove from it until it disappears from view. Even at night, one must remove the same distance as if it were daytime. If it is on the side of one, one must keep away the same distance as if it were in front of one, and one should then turn aside so that it will remain in the back.

9. If excrement is found in a house where a congregation of people pray, the *ḥazan* (Reader) must at once stop praying until the excrement is either removed or covered. This is true even when the unclean matter lies behind him, and it is more than four cubits from the place where the bad odor ceases, because it is impossible that there should not be at least one worshiper in the congregation within the four cubits from the place where the odor ceases, and this worshiper is not allowed to listen and to pay attention to what the *ḥazan* is reciting.

10. If one discovers excrement after one had finished praying, then, if there was ground to suspect that the place contained excrement, yet he flagrantly failed to investigate such a possibility, inasmuch as the *Shemoneh esreh* (silent prayer) is in lieu of a sacrifice, the Scriptural verse (Proverbs 21:27): "The sacrifice of the wicked is an abomination," may be applied to this man's prayer, and he must repeat the *Shemoneh esreh*. He must also repeat the reading of the *shema* in such a case, since the reading of it is a Divine Command. However, he must omit the benedictions preceding and following the *shema*; neither must he repeat the benedictions or Grace after meals, recited in such a place. If, however, there was no ground to suspect that the place contained excrement, he has discharged his duty, even in as far as the *Shemoneh esreh* is concerned, for the reason that he is not considered as being negligent. If urine is found, even in a place where its existence should have been suspected, his duty is discharged even as regards the *Shemoneh esreh*, it being post facto.

11. If one had let wind, one is forbidden to utter anything holy until bad odor had ceased; the same applies to a case where the bad odor had issued from his neighbor. But if one is engaged in the study of the Torah, one need not interrupt his study on account of a bad odor that had issued from his neighbor.

12. We must keep away from a lavatory (when praying), even though it is enclosed by partitions and does not contain any unclean matter. A bench with a hole in it, under which a pot is put for one to do his needs, is considered as a lavatory, although the pot has been removed and the hole has been covered with a board. The bench, therefore, must be either removed from the house or completely covered. However, if a chair is made primarily to sit upon, and is covered with a cushion for this purpose, but on occasion the cushion is removed and the chair is used for easing oneself, after which the cushion is restored to its place, such a chair is not considered as a lavatory.

13. A night-pot for excrement or urine, if made of clay or wood, even though it is clean and has no bad odor, is regarded as a lavatory. Even if water is poured into such a vessel or is inverted, or put underneath a bed, it is of no avail; it must be either removed from the house or completely covered.

14. It is forbidden to speak or to think of any holy matter in the bath-house. It is forbidden to utter any name by which the Holy One, blessed be He, is known, either in a bath-house or in a filthy alley, even when it is uttered in a secular tongue, like *Gott* in German or *Boga* in Polish. It is forbidden to say *Shalom* (peace) to a friend in a bath-house, for *Shalom* is the name of the Holy One, blessed be He; as it is written (Judges 6:24): "And he called it, *Adonai-Shalom.*" Some authorities are of the opinion that if a man's name is *Shalom,* he must not be addressed by his name in the places mentioned above. Others permit it, because there is no intention of saying anything pertaining to peace, but simply to call the man by his name. The general custom is to be lenient in this regard, but the God-fearing should follow the stricter opinion.

15. It is forbidden to discuss subjects of the Torah or to utter anything holy, in view of a genital organ, whether his own or anyone else's, even that of a minor male or female. It is permissible only at a *Brith Milah.* Just to close the eyes, not to look at it does not suffice, since it is in front of him; but he must turn away his face and body from it.

16. The uncovered part of a woman's body that is ordinarily covered; if it is one handbreadth (four inches) is in the same category as a genital organ; and the hair of a married woman which must always be covered, is

treated as a part of her body. It is immaterial whether it is that of one's wife or of any other woman. However, when it is exposed in the presence of another woman, it is not regarded as nakedness. The singing of a woman is akin to nakedness (as regards the reading of the *Shema*, etc.). However, when a man hears a woman sing and he is unable to stop her, he must not, because of that, refrain from reading the *Shema*, the *Shemoneh esreh* (silent prayer), or the study of the Torah, but he shall concentrate upon the holy subjects with which he is occupied and pay no heed to her singing.

17. If a man's heart could view his genital organ (that is, if no garment or girdle separates the upper part of the body from the lower), he is not allowed to utter anything holy, even though his nakedness is covered. He must either put on trousers which are tight on his body, gird himself with a belt, or place his arms on the robe in order to make a separation between his heart and his organ. There is no need for a woman to do that.

CHAPTER 6

Laws Relating to Benedictions

1. Before uttering any benediction, we must make sure which one it is, so that when we mention God's name, which is the most important part of the benediction, we shall know what we are thanking Him for. It is forbidden to do anything else while reciting a benediction; and it must not be uttered hurriedly; but attention must be paid to the meaning of the words. And this is what the "Book of the Pious" (*Sefer Ḥasidim* says): "When we wash our hands, or utter a benediction over fruit, or over a precept—benedictions which everybody knows, we must direct our attention to praise the name of our Creator, who was wondrously kind to us in giving us the fruit or the bread of which we partake, and in commanding us to perform this precept. We must not do it automatically out of sheer habit, spouting words thoughtlessly. On account of this, the anger of God was kindled, and He sent us word by Isaiah His Prophet, saying (Isaiah 29:13): 'Forasmuch as this people draw near, with their mouths and their lips do honor Me, and their fear of Me is but the acquired precept of men.' The Holy One, blessed be He, said to Isaiah: 'Look at the deeds of My children, and see that they do it only outwardly, and hold on to it just as a man clings to the practices of his forefathers; they enter My house and pray to Me the fixed prayers, in accordance with the customs of their fathers, but not with their whole hearts; they wash their hands and utter the benediction for the occasion; they cut off a piece of bread and utter the benediction *Hamotsi*; they drink and pronounce benedictions habitually; but at the time they do not intend to praise Me by it.' Therefore, His wrath was kindled and He swore by His great name to destroy

the wisdom of their wise men, who know Him and praise Him because of established customs, but not wholeheartedly; as it is written thereafter (loco citato 14): 'Therefore, behold, I will do yet farther . . . so that the wisdom of their wise men shall be lost,' etc. Therefore have the Sages warned us concerning this matter, saying (Nedarim 62a): 'Do things for the sake of their Maker,' etc." A man should accustom himself to say the benedictions aloud, because an audible voice is conducive to concentration of mind.

2. When we say a benediction, our mouths must be free of saliva, nor should anything else be in our mouths; for it is said (Psalms 71:8): "My mouth shall be filled with Thy praise."

3. It is forbidden to utter the name of God in vain, and whoever utters it in vain is guilty of violating a Divine Command, for it is written (Deuteronomy 6: 13): "Thou shalt fear the Lord thy God;" and it is written again (Deuteronomy 28:58): "If thou wilt not observe . . . to fear this glorious and fearful Name." Included in the concept of fear is, that one should not mention His great Name unless it is by the way of praise or blessing whenever required, or when studying the Torah. One's entire body must tremble upon mentioning the name of God, blessed be His name, but one should not mention it in vain, God forbid. This injunction applies not only to the ineffable Name (the four letters, *Yod, He, Vav, He,* the Tetragrammaton), but to all attributes of Him, blessed be He. It is forbidden to mention the Name not only in the Holy Tongue (Hebrew), but in any language. He who in any language, curses himself or his neighbor by pronouncing the ineffable Name or one of His attributes (an "attribute" is a word or phrase by which we praise the Holy One, blessed be He, such as, "the Great, "the Mighty," "the Revered," "the Faithful," "the Glorious," "the Strong," "the Steadfast," "the Omnipotent," "the Gracious," "the Merciful," " the Zealous," "the Long-suffering," "the Abundant in mercy,") is liable to the penalty of lashes. Due to our sinful propensities, most people are careless and say in the vernacular, "God shall punish him," or the like, thus violating a Divine Command. If one curses without mentioning the ineffable Name of God, or one of His attributes, or if the curse can be inferred from the contents of one's words, as for instance when one says: "May that man not be blessed by God," or using expressions of similar nature, although one does not incur the punishment of lashes in this instance, nevertheless, it constitutes a violation. It is likewise forbidden to incorporate His name, may He be blessed, in a letter, no matter in what language it is written. Many people erroneously write His name, may He be blessed, in the vernacular, or they write the word *adieu,* which in the French language means "with God;" this constitutes a clear violation, for in the course of time, this letter will be thrown on a dunghill. The mentioning of God's name frequently, especially when mentioned disdainfully, God forbid, causes poverty in Israel; and wisdom and endeavor are required to abolish this evil. When saliva accumulates in one's mouth, one should spit it out first and then mention the name of God. Likewise, when one is about to kiss the Scroll of the Law, one should first spit out his saliva.

When we wish to mention the name of God in our daily talk, we are to say *Hashem* ("the Name"), and not as the common people say *Adoshem*, for this is undignified when referring to Heaven.

4. Great care should be taken not to utter a benediction in vain, God forbid; nor should one create for oneself an occasion over which to utter an unnecessary benediction. If by inadvertence we do utter a benediction in vain, or we mention the name of God unnecessarily, we should thereafter say: *Baruḥ shem kevod malḥuto leolam vaed* (blessed be the name of His glorious kingdom forever and ever). If immediately after pronouncing the the name of God (in a benediction), we remember that there is no need for the benediction, we must conclude it with the verse *Lamdeni ḥukeḥa* (Psalm 119:12) "Teach me Thy statutes." As this is a complete verse in itself, it is as though he had recited the Psalms, and the Name, consequently, was not mentioned in vain. If we have also begun the word *Elohenu* (our God), but after saying *Elohe* (meaning the God of), and have not uttered the last part of the word *nu* (our), then we should conclude with the verse *Yisrael Avinu meolam vead olam*" (I. Chronicles 29:10) "Israel our Father, forever and ever." At any rate, we are to add: "Blessed be the name of His glorious kingdom forever and ever."

5. If a person utters a benediction over water and then he becomes aware that someone in the neighborhood had died, when it is customary to spill out the water stored in the houses of the neighborhood, because drinking such water is considered dangerous, he must nevertheless taste some of the water, so that his benediction shall not be uttered in vain. He need not be concerned about the danger, as the Scriptures say (Ecclesiastes 8:5): "Whoso keepeth the commandment shall know no evil." After drinking a little of it, he shall spill out the rest.

6. If a person is in doubt whether he said any one of the benedictions, he is not bound to repeat it, except Grace after meals.

7. A man must pronounce at least one hundred benedictions daily. This law was enacted by King David. A hint to this effect is found in the Scriptures (II Samuel 23:1): "The saying of the man who was raised (Hebrew, *al*) on high," The numerical value of the letters in the word *al*, is one hundred. A support for this is found in the Pentateuch (Deuteronomy 10:12): "Now, O Israel, what (Hebrew, *mah*) does the Lord thy God require of thee? But to fear the Lord," etc. Do not read *mah* (what), but *meah* (one hundred), and it refers to the one-hundred benedictions." The recitation of the benedictions will cause one to fear the Lord, to loving Him and to constantly remember Him. The curses contained in Deuteronomy (28:15-61) number ninety-eight, and adding to them (loco citato 63): "Every sickness" and "every plague," the number is increased to one hundred. Now, the one hundred benedictions we utter daily, shield us from these one hundred curses. On the Sabbath, festivals and fast days, when the number of benedictions is re-

duced, the deficiency is filled by paying attention to the benedictions recited by the *ḥazan*, when he repeats the *Shemoneh esreh*, and by the benedictions pronounced over the reading of the Torah and the Prophets, after which we respond *Amen*. The number may also be increased by blessings over extra dainties.

8. Upon hearing a benediction pronounced by one's fellow, one must say: *Baruḥ hu ubaruḥ shemo* (Blessed be He and blessed be His name) at the utterance of the Name (*Adonai*), and respond *Amen* at the conclusion of the benediction. *Amen* means *it is true*, and therefore when saying *Amen*, we must have in mind these two things: that what the benediction says is true, and that we believe in it explicitly. In responding *Amen* to benedictions which also include a prayer, for instance, the benedictions in the *Shemoneh esreh* beginning with *Attah ḥonen leadam daat* (Thou favorest man with knowledge) until *Hamaḥazir sheḥinato letziyon* (He who restores His divine presence to Zion), and *Sim shalom* (bestow peace), we must have in mind these two things: that the contents of the benediction is true, and that it may be the will of God that the prayer be accepted soon. In responding *Amen* to the *kaddish*, which contains a prayer for the future only, we have in mind that the prayer be accepted soon.

9. If we are reading that portion of the prayers, during which no interruption may be made, we should not say *Baruḥ hu ubaruḥ shemo* (blessed be He and blessed be His name). Also, when we hear a benediction to which we need only listen in order to fulfill our obligation, as for instance, the benediction said before the sounding of the *Shofar*, or the reading of the *Megillah* (Scroll of Esther), we must not say *Baruḥ hu ubaruḥ shemo*, because such a response would be a break in the benedictions. (The laws relating to the responding of *Amen*, when reading that portion of the prayers, during which no interruption may be made, will be discussed, God willing, in chapters 14 and 16).

10. We must be careful to pronounce the word *Amen* correctly, not to pronounce the letter *Aleph* hastily, nor to leave the letter *Nun* unpronounced. We should likewise be careful not to respond *Amen* before the entire benediction is concluded, for this is termed "A hasty *Amen*;" neither should we wait too long in responding *Amen*, for this is called "An orphaned *Amen*;" but we must respond immediately upon the conclusion of the benediction. We must not raise our voices louder than the one who utters the benediction, for it is said (Psalms 34:4): "O magnify the Lord with me, and let us exalt His name together."

11. We must not respond *Amen* to our own benediction (except in Grace after meals, when we conclude *Bone yerushalayim, the Builder of Jerusalem*). Even if we finish a benediction together with the *ḥazan*, we need not respond *Amen*. But if we are uttering one benediction and the *ḥazan* another, and we conclude them at the same time, we must respond *Amen* to the *ḥazan's* benediction. We must respond *Amen* upon concluding together with the *ḥazan* the benedictions *Yishtabaḥ* (let Him be praised), *Shomer ammo yisrael laad*

(He guards His people Israel forever), and *Yehaluluḥa* (Let them praise Thee) after *Hallel*. (For many authorities hold that even when we ourselves conclude these benedictions, we must say *Amen*).

CHAPTER 7

The Morning Benedictions

1. There is disagreement among authorities as to whether or not the listener should respond *Amen* to the benediction *Laasok bedivre Torah* (to engage in the study of the Torah). Some authorities hold that the benediction does not end there, but that *Vehaarev na* (and make pleasant) is a continuation of it, and it is all one benediction; therefore no *Amen* should be responded to it. Others hold that the benediction ends there, and that *Vehaarev na* is a separate benediction, and therefore *Amen* must be responded to the first. One should, therefore, pronounce that benediction in silence, so that no one shall hear it, thus averting the moot question.

2. The benediction *Asher natan lasehvi binah* (He that gives the cock understanding) should not be uttered before daylight.

3. The benediction *Pokeaḥ ivrim* (Who opens the eyes of the blind) may be said even by a blind person, for he, too, is benefitted by sight, in that others can show him the way. If one happens to say the benediction *Zokef kefufim* (Who raises the bowed down) before the benediction *Mattir asurim* (Who sets the captives free), that is, loosens the joints of one's body to give one free movement and co-ordination of muscles, one need not repeat the latter, as it has already been covered by the former.

4. No *Amen* should be responded to after the benediction *Hamaavir shenah meenai*, etc. (He who removes sleep from my eyes), because this is not the end of the benediction. *Yehi ratzon* (may it be Thy will) concludes the benediction, ending with *Gomel ḥasadim tovim leamo yisrael*" (He who bestows kindly favors upon His people Israel).

5. Even he who is awake all night must say all the morning benedictions, except the benediction *Al netilat yadayim* (concerning the washing of the hands). It is doubtful whether or not he has to say the benedictions, *Elohai neshamah* (my God, the soul, etc.), and *Hamaavir shenah* (He who takes sleep away). It is also doubtful whether he should say the benedictions over the Law. It is, therefore, a good practice to hear others say these benedictions and respond *Amen* to them.

6. If one has not said the morning benedictions before praying, he must say them after that, except the benediction *Al netilat yadaim* (for some authorities hold that the washing of the hands in the morning was ordained primarily because of the prayers, but when the praying is done already, there

is no longer any need for this benediction). Neither should he say *Elohai neshamah* (my God, the soul, etc.,) (for this theme had already been covered in the benediction, "Who quickenest the dead").

7. If, before praying, one has omitted the benedictions over the Torah, the authorities disagree as to whether one need say them after the prayer. Some hold that he should not say them, because he had already done it by reading the prayer *Ahavah rabbah* ("With abounding love,") which is somewhat similar to the benedictions over the Torah, for it reads: "And put it into our hearts to understand and to discern, to hearken, learn and teach," etc. There are others who hold that the reading of the prayer *Ahavah rabbah* does not exempt him from reciting the former benedictions, unless he immediately engages in the study of the Torah. We must, therefore, be careful to recite the benedictions of the Torah before praying, but post facto, if we forget to recite them, we should study something of the Torah immediately after praying. If we forget to do this, too, then due to the divergence of opinion, we need not say those benedictions any longer.

8. If, before saying the morning benedictions, one is called to go up to the Torah, one if possible should first say the morning benedictions of the Torah, then read at least one Torah verse, like, for instance, *Yevareḥeḥa* (May He bless thee), etc., and then go up to the reading of the Torah. But if it's impossible to do so, one should go straightway to the Torah. And, since one had already recited the benediction *Asher baḥar banu* (Who has chosen us), etc., one need not repeat it again privately, but read: *Asher kideshanu* (Who has sanctified us) and *Vehaarev na* (And make pleasant), up to *Leamo yisrael* (to His people Israel), and then say *Yevareḥeḥa* (The Lord bless thee), etc.

CHAPTER 8

What May Not Be Done From Dawn Until Praying Time

1. As soon as the day dawns, that is, when the first light of the sun is seen in the East—since this is the time when prayers may begin (if one had by chance prayed at that early hour, one had complied with his duty) we are not permitted to begin any kind of work, or transact business, or start a journey until one had prayed, as it is said (Psalms 85:14): "Righteousness shall go before him; and he shall make its footsteps a way to walk in." "Righteousness" means prayer, wherein we declare the righteousness of our Creator, and only afterward are we to direct our footsteps on the road of our material desires.

2. One is not allowed to eat or drink before praying, as it is said (Leviticus 19: 26): "Ye shall not eat with the blood," which means, that you shall not eat before you pray for your lives. To one who first eats and drinks and

then prays, the following Scriptural text applies (I Kings 14:9): "And hast cast Me behind thy back." Do not read *Geveḥa* (thy back), but read *Geeḥa* (thy pride); the Holy One, blessed be He, said: "After this man had catered to his pride, he then vouchsafed to accept the yoke of the Kingdom of Heaven." Before praying, it is forbidden even to drink coffee or tea with sugar and milk. But if one is old or feeble and cannot wait for his food until the congregation leaves the synagogue, especially on Sabbaths and festivals, when the services are prolonged, one may pray the *Shaḥarit* (morning prayer) at home, then recite the *kiddush,* and partake of some food. Then he should go to the synagogue, listen attentively while the congregation prays the *Shaḥarit,* and afterwards pray with them the *Musaph* (additional prayers); but one should not drink coffee with sugar, or the like, without first accepting the yoke of the Kingdom of Heaven. However, if one is ill, this is not an act of pampering one's ego. If one cannot concentrate upon the prayers while hungry or thirsty, one may eat and drink before praying.

3. There are some authorities who hold that even if a man awakes at midnight, he is not allowed to taste any food before praying; and it is proper to follow this stricter opinion. But if he has a weak heart, he may partake of food and drink to fortify himself for the Divine Commands.

4. Water, tea or coffee without sugar or milk may be taken before praying, even after dawn, because there is no trace of egotistic indulgence in this. This may be done even on the Sabbath and festivals when the *kiddush* must be recited before meals, because the time for reciting the *kiddush* is immediately before a meal, and since it is not permissible to partake of any food before saying the morning prayers, then the proper time for saying the *kiddush* has not yet come.

5. Before praying in the morning, we are not allowed to go to a neighbor, to meet him or to say "good morning" as it is said (Isaiah 2:22): "Withdraw yourselves from man, whose breath is still in his nostrils; because for what is he to be esteemed?" This means, what is his importance, that you have honored him before you have honored Me? But if we meet a neighbor casually, we are allowed to salute him. It is proper, however, to alter somewhat the usual form of salutation, so that we remember that we must not engage in other matters before praying.

6. It is forbidden even to begin the study of the Torah after dawn. But if one is accustomed to attend regularly the synagogue service and there is no likelihood that he will overlook the time, one may begin studying after the rise of dawn. One may also study the Torah together with others before praying, if they will have no chance to study later, because the collective merit of a group is very great. They must take care, however, not to overlook the time set for praying.

CHAPTER 9

The Tzitzit (Fringes)

1. The precept to wear the *tzitzit* (a fringed garment) is of great importance; for all the commandments of the Scriptures were dependent on it, as it is said (Numbers 15:39): "That ye may look upon it, and remember all the commandments of the Lord." The numerical value of the letters spelling out the word *tzitzit* is six hundred, and taken together with the eight threads and the five knots which make up the *tzitzit*, it makes a total of six hundred and thirteen (the number of the Divine Commandments contained in the Torah). Therefore, every Jew must take care to wear a *tallit katan* (a small fringed garment)all day. This must be made of white lamb's wool, measuring about three-fourths of a cubit in length and half a cubit in width (13½ inches by 9 inches); other authorities hold that it must measure one cubit square (18 by 18 inches). Those who sew together the sides of the *tallit katan*, should take care to leave the greater part of both sides open, and it is not permissible to join the open parts by means of hooks. Every man must also provide himself with a large fringed *tallit*, with which to enfold himself while praying, and he should take care that the *tallit* be handsome. For every religious deed must be performed in the grandest manner, as it is written (Exodus 15:2): "This is my God, and I will glorify Him," and it is explained to mean: Show yourself glorious before Him when performing His Commandments. One must also be careful to buy the fringes from a trustworthy person, so as to be certain that they were spun and twined for that specific purpose in accordance with the provisions of the law, and that they are of the prescribed length.

2. If one can afford only a linen *tallit*, to which no woolen fringes may be attached on account of the law prohibiting *shatnez* (mixture of wool and linen), then according to one authority, one should make the corners of the *tallit* out of leather and attach woolen fringes to them; but other authorities disagree with this opinion.

3. The aperture into which the fringes are inserted must be within three thumb-breadths, both from the vertical and horizontal edges of the *tallit*. (Some authorities maintain that the measurement of a thumb-breadth is the short joint of the thumb, which is at its top, and it is proper to follow this stricter opinion, because above three thumb-breadths from the edge is

not called *corner*, but it is the garment proper.) If one has made the aperture more than three thumb-breadths removed from the edge of the *tallit*, even though, when tying on the fringes, he pulls the knot tightly so that the *tallit* is contracted and the aperture comes within the prescribed distance from the edge, it is still invalid. If one inserts the fringes into apertures that are removed from the edge of the *tallit* above the prescribed limit, and then makes the apertures larger to make the fringes hang within the three thumb-breadths, it is invalid; for, it reads (Deuteronomy 22:12): "Thou shalt *make* the fringes," which means, they must be valid while putting them in, and not made legal by a subsequent act. The aperture must not be too near the vertical or horizontal edge, measuring less than the size of the first phalanx of the thumb, because if it measures less than that it can no longer be called the *corner*, but below the corner. If the aperture is made at the prescribed edge of the *tallit*, but by pulling the knot of the fringe, the edge has become contracted, and the aperture is now removed from the edge, less than the prescribed measure, it is nevertheless valid. It is doubtful whether or not the unwoven threads at the end of a *tallit* should be included in the measurements mentioned before; they must therefore be cut off before the fringes are tied on. Some people are accustomed to make two horizontal apertures, like the Hebrew vowel point *tzere*, and in these two they insert the fringes, suspending them on the outside of the *tallit*.

4. If, when the fringes are tied on, the apertures are at the prescribed distance from the edge, but in time the apertures become enlarged or the edges of the *tallit* are worn-out to the extent that the fringes are no longer within the necessary distance from the edge, they are still valid, because the Torah only provides that the fringes shall not be made below the corner, when they are tied on, as it is said (Numbers 15:38): "And they shall make for themselves fringes at the corner of their garments." Nevertheless, it is best to make a seam around the aperture and on the border of the *tallit*, so that the required measurements may not in time be diminished.

5. It is the general custom to make five double knots in the fringes, between which there are four spaces. It is done in this manner: We put the four threads through the aperture and make two knots; we then take the longest thread, that is called the *shamesh* (servant), and coil it around the threads seven times, and make two knots; we coil it around again eight times, and make two knots; then we coil it around again eleven times, and make two knots; and finally we coil it around thirteen times, and make two knots. Since the beauty of the fringes lies in that all the spaces be of equal dimensions, we make the threads far apart in the first space where the number of coils is the smallest; in the second, we make them somewhat closer, and in the third and in the fourth still closer. The prescribed length of the fringe,

that is, beginning with the first knot to the ends of the thread, must be no less than twelve thumb-breadths. For the same reason of symmetry, it is proper that all the spaces together be one-third of the prescribed length, and the loose threads two-thirds thereof; we should, therefore, take care that every space shall be of the size of a thumb-breadth; then all the spaces taken together will equal four thumb-breadths, and the threads that remain loose will equal eight thumb-breadths in length. If the threads are longer we should make the spaces a little larger. It is advisable to make all the knots by tying together the four threads on the one side with the four threads on the other side, so that each of the four inserted threads is divided, one-half on one side and the other half on the other side.

6. If one does not take four separate threads, but takes one long thread, folds it into four, puts it through the aperture, makes a knot, and thereafter cuts apart the threads, it is invalid, because it is written (Deuteronomy 22:12): "Thou shalt make thyself fringes," which means, you must *make* the fringes in the manner prescribed by law, before putting them on, and not put them in first unlawfully and thereafter legalize them by a subsequent act. Likewise, if one puts in the fringes on one garment, in the manner prescribed by law and the garment becomes torn, and one desires to put them on a different garment, or even in the same garment, as when for instance, the corner of the garment becomes torn and the fringes fall off, and one desires to replace them and we mend the rent up to the aperture—this is invalid, because the Divine Command is: "Thou shalt make," and not use what has already been made. Likewise, if one puts in the fringes into a garment which is legally unfit to put fringes in it, as for instance, when most of the sides of the garment is sewed up, and after that one opens up the seams and thus rendered the garment valid for *tzitzit*, it is invalid, for the reason stated before, that the *tzitzit* must be made, and not use what has already been made. But in the above cases, and in instances similar to them, one must first untie the *tzitzit*, and put them on again as prescribed by law.

7. Before wrapping oneself with the *tallit* one must examine the *tzitzit*, the threads and the coils, to see if they are in order, and separate the threads from one another, if they are entangled. However, if one comes late to the synagogue, and by examining and separating the threads, one will lose the opportunity to pray together with the congregation, one may dispense with the examination and separation.

8. The appropriate benediction must be pronounced before the actual performance of any precept, and the precept must be performed immediately afterward. Therefore, we must take the *tallit* with both hands, and bear in

mind that the Holy One, blessed be He, commanded us to wrap ourselves with the *tzitzit* in order that we may remember to perform *all* His commandments, as it is said (Numbers 15:39): "That ye may look upon it and remember all the commandments of the Lord." Then while still standing, we say the benediction *Lehitateph batzitzit* (to wrap ourselves with the *tzitzit*), and immediately cover our heads all the way down to our mouth. After that we raise the four corners of the *tallit,* wrap them around the neck, after the fashion of the Arabs, and remain standing like this as long as it takes one to walk four cubits (six feet), while reciting the verses: *Mah yakar* (how precious), etc. After this we may remove it from our head. It is proper to take care not to let the *tzitzit* drag on the floor, as it constitutes contempt of the precept; we must, therefore, raise them and stick them under the belt.

9. The benediction over the *tzitzit* should be pronounced only during the day and not during the night. Care should be taken not to say it before one is able to distinguish between blue and white. If one puts on the small *tallit* while it is still night, or while one's hands are still unwashed, when no benediction may be said over it, then upon putting on the large *tallit,* one should have in mind to include the small *tallit* as well. If one has no large *tallit,* then upon putting on the small *tallit* in the daytime, with hands already washed, one should say over it the benediction, *Al mitzvat tzitzit* (concerning the commandment of the *tzitzit*). If one puts on the small *tallit* when no benediction may be said over it, then when it is already daytime and one's hands are washed one should take the fringes in one's hands and say the benediction, *Al mitzvat tzitzit.* If one sleeps with the small *tallit* on, one should say no benediction over it in the morning, but upon saying the benediction over the large *tallit,* one should have in mind to include the small one as well.

10. If one takes off the *tallit,* intending to put it on again soon, even if one went to the lavatory, one need not say the benediction upon putting it on again. But if one does not intend to put it on soon again, and thereafter one changes one's mind and puts it on again, one must repeat the benediction. If the *tallit* slips off the back, but a part of it still remains on the body, even though most of it fell off, there is no need to repeat the benediction upon adjusting it, but if no part of it was left on the body, even though one is holding on to it with the hands, the benediction must be repeated upon putting it on; for, the intent of the precept is not that we should hold the *tallit* in our hands, but that we should enfold our bodies with it. If the *tallit* falls off while reciting a prayer which may not be interrupted, one should not

say the benediction upon adjusting it, but after finishing the prayer one takes the *tzitzit* in the hands and says the benediction.

11. It is permissible occasionally to borrow the *tallit* belonging to someone else, even without his knowledge, to pray in it and say the benediction, because it is presumed that a person is glad if a precept is performed with his property when no pecuniary loss is involved. But the *tallit* must not be carried out of the premises, because the owner might object to that. If the *tallit* was folded, the borrower must leave it folded. On the Sabbath, the borrower need not fold it; for, since no *tallit* may be folded on the Sabbath, the owner will forgive him. If he borrows somebody's *tallit* for the purpose of going up to the reading of the Torah, it is doubtful whether one must say a benediction over it. The borrower should, therefore, have it in mind that he does not intend to acquire even temporary possession of the *tallit*, and in such event all authorities agree that no benediction need be said. But if one takes a *tallit* belonging to the congregation, even if only for the purpose of going up to the reading of the Torah, one must say the benediction, because it is considered like his own property.

12. The word "wool" mentioned either in the Torah or by the legal authorities ordinarily means either lamb's or ram's wool. If the warp of the *tallit* is of wool and the woof is cotton or silk; or if the woof is of wool and the warp is of another kind, a God-fearing man should not pronounce the benediction over such a *tallit*. Some authorities hold that even if the *tzitzit* and the *tallit* are of diverse fabrics, one may not say the benediction over such a *tallit*. If the *tallit* is of silk and the fringes of wool, one is not allowed to say the benediction over it, but one must first say the benediction over a woolen *tallit* and then one may remove it and put on the silk one. However, a benediction may be said over a silk *tallit* with silk *tzitzit*. If some of the *tzitzit* are of wool and some of silk, it is still worse; no *tzitzit* should ever be made in this manner.

13. If one part of the four threads (which are folded to form eight fringes) has been torn off, and there is enough left of it to make a loop, the size of four thumb-breadths, or even if parts of two threads have been torn off and four thumb-breadths is left of each, but the other two threads are perfect, such *tzitzit* are still valid. But if three threads have been damaged, even though there is four thumb-breadths left of each and the fourth one is perfect; or if only one thread has been damaged so that less than a thumb-breadth is left of it, even though the remaining three threads are perfect, the *tzitzit* are unfit. It follows that if one of the eight fringes has been even en-

tirely torn off to the very links, the *tzitzit* are valid beyond any doubt, since in reality, this is only one-half of the thread, and of the other half there is still enough left to make a loop with it. If two of the fringes have been torn off and less than four thumb-breadths is left of each, the *tzitzit* are rendered unfit, since it is likely that the two torn fringes belong to one and the same thread. However, if one is certain that they belong to two different threads, as for instance when tying the *tzitzit*, one has always been careful to tie four ends of one side and four ends of the other side (never mixing them up), and now the two fringes that have been torn off are both on one side of the knot, then these two torn fringes surely belong to the other group of four; and since there is still left of each thread no less than the length of four thumb-breadths on the other side of the knot, and the remaining two threads are perfect, the *tzitzit* are considered valid. If one of the threads is torn where it is inserted in the aperture, the *tzitzit* are rendered unfit. The law that if one thread is torn off and there is enough left of it with which to make a loop the *tzitzit* are still valid, is true only when all the threads have been of the prescribed length when originally put in, but if at the time of putting in the *tzitzit*, one of the threads is shorter than the prescribed length, no matter to what extent, the *tzitzit* are unfit for the purpose.

14. The threads of the *tzitzit* must be twisted, and if any thread has become untwisted, the untwisted part is considered as entirely cut off and non-existent.

15. At times a *tallit* consists of two parts, as is the case with many of our *talliyot* (fringed garments). Occasionally such a *tallit* is taken apart for washing or mending it, and after that it is joined again by means of a seam. If each part is large enough to wrap oneself with it, then it suffices to remove the two *tzitzit* from either of the parts, and after joining the two parts together the *tzitzit* may be put in again. But if each part is not large enough to wrap oneself with it, then the *tzitzit* from both parts must be removed. If one part is large enough and the other part is not, then the *tzitzit* should be removed from the smaller part.

16. Some authorities are of the opinion that if a corner was severed from the *tallit* and the severed piece measures less than three thumb-breadths square, then even though this piece is sewed on to the *tallit*, it is unfit to put the *tzitzit* in it, because the detached piece, measuring less than three thumb-

breadths square, cannot legally be called "garment," and even when attached to the *tallit* it is still considered in the eyes of the law as severed. And it is proper to follow this opinion. But if the piece torn off is not entirely severed from the *tallit,* then the sewing it on makes it a part of the *tallit* itself, and the *tzitzit* put in afterward are valid. It is customary to sew on a piece of extra cloth at the corners of the *tallit,* because there are many garments, even new ones, that are made up of several pieces joined together, measuring less than three thumb-breadths square; therefore, we put on a piece of cloth measuring three thumb-breadths square in the place where the *tzitzit* are put in.

17. Some authorities are of the opinion that in the entire area of the corner where the *tzitzit* may be inserted, that is, from the edge above the width of the first phalanx of the thumb, up to three thumb-breadths, no seam, no matter how small, should be made of thread which is suitable for the *tzitzit* of this particular *tallit.* For instance, if the *tallit* is of flax, we must not make a seam with flax threads, only with silk threads, or if the *tallit* is of silk, no silk threads may be used; and if the *tallit* is of wool, no woolen threads may be used, only silk threads, or the like. It is proper to observe this rule of law also as regards the seam made to strengthen the apertures. All these laws apply only to a case where white thread is being used, but if colored thread is used, it does not matter.

18. One may remove the *tzitzit* from the *tallit* in order to repalce them with better ones, or if one of the threads has been torn off and one desires to put in perfect ones in their place, although the first ones are still fit. This is permissible because one does not intend to free the *tallit* from the requirement of *tzitzit*; on the contrary, one intends to put in better ones. But one must take care not to throw out the discarded *tzitzit* into a filthy place.

19. Even *tzitzit* that fall off and are removed from the *tallit* must not be thrown into a rubbish heap, because we slight thereby a Divine Command. Some people are strict about discarded *tzitzit* and place them in a book to serve as a bookmark, because, since they have once been used for the performance of a precept, let another precept be performed with them. Nor must one make any unworthy use of an old *tallit* which is no longer used for the performance of a religious duty.

20. If upon entering the synagogue on the Sabbath one discovers that one of the *tzitzit* in his *tallit* has become unfit, and he is unable to procure another *tallit,* and one feels embarrassed to remain there without a *tallit,* since it is impossible on this day to replace it by another *tzitzit,* one may as a matter of decorum, put on the *tallit* as it is, without saying the benediction over it.

This rule of law applies only to a case where one was not aware of it before the Sabbath, but if one has been aware of it before the Sabbath but failed to take care of it, one is not allowed to put it on now.

21. He who puts on a garment requiring *tzitzit*, and he neglects to do so, is guilty of violating a Command of the Torah. Garments having four square corners; one of these corners must be cut off and made round in order not to require *tzitzit*; but one does not exempt the garment from *tzitzit* by simply folding up one of the corners and sewing it up, for as long as it has not been cut off, it is still considered a part of the garment. Severe is the punishment of the one who neglects the performance of the Divine Command in putting on the *tzitzit*. He who is scrupulous in performing this Commandment will be worthy of beholding the Divine Presence.

CHAPTER 10

The Tefillin (Phylacteries)

1. The Divine Command regarding *tefillin* is likewise a very precious precept, because the whole Torah is compared to the *tefillin*, as it is written (Exodus 13:9): "In order that the law of the Lord may be in your mouth." They who fail to put on the *tefillin* are reckoned the transgressors in Israel who sin with their bodies, because they refuse to subjugate their bodies to the worship of the Almighty. They who put on defective *tefillin* not only fail to observe the Divine Command, but also utter many benedictions in vain, which constitutes a grave crime. Therefore, we must take care to buy our *tefillin* from a competent and God-fearing scribe. We must also buy the straps for the *tefillin* from a trustworthy person to be sure that they were prepared for this particular purpose from the skin of a clean animal. But due to our woeful shortcomings, this gross blunder is on the increase, in that people generally buy their *tefillin* and the straps from anyone who sells them cheaply, although they are unfit. Every God-fearing person should consider this: if he is spending money liberally for his clothes and utensils, so that they be of the right kind, how much more, then, should he do so with the objects required by the Almighty, blessed be His name. He should not economize and worry about money, but buy those holy objects only when certain that they are fit for the purpose, although the price may be high. He should always take care of the *tefillin* that they be in proper condition, and that the cases and the straps be black. It is proper to smear the straps with a little oil, so that they are always black. But the oil must not come from a non-kosher fish. If the *tefillin* become defective, even in the slightest degree, or if the stitches become loose, we should immediately consult a competent scholar to ascertain whether they are still fit. We must particularly be careful regarding the edges of the cases, and especially so with the edges of the one for the head, because these generally become frayed and form holes therein, as a result of which they are rendered unfit. Very frequently, when the *tefillin* become old, some part of the upper skin of the *tefillin* of the head becomes separated, as a result of which the *tefillin* are rendered unfit. It is,

therefore, important that we take great care regarding this matter. If we are careful in performing the precept of the *tefillin* and treat the *tefillin* with respect, our days will be prolonged, and we are certain of having a share in the world to come, as it is written (Isaiah 28:16): "O Lord, by these things men will live, and in all these things is the life of my spirit; so wilt Thou give me health and cause me to live." The word *tefillin* connotes judgment and admonition, because the *tefillin* serve as evidence and convincing proof that the Divine Presence rests on us, as it is written (Deuteronomy 28:10): "And all the nations of the earth shall see that Thou art called by the name of the Lord;" and our Rabbis, of blessed memory, explained that this refers to the *tefillah* of the head upon which is embossed the letter *shin,* the first letter spelling out the word *Shaddai* (Almighty). Therefore, it is forbidden to cover entirely the *tefillah* of the head with the *tallit.*

2. The time for putting on the *tefillin* begins from that hour of morning when a man can recognize his neighbor, with whom he is slightly acquainted, at a distance of four cubits. The *tefillin* are put on after the *tallit.* The reason the *tzitzit* have precedence over the *tefillin* is that the precept of the *tzitzit* is to be performed daily, including Sabbaths and festivals, while the precept of the *tefillin* is to be performed on weekdays only. And this rule is well established; that a precept which is observed regularly takes precedence over a precept which is not observed regularly. However, if one happens to take hold of the *tefillin* first, although they are still in the bag, one must put them on first and then enfold oneself with the *tallit,* because a mitzvah must not be passed by, as it is written (Exodus 12:17): "And ye shall observe the *matzot,*" read instead *mitzvot* (commandments): that is, if an opportunity of performing a Divine Command presents itself, do not allow it to sour by delaying its performance.

3. It is written (Exodus 13:16): "And it shall be as a sign upon thy hand" (Hebrew, *yadḥah*), written with the superfluous letter *he* at the end of the word. Our Rabbis, of blessed memory, said that this is to be interpreted as meaning *yad kehah,* the left hand, which is weaker and feebler. We must put the *tefillah* on the elevated part of the biceps, as it is written (Deuteronomy 11:18): "Therefore, shall ye lay up these My words in your heart," which means that it shall be put physically opposite the heart. Therefore, we must place the *tefillah* in the place mentioned and incline it slightly towards the side, so that when we let our arm down, the *tefillah* would be on a level with the heart. Regarding the *tefillah* of the head, it is written (Deuteronomy 7:8): "Between your eyes," and our Rabbis, of blessed memory, received it by tradition, that it does not mean literally *between the eyes,* but on the head midway between the eyes. And the place is from where the hair begins to

grow, up to the spot where the child's skull is soft; which means that the lower edge of the *tefillah* should not be lower than the place where the hair begins to grow, and the upper edge not higher than the place where a child's skull is soft. Great care should be taken to watch that the *tefillah* should always lie in its proper place. Even if only a small part of the *tefillah* is on the forehead where no hair grows, or if it inclines to the side and it is not exactly midway between the eyes, the precept is not fulfilled, and the benediction is pronounced in vain. The knot in the strap must be placed on the back of the head, above the nape of the neck, at the base of the skull, and the *tefillah* must not incline either towards one side or another. The strap should be fastened on the head; but when the case and the base are wide, it is diffi cult to have it tightened properly. It is, therefore, urgent to be very careful regarding this matter.

4. The *tefillin* must be put on while standing. We must not shake the *tefillin* out of the bag, because it is an act of contempt toward a *mitzvah*; but we must take them out with our hand. We first put on the *tefillah* of the hand, and before tightening the knot we say the benediction *Lehaniaḥ tefillin* (to put on the *tefillin*). We then tighten the knot and make seven coils on our forearm. Thereafter, we put on the *tefillah* of the head, and before we tighten it we say the benediction, *Al mitzvat tefillin* (Concerning the commandment of the *tefillin*). We then tighten the strap on our head and say: *Baruḥ shem kevod malleḥuto leolam vaed* (blessed be His glorious kingdom forever and and ever). The reason for saying this last verse is because there is some doubt whether this benediction should be said. Because of this uncertainty, it is also doubtful whether or not a listener is bound to respond *Amen* to it. It seems to me, therefore, that this benediction should be uttered silently. After we put on the *tefillah* of the head we make three coils on the middle finger, one around the middle phalanx, and two around the lower phalanx.

5. If one happens to take from the bag the *tefillah* of the head first, one must put it down, cover it up, and put on the *tefillah* of the hand first. Since the precedence of the *tefillah* of the hand, over the one of the head, is ordained in the Torah, as it is written (Deuteronomy 6:8): "And thou shalt bind them

for a sign upon thy hand, and they shall be frontlets between thy eyes." Hence, we are to disregard in this case, the apparent neglect of a religious object.

6. Nothing must intervene between the flesh and the *tefillin*, and it makes no difference whether it is the one of the hand or of the head. Short hair is not considered an interposition since it is customary to wear the hair like that. But a thick tuft of hair, not only indicates brazenness and vanity, but it also constitutes an imposition between the head and the *tefillah*.

7. Care should be taken that the knot of the *tifillah* of the hand should not be shifted from the case (even when in the bag), and the *yod* of the knot must always be facing the heart. The base in which the strap is inserted should be upward and the case downward. In an emergency, for instance, when a left-handed person, who puts on the *tefillah* on the right hand, has no *tefillin* of his own and he borrows from a person who puts it on his left, if he is unable to change the knot and he puts them on as they are with the base upward and the case downward, then the *yod* and the knot will be facing outward. In such a case, he may invert the *tefillah*, and put it on with the base being downward and the case upward, so that the *yod* and the knot may be facing the heart.

8. No conversation is permitted between the putting on of the *tefillah* of the hand and that of the head. It is even forbidden to wink the eyes or motion with the hands. For it is written (Exodus 13:9): "And it shall be unto thee for a sign upon thy hand and for a memorial between thy eyes," it is necessary that the memorial must be instantaneous between the *tefillah* of the hand and that of the head, so that both of them may constitute one unit. Even if we hear the *kaddish* or the *kedushah*, we must not interrupt to respond with the congregation, but we must keep silent and listen to what the worshipers say. If, however, we hear someone utter the benediction, *Lehaniaḥ tefillin* (to put on the *tefillin*), we should respond *Amen* to it, because this *Amen* is a corroboration that we believe in the precept of the *tefillin*; and is therefore, not an interruption. When putting on the *tefillin*, arranged according to the view of Rabbenu Tam, it is likewise forbidden to interrupt between putting on the *tefillah* of the hand and that of the head; but it may be interrupted with responding to the *kaddish* and the *kedushah*.

9. If by error we do interrupt, we must touch the *tefillah* of the hand, repeat the benediction, *Lehaniaḥ tefillin*, tighten the knot and thereafter put on the *tefillah* of the head and say the required benediction. If, however, the interruption has been for the need of the *tefillin*, we need not repeat the benediction.

10. When we put on the *tefillin*, we must reflect that by doing this, we fulfill the command of the Holy One, blessed be He, who commanded us to do so. The *tefillin* contain four sections of the Torah which speak of the unity of God, blessed be His name, and of the exodus of the Israelites from the land of Egypt. The *tefillin* are put on the arm nearest the heart and on the head near the brain, in order that we should always remember the miracles and wonders that He has wrought for us, which signify His Unity and His might and dominion over those who are above and below, who can do with them as He pleases; also, that we should submit to Him both the soul which resides in the brain, and the heart, which is the seat of our desires and passions. In so doing, we become mindful of our Creator, restrain our pleasures, and also fulfill that which is written (Numbers 15:39): "And that ye seek not after the inclination of your heart and the delight of your own soul." This is the reason why, concerning the *tefillin*, it is written, "Between thy eyes."

11. The *tefillin* of the hand and of the head are two separate and distinct precepts, and the inability to observe one does not bar the observance of the other. Therefore, if we have only one *tefillah* available, or if by reason of some accident we are able to put on only one, we are bound to put that one on. If it is the one for the hand, we say only the benediction *Lehaniaḥ tefillin* (to put on the *tefillin*); but if it is the one for the head, we say both benedictions, *Lehaniaḥ tefillin* and *Al mitzvat tefillin;* and we say also *Baruḥ shem kevod maleḥuto leolam vaed* (blessed be the name of His glorious kingdom forever and ever.)

12. A fully left-handed man, although he has become left-handed by mere habit, must put on the *tefillah* on the right hand which is equivalent to everyone's left. If he does all work with his right hand but he writes with his left, or vice versa, then the hand with which he writes is considered the right one, and the *tefillah* is placed on the other. An ambidextrous person puts the *tefillah* on the left hand. A man not born left-handed, who has accustomed himself to write with the left but does all his other work with the right hand, must bind the *tefillah* on the left hand.

13. The preseribed width of the straps, whether of the *tefillah* of the head or of the hand, is no less than the length of a barley. The prescribed length of both straps for the *tefillah* of the head, is to reach down to a man's navel, or a trifle above that. There is an opinion that holds that the strap on the right hand side should reach down to below a man's abdomen. And it is proper to follow this stricter view in the first instance. The strap of the *tefillah* of the hand should be long enough to make seven coils around the arm, and three windings around the middle finger, with enough left to tighten it. If the strap be torn, whether it be of the head or of the hand, an authority should be consulted.

14. Care should be taken that the straps always be with their black side out. If it happens that the strap around his hand or around his head

becomes inverted accidently, he must either fast or redeem himself by giving charity. If the *tefillin,* when not in the bag, fall to the ground, we must likewise fast. But if they fall down while in the bag, we need not fast, but we must give charity.

15. If one has removed the *tefillin* in order to go to the lavatory, one must repeat the benediction upon putting them on again. But if one has removed them in the middle of the benedictions belonging to the *shema,* that is, from the benediction *Yotzer or* (who forms the light) and onward, one must not interrupt by uttering the benediction over the *tefillin;* but one must wait until after the reading of the *Shemoneh esreh* (silent prayer), then touch the *tefillin* and say the benediction over them.

16. As long as we have the *tefillin* on, our attention must not be diverted from them even for a moment, except during the *Shemoneh esreh* prayer and while studying the Torah. We are forbidden to eat a regular meal while having the *tefillin* on, but we may have light refreshments. Sleep, even for a little while, while wearing the *tefillin,* is prohibited.

17. We must touch the *tefillin* whenever we think of them, because by so doing, our minds will not be diverted from them. We should first touch the *tefillah* of the hand and then the one of the head. It is a beautiful custom to touch the *tefillin* when mentioning the precept concerning them in the reading of the *Shema.* When saying (Deuteronomy 6:8): "And thou shalt bind them as a sign upon thy hand," we touch the *tefillah* of the hand and kiss (that object with which we have touched it), and when saying: "And they shall be as frontlets between thy eyes," we touch the *tefillah* of the head and kiss (that object with which we have touched it).

18. We may elevate a holy thing to a higher grade of sanctity but not degrade it. Since the *tefillah* of the head is more sacred than the one of the hand, for it is composed of four compartments and the letter *shin;* therefore, the strap that was in the former may not be used for the latter, but the strap that was in the latter may be used for the former. If the strap of the *tefillah* of the hand breaks above the knot, it is forbidden to reverse it and make the knot out of the lower end of the strap, but the knot must be made at the place it has been broken off. The same applies to the strap of the *tefillah* of the head. A bag made for the purpose of keeping the *tefillin,* and the *tefillin* had already been held therein, must not be used for any secular purpose.

19. The *tefillin* should not be taken off until we recite *Yehi ratzon shenishmor ḥukeḥa* (may it be Thy will, O Lord, that we keep Thy statutes), contained in the prayer *Uva letziyon goel* (and a redeemer shall come to Zion). But in communities where it is customary, that on the day the Torah is read,

the holy scroll is not replaced in the ark until after the prayer *Uva letziyon* had been completed, the *tefillin* should not be taken off before the scroll is returned to the ark. A Biblical hint to this rule is found (Micah 2:13): "And their king passeth on before them, and the Lord at their head." If there is a circumcision in the synagogue, the *tefillin* should not be removed until after the circumcision. On *Rosh Ḥodesh* (the New Moon), the *tefillin* are removed before the *Musaph* (additional) service; on *Ḥol Hammoed Sukkot* (the Intermediate Days of Tabernacles), they are taken off before *Hallel*; but on *Ḥol Hammoed Pesaḥ* (Intermediate Days of Passover), the congregation removes the *tefillin* before *Hallel* and the *ḥazan* (Reader) thereafter.

20. The *tefillin* must be removed while standing. First we unwind the coils around the middle finger and two or three coils from around the arm, then we remove the *tefillah* of the head, and finally the *tefillah* of the hand, because it is written (Deuteronomy 6:8): "And they shall be for frontlets between thy eyes," and our Rabbis, of blessed memory, explained that since it is written in the plural, "And they shall be," it signifies that as long as the *tefillah* is midway between the eyes the two *tefillahs* must always be on. Therefore, we first put on the *tefillah* of the hand and remove the *tefillah* of the head first, so that whenever the *tefillah* of the head is on the one of the hand should also be on. It is proper to remove the *tefillah* from the head with the left hand, which is the weaker one, in order to indicate that we are reluctant to remove it; for in reality we should wear the *tefillin* the whole day, but because our bodies are not always clean we take them off immediately after we are through praying. We must not remove the *tefillin* in the presence of a *sefer torah* (Holy Scroll), nor in the presence of our teacher; we must turn aside and remove them. It is the custom of sages to kiss the *tefillin* when putting them on and when taking them off. The *tallit* is not taken off before we remove the *tefillin*.

21. The *tefillin* must be placed in the bag in a way that we may be certain the following day of taking out the *tefillah* of the hand first. It is not permissible to place the *tefillah* of the hand on top of one of the head, since the latter is more sacred than the former, but they must be placed side by side. The bag containing the *tefillin* should be placed in the *tallit* bag, with the *tallit* above them, so that the *tallit* is first at hand.

22. If a man who has no *tefillin* of his own arrives at the synagogue when the congregation is already praying, he should wait till the end of the service and then borrow *tefillin* from someone, so that he can read the *Shema* and the *Shemoneh esreh* wearing *tefillin*, rather than pray together with the congregation without *tefillin*. If he is afraid that by waiting for the *tefillin* the time limit set for the praying of the *Shema* will pass, he should read the *Shema* without *tefillin*. If he is afraid that the time limit set for praying will like-

wise be over, he should also pray without *tefillin*. But upon obtaining *tefillin* later, he shall put them on, pronouncing the necessary benedictions over them, then recite some Psalms, or put them on at the *Minḥah* (afternoon) service. It is forbidden to put the *tefillin* on in the nighttime. It is permissible to take someone else's *tefillin*, without his knowledge, put them on and say the benedictions over them. (As is provided in chapter 9, 11, relating to the law of the *tallit*.)

23. The body of the one having the *tefillin* on must be kept clean; therefore one should be careful not to do anything unseemly while having them on. A person suffering with diarrhea, although he has no actual pain, is exempt from putting on the *tefillin*, since he is unable to keep himself properly clean. However, if he is under the impression that he will be able to keep his body clean when reading the *Shema* and the *Shemoneh esreh*, he may then put them on. As regards any other patient, if he suffers pain and his mind is disturbed by it, he is exempt from putting them on, because we are forbidden to divert attention from them; if no such condition exists, he is bound to put them on.

24. A father must provide his minor son (below the age of thirteen) with *tefillin*, if he knows how to take care of them, not to do anything unseemly and not to sleep while having them on. It is now the prevailing custom that a minor begins putting on *tefillin* two or three months before he becomes thirteen years old.

25. As regards to wearing the *tefillin* on *Ḥol Hammoed* (Intermediate Days of festivals), there is disagreement among the authorities and divergent customs. In some communities, they do not put on *tefillin* on *Ḥol Hamoed*, while in other communities, they do, but do not say the benedictions over them aloud at the synagogue as it is done on weekdays. In still other communities, they have made it a custom not to say the benedictions at all (then one must have in mind, that if *Ḥol Hammoed* is not the appropriate time for putting on the *tefillin*, they should be considered merely as ordinary straps). And although no benediction is said over them, one is not allowed to interrupt (by talking or otherwise) between putting on the *tefillah* of the hand and that of the head, but one may interrupt for *kaddish* and *kedushah*. Care must be taken that among those who worship in one synagogue there should not be some who put on the *tefillin* and others who do not.

26. *Tefillin* that are known to be ritually fit need not be examined to ascertain their validity. As long as the cases are in perfect condition, the written parchments, too, are presumed to be valid. Nevertheless, it is proper

to have them examined occasionally, because at times they become spoiled through perspiration. If the *tefillin* are being used only occasionally, they should be examined twice in seven years, because there is a possibility that they have become moldy. If the cases are torn, the parchment must be examined. An examination is also called for when the *tefillin* fall into water. However, if there is no competent person to examine them and sew them up again, one should put them on without having them examined, but without saying the benedictions.

CHAPTER 11

The Mezuzah

1. It is a Divine Command to affix a *mezuzah* to every door of the house. Even if one has many rooms, and in every room there are many doors for ingress and egress, one must affix a *mezuzah* to each one of the doors, even though only one of the doors is ordinarily used. Even if the number of tenants was reduced and only one door is being used, nevertheless, *mezuzot* must be affixed to all doors. If a door has been made for occasional deliveries, and there is another door for entrance and exit, no *mezuzah* need be affixed to the door used for deliveries.

2. *Mezuzot* must be affixed also to the gates of courts, alleys, cities and provinces, as it is written (Deuteronomy 6:9): "And upon thy gates."

3. The *mezuzah* must be affixed to the right hand side as one enters. If it is affixed to the left hand side, it is invalid. It must be removed and affixed to the right hand side, and the benediction repeated upon fastening it. As regards the affixing of the *mezuzah,* it is immaterial whether one is left-handed or right-handed.

4. If there are two houses, each of which has a door opening either into the street or into a court, and the space between the two houses, too, has a door, and it is doubtful to which side of this door the *mezuzah* should be affixed, then we are guided by the location of the hinges, that is, the place where the hinges are affixed and toward which the door opens, is to be considered as a part of that house, and the *mezuzah* should accordingly be affixed to the right side where one enters. This rule applies only to a case where both houses are used equally, but if one of the two is used more frequently,

then we are not to be guided by the position of the hinges, but the *mezuzah* must be affixed to the right side of the entrance to the house which is more often used, even though the door opens into the other house.

5. The *mezuzah* must be affixed within the upper third of the door-post. If we affix it higher than this limit, it is valid, providing it is one hand-breadth from the lintel. But if we affix it lower than the upper one-third, it is invalid, and we must remove it, affix it to the proper place and pronounce the necessary benediction. If we place it above the one hand-breadth limit, we must remove it and affix it to the proper place without saying the benediction. It is best to affix the *mezuzah* within the outside hand-breadth of the door-post, but if one deviates from the rule, it does not matter.

6. How should the *mezuzah* be affixed? We roll the parchment from the end of the sentence to the beginning, that is, from the last word *Eḥad* (One) towards the first word *Shema* (Hear), so that the word *Shema* be on the top. Then we put it in the tube or other receptacle, and fasten it with nails to the door-post diagonally, having the top line containing the first word *Shema* towards the house, and the last line towards the outside. If the door-post is not wide enough, we may fasten the *mezuzah* vertically. If we simply suspend the *mezuzah*, it is not valid. We must fasten it with nails at the top and at the bottom, so that it should not remain suspended.

7. Before affixing the *mezuzah*, we say the benediction: "Blessed art Thou, O Lord our God, King of the universe, who hath sanctified us by His commandments, and hath commanded us to affix the *mezuzah*." If several *mezuzot* are to be affixed at the time, one benediction suffices for all. If a *mezuzah* fell off the door-post, the benediction must be repeated when we attach it again; but if we remove it in order to have it examined, it is doubtful whether or not we need repeat the benediction upon affixing it.

8. Some courts have a small door by the big gate, through which people pass in and out, whereas the big gate is used only occasionally. Since these are two separate entrances, having between them a post one hand-breadth wide, a *mezuzah* must be affixed to each.

9. In a place where we suspect that the *mezuzah* might be stolen, then if possible, one should make a groove in the door-post and place the *mezuzah* in it; but the groove must not be more than one hand-breadth deep, because

if it is deeper, then the *mezuzah* is not *on the door-post of thy house* but *in* the door-post. One must, however, make some mark to indicate where the *mezuzah* is placed. If it is impossible to make a groove in the door-post, one may affix it inside the house behind the door, but it must be affixed to the door-post and not to the wall, and it must be affixed not more than one hand-breadth away from the opening of the door. If it is more than one hand-breadth from the door, it is invalid.

10. A house requires a *mezuzah* only when it measures no less than four cubits (six feet) square. If it is not square, but it occupies an area of sixteen cubits, the same as four by four, as for instance when the house is long and narrow, or it is circular, it requires a *mezuzah* according to the opinion of some authorities, while others hold that it does not require a *mezuzah*, unless it is four cubits wide.

11. Only doors which have two door-posts at least ten hand-breadths high, and lintel above them, require *mezuzot*. Even when the door-posts are not made of special wood or stone, but the walls of the structure themselves form the door-posts and above them is the ceiling, a *mezuzah* must be affixed to it. If the house has only one door-post, for instance where the wall extends beyond the door on one side, like this 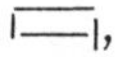, then if the door-post is on the left side of the entrance, no *mezuzah* is required; if the door-post is on the right side of the entrance, it is doubtful whether a *mezuzah* is required. In such a case, we should either affix the *mezuzah* without saying the benediction, or first affix one to a door which definitely requires a *mezuzah*, and then to the doubtful door. Thus the benediction said over the former, covers the latter. (See section 7, above). This rule is to be applied to all doubtful cases.

12. If the two door-posts have no lintel above them, but they have an arched top, like a bow, or even if there are no door-posts at all, but the vault itself begins from the ground, then if the wall is ten hand-breadths high and four hand-breadths wide, a *mezuzah* must be affixed in either case. In the case of stores, where one door-post is made to reach from the ground to the lintel, but the other door-post does not reach to the lintel, but a wall is made to protrude to about a cubit (one foot and a half) or more, like this 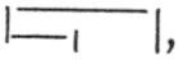, then if the door-post which reaches to the upper one is to the right of the entrance, a *mezuzah* must be affixed to it; and if the lower door-post is to the right of the entrance, then if this door-post is ten hand-breadths high, a *mezuzah* must be affixed to it, but if it is less than ten hand-breadths high, it should be affixed to the wider part of the wall.

13. There are some authorities who hold that if an entrance has no door, it nevertheless requires a *mezuzah*, and there are others who hold that there must be a door. Therefore, the *mezuzah* should not be affixed before the door

is put in. But one should never first affix the *mezuzah* and put in the door thereafter, because a precept must be performed on an occasion already existing, and not perform the precept first and thereafter create the occasion for it.

14. A house used as a temporary residence needs no *mezuzah.* Therefore, the *sukkah* erected for the Feast of Tabernacles, requires no *mezuzah* during the days of the Feast. Stores erected for the duration of a bazaar, and are thereafter, either taken apart or they remain entirely unoccupied, likewise require no *mezuzah.* But stores which are permanently occupied with merchandise, do require a *mezuzah.*

15. A corridor which has three walls with a ceiling above them, and the fourth side is open, but it has two columns resembling an entrance, requires no *mezuzah,* because these columns have not been made to serve as door-posts, but rather to support the ceiling. However, if it has a wall on the fourth side as well, although the wall is low and does not reach to the ceiling, or even though it is made up of windows, a *mezuzah* is required.

16. A gate-house, that is, a small hut by the gate of a court in which the watchman stays, or a porch used as an entrance to an attic, a garden-hut, and a shed, require no *mezuzah,* because they are not used as residences. However, if a house requiring a *mezuzah* opens into any of these structures or into the corridor, a *mezuzah* must be affixed to the door leading from any of these structures into the public thoroughfare. Therefore, the gates of courts, alleys, provinces and towns require a *mezuzah,* since houses requiring *mezuzot* open into them. Even if ten houses open into one another and only the inner one requires a *mezuzah, mezuzot* must be affixed to the nine outer ones. Therefore, a gate opening from a garden-house into a court, does require a *mezuzah.* Some authorities are of the opinion that a gate-house and a porch require a *mezuzah,* even if there is no house opening into them. It is therefore, best to affix the *mezuzah* to such structures without saying the benediction.

17. Bath-houses, canneries and immersion houses (containing pools for ritual purification), require no *mezuzah,* since they are not made for respectable dwellings. However, stables, houses where fowl are raised, barns for

straw, and cellars where wine or other beverages are kept, provided they have the required legal size of a house (see section 10, above), do require *mezuzot.* Some authorities hold that even these are exempt from a *mezuzah.*

18. The *mezuzah* in a room where children are usually found, or in a room where people at times, wash themselves or urinate, should be covered. The covering of the *mezuzah* suffices only when these practices are occasional, but when something for loathsome usage is regularly kept near the *mezuzah,* as for instance, a urinal, it does not suffice.

19. A house or a court in which non-Jews as well as Jews dwell, is exempt from a *mezuzah.*

20. A cellar having doors and door-post lying in the ground, is exempt from a *mezuzah,* because the term 'door-post' applies only to one standing vertically.

21. If a man rents a house outside the land of Israel, he need not affix *mezuzot* to its doors for the first thirty days, because it is not considered a permanent dwelling.

22. If a man moves from a house and it is to be occupied by another Jew, he must not remove the *mezuzot,* but must leave them there, and the new occupant is to pay for them.

23. One must take special care to observe the precept of *mezuzah,* because it is a continuous obligation. Whenever we enter or leave our house, we are confronted with His name, the Name of the Holy One, blessed be He. And remembering His love, we will awaken from our lethargy, and will cease going astray after the vanities of the time. We will be aware that nothing in this world endures forever, except the knowledge of the Rock of the world, and we will at once come to our senses and walk in the path of the righteous. Our Rabbis, of blessed memory, said (Menaḥot 43b): "He who has *tefillin* on his head and on his arm, *tzitzit* in his garment, and a *mezuzah* upon his door, is sure not to sin, because he has many reminders; and these are the very guardian angels who protect him from sinning, as it is written (Psalms 34:8): 'The angel of the Lord encampeth round about them that fear Him and delivereth them.'" Our Rabbis, of blessed memory said again (Shabbat 32b): "For the sin of one's failure to observe the precept of the *mezuzah,* one's children die when young; but the children of one who strictly observes it, will live to a ripe old age, for it is said (Deuteronomy 11:21): 'That your days may be multiplied, and the days of your children.'"

24. Because the purpose of the *mezuzah* is to remind us of His name, blessed be He, therefore, we should kiss the *mezuzah* upon leaving the house and upon entering it. But we are not allowed to put our hand upon the *mezuzah* proper; we must, therefore, cover the Name (Shaddai) with glass. Upon leaving the house and placing our hand on the *mezuzah*, we say: "The Lord is my keeper, the Lord is my shade upon my right hand; the Lord shall preserve my going out and my coming in, from this time forth and forever."

25. The *mezuzah* of a private dwelling should be examined twice in seven years, but that of a public building should be examined only twice in a jubilee (fifty years).

CHAPTER 12

Purity of Body, and Places for Holding Services

1. It is written (Amos 4:12): "Prepare to meet thy God, O Israel;" this means, that we should prepare ourselves before coming into the presence of His name, blessed be He, and put on decent garments when going to pray, as we do when we are to meet an august prince. Even when we pray privately, at home, we must be properly dressed. In communities where it is customary to wear sashes, one is not allowed to pray before girding oneself with a sash.

2. It is well to give charity before praying, as it is written (Psalms 17:15): "As for me, in righteousness shall I behold Thy face;" and also to resolve to observe the Divine Command (Leviticus 19:18): "And thou shalt love thy neighbor as thyself;" and we should determine to love every Jew as we love ourselves. For, if there is, God forbid, dissension among Israel on earth, there is no harmony above. Bodily unity of the people on earth, causes unity and concord of their souls in heaven above. By means of this, their prayers also become united as one, and united into one, they are acceptable before Him, blessed be His name.

3. It is written (Ecclesiastes 4:17): "Watch thy foot when thou goest to the house of God;" and our Rabbis, of blessed memory, explained that this verse, refers to the orifices that are near the legs. Therefore, before praying, it is the duty of every man to ascertain whether he needs to respond to

the call of nature. Even if he feels the slightest need for it, he is forbidden to pray or to study the Torah, as long as his body remains impure. If a person did pray at a time when he had to respond to the call of nature, if he had felt that he could abstain himself for the length of time within which he could walk a parasang (about one hour and a fifth), his prayer is considered as valid, otherwise his prayer is a mere abomination, and he must pray over again. Some authorities hold that if one can abstain oneself for the length of time mentioned above, one may start praying in the first instance. One may rely on the latter opinion in the event that by responding to the call of nature, the legal time limit set for praying will have passed.

4. If one is certain that one will be unable to keep his body in a pure state before finishing the reading of the *Shema* and the prayer, it is preferable that one should allow the time limit set for the *Shema* and the prayer to pass, than pray while the body is impure. If the time for prayer is over in such a case, then one is considered as being the victim of an accident (and one may complete the prayer, as is provided in chapter 21, below). If one thinks that he can stay pure during the reading of the *Shema,* one should put on the *tefillin* when finishing the benediction before the *Shema, "Haboḥer beamo yisrael beahabah"* (who hast chosen Thy people Israel in love), and say the necessary benediction over the *tefillin.*

5. Before praying, the hands must be washed up to the wrist. Even though one has already washed one's hands in the morning (as provided for in chapter 2), but thereafter touched an unclean spot, like some part of the body which is customarily covered, and where at times beads of perspiration are found, or when one scratched one's head, or when one has not washed one's hands up to the wrist in the morning, then one must wash them again before praying. If there is no water available, one must look for it; when on a journey, one must walk four miles forward, or one mile backward to look for it. If one fears that, by searching for water, the time limit for praying will pass, one may clean one's hands with chips of wood, with earth, or with any other substance that cleans, and one may pray; for it is written (Psalms 26:6): "I will wash my hands in innocency (Hebrew, *nikkayon,* also meaning *cleanliness,"* etc)., which signifies: "I will wash my hands with water if possible, and if not with *nikkayon,* any substance that cleans.

6. If one washed his hands properly in the morning, but does not know whether or not his hands have become soiled, since his mind has become diverted in the meantime, he must wash his hands again for the purpose of praying. Even if he had studied the Torah, between the morning hand-washing and praying, it constitutes a diversion of mind, and he must wash his hands before praying. In this case, however, one need not necessar-

ily go searching for water. If there is no water available, and if by searching for water, he will miss the opportunity of praying together with the congregation, he should not search for it, but should clean the hands with any cleansing substance, and pray with the congregation.

7. One must make a serious effort to join his prayer with the congregation, for it is written (Psalms 69:14): "But as for me, let my prayer be unto Thee, O Lord, in acceptable time." And it is written again (Isaiah 49:8): "Thus saith the Lord, in an acceptable time have I answered thee." The Holy One, blessed be He, does not despise the prayer of the multitude, even though there are sinful men in their midst, for it is written (Job 36:5): "Behold, God is mighty (Hebrew, *kabbir*, which also means *many*), yet He despiseth not any." And it is written again (Psalms 55:19): "He hath redeemed my soul in peace so that none come nigh me; for there were multitudes that strove with me."

8. If a person is on the road, and he arrives at a certain place where he desires to stay overnight, if farther on the road, within a distance of four miles, there is a place where public prayers are held, he must try to reach that community to pray with the congregation, provided that he can reach there while it is still light, so that it should not be necessary for him to walk all alone in the nighttime. If the congregation is in the rear of him, he must turn back one mile in order to pray with the congregation. Needless to say, that one should not walk away from a community where they hold public prayer, if one can arrive at one's desired destination while it is still daylight.

9. It is a highly meritorious act to pray in a synagogue or in the House of Study, as these are sacred places. Even if it happens that at times there is no *minyan* (a quorum of ten male adults) for prayer, it is nevertheless meritorious to pray there even by oneself, since they are hallowed places. He who is accustomed to study the Torah in the House of Study, should also pray there with a *minyan*. But if one does not customarily study there, one should pray in the synagogue where there are a great number of people, for "In the multitude of people is the king's glory" (Proverbs 14:28). If there are two synagogues in the community, one should go to the farthest, in order to earn a reward for the extra walk. Said Rabbi Judah ben Levi (Beraḥot 47b): "A man should always come early to the synagogue, in order that he may be of the first ten, for even if one hundred come after him, he receives a reward equal to the combined reward of all." Our Rabbis, of blessed memory, also said (Beraḥot 8a): "Whoever comes to worship in the synagogue or in the House of Study, morning and evening at the proper time, and tarries there the proper length of time, and conducts himself with proper respect, will merit long life, for it is written (Proverbs 8:34): "Happy is the man

that hearkeneth to Me, watching daily at My gates, waiting at the posts of My doors;" and thereafter it is written (Ibidem 8:35): "For he who findeth Me findeth life."

10. It is the duty of every man to select a synagogue, or a House of Study, where to pray regularly; and he should also select a permanent seat for worship. The space within a radius of four cubits (six feet) is considered as one and the same place in this regard. It is well to select a seat by the wall, as we find it to be the case of King Hezekiah, for it is written (Isaiah 38:2): "Then Hezekiah turned his face to the wall," etc. While praying, one should try not to sit next to a godless person; and when praying privately at home, one should also choose a regular place, so that one be not disturbed by the members of one's family.

11. It is obligatory to hasten while going to the synagogue or to the House of Study, or when going to perform some other religious duty, for it is said (Hosea 6:3): "Let us know, let us press on to know the Lord;" and it is written further (Psalms 119:32): "I will run the way of Thy commandments." Therefore, it is permissible to speed, even on the Sabbath, to perform a religious act, but it is forbidden to rush in the synagogue or in the House of Study. On arriving at the entrance of the house of worship, one should tarry awhile, and not enter suddenly; and one should tremble with awe before the splendor of His glory, blessed be His name, and recite the verse (Psalms 5:8): *Vaani berov ḥasdeḥa* (but as for me, in the abundance of Thy kindness, etc.), which recitation is tantamount to begging permission to enter. Thereafter, one should proceed with fear and awe, as when walking before a king. In communities where Jews dwell in streets for themselves, one should wrap himself in the *tallit* and put on the *tefillin* at his house, and thus walk to the house of worship. In a community where Jews live among other nationalities, or in the event one has to pass through filthy alleys, one should put on the *tallit* and the *tefillin* in the corridor of the house of worship, for it is of great merit to enter the synagogue enfolded in the *tallit* and crowned with the *tefillin*.

12. If because of some emergency, one is unable to go to the synagogue or to any other place where a *minyan* congregates to pray, one should get ten male adults together, and have a communal service at home. If this too, is impossible, one should at least, pray at the same time that the congregation prays, for that is a propitious moment. Likewise, if one dwells in a place where there is no *minyan*, one should pray at the time when the town congregations pray. But if one desires to study, or to begin doing some necessary

work, and since as it is explained in chapter 8, one is not allowed to begin those things before praying, then one may pray earlier, at sunrise.

13. If one has a weak heart and cannot wait for one's meal until the congregation is through praying, one is allowed to pray earlier at home (as stated in chapter 8). Only in one's house may one pray earlier in this manner, but if one has already come into the synagogue where they pray as a congregation, one is forbidden to pray before the congregation prays. Even if one wants to go out of the synagogue and pray elsewhere, before the congregation starts praying, it is forbidden. But if the congregation is late in praying, one may pray alone, in order that the legal time set for praying may not go by. Likewise, if one is sick or has met with some accident, one may pray before the congregation does even in the house of worship. It is, however, best in such a case to go home and pray.

14. Some authorities hold that if one *minyan* had prayed in the synagogue, and then another *minyan* comes in to pray, the second *ḥazan* is not allowed to stand in the same place where the first one stood, because it is an affront to the first people, if they have not as yet left the synagogue. If the first *minyan* had taken out a *Sefer torah* (Scroll of the Law) and read from it, the second *minyan* is not allowed to take it out again for reading from it in the same synagogue. In many communities, however, they are not particular about these matters; and it all depends upon the custom of the community.

15. The inhabitants of a community may compel one another to build a synagogue or a House of Study, and to buy books for studying purposes. In communities where there is no steady *minyan*, the inhabitants may compel one another by imposing fines to assemble regularly for a *minyan*, so that the regular daily service might be continued without interruption. Even scholars can be compelled to come to form a *minyan*, although they are prevented by this from studying the Torah; for there is a time for study and a time for prayer.

Chapter 13

The Sanctity of the Synagogue and the House of Study

1. The sanctity of the synagogue and the House of Study is very great, and we are enjoined to fear the One who dwells in them, blessed be His name; as it is written (Leviticus 19:30): "And My sanctuary shall ye reverence."

The synagogue and the House of Study are also called "sanctuaries" as it is written (Ezekiel 11:16): "Yet will I be to them as a minor sanctuary;" and it is explained that this verse refers to the synagogue and to the House of Study. Therefore, it is forbidden to engage there in gossip or to make there any calculations, except those pertaining to religious matters, such as the counting of charity money, or the like. Such places must be respected, kept perfectly clean, and candles should be lit therein to show our reverence for the place. One should not kiss one's little children there, because no other love must be shown in a house of worship except the love of God, blessed be His name.

2. Before entering such holy places, we must wipe the mud off our shoes, and we must take care that there be no dirt, either on our bodies or on our garments. If need be, it is permissible to spit on the floor there, but it must be immediately rubbed out with the feet.

3. We must not enter a holy place merely for the purpose of taking shelter from the heat or from the rain. We may enter there to call our friend, but we must first read there some Biblical verses, or study some *Mishnah*, or offer some prayer, or listen to some religious discourse, or at least sit down for a while, for even just sitting in a holy place is considered meritorious. Thereafter, we may call our friend.

4. It is forbidden to eat, drink, or sleep in places of worship, even if it is only a short nap. But it is permissible to sleep there for the sake of a meritorious act, when one, for instance, wishes to spend the night of *Yom Kippur* in the synagogue. But one must keep at a distance from the holy ark. It is likewise permissible to have in the synagogue a sacramental meal, provided there is no drunkenness and no frivolity connected with it. Those who study in the synagogue regularly are likewise allowed to eat and sleep there even regularly, in order that they may not lose time.

5. When a synagogue is to be erected, it is necessary to consult a learned man as to how and in what manner it is to be built.

CHAPTER 14

Pesuke Dezimerah (Special Verses of Psalms)

1. The prayers from *Hodu* (praise ye) to the end of *Az yashir* (then sang Moses), are called *Pesuke dezimerah* (special verses of psalms). *Baruḥ sheamar* (blessed be He who said) is the benediction preceding them, and *Yishtabaḥ* (praised be) is the benediction following them. The prayers from *Baruḥ sheamar* through the *Shemoneh esreh* (silent prayer) must not be interrupted with conversation, even when held in the Holy Tongue. With reference to interrupting for the purpose of performing a religious duty, a distinction is to be drawn between the *Pesuke dezimerah* and its concomitant benedictions, and the reading of the *Shema* and its benedictions. Regarding the former, even while one is in the midst of *Baruḥ sheamar*, or in the midst of *Yishtabaḥ*, one may respond *Amen* upon hearing a benediction. Likewise, if one hears the congregation reading the *Shema*, he may read with them the verse *Shema yisrael* (hear O Israel). Especially may one interrupt the prayer to recite with the congregation the *kaddish, kedushah* and *barḥu*. Nevertheless, if possible, one should endeavor to do so at an intermission, for instance, between Psalms or between verses. While reading the *Pesuke dezimerah*, we are not allowed to say *Baruḥ hu ubaruḥ shemo* (blessed be He and blessed be His name), even at a pause; nor should we then recite the prayer *Yitbaraḥ veyishtabaḥ* (let Him be blessed and praised), usually recited when the *ḥazan* chants *barḥu*, since the saying of this prayer is merely a custom (not prescribed by law). It seems to me that, during the reading of the *Pesuke dezimerah*, we should not say the benediction *Asher yatzar* (He who formed), after washing the hands upon leaving the lavatory, since it may be recited afterwards.

2. While reciting *Baruḥ sheamar*, we take the two front *tzitzit* of the *tallit* and stand up. Upon concluding the benediction with the words *Mehullal batishbaḥot* (extolled with praises), we kiss the *tzitzit* and release them from our hands. All *Pesuke dezimerah* should be recited in a moderate, pleasant voice and not hurriedly. Attention should be paid to each and every word, as though we were counting money, and we should bear in mind the significance of the words. The verse *Poteaḥ et yadeḥa* (Thou openest Thy hand) etc., especially should be read with great fervor, inasmuch as we beseech God for our own food and for the food of all Israel. If we happen to read this verse absent-mindedly, we must read it again attentively. In the prayer *Hodu ladonai* (praise ye the Lord), we must pause briefly between the words *Elilim* (idols) and *Vadonai* (and the Lord), so that it may not sound as if *Vadonai* is connected with *Elilim*.

3. While reciting the *Pesuke dezimerah*, we must take care not to touch any part of the body or head, which is generally covered, and needless to say that it must not be done during the subsequent prayers. It is likewise forbidden to touch the phlegm of the nose or the wax of the ear, except by means of a handkerchief. If we do happen to touch it, we must wash our hands. If

we are then in the midst of a prayer and we are unable to go about looking for water, we may clean our hands with pebbles, or rub them against the wall, and the like.

4. *Mizemor letodah* (a Psalm of thanksgiving offering) should be recited while standing and in a cheerful tone, for it is in place of a thanksgiving offering. From *Vayevareḥ david* (and David blessed) as far as *Attah hu adonai haelohim* (Thou art the Lord God), should also be recited while standing. The *Shirah* (Song of Moses, *Az yashir*), should likewise be recited while standing, and with joy and fervor. One should also stand up while reciting the benediction *Yishtabaḥ* (praised be).

5. The Psalm *Mizemor letodah* (a Psalm of thanksgiving) is omitted on Sabbaths and on festivals, because it is in lieu of a freewill thanksgiving offering, and neither vows nor freewill sacrifices may be offered on these days. This Psalm is also omitted during *Ḥol Hamoed* (Intermediate Days) of Passover, as no thanksgiving sacrifice can be offered during those days, for the reason that with the thanksgiving sacrifice, ten leavened loaves must be offered; nor can this sacrifice be brought on the day preceding the Passover, for the reason that they may not be able to finish the breads before the time limit set for eating *ḥametz*, and then they will have to be burnt; nor can it be brought on the day before the Day of Atonement, because there is not sufficient time for the consumption of the breads, thereby causing holy things to become defective.

6. If a man arrives late in the synagogue, after the congregation started to pray, and if by praying according to the prescribed order, he will not be able to read the *Shemoneh esreh* together with the congregation, since reciting the *Shemoneh esreh* with the congregation is of primary importance, he may omit some parts of the prayers, (as will be explained herein below) and join the congregational prayer. However, the benediction *Al netilat yadayim* (concerning the washing of the hands), the blessings over the Torah, and the benediction *Elohai neshamah* (O my God, the soul, etc)., must always be recited before the *Shemoneh esreh*. Therefore, if he neglected to recite these benedictions at home, he must recite them at the synagogue, even if on that account he will not be able to recite the *Shemoneh esreh* simultaneously with the congregation. The morning *Shema*, together with the benedictions, must also be recited before the *Shemoneh esreh*; that is, we must begin with the benediction *Yotzer or* (who formest light, etc)., and then continue to pray according to the order given in the prayer book, till after the *Shemoneh esreh* without interruption. But the other benedictions, the whole order of prayers, and the *Pesuke dezimerah* except the benedictions *Baruḥ sheamar* (blessed be He who said), and *Yishtabaḥ* (praised be) may be read, even after the *Shemoneh esreh*.

7. Therefore, if after having recited the three benedictions mentioned above (*Al netilat yadayim*, the blessings over the Torah, and *Elohai neshamah*) and having put on the *tallit* and the *tefillin*, the worshiper sees that he will be unable to pray the *Shemoneh esreh* with the congregation, unless he omits everything else and begins with *Yotzer or* (who formest the light), he may begin from there. If he has enough time, he should also recite *Baruḥ sheamar*, and *Tehillah ledavid* (a Psalm of praise of David) to the end, that is, to *Shem*

kadsho leolam vaed (His holy name forever and ever); if he has more time, he should also recite *Haleluyah, halelu el bekadsho* (praise ye the Lord, praise God in His sanctuary), up to *Kal haneshamah tehallel yah, haleluyah* (let everything that hath breath praise the Lord; praise ye the Lord); if he has more time, he should also recite *Haleluyah, halelu et adonai min hashamayim* (praise ye the Lord. Praise ye the Lord from the heavens), etc.; if he has more time, he should recite the rest of the *Haleluyot*; if he has still more time, he should also recite *Vayevareḥ david* (and David blessed) up to *Leshem tifarteḥa* (Thy glorious name); and if he has yet more time, he should also recite *Hodu* (O give thanks) up to *Vehu raḥum* and then skip up to *Vehu raḥum* which precedes *Ashre* (happy are they), and begin to read from there. If he has not enough time to read all the special Psalms that are added on the Sabbath and on the festivals, then all the Psalms and verses read daily have preference. If the worshiper can spare some time to recite a part of the special additions, it seems to me, that on the Sabbath and on the Day of Atonement, preference is to be given to the Psalm *Mizemor shir leyom hashabbat* (a Psalm, a Song, for the Sabbath day) and the great *Hallel*, that is, *Hodu ladonai ki tov* (O give thanks unto the Lord, for He is good), etc. On any other festival, the great *Hallel* alone has the preference. Thereafter, the following order is to be observed; the Psalm *Lamenatzeaḥ* (for the chief musician), *Ledavid beshanoto* (a Psalm of David, when he changed) etc., and *Tefillah lemoshe* (a prayer of Moses). All these Psalms and verses should be read before reciting *Yishtabaḥ*; but after concluding the prayers, the worshiper should complete the omitted parts. Only the benedictions *Baruḥ sheamar* and *Yishtabaḥ* cannot be read after the prayers. If the worshiper sees that even if he begins with the benediction *Yotzer or* he will not be able to read the *Shemoneh esreh* with the congregation, unless he reads the prayers very quickly, then it is best that he pray by himself, according to the prescribed order, slowly and meditatively.

8. If one comes to the synagogue when the congregation begins to recite the *Pesuke dezimerah*, and one has no *tallit* and *tefillin*, but expects to get them later, one may recite the *Pesuke dezimerah* with the congregation, and put the *tallit* and *tefillin* on later when they come, after saying *Yishtabaḥ* (praised be), before the benediction *Yotzer or* (who formest light), pronouncing the necessary benedictions. If one thinks that by putting them on, one will be prevented from praying the *Shemoneh esreh* with the congregation, one may omit the prayers from *Vehu raḥum* contained in *Hodu* (O give thanks) up to *Vehu raḥum* preceding *Ashre* (happy are they); or omit from *Vayosha adonai* (thus the Lord saved) up to *Yishtabaḥ*; and he should recite only the most important Psalms, as is provided for in the preceding Section, so as to have sufficient time to put them on after he has recited *Yishtabaḥ* and before the Reader has said the *kaddish*.

Chapter 15

Kaddish, Barḥu, Minyan and Ḥazan

1. After *Yishtabaḥ*, the *ḥazan* recites the half-*kaddish*. But neither *kaddish*, nor *Barḥu*, nor *kedushah* may be said, nor may the Torah be read, unless ten male adults are present. If fewer than ten are present during the

recital of *Yishtabaḥ*, and the number is completed later, the *ḥazan* should not recite the half-*kaddish*, because *kaddish* is to be said only after a prayer is recited by ten. The worshipers should therefore, wait until ten assemble before saying *Yishtabaḥ*. They must wait about half an hour but no longer, then say *Yishtabaḥ* and thereafter wait, and when ten men assemble, they first recite some Biblical verses, and then the *ḥazan* recites the half-*kaddish*.

2. A male adult is one who is thirteen years old, and is going on his fourteenth year; for instance, if he was born on *Rosh Ḥodesh* (New Moon) of the month of *Nisan*, then at the beginning of the night of the month of *Nisan*, after thirteen years, he becomes an adult. If a male was born in the month of *Adar* in a regular year, and when he is to become an adult, it is an intercalated year, when there are two *Adars*, he does not reach his majority before the second *Adar*; but if he were born in an intercalated year in the first *Adar*, he becomes an adult in the first *Adar*. If he were born in an intercalated year, and when he becomes an adult, it is a regular year, then whether he was born in the first *Adar* or in the second *Adar*, he becomes an adult on the date of the present *Adar*. It follows, then, that sometimes a male, born before another, may become an adult later than the other; for instance, if both males were born in an intercalated year, one on the twentieth day of the first *Adar* and the other on the tenth day of the second *Adar*, and they reach their majority in a plain year, then the former who was born first will become an adult on the twentieth day of the month, while the other who was born later will become an adult on the tenth day.

3. We must take care not to count people by their polls (in a direct manner), when we wish to ascertain if there is a *minyan*. It is forbidden to count in such a manner, even for the purpose of performing a religious duty, for it is written (I Samuel 15:4): "And Saul summoned the people, and he numbered them *with lambs*." It is customary to do the counting, by reciting the Biblical verse (Psalms 28:9): *Hoshiah et ameḥa* (save Thy people) etc., which verse contains ten Hebrew words.

4. It is necessary that all ten worshipers, and the *ḥazan* be in one room, If some of them are in one room and others in another, they do not constitute a quorum, even though there is an open door between them. Even if the majority of the *minyan* are in the synagogue and a minority are outside in the front of the synagogue, the latter do not combine with the majority to complete a *minyan*; even if the latter are standing on the outer part of the

threshold, that is, when the door closes, this spot remains outside, even though at present the door is open, it is considered as an outside place. All this is true only with reference to completing the *minyan,* but if there are ten people in one room reciting the *kaddish, barḥu,* or the *kedushah,* then any one who hears their voices may join them in the responsive passages, even when many houses are intervening between them. "Not even an iron partition can separate Israel from their Father in Heaven" (Sotah 38b), provided there is no excrement or idols in the spot (where the listener is standing).

5. One must listen carefully to the reciting of the *kaddish* and to make all responses with zeal, especially so when responding *Amen, yehe shemeh rabba* (*Amen,* let His great name, etc.). It is well to respond *Amen, yehe shemeh rabba* in a loud voice, because by doing so, one will frustrate all Satanic malingers and nullify even a seventy-year old evil decree. Nevertheless, one should not scream too loud, so as not to cause people to mock at him and thereby cause them to commit a sin. *Amen, yehe shemeh rabba* should be quickly joined with the word *Yitbaraḥ* (blessed), and then listen when the *ḥazan* repeats it and respond *Amen.*

6. Some authorities hold that it is not necessary to stand at the recital of the *kaddish;* but when the *kaddish* is recited after a prayer which is being said standing, like the *hallel,* for instance, then it is necessary to remain standing till after *Amen, yehe shemeh rabba.* Some authorities hold that it is always necessary to stand while the *kaddish* is recited, as well as for any other sacred matter. This rule of law can be inferred by a deduction from minor to major, from the case of Eglon the king of Moab. For it is written (Judges 3:20): "And Ehud came unto him. . . and Ehud said: I have a message from God unto thee; and he arose from his seat." Now, if Eglon the king of Moab, who was an idol-worshiper, rose for the message of God, how much more so should we, His people, be careful to do so. And it is advisable to follow the more scrupulous view.

7. If there are not nine persons to listen to the *ḥazan,* no *kaddish* should be said, because no communal sanctification may be recited if there are fewer than ten male adults; that is, one to officiate and nine to listen and respond. Nevertheless, if one of the ten is praying the *Shemoneh esreh,* although he may not respond with them, he may be counted in the quorum; and the same is true even if there are two, or three, or four of them praying the *Shemoneh esreh,* for so long as there remains a majority of the *minyan* who can respond, the minority constitutes no hindrance. But if one of them is asleep, he must be awakened, because a sleeping person cannot be counted in the quorum of ten.

8. After the *ḥazan* finishes the half-*kaddish* (after *Yishtabaḥ*), he recites aloud: *Barḥu et adonai hamevoraḥ* (bless ye the Lord who is to be blessed), and the congregation responds: *Baruḥ adonai hamevoraḥ leolam vaed* (Blessed is the Lord who is to be blessed forever and ever); then the *ḥzzan* repeats the last verse; for he should not exclude himself from the congregation whom he invites to bless the Lord, while he himself does not do so. Some people are accustomed to respond *Amen* (after the *ḥazan* concludes the above verse), but the *ḥazan* should in no event respond *Amen* after the congregation concludes the same verse. If the *ḥazan* prolongs the singing of *barḥu*, the congregation should recite *Yitbaraḥ*. This should be recited only when the *ḥazan* is singing, but when he utters the words, nothing should be said by them; they must keep silent and listen to what he says. Even though one has not heard the *ḥazan* say *barḥu*, but hears the congregation respond *Baruḥ adonai*, etc., one may respond with them.

9. It is proper to recite the *kedushah* contained in the prayer *Yotzer or* (who formest light) together with the congregation; but if that is impossible, one may recite it privately.

10. If there is a quorum of only ten present in the synagogue, no one of the ten persons is allowed to leave; and concerning those who do leave, it is written (Isaiah 1:28): "And they that forsake the Lord shall be consumed;" but if a quorum of ten remains, the others may leave if they have already heard *barḥu*, *kedushah*, and all the *kaddishim* till after the prayer *Alenu* (it is our duty to praise). However, even if no quorum of ten remains, the congregation may finish that portion of the service which has been commenced when there were ten (provided that there is still a majority of the quorum left). If the *ḥazan* has commenced the repetition of the *Shemoneh esreh*, he may finish reading it, and the congregation may recite the *kedushah*, and the *ḥazan* may also say: *Elohenu veloheh avotenu barḥenu vaberaḥa* (our God and the God of our fathers, bless us with the threefold blessing), etc., but the *kohanim* (priests) should not raise their hands to pronounce the blessing, and the *kaddish* after the *Shemoneh esreh* should not be recited by the *ḥazan*, for these are not parts of the *Shemoneh esreh*, but different subjects of the service. If the reading of the Torah has been begun with a quorum of ten, and in the meantime some of them left, the reading may be completed, but no additional people should be called up to the number required on that day. Neither should anyone be called up for the *maftir*, but the last one of the ones called, should read the *haftorah* (a section of the Prophets), without pronouncing the benedictions.

11. The *ḥazan* should be a worthy person, as it is written (Jeremiah 12:8): "It sent forth its voice against me; therefore, do I hate it." And our Rabbis, of blessed memory, said that this verse refers to a *ḥazan* who is unworthy and officiates before the public. Who is considered worthy? One who is sinless, whose puberty was unblemished, that is, he did not have a tarnished reputation even as a youth; he must be modest and agreeable to the congrega-

tion, so that they desire his services. He must have a pleasant, melodious voice which appeals to the worshipers, he must be conversant with the Torah, Prophets and the Hagiographa, so that he be well familiar with the Scriptural texts of the prayer. If, however, one possessing all these qualifications is unavailable, the best among them, with respect to wisdom and good deeds should be chosen.

12. No one should officiate without the consent of the congregation. If one officiates without consent, by sheer force and arrogance, no *Amen* should be responded to after his benedictions, for it is written (Psalms 10:3): "And the covetous blesseth himself though he despises the Lord."

13. None should be appointed as permanent *ḥazan* whose beard is not fully grown; but on occasions, any male adult, thirteen years and one day old may officiate.

CHAPTER 16

The Shema and its Benedictions

1. The *Shema* and its three benedictions: *Yotzer or* (who formest light), *Ahavah rabbah* (with abounding love), and *Emet veyatziv* (true and firm), are much more important than the *Pesuke dezimerah.* This also applies to the *Shema* and its benedictions in the *Maariv* (evening) service. The former are divided into sections, and the following are the intervening parts: between *Yotzer hameorot* (the Creator of the luminaries) and *Ahavah rabbah*; between *Haboḥer beamo yisrael beahavah* (who hath chosen Thy people Israel in love) and *Shema yisrael*; between *Ubisheareḥa* (and upon thy gates) and *Vehayah im shamoa* (and it shall come to pass if ye shall hearken); and between *Al haaretz* (upon the earth) and *Vayomer adonai* (and the Lord spoke).

2. Between these sections, it is permissible to respond *Amen* to every benediction that one may hear; and it is certainly permissible to respond to *kedushah, kaddish* and *barḥu*; but one is not allowed to say, *Baruḥ hu ubaruḥ shemo* (blessed be He and blessed be His name). Upon hearing the congregation reading the *Shema,* one should not recite with them the verse *Shema yisrael,* but one should say aloud whatever part one may happen to read, in the same manner of voice that the congregation recites *Shema yisrael,* so as to appear as if one was reading with them.

3. In the middle of a section, no *Amen* should be responded, except after the benediction *Hael hakkadosh* (the holy God), and after the benediction *Shomea tefillah* (who hearkenest unto prayer); upon hearing the recital of the *kaddish,* one may respond *Amen, yehe shemeh rabba mevoraḥ leolam ulealme almaya* (*Amen;* let His great name be blessed forever and ever); and

when the *ḥazan* says, *Daamiran bealma, veimeru amen* (which are uttered in the world; and say ye, *Amen*) one should also say *Amen.* But it is not permissible to respond any other *Amen* in the *kaddish,* because these are not essential parts of the *kaddish.* Upon hearing the recital of the *kedushah,* one should keep quiet, listen to the *ḥazan,* and say with the congregation, *Kadosh, kadosh, kadosh, adonai tzebaot, melo kal haaretz kevodo* (holy, holy, holy is the Lord of hosts; the whole world is full of His glory); one should keep quiet again, and then say with the congregation: *Baruḥ kevod adonai mimekomo* (blessed be the glory of the Lord from His place). One is not allowed to say any more, because the rest is not an essential part of the *kedushah.* Upon hearing the recital of *barḥu,* either by the *ḥazan* or by the one that is called up to the Torah, one is to recite: *Baruḥ adonai hamevoraḥ leolam vaed* (blessed be the Lord who is to be blessed forever and ever). And one must also respond *Amen* upon hearing the benedictions of one that is called up to the Torah. Upon hearing the congregation recite *Modim* (we give thanks), the worshiper, too, should bow and say only *Modim anaḥnu laḥ* (we give thanks unto Thee), but should say no more. Some authorities hold that one may pause upon hearing the sound of thunder, to say the prescribed benediction. Others disapprove of this interposition.

4. The above are the interruptions which one may make in the middle of a chapter. If the worshiper is then reciting the benedictions, he should manage to make the interruption at the conclusion of a phrase; and if he is reading the *Shema,* he should make the interruption between verses. If this is impossible, he may make the interruption even in the middle of a verse, and thereafter, repeat it from the beginning.

5. The rule that no one may interrupt in the middle of a chapter for the stated occasions, does not apply to the verse *Shema yisrael* and to the verse *Baruḥ shem kevod malḥuto leolam vaed.* No interruption may be made, under any circumstances, while reciting these verses. No response may be made, even to a king's greetings. No interruption whatever should be made between *Ani adonai eloheḥem* (I am the Lord your God) and *Emet veyatziv* (true and firm), because it is written (Jeremiah 10:10): "But the Lord your God is the true God." Therefore, no interruption may be made between the words *Eloheḥem* (your God) and *Emet* (true). It is best not to interrupt until after one has also said the word *Veyatziv* (and firm) because *Veyatziv* also connotes *truth.* Thereafter, one may interrupt, as when reading any other chapter. (Nowadays, people are not ceremonious about salutations, and therefore, no interruption for this purpose should be made, even between sections.)

CHAPTER 17

Laws Regarding the Reading of Shema

1. The time when we may begin the reading of the morning *Shema* is the same as that of putting on the *tefillin* (see chapter 10, section 2, above), and it extends to the end of the first quarter of the day, whether the day is long or short. The length of the day is reckoned from daybreak until the

stars become visible to the naked eye. The ideal fulfillment of the precept is to do as the pious men of old, who began the reading, a short time before sunrise, in order to finish the *Shema* and its benedictions at sunrise, and proceed with the prayer immediately thereafter. He who can manage to follow their example will merit great reward. Under no circumstances should the reading be delayed past the first quarter of the day. One should be especailly careful in the summer, when the days are long, and at times the end of the period for reading the *Shema* is before seven o'clock in the morning. Nevertheless, if the time limit has passed, it is permissible to read the *Shema* and its benedictions up to a third of the day. After that time, it is no longer permissible to say the benedictions, but the *Shema* alone, may be read at any hour of the day. (Some authorities hold that even the benedictions may be said all day.)

2. The *Shema* may be read either sitting or standing. If the worshiper happens to be seated, he is not permitted to rise; but it must not be read while lying; and if he is already lying, he should recline to one side. If he is ill and it is difficult for him to lie on his side, then he should at least incline a little to one side.

3. Before we begin reading it, we should be conscious of the fact that we are about to perform the precept of reading the *Shema*, as the Holy One, blessed be He, has commanded us. When we say *Shema yisrael* (hear, O Israel), we must pay heed to the meaning of the verse, namely, that the Lord, who is our God, is the only One, one and alone in heaven and on earth. We should prolong the sound of the letter *ḥet* in the word *eḥad*, so that there be enough time within which to acknowledge the kingdom of the Holy One, blessed be He, in heaven and on earth; and we should also somewhat prolong the sound of the letter *dalet*, enough time within which to think that the Holy One, blessed be He, is the only one in His world and is the Ruler of the four corners of the world (the numerical value of the letter *dalet*), but we must not prolong the sounds longer than that. We must take care not to spoil the pronunciation of the word *eḥad*, by the over-emphasis of the letters. For some of the common people do spoil the pronunciation of the word; some pronounce it *eḥ-ad*, while others pronounce it *eḥadde;* and it is better not to prolong the letters at all than to prolong them and spoil the pronunciation of the word. It is customary to recite aloud the verse *Shema yisrael*, in order to stimulate zeal, and to place the right hand upon the eyes. After saying *eḥad*, we pause a little and then say: *Baruḥ shem kevod maleḥuto leolam vaed* (blessed be the name of His glorious kingdom forever and ever) quietly (except on *Yom Kippur*, when it is read aloud), and we must likewise concentrate on the meaning of the words.

4. We make a short pause, and then recite *Veahavta* (and thou shalt love), and we make a pause between this section and the one that follows: *Vehayah im shamoa* (and it shall come to pass, if ye will listen) etc. We likewise make a brief pause before the section *Vayomer adonai* (and the Lord said), and we must bear in mind that by reading this section, we fulfill the Divine Precept of commemorating the departure of Israel from the land of Egypt.

5. The prayer *Shema* must be read very carefully out of a well-revised prayer book, and attention must be paid to the words uttered. We should take heed not to pronounce a hard letter (with a *dagesh*) in the place of a soft letter (without a *dagesh*), and conversely, a soft letter in place of a hard one. We must make a short pause wherever there is an accent mark: a vertical line like this (|). These rules of law apply also to the *Pesuke dezimerah* (verses of the Psalms; chapter 14, above). We should also accentuate the letter *ayin* in the word *nishba* (He swore), so that it should not sound like the word *nishbah* (he was taken captive). We must also accentuate the letter *zain* in the words *tizkeru* (ye shall remember) and *uzḥartem* (and ye shall remember), so that it should not sound as if we have pronounced them with the letter *sin* (which would then connote, *and ye shall hire*).

6. When reading the prayer *Shema*, we must not wink our eyes, twitch our lips, or point with the fingers; but for the purpose of performing a religious duty, we are permitted to do so when reading the second section of the *Shema*.

7. When we say *Vahavienu leshalom* (O bring us in peace), before reading the *Shema*, we take the fringes of the *tallit*, and hold them opposite the heart while reading the *Shema* in the left hand, between the ring finger and the little finger, and when we read the section *Vayomer adonai* (and the Lord said), which section deals with the fringes, we must also hold the fringes with our right hand. When we say *Ureitem oiso* (that ye may look upon them), we place the fringes on our eyes, look at them, and kiss them. It is customary to kiss the fringes whenever we mention the word *tzitzit*, and hold them until we say the words *Veneemanim laad* (and desirable forever), when we kiss them again and release them from our hands.

8. When we say *Ani adonai eloheḥem* (I am the Lord your God), we must immediately add the following word *Emet* (true). The *ḥazan*, too, must privately conclude the *Shema* in like manner, but thereafter, repeats aloud *Adonai eloheḥem emet.* Everyone must listen attentively to these three words recited by the *ḥazan*, for with these three words are completed the two hundred and forty-eight words in the *Shema* prayer, corresponding to the two hundred and forty-eight limbs in a man's body. Thereafter, we begin with *Veyatziv* (and form), but we do not repeat the word *Emet* again. If we pray privately, we must add before the *Shema* the three words *El meleḥ neeman* (God is a true King), in order to supply the three words we did not hear from the *ḥazan* and thereby we complete the number of two hundred and forty-eight words.

9. If one has been forced to interrupt the reading of the *Shema*, due to an accident, for instance, when one went out to respond to the call of nature,

or when something unseemly has been discovered in the place where he worships, if the interruption has lasted as long as it takes to read the entire *Shema* prayer, he must repeat the *Shema* from its very beginning.

10. If one has read the *Shema* privately and then entered the synagogue and found the congregation reading the *Shema,* he must read the entire *Shema* with them, so that he may not appear as if he does not wish to accept the yoke of the kingdom of heaven, and he will be rewarded for reading a portion of the Torah. The same rule applies to a case when one is at the synagogue and is reciting supplications or other verses where interruptions are allowed, then if he has not yet read the *Shema,* he must read it, together with the congregation, but he must intend not to fulfill by this, the obligation of reading the *Shema,* in order that he may read it thereafter, together with its benedictions. This rule applies also to other things that the congregation may be reciting, for instance the Psalm *Tehillah ledavid* (a Psalm of praise of David), and *Alenu* (it is our duty), and the like. We should read with them even the special festival hymns, so as not to keep aloof from the congregation.

CHAPTER 18

The Shemoneh Esreh (Silent Prayer)

1. The time for saying the morning prayers begins at sunrise, as it is written (Psalms 72:5): "They shall fear Thee when the sun shineth." Nevertheless, if we said the prayers at dawn, we have performed our duty. The time for prayer is until the first third of the day. If, however, we have neglected to say the prayers within this time, even wittingly, we may pray till midday. If we wilfully delayed our prayers until after midday, we can no longer make up for it, and concerning such a man it is said (Ecclesiastes 1:15): "What is crooked cannot be made straight." (Cases where the delay is caused through ignorance or emergency, will be discussed in chapter 21.)

2. On saying *Tehillot leel elyon* (praises to the most high God), before the *Shemoneh esreh,* we rise and prepare ourselves for the prayer of the *Shemoneh esreh.* We must remove the phlegm and saliva or anything that tends to distract our thoughts. Then we walk three paces backward and say *Tehillot leel elyon* up to *Gaal yisrael* (who redeemed Israel). Then we walk three paces forward, in the manner of one approaching a king. We should

make no interruption between *Gaal yisrael* and the *Shemoneh esreh*, not even for the *Kaddish*, the *Kedushah*, or *Barḥu*, because we must closely connect redemption with prayer. It is best to conclude the benediction *Gaal yisrael* simultaneously with the *ḥazan;* for, if we finish it first, it is doubtful whether we need respond *Amen* to the benediction said by the *ḥazan*. But if we conclude the benediction simultaneously with him, then there is no doubt, because no *Amen* is to be responded to our own benedictions. In the *Maariv* (evening) prayer, since the benediction preceding the *Shemoneh esreh* does not end with *Gaal yisrael*, it is permissible to make an interruption, the same as at any other place between one section and another. Before reciting the *Shemoneh esreh*, we say the verse (Psalms 51:17): *Adonai sefatai tiftaḥ* (O Lord, open Thou) etc.; this recitation is not considered an interruption, but a part of the prayer. We should not say the verse (Deuteronomy 32:3): *Ki shem adonai ekra* (when I call upon the name of the Lord) etc. We only say it at the *Musaph* (additional) service and at the *Minḥah* (afternoon) service before reciting *Adonai sefatai tiftaḥ*.

3. The worshiper should be mindful of the fact that the Divine Presence is before him, as it is written (Lamentations 2:19): "Pour out thy heart like water before the face of the Lord." He should concentrate on the prayers, and banish from his mind all thoughts that may trouble him. Let him think: if he were to speak to a mortal king, he would properly prepare his speech and take care not to blunder. How much more, should he concentrate his thoughts when speaking to the Supreme King of kings, blessed be He, because to Him, blessed be His name, thoughts are like spoken words, and He examines all thoughts. Before praying, he should think of the majesty of God, blessed be His name, and of the low state of man, and banish from his mind all thoughts of human pleasures.

4. The worshiper should think of the meaning of the words that he utters with his lips, for it is written (Psalms 10:17): "Thou wilt strengthen their heart, Thou wilt cause Thy ear to listen." Many prayer books with translations have been published, and every one is able to study and understand what he is praying. If he is unable to understand the meaning of the words, he should at least think of matters that humble the heart and direct his thoughts toward his Father in heaven. Should any profane thought enter into his mind, he must cease praying and wait until the thought passes away.

5. He should place his feet close together as if they were but one, simulating the angels, of whom it is written (Ezekiel 1:7): "And their feet were straight feet," (in Hebrew, *regel* foot) that is, their feet appeared as though they were one foot. He should droop his head slightly, and close his eyes so

as not to look at anything; and if he reads from a *Siddur*, he should not take his eyes off the book. He should place his hands over his heart, the right hand over the left, and pray wholeheartedly, with fear and reverence and humility, in the manner of a poor man standing at the door begging for alms, and he should pronounce the words feelingly and correctly. Every one should read the prayers according to his own text, whether it be Ashkenazic or Sephardic; they are both of sacred origin. But one must not confuse the texts, because the words of each text are numbered and in accordance with profound mystic speculations, and nothing should be either added or subtracted.

6. He should be careful to pray the *Shemoneh esreh* quietly, so that only he himself may hear what he says, but not the one standing next to him, as it is written of Hannah (I Samuel 1:13): "Only her lips moved, but her voice could not be heard."

7. He should not lean against anything while praying the *Shemoneh esreh*, unless he is ill, in which case he may read it sitting or even lying down, provided that he concentrates his thoughts upon the prayers. If he is too ill to articulate the words, he should meditate the prayers in his heart.

8. When praying the *Shemoneh esreh*, he should have nothing in his hand except the *Siddur*, or the *Maḥzor* (festival prayer book). Before commencing to pray, he should mark the places to be read, so that he should not have to look for them in the midst of his praying. There should be no barrier between him and the wall, for it is written (Isaiah 38:2): "Then Hezekiah turned his face to the wall, and he prayed unto the Lord." A thing is called a barrier only when it measures no less than ten hand-breadths (forty inches) high and four hand-breadths (sixteen inches) wide, but smaller than this size is not called a barrier. However, anything which is affixed permanently to the wall, for instance, a closet or a chest, is not considered a barrier, no matter how big it may be; neither is a human being considered a barrier. At any rate, in case of necessity, he should disregard it, as long as he closes his eyes, or prays out of a prayer book, so that his mind is not diverted. He must not pray in front of a picture, and if he happens to pray in front of a cloth or a wall decorated with pictures, he should close his eyes. It is forbidden to pray in front of a mirror, even with closed eyes. A man must not pray in open spaces, such as fields, because when we pray in a private place, we are imbued with the awe of the King and our hearts are contrite and humble. However, if we are on the road, we may pray in the open field. If possible, however, we should pray among trees.

9. When praying the *Shemoneh esreh,* one must not belch, or stretch or yawn. If he must do so, he should place his hand over the mouth, and cover it. He must not spit or expectorate, but if there is saliva in his mouth and he is annoyed by it to the extent that he cannot concentrate on the prayer, he should eject it in a handkerchief; and if this is loathsome to him, he should turn to the left and expectorate behind him. If he cannot expectorate behind him, he shall expectorate on his left side. If he cannot do it on the left, he may do it on the right. If he is stung by a vermin, he may remove it from his clothes, so that his attention be not diverted, but he must not remove it with his bare hands. If the *tallit* happens to slip from his shoulders, he may replace it, even when the greater part of it has slipped off; but if it falls off completely, he is not allowed to put it on during the *Amidah,* because it constitutes an interruption. If a book falls on the floor in front of him and causes distraction, he may pick it up between one benediction and another. All things forbidden during the *Shemoneh esreh,* may not be done until after he had stepped three paces backward.

10. When praying the *Shemoneh esreh,* we must stand facing the Land of Israel, as it is written (I Kings 8:48): "And they pray unto Thee toward their land." We should also face Jerusalem, the Holy Temple, and the Holy of Holies. Therefore, we who dwell West of the Land of Israel, turn towards the East (not exactly East, but Southeast). People living North of the Land of Israel, turn towards the South; those living East, turn towards the West; and those living South, turn towards the North. Thus all Israelites turn their faces towards one place, namely towards Jerusalem and the Holy of Holies, because there is the Heavenly Gate, through which all prayers ascend. Therefore, is the Temple called *Talpiyot,* (Canticles 4:4): "Thy neck is like the tower of David built Talpiyot." *Tel,* means a hill, and *Piyot* means mouths, which means, the hill to which all mouths (prayers) turn. If a worshiper prays in a place from which he is unable to turn towards the Land of Israel, he should direct his thoughts to his Father in heaven, as it is written (I Kings 8:48): "And they shall pray unto Thee." If he has been facing either North

or South, and in the midst of the prayer, he remembered that he was not standing properly, he is not allowed to shift his feet, but he should just turn his face eastward. If he is unable to do that, as for instance, when he faces toward the West, he may conclude his prayer in this position, and he should direct his thoughts towards the Holy of Holies, but he should not shift his feet. If one prays in a place where there are pictures drawn on the Eastern wall, one may turn towards any side, although it is not the East.

11. It is necessary to bend the knees and bow four times while saying the *Shemoneh esreh,* at the beginning and at the end of the first benediction, and at the beginning and the end of the benediction *Modim* (we give thanks). When we say *Baruḥ* (blessed art) we bend the knees, and then we say *attah* (Thou) we bow, so that the vertebrae of the spinal column protrude, and we also bow our heads. Before pronouncing the Name (*adonai*), we slowly raise ourselves to an erect position, for it is written (Psalms 146:8): "The Lord raises up them that are bowed down." So at *Modim,* we bend the knees and bow, and before uttering the name of God, we straighten up. We must not bow down too much, so that the mouth be opposite the girdle, because this is an act of ostentation. Old people and invalids, to whom bending the knees is painful, should merely incline their heads. Additional genuflections for the other benedictions, either at their beginning or their end are forbidden.

12. On concluding the *Shemoneh esreh,* we recite *Elohai netzor* (O my God, guard), and before saying *Oseh shalom* (He who maketh peace), we should bow and walk only three steps backward after the manner of a servant who takes leave of his master. The steps should be of average size, the minimum of which is that the toe should touch the heel. We should not take big strides and not take more than three steps, taking the first step with our left foot, the second with our right, and the third again with our left. While still bowed, we should turn our face towards the left, which is the right of the Divine Presence, who is before us while we are praying. Upon concluding our prayer, we should say: *Oseh shalom bimeromav* (He who maketh peace in His high places); and we turn our face towards our right, which is towards the left of the Divine Presence, and we say: *Hu yaaseh shalom alenu* (may He make peace for us). Thereafter, we bow towards the front, and say: *Veal kal yisrael, veimeru, amen* (And for all Israel, and say ye, Amen). After this we stand erect, and say: *Yehi ratzon . . . sheyibaneh bet hamikdash,* etc. (may it be Thy will . . . that the Temple be rebuilt speedily in our days, etc.), because the prayers take the place of the sacrifices in the Temple, therefore, we pray for the rebuilding of the Temple, so that we shall be able to do the actual service there speedily in our days. The reason we take our first step with our left foot, is because people generally take their first step with their right foot, and on this occasion we indicate that it is hard for us to leave the presence of God, blessed be His name. A left-handed person should therefore take the first step with his left foot, which is everybody else's right.

13. Retreating the three steps, we remain standing with our feet close together, as when praying, and we should not turn our face toward the West, nor return to our place, until the *ḥazan* reaches the *kedushah*. When a person prays privately, he should also remain standing that same length of time that would take the *ḥazan* to reach the *kedushah*. If the place is narrow and crowded, or on the day of the festival, compositions are read, we may return to our place as soon as the *ḥazan* begins the prayer.

14. While saying the *Shemoneh esreh*, the worshiper should not blink his eyes, nor twitch his lips, nor point his finger, nor interrupt for the *kaddish*, *kedushah* or *barḥu*. He must remain silent and pay attention to what the *ḥazan* and the congregation are saying, and this will be accounted to him as if he had actually participated in the response of the congregation, albeit not considered an interruption.

15. While reciting *Elohai netzor* (O my God, guard), one is allowed to interrupt for all those things with which one may interrupt in the middle of a section of the *Shema* and its benedictions (chapter 36, above). Nevertheless, if possible, one should first recite *Yiheyu leratzon imre fi* (let the words of my mouth), and if he still has time, one should take. three steps backward (before making the interruption). Some people are accustomed to say the verse *Yiheyu leratzon imre fi* immediately after saying the benediction *Hamebareḥ et ammo yisrael bashalom* (who blessest Thy people Israel with peace), then they recite *Elohai netzor*, concluding it with *Yiheyu leratzon imre fi*, and this is the proper thing to do. It seems to me that in such an event, it is permissible to interrupt while reading *Elohai netzor* with responding any *Amen*. Some authorities hold that before saying *Yiheyu leratzon imre fi*, it is advisable to recite one verse from the Torah, the Prophets, or the Hagiogripha, which begins with the same letter that his name begins, and ends with the same letter with which his name ends. It seems to me that when one repeats *Yiheu leratzon imre fi* twice, one should say the aforesaid verse before the second reading of *Yiheyu leratzon*.

16. It has already been stated before (chapter 12:3), that if a person feels the slightest need to respond to the call of nature, he is not allowed to begin his prayers until he does so. So much more so, a person is forbidden to commence the *Shemoneh esreh*, if he has the slightest feeling that he needs to respond to the call of nature. However, if he had not felt need for it at first, and begins to feel it while saying the *Shemoneh esreh*, whether it be bowel movement or urinating, he should restrain himself until the end of the *Shemoneh esreh*. Even if the need be great, he should nevertheless try to restrain himself as long as possible and not go out before he had said *Hamebareḥ et ammo Yisrael bashalom* (who blesseth His people Israel with peace).

17. If a worshiper feels that a bad odor is about to come out of him, and he cannot restrain himself, then if he prays privately at his own house, he should walk four cubits either backwards or to his side, let off wind, wait until the odor vanishes, and then return to his place and say: "Master of the Worlds! Thou hast created us full of orifices and vessels. Our shame and disgrace are revealed and known unto Thee. We are a shame and a disgrace while we are alive, and worms when we are dead." After that he may conclude his prayer. If a person lets off wind accidently at the place where he prays, or when he prays with a congregation and he would be embarrassed to walk backward, then he need not walk away from his place, nor need he say "Master," etc., but he should wait until the odor vanishes and conclude his prayer.

18. It is forbidden to sit within four cubits of one praying the *Shemoneh esreh,* either in front of him, in the back of him, or at his side. If the one seated is engaged in something which pertains to the prayer, then he need not keep away. Some authorities are more lenient about this and hold that even if the one seated is not engaged in something appertaining to prayer, but is engaged in the study of the Law, he need not keep away. The God-fearing should not sit in front of one praying the *Shemoneh esreh,* as far as his eyes can see, even when engaged in reading the prayer *Shema,* but one may sit in the back of him or at his side. In any case, one is allowed to stand in front of one praying the *Shemoneh esreh.*

19. A feeble person should not be prevented from remaining seated within four cubits of one praying the *Shemoneh esreh.*

20. If a person is sitting down, and another one comes along and starts praying either at his side or in front of him, so that the one seated is now behind the one who prays, the former need not rise, since the latter came within his limits. If, however, the latter has started praying behind the one seated, so that the former is now in front of him, the former must rise. All this is true only when the praying is done in his own house, but if he prays in a house designated for a permanent quorum of ten to pray, and especially in a synagogue which is designated for public prayers, then even if he has sat down at first, he must rise.

21. It is forbidden to pass within four cubits in front of one praying the *Shemoneh esreh.* Therefore, if one concludes his prayer and the one standing behind him is still praying, the former must not step backward the required three steps, because it is equivalent to passing in front of a praying man. It is permissible, however, to pass at his side and certainly behind him.

22. If a person is intoxicated to the extent that he would not be able to speak with the deference due a great and respected person, he is not permitted to say the *Shemoneh esreh.* If a man does say the *Shemoneh esreh,* in such a condition, his prayer is considered an abomination, and he is obliged to repeat the prayer when he is sober. If the time limit for prayer has passed, then he

must make up for it by incorporating the *Shemoneh esreh* in the next prayer, in accordance with the rules of law applying to one who neglects to pray, unwittingly and by force. (See chapter 21, below.)

CHAPTER 19

Laws Concerning "Mashiv Haruaḥ" and "Tal Umatar"

1. During the winter, we include in the *Shemoneh esreh, Mashiv haruaḥ umorid hageshem* (Thou causest the wind to blow and the rain to fall). We begin saying it at the *Musaph* service of *Shemini atzeret* (Eighth Day of Solemn Assembly). Before beginning the *Shemoneh esreh,* the *shamesh* announces: *Mashiv haruaḥ umorid hageshem* (as a reminder to the congregation). If he has failed to make the announcement, it is not included in the *Musaph* (silent prayer). A sick person who prays privately, also villagers who have no quorum for praying, should defer praying the *Musaph* until such time as they may be reasonably certain that the townsmen have already prayed the *Musaph,* then they, too, pray the *Musaph* and include *Mashiv haruaḥ. Mashiv haruaḥ* is said through the *Musaph* service on the first day of Passover, when the congregation including the *ḥazan* say it at the silent prayer, but on repeating the *Shemoneh esreh,* the *ḥazan* no longer says it. The congregation then omits it at the *Minḥah* service on the same day, since they have already heard that the *ḥazan* no longer said it. He who prays privately (on the first day of Passover) should pray the *Musaph* before the congregations in the towns do, when the *ḥazan* has not yet ceased saying it. For the one who prays the *Musaph* after the *ḥazan* has stopped saying *Mashiv haruaḥ,* need not say it any longer. There are communities where the custom prevails to say during the summer months: *Mashiv haruaḥ umorid hattal* (Thou causest the wind to blow and the dew to descend). The *shamesh* should make an announcement to this effect before the *Musaph* service on the first day of Passover, then the congregation begins saying it at the *Musaph Shemoneh esreh,* when they stop saying, *umorid hageshem.*

2. If one has neglected to say *Mashiv haruaḥ umorid hageshem,* and one becomes aware of the omission before reciting the benediction, *Meḥayeh hammetim* (Thou quickenest the dead), one may say it at the place where he becomes aware of the omission, providing that it is not in the middle of a sentence. Thus if one becomes aware of the omission after saying, *Umekayem emunato* (Thou keepest Thy faith), one must first add the words, *Lishene afar* (to them that sleep in the dust), then say *Mashiv haruaḥ,* and continue with the prayer *Mi ḥamoḥa* (who is like unto Thee), etc. If one prefers, one may repeat the whole paragraph, that is, say *Mashiv haruaḥ umorid hageshem,* and then continue in the regular order *Meḥalkel ḥayyim* (Thou sustainest the living), etc. But if one has not become aware of it until one has concluded the benediction, *Meḥayeh hammetim,* one must repeat the *Shemoneh esreh* from the beginning. (And it would not suffice to begin with *Attah gibbor,* Thou art mighty, O Lord, because the first three benedictions are in this case, considered as one, so that if we conclude the benediction improperly, we must begin from the beginning of the prayer.) If one forgets to say *Mashiv haruaḥ* at the *Maariv* prayer, or at the *Shaḥarit* (morning) prayer, or at the *Musaph* service on the first day of Passover, one need not repeat the *Shemoneh esreh.*

3. In communities where they say in the summer, *Mashiv haruaḥ umorid hattal* (Thou causest the wind to blow and the dew to fall), if by error one recited the same version during the winter, and does not become aware of the error until after he has said *Baruḥ attah adonai* (blessed art Thou, O Lord), one should conclude the benediction with *Meḥayeh hammetim* (who quickenest the dead). One need not repeat the prayer for the purpose of mentioning *rain*, since one had already mentioned *dew*. But if one becomes aware of the error before uttering the Name (*Adonai*), one should say at the end of the sentence *Morid hageshem.*

4. If by error, one said in the summer *Mashiv haruaḥ umorid hageshem*, if he becomes aware of the error before saying the benediction *Meḥayeh hammetim*, he should repeat from *Attah gibbor* (Thou, O Lord, art mighty), etc. (This is done not because the law requires that it be repeated, but it is simply to make it more evident that *Mashiv haruaḥ* is not to be incorporated in this benediction.) But if he becomes aware of the error after concluding the benediction *Meḥayeh hammetim*, he must repeat from the beginning of the *Shemoneh esreh*. If he only says *Mashiv haruaḥ* and omits *Umorid hageshem*, it does not matter, and he may proceed with *Meḥalkel ḥayyim* (Thou sustainest the living). If by error he says *Mashiv haruaḥ* in the evening prayer or in morning prayer of *Shemini Atzeret* (Eighth Day of Sukkot), he need not repeat the *Shemoneh esreh*.

5. We begin including *Tal umatar* (rain and dew) in the *Shemoneh esreh* at the *Maariv* service of the sixtieth day after the *Tishre tekupha* (cycle), which is about the fourth or fifth day of December, and we say it until Passover.

6. If we neglect to say *Tal umatar*, then if we become aware of the omission before concluding the benediction *Mevareḥ hashanim* (who blesseth the years), we may say at that place *Vetain tal umatar al pene haadamah, vesabenu* (and give dew and rain for a blessing upon the face of the earth, and satisfy us), and conclude the benediction. If we become aware of the omission after concluding the benediction, we should continue the prayer, and when saying the benediction, *Shema kolenu* (Hear our voice), after the words *Rekam al teshivenu* (turn us not away empty-handed) we say, *Veten tal umatar libraḥa, ki attah shomea* (and give dew and rain for a blessing, for Thou hearkenest), etc. And even if we become aware of our error after we have said *Baruḥ attah* (blessed art Thou), as long as we have not uttered the Name (*Adonai*), we may say, *Veten tal umatar libraḥa, ki attah shomea*, etc. But if we become aware of the error after we have concluded the benediction, *Shomea tefillah* (who hearkenest unto prayer), we must repeat from *Bareḥ alenu* (bless this year unto us), etc. If we become aware of the error after saying *Yiheyu leratzon* (let the words of my mouth), etc., we must repeat from the beginning of the *Shemoneh esreh.*

7. If by error we say *Tal umatar* during the summer, we must repeat the benediction *Bareḥ alenu* (bless this year); but if we become aware of the error after saying *Yiheyu leratzon* (let the words of my mouth), we must repeat the *Shemoneh esreh.*

8. If one is in doubt whether he had said *Mashiv haruaḥ*, then if more than thirty days have elapsed from the time this phrase was to be included

in the prayer, so that he had prayed ninety times as is required, the presumption is that he has prayed properly this time, too. If this doubt arises within ninety days, he must repeat the *Shemoneh esreh.* The same rule applies to the including of *Tal umatar;* if the doubt arises after one had already said it ninety times, we presume that now, too, he had prayed properly; but if it is within the thirty days, he must repeat the *Shemoneh esreh.*

9. If by error one read the weekday *Shemoneh esreh* on the first day of Passover, and became aware of the error after he started reading *Bareḥ alenu* (bless this year for us), which, according to law (chapter 76:16, below) he must conclude the entire benediction, he need not say *Tal umatar,* since the congregation also omits it. If the day on which we begin to say *Tal umatar* falls on the Sabbath, and by error he recites the weekday *Shemoneh esreh,* if he began reciting the benediction *Bareḥ alenu,* he need not include *Tal umatar* since the congregation has not begun saying it yet, and the individual must always follow the congregation.

10. If one forgot to include *Yaaleh veyavo* (may our remembrance rise, come), etc., in the *Shemoneh esreh* on *Rosh Ḥodesh* (new moon) either in the morning or in the afternoon services, or in any of the daily services of *Ḥol hammoed* (the Intermediate Days of Festivals), if he became aware of the omission before saying *Yiheyu leratzon* (let the words of my mouth) etc., he must start again from *Retzeh* (accept, O Lord our God); even if he became aware of the omission before he began reciting *Modim* (we give thanks), since he has already concluded the benediction *Hamaḥazir sheḥinato letziyon* (who restorest Thy Divine Presence unto Zion), he must repeat from *Retzeh;* but if he becomes aware of the omission before reciting the benediction, *Hamaḥazir sheḥinato letziyon,* he says, *Yaaleh veyavo,* where he became aware of the omission, and concludes with *Veteḥezenah enenu* (and our eyes behold), etc. If he became aware of the omission after reciting *Yiheyu leratzon,* he must repeat the whole *Shemoneh esreh.* And on *Rosh Ḥodesh,* if he forgets to say *Yaaleh veyavo* in the *Maariv* service, whether *Rosh Ḥodesh* consists of one or two days, as soon as he had said *Baruḥ attah adonai* (blessed art Thou, O Lord), mentioning the Divine Name, he may not repeat that benediction, but must conclude with, *Hamaḥazir sheḥinato letziyon,* and finish to the end of the *Shemoneh esreh.* The reason for this procedure (that we need not repeat the whole *Shemoneh esreh*), is that the ceremony of proclaiming the New Moon was not performed at night.

11. If one forgot to say *Yaaleh veyavo* on *Rosh Ḥodesh* or on *Ḥol hammoed* in the morning service, although one became aware of the omission after praying the *Musaph* (in which we have already made reference to the New Moon or the festival), he must nevertheless repeat the *Shemoneh esreh.* If the time for praying the morning service has passed, he must make up for it at the *Minḥah* service. (See chapter 21, and chapter 20:10, below.)

12. Whenever we are required to repeat the *Shemoneh esreh,* we must wait (before beginning the repetition) as long as it takes one to walk four cubits.

13. If the *ḥazan* makes an error while reading the silent *Shemoneh esreh,* he need not repeat it, so as not to inconvenience the congregation by the delay, and he may depend on his public repetition of the *Shemoneh esreh* (to make up for the error). But if he makes the error in the first three benedictions, he must repeat from the beginning of the *Shemoneh esreh.*

14. On a public or private fast day, we must say the prayer *Anenu* (Answer us) in the *Shemoneh esreh* of the *Minḥah* service in the benediction *Shema kolenu* (hear our voice), and when reciting the words *Beḥal et tzarah vetzukah* (all times of trouble and distress), we conclude with *Ki attah shomea* (for Thou hearkenest), etc. If one forgot to include *Anenu,* and became aware of the omission after uttering the Divine Name in the benediction *Shomea tefillah* (who hearkenest unto prayer), one need not repeat the benediction (in order to include *Anenu*), but after reciting *Elohai netzor* (O my God) at the conclusion of the *Shemoneh esreh* and before leaving one's position, one must say *Anenu* up to *Beḥal et tzarah vetzukah,* and conclude with the verse *Yiheyu leratzon.* If one becomes aware of the error after removing the feet, one need not say it at all.

CHAPTER 20

The Ḥazan's Repetition of the Shemoneh Esreh

1. Upon concluding the silent reading of the *Shemoneh esreh,* the *ḥazan* walks backwards three steps, and remains standing as long as it takes one to walk four cubits. Then he returns to his place and says in an undertone, *Adonai sefatai tiftaḥ* (O Lord, open Thou my lips), etc., and begins in a loud tone *Baruḥ attah* (blessed art Thou), etc. Every one present must be silent and listen with attention and devotion to what the *ḥazan* is saying, and respond *Baruḥ hu ubaruḥ shemo* (blessed be He and blessed be His name) and *Amen* to every benediction as is required. Even studying holy subjects is forbidden during the *ḥazan's* repetition of the *Shemoneh esreh;* and needless to say that there must be no idle conversation. Whoever is able, should remain standing, just as though he himself were praying the *Shemoneh esreh,* either with his eyes closed, or following attentively in the prayer book, what the *ḥazan* is saying. After the *kedushah,* some people are accustomed to remove *Rashi's tefillin* and put on *Rabbenu Tam's tefillin,* but they are not acting according to law.

2. Since the *ḥazan* has already said the silent *Shemoneh esreh* for himself, and he repeats it only for the sake of the listeners, it is necessary that there be at least nine people in the congregation to listen and respond, so that the *ḥazan's* benedictions may not be uttered in vain. Therefore, if there

is no more than an even quorum of ten, the *ḥazan* should not begin the recitiation until all of them have finished praying, so that all might be able to respond.

3. The *ḥazan* must take care that upon concluding a benediction, he should not begin another one before most of the worshipers have responded *Amen.* If he immediately begins another benediction, for instance when he concludes the benediction *Magen Avraham* (the shield of Abraham), he immediately begins reciting the benediction *Attah gibbor* (Thou art mighty), no *Amen* may be responded to the former benediction; and the sin for depriving the worshipers from responding *Amen,* will rest on the *ḥazan.*

4. While reciting the *Kedushah,* every one should keep his feet close together, and when saying *Kadosh, kadosh, kadosh* (holy, holy, holy), and *Baruḥ* (blessed be), and *Yimeloḥ* (the Lord shall reign), he should raise himself on his toes, and it is customary to lift the eyes, and it is best that they be closed.

5. When the *ḥazan* recites *Modim* (we give thanks), all worshipers must bow and recite the *Modim* of the Rabbis while in a bowing posture. If a worshiper recites the *Shemoneh esreh,* and hears the *ḥazan* say *Modim,* if he is in the middle of a benediction, he too, should bow, but if he is either at the beginning or at the end of a benediction, he should not bow, for it is forbidden to make additional bows either at the beginning or at the end of any benediction, besides those provided for by the Rabbis, of blessed memory. (See chapter 18:11.)

6. Before the *ḥazan* says the benediction *Sim shalom* (grant peace), he should recite the priestly blessing *Elohenu velohe avotenu, barḥenu* (our God and God of our fathers, bless us). When he says *Veyishmereḥa* (the Lord keep thee), the congregation says *Ken yehi ratzon* (thus may it be His will), but no *Amen* should be said; the same procedure is followed when he says *Viḥuneka* (and be gracious unto thee), and *Veyasem leḥa shalom* (and give thee peace). This benediction is included only in the *Shaḥarit* (morning) and *Musaph* (additional) services, but not in the *Minḥah* (afternoon) service. On a public fast day when the benediction *Sim shalom* is also included in the *Minḥah* service, then the *ḥazan* also recites *Elohenu velohe avotenu.* But it is not said in the house of a mourner or on *Tisheah beab* (the ninth day of *Ab*) in the morning service.

7. On concluding the repetition of the *Shemoneh esreh,* the *ḥazan* should recite silently *Yiheyu leratzon* (let the words of my mouth), etc., but he need not take three steps backward; the three steps taken by him at the end of the complete *Kaddish,* are sufficient.

8. On a public fast day, if there are ten worshipers who are fasting the whole day, the *ḥazan* should recite *Anenu* before the benediction *Refaenu adonai* (heal us, O Lord), in the morning and afternoon services. If he forgot to recite it, and becomes aware of the omission before he uttered the Divine Name (*adonai*) in the benediction *Rofe ḥole* (who healeth the sick), he should recite *Anenu* there and repeat the benediction *Refaenu* (heal us). If he becomes aware of the omission after uttering the Divine Name, he concludes the benediction *Rofe ḥole ammo yisrael* (who healeth the sick of His people), and then includes *Anenu* in the benediction *Shomea tefillah* (who hearest prayer), and concludes with *Shomea tefillah*, like the individual worshiper. If he forgets to recite it even there, he must say it after the conclusion of the *Shemoneh esreh* without the concluding benediction.

9. The *Shemoneh esreh* is not repeated aloud by the *ḥazan*, unless at least six male adults who have just said the *Shemoneh esreh* are present, since six constitute a majority of the quorum. But if there are fewer than six who have just said the *Shemoneh esreh*, the entire *Shemoneh esreh* is not repeated aloud, but one of them reads aloud up to *Hael hakkadosh* (the holy God), and the *Kedushah* is said, and then he concludes the *Shemoneh esreh* silently.

10. Even as an individual worshiper, the *ḥazan* must repeat if he made an error in the public recitation of the *Shemoneh esreh*. However, if he omits *Yaaleh veyavo* (may our remembrance rise, come), at the morning service of *Rosh Ḥodesh* and *Ḥol hammoed* and has become aware of the omission after he has finished the *Shemoneh esreh*, he need not repeat it, because of the inconvenience the repetition will cause to the congregation. We may content ourselves with the special reference to the day he will make in the *Musaph* service. But if he becomes aware of it before he has completed the *Shemoneh esreh*, he should resume from *Retzeh* (accept, O Lord), as this will not inconvenience the congregation.

11. Every man is duty-bound to recite the *Kedushah* with the congregation and respond *Amen* after the benedictions *Hael hakkadosh* (O Lord, the holy God), and *Shomea tefillah* (who hearkeneth unto prayer). He is also bound to respond *Amen* to all the *kaddishim*, and to bow with the congregation at *Modim*. Therefore, if a worshiper comes so late at the synagogue that he is unable to pray together with the congregation and he is compelled to pray privately, then if the time limit for praying will not pass in the meantime, he should be careful not to pray the *Shemoneh esreh* at such time, when he can lose the opportunity of saying any one of the things mentioned above. He should wait until he makes the necessary responses, and thereafter continue with his prayers. But he must make no pause for this purpose between *Gaal yisrael* and the *Shemoneh esreh*, because the "Redemption" and the *Shemoneh esreh* must be closely connected, he should, therefore, wait before saying *Shirah ḥadashah* (with a new song).

12. When a worshiper prays the *Shemoneh esreh* singly, and when he concludes the benediction *Meḥayeh hammetim* (who quickenest the dead), the congregation happens to say *Kedushah* contained either in *Uva letziyon* (and a redeemer shall come to Zion) or in the benediction *Yotzer* (who formest light), he must not say *Kadosh* (holy) with them, because these *Kedushot* are not similar (to the one contained in the *Shemoneh esreh*). But if the congregation is saying the *Kedushah* of the *Musaph*, although he is reading the *Shaḥarit* prayer, or vice versa (that is, he reads the *Musaph*, and the congregation the *Shaḥarit*), he should respond *Kadosh* with them, because both *Kedushot* are similar.

CHAPTER 21

The Making Up of Omitted Prayers

1. It has already been explained (chapter 18, above), that if we have wilfully delayed our prayers until the time limit has passed, we cannot make up for it. But if the delay was due to a mistake or a mishap, or when we must repeat the *Shemoneh esreh* because of an error made in the prayer, we may make up for it in the following service. In such an event, we first say the prayer which is required to be said at the time, and then we say the overdue prayer; for instance, if we omit the morning prayer, then when the time for the *Minḥah* service comes, we first say the *Minḥah* service, say *Taḥanun* (petition for grace), and immediately thereafter, we say *Ashre* (happy are they), and then repeat the *Shemoneh esreh* to make up for the morning prayer. If we omit the *Minḥah* service, then, in the evening we first read the *Marriv* prayer, wait thereafter only as long as it takes one to walk four cubits, and immediately say the *Shemoneh esreh* for the afternoon prayer, without reciting *Ashre*. If we omit the *Maariv* prayer, then after the morning *Shemoneh esreh* (of the following day), we say *Taḥanun* and *Ashre*, and then read the *Shemoneh esreh* for the omitted evening prayer, and after that we say *Lamenatzeaḥ* (for the chief musicain) and *Uva letziyon* (a redeemer shall come). We are not allowed to taste any food until we have also said the *Shemoneh esreh* for last night's *Maariv*.

2. If one did not pray within the prescribed time, because he thought that he would have sufficient time after finishing a certain transaction, and in the meantime the time set for praying has passed; or if he was occupied with some matter in order not to sustain a loss, and because of that, the time limit for prayer has passed, although it is forbidden to miss the time for praying in order to prevent a monetary loss, it is still considered a mishap, and he is allowed to make up for it. If a person is intoxicated to the extent that it is improper for him to pray, this, too, is considered a mishap, although he began his drinking illegally, when the time for praying was already due.

3. We can make up for omitted prayers only during the service that immediately follows, but if they are delayed longer, we cannot make up for

them; for instance, if we omit the morning and the afternoon prayers, then we can make up for the afternoon prayer during the following evening service, but we can no longer make up for the morning prayers, since two prayer periods have passed, the original morning period, and the following afternoon period.

4. If we omit the morning prayer, on the day when the *Musaph* service is said, we can make up for it after concluding the *Minḥah* (afternoon) service (since the time for praying the *Musaph* is the whole day until the evening, as is the case with the *Minḥah* service, consequently no two prayer periods have passed). However, if we have already said the *Musaph* prayer, we can no longer make up for it, (since we mention the *Musaph* sacrifice in it, it is inappropriate that it should make up for morning prayers). But if the time for the morning service has not yet passed, we may read the morning *Shemoneh esreh,* although we have already said the *Musaph* prayers.

5. One can make up for an omitted prayer only at the time that he offers the subsequent current prayer. But if one has waited a long time after saying the current prayer, he can no longer make up for the omitted prayer.

6. The version of the complementary prayer must be the same as that of the current prayer; thus, if we omit the afternoon prayer on a Friday, then in the evening, we must say twice the *Shemoneh esreh* of the Sabbath, although the second one is read to make up for a weekday prayer, but since it is Sabbath now, we must read the Sabbath prayer, and if by error we read the weekday prayer, we must repeat the *Shemoneh esreh* of the Sabbath. Or, if we omit the *Minḥah* prayer on the day before *Rosh Ḥodesh,* we must read twice the *Shemoneh esreh* at the *Maariv* prayer and include *Yaaleh veyavo* in both. If we omit the evening prayer of *Rosh Ḥodesh,* and we make up for it the following morning, if we forget to include *Yaaleh veyavo* in the second reading of the *Shemoneh esreh,* we must repeat it (although if we forget to include *Yaaleh veyavo* in the evening *Shemoneh esreh,* we are not bound to repeat it). If we omit the *Minḥah* prayer on the Sabbath, then in the evening, we read the weekday *Shemoneh esreh* twice, but with this variation, that in the first reading we include *Attah ḥonantanu* (Thou hast favored us), and in the second reading we omit it. The reason for this rule is, that the prayer *Attah ḥonantanu* is like the *Havdalah* (separating the Sabbath from weekdays), and we do not read the *Havdalah* twice in the prayers. And conversely; if we omitted the *Maariv* prayer on Saturday night, and on the following morning we read the *Shemoneh esreh* twice, we include in the second reading *Attah ḥonantanu,* because the *Havdalah* must be recited in the prayer following the Sabbath.

7. If we neglect to say *Yaaleh veyavo* at the afternoon service of *Rosh Ḥodesh,* and the following day is no longer *Rosh Ḥodesh,* so that even if we do repeat the *Shemoneh esreh* at the evening service, we will gain nothing by it, because we can no longer say the *Yaaleh veyavo,* and without this prayer we have already prayed our afternoon service, therefore, we need not say anything additional in order to make up for the omitted prayer.

8. Although the time for reading the *Musaph* prayer is the whole day, and the *Maariv* prayer is the one that immediately follows it, nevertheless, if we omit the *Musaph* we cannot make up for it at night, because the *Musaph* was instituted in accordance with the prophetic verse (Hosea 14:3): "So will we render for bullocks the offering of our lips," and since the time has passed, no offering can be sacrificed.

9. If the *ḥazan* must recite either the morning or the afternoon *Shemoneh esreh* twice to make up for an omitted prayer, he fulfills his duty by his repeating the audible *Shemoneh esreh* for the congregation.

10. If one is in doubt whether one has read the *Shemoneh esreh,* one need not repeat it. (For voluntary *Amidah* prayers are not offered nowadays.)

Chapter 22

The Taḥanun (Petition for Grace)

1. After the *Shemoneh esreh* we recite the *Taḥanun* (petition for grace), while reposing the head on the arm. And it is not permissible to indulge in secular conversation between the *Shemoneh esreh* and the *Taḥanun.*

2. At the morning service, since the *tefillin* is on the left arm, we rest the head on the right arm, in deference to the *tefillin,* but at the *Minḥah* service, we rest the head on the left arm.

3. The rite of resting the head on the arm, is to be performed while sitting, but in the case of expediency, it may be done while standing. After the *Taḥanun* we say *Vaanaḥnu lo neda* (and we do not know), which is likewise to be recited while sitting, and thereafter we stand up and continue with the phrase of *Mah naaseh* (what to do).

4. The rite of reposing the head on the arm is performed only in a place where a *sefer torah* (Scroll of the Law) is found, but in a place where there is no *sefer torah,* although some other holy books are found there, we do not rest the head on the arm, but we recite the Psalm without doing it. If we pray in the corridor of a synagogue and the door of the synagogue is open, it is considered as though the *sefer torah* is there.

5. Those who pray in the house of a mourner, or in a house where a death has occurred, even if there is no mourner do not recite the *taḥanun* during the seven days of mourning, even at the *Minḥah* service of the seventh day.

It is customary that even when they return home, they do not say it. If a mourner prays in a synagogue, the congregation reads the *taḥanun,* while the mourner himself omits it.

6. The *taḥanun* is not recited in the synagogue if a circumcision takes place there, or when the father of the child, or the *sandek* (godfather), or the *mohel* (circumciser) pray there, even though the circumcision took place elsewhere. If the *Minḥah* prayer is recited in the house where the circumcision took place, either before the feast or during the feast, the *taḥanun* is omitted. But if the *Minḥah* service is said after Grace, the *taḥanun* should be recited. However, the father of the child, the *sandek* and the *mohel* do not say it, even after Grace, because the entire day is considered their holiday.

7. The *taḥanun* is likewise omitted in a synagogue when a bridegroom is present, during the seven days of bridal festivity. This applies, however, only when either the bridegroom or the bride has not been married previously. If a widower marries a widow, the *taḥanun* is omitted only on the first three days. On the day of the wedding, the *taḥanun* is said at the morning prayers, but is omitted at the *Minḥah* service immediately preceding the wedding.

8. The *taḥanun* is omitted on *Rosh Ḥodesh,* on the fifteenth day of the month of *Ab,* on the fifteenth day of *Shevat,* on *Ḥanukkah, Purim, Shushan Purim,* and the two days of *Purim Katan* (the "Small *Purim,*" on the first *Adar* in a leap year), on *Lag Baomer* (thirty-third day of counting the Omer), during the entire month of *Nisan,* on the ninth of *Ab,* on the days between *Yom Kippur* and *Sukkot,* from *Rosh Ḥodesh Sivan* till after the day following *Shavuot,* and on the day after *Sukkot.* The *taḥanun* is omitted at the *Minḥah* service preceding the aforesaid days, but it is read at the *Minḥah* service preceding the day before *Rosh Hashanah* and the day before *Yom Kippur.* The *taḥanun* is also read at the *seliḥot* (supplication for forgiveness) on the day before *Rosh Hashanah,* but is omitted thereafter (in the morning service).

9. Monday and Thursday are days of grace because, during the forty days of receiving the Second Tablets, Moses our Teacher, ascended to heaven on Thursday and descended from there on Monday. We therefore, augment our supplications on these days and we read before the *taḥanun,* Special Supplications, known as *Vehu raḥum.* These are to be read while standing, with great devotion and slowly in the manner of petitions. On days when the *taḥanun* is omitted, these Supplications are likewise omitted.

10. After the *taḥanun,* the half-*kaddish* is recited by the *ḥazan,* and on Mondays and Thursdays, we read while standing, *El ereḥ appayim* (God who art long-suffering)

CHAPTER 23

The Reading of The Torah

1. The person who takes the *sefer torah* out of the holy ark to carry it to the reading desk, should walk with it northward, which is on his right side, and when he takes it back to the ark, he should walk with it southward. The *sefer torah*, however, should always be carried on the right arm. It is the duty of every person past whom the *sefer torah* is carried, to accompany it to the reading desk.

2. He, who is called up to the reading of the Torah should wrap himself in a fringed *tallit*, and take the shortest way going up to the reading desk, and the longest way going down. If the two ways are of equal distance, he ascends at his right and descends at his left. It is customary for the person called up to the Torah, not to descend until after the one called up after him had said the last benediction.

3. The Scroll is opened, and the one who is called up, looks at the passage to be read, and taking hold of the two handles, he closes his eyes, and says: *Barḥu et adonai hamevoraḥ* (Bless ye the Lord who is to be blessed). He should recite this aloud, so that the entire congregation may hear and respond: *Baruḥ adonai hamevoraḥ leolam vaed* (Blessed is the Lord who is to be blessed forever and ever). If the congregation has not heard the person who recites the benediction, even though they hear the Reader responding, they must not respond with him, but wait until he concludes it, and then respond *Amen*. After the congregation responds: *Baruḥ adonai hamevoraḥ leolam vaed*, the person called repeats it, and continues with the benediction: *Asher baḥar banu* (He who has chosen us) etc., to which the congregation responds *Amen*. He then removes his left hand from the Scroll and holds on to it with his right hand only. The Reader then reads the prescribed portion and the one who is called up, follows him silently. The Reader is not allowed to begin reading the portion until the entire congregation has responded *Amen*. It is the duty of the congregation to listen with close attention to the reading of the Torah. After the reading, the one called up takes hold of the Scroll with his left hand also, rolls it up and says the benediction: *Asher natan lanu* (Who hast given us), etc.

4. It is forbidden to take hold of the Scroll with bare hands. It must be held either by means of the *tallit* or by its rollers. Some are more strict about it, and do not touch even the rollers with their bare hands, but by means of the *tallit*.

5. Both the one called up and the Reader, must stand while the Torah is read. They are forbidden to lean against anything, but must stand erect with awe; for, just as the Torah was given in an atmosphere of awe, so must we stand before it in awe. But a feeble person is permitted to lean slightly if necessary.

6. When the one that is called up says *Barḥu* (bless ye) the congregation responding: *Baruḥ adonai hamevoraḥ leolam vaed,* must remain standing, but when he recites the benediction: *Asher baḥar banu,* also while the Torah is read, and during the reciting of the last benediction, the congregation need not stand. However, people who are meticulous in the performance of precepts remain standing, and this is the proper thing to do. However, at the interval between the calling up of persons, it is not necessary to be so strict.

7. If the Reader himself is called to the benediction of the Torah, somebody must stand along side of him; for, just as the Torah was given through an intermediary, our teacher Moses, peace be unto him, so we, too, must proceed in the same manner.

8. During the reading of the Torah, it is forbidden to indulge in conversation, even regarding matters of the Law, and even between the calling up of persons. It is forbidden to leave the synagogue when the Torah is read, but between the calling up of persons, when the Scroll is rolled up, one may leave the synagogue, if very urgent.

9. If there is a *Kohen* in the synagogue, he must be called up first. Even if he is an unlearned person, but an honest man, he has preference over a sage. Even if the *Kohen* is willing to waive his right to be called first, it is of no avail. After the *Kohen* a *Levi* is called, and if there is no *Levi*, the *Kohen* is called again in his stead, and we say *Bimekom levi* (in the stead of the Levi). If there is no *Kohen* present, a *Levi* or an Israelite is called in his stead, but it is proper that the one who is the most learned among those present should be called. And we say: *Im en kan kohen, levi bimekon kohen* (if there is no *Kohen,* a *Levi* in the stead of a *Kohen*) or *Yisrael bimekom kohen* (an Israelite in the stead of a *Kohen*). If an Israelite is called up instead of a *Kohen,* then a *Levi* should not be called after him. In a community where all inhabitants are *Kohanim* or *Leviim,* a competent Rabbi should be consulted how to act in such a case.

10. If a *Kohen* is reciting *Shema* or the *Shemoneh esreh,* he must not be called to the Torah, even if there is no other *Kohen* present. It is not necessary

to wait for him, for it will inconvenience the congregation. We then call up a *Levi* or an Israelite in his stead, but we do not say *Im en kan kohen* (if there is no *Kohen*), but we say *Levi* or *Yisrael bimekom kohen.* Should, however, the *Kohen* be called while he is reading the *Shema* or its benedictions, he goes up to say the benediction, but he must not read together with the Reader, only listen to him. Nevertheless, before he ascends to the *bimah,* he should pause, if possible at a place where the subject ends. If he is reading the *Shemoneh esreh,* or if he is at the place between the benedictions of redemption (*Gaal yisrael*) and the *Shemoneh esreh,* he should not go up, even if he is called; but if he is reading the prayer *Elohai netzor* (O my God, guard), he should go up. If he is reading *Pesuke dezimerah,* and there is no other *Kohen* present, he may be called, but he should not read together with the Reader. If there is another *Kohen* present, the former should not be called up. And these rules apply to a *Levi* as well.

11. If a *Kohen* or a *Levi,* is called and he is not in the synagogue, the person taking his place should not be called by name, but he should simply be requested to go up, lest people may suspect that the former one was unfit. However, the son of the absent *Kohen* may be called up by his name, for this will no longer be a reflection upon the father, because if the father were unfit, his son would likewise be unfit. If the *Kohen* or the *Levi* cannot go up because he is saying the *Shemoneh esreh,* someone else may be called up by his name, because all can see that the former does not go up for the reason that he is not allowed to do so. If an Israelite who is not present is called, another Israelite may be called up by name, because no question of being unfit may arise in this case. If a *Kohen* or a *Levi* who is not present is called to the last portion of the reading of the Torah or as *Maftir,* someone else may be called up by his name.

12. If there is no *Kohen* in the synagogue, or if a *Kohen* is present but it is not known to the worshipers, and an Israelite who is called up, has already gone up and recited *Barḥu et adonai hamevoraḥ* (bless ye the Lord who is to be blessed), but he has not as yet commenced reciting the benediction *Asher baḥar banu* (who hast chosen us), then if a *Kohen* enters the synagogue, or his presence there becomes known, he must be called, and when going up to the Torah, he, too, says *Barḥu.* As for the Israelite, in order not to be embarrassed, he remains standing there until after the *Kohen* and the *Levi* have been called, and then he is called. But if the Israelite has already uttered the Name in the benediction, that is, he has already said: *Baruḥ attah adonai,* the *Kohen* can no longer be called up. The same rule of law applies to a case where a *Levi* is called up instead of a *Kohen,* and a *Kohen* enters the synagogue before the *Levi* has said *Baruḥ attah adonai,* then the *Kohen* goes up and the *Levi* remains and he is called up thereafter. The same rule of law also applies to a case where there is no *Levi* present and the *Kohen*

is also called in lieu of the *Levi*, and thereafter the *Levi* comes in before the *Kohen* has said *Baruḥ attah adonai*, then the *Levi* must be called up.

13. Two brothers, whether of one father or of one mother, may not be called up to the Torah in succession; nor could a father and son, or grandson be called up in succession, because of an evil eye. Even if they say that they have no apprehension about it, and even if one is called up for the last section and the other is called as *maftir*, they may not come up in succession. The last rule of law applies only to the Sabbath, when no other Scroll is taken out for the reading of the *maftir*, but when another Scroll is taken out for the *maftir*, it is permissible. It is also permissible, when the one called up as *maftir* is not yet *Bar Mitzvah*. In all these cases, if they are by chance called up, and have already gone up to the Torah, they need not come down. Two brothers of one mother, and a grandfather and his grandson should not refuse to go up, if they are called up in succession, and where the occasion requires it, they may be called up in succession in the first instance.

14. If a person is called up to the Torah in one synagogue, and then upon visiting another synagogue he is called up again, he should go and say the benediction, even in the event he is called up to the same section to which he has already been called up before.

15. On a public fast day, when the section *Vayeḥal* (and he supplicated) (Exodus 32:11) is read, only those who fast are to be called up to the Torah. If the only *Kohen* who is present either does not fast at all, or he does not intend to complete the fast after the service, then an Israelite or a *Levi* should be called in his stead. In such an event, it is best that the *Kohen* should leave the synagogue. If another *Kohen* is present, the former need not leave, but he must notify them that he should not be called up. If he is called he should not go up. If the fast falls on a Monday or Thursday, although the section *Vayeḥal* is read, nevertheless, since the Torah is always read on these days, if he has not left the synagogue and he is called up, he should go.

16. Likewise, if a person who resides in Israel where only one festival day is observed, comes to another country where he attends a synagogue on the second day of a festival, he should not be called up to the Torah. The law in such a case is the same as that laid down in the preceding section.

17. It is customary to call up a blind person to the Torah. And although the law is that (Gittin 60b): "The Written Torah must not be recited by heart," since nowadays the Reader chants the portion to him, it is permissible. It is the custom not to investigate whether the blind person is learned or unlearned; it is presumed that he is able to follow the Reader.

18. If a person who is called up to the Torah is shown the wrong place where the Reader is supposed to begin, and he recited the benediction, then the error is discovered, he need not repeat the benediction, whether or not the reading has begun, if the proper place to be read is also unrolled before him, even though it is in a different column, but it follows the place that has been shown to him, because his intention was to say the benediction over whatever is unrolled before him. But if the proper place has not been unrolled before him, but the Torah must be rolled to find the proper place, or even if the place has been unrolled before him but it precedes the place shown to him, he must repeat the benediction *Asher baḥar banu* (who hast chosen us), but he need not repeat *Barḥu* (bless ye), and before repeating the benediction, he should say, *Baruḥ shem kevod maleḥuto leolam vaed* (blessed be the name of the glory of His kingdom forever and ever) for the first benediction which he has said in vain. If he has only said *Baruḥ attah adonai* (before the error has been discovered), he should conclude the benediction with the verse (Psalms 119:12), *Lamedeni ḥukeḥa* (teach me Thy statutes). If the place to be read precedes the place improperly shown to him, by three verses, the Reader starts from the place over which the benediction was pronounced, continuing with the rest of the portion, and the person need not repeat the benediction.

19. No less than three verses should be read to every person called up. Monday and Thursday and at the Sabbath *Minḥah* service, no less than ten verses in all should be read, and it is proper to read to the third one, no less than four verses. But if only nine verses have been read in all, three to each one, they have complied with the law. On *Purim*, only nine verses are read in all, because the subject matter ends there.

20. The Reader should not stop at a place where there are less than three verses to the end of the section, whether it is a *petuḥah* (having the letter *pe*) or a *setumah* (having the letter *sameḥ* at the end of the section). If the pause is made where there are less than three verses left before the next section, and the person called up has already said the benediction after the reading, it is not necessary to commence for the next person called up from the preceding verse. The Reader should commence where he left off, and read three additional verses from the next section. The Reader may stop before a section that contains only two verses. If the section ends in the middle of a verse, for instance, at the beginning of the Sidrah *Pineḥas* (Numbers 25:19), it is permissible to end the reading, even with the verse adjoining it.

21. The Reader may not begin in fewer than three verses removed from the beginning of a section, and therefore, the reading to the one called up before, should not end fewer than three verses from the beginning of a section.

22. The Reader should always begin and end with a subject favorable to Israel, and he should not end where the evil deed of someone is recorded.

23. If only two verses were read, and the person called up has already said the last benediction, the reading must be repeated, and he must say once more both the first and the last benedictions; and since the saying of the second benediction constitutes a distraction, he must again begin with *Barḥu.* The Reader then repeats the two verses and adds a third one. If this happens to the reading of the third person that is called up (and the two persons before him had only three verses read to each), then two additional verses must be read, making a total of four verses. If only two verses are read to a *Kohen,* and the error has been discovered after a *Levi* was called up, then the law is as follows: If the *Levi* has not yet said the first benediction, even if he has said *Barḥu,* this does not constitute the beginning of the benediction and three verses must be read to the *Kohen,* who says the necessary benedictions, and the *Levi* is to wait to be called thereafter. But if the *Levi* has already said the benediction, then the Reader, reads to the *Levi* from the place where the *Kohen* left off (because if the verses read to the *Kohen* should be repeated to the *Levi,* it would be a disparagement to the *Kohanim* that are present in the synagogue, inasmuch as it would seem as though a *Levi* has been honored first). Then after the *Levi* two Israelites should be called, to complete the necessary number of three that are to be called up, because the *Kohen* does not count (since only two verses have been read to him). If only two verses are read to a *Levi,* and the Israelite called up after him has already said the benediction, the two verses read to the *Levi* should be repeated, adding one more verse to them, and then another Israelite should be called to complete the necessary number of three. If there is no *Kohen* in the synagogue, and they called up an Israelite, to whom only two verses were read, and the error was not discovered until after another Israelite was called and said the benedictions, then the reading must be repeated from the beginning of the section for the second Israelite, and the first Israelite should wait to be called as the next one, and after him a third Israelite is called up.

24. A minor should not be a Reader of the Torah, neither should he be called up to say the benedictions over the Torah. (See chapter 79:9.)

25. After the reading of the Torah, half-*kaddish* is said and the Scroll is raised. The one who raises the Scroll should open it so that three columns of the script should be visible, and while it is open, he must show it to the people on the right, on the left, in front of him and behind him, for it is the duty of every worshiper to see the script and say *Vezot hattorah* (and this is the Torah), etc. Then the Scroll is rolled up, and it should be so rolled that the nearest seam be in the center, between the two rolls; if the seam preceding the part read is the nearest, it should be rolled towards there, and if the seam after is the nearest, it should be rolled in that direction, for it is best to lessen the rolling, in deference to the Torah.

26. At the conclusion of reading the Torah, half-*kaddish* is always recited, except at the Sabbath *Minḥah* service and at the *Minḥah* service of a fast day; on these occasions we are content with the half-*kaddish*, said before the *Shemoneh esreh*.

27. After raising the Scroll on Mondays and Thursdays, *Yehi ratzon* (may it be Thy will), is read, to which the congregation listens and responds *Amen.* Whenever the *Taḥanun* is omitted, *Yehi ratzon* is likewise omitted.

28. The Scroll is then replaced in the Holy Ark. It is the duty of all, before whom the Scroll is carried, and also of the one who has raised it and of the one who has rolled it up to accompany it to the Holy Ark.

29. In a place where there is no Scroll, someone should read aloud, out of a *Ḥumash* (Pentateuch) and the congregation should listen, so that the practice of reading the Torah be not forgotten.

30. If a quorum of ten pray and they have no Scroll, none should be brought to them for the purpose of reading out of it, even if they are confined in prison, and even if it is *Rosh Hashanah* or *Yom Kippur.* But if they have prepared an ark or a reading desk a day or two before, so that they have a fixed place for the Scroll, it is permissible to bring one there. For a worthy man who is ill, it is permissible to bring a Scroll for the purpose of reading out of it. Some authorities hold that for a worthy person, even if he is not ill, and for an ill person even if he is not worthy, a Scroll may be brought for them. This rule against transporting a Scroll may be relaxed on the Sabbath when the section *Zaḥor* or the section *Parah* is read, because some authorities hold that these readings are prescribed by Biblical law.

CHAPTER 24

Laws Concerning Errors and Defects in a Sefer Torah

1. If a *sefer torah* is found to be defective due to an error, if the error is a serious one, we are not permitted to read out of it, and we must read out of another one. What constitutes a serious error? A superfluous or missing letter, or if a letter is interchanged so as to alter the reading, for instance, when the word *teomim* (twins) is written without the letter *aleph*, or the word *migreshehem* (with the letter *mem* at the end) is written *migreshehen* (with the letter *nun* at the end), although the meaning of the word is the same, nevertheless since the reading of it is not the same, it is considered a serious error. If the error is such that the word may be pronounced properly as it should be, but it is so written that the meaning of the word is changed by it, for instance, in the verse (Exodus 25:10): *Ammah vaḥetzi raḥbo* (and a cubit and one half its width), if instead of *Raḥbo* (with the letter *vav* at the end), it is written *Raḥbah* (with the letter *he* at the end), although even as it is written,

the letter *bet* (with the *he*) can be pronounced with a *Ḥolem* (a vowel having the *o* sound), nevertheless, since as it is written now, the meaning of the word is different, it constitutes a serious error. But if the error is such that it changes neither the pronunciation nor the meaning of the word, for instance, when the word *avotam* (their fathers) with the letter *vav* after the *bet*, is written without the *vav*, or vice versa; or a word which should be spelled with the additive letter *yod* (to designate the plural), is written without the *yod*, as *avoteḥem* (your fathers), is written without the *yod*, or vice versa, another Scroll need not be taken out because nowadays the Scrolls are not so perfect that we can be sure that one is more fit than the other. But if a radical *yod* is missing, as in the verse (Genesis 21:17): *Mah laḥ Hagar, al tirei* (What ails thee, Hagar, fear thou not), the word *tirei* is found to be written without a *yod* after the *tav*; or in the verse (Genesis 15:1): *Al tira Avraham* (fear not Abraham), the word *tira* is written without a *yod* (which in both instances changes the meaning of the word from *fear* to *see*), then another Scroll should be taken out.

2. If a single word is divided so that it looks like two separate words, or if two words are so close to each other that they look like one word to a child (see section 5, below), or if there is a superfluous word which is either entirely out of place or it is a duplication, or if there is a change in the division of sections, as a *pe* instead of a *sammeḥ*, or a *sammeḥ* instead of a *pe*, or there is an unnecessary division in a portion, or if a necessary division is wanting, all these errors constitute serious defects, and another Scroll must be used.

3. If one letter is joined to another and it is obvious that they were joined after the Scroll was written, it may be used, provided that the shapes of the letters were not changed. However, if it is evident that this has happened while it was being written, then if the letters were joined before they were completely finished, as, when the letter *nun* is connected with the leg of the *tav*, the Scroll is unfit for use. However, on weekdays it is permissible to make an erasure to separate them.

4. If a letter has lost its shape on account of a hole, whether this happened at the time the Scroll was written, or thereafter, the Scroll is unfit for use. If the hole is in the middle of the letter or outside of it, so that the letter has the proper shape but it is not completely surrounded by parchment, and it is obvious that the hole has been made after the letter was written,

then the Scroll is fit for use, because at the time the letter was written it was fully surrounded by parchment. If the ink has faded from any letter so that it is not properly black, the Scroll is unfit for use.

5. If there is any doubt as to whether a letter has its proper shape, it is shown to a child who is neither precocious nor retarded (that is, one who does not understand the contents but knows and understands the letters), and if he reads it properly, the Scroll may be used, otherwise it is unfit for use. If shown to several children and they differ, the view of the majority prevails. It is only when we are in doubt that we may depend on the opinion of a child, but when we are certain that the letter is not as it should be, or when the upper part of the *ayin* or of the *shin*, or the lower part of the *tav* or of similar letters is missing, the Scroll may not be used, even when a child is able to identify it.

6. When the letter is shown to a child, it is not necessary to cover the letters that follow, but it is the practice to cover the letters that precede it. If a letter is severed by a hole and a part of the letter is left below the hole, and we are in doubt whether there is enough of the letter above the hole to make it valid, it is necessary to cover the part below the hole, because the child will naturally combine the parts, whereas in reality it has no connection with the upper part. Also, if the ink of a part of a letter is faded and some trace of it is left, it must be covered so that the child may not connect it (with what is left).

7. If because of a defect, another Scroll must be taken out, if the defect is discovered between the calling of two persons, another Scroll is taken out and the reading is resumed from where it was left off, and the number of men to be called up is completed. And those who have been called up to the defective Scroll are included in the required number. On the Sabbath, however, seven people should be called up to the second Scroll, if possible, because in any event it is the general custom to call up more than the required number. (It will also be in accordance with some authorities who maintain that the first group cannot be included in the required number.)

8. There are diverse opinions and customs regarding the case where a defect in the Scroll is discovered while we are reading out of it, and every community must abide by its prevailing customs. It seems to me, that in a community where there is no fixed custom, it is proper to follow the provisions as laid down in the *Shulḥan Aruḥ;* namely, not to say the benedictions over the defective Scroll. The reading should be stopped immediately, another Scroll should be taken out, and the reading should be commenced from where it has been left off in the other Scroll. It seems to me, that if the reading was stopped in the middle of a verse, the reading in the other Torah should be started from the beginning of that verse, and the portion is concluded. It

would seem that at least three verses should be read out of the correct Scroll. If no three verses are left in the portion of the week, we should begin reading from a verse preceding the one where the reading stopped, and the second benediction should be said. The first benediction need not be repeated, although it was pronounced over the defective Scroll. (And it is self-evident that, if possible, seven persons should be called up to the correct Scroll, as provided for in the preceding section.) The same rule is applied to a case where the reading has not commenced at all, when the defect was discovered immediately after the first benediction. We then take out another Scroll, and the first benediction need not be repeated. In this regard, no distinction is drawn between the last portion of the reading and the other portions.

9. If a defect is discovered in the Scroll, and no other Scroll is available, the reading should be completed to the required number of persons, but without pronouncing the benedictions.

10. Some authorities are of the opinion, that if a defect is discovered in one of the Five Books of Moses, it is permissible to read out of another Book; for instance, if the defect is in the Book of Genesis, we may read from Exodus, and say the benedictions over those chapters. This opinion may be relied upon in cases of emergency, that is, when either there is not sufficient time to mend the defect, or the defect is discovered on a Sabbath or on a festival. However, this Scroll may not be used at the *Minḥah* (afternoon) service on the Sabbath, because this reading is not so essential, as it was instituted merely for the sake of those who do not come to the synagogue on Monday and Thursday.

11. If the seam between two columns of the Scroll is rent, we may read out of it if the greater part of the seam has remained; if not, we must take out another Scroll. If no other Scroll is available, then if the rent is in that book of the Pentateuch out of which we are to read, we may not use it unless at least five stitches have remained; but if the rent is in another Book, we may read out of this Scroll even though only two stitches have remained.

12. If there is a drop of wax or fat upon a letter or a word, it may be removed on a weekday, but on the Sabbath or a festival, the Scroll may be used only if the covered letters are visible; but if the letters are so thickly covered that they are no longer visible, then the Scroll may be used and the benedictions may be said if the letters are not in the place where the reading occurs; if they are in the place where the reading occurs—since it is forbidden to read even one single word from memory—the wax or the fat should be removed indirectly, that is, if the substance is so thoroughly dry that by bend-

ing the parchment it would come off, then it may be so done; otherwise, we may not read out of it. When the fat or the wax covering the Divine Name, is removed on weekdays, care must be taken that none of the letters be erased, God forbid, but the reverse side of the parchment should be slightly warmed so that the wax or the fat comes off of itself.

CHAPTER 25

Laws Concerning Ashre and Uva Letziyon

1. *Ashre* (Happy are they) and *Tehillah ledavid* (A Psalm of Praise of David) (Psalms 145) are then recited, and we must concentrate well while so doing, especially when we read the verse *Poteaḥ et yadeḥa* (Thou openest Thy hand).

2. Thereafter, we read (Psalm 20) *Lamenatzeaḥ* (For the Chief Musician). This Psalm is omitted on the following days: *Rosh Ḥodesh, Ḥanukkah, Purim,* (the same applies to the fourteenth and fifteenth days of the month *Adar I* in an intercalated year), the day before Passover, the day before *Yom Kippur,* and on *Tisheah Beav.* Neither is it said in the house of a mourner. On the day the Psalm *Lamenatzeaḥ* is omitted, *El ereḥ appayim* (O God who art long-suffering) is likewise omitted.

3. The *kedushah* contained in the prayer *Uva letziyon* (and a redeemer shall come to Zion) should be recited with the *Targum* (Aramaic translation). Care should be taken to recite it with great devotion; and the *Targum* should be recited silently.

4. No one should leave the synagogue before reciting this *kedushah.*

5. One should strive to recite this *Kedushah* together with the congregation, and therefore, if a worshiper arrives at the synagogue when the congregation is reciting it, he should recite it with them even before he has said his prayers. He may recite this *kedushah* even before saying the two verses that precede it: *Uva letziyon goel* and *Vaani zot beriti* (And as for Me, this is My covenant), and upon concluding the *kedushah,* he says these two verses. Needless to add, that he may skip *Ashre* and *Lamenatzeaḥ* in order to say this *kedushah* together with the congregation, and say afterwards what he had omitted.

6. Then we say the prayer *Alenu leshabeaḥ* (it is our duty to praise), and this should be said with great awe and reverence. This prayer was instituted by Joshua upon the conquest of Jericho. Thereafter, we recite the *Yom* (Psalm for the day) and the other Psalms, every one according to the custom prevailing in the community.

7. Upon leaving the synagogue, we recite the verse (Psalms 5:9): *Adonai naḥeni* (O Lord, lead me) etc., and we bow toward the Ark, in the manner of a pupil taking leave of his master. When leaving the synagogue, we must not turn our backs towards the Ark, but we must walk out sideways; and so must it be done when moving away from the reading desk (after being called up to the Torah).

8. Upon leaving the synagogue, one must neither run nor walk with great strides, because this would indicate that his stay at the synagogue was a burden to him. This applies only to a case where one goes to attend to his business. But when he heads for the house of study, it is meritorious to hasten.

CHAPTER 26

The Mourner's Kaddish

1. Many stories are told in the *Midrashim* to the effect that because the son said the *kaddish* for his departed father or mother, they were saved from judgment. It is therefore, customary for a mourner to say *kaddish*, to be called up to *maftir*, and to act as *ḥazan* before the congregation, and particularly so at the termination of the Sabbath when the souls are returning to Gehenna; and this is true of every evening, because the judgment is then rigorous. There are many diverse opinions regarding the *kaddish*, based on prevailing customs.

2. During the first seven days of mourning, whether the mourner is a minor or an adult, a resident or a stranger, he is entitled to say all the *kaddishim*, precluding all other mourners. Even if a festival occurs within the seven days of mourning, which has the effect of annulling the seven day mourning period, or if the festival occurs after the seven days of mourning which has the effect of annulling the first thirty days of mourning, the law regarding the *kaddish* remains unchanged. The principle that a part of the day is considered as the entire day (chapter 216, below), likewise has no application to the *kaddish;* so that even at the *Minḥah* service of the seventh day, the mourner has the preference of saying all the *kaddishim*. The first seven days of mourning as well as the first thirty days are counted from the day of the burial. If the mourner does not become aware of his loss immediately and thereafter begins to observe the seven days of mourning, he has no preference in as far as the saying of *kaddish* is concerned during such period of mourning. If the death occurs on a festival, we likewise count, as regards the *kaddish*, from the day of the burial (and not from the day they begin the seven days of mourning after the festival).

3. If there is also a *Jahrzeit* at the synagogue, and the mourner who observes the seven days of mourning is a minor who attends services daily at the synagogue, the *Jahrzeit* may say one *kaddish*. If there are many people observing the *Jahrzeit*, each one may say one *kaddish*, even if on account of that the minor is entirely deprived from saying *kaddish*; but if there are many who observe the thirty days of mourning, the minor who observes the seven days of mourning is not entirely debarred because of them. If the mourner is an adult who does not attend the service at the synagogue during the first seven days of mourning, even though he prays at his home with a quorum of ten, nevertheless, when he comes to the synagogue on the Sabbath, he is entitled to all the *kaddishim*. Even if there is another one observing *Jahrzeit*, the former is entitled to say all the *kaddishim*, except one *kaddish* over which

lots have to be cast (to determine who should recite it). But if the seven day mourning period is interrupted either by the intervention of a festival or when the death occurs on a festival, then the law concerning a minor is to be applied to him, since he may attend services at the synagogue daily.

4. A minor and an adult, observing the first seven days of mourning, upon coming to the synagogue on the Sabbath, have equal privileges as regards the saying of *kaddish,* and if there is also one who observes *Jahrzeit,* he is debarred on account of the adult, and therefore, the adult recites one *kaddish* more than the minor in this case, that is, the one *kaddish* which the minor was supposed to relinquish to the observer of the *Jahrzeit.*

5. The one who observes *Jahrzeit* and a mourner who observes the first thirty days of mourning, have preference over mourners who observe the rest of the year of mourning; nevertheless, some of the *kaddishim* should be relinquished to them. It is proper to make it a custom that the *kaddish of the Rabbis* and also the *kaddish* recited after the prayer *Alenu,* should be said by the one observing *Jahrzeit* or by the one observing the first thirty days of mourning, while the rest of the *kaddishim* should be recited by the other mourners, if their number equals that of the *kaddishim.*

6. As between one observing *Jarhzeit* and one who observes the first thirty days of mourning, the latter is favored and the former recites only one *kaddish.* If there are many who observe *Jahrzeit,* every one of them is entitled to recite one *kaddish,* even if the one who observes the thirty days of mourning will be entirely deprived from saying any *kaddish,* because the latter will have an opportunity to say *kaddish* on the morrow, but if the former do not say it today, their opportunity is gone.

7. If there are two mourners with equal rights, they cast lots. If one of them won by lot, the right to recite the *kaddish* at the *Maariv* service, the other is entitled to say one *kaddish* at the morning service on the morrow without casting lots, and lots are cast for the third *kaddish* that remains. Lots should also be cast when there are many mourners, and one who won in a lot is excluded from subsequent lots until each mourner has said one *kaddish.*

8. A resident mourner has preference over a stranger (if he is not observing the first seven days of mourning). Between a resident and a stranger, both of whom are observing *Jahrzeit,* the latter has no claim whatsoever. If there is a resident who observes either the first thirty days of mourning, or the rest of the year, and there is a stranger who observes *Jahrzeit,* the latter is entitled to say one *kaddish.* If there is one resident who observes *Jahrzeit* and another one who observes the first thirty days of mourning, and a stranger who observes *Jahrzeit,* the last named recites one *kaddish,* and the resident who observes *Jahrzeit* cannot say to the stranger: "I am entitled to it," for the latter can reply: "I do not take this *kaddish* from you, but from the one who observes the thirty days." The one who observes *Jahrzeit* says the first *kaddish,* the stranger says the second, and the one who observes the thirty days the third.

9. A stranger observing the thirty days of mourning, and a resident observing the rest of the year, have equal rights.

10. If there is a resident who observes *Jahrzeit,* and a stranger who observes the thirty days of mourning, the former says the first and second *kaddish,* and the latter the third one.

11. A stranger observing the rest of the year of mourning is entitled to one *kaddish* among residents if they, too, observe the rest of the year of mourning.

12. A resident in this regard, is one who has a permanent residence in the community, even though he pays no taxes, or if he pays taxes in the community, even though he does not reside there. If a person comes from a different community to say *kaddish* after his father and mother where they have resided, although they have been legal residents there, this son who neither resides nor pays taxes there, does not have the status of a resident. If a resident employs a teacher or a servant who is single, they are considered as residents of the community, but if they have wives residing elsewhere, they are considered strangers. A student at college and a teacher who instructs the children of many residents, although they have wives residing elsewhere, are considered residents of this community. If a resident raises a fatherless and motherless orphan, even for a remuneration, the orphan is considered a resident of this community; but if the orphan has either a father or mother elsewhere, although he raised him as a charitable act, is considered a stranger.

13. If a person who prays regularly at one synagogue or at a House of Study, comes to another place of worship, the mourners there may debar him from saying any *kaddish,* even if he is observing the first seven days of mourning. Such a one has less rights than a stranger, because the latter has no other place where to say *kaddish,* while the former has.

14. A mourner who is competent to act as *ḥazan* should do so, for this is preferable to the saying of *kaddish,* which was originally instituted for minors. A mourner who is unable to read the whole service, should begin at least from *Ashre* (Happy are they) and *Uva letziyon* (A redeemer shall come to Zion), etc. A mourner who has priority rights as regards the saying of the *kaddish,* for instance, one observing the first seven days of mourning or the first thirty days, also has priority rights as regards the acting as *ḥazan.* It is customary that a mourner does not officiate on the Sabbath and on festivals. However, if before he has become a mourner he was accustomed to act as *ḥazan* on Sabbath and festivals, he may also act as such during the mourning period.

15. If two mourners have equal rights as regards the saying of *kaddish,* and both of them are able to act as *ḥazan* and are also equally acceptable to the congregation, lots should be cast between them as to who should officiate up to *Ashre* and *Uva letziyon* and who should conclude it. If one mourner is unable to officiate, or he is unacceptable to the congregation, and the other mourner has officiated, the one who officiated does not thereby lose his rights to the *kaddishim.* Nevertheless, it is proper for him to forego his right and let the one who has not acted as *ḥazan* to say the *kaddish;* especially should he forego such rights when the other mourners are minors.

16. He who mourns the loss of his father and his mother, enjoys no more rights than any other mourner with regards to officiating or the saying of *kaddish,* because one memorial suffices for both parents.

17. It is customary to say *kaddish,* no longer than eleven months after the parents' death, in order not to make the departed appear as evildoers, for the wicked are judged by the Heavenly Court during the first twelve months; for instance, if a death occurs on the tenth day of the month of *Shevat,* the mourner ceases to say *kaddish* on the ninth day of the month of *Tevet.* One should not say any *kaddish* on the tenth of *Tevet,* for this is the first day of the twelfth month, and as only one day in a month is considered as the entire month, then it will appear that he has said *kaddish* for twelve months. As regards the saying of *kaddish,* we count from the day of the burial and not from the day of the death, so that, if the burial has taken place on the eleventh day of the month of *Shevat,* the mourner ceases saying the *kaddish* on the tenth of *Tevet,* because the Heavenly judgment begins only after burial. If it was an intercalated year, the mourner ceases saying *kaddish* on the tenth of *Kislev.* On the day the mourner ceases saying *kaddish,* he is entitled to say all the *kaddishim,* and one who observes *Jahrzeit* or one who observes the first thirty days of mourning may say only one *kaddish.* If there are many who observe *Jahrzeit* or the first thirty days, then he is debarred entirely on account of them. If a mourner knows that his father and mother have been evildoers, belonging to those who are judged by the Heavenly Court for twelve months, it is proper and obligatory for him to say *kaddish* for twelve months.

18. If there are many mourners, God forbid, then, in order to avoid quarrels and strifes, it is customary in many communities for two or three mourners to say the *kaddish* together.

19. If there are no mourners for a father or a mother in the synagogue, any one who has neither father nor mother shall recite the mourner's *kaddish,* in memory of all the departed in Israel. The custom prevails in some communities that any relative says *kaddish* for the next of kin when there is no one present at the synagogue who mourns the loss of father or mother. Even when there are mourners for fathers or mothers, if one desires to say *kaddish* in memory of his grandfather or his grandmother who have died without leaving any sons, or for his son or his daughter who died childless, the other mourners should permit him to say one *kaddish,* after all of them have said *kaddish.* The custom prevails in some communities, that any relative says *kaddish* for his next of kin, even if mourners for fathers and mothers are present; but a compromise is reached between them that the former does not say as many *kaddishim* as the latter. In this respect we must follow the prevailing custom of the community, provided it is fixed and invariable.

20. A daughter should not say *kaddish* at the synagogue. Some authorities hold that a quorum of ten male adults may meet in her home, so that she may say *kaddish*. Other authorities hold that even this is not permissible.

21. If a person is unable to say *kaddish* on the day he observes *Jahrzeit*, either because he is on the road or because there are not enough *kaddishim* to go around, then he may say *kaddish* at the *Maariv* service following the day of *Jahrzeit*.

22. Although the saying of *kaddish* is helpful to the departed parents, it is not the most essential thing. It is far more important, that the children should walk in the path of righteousness, because through this, they obtain Divine Grace for their parents. Thus it is stated in the holy *Zohar* (Beḥukotai, end): "It is written (Malaḥi 1:6): 'A son honoreth his father,' in accordance with the injunction (Exodus 20:12): 'Honor thy father and thy mother.' This is explained to mean that the son must provide them during their lifetime with food, drink and clothes. One would suppose that after their death he is exempt, but this is not so. After their death the son is obligated to honor them even more; for it is written 'Honor thy father,' and if the son walks in the wrong path, he surely dishonors his father and brings disgrace upon him. But, if the son walks in the path of righteousness and his behavior is proper, he thereby honors his father in this world in the esteem of men, and brings him glory in the other world before the Holy One, blessed be He. And the Holy One, blessed be He, has pity on the departed and places him on a throne of glory." A man should therefore, charge his children to adhere, especially to a certain precept. Its fulfillment shall stand him in better stead than the saying of *kaddish*. This is also a good rule to one who has only daughters.

CHAPTER 27

The Study of the Torah

1. Every man should set a certain time for the study of the Torah after praying, and he should not utilize it for any other purpose, even when he expects to make big profits by a transaction. If he has very important business to transact, he should first study at least one verse of the Torah or one law, then attend to his affairs and thereafter, complete his regular assignment. In some holy communities, societies have been formed for the purpose of studying the Torah in public, immediately after praying; and every God-fearing man should join them.

2. Every Israelite, whether rich or poor, healthy or afflicted, young or old, must study the Torah. Even a beggar is bound to set a time for the study of the Torah during the day and night; for it is written (Joshua 1:8): "And thou shalt meditate in it day and night." If a person is unable to study the Torah, because he either lacks the knowledge or he is very much occupied with his affairs, he should at least help support others who devote their time to study, and this will be credited to him as though he himself had studied, as our Rabbis, of blessed memory, explained the verse (Deuteronomy 33:18): "Rejoice, O Zebulun on thy going out and Issaḥar in thy tents." Zebulun and Issaḥar entered into a partnership agreement, by which Zebulun engaged himself in commerce, and supported Issaḥar, so that he could have time to devote himself to the study of the Torah. For this reason, the Biblical verse mentions Zebulun before Issaḥar, because Issaḥar's learning has been acquired through Zebulun. Thus we also find in the *Mishnah* (Zevaḥim 1:2): "Simeon the brother of Azariah said:" etc. Simeon is designated as the brother of Azariah, because the latter was engaged in business and he provided the needs of his brother Simeon, who devoted his time to the study of the Torah, and they agreed between them that Azariah should have a share in Simeon's reward for his study. Nevertheless, every person should strive to study the Torah by himself, be it ever so little, every day and every night.

3. He who is unable to devote all his time to the study of the Torah, but sets certain periods for study, should utilize those periods for the study of recurrent laws which every Israelite must know. He should likewise study the *Agadot* and the *Midrashim* and the books of ethics that are based upon the *Midrashim* of the Rabbis, of blessed memory, and which are instrumental in subduing the evil impulses in man. Happy is he who has set an inflexible rule to study daily, a portion of the book entitled *Ḥok Leyisrael*, and whosoever extends his studies, Heaven extends blessings to him.

4. When a person interrupts his studies, he should not leave the book open, because this causes him to forget what he learned.

5. A person should take care to pronounce with his lips and make audible to his ears, whatever he studies, and he should concentrate his mind upon it, for it is written (Joshua 1:8): "This Torah shall not depart from thy

mouth, and thou shalt meditate on it," etc. The person who pronounces the words with his lips fulfills the precept of "And ye shall study them," although he does not understand the meaning of the words. Therefore, every unlearned person pronounces the benediction over the Torah every morning before reading the verses, and also when he is called up to the reading of the Torah. Whoever makes an endeavor to study the Torah, but is unable to understand it will merit the reward, to understand it in the world to come.

CHAPTER 28

The Scroll and Other Holy Books

1. It is a definite precept devolving upon every Israelite to write for himself a *sefer torah* (Scroll of the Law), for it is written (Deuteronomy 31:19): "And ye shall write for yourselves this song," and our Rabbis, of blessed memory, received it by tradition that the meaning of this command is, that we must write the whole Torah which contains this song (of Moses). If a person inherits a Scroll from his father, he must, nevertheless, write another one for himself. If a person hires one to write a Scroll for him, or if he has bought one and found it defective and he corrected it, it is accounted as though he had written it. A *sefer torah* must not be sold, but in case of dire need, one should consult a competent rabbi.

2. It is also the duty of every man to buy other holy books, such as the Holy Scriptures, the *Mishnah*, the *Talmud*, and commentaries for himself to study and to lend them to others. If one cannot afford to buy both a *sefer torah* and other books for study, then the latter should have preference. Our Rabbis, of blessed memory, said: "It is written (Psalms 111:3): 'And this righteousness endureth forever,' this refers to one who writes or buys books and lends them to others."

3. A man must treat the *sefer torah* with the utmost respect, and he must assign to it a special place which must be treated with reverence, and beautifully decorated. He must not expectorate in front of the *sefer torah*, and he must not handle the *sefer torah* without its cover or mantle. When he sees a *sefer torah* being carried, he must rise and remain standing until it is brought to its place or until it is out of sight. In the synagogue, when the *sefer torah* is taken out or replaced, it must be followed by those before whom it is being carried until it reaches its destination. Also, the one who has raised it and the one who has rolled it up must follow it.

4. Other sacred books, also must be treated with respect. If they are on a bench, it is forbidden to sit on this bench unless they are placed on something which is at least one hand-breadth (four inches) in height. Needless to say, it is forbidden to place sacred books on the floor. It is forbidden to place

a sacred book upon one's knees and rest one's arms upon it. In an emergency, one may sit on a chest containing sacred books, but if it contains a *sefer torah* it is forbidden to do so. The Pentateuch may be placed upon the Books of the Prophets or upon the Books of the Hagiographa, and the Books of Hagiographa upon the Books of the Prophets, or vice versa, but the Books of the Prophets and the Hagiographa may not be placed upon the Pentateuch.

5. The *sefer torah*, or any sacred book or writing, or anything which has served a holy purpose, which has become worn out, must not be burned but secreted.

6. Sacred books should not be thrown around, be they even merely books of law and *Aggada*, nor should they be placed wrong side up; should we find them inverted, we must put them back in the proper position.

7. It is forbidden to urinate before sacred books, but in cases of extreme emergency, they should be placed at least ten hand-breadths (forty inches) high.

8. It is forbidden to make a covering or a mantle for any sacred object out of material used for common purposes. But post facto, if it has already been made, it may be used. However, material used for idolatrous purposes may never be used for sacred objects.

9. It is forbidden to utilize a sacred book for one's own personal convenience, like using it as a screen against the sun, or that people may not see what one does. However, if the sun shines on the book out of which one is studying, one may screen it with another book, since it is not for one's material benefit. One is likewise allowed to place one book beneath the other, in order to raise it for the purpose of studying; but one is not allowed to place one book within another, as a bookmark. A copybook must not be placed on a sacred book for the purpose of ruling it, because a copybook is not sacred before something sacred is written in it; nor is one allowed to put in a book, a sheet of paper or anything similar to it, for the purpose of preserving it.

10. He who destroys sacred writings is guilty of violating the Divine Command (Deuteronomy 12:4): "Ye shall not do thus to the Lord your God." We should protest against some bookbinders who paste sacred writings in the covers. Upon giving sacred books to a non-Jewish bookbinder to

have them rebound, one must be careful to remove the old covers from the books, and hide them away, thus preventing them from being used on secular books by the bookbinder.

11. We are forbidden to buy a *sefer torah, tefillin,* or *mezuzot* from non-Jews at an exorbitant price, in order not to encourage them to steal them, but it is our duty to buy them at their proper value. If the non-Jew wants an exorbitant price for them, we must bargain with him and coax him to sell them at their proper value. If he is insistent, we should let him keep them. We must not ask the non-Jew to sell them at a very low price, lest he become angry and throw them away or destroy them.

12. If one should drop a *sefer torah,* even if it is covered by a mantle, one must fast; and it is customary that those who see it fall, also fast.

13. One must not write a Biblical verse (in the *sefer torah*) without lines. Some authorities hold that one must not write secular words in the Assyrian (*Chaldaic*) type in which the *sefer torah* is written.

CHAPTER 29

Moral Laws

1. Men differ widely in their temperaments: Some are chronically angry, others are of a placid disposition who never become angry, or become angry once in many years; some are too haughty and others too humble; some are sensuous, never satiated with pleasure, others are ascetic, having no desire even for small things which are the necessities of life; some possess unbounded greed, not satisfied with all the wealth in the world, as it is written (Ecclesiastes 5:9): "He that loveth money will not be satisfied with money;" others are improvident, satisfied with the little they have, and they do not even seek to earn enough for their necessities; some are avaricious, afflicting themselves with hunger, keep on hoarding money, and whatever they spend for their food they do so grudgingly, others are spendthrifts, spending all their money lavishly; and the same is true with other dispositions and views: the naturally melancholy and the gay; the villain and the noble; the cruel and the compassionate; the gentle and the hard-hearted, and so forth.

2. The good and right course for one to follow is the happy mean, and not the extreme. One should desire only those things which are actually needed for a healthy existence, and without which it is impossible to live, as

it is written (Proverbs 13:25): "The righteous eateth to satisfy his desire." Neither should a person be too much absorbed in his business, but only sufficiently to obtain things that are required for his current necessities, as it is written (Psalms 37:16): "Better is the little that the righteous hath." Neither should one be tight-fisted or extravagant, but should give charity according to one's means and lend liberally to the needy. One should neither be too jocular and gay, nor too morose and melancholy; but should strive at all times to be happy, contented and friendly. And so with regard to other attributes a person who adopts the middle course is called wise.

3. Pride is an extremely wicked trait, and a person must not betray it even in the slightest degree, but he should accustom himself to be humble in spirit, as the Sages, of blessed memory, have ordained (Mishnah, Abot 4:4): "Be exceedingly humble of spirit." And how can we accustom ourselves to be modest and humble? All our words should be uttered quietly; our heads bent down; our eyes should look downward, but our hearts upward; and we should consider every man greater than we are. If he is more learned than we, then we are duty-bound to honor him; if he is richer than we, we must also honor him, as we are told in the *Talmud* (Erubin 86a): "Rabbi used to nonor the rich;" for we should consider that since the Almighty, blessed be He, has given him riches, he is evidently worthy of it. If he is inferior to us in wisdom or in riches, then we should consider him as being more righteous than we, because if he commits a sin he is considered as an involuntary and accidental violator of the law, but as for us, when we transgress the law, we are considered intentional violators. If we bear this constantly in our minds, we will shun pride and it will be well with us.

4. Anger is also an extremely wicked characteristic, and we must not betray it in the slightest way. We must learn to exercise self control, and not become angry even when a rightful cause exists. When it is necessary for us to exercise our authority over our children and our household, we may pretend to be angry in their presence in order to chastise them, while inwardly we should retain our composure. Our Talmudic sages say (Beraḥot 29b): "Said Elijah to Rabbi Judah, the brother of Rabbi Salla the Pious; 'Do not become angry and you will not sin; do not become intoxicated and you will not sin.'" Again said our Rabbis, of blessed memory (Maimonides, Hilḥot Deot, chapter 2; Zohar Bereshit 27): "If a person becomes angry, it is accounted to him as if he had worshiped idols, and Gehenna will have dominion over him;" as it is said (Ecclesiastes 11:10): "And remove vexation from thy heart, and cause evil to pass away from thy body." The word 'evil' connotes nothing else but Gehenna, for it is said (Proverbs 16:4): "Yea, even the wicked for the day of evil." The life of those who are chronically angry is not considered life at all. Therefore, have our Sages ordained that we should so control our passions as not to become angry even when a rightful cause for anger exists. This is the proper path for man to follow, and it is the way of

the righteous; as our Sages say (Yoma 23a): "Those who are insulted and do not insult; those who hear themselves being reviled and answer not; those who do things for love's sake, and rejoice even when suffering pain, concerning them the Scriptures says (Judges 5:31): 'But they that love Him are as the sun when it goeth forth in its might.'"

5. A man should cultivate the virtue of silence, and should converse only on matters appertaining to the study of the Torah and the necessities of life, and even when talking of the latter, he should not talk too much about them. Our Rabbis, of blessed memory, have already said (Abot 1:17): "And whoso is profuse of words causes sin;" and they said again (loco citato): "I have found nothing better for a person than silence." Rabba said (Araḥin 15b): "What is the meaning of the verse (Proverbs 38:21): 'Death and life are in the power of the tongue'? He who desires life will find it in the tongue, and he who desires death will likewise find it in the tongue."

6. We must neither be frivolous and jesting nor morose and gloomy, but rather happy. Thus said our Rabbis, of blessed memory (Abot 3:17): "Jesting and levity lead a man to lewdness." We must also shun avarice, that unbounded greed for wealth, nor be dejected and idle; but we must learn to look with a friendly eye upon the happiness of others, to be less occupied with business affairs, and devote some of our time to the study of the Torah, and to be content with that little which has been allotted to us; as our sages said (Abot 4:28): "Envy, lust and ambition shorten a man's life." Therefore, a man must shun these vices.

7. Perhaps a man will say: "Since envy, lust and ambition and similar vices, shorten a man's life, I will shun them to an extreme," with the result that he would not partake of meat, nor drink wine, nor marry a woman, nor live in a comfortable abode, nor wear respectable clothes, but he will put on sackcloth, or something similar to it; this, too, is an improper way of life, and it is forbidden to follow it. He who adopts such a manner of life, is called a sinner; for in the case of the Nazarite it is written (Numbers 6:11): "And he shall make atonement for him, for that he sinned by the dead" (written *nefesh,* also meaning *soul*), and our Rabbis, of blessed memory, said (Taanit 11a): "If a Nazarite who abstained only from drinking wine requires an atonement, how much more so does one need it when he abstains himself from everything." Therefore, have our Rabbis, of blessed memory, ordained that we should abstain ourselves only from those things which are forbidden to us by the Divine Law, but not abstain by vows and oaths from things which we are allowed to enjoy. Thus said our Rabbis, of blessed memory (Jerushalmi Nedarim 9:1): "Does not what the Torah has forbidden us suf-

fice thee, that thou hast to vow abstinence from things permissible?" And the Rabbis, of blessed memory, have forbidden us to torment ourselves with fast days more than is required; and concerning all these matters, and things similar to them, King Solomon, peace be unto him, said (Ecclesiastes 7:16): "Be not righteous overmuch; neither show thyself overwise; why wouldst thou destroy thyself?" And he said again (Proverbs 4:26): "Balance well the track of thy foot, and let all thy ways be firmly right."

8. We have already quoted (chapter 1, section 3, above) the passage of Rabbi Judah, the son of Tema (Abot 5:3): "Be bold as a leopard," etc., which means that we should not be ashamed before people who mock us when we are worshiping God, blessed be His name; nevertheless, we should not speak to them harshly, so that we may not develop a disposition of insolence even in matters not appertaining to the worship of God, blessed be His name.

9. We must not quarrel over the privilege to perform a precept, such as, to officiate as *ḥazan*, or to be called up to the Torah, or the like. Just as we find it to be the case with the Shew-bread, that although it was a meritorious deed to partake of it, nevertheless, it is stated (Yoma 39a): "The modest used to withdraw, while the gluttons used to grab and eat."

10. It is in the nature of man to follow the example of his friends, and townfolk. A man should, therefore, associate himself with the righteous, and be in the company of sages in order to learn their ways, shunning the company of the wicked who walk in the dark, in order that one may not learn to act as they do. Said King Solomon, peace be unto him (Proverbs 13:20): "He that walketh with wise men will become wise; but he that associateth with fools will be destroyed;" and it said again (Psalms 1:1): "Happy is the man who walketh not," etc. If one dwells in a community the leaders of which are wicked, and its inhabitants do not walk in the right path, he should move away from there to dwell in a place where its inhabitants are righteous men and conduct themselves properly.

11. It is a Divine Command that we should associate ourselves with the learned, so that we learn to act as they do, as it is written (Deuteronomy 10:20): "And unto Him shalt thou cleave." Is it possible for man to cleave to the Divine Presence? But our Rabbis, of blessed memory, explained it thus (Ketubot 111b): "Cleave unto the learned in the Law." Therefore, it is the duty of every man to make an endeavor to marry the daughter of one learned in the Law, to give his daughter in marriage to a learned man, to eat and drink with the learned, do business with them and associate with them in every possible manner. For it is written: "And to cleave unto Him." And thus commanded our Rabbis, of blessed memory (Abot 1:4): "Sit at their feet in the dust and drink their words with thirst."

12. Every Jew is bound by the Divine Command to love his neighbor as he loves himself, as it is written (Leviticus 19:18): "And thou shalt love thy neighbor as thyself." He is therefore, bound to have the same regard for his neighbor's honor and property as for his own. He who glorifies himself by defaming his neighbor, even though his neighbor is not present, and the insult has not reached him, or even if he does not expressly vilify him, but he compares his own good deeds and wisdom with that of his neighbor, so that it may be inferred from his statement that he is an honorable man while his neighbor is a contemptible person, he has no share in the world to come unless he fully repents.

13. He who hates a fellow-Jew in his heart is guilty of violating God's Law, for it is written (Leviticus 19:17): "Thou shalt not hate thy brother in thy heart." If anybody has wronged you, you must not hate him in your heart and keep silent about it; as it is written concerning the wicked (II Samuel 13:22): "And Absalom hath not spoken with Amnon either bad or good, for Absalom hated Amnon;" but it is your duty to seek him out and say openly to him: "Why have you done this to me, and why have you sinned against me by doing this thing?" If the wrongdoer repents and requests your pardon, you are bound to pardon him and not to be obdurate, as it is said (Genesis 20:17): "And Abraham prayed unto God." In Abot d'Rabbi Nathan (Chapter 16, end) it is stated: "What is meant by 'hatred of people?' One should not say: 'I will love the sages and hate the disciples; I will love the disciples and hate the unlearned;' but it is his duty to love them all, and only hate the heretics, those who entice people to worship idols, the seducers, and the informers." And thus did David say (Psalms 139:21-22): "Those who hate Thee I ever hate, O Lord; and those who rise against Thee do I feel loathing. With the utmost hatred do I hate them; enemies are they become unto me." Is it not said (Leviticus 19:18): "And thou shalt love thy neighbor as thyself, I am the Lord?" What is the reason thereof? Because I (the Lord) have created them. If a person abides by the laws of your people, you must love him; if not, you are not bound to love him.

14. A man is forbidden to invoke the judgment of Heaven against the one who wronged him; but this is true only when he can have redress in a human court. He who prays for Divine judgment to come upon his fellowman, will himself be the first to be punished. Some authorities hold that even if he can have no redress in a human court of law, he is not allowed to invoke the judgment of Heaven against the one who wronged him, unless he first notifies him of his intention.

15. If a man sees anyone committing a sin, or following a wrongful course, it is his duty to convince him that he is doing wrong and cause him to improve his ways, for it is written (Leviticus 19:17): "Thou shalt surely rebuke thy neighbor." But when one rebukes his fellowman, whether it concerns a personal matter, or something which concerns his relations to God,

one must rebuke him privately and gently, and tell him that he is doing it only for his good and to bring him to the life of the world to come. He who has the opportunity of preventing the commission of a sin and fails to do so, will himself be held responsible for this crime.

16. The above rule of law applies only to a case where one thinks that the sinner would listen to him, but if one is certain that the sinner will not heed his words, then he must refrain from rebuking him. For Rabbi Ilaah, in the name of Rabbi Eliezer ben Simeon, said (Yebamot 65b): "Just as it is meritorious for one to say something which will be heeded, even so is it meritorious to refrain from saying anything which will not be heeded." Rabbi Abba says: "To refrain from saying anything is one's duty, for it is written (Proverbs 9:8): 'Do not correct a scorner, lest he hate thee; reprove a wise man and he will love thee.'"

17. It is forbidden to insult anyone either by word or by deed, especially in public. Our Rabbis, of blessed memory, said (Baba Metzia 58b): "He who insults his fellowman in public will have no share in the world to come." And our Rabbis, of blessed memory, said again (loco citato 59a): "It is better for man to be thrown in a fiery furnace than insult his fellowman in public, for it is written (Genesis 38:25): 'And when she was brought forth, she said to her father-in-law, saying: He to whom these things belong, of him am I conceived;' she did not expressly say that it was of him (Judah); she merely hinted, thinking, if he admits it, good and well, if not, I will not expose him." Therefore, we must be very careful not to insult anybody in public whether he be small or great, and we must refrain from calling anyone by an offensive name, or from narrating in his presence, anything of which he feels ashamed. And if anyone has sinned against us and we need to rebuke him for it, we must not insult him, for it is said (Leviticus 19:17): "And thou shalt not bear a sin because of him." This rule of law applies only to a case where the sin is committed against a fellowman, but if one is guilty of transgressing a law relating between him and God, and he refuses to retract, upon being rebuked privately, we may berate him publicly and make his sin public, and we may abuse him in his presence, insult and denounce him until he repents, as all the prophets in Israel have done. As regards such a one, the law forbidding taunting does not apply; for it is said (Leviticus 25:17): "And ye shall not deceive one another (*amito*)," and the Rabbis, of blessed memory, explained that the term *amito*, applies to anyone who is in accord with us in performing the precepts and obeying the injunctions of the Torah. Only as regards such a one has the Torah warned us against grieving him with words, but not against the one who violates the Law of God and refuses to repent after he has been rebuked privately and gently.

18. If any man was wronged by another and he neither rebukes, nor hates, nor bears a grudge against him, but forgives him with his whole heart, this is a saintly virtue, for the Torah only forbids hatred.

19. One must be especially careful to speak kindly to orphans and widows, to treat them respectfully, and not to vex them even with words, because their souls are downcast and their spirits are low, even if they are wealthy. We are thus warned even as regards the widow and the orphan of a king, for it is written (Exodus 22:21): "Any widow or orphan ye shall not afflict." He, by whose word the world was called into being, made a covenant with orphans and widows, that whenever they are crying to Him because of their being wronged, their prayers will be answered, for it is written (loco citato 22): "For if he cry unto Me, I shall hearken unto his cry." All this refers to a case where one afflicts them for one's own advantage, but not when one afflicts them for the purpose of teaching them the Law of God or a trade, or to lead them upon the right path. But even then one must direct them with kindness and mercy, for it is written (Proverbs 23:11): "For the Lord will plead their cause." In this regard, it is immaterial whether he is an orphan from his father or his mother. And how long are they to be considered as orphans in this matter? Until they are able to attend to all their needs by themselves like all adults.

20. A person must be careful not to do anything which may tend to arouse suspicion. As we find it in the case of the *Kohen* (priest) who cleaned the chamber in the Temple, that he did not enter robed in a garb wherein he could hide something; for it is man's duty to please humanity as well as the Almighty, blessed be He; for it is written (Numbers 32:22): "And ye shall be guiltless from God and from Israel." And it is written again (Proverbs 3:4): "So shalt thou find grace and good favor in the sight of God and man."

21. It is a saintly virtue not to accept gifts, for we must have confidence in God, that He will sufficiently supply our needs, for it is written (Proverbs 15:27): "But he that hateth gifts shall live."

CHAPTER 30

Talebearing, Slander, Vengeance and Bearing a Grudge

1. It is written (Leviticus 19:16): "Thou shalt not go up and down as a talebearer among thy people." What constitutes talebearing? A tell-tale is he who goes from one to another saying: "Thus spoke so and so; I have heard concerning him thus and so;" even if the gossip he spreads is true and there is no odium attached to it, it is, nevertheless, a violation of the Divine Command, and it is a grave sin, which may cause death to some people in Israel. For this reason, this command is followed by (loco citato): "And thou shalt not stand by the blood of thy neighbor." Take for example what happened in the case of Doeg the Edomite who told Saul that Aḥimeleḥ had

given to David, food and a sword. Although the thing he told was true and he cast no aspersions on Aḥimeleḥ, for he had done no wrong by it, and even if Saul himself had asked Aḥimeleḥ, he would have told him what he had done, for he had no intention to sin against Saul by this, nevertheless, the talebearing of Doeg caused the death of many Priests.

2. There is a much graver sin than talebearing, and this is slander, that is, when a man talks disparagingly about someone, although he is telling the truth. If one maliciously invents untruths about a person, he is guilty of defamation of character as well. A slanderer is one who says: "So and so has done such and such a thing; so and so were his parents; such and such a thing have I heard about him;" and the nature of the thing tends to disgrace him. To the slanderer the words of the Psalmist applies (Psalms 12:4): "May the Lord cut off all the flattering lips, the tongue that speaketh boastful things." He who listens to slanderous reports is much worse than the one who spreads them. The decree of annihilation against our forefathers in the wilderness was sealed only on account of their tendency to slander.

3. To what extent must one refrain from slander? A man asks of his fellow man: "Where can I find fire?" And the reply is: "Fire can be found in the house of so and so, where there is plenty of meat and fish, and where they are always cooking something," this constitutes slander.

4. There are certain "shades of slander;" for instance, one says: "Silence about that man; I do not wish to tell what happened," or words to that effect. If one speaks of the virtues of a person in the presence of his enemies, this also constitutes "shades of slander," because this will provoke the enemies to tell of things which will disgrace him. Concerning this, Solomon said (Proverbs 27:14): "When one saluteth his friend with a loud voice, when rising early in the morning, it will be counted a curse unto him." Also the one who slanders in a jesting, jocular manner as if he were free from hatred, about him Solomon in his wisdom said (Proverbs 26:18-19): "As one fatigueth himself shooting off fire-brands, arrows and death; so is the man that cheateth his neighbor and saith: 'Behold, I am only jesting.'" One is also a slanderer if he slanders slyly, pretending to speak innocently; and when he is rebuked for that, he says: "I did not know that this was slander."

5. If one utters slanderous words, either in the presence or in the absence of his fellow man; or if one tells things that, if circulated, may cause some damage, either to the person or the property of his fellow man, or even if only for the purpose of vexing or frightening him, this constitutes slander. If those things have already been told in the presence of three persons, it is to be presumed that they have already become known, and if one of the three repeats them to someone else, it no longer constitutes slander, provided he does not say it with the intention of spreading it still further. What effective

precaution shall a man take to refrain from slander? If he is a scholar, he shall busy himself with the study of the Torah, and if he is unlearned, he shall cultivate humility.

6. Said Jeremiah bar Abba (Sotah 42a): "These four classes of people will never behold the Divine Presence: scorners, hypocrites, liars, and slanderers. The scorners may be inferred from the Biblical verse (Hosea 7:5): 'He who stretches (*moshaḥ*) His hand from the scorners.' (According to Rashi, the meaning of the Hebrew word *moshaḥ* in this case is, *pulled away*); the hypocrites we may infer from the verse (Job 13:16): 'For a hypocrite cannot come before Him;' the liar may be inferred from the verse (Psalms 101:7): 'He that speaketh falsehoods shall not succeed before My eyes;' the slanderer may be inferred from the verse (Psalms 5:5): 'For Thou art a God that hath no pleasure in wickedness; evil shall not abide with Thee' (according to Rashi's interpretation of the verse, the word *evil* refers to the slanderer, because in verse 10 of this chapter, it is written: 'For there is no sincerity in their mouth')." Our Rabbis, of blessed memory, said (Sanhedrin 63b): "All jesting is forbidden, except jesting about idols, for it is written (I Kings 18:27): 'And Elijah mocked them,' etc."

7. He who takes revenge upon his fellow man violates a precept, for it is written (Leviticus 19:18): "Thou shalt take no vengeance," And what constitutes vengeance? One person says to his fellowman: "Lend me your hatchet," and the latter says: "I will not lend it to you, for you refused to lend me one when I requested it of you;" this constitutes vengeance, and he is guilty of violating the Law of God. When the latter comes to borrow anything from him, he should give it to him wholeheartedly, and not requite him according to his deeds. It is the duty of every man not to retaliate in mundane matters, for to the thinking person all material things are nothing but vanity, and it is not worth one's while to take vengeance concerning them. And thus said King David (Psalms 7:5): "If I have rewarded him that did evil unto me," etc.

8. There is but one good way to take vengeance upon your enemy, it is to acquire good virtues and walk in the path of the righteous, and you will indirectly take vengeance upon your enemies, for they will be grieved because of your excellent qualities and good reputation. If you will do contemptible deeds, then your enemies will rejoice over your disgrace and shame, and the true vengeance will be theirs.

9. He who bears a grudge against his fellow man violates a precept, for it is written (Leviticus 19:18): "Thou shalt not bear a grudge against the sons of thy people." What constitutes a grudge? Reuben said to Simeon: "Lend me such and such a thing," and Simeon refused to do it. After some time, Simeon came to borrow something from Reuben, and the latter said:

"I will lend it to you, for I am not like you." He who acts like that violates the Law of God: "Thou shalt not bear a grudge." One must obliterate the entire incident from his mind, and not to mention it at all. This is the proper attitude by which the social welfare of the land and commerce among people will be firmly established.

CHAPTER 31

All of Man's Intentions Must be for the Sake of Heaven

1. Our Rabbis, of blessed memory, said (Beraḥot 63a): "Which is a short verse upon which all the principles of the Torah depend. It is (Proverbs 3:6): 'In all thy ways acknowledge Him.'" This means, that in all our actions, even those which we must do in order to sustain life, we must acknowledge the Lord, and do them for the sake of His name, blessed be He. For instance, eating, drinking, walking, sitting, lying down, rising, having sexual intersourse, talking—all acts performed to sustain life, should be done for the sake of worshiping our Creator, or for the purpose of doing something that will be conducive to the service of Him.

2. What is meant by "eating" and "drinking?" Needless to say that we must not, God forbid, eat or drink things that are forbidden. But when we partake of things that are not forbidden, and we eat and drink just to satisfy our hunger or thirst, this is not praiseworthy. While eating and drinking, our purpose must be to gain strength to worship the Creator. Therefore, we must not eat whatever is palatable just like the dog and the ass do, but we should eat only the things that are helpful to, and good for, the health of the body. There are some saintly people who, before partaking of food or drink, say: "I am ready to eat and drink in order that I may gain health and strength to worship the Creator, blessed be His name."

3. What is meant by "sitting," "rising" and "walking?" Superfluous to state, that one should not sit among scoffers, nor stand in the way of sinners, nor walk in the councils of the wicked. But even sitting in the council of the honorable, and standing in the place of the righteous, and walking in the council of the perfect, are not praisworthy if done for one's own gratification. It should be done for the sake of Heaven. Nevertheless, if one is unable to concentrate one's thoughts for the purpose of Heaven only, one should not abstain from doing these things, for work done for a selfish purpose, will eventually lead to doing good for its own sake.

4. What is meant by "lying down?" Needless to say, that it is improper to indulge in sleep for one's own pleasure, at a time when one is able to occupy oneself with the Torah and good deeds. But it is not right to sleep for one's own gratification, even when one is weary and one must sleep in order to rest up from one's toil. One should always sleep and rest for the purpose of gaining good health, so that one's mind should not wander when studying the Law of God.

5. What is meant by "having sexual intercourse?" Superfluous to state, that one should not, God forbid, commit a sin, but it is improper to have sexual intercourse for one's own gratification, even during periods spoken of in the Torah. Nor is it right for one to have it in mind, when having intercourse, to beget children who can be of service to him and to take his place. But one's intention should be to have children to worship the Creator, or to strengthen the body, also to perform the act as an obligation to his wife.

6. What is meant by "talking?" Needless to say that one must not slander, go about talebearing, scoff or engage in lewd tales, God forbid; but even in quoting the words of the sages, one's intentions must be to worship the Creator, or do something conducive to worshiping Him.

7. When a man is engaged in business or in doing some manual labor for his livelihood, his intention should not be merely to accumulate wealth, but to support his family, to give charity, and to raise his children to study God's Law. The general principle of the foregoing is, that it is the duty of every man to well consider his ways and weigh his deeds in the scales of reason. If the thing to be performed may be conducive to the worship of the Creator, he shall do it, but not otherwise. He who accustoms himself to do this, will, as a result, worship God all his days, even when sitting, rising, walking, transacting business, eating, drinking, having intercourse, and so forth. All this was ordained by our Rabbis, of blessed menory, who said (Abot 2:17): "And let all thy deeds be done for the sake of Heaven." And in like manner did Rabbenu Hakkadosh, as told in the Talmud (Ketubot 104a): "When the Rabbi was about to depart, he raised his fingers heavenward and said: 'It is revealed and known to Thee that I have derived no personal gain from them other than what I have done for the sake of Heaven.'"

CHAPTER 32

Rules Concerning Physical Wellbeing

1. Since it is the will of the Almighty that man's body be kept healthy and strong, because it is impossible for a man to have any knowledge of his Creator, when ill, it is, therefore, his duty to shun anything which may waste his body, and to strive to acquire habits that will help him to become healthy. Thus it is written (Deuteronomy 4:15): "Take you, therefore, good heed of your souls."

2. The Creator, blessed be He, and blessed be His name, created man and gave him the natural warmth which is the essence of life, for, it the natural warmth of the body should be cooled off, life would cease. This warmth of the body is maintained by means of the food which the man consumes. Just as in the case of fire, if wood is not added to it, it will be ex-

tinguished, so it is with a man, if he would stop eating, the heat within him would cool off, and he would die. The food is first ground between the teeth and becomes mixed with juice and saliva. From there it goes down into the stomach where it is likewise ground and mixed with juices, the juice of the stomach and the juice of the gall, and is reduced to dregs, and it is boiled by means of the heat and the juice, and thus becomes digested. The limbs are nourished by the pure parts of the food, and this sustains the life of the man, and the impure substance which is unnecessary, is pushed towards the outside. And concerning this process, we say in the benediction *Asher yatzar* (who formest), the following: *Umafli lassot* (and doest wonderfully), which means, that the Holy One, blessed be He, has endowed the man with the nature to select the good part of the food, and every limb selects for itself the nourishment that is suitable for it, and rejects the waste out of the body; for, if the waste should remain in the body, it would cause many diseases, God forbid. Therefore, the good health of the body depends upon the digestion of the food; if it is easily digested, the man is healthy and vigorous, but if the digestive system does not function properly, the man becomes weak, and this may cause a dangerous state of health, God forbid.

3. Food can be easily digested when it is not too much and it is the easily digested kind. When a person eats too much and his stomach is full, the digestion is difficult for the reason that the stomach cannot expand and contract properly and grind the food as necessary; just as in the case with fire, if too much wood is placed on it, it will not burn well; so it is the case with the food in the stomach. Therefore, the person who wishes to preserve his physical wellbeing, must take care to adopt the happy mean, eating neither too little nor too much, all depending upon the nature of his body. Most of the maladies which plague man arise either from eating unwholesome food, or from the excessive eating, even of wholesome food. To this, Solomon wisely alludes (Proverbs 21:23): "Whosoever keepeth his mouth and his tongue, keepeth his life from trouble;" this refers to the person who keeps his mouth from eating unwholesome food and from gluttony, and keeps his tongue from speaking, except what is necessary for his daily needs. A certain sage said: "He who eats little from unwholesome food is not harmed as much as the one who eats excessively from wholesome food."

4. When a person is young, his digestive system is strong; therefore, he is in greater need of regular meals than the middle-aged person. The aged man, because of his weakness, requires light food, little in quantity and rich in quality to sustain his strength.

5. On hot days the digestive system is weak on account of the heat, therefore less food should be consumed than on cool days. Medical scientists have suggested that in the summer, a person should eat only two-thirds of what he eats in the winter.

6. It is a known rule in medical science, that before eating, a man should have some exercise, by walking or by working until his body becomes warm, and thereafter eat. And concerning this it is written (Genesis 3:19): "With the sweat of thy face thou shalt eat bread." And again (Proverbs 31:27): "And the bread of idleness she doeth not eat." A person should loosen his belt before eating; (those fond of *nutarikin* found reference to it in the verse (Genesis 18:5): ואקחה פת לחם. The letters of אקחה read backward are the initials of התר חגורה קודם אכילה "loosen the belt before eating." And the letters of פת לחם are the initials of פן תבוא לידי חולי מעיים "lest you contract a pain in the inwards,") and while he is eating, he should be seated or recline on his left side; and after the meal, he should not move about too much, so that the food may not reach the stomach before it is well conditioned and cause him harm. He should walk a little and then rest; but he should not take a long walk or tire himself out too much after the meal; neither should he take a nap immediately after the meal, before the expiration of at least two hours, so that the gases may not penetrate the brain and cause him injury. Immediately after a meal, it is not good to bathe, let blood, or have sexual intercourse.

7. Men differ with respect to their temperaments; some are hot-tempered, some cold, and others medium. Foods also differ with respect to applying bodily heat, and one whose temperament is medium should eat food which is medium. But one whose temperament is not medium should eat food which is a trifle reverse to his temperament. One whose temperament is hot should not eat hot foods, such as spices and balsam plants, but food which is cool and somewhat fermented; and one whose temperament is cool, should eat food which is a little warm. The food should likewise be prepared according to the season of the year and the place; in the summer, one should eat cool foods, for instance, the meat of tender lambs and goats and spring chicken, and also a little of fermented foods; but in the winter, one should eat food that generates heat. In a cold climate one should also eat hot food, but in a warm climate, cool food.

8. The medium food is wheat bread, but not the kind made out of pure fine flour, because fine flour takes long to digest; but it should contain some of the bran, moderately leavened and salted, and baked in an oven; the other kinds of food made out of wheat are not good. The best kind of meat is that from lamb, one year old and from suckling kids, but the intestines and the heads are not good. Goats, old cows, and old cheese make bad and heavy food. Poultry meat is more easily digested than the meat of cattle, and the best of poultry is that of the hen. Physicians say, however, that the food to which man is accustomed is never harmful even if it is bad, because habit becomes second nature, provided he does not eat to excess.

9. One should not eat the heart of an animal or of fowl, because it is harmful to the memory; neither should one eat any food which has been partly eaten by a cat or a mouse, for the like reason that it is harmful to the memory.

10. A person should eat only when he has a natural desire for food, and not an indulgent desire. A natural desire for food occurs when the stomach is empty; and an indulgent desire is a longing for a particular kind of food. In general, a healthy, strong person should eat twice a day, and the feeble and the aged should eat little at a time, several times during the day, because excessive eating at one time weakens the stomach. He who desires to preserve his physical condition, should not eat before his stomach is purged of the previous food. The ordinary length of time for the digestion of food, for people who eat moderately and have moderate exercises, is six hours. It is best to omit one meal during the week, in order that the stomach may have a rest from its work, thus strengthening its digestive power. And it would seem that this omission should take place on Friday.

11. It is advisable that a person should accustom himself to have breakfast in the morning.

12. If one desires to have several kinds of food at one meal, he should first eat the foods which possess laxative qualities, but he should not mix them with the other food. He should wait a while between the two kinds of food. One should likewise eat first light foods which are easily digested; for instance, fowl meat should be eaten before the meat of cattle, and the meat of small cattle before the meat of big cattle. Food possessing costive qualities should be eaten directly after the meal, and not too much.

13. Since the digestive process begins with grinding the food with the teeth and by mixing it with the juice of the saliva, one should not swallow any food without masticating it well, because it will overtax the stomach and make digestion difficult.

14. It has already been stated (section 7), above that people differ with respect to their temperaments, and therefore, every person should, on the advice of a physician, choose the food according to his temperament, the climate and the season. In general, the ancient medical scientists have divided foods into various classifications. Some foods are extremely injurious, and it is advisable not to eat them at all, for instance, large stale salted fish, stale salted cheese, mushrooms and truffles, stale salted meat, wine fresh from the press, cooked food which has lost its flavor, and any kind of food which has a bad odor or a bitter taste; all of these are like deadly poison to the body. There

is another class of food which is also injurious, although not as bad as the former; therefore, one should eat little of these and only on rare occasions. One should not become accustomed to eat them as one's steady diet, or even eat a little at every meal. These are: large fish, cheese, milk twenty-four hours after the milking, meat of large oxen or large he-goats, barley bread, unleavened bread, cabbage, leek, onions, garlic, mustard and radishes; all of these are unwholesome, and one should eat very little of them in the winter, but in the summer they should be entirely avoided.

15. There are other kinds of food which are unwholesome, but less injurious than the former. They are the following: aquatic fowl, small young pigeons, dates, bread kneaded in oil, and fine flour which has been so thoroughly sifted that even the odor of the bran disappeared. One should not eat too much of these.

16. One should always abstain from eating fruit of the trees, and one should not eat too much of them even when they are dried, much less before they are fully ripened on the tree, they are just like swords to the body. Carobs are always injurious. Pickled fruits are bad, and one should eat very little of them during the summer or in warm climates. Figs, grapes, almonds and pomegranates are always wholesome, whether fresh or dried, and one may eat of them to one's fill. Yet one must not eat them steadily as one's daily diet, although they are the most wholesome of all the fruits.

17. As regards drinking, water is the natural drink for a person and it is healthful. If the water is clean and pure, it is helpful in that it preserves the moisture of the body and hastens the ejection of waste. One should choose cool water for drinking, because it satisfies the thirst and helps the digestion more than water which is not cold. But the water should not be too cold, because it diminishes the natural warmth of the body. Especially when a man is tired and weary, he should be careful not to drink very cold water; because the fat of the heart at such a time is hot and it becomes dissolved, and cold water may cause such harm as to prove fatal, God forbid. Although water is good for the health, it should not be drunk to excess. One should drink no water before the meal, because when the stomach becomes cooled off, it will not digest the food properly. Only a little water mixed with wine should one drink in the middle of the meal, and only when the food begins to become digested, may one drink a moderate portion of water. One should drink no water upon leaving the bath-house, so that the liver may not become cooled off, and surely one should abstain from drinking water, while being in the bath-house. Neither should one drink water immediately after having sexual intercourse, because the natural warmth of the body is then weakened, and it may cause paralysis of the limbs.

18. Wine preserves the natural warmth of the body, improves digestion, helps the expulsion of waste, and is good for the health, provided it is used moderately. A person who suffers from headaches, should abstain from drinking wine, because it fills the head with gases and may aggravate this condition. Wine is good for the aged but injurious to the young, because it increases the warmth of the body, and it is like adding fuel to fire. It is advisable for one to abstain from wine up to the age of twenty-one. A little wine should be drunk before the meal, in order to open up the intestines. Wine should not be drunk when hungry, or after a bath, or after perspiring, or while being tired and weary. It should be drunk sparingly during meals.

19. A person should eat only when he is hungry, and drink when he is thirsty, and should not neglect the call of nature even for one moment, and should not begin consuming food before he ascertains whether he has an urge to purge.

20. A man should ever endeavor to keep his bowels lax, even approaching a diarrhetic state; for this is a leading rule in hygiene, that as long as the bowels are constipated or when they act with difficulty, serious diseases may result. Therefore, when a person observes that his bowels do not function properly, he should consult a physician.

21. Toil in a moderate degree is good for the physical health, but excessive toil, as well as idleness, are injurious to the body. In the hot season, a little exercise will suffice, but in the cold season, more is required. A fat person requires more exercise than a lean person.

22. One who desires to preserve his health, must learn about his psychological reactions and control them; joy, worry, anger and fright are psychological reactions. A wise man must always be satisfied with his portion during the time of his vain existence, and should not grieve over a world that does not belong to him. He should not look for luxuries, and he should be in good spirits and joyous to a moderate extent at all times, because these characteristics help increase the natural warmth of the body, to digest the food, to eliminate the superfluous matter, to strengthen the eyesight and the other faculties, and to strengthen the power of reasoning. But one should not try to stimulate the joy of life by means of eating or drinking, as the fools do, for the reason that by too much joy, the warmth of the heart is diffused over the entire body, and the natural warmth of the heart is cooled off, with the result that it may cause sudden death. Especailly can that happen to fat persons, because the natural warmth in their bodies is little, for the reason that the blood vessels in their bodies are narrow, and the circulation of the blood, which is the main cause of the warmth, is slow. Grief, which is the reverse of joy, is likewise injurious, because it cools off the body

and the natural warmth centralizes into the heart, which condition may cause death. Anger stirs up the warmth of the body, so that it produces a kind of fever. Fright causes coolness in the body, and therefore, it happens that the frightened person begins to shiver, and when the coolness increases, it may cause death. And how much more must one take care not to eat when angry, frightened, or worried, but eat when only moderately happy.

23. Moderate sleep is good for the physical wellbeing, because it helps digest food and rest the senses; and if one is unable to sleep because of illness, one should eat such foods that stimulate sleep. Too much sleep, however, is injurious, because it increases the gases that come up from the belly, fill up the head with them, and causes serious harm to the body. Just as one must be careful not to sleep immediately after eating, so must one take care not to go to sleep when one is hungry, because when there is no food in the body, the natural warmth works in the superfluous matter producing foul gases which enter the head. When sleeping, the head should be higher than the rest of the body, because it will help the food come down from the stomach, and it will diminish the gases that come up into the head. The natural sleep is the one at night; sleep in the daytime is harmful, and is good only for those who are accustomed to it.

24. The proper way of washing oneself is to take a bath regularly every week. One should not enter the bath-house when one is either hungry or full, but when the food is beginning to become digested. One should wash the body with hot water, afterward with tepid water, then with water some degrees cooler, and finally with cold water. Upon leaving the bath-house, one should put on one's clothes and cover the head well, thereby avoiding catching a cold; it is necessary to take this precaution even in the summer time. One should not eat immediately upon leaving the bath-house, but one should wait until one regains his mental and physical composure, and allow the heat to subside, and then eat. If one can take a nap upon leaving the bath-house, before his meal, so much the better.

25. A person should endeavor to dwell where the air is pure and clear, on elevated ground, and in a house of ample proportions. If possible, he should not dwell in a house having either a northern or an eastern exposure, and that there should be no decayed matter around. It is very beneficial to continually purify the air of the house with fragrant substances and by proper fumigation.

26. The air best for the physical wellbeing is that of even temperature, neither too hot nor too cold. Therefore, precautions should be taken not to overheat the house in the winter as many senseless people do, because excessive heat occasions many illnesses, God forbid. A house should be heated just enough so that the cold should not be felt, but it should not be too hot.

27. To preserve one's eyesight, one should guard against the following: not to enter suddenly from a dark place into a well illuminated place. He should first open the door of the well-lighted room slightly, and look at that dim light for a moment, then open it a little more, and finally open it completely. One should also take the same precaution when coming from a well-lighted place into a dark one. The change from light to darkness and from darkness to light, without a medium, is injurious to the eyesight. Therefore, the Holy One, blessed be His name, has in His mercy so created the world that the sun should begin shining upon the earth gradually, not at once, and so does it set gradually. On account of this, we say the benediction *Hammeir laaretz veladarim aleha beraḥamim* (who in mercy giveth light to the earth and to them that dwell thereon); which means, that in His mercy He gives us light gradually and not suddenly, at once. The light that is reflected from the light of the sun, that is, when the sun shines down on some place and from there the light is reflected, is very injurious to the eyes. Therefore, one should not dwell in a house, the windows of which face to the north only, because the sun never shines from the north, and whatever light there is in such house is obtained only by reflection. Even if the windows face east, south or west, but if the open sky cannot be seen through them, being obstructed by high walls, the light that penetrates through them is likewise only a reflection. One should not write, read, or do any delicate work in the dusk of twilight, nor in the middle of the day when the sun shines the brightest. Neither should one write or read too much small print or do any delicate work before candle light at night. Gazing steadily at a white color is likewise harmful to the eyes; therefore, is the color of the sky blue, not white, in order not to hurt the eyes. Gazing steadily at bright red colors or at fire is also injurious. Smoke, sulphurous odors, fine dust and strong wind blowing in the face, excessive or rapid walking, and excessive weeping are injurious to the eyes; for it is written (Lamentations 2:11): "My eyes do fail with tears." The most injurious of all is excessive copulation; but "The precept of the Lord is pure, enlightening the eyes" (Psalms 19:9).

CHAPTER 33

Things Forbidden Because They are Dangerous

1. It is forbidden to eat fish together with meat, even with poultry fat, because it is dangerous. One should not roast meat and bake fish at the same time in a small oven, unless either one or the other is covered; but it may be done in our ovens which are large.

2. If one eats fish immediately after eating meat, or vice versa, one should eat some bread or drink some beverage between them, which will serve to wash the food down and to rinse the mouth.

3. One should guard oneself against human perspiration, because human perspiration is deadly poison, except that of the face. Therefore, no food should be placed underneath one's clothes where it may touch the body, neither should one place coins in one's mouth, as some perspiration may have clung to it. Moreover, since they have passed through many hands, they might have been handled by sick people.

4. A man should be careful to cleanse his mouth of all saliva and not swallow it, when he smells the odor of some food, because if he swallows it, it may be dangerous to him, God forbid.

5. It is advisable not to drink water that has remained uncovered.

6. It is forbidden to place any food or drink underneath the bed, even if they are covered, because an evil spirit descends upon them. In villages, some people keep potatoes and other foodstuffs underneath the beds; and they should be warned against it.

7. One should guard oneself against all things that are dangerous, because "Regulations concerning health and life are made more stringent than ritual laws" (Ḥullin 10a); and the risk of danger is to be apprehended even more than the risk of infringing upon a precept. Therefore, it is forbidden to walk in a dangerous place, for instance, beside a shaky wall or over a broken bridge. Nor should one go out alone at night, nor sleep alone in a room at night, nor drink water from rivers at night, nor put the mouth under a jet of water to drink, lest he swallow something harmful.

8. At the time of the equinox, it is customary to place some iron over all beverages or food; but it need not be placed over food that is cooked, or pickled, or preserved in salt.

9. We are not allowed to partake of any food or drink which we dislike, or eat or drink out of unclean vessels that are loathsome; nor should we eat with soiled hands, for all these things come under the Biblical injunction (Leviticus 11:43): "And ye shall not make yourselves abominable;" even if a person should assert that it is not loathsome to him, his opinion is voided by the majority.

10. If beasts or fowl are slaughtered after they became seriously sick, although it is lawful to slaughter them, still the scrupulous avoid partaking of their meat.

11. It is forbidden to cut down a fruit tree bearing fruit—for instance, an olive tree producing a quarter of a *kav* of olives, and a date tree producing a *kav* of dates—because it is dangerous. However, if it grows near other more valuable trees and they are debilitated by its close proximity, or if one needs the space it occupies, or if its timber is more valuable than its fruit, it may be cut down.

12. One who has abdominal trouble is not allowed to make use of the remedy that is recommended by some people, that of placing a vessel of hot water on the abdomen, as it is dangerous to do so.

13. One is not allowed to cross a stream when the water is rising, if it reaches above the loins, as there is danger of being swept away by the current.

14. It is forbidden to utter an ominous phrase against a fellow Jew, even merely to say about a missing person: "If he were alive, he would have come here;" for "A covenant is made with the lips" say our Rabbis (Moed Katan 18a); nor should one scare a child by an unclean thing; like saying that a cat or a dog will seize him. One should avoid uttering any words of a similar nature.

CHAPTER 34

Laws Concerning Charity

1. It is a religious duty to give alms to the poor of Israel, as it is written (Deuteronomy 15:8): "Thou shalt surely open thy hand unto him;" and it is written again (Leviticus 25:36): "That thy brother may live with thee." If a poor man asks for help and we disregard his supplications and give him no relief, we transgress God's command, for He ordered (Deuteronomy 15:7): "Thou shalt not harden thy heart nor shut thy hand from thy poor brother." The giving of charity is a characteristic of the descendants of our father Abraham, for it is said (Genesis 18:19): "For I know him that he will command his children . . . to do *tzedakah* (charity)." The glory of Israel is attested and the law of truth is confirmed only by means of charity, for it is written (Isaiah 54:14): "*Bitzedakah* (by charity) shalt thou be established." The giving of charity is more important than all the sacrifices, for it is said (Proverbs 21:3): "To exercise *tzedakah* (charity) and justice is more acceptable to the Lord than sacrifice." And Israel will be redeemed only by means of charity, for it is written (Isaiah 1:27): "Zion shall be redeemed by justice, and those that return to her with *tzedakah* (charity)." No man ever becomes poor by giving charity, nor will any harm result from its practice, as it is said (Isaiah 32:17): "And the work of charity is peace." Mercy will be shown to him that is merciful, as it is said (Deuteronomy 13:18): "And He will show thee mercy, and have compassion on thee and multiply thee." If a person is cruel, his lineage is under suspicion. The Holy One, blessed be He, heeds the cry of the poor, as it is said (Job 34:28): "And the cry of the poor will He hear."

Therefore, should one beware of their cry (to the Lord), who has made a covenant with them, as it is written (Exodus 22:26): "And it shall come to pass when he crieth unto Me, that I will hear, for I am gracious." In the Jerusalem Talmud it is said: "A door which opens not for the poor will open for the physician." A man should suppose, that he is continually begging for sustenance from the Holy One, blessed be He, and just as he prays that the Holy One listens to his cries and supplications, so shall he listen to the supplication of the poor. A man should also consider, that the wheel of fortune is ever revolving, and that either he himself, or his son, or his grandson may eventually beg for charity. Let no man say: "Why should I dissipate my wealth by giving it to the poor?" He must bear in mind that the wealth really belongs not to him, but that it was simply given to him as a trust with which to execute the will of the One who has entrusted his fund to him. And this (charity-giving) is man's real portion which he has saved from all his toil in this world, as it is written (Isaiah 58:8): "And before thee shall go thy *tzedakah* (charity)." Charity wards off evil decrees and prolongs life.

2. Every man must contribute to charity according to his means. Even a person who is supported by charity, as a person who has some money of his own but does not invest it in business, is allowed to receive charity if the increment is not sufficient for his livelihood, must donate to charity from what is given to him. Even if a person can give but very little, he should not refrain from giving it, for the little he gives is just as worthy as the large contributions of the wealthy. Thus our Rabbis, of blessed memory, say (Menaḥot 110a): "Concerning the burnt offering of an animal, it is written (Leviticus 1:9): 'A fire offering of sweet savor;' concerning the burnt offering of fowl, it is written (loco citato 17): 'A fire-offering of sweet savor;' and concerning a meal-offering it is likewise written (loco citato 2): 'A fire-offering of sweet savor;' this is to teach us, that it is the same whether one gives much or little, provided that one turns his heart towards his Father in Heaven." But he who has barely sufficient for his own needs, is not obligated to give charity, for his own sustenance takes precedence over another's.

3. How much should a poor man be given? Sufficient to supply his needs. That applies to a man receiving charity in secrecy, then the town folks must supply him with all his wants, even to the extent of maintaining him in the same style that he had been accustomed to live before he became poor; but to the poor man who goes begging from door to door, a small sum may be given, in accordance with his worth. In any event, a poor man should be given in each town, at least enough food for two meals and a place to stay overnight. The poor of all nations must be supported like poor Israelites, for the sake of peace.

4. How much must a man contribute to charity? The first year he should donate the tithe of his capital, and thereafter the tithe of his annual net profits; this, however, is but the average way of giving charity, but the most preferable way of performing this precept, is to give a fifth of the capital the first year, and thereafter, a fifth of the net annual profit. A person must not give more than one-fifth, so that he himself may not eventually need the support of others. This rule applies only to charity given during a man's lifetime, but at the time of his death, he may donate even one-third of his fortune to charity. The tithe-money (set aside for charity), must not be used for the purpose of any other religious act, like buying candles for the synagogue, and so forth; but it must be given to the poor. However, when one has a son to be circumcised, or wishes to dower a poor groom and bride, to enable them to get married, or to purchase religious books out of which he himself will study, and also lend them to others for study, then if one cannot afford to spend additional money, and consequently would be unable to perform any of these religious duties, one may use the tithe-money for these purposes. When buying religious books with the tithe-money, one must be careful to lend them to others, unless one needs them for one's own use. One must also write on the books that they have been bought with the tithe-money, so that one's children may not take possession of them after one's death.

5. He who desires to make himself worthy, must not stint when buying anything for the glory of God; he should open wide his hand and buy everything of the best. If he builds a synagogue, it must be more beautiful than his own home; when he feeds the hungry, he must serve them with the best food from his table; when he clothes the naked, he must clothe them with the best garments, and when he consecrates something, he must consecrate the best of his possessions; for thus it is written (Leviticus 3:16): "All the fat is unto the Lord."

6. Supporting sons and daughters, who have no claim to support (being over six years old), in order to teach the Torah to his male children, and moral conduct to his female children is classed as charity. Also making gifts to parents (whom he can support only from his charity fund), is included in charity giving. Moreover, they take precedence over others. Even other kinsmen, take precedence over strangers. The poor living in his own house have precedence over the poor of the town, and the poor of his town have precedence over the poor of another town. For it is written (Deuteronomy 15:11): "To thy brother, to thy poor and to thy needy, in thy land." But a warden of charity must not give preference to his own relatives.

7. He who gives alms to the poor with an unfriendly mien, even if he give as much as a thousand pieces of gold, his deed is without merit; he nullifies it by his ill-will, and he violates the Divine Command (Deuteronomy

15:10): "And thy heart shall not be grieved when thou givest it to them." But he must give it with a cheerful countenance and a joyful feeling. He should also condole with them and cheer them, as Job said (Job 30:25): "Did I not weep for him that was in trouble? Was not my soul grieved for the needy?" And it is written (Job 29:13): "And the heart of the widow I caused to sing for joy."

8. We must not turn away empty-handed, anyone who comes to us for help, even if all we are able to give is one dried fig or a morsel of bread, for it is written (Psalms 74:21): "O let not the oppressed return confounded." If we have nothing in our possession to give him, then let us at least speak to him kind words. We must neither rebuke nor speak harshly to the poor, for their hearts are broken and humbled, and it is written (Psalms 51:19): "A broken and contrite heart, O God, wilt Thou not despise." Woe unto him who puts the poor to disgrace. We must be like parents to the poor and show them mercy by deed as well as by words, for it is written (Job 29:16): "I was a father to the needy."

9. A promise of charity is in the nature of a vow. Therefore, if we say: "We shall give a *sela* (a coin, equal to one sacred or two common *shekels*) as charity," or if we say: "We shall give this *sela* as charity," we must give it to the poor without delay, and if we do delay giving it, we are guilty of transgressing the Divine Command (Deuteronomy 23:22): "Thou shalt not delay," since we could have given it forthwith. If no poor are around, we must lay that money aside until we find some poor people. When we make a charity vow at the synagogue, where the money is given to the collector of charities, we are not violating the Law unless the latter demands payment. If we postpone giving it to him, we are immediately guilty of a violation, unless we know that the collector does not at the moment need the money for distribution, but he would only keep it in his possession.

10. If a person says: "I shall give a *sela* as charity to such and such a poor man," he does not violate the Law before that particular person comes. Anyone may set aside a certain sum of money for charitable purposes, keep it in his possession, and distribute it little by little to whomever he sees fit.

11. He who urges others to give charity and causes them to practice it, deserves greater reward than the one who merely gives charity; as it is written (Isaiah 32:17): "And the work of charity shall be peace," and concerning the collector of charity and others like him, it is written (Daniel 12:3): "And they that turn the many to righteousness (shall shine) as the stars forever and ever." The collector should not mind it, if at times he is insulted by the poor, because on account of this his merit is the greater.

12. The highest merit in giving charity is attained by the person who comes to the aid of a fellow man in bad circumstances, before he reaches the stage of actual poverty. Such aid may be in the form of a substantial gift

presented in an honorable manner, or by a loan, or by entering into partnership with him for the transaction of some business enterprise, or by assistance in obtaining some employment for him, so that he would not be forced to seek charity from his fellow men. Concerning this it is written (Leviticus 25:35): "Thou shalt strengthen him," which means, assist him so that he fall not.

13. It is urgent to make charitable contributions secretly, and if possible in such a way that the giver is not aware to whom he is giving it, and the recipient does not know from whom he is receiving it. At any rate, no man should ever boast of the charitable contributions he makes. But if a man donates a certain object for a charitable purpose, he may write his name on it that it may serve as a memorial.

14. We must take special care in the treatment of a poor scholar who studies the Law, and to offer gifts to him in a manner that accords with his dignity. If he is unwilling to accept money in the form of charity, some business should be procured for him by obtaining merchandise for him at a low price, and purchasing it back from him at a higher price. Our Rabbis, of blessed memory, said (Pesaḥim 53b): "He who supplies a scholar with merchandise (that is, he gives a scholar an opportunity to gain a livelihood), merits to sit in the divine court." They said again (Beraḥot 34b): "The glorious prophecies predicted by all the prophets were for the man who establishes a scholar in business, and who gives his daughter in marriage to a scholar."

15. A man should avoid charity. He should rather suffer hardship than depend on men. Our sages, of blessed memory, enjoined (Shabbat 118a): "Rather make thy Sabbath a weekday (as regards festive meals) than be dependent on men." Even if an honored sage becomes poor, he should find some occupation, even of a menial kind, rather than depend on men.

16. Whoever has no need for charity and gets it by deceit, shall live to become dependent on the charity of his fellow men. On the other hand, one who is in need of charity, and cannot exist without help, either because of old age or sickness, and yet refuses to accept it because of pride, is guilty of bloodshed and forfeits his own life, and he has nothing for his suffering but sins and transgressions. He, however, who is in need of charity, and suffers distress and hardship, not because of pride but because he does not wish to become a burden to the public, shall live to acquire the means of supporting others. And of him it is written (Jeremiah 17:7): "Blessed is the man who trusts in the Lord."

CHAPTER 35

The Separation of Ḥallah (First Portion of the Dough)

1. From the dough made of one of the five species of grain (wheat, barley, spelt, rye, and oats), the *ḥallah* portion must be separated. Immediately before separating the *ḥallah*, the following benediction is recited: "Blessed art Thou, O Lord our God, King of the universe, who hath sanctified us by His commandments, and hath commanded us to separate *ḥallah*." Then dough no less than the size of an olive is separated and burned. The custom is to burn it in the oven where the bread is being baked.

2. What is the quantity of dough which becomes subject to the law of separating *ḥallah*? Whatever is made out of no less than five quarters of flour, which is equivalent to the weight of forty-three and one-fifth eggs (two and a half quarts, or three and one-half pounds).

3. As regards the *matzah* baked for the Passover, although each mass of dough in itself does not contain the necessary quantity of flour to make it subject to the law of *ḥallah*, yet by placing them into one vessel after baking it becomes one unit and makes the separation of *ḥallah* obligatory. Care must be taken to place all the *matzot* inside the vessel; yet if some of the *matzot* protrude partly outside the vessel, they are counted as one unit. However, if some *matzot* lie wholly on the top of the vessel, they do not count as one unit, even if they have been covered with a cloth. If one places the *matzot* into a cloth and covers them with the folds of the same cloth, the cloth is considered as though it were a vessel and it makes the *matzot* count as one unit, even though some of the *matzot* remain uncovered in the middle. Only care must be taken that whole *matzot* should not remain outside the covering.

4. The leaven taken from dough for fermenting other dough, should be removed before *ḥallah* has been separated. But the leaven taken for fermenting liquids, which we call *borsht*, should be removed after the separation of *ḥallah*.

5. After Passover, when leaven is bought from a non-Jew for fermenting dough with it, care should be taken that the slice of dough separated from it as *ḥallah* should be larger than the leaven bought from the non-Jew.

6. If dough is prepared for cooking, or frying, the *ḥallah* should be separated without saying the benediction. If, however, any part of such dough is intended to be used for baking, the benediction must be recited upon separating the *ḥallah*.

7. Regarding dough kneaded with eggs or with any kind of fruit-juice, there are doubts (whether *ḥallah* should be separated from it). It is, therefore, best to add a little water, milk, honey, wine, or olive oil to it while kneading the dough. Then the *ḥallah* may be separated from it and the proper benediction recited.

8. The precept concerning the separation of *ḥallah* belongs to the mistress of the house. But if she is not at home and there is a likelihood that the dough may spoil before she returns, then the maid or any other person may separate the *ḥallah*.

9. If one forgets to separate *ḥallah* on Friday from the bread to be eaten on the Sabbath, then in countries outside Israel, the bread may be eaten on the Sabbath, and a portion of it left over; and at the termination of the Sabbath the *ḥallah* portion is to be taken from it. The portion thus left over must be large enough for the separation of *ḥallah*, and the piece left over must be of substantial quantity. If the day preceding the Passover is a Sabbath, and one forgets to separate the *ḥallah* from the bread which has been baked in honor of the Sabbath, there is a great diversity of opinion as to what procedure to adopt in such a case. Therefore, every man must be very careful to remind his family on Friday, concerning the separation of the *ḥallah*.

CHAPTER 36

The Salting of Meat

1. Before the meat is salted it must be thoroughly rinsed with water. The meat should be soaked and entirely submerged in water for half an hour. Wherever a particle of blood is visible it must be thoroughly washed with the water in which it is soaked. In the case of fowl, the place where the incision was made in killing it, should also be thoroughly washed, and the blood visible inside the fowl must be washed off. Lumps of coagulated blood due to a wound are at times found in cattle and fowl; these must be cut away and removed before the meat is soaked. If the water is very cold, it should be put in a warm place to take the cold out before the meat is soaked in it, because in cold water, meat becomes hardened and the blood is not easily drawn out when the meat is salted.

2. If by error one allows meat to soak in water for twenty-four hours, the meat as well as the vessel in which it has soaked must not be used. If liver is soaked in water for twenty-four hours, a competent rabbi must be consulted.

3. Before the approach of the Sabbath, when there is not much time to spare, or on any other occasion when one is pressed for time, it suffices to wash the meat thoroughly and then let it soak in water a short time; when the water no longer becomes reddened by the blood, the meat may be salted.

4. If a piece of meat is cut up again after soaking, the new surfaces produced by the cut must be thoroughly washed of the surface blood.

5. Frozen meat must be allowed to thaw out before being salted, but it must not be placed near a hot stove nor put in hot water. In cases of emergency, the frozen meat may be soaked in tepid water.

6. The vessel specifically used for the purpose of soaking meat may not be used for the preparation of any other food.

7. After the meat has been soaked, the water must be allowed to drain off, so that the salt may not be dissolved at once and become ineffective in drawing out the blood. The meat should not be allowed to become thoroughly dry, for then the salt would not adhere to it, and would fail to drain the blood from it.

8. The salt should not be as fine as flour, as it would dissolve too quickly and would not properly drain the blood. Neither should the salt be too coarse as it may drop from the meat. The salt should be of medium size, like that used for cooking, and should be kept dry enough to be easily sprinkled.

9. The salt must be sprinkled on all sides of the meat, so that no part of the surface is left unsalted. Care should be taken to open poultry properly so that it may be well salted within.

10. The meat that has been salted must be placed where the blood can easily drain off; therefore, the basket containing the meat must not be placed on the ground, as the flow of blood will be impeded by it. Even though the meat remained in salt for the proper length of time (one hour) before washing it, it should not be placed where the blood cannot flow freely from it. If the meat is salted on a board, the board must be placed in a sloping position, so that the blood may flow freely. There should be no hollow part or cavity in the salting board where the brine may accumulate. Poultry or an entire side of an animal having a cavity, must be turned with the hollow part downward when placed on the board after salting, in order that the blood may drain freely.

11. The meat should remain in the salt for one hour; but in case of emergency, twenty-four minutes is sufficient.

12. After the meat has remained in the salt for the proper length of time, the salt should be thoroughly shaken off and the meat rinsed three times. A God-fearing woman should personally supervise the rinsing of the meat, because her servant, who brings in the water from the well on her shoulder, may be inclined to be economical in using the water, and thus, God forbid, cause the transgression of the Divine Law, forbidding the use of blood. Care should be taken, never to put the meat immediately after salting, into an empty vessel containing no water before it is rinsed.

13. The heads of poultry must be severed before the poultry is soaked; and if they have been salted with the heads attached, a competent rabbi should be consulted.

14. Unsalted meat must not be put in a place where salt is sometimes kept. A special vessel in which to keep unsoaked and unsalted meat must be set aside, and in such a vessel one must not put vegetables, or fruit, or any other article of food which is generally eaten without first being washed, because the blood of the meat clings to the vessel, and from the vessel it is communicated to the articles of food.

15. Before soaking the head, it must be split open, the brain removed, and its membrane torn off. The head must be soaked and salted. The head must be salted within and without, and may be salted while it still has the hair on.

16. Bones which contain marrow and are still attached to the meat may be salted together with other meat; but if the bones are bare, they should be salted separately, and should not even be placed near the other meat when in the salt.

17. The tips of the hoofs of animals must be cut off before soaking the legs in water, so that the blood can flow out. When in the salt, the legs must be placed hoofs downward, so that the blood may drain out easily. It is permissible to salt the legs before removing the hair.

18. It is necessary to cut open the heart of an animal before soaking it in water, so that the blood may issue from it.

19. It is customary to cut the lungs of an animal and to open the large tubes before soaking them in water.

20. Liver, because it contains a large quantity of blood, may not be made *kosher* in the same manner as ordinary meat. It must first be cut open, and then broiled over a fire, with the open parts downward so that the blood may drain from them. Before the liver is placed over the fire, it must be rinsed, and while being broiled it must be lightly sprinkled with salt. It must be broiled until it is fit to be eaten. After broiling, it should be rinsed three times of the blood which has been discharged. After that it may be boiled, if desired.

21. Liver must be broiled over a flame, and not in an oven out of which the ashes and coals have been removed. When being broiled, it must not be wrapped in any kind of paper, be it even of the flimsiest kind.

22. It is forbidden to salt liver in the same manner as ordinary meat, and it certainly must not be salted together with meat.

23. The *koshering* of the spleen is done in the same manner as ordinary meat; with the exception, however, that the membrane must be removed before soaking it, because it is classed as forbidden fat, and so must the spleenic vein be removed. The spleenic vein should be pulled out by its head along with the three cords that are contained in it. Care should be taken not to sever any of these cords, and if it happens to become severed, it is necessary to eradicate it.

24. The mesentery (membrane keeping the bowels in position) and other entrails, should be salted on their exterior to which the fat clings.

25. The milk contained at times in the stomach of a calf must be spilled out before soaking the stomach in water, and it is then treated like ordinary meat.

26. Eggs found in poultry, no matter what their stage of development, must be soaked, salted and rinsed as if they were meat. They must not, however, be salted together with meat, and they must not be placed in a position where blood can drain on them. Such eggs, even though they are fully developed, must not be eaten or boiled together with milk, because they are considered as meat.

27. Meat that was kept for three full days, may not be boiled, unless it has been soaked before the three days were over.

28. It is customary to singe poultry after being plucked in order to remove the feathers that have been left. Care should be taken to singe them over a small flame and to be moved too and fro over the flame, so that they may not be heated.

CHAPTER 37

The Immersion of Vessels

1. Glass and metal utensils bought from a heathen for culinary purposes, even when new, must not be used even for holding cold victuals before they are immersed in a pool that would be approved for the ritual immersion of a woman after her period of menstruation. Before the immersion, the following benediction is pronounced: "Blessed art Thou, O Lord our God, King of the universe, who hath sanctified us by His commandments, and

commanded us concerning the immersion of *a vessel,*" (or "vessels" if more than one are immersed).

2. Since the vessels must be immersed in a stream valid for the ritual immersion of women, therefore, care should be taken not to immerse in streams at the time they are swelled by excessive rain or by the thaw. It occurs very frequently that people do immerse vessels in streams before the Passover when the rivers swell up; this is an improper practice. (See chapter 162:12-13.)

3. Wooden vessels need not be immersed, but if they have metal hoops, they are to be immersed without pronouncing the benediction. Clay vessels need not be immersed, but if they are glazed on the inside, they are to be immersed without pronouncing the benediction; the same law applies to porcelain vessels.

4. An old vessel which has been used by a non-Jew and it is necessary to put it in boiling water or made red hot, must be done before it is immersed.

5. Vessels hired or borrowed from a non-Jew need not be immersed; but vessels hired or borrowed from Jewish dealers should be immersed without pronouncing the benediction. The dealer must make the fact of the immersion known to the one who subsequently buys the vessels, so that the latter might not immerse them again and pronounce the benediction in vain.

6. Glassware manufactured by an Israelite who employs non-Jewish workmen, should be immersed without pronouncing the benediction.

7. If an Israelite has given silver or any other kind of metal to a non-Jewish artisan to make a vessel out of it, or he has given to repair a leaky vessel not large enough to hold a fourth of a *lug* (a quantity equal to the capacity of one and one-half egg shells), such vessels should be immersed without the benediction.

8. Only vessels used to hold food ready to be eaten without any further preparation need be immersed. The iron tools with which the *matzot* are prepared, and with which the dough is cut, and the needle with which stuffed birds or parts of animals are sewn, need not be immersed. A slaughtering knife, or a knife with which animals are skinned, since it may be used to cut with it food fit to eat without any further preparation, also trays upon which *matzot* are placed, should be immersed but without pronouncing the benediction. A tripod upon which cooking utensils are placed, because it

is not touched by the food, need not be immersed. A metal spit used for roasting meat, must be immersed and the benediction pronounced. Some authorities hold that large glass bottles in which liquids are kept to be poured out into drinking glasses, are not classed as table utensils, and need not be immersed; while other authorities hold that they should be immersed; they should, therefore, be immersed without the benediction.

9. Pepper grinders should be immersed, because they have some metal parts, but their lower parts which receive the ground pepper need not be immersed since they are made of wood. Coffee grinders should be immersed without the benediction.

10. Before immersing the vessel, it must be thoroughly cleansed, so that neither rust nor dirt be found on it. (A small particle of rust or a black spot, usually found on such vessels, and regarding which people are not fastidious, may be disregarded). The whole vessel must be submerged at one time, so that the whole of it should be in the water. A vessel with a handle, must be submerged with the handle and all at one time. If the vessel is held in the hand during the immersion, the hand should first be dipped into the water; and the vessel be held not tightly, but with an ordinary grip. If the vessel is immersed by means of a cord, as when it is immersed in a well, the cord should be knotted loosely, so that the water may reach every part of the vessel.

11. If we immerse vessels with narrow openings, we must keep them in the water until the water fills them entirely.

12. A minor, whether male or female, may not be entrusted with the ritual of immersing vessels.

13. It is forbidden to immerse vessels either on the Sabbath or on a festival. If we neglect to immerse a vessel before those days, we should give it as a gift to a non-Jew, and then borrow it from him. If it is a vessel fit to carry water in it, and we live in a community where it is permissible to carry things on the Sabbath, we should draw water with it and bring the water into the house, so that it may not appear as if we have immersed it, but we should not say the benediction.

CHAPTER 38

Laws Concerning Bread, Cooked Food, and Milk of a Non-Jew

1. The sages have forbidden us to eat the bread of a non-Jew. In some localities, they do buy bread of a non-Jewish baker, either when there is no Jewish baker in that locality, or when there is one, but his bread is inferior to

that of the non-Jewish baker. However, they are more strict regarding the bread of a non-Jewish private person, and they permit the use of such bread only in cases of emergency. When we are on the road, we should wait for *kosher* bread, if it can be obtained within the distance of a mile. Only bread baked especially for the family, is called *private bread,* but if it is made for the purpose of being sold, it is called a *baker's bread,* even though ordinarily he does not bake for the trade; if a baker bakes bread for his own family, it is called *private bread.* One authority holds that in a locality where no baker can be found, it is even permissible to partake of the bread of a non-Jewish private person, and one need not wait for *kosher* bread; and this opinion is generally followed.

2. If a Jew has thrown even one piece of wood into a non-Jewish oven at the time it was heated, the bread baked in that oven is no longer considered as the bread of a non-Jew.

3. The bread of a non-Jew is forbidden only when it is made of one of the five species of grain: wheat, barley, spelt, rye and oats, but bread made of pulse, like beans, peas, etc., is not considered bread; neither can it be forbidden as food cooked by a non-Jew, since such food is not fit to be served on "the table of a king."

4. Non-Jewish bread smeared over with eggs is forbidden on account of the eggs, for it is then considered as the cooking of a non-Jew. Those cakes which are baked on iron pans are forbidden in any event, because there is a possibility that the iron has been smeared with some kind of forbidden fat, and that the pan has absorbed some of the fat.

5. Jewish bread baked by a non-Jew is much worse than the bread of a non-Jew, and it is forbidden as food cooked by a non-Jew, unless the owner of the bread has prepared the oven by throwing a piece of wood in it. When we send something to be baked or roasted in an oven of a non-Jewish baker, we must be careful to have a Jew throw a piece of wood into the oven, or that a Jew put the bread or the pan into the oven.

6. An article of food that is not eaten raw and is also fit to be served at the table of a king, either as a relish eaten with bread or as a dessert, if cooked or roasted by a non-Jew, even in the vessels and in the house of a Jew, is forbidden, inasmuch as it was cooked by a non-Jew. However, an article of food that is eaten when raw, or if it is not a delicacy fit to be served at the table of a king, is not forbidden as the cooking of a non-Jew. Nor need any scruples be felt regarding the gentile's vessels, because it is assumed that ordinarily no cooking had been done in them in the past twenty-four hours.

7. A Jewish household employing a non-Jewish servant who also does the cooking, the cooking is not forbidden, since it seems unlikely that some member of the household will not rake the fire while the cooking is being done.

8. However, if the servant cooks food for herself only, it is not likely that any member of the Jewish family would rake the fire—and it is possible that even raking the fire would be of no avail; it is worse than when she cooks for a Jew. Therefore, if she cooks food which is subject to the rules of non-Jewish cooking, then not only the food but also the use of the pots is forbidden, and if we happen to use them, we must consult a competent rabbi about it.

9. The food cooked by a non-Jew for a sick person on the Sabbath, may not be eaten at the close of the Sabbath even by the sick person himself, if it is possible to cook other food for him. The vessels, however, may be used after the expiration of twenty-four hours.

10. Although an egg is fit to be swallowed raw, yet if it is cooked by a non-Jew, it becomes forbidden food. This rule of law applies also to anything similar to it.

11. Fruits, not fully ripened and are eaten raw only in cases of emergency, are forbidden as food cooked by a non-Jew, if they are expertly preserved in sugar.

12. It is customary to permit the drinking of beer made either of grain or of honey, even when sold in the house of a non-Jew. This is not subject to the law of non-Jewish cooking, because the grain loses its identity in the water. It is only necessary to investigate whether or not it has been made with wine-yeast. In a locality where Jews trifle with the law and permit the use of non-Jewish wine, a scrupulous person should refrain from the use of beer. A scrupulous Jew should avoid the drinking of coffee (without milk, for with milk it is surely forbidden), chocolate or tea of a non-Jew. Some authorities permit to drink the above only occasionally, but not to make it a regular practice.

13. It is forbidden to use the milk which has been milked by a non-Jew, not under the supervision of a Jew; and it is even forbidden to make cheese from it. It is necessary that a Jew be present when the milking is begun and

to see to it that the vessel into which it is milked be clean. It is customary to refrain from milking into a vessel generally used for milking by a non-Jew. It is permissible to let non-Jewish servants milk the cows either in the premises of a Jew or in a barn belonging to them, if there is no house belonging to a non-Jew obstructing the milking from view, and there is no danger of their drawing milk from an unclean animal. However, if the milking is obstructed from view by a house belonging to a non-Jew, it is necessary that a Jew be present at the milking; even a minor male or female, nine years of age is considered competent for that purpose.

14. The cheese of a non-Jew is forbidden food. If, however, a Jew has supervised the milking as well as the making of the cheese, then if during the process the cheese belonged to a Jew, it is permissible to partake of it; but if during the process it still belonged to a non-Jew, it is forbidden food.

15. As to non-Jewish butter, it depends upon the custom of the place. There are certain communities where such butter is not used, and others where it is used. He who goes from a community where it is not used, to a place where it is used, is allowed to eat it with them even though he intends to return to his own community, he who goes from a place where it is used to a place where it is not used, is not allowed to eat it there. Nowadays, as it is rumored that non-Jews mix the butter with lard, the scrupulous should avoid using their butter.

CHAPTER 39

Eating and Drinking Before the Regular Meals

1. If one desires to eat before the washing of the hands of a regular meal, any food that will be served during the meal (regardless whether such food requires an extra benediction when eaten during the meal, such as fruits, or it is the kind of food that requires no extra benediction when eaten during the meal, such as all kinds of vegetables, pods or potatoes); or if one desires to drink any beverage (except wine) before washing the hands, and he also intends to drink such beverage during the meal; authorities disagree as to whether or not the things thus eaten or drunk are exempted from the concluding benediction and are covered by the Grace after meals, just as those foods eaten during the meal are exempted. Therefore, it is best to eat or drink those things before the meal only, and thereafter, pronounce the concluding benediction, and to avoid eating or drinking of the same during the meal. If we neglect to say the concluding benediction before the meal, we may say it either during the course of the meal or even after Grace. If we eat or drink

of these kinds also during the course of the meal, then we must eat and drink some of it also after the meal and then recite the concluding benediction which will cover whatever we have eaten or drunk before the meal.

2. Some authorities are of the opinion that one may drink wine before washing the hands, even though one does not intend to drink any wine during the meal; for, since wine is used only as a stimulant, it is included in the meal, and is exempted from the concluding benediction by the recitation of Grace after the meal. Other authorities hold that even if one drinks wine during the meal, yet the wine drunk before washing the hands is not exempt from the benediction by the Grace. Therefore, one should abstain from drinking any wine before washing the hands, unless one drinks some wine also after reciting the Grace and pronounces thereafter the benediction *Al haggefen* (for the vine), etc., and thereby also exempts the wine drunk before washing the hands. If one desires to drink some brandy before the meal, one should be careful to drink less the quantity of the size of an olive, whether or not one intends to drink some more during the course of the meal; but if one drinks as much as the quantity of an olive or more, it is doubtful whether or not the concluding benediction should be recited.

3. If before washing the hands, one desires to eat food, such as honey cakes and egg cakes, after the eating of which we say the benediction *Al hamiḥeyah* (for the sustenance), etc., the Grace after meals exempts one from reciting the benediction whether or not one intends to eat of the same during the meal, provided, however, there is no long delay between the eating of the cake and the washing of the hands. If one does allow a long interval to elapse, one should first say the benediction *Al hamiḥeyah*, even though one intends to eat the same kinds of food during the meal.

Chapter 40

Washing the Hands Before Meals

1. Before eating bread over which the benediction *Hamotzi* (who bringeth forth) is said, one must wash his hands first. If the bread is no less than the size of an egg, he must say the benediction for washing hands; but if it is less than that, he need not say the benediction.

2. The water used for washing the hands must be poured out of a vessel that is perfect, having neither a hole nor a crack. It must also be even at the top without any indents or projecting parts. When using a vessel having a spout, we must not let the water run through the spout, because that

part is not the vessel proper since it does not hold any liquid. We must, therefore, pour the water from the edge of the vessel which contains the liquid.

3. A vessel that has been originally made to stand only by means of a support, is considered a vessel, but if it has not been originally made to be so used, for instance, when it is a cover of some vessel, the hands may not be washed from it. Concerning this, there are many different opinions in the *Shulḥan Aruḥ*.

4. It is difficult to ascertain the exact quantity of water required for washing the hands. We should, therefore, pour water lavishly on our hands, for Rab Ḥisda said (Shabbat 62b): "I wash with handsful of water and handsful of goodness are given me." We first wash our right hand and then our left. The water must cover the entire hand up to the wrist. No part of the hands should be left unwashed; therefore, the fingers must be slightly parted, and raised somewhat upward, in order that the water may run down the entire length of the fingers. It must also cover the finger tips and the full circumference of the fingers. The entire hand should be covered with one outpouring of water. We should, therefore, not wash the hands out of a vessel with a narrow opening through which the water cannot flow out freely. It is best to pour water twice on each hand.

5. After washing both hands, we rub them together and then raise them upward, as it is written (Psalms 134:2): "Lift up your hands," etc. Then, before drying them, we recite the benediction: "Blessed art Thou, O Lord our God, King of the universe, who hath sanctified us by His commandments and hath commanded us concerning the washing of the hands." (And although the benediction must be pronounced in every other case before the performance of the precept, as has been stated in chapter 8, section 8, above, yet in the case of washing the hands, since one's hands are at times unclean, it has been enacted that the benediction should be recited after the washing. Moreover, the drying of the hands is also a part of performing the precept). He who is accustomed to pour water twice on each hand, should first pour once on each hand, rub them together, pronounce the benediction, and thereafter pour a second time. We must be careful to have our hands thoroughly dried, and we should not dry them with our shirts, because it is harmful to the memory.

6. If after pouring the water upon one hand, he touched it with the other hand, or someone else had touched it, the water on the hand becomes contaminated by the contact. The hand must, therefore, be dried and then washed a second time. But if that happens after he had pronounced the benediction, the benediction need not be repeated.

7. If there is no vessel available, we may dip our hands into a stream, or into a tank ritually fit for the immersion of women, or into a well, even though there are no forty *seahs* of water (approximately twenty-four cubic feet) in it, but as long as there is enough water to cover both of our hands at one time, we may pronounce the benediction *Al netilat yadayim* (concerning the washing of the hands). In case of emergency, we may dip our hands into snow, if there is enough of it on the ground to make up the forty *seahs* required for a ritual immersion tank. If we wash our hands from a pump, we should put one hand near the ground, pump the water with the other hand, and then alternate our hands; or someone else should pump the water for us. But if the hands are high above the ground, the washing from the pump is invalid.

8. If the color of the water has changed, either because of the place or because something fell into it, it is unfit for the ritual washing of the hands; but if the change was due to natural causes, the water is fit. Water which has been used for washing utensils, or for soaking vegetables, or for placing in it vessels containing beverages for the purpose of keeping them cool, or for testing the capacity of some measures, is unfit for the ritual washing. Some authorities declare that water which has become loathsome, for instance, when a dog, or a pig, has drunk out of it, is considered as dirty water; and it is well to pay heed to their opinion.

9. If one touches water before washing the hands, the water does not become defiled by it. Therefore, upon leaving the lavatory, one may take a handful of water out of the barrel to wash the hands with it; and the remainder may be used for washing the hands before meals. However, if we dip the hands in the water to clean them, even if we have dipped in it only our little finger for the purpose of cleaning it, all the water becomes invalid for the ritual washing, since some work has been done with it.

10. Salt water, or water that is foul, or bitter, or turbid, which is not fit for a dog to drink, is unfit for the purpose of washing the hands before meals.

11. Before washing the hands, we must examine them to make sure that there is no coating on them, as that would be an obstruction between the hands and the water. If we have big nails, we must clean them well, so that there would be no clay or dirt under them, as that, too, is considered an obstruction. We must also remove the rings from the fingers before the washing.

12. If one's hands are colored by dye, but there is no crust of dye on them, it is not considered an obstruction. However, even a small quantity of dye-stuff on them, is considered an obstruction. If a man is a painter by trade, or a butcher, and his hands are stained with blood, or if he is a scribe

and his fingers are stained with ink, and he is accustomed to it, and members of his craft are not particular about it, it is not considered as an obstruction, unless it covers the greater part of the hand. If one has a bruise on his hand, upon which there is a plaster, and it would be painful to remove it, it is not considered an obstruction. (See chapter 161, dealing with the laws of obstruction in the immersion of women, as those laws apply also to the washing of hands).

13. The water must come down upon the hands by manual power; if it comes down spontaneously, it is invalid for the ritual washing. If the spigot is removed from a barrel that has a vent-hole, the first gush of water only is considered as poured by human agency, but the water flowing out thereafter is considered as if poured spontaneously. Therefore, if we desire to wash our hands with the water coming through the vent-hole, we must be sure that the entire hand is covered with the first gush; then we must close the hole, and open it again for the second outpour. If we are unable to judge these measurements, we must not wash our hands in this manner; needless to say that we should not wash our hands with water coming out of a wash-barrel that has a small hole and the outflow is light.

14. It is forbidden to eat without first washing the hands, even if they are wrapped in a cloth. If one is on a journey and has no water, but water can be obtained either within four miles ahead or within a mile in the rear, one must travel that distance, in order to wash the hands before eating. But if no water can be obtained even within such distances, or if one travels with a group and is afraid to separate oneself from them, or if one is prevented from washing the hands through some other cause, one may wrap the hands in a cloth or put on gloves and eat.

15. Regarding a person who responded to the call of nature before a meal, when he must wash his hands and recite the benediction *Asher yatzar*, and he also has to wash his hands for the meal, there are many conflicting opinions. Therefore, the proper thing to do is to wash his hands first in a manner insufficient for the pre-meal washing: that is, he should pour a little water into the palm of one hand and with that rub both hands together, then dry them well, and say the benediction *Asher yatzar*. Thereafter, he shall wash his hands as prescribed for the pre-meal washing and pronounce the benediction *Al netilat yadayim*.

16. If one touched during the meal a part of the body which is usually covered, or scratched the head, or urinated, one must wash the hands again, but without saying the benediction. Even if one has defecated during the

meal, one is to wash the hands without saying the benediction *Al netilat yadayim.*

17. If one eats some food which has been dipped in a liquid (see section that follows), or if a liquid has been poured on the food, even though one does not touch that part of the food where the liquid is, yet one must wash the hands first, but without saying the benediction *Al netilat yadayim.* Many persons are lenient in this matter; but every God-fearing person should be stringent about it.

18. Liquids with regard to the above law, are seven in number, and they are: wine including vinegar from wine, honey from bees, olive oil, milk including whey, dew, blood of cattle, animals and fowl (when taken for medicinal purpose), and water. Other fruit juices, even in localities where it is customary to make liquids for drinking purposes by squeezing out some fruit, are not considered as liquids, as regards this rule of law.

19. Fruits preserved in sugar do not require the ritual washing of the hands, because sugar is not a liquid. Neither is the moisture that comes out of fruit considered a liquid, because it is fruit juice. However, if the fruit is preserved in honey, and the honey is well congealed, it is no longer regarded as a liquid but as solid food, and therefore, does not require the washing of the hands. But if the honey is not well congealed, but has become thickened a little and is still fluid, it does require the washing of the hands. Butter, which is generally included in *milk,* is not considered a liquid but a solid food if it is congealed, but if it is melted, it is liquid.

20. Things that are generally eaten without either a spoon or a fork, even if one does eat it with a spoon or a fork, require the washing of the hands. But things which are generally eaten with a spoon or with a fork, for instance, pancakes, also fruits preserved in honey, in localities where it is generally eaten only with a spoon or a fork, do not require the washing of the hands.

21. Every substance that has been formed out of water is regarded as water (because water even when solidified is still regarded as a liquid). If, therefore, we dip radishes or anything similar to it in salt, we must wash our hands. Brandy made out of corn or fruit, is not regarded as a liquid with respect to this law, because it is nothing more than the vapor of the corn or of the fruit. And although it contains some water, and it is also mixed with some water, nevertheless, it is only a minor part of it; therefore, if we dip

something in it and eat it, we need not wash our hands. But whiskey made out of the kernels or shells of grapes, or from the lees of wine, should obviously be regarded as a liquid.

CHALTER 41

The Breaking of Bread and Hamotzi

1. Over true bread made of one of the five species of grain (wheat, spelt, oats, barley or rye), we say the benediction *Hamotzi*, and after eating it, we say Grace after meals.

2. One must be careful not to linger between washing the hands and the benediction *Hamotzi*, but one may respond *Amen* to any benediction one may happen to hear. A pause lasting as long as it takes to walk twenty-two cubits (thirty-three feet), or from one house to another even a short distance, or talking about something that appertains not to the meal, constitutes an interruption. However, if one inadvertently makes such an interruption, it does not matter, provided one does not perform some task or engage in a lengthy conversation, for then it constitutes a distraction and one must wash the hands again.

3. As a token of respect to the benediction *Hamotzi*, one should break off at the choicest spot of the bread. The hardest part of the bread is considered the choicest, and that is the opposite of the part where it breaks open, for the reason that at the part it begins to bake, there is pressure due to the expansion of the dough and the opposite end breaks open. Nevertheless, an old person, for whom it is difficult to eat hard bread, may break off the soft part. As it is improper to pause too long between the benediction *Hamotzi* and the eating of the bread, therefore, before reciting the benediction, one must make a slight circular incision in the bread in a manner that by raising one end, the other end will be lifted too, and after the benediction, complete the cut. Thus the benediction will be concluded while the loaf is still whole. Also, in breaking off a piece from the loaf which is not whole, one should not cut it entirely before saying the *Hamotzi*, so that when the benediction is said, the bread would be as large as possible. On the Sabbath, one should not cut the loaf at all until after the benediction, so that both loaves be perfectly whole. Also on a weekday, if it is a thin roll, we should say the *Hamotzi* before cutting it, since the cutting does not consume much time.

4. One should not break off too small a portion of the bread, so that one may not appear miserly, nor should one break off a portion larger than the size of an egg, so that one may not appear gluttonous. The above rule applies only to the case where one eats all alone, but when one eats in the company of other people and is required to give each a portion of the bread no less than the size of an olive, one may divide the loaf in such a manner as is best suited to the occasion. On the Sabbath, even when one eats all alone, one may cut a portion large enough to last for the entire meal. This is to evince respect for the Sabbath-meal by a desire to partake liberally of food.

It is proper to eat first of the portion which was broken off for the *Hamotzi* before eating any other morsel, and this is to show respect for a religious act, since over this portion one has pronounced the benediction. It is well to take care not to give any part of it to a non-Jew, a beast or a fowl.

5. Before saying the *Hamotzi*, we should place both hands upon the bread; the ten fingers being typical of the ten Divine Commands concerning bread; they are (Deuteronomy 22:10): "Thou shalt not plow with an ox and an ass together;" sowing divers seeds (loco citato 9); gleanings (Leviticus 19:9); leaving a forgotten sheaf in the field (Deuteronomy 24:19); leaving a corner of the field unreaped (Leviticus 19:9); not to muzzle an ox while threshing (Deuteronomy 25:4); the heave-offering (Numbers 15:19); the first tithe; the second tithe; and the separation of *ḥallah* (Numbers 15:21). Therefore, there are ten words in the benediction *Hamotzi*; ten Hebrew words in the verse (Psalms 145:15): "The eyes of all wait upon Thee;" ten words in the verse (Deuteronomy 8:8): "A land of wheat and barley," etc., and ten words in the verse (Genesis 27:28): "May God give thee," etc. When we pronounce the Divine Name, we should raise the bread, and on the Sabbath we should raise both loaves. We must recite the *Hamotzi* very devoutly; and aspirate distinctly the letter *he* from the word *hamotsi;* and allow a short pause between the words *leḥem* and *min,* in order not to slur over the letter *mem.* Immediately after pronouncing the benediction, we should eat, as it is forbidden to make any pause between the benediction and the eating, even for the purpose of responding *Amen.* It is proper to eat bread of no less than the size of an olive before making an interruption.

6. It is required to have salt set on the table before breaking bread, and to dip into the salt the piece of bread over which the *Hamotzi* is said, because the table represents the altar and the food symbolizes the offerings, and it is said (Leviticus 2:13): "With all thine offerings thou shalt offer salt." And because a table is likened to an altar, it is best to take care not to kill any vermin on it.

7. When distributing the portions of bread among those who are at the table, we must not throw it, as it is forbidden to throw bread; neither shall we give it into their hands, but we should place it before them.

8. It is meritorious to say *Hamotzi* over the bread that is more important. Therefore, if we have a part of a loaf and a whole loaf made of the same kind of grain, and we intend to partake of both in the course of the meal, even if the whole one is smaller in size and it is not as pure as the piece, we should, nevertheless, break off the whole one, because it is the more desirable. However, if they are not of the same kind of grain, and the whole one is of an inferior grade, for instance, when the whole one is made of spelt and the piece is made of wheat, we should pronounce the *Hamotzi* over the one made of wheat even though it is smaller. If the whole one is made of barley, although barley is inferior to wheat, nevertheless, since barley, too, is mentioned in the Biblical text (Deuteronomy 8:8), and since the loaf is a whole one, the God-fearing should show respect to the barley loaf. What do we do in such a case? We lay the piece underneath the whole one, and break

off from both at the same time. If both are whole ones or both are pieces and are made of the same kind of grain, we should say the *Hamotzi* over the one that is purer; and if both are equally pure, we should say the *Hamotzi* over the larger one.

9. If we have bread baked by a Jew and bread baked by a non-Jew, and we do not abstain from eating the bread baked by a non-Jew, if both of them are either whole or pieces, and are also of the same size and baked of the same kind of grain, we should say the *Hamotzi* over the bread baked by the Jew. If the bread baked by the Jew is not as pure as that of the non-Jew, we may say the *Hamotzi* over whichever bread we prefer. If the master of the house abstains from eating the bread of a non-Jew, but this time non-Jewish bread has been brought for the sake of a guest, it should be removed from the table until after the *Hamotzi* has been said.

10. The law concerning the preferable treatment of bread, applies only to a case where we intend to partake of the two kinds of bread in the course of the meal; but when we intend to partake of only one kind of bread, we should say the *Hamotzi* over the one we intend to eat, and the preference should be entirely disregarded.

CHAPTER 42

Laws Concerning Meals

1. If we possess cattle or poultry which we must feed, we are forbidden to partake of any food before we provide them with food, for it is written (Deuteronomy 11:15): "And I will give grass in thy field for thy cattle, that thou mayest eat and be full." Thus has the Torah given precedence in feeding the beast to the man. However, as regards drinking, the man takes precedence, for it is written (Genesis 24:46): "Drink, and I will give thy camels drink also;" and it is written again (Numbers 20:8): "So shalt thou give the congregation and the cattle drink."

2. We must neither eat nor drink voraciously, nor while standing, and our table should be immaculate and nicely covered, even though we have but common fare. We should not take a portion as large as an egg and eat of it, nor should we hold the food in one hand and break it off with the other. We must not drink a glassful of wine at one draught; one who does so is a guzzler. It is polite usage to drink a glass of wine in two draughts, but to drink it in three draughts is squeamish. However, if the glass is extra large, we may drink it in several draughts; if it is a small glass, we may drink it all in one draught.

3. We should not take a bite of a piece of bread and then put it on the table, or give it to someone else, or put it in the dish, because it may be repulsive to our neighbor. We should not drink a part of a cup and then give

the rest to our neighbor to drink, for utmost care should be taken not to drink of the residue of a cup that someone else has drunk, for the one to whom it has been tendered might be bashful and drink it against his will.

4. A person must not be irritable while eating, because the invited guests and the members of the household are then ashamed to eat, thinking that he is raging because he begrudges them their eating.

5. Conversation, even about matters relating to the Torah, must not be indulged in while eating, owing to the danger of choking, arising from the simultaneous use of the windpipe and the gullet. It is even forbidden to say "Good health" to the one who sneezes. However, when not actually engaged in eating, it is a duty to discourse at the table matters relating to the Torah; and we must be very careful to observe this rule. It is a good custom to recite (Psalm 23): "A Psalm of David, the Lord is my shepherd, I shall not want," which is Torah (Scripture) as well as a prayer for one's sustenance. At the conclusion of the meal, it is customary to recite on weekdays (Psalm 137): "By the rivers of Babylon" etc., and on Sabbath and festivals and on such days when the *Taḥanun* is not recited, it is customary to say (Psalm 126): "A song of degrees, when the Lord turned again the captivity of Zion," etc. When studying out of a book upon the table, we must be very careful, as books are likely to have little worms, and we might, God forbid, violate thereby a Divine Command (the prohibition against worms in food).

6. When two persons eat at one table, even if each one eats out of his own plate, or if they eat fruit and each one has his own portion before him, it is proper to allow the elder of the two to commence eating first. The one who eats before his elder is considered a glutton.

7. If two persons eat out of one bowl, and one of them interrupts his eating in order to drink or to perform some other trivial thing, it is polite usage for the other to wait until his companion resumes eating; but if there are three eating and one of them leaves off eating, the other two need not wait for the third.

8. We may utilize bread for any purpose, provided it does not become loathsome thereby. Therefore, we may not prop up a plate with it which contains something that may render the bread loathsome if it spills on it. If we eat anything by means of a slice of bread, using it as a spoon, we must eat some of the bread with every mouthful of the other food; and whatever is left of the bread should also be eaten.

9. It is forbidden to throw bread even in a place where it will not become loathsome, for the very act of throwing it is a degrading act. We may not throw any other kind of food, when it becomes loathsome by it; but we may throw articles of food which are not affected by it, such as nuts and the like. We should not sit upon a bag containing fruit, because they would be-

come loathsome by it. We should not wash our hands with wine or any other beverage as it tends to degrade them. When we see food lying on the ground, we must pick it up. Food suitable for the consumption of human beings must not be fed to beasts, as the food is degraded by it.

10. If we have to use bread or any other kind of food as a medicament, we are allowed to use it even if it makes it loathsome.

11. We should be careful not to throw crumbs about, for it causes poverty; we should instead gather them up and feed them to the fowl.

12. We should not drink any water in the presence of others; we should turn our face away; but we need not do so, when we drink other beverages.

13. We should neither stare at the face of a person who is eating or drinking nor at the portion set before him, so that we may not embarrass him.

14. If we are served savory food or drink that creates a craving for it, we must immediately give some of it to the person who served it as it is harmful to see food for which one has a longing and yet is unable to eat of it.

15. We should not give any food to any person unless we are certain that he will wash his hands and say the appropriate benediction.

16. A woman whose husband is not present should drink no wine; and if she is in a different place, not in her own house, she may drink no wine even if her husband is present. This law applies to other intoxicating beverages as well. If, however, she is accustomed to drink some wine in the presence of her husband, she may drink a little of it in her husband's absence.

17. Guests are not allowed to give to the children of the host of the food that has been set before them. For the host may have no more food than what has been set before them, and he will feel embarrassed if they will not have enough for themselves. However, if there is abundant food on the table, they are permitted to do so.

18. When a man comes into a house, he should not say: "Give me something to eat," but he should wait until they invite him. One must not partake of food which does not suffice for the host, for this is considered a shade of robbery, even though the host invites us to dine with him. The violation of this rule is a grievous sin, and it is one for which it is difficult to obtain forgiveness.

19. We are not allowed to leave our seats at the table before saying Grace. We may not go into another room to finish our meal there; nor may we leave with the intention of returning to finish our meal at the same table; nor may we cross the threshold of our door, even with the intention of returning to the same table to finish our meal. Nevertheless, if we do transgress by leaving our seat, whether we finish our meal at the present place, or we return to our original place to finish it there, we need not repeat the benediction *Hamotzi*. For, since we have established the place of the repast by means of eating bread, although we have thereafter changed our place, it is nevertheless considered as one meal; we must only be careful to eat a slice of bread of no less than the size of an olive at the place we intend to recite Grace. The above rule of law does not apply to other matters.

20. If several people eat together in company and some of them leave with the intention of returning, as long as there remains one in the original place, the status of the place that they have established does not cease and is resumed when they return, and it is not considered an interruption.

21. If at the time we say the *Hamotzi*, we intend to go thereafter to another room to say Grace there, it is permissible to do so, provided we eat there a slice of bread no less than the size of an olive. This, however, may be done only in cases of emergency, as when we need attend to a religious feast.

22. If we say our prayers in the middle of the meal, we need not repeat the *Hamotzi* when we resume eating. If we take a nap in the middle of the meal, even though it is prolonged for some time, it does not constitute an interruption. If we interrupt to attend to secular matters, for instance, to attend to the call of nature, or the like, it likewise does not constitute an interruption. In all these cases, however, we must wash our hands anew, since there has been a diversion of mind, unless we have taken care of our hands (not to become unclean), but we need not pronounce the benediction over washing the hands because we are not required to repeat the benediction over washing the hands on account of a diversion of mind.

23. If upon finishing our meal, we have resolved to recite Grace, but thereafter we have changed our mind and desire to eat or drink something, there are divergent opinions regarding the benedictions applying to such a case. Therefore, an act like this should be avoided, and we should recite the Grace immediately upon resolving to do so.

CHAPTER 43

Benedictions Over Special Courses, During Meals

1. We need not say a special benediction before or after eating any kind of food which is generally eaten in the course of the meal, such as meat, fish, relishes, porridge, soup, pancakes, and the like, even food which is generally eaten without bread. For since we usually partake of such food during a meal, it forms a part of the meal, and it is, therefore, blessed by the *Hamotzi*

said over the bread, as well as by the Grace recited after the meal. Even if the articles of food have been brought in from another house during the course of the meal, we need not say the special benediction over them, it being assumed that we are prepared to eat whatever will be served to us.

2. Neither do we have to say a benediction over the beverages drunk during the course of the meal, for it is not customary to eat a meal without drinking. Wine, however, is an exception because of its importance (inasmuch as there are many occasions when we must say a benediction over wine, even when we have no desire to drink it, as at the *Kiddush* and the *Havdalah*). We must, therefore, say a benediction over it when we drink it during the course of the meal. If we recite the benediction over wine before washing the hands, and we intend to drink some wine also during the course of the meal, or if we are accustomed to drink wine in the course of the meal, we need not repeat the benediction, for it has already been blessed by the benediction said over it before the meal. As it is not the prevalent custom in our country to drink brandy in the course of a meal, it is doubtful whether this beverage is included in the meal. Therefore, if we intend to drink some brandy during the course of the meal, we should drink some of it, no less than the quantity of an olive, before washing our hands, say the benediction over it, and have it in mind to exempt thereby also what we will drink during the course of the meal. If we fail to do that, we should first say a benediction over sugar, and by this benediction, exempt the brandy. Some are accustomed to dip some bread in the brandy, but others have scruples about it.

3. We must say a benediction over fruit eaten during the course of the meal without bread, even if they have been on the table before we said the benediction *Hamotzi*, for since they are not an essential part of the meal, they are not exempt from their particular benediction through the *Hamotzi;* but we need not say the concluding benediction recited after eating fruit, for they are exempted by reciting the Grace after meals. However, if we do not eat the fruit without bread, we need not say a benediction over them, as the fruit then becomes an accessory to the bread. If we desire to eat some fruit with bread and some without it, we should take care to eat first some fruit without bread and say the necessary benediction, and then we can eat some with bread. Should we happen to eat first some fruit with bread and thereafter eat some without bread, it is doubtful whether we need say the benediction. Some people are accustomed to eat between courses, certain appetizers, such as salted olives, lemons, radishes, and the like. These are considered as a part of the meal, as through these the appetite increases; therefore the benediction need not be said over them, because the *Hamotzi* exempts them.

4. If the principal part of our meal consists of fruit eaten with bread, since the fruit is the principal part of our meal, they are exempted by the benediction *Hamotzi* even if they have not been on the table when the benediction was pronounced. However, in such an event it is necessary that we first eat some of the fruit with bread, and thereafter we need not say a special benediction when we eat it without bread.

5. If we eat cooked fruit as part of the meal, as a dessert is generally cooked, whether it is cooked with or without meat, we should eat some of it at the beginning and at the end of the meal with bread, then we may eat it during the meal without bread and need not say the benediction over it.

6. If we eat pastry during the meal, such as sponge cakes, almond cakes, and the like, to satisfy our hunger, it is doubtful whether we need say the benediction. Therefore, it is good practice that when we say the benediction *Hamotzi*, to have it in mind to exempt thereby whatever we will eat of these sorts of food.

7. If after finishing the meal and before reciting Grace, we drink some coffee to help digest the food, we must say the first benediction over it. For whatever serves to aid digestion is not considered as an essential element of the meal. Nevertheless, it is best to say the benediction *Shehakol* (all things exist) over a piece of sugar, in order to exempt the coffee by it.

Chapter 44

Laws Concerning the Washing of Hands and the Saying of Grace After Meals

1. Many people are lenient regarding the washing of hands after meals, but the God-fearing should be careful to observe it scrupulously. We are required to wash only the first two joints of our fingers, holding our hands downward before drying them. He who leads in saying the Grace should wash his hands first.

2. We must not pour this water on the ground where people walk, because an evil spirit rests upon it. We must wash into a vessel or underneath the table. We dry our hands before reciting Grace, and we must not pause between the washing and the reciting of Grace.

3. The table cloth and the bread must still remain upon the table when Grace is recited, this is to indicate the abundance of food which the Lord, blessed be His name, has supplied for us, in that He gives enough to eat and to spare; as Elisha said to his servant (II Kings 4:43): "Because thus saith the Lord, one should eat and leave over." Another reason is, because the

blessing of God comes only on some existing substance and not upon an empty space, as Elisha said to the wife of Obadiah (loco citato 2): "What hast thou in the house?"

4. It is customary either to remove the knives left on the table before reciting Grace, or else to cover them. For the table is compared to an altar, and concerning the altar, it is written (Deuteronomy 27:5): "Thou shalt not lift up any iron upon them." For iron shortens the life of man while the altar prolongs life, and it is improper that one which shortens life should be raised on one that prolongs it. The table also prolongs the days of man and atones for his sins if one invites poor wayfarers at his table. The power of hospitality is so great that it causes the Divine Presence to be in our midst. The custom prevails in many communities not to cover the knives on the Sabbath or on festivals; for on weekdays they represent the brutal might of Esau, but on the Sabbath and festivals there is no Satan or evil occurence. And a custom in Israel is as valid as Law.

5. Even if we have eaten only a piece of bread no larger than the size of an olive, we must say the Grace thereafter.

6. Grace after meals should be recited neither standing nor walking, but sitting. If we have walked to and fro in the house while eating, or if we have been standing or reclining, we must sit when reciting the Grace, in order that we may recite it with devotion. While saying Grace, we should not recline on our seats, because it is indicative of pride, but we should sit erect, put on the coat and hat, in order that the fear of Heaven be upon us, and that our minds be concentrated upon saying the Grace with reverence and awe. We are not allowed to do anything else while reciting Grace.

7. It is the custom to respond *Amen* to all the prayers beginning with *Haraḥaman* (the All-merciful) contained in the Grace, for it is stated in the *Midrash* that when we hear someone pray for a certain thing or bless an Israelite, even not mentioning the Divine Name, we are bound to respond *Amen* to it.

8. If we neglect to recite Grace up to the time the food has become digested, that is, when we begin to feel hungry, we can no longer make amends and say Grace. Some are of the opinion that food is digested in one and one-fifth hours. Nevertheless, at big feasts, people occasionally tarry longer than this time limit between the eating and the saying of Grace, for the reason that also in the interim they drink and eat desserts. However, it is best not to wait too long.

9. If we violate the law and leave the table before reciting Grace, then if at the place where we are now there is a piece of bread, we should partake thereof without saying the benediction *Hamotzi*, and thereafter say Grace. If no bread is to be obtained in that place, we must return to the original

place to say Grace. But if we are so far away from the original place that before we return the food might be digested, we may say Grace in the place where we are.

10. On the Sabbath upon which either the New Moon, or a festival, or an intermediate day of a festival occurs, *Retzeh* (be pleased, O Lord our God) should be recited first, and *Yaaleh veyavo* (may our remembrance rise), etc., later, because the Sabbath is more constant and more sacred than the festival.

11. If we are in doubt as to whether or not we have recited Grace, then if we are still satiated, we must recite Grace again (for the saying of Grace is then a Mosaic ordinance). If we happen to fall asleep in the middle of reciting Grace, and upon awakening we do not know where we left off, we must repeat from the beginning. If a woman is in doubt as to whether she has said Grace, she need not repeat it.

12. If we omit *Retzeh* on the Sabbath or *Yaaleh veyavo* on a festival, and we become aware of the omission before pronouncing the Divine Name in the benediction, "Blessed be Thou, O Lord, who in Thy compassion rebuildest Jerusalem," we should recite *Retzeh* or *Yaaleh veyavo*, and thereafter recite *Uveneh* (and rebuild Jerusalem). But if we become aware of the omission after pronouncing the Divine Name, we should conclude the benediction *Boneh beraḥamav yerushalayim, Amen* (who in Thy compassion rebuildest Jerusalem, Amen), and then on the Sabbath we say: "Blessed art Thou, O Lord our God, King of the universe, who in His love gave Sabbaths for rest to His people Israel, for a sign and for a covenant, blessed art Thou, O Lord, who hallowest the Sabbath." On a festival we say there: "Blessed art Thou, O Lord our God, King of the universe, who gave festivals to His people Israel for gladness and for joy, this day of (naming the particular festival). Blessed art Thou, O Lord our God, who hallowest Israel and the seasons." If the festival occurs on a Sabbath and we forget to recite *Retzeh* and *Yaaleh veyavo*, we should say: "Blessed art Thou, O Lord our God, King of the universe, who in love gave Sabbaths for rest to His people Israel for a sign and for a covenant, and festivals for gladness and joy, this day of (naming the festival), blessed art Thou, O Lord, who hallowest the Sabbath and Israel and the seasons." If we have recited *Retzeh* but have omitted *Yaaleh veyavo*, we should say what is to be said on a festival only. If we have recited *Yaaleh veyavo* but have omitted *Retzeh*, we should recite what is to be said on the Sabbath only.

13. If we become aware of the omissions mentioned above after having begun the benediction that follows: "Blessed art Thou, O Lord our God, King of the universe, O God our Father," etc., even if we have only said the word *Baruḥ* (blessed), we can no longer remedy the omission by saying the benediction "Who gave," etc. Therefore, if this occurs during the first two meals, we must repeat the Grace from the beginning. If we have said: "Blessed art Thou, O Lord," and became aware of the omission, we must conclude the benediction with *Lamedeni ḥukkeḥa* (teach me Thy statutes), so that the benediction would not be pronounced in vain, and then repeat the Grace from the beginning. But if this occurs in the third meal at which we

are not bound to eat bread even on the Sabbath, and much less so on a festival, and the saying of Grace on that particular time is not obligatory, therefore we need not repeat Grace from the beginning, but conclude it without it. Nevertheless, if we become aware of the omission at a place where it is still possible to remedy it by saying the benediction "Who gave," etc., we must do so even if it happens after any number of meals.

14. If we omit *Yaaleh veyavo* on *Rosh Ḥodesh,* we should say: "Blessed art Thou, O Lord our God, King of the universe, who gave New Moons to His people Israel for a memorial," but we must not conclude it. (It is immaterial whether it is during the day or night). If we omit *Yaaleh veyavo* during the Intermediate Days of the festivals, we should say: "Blessed art Thou, O Lord our God, King of the universe, who gave appointed times to His people Israel for gladness and for joy this day of (naming the festival), blessed art Thou, O Lord, who hallowest Israel and the seasons." On *Rosh Hashanah,* we say: "Blessed art Thou, O Lord our God, King of the universe, who gave festivals to His people Israel on this Day of Memorial; blessed art Thou, who hallowest Israel and the Day of Memorial." If we become aware of the omission after we have begun the benediction that follows, we need not then repeat Grace from the beginning, because on *Rosh Hashanah, Rosh Ḥodesh* and *Ḥol Hammoed,* the eating of bread is not obligatory.

15. If *Rosh Ḥodesh* occurs on the Sabbath, and we forget to say both *Retzeh* and *Yaaleh veyavo,* then when we become aware of the omission, we should say: "Blessed art Thou, O Lord our God, King of the universe, who gave Sabbaths for rest to His people Israel in love, for a sign of a covenant, and New Moons as a memorial." For although on *Rosh Ḥodesh* that benediction is not included, in this case, however, since we recite the benediction also for the sake of the Sabbath, we must also mention *Rosh Ḥodesh.* If we have recited *Retzeh* but omitted *Yaaleh veyavo,* and became aware of the omission after beginning the benediction which follows it, we need not repeat the Grace from the beginning, for that which belongs to the Sabbath we have recited, and for the sake of *Rosh Ḥodesh* alone we need not repeat it. But if we have said *Yaaleh veyavo,* but have omitted *Retzeh,* as a result of which we must repeat Grace from the beginning, then we must also include *Yaaleh veyavo.* The same law applies to the Intermediate Days of festivals and *Rosh Hashanah.*

16. If we forget to include *Al hannisim* (for the miracles) in Grace, either on *Ḥanukkah* or on *Purim,* and we become aware of the omission after pronouncing the Divine Name in the concluding benediction, that is, we have already said "Blessed art Thou, O Lord," we need not repeat the Grace. But while reciting the *Haraḥaman* (May the All-merciful), we include: "May the All-merciful perform for us miracles and wonders as He hath wrought for our ancestors in days of old, at this season," and then add: "In the days of Mattathias," or "In the days of Mordecai."

17. If we commence eating a meal on the Sabbath, and continue to eat until dark, we must include *Retzeh* in the Grace, since we have not yet recited the *Maariv* service. Likewise on a festival, *Rosh Ḥodesh, Ḥanukkah* and *Purim,* if we begin our meal while it is yet day, we must mention the special

prayer applying to that day, even if it is already night when we recite Grace. Also, if we begin eating our meal before *Rosh Ḥodesh* has set in, and continue eating during the night when we eat bread no less than the size of an olive, we must recite *Yaaleh veyavo*. This rule also applies to *Ḥanukkah* and *Purim*. If we begin eating a meal on the Sabbath and continue eating it during the night, when we eat bread no less than the size of an olive, and Sunday is *Rosh Ḥodesh*, we must include both *Retzeh* and *Yaaleh veyavo* in the Grace. The same rule applies to *Ḥanukkah* and *Purim*. There are dissenting opinions to this rule of law, because they consider it as self-contradictory. It is, therefore, best to avoid continuing the meal at night on such occasions.

18. If a non-Jew is present in the room when Grace is recited, we should add: "Us the sons of the Covenant, all of us together."

CHAPTER 45

Formal Grace (of Three or More)

1. If three male persons have eaten together, they have to unite in saying Grace after meals, and they must recite it over a cup of wine, if possible. If it is impossible to obtain wine, then beer, mead or brandy may be used, when such liquid is the common beverage of the locality; that is, where vine culture does not obtain and one must walk all day to obtain it, as a result of which wine is expensive and these beverages are substituted for wine. Some authorities hold that even a lone person is required to recite Grace over a cup. When reciting Grace alone, meticulous people do not hold the cup in their hands, but place it on the table in front of them.

2. The cup is filled first and thereafter the hands are washed.

3. If we drink some of the wine out of a vessel, whatever remains in it becomes unfit for use at the Grace, unless we add a little water or wine, that has not been disqualified. Since the cup must be filled for the express purpose of using it for the benediction, therefore, if the contents of the cup is unfit, we must first pour it into a vessel and from there into the cup for the special purpose mentioned.

4. The cup used for Grace must be whole, and even if only its base is broken it is unfit. Even the least defect in the rim of the cup, or a crack, renders it unfit. The cup must be rinsed inside and washed outside, or it may be wiped well so that it is clean. The liquid should be poured from the vessel into the cup for the purpose of reciting the Grace, and the cup must be full.

The person who is to lead in saying the Grace, should take the cup with both hands (to indicate his affection for the cup, in that he longs to accept it with all his might) and as it is written (Psalms 134:2): "Lift up your hands towards the sanctuary, and bless the Lord." Afterward he removes his left hand and holds it only with his right, without any help of the left (so that it should not appear as being burdensome to him). He should look at the cup in order not to divert his attention from it; and he should hold it one hand-breadth (four inches) above the table, as it is written (Psalms 116:13): "I will lift the cup of salvation and call upon the name of the Lord." A left-handed person should keep it in the left hand, which is like everybody's right. It is proper to remove the empty dishes from the table before reciting Grace.

5. If all those who sit at the table are of equal rank, and there is a *Kohen* among them, it is a religious duty to honor him with leading in saying Grace, as it is written (Leviticus 21:8): "Thou shalt sanctify him." However, if there is a worthy and eminent man among them, he should lead in saying Grace. It is customary to let a mourner lead in saying Grace, but only when all are of equal rank. It is proper to confer the honor of leading in saying Grace upon one who is kind and hates ill-gotten profit, and dispenses charity of his own money, for it is written (Proverbs 22:9): "A man of benevolent eye will indeed be blessed." Do not read *Yevoraḥ* (shall be blessed), but *Yevareḥ* (shall bless).

6. The person who leads in saying Grace, begins by saying: *Hav lan unevareḥ* (let us say Grace), for every sacred function requires attention. Or he may say, as is the prevailing custom, in the Yiddish language: *Rabbotai, mir villen bentshen* (gentlemen, let us say Grace), and the rest of the company respond: "Blessed be the name of the Lord henceforth and forever." Then the leader continues: "With the sanction of these honored guests, we will bless Him, of whose bounty we have eaten." Those present reply: "Blessed be He of whose bounty we have eaten, and through whose goodness we live." The leader repeats the last sentence. In some communities it is the custom that those present respond *Amen* after the leader says: "And through whose goodness we live;" while in other communities no such custom prevails. There are also various customs with regards to saying, *Baruḥ hu ubaruḥ shemo* (blessed be He and blessed be His name). In some communities, the one who leads in saying Grace, says it even when there are only three persons, while in others, he says it only when there are ten who say the Grace, because the Divine Name is then mentioned; and it is proper to follow the latter custom. Those present, however, should not say it in any event, and needless to say that the one saying the Grace privately should not say it.

7. The leader then recites the Grace aloud, while those present, quietly repeat every word with him and they hasten to finish the benediction before he does, so that they may respond *Amen.*

8. Upon concluding Grace, the leader pronounces the benediction on the cup over which he has said the Grace, and drinks of it a quantity equal to the capacity of one and a half eggshells, so that he may pronounce the concluding benediction said after drinking wine. If the contents of the cups of those seated at the table has become defective, the one who led in saying Grace should, after pronouncing the benediction, "Who hath created the

fruit of the vine," and before drinking of it, pour a little of his wine unto their cups, so that they, too, may pronounce the benediction. If their cups are empty, he should likewise pour in them a little of his wine, and they should not taste of it before the leader has tasted his. But if each of them has a cup which is not unfit, the leader need not give them any of his wine, and they may taste of theirs before he tastes of his. And this is the proper way. It is best that each guest should have a full cup, if possible.

9. Some authorities hold that if the person who is leading in saying Grace, does not wish to drink of his cup, he may let one of those present say the benediction, "Who created the fruit of the vine," and this one should drink a quarter of a *lug* (one and a half eggshells) and say the concluding benediction. Other authorities hold that this is an improper practice, and that only the leader may say the benediction over the cup of wine. The latter view prevails.

10. If two persons have eaten together, they should invite a third one to join them in saying Grace. Even if that third person comes after the two have already finished their meal, yet, if some food were brought to them as a dessert, that they would eat of, it is proper to invite the third person to join them in saying Grace. They should give him bread, no less than the size of an olive, so that he should be required to recite Grace. Some authorities hold that he must be given bread; some hold that any kind of grain suffices; others hold that even fruit or vegetables are sufficient; while others still are of the opinion that even if he eats nothing at all, but he drinks any kind of beverage except water, a quantity equal to the capacity of an egg and a half, he may join them in saying the formal Grace. And this is the accepted view. He may in such a case say: "Blessed be He of whose bounty we have eaten," even though he has not eaten any food but drunk liquids, because drinking is included in the term "eating." After they have said: *Hazzan et hakkol* (who giveth food unto all), the third person should say the concluding benediction over whatever he has eaten or drunk. However, if the third person has arrived after the other two washed their hands, he may no longer join them in saying Grace.

11. If three people eat together, inasmuch as they are obliged to join in saying the formal Grace, they are not allowed to separate. And so if four or five persons eat together, not one of them is allowed to recite the Grace privately, for all of them must unite in saying Grace. If the company consists of six or more persons, but less than ten, they may separate in such a manner that the requisite number of three for reciting the formal Grace remains in each group.

12. If ten males have eaten together, they must add in the Grace the Divine Name; that is, the person who leads in saying Grace says: "We will bless our God, He of whose bounty we have eaten," etc. Those present respond: "Blessed be our God, He of whose bounty," etc. Since the ten must mention the Divine Name, they must not separate into smaller groups unless there are twenty or more, when they may divide into two groups (of ten each), and then each group can unite in reciting the Grace, mentioning the Divine Name.

13. If ten males unite in saying Grace and they neglect to mention the Divine Name, they may not repeat it in order to mention the Divine Name, for their duty of uniting in saying the Grace has already been fulfilled, and their neglect to mention the Divine Name is an error which cannot be rectified. But if the rest of the company have not responded to the leader's invitation to say Grace, the leader must repeat the invitation and include the Divine Name.

14. If seven of the company have eaten bread, and three of them have eaten fruit or have drunk sufficient liquor so as to be required to say the concluding benediction thereafter, they may unite in saying Grace and mention the Divine Name. (In this case all authorities agree that the eating of fruit or the drinking of liquor is sufficient). It is meritorious to seek after ten males to unite in saying the Grace so that the Divine Name may be mentioned. But if only six of the ten have eaten bread, they cannot unite with four who have eaten only fruit or have drunk liquor, because a substantial majority is required.

15. All who have eaten together, whether three or ten, even though they have not eaten the entire meal together, but have sat down to eat and have said the benediction *Hamotzi*, and each one has subsequently eaten from his own lunch, they must say Grace together, inasmuch as they have united as one body; they are not allowed to separate. Even if one of them wishes to finish his meal before the others, they still are not allowed to separate. But if they have not started together at the beginning of the meal, but after two persons have eaten already, were it even no more than the size of an olive, and a third person came along and joined them, then if he has finished his meal with them, they are obliged to unite in saying Grace; but if he wishes to finish his meal before them, he is allowed to separate and recite the Grace privately. Nevertheless, it is proper for the third person to wait and unite in saying the Grace. If one of them is forced by circumstances, or if he fears the possibility of suffering a loss, even if he has joined them at the beginning, he is allowed to finish his meal before the others and to recite the Grace privately. However, if the case is not urgent, it is proper for him to wait.

16. If three males eat in company and one of them forgets and recites the Grace privately, the rest may yet unite with him, even after he had concluded the Grace, and he may also respond: "We will bless Him of whose bounty we have eaten," etc. However, if he has united with two others in saying the Grace, he can no longer be counted with the former two. If two of the three have said the Grace, even privately, they can no longer unite in saying Grace formally.

17. If three males eat in company and two finish their meal and wish to say Grace, while the third one has not yet finished his meal, he must interrupt his meal, so that they may say formal Grace. He must respond with them, and thus he discharges his duty of saying formal Grace. Then he waits until the person who leads in saying Grace concludes *Hazzan et hakkol* (who giveth food unto all), and resume his meal without saying the benediction *Hamotzi*,

since it has been his intention to eat some more. After finishing his meal, he should recite the Grace privately. But two persons need not interrupt their meal for the sake of one, unless they wish to honor him more than is actually demanded by law. If ten persons eat together, four are obliged to interrupt their meal for the sake of six, and they need only wait until the leader has said: *Baruḥ elohenu* (blessed be our God) before resuming their meal. After their meal, they should unite in saying Grace together, without mentioning the Divine Name in the introduction.

18. At large banquets where many guests are present, it is proper to choose someone to lead in saying Grace in a powerful voice, so that all present can hear him, at least up to *Hazzan et hakkol* (who giveth food to all). If this is impossible, they should form groups of ten each to say Grace.

19. If two separate groups eat in one house, or if they eat in two separate houses but some of them can see one another, they are considered as one company and may combine in saying Grace. However, if they cannot see one another, each group must unite separately. Nevertheless, if one person waits upon both groups, he is the means of combining them, provided they have originally entered with the intention of being considered as one company. In whatever manner they unite, it is essential that they all hear the person leading in saying the Grace, at least up to *Hazzan et hakkol.*

20. If we hear others saying Grace who have united for this purpose, but we have neither eaten nor drunk with them, we should respond: "Blessed be He and blessed be His name continuously and forever," when we hear the leader say: "We will bless Him." If a party of ten have united in saying Grace, and we hear the leader say: "We will bless our God," we should then respond: "Blessed be our God and blessed be His name continuously forever." But if we arrive after the leader had already said: "We will bless," etc., and we hear the rest of the company respond: "We will bless," etc., we should only say *Amen* at the conclusion of their response.

21. When three persons eat together, each one having his own loaf, and one of them has bread baked by a non-Jew, whereas the other two avoid eating such bread, they may, nevertheless, unite in saying Grace, and the one who has eaten the non-Jewish bread should lead in saying Grace, because he could eat the bread of the other two, while the other two could not eat his. Likewise, if one has eaten dairy foods, and the other two have eaten meat, they may unite in saying Grace, and the former should be the leader, because he may eat of the food of the other two. If such a person drinks no wine, or if only "new" beer is available, and he avoids drinking "new" beer, then it is better that one of the two who have eaten meat, should lead in saying Grace over a cup of beverage. If one has eaten hard cheese, and two have eaten meat, some authorities hold that these cannot unite in saying Grace, while others hold that they may unite, because they could all eat of the same loaf of bread. And it is well to accept the more lenient opinion.

22. If women eat together with men who are obliged to unite in saying Grace, they must listen to its recital. It is the custom not to include a minor in the quorum for reciting the formal Grace, unless he is thirteen years and one day old, even though it has not been ascertained whether or not he brought forth at least two hairs indicating purberty.

23. A person who does not read the *Shema* morning and evening, or the one who publicly violates the Divine Commands should not be counted in with those who unite in saying Grace. A true proselyte may join others to recite Grace, and he may also recite the verse: "Who has caused our fathers to inherit," for it is written concerning Abraham (Genesis 17:5): "For a father of many nations have I made thee," and this verse is interpreted to mean: In the past he had been the father of Assyria only, but thenceforth the father of all nations.

CHAPTER 46

Forbidden Foods

1. The blood found in eggs is forbidden. Occasionally it is forbidden to eat the entire egg on account of blood-spots. Therefore, the egg should be examined before using it in the preparation of food.

2. The use of the blood of fish is permitted, but if it is collected into a vessel, its use is forbidden for the sake of appearance, because people might think that it is forbidden blood. If, however, it is evident that it is the blood of a fish, as when it contains scales, then its use is permissible.

3. If we bite off a piece of bread or any other food, and blood from our gums is upon it, we must cut off the tinted part and throw it away. The blood from the gums may be soaked up on a weekday, since it has not discharged itself, but not on a Sabbath. (See chapter 80, section 54, below).

4. Blood is sometimes found in milk, which comes out of the cow's udder together with the milk; when that occurs, a rabbi should be consulted.

5. Meat and dairy products may not be eaten or cooked together, nor is it permissible to derive any benefit from such mixed foods. If, therefore, meat and dairy products happen to become mixed together, a rabbi should be consulted, as in certain instances a benefit may be derived from it, while in others it may not.

6. Two Jewish acquaintances may not eat at one table, if one eats meat and the other dairy products, even though they are at odds, unless they make a noticeable mark between them, for instance, by having a separate cover laid for each, or by placing upon the table a certain article that generally does not belong there, between their respective food. They must be careful not to drink any liquid out of the same vessel, as the food clings to it.

7. We must not eat of the same loaf of bread with both meat and dairy products. It is customary to have two salt-cellars, one for meat and another for dairy products, because at times the food is dipped into the salt, and part of the food may have remained in it.

8. It is customary to mark all utensils used for dairy foods, so that they might not be interchanged with those used for meat.

9. After eating meat or a dish prepared with meat, we should wait six hours before eating dairy food, and the one who masticates food for an infant is also obliged to wait that length of time. If after waiting six hours, we find particles of meat between our teeth, we must remove it, but we need not wait thereafter. We should cleanse our mouth and rinse it, that is, we should eat a little bread to cleanse our mouth with it, and then rinse our mouth with water or any other liquid.

10. If one has eaten food which contained neither meat nor animal fat, but was cooked in a pot used for boiling meat, even if that pot has not been cleansed beforehand, it is permissible to eat dairy food immediately thereafter.

11. After eating cheese, we may eat meat immediately thereafter at another meal, but we must carefully examine our hands to make sure that no particles of cheese cling to them; we must also cleanse the teeth and rinse the mouth. If the cheese was hard, that is to say, it was curdled by rennet and was six months old, or if it had worms, we must wait six hours before eating meat.

12. If we desire to eat meat after eating cheese, we must remove from the table the rest of the bread of which we ate with the cheese. Cheese should not be eaten upon the tablecloth on which we have eaten meat, and conversely, no meat should be eaten upon the tablecloth upon which we have eaten cheese; nor should we cut bread to eat with cheese, with a knife used for cutting meat, or vice versa, even if the knife is clean. However, in an emergency, as when we are on a journey, we are allowed to cut the bread to eat with cheese with a knife that has been used for cutting meat, or vice versa, if the knife is thoroughly clean.

13. If we cut onions or some other pungent things with a knife used for cutting meat, and put it in food made of milk, or vice versa, a rabbi should be consulted as to the fitness of the food.

14. If we prepare a dish of meat with the extract of almonds, we must put whole almonds in it on account of its deceptive appearance (because it looks like milk, thus averting the suspicion of having transgressed the law, by having boiled meat and milk together).

15. It is not customary ritually to purify utensils used for dairy food, to make them fit for use of meat, or vice versa.

16. If we give wine, meat or a piece of fish into the care of a non-Jew, without making any special mark (by which it may be recognized, and especially so when given to an Israelite who is suspected of tampering with it,) either to store it or to forward it, we must put a double seal on it. But one seal suffices for boiled wine, wine-vinegar, bread or cheese.

17. If we give something in a sack to a non-Jew, either to be forwarded or to be stored, it is necessary that the stitches of the sack be on the inside and it must be tied and sealed.

18. If we happen to forward, through a non-Jew, a slaughtered beast or fowl or anything else without a seal, then we must consult a rabbi about it.

19. Cheese or other articles of food which are in the hands of a non-Jew, although they are sealed or stamped, stating that they are ritually fit for food, are, neverthelesss, unfit for use as long as we do not know who has sealed them.

20. Care should be taken that a Jew and a non-Jew should not cook or fry, together in uncovered pots or frying pans, one pot containing food which is ritually fit, and the other containing ritually unfit food. Care should also be taken not to leave any pots in the care of non-Jewish servants, when there is no Jew in the house, or when there is no Jew going in and out.

21. It is forbidden to purchase wine or any food, the ritual fitness of which may be doubtful, from one who does not have a reputation for complying with the dietary laws. However, if we become such a person's guest, we may eat with him as long as we are not certain that there is ground for suspicion.

22. Care must be taken not to leave culinary utensils in the house of a non-Jew, lest he make use of them. Even when we give such utensils to a non-Jew to be repaired, we must consult a rabbi, if there is a possibility that he has made use of them.

23. Occasionally people buy a live fowl with its legs trussed, they throw it to the ground, and subsequently have it ritually killed. It is strictly forbidden to eat of such fowl; because when a beast or a fowl has fallen, its meat is unfit for use unless we see it walk thereafter at least four cubits (six feet). It is well to be extremely careful in regard to this matter with lambs and calves as well.

24. During the summer, slight swellings like warts are at times found upon the intestines of ducks and many of them become ritually unfit for food because of that. It is, therefore, advisable to examine the intestines, and if such swellings are found, a rabbi should be consulted.

25. We must not knead dough with milk, lest it be eaten with meat, and for this reason it is even forbidden to eat the bread itself, if it has been entirely prepared in that manner. If, however, it was only in a small quantity, sufficient only for one meal, or if the bread has been shaped in such a manner that it can be easily discerned that it is not to be eaten with meat, it is permissible to prepare it with milk. The same law applies to the use of animal fat in the kneading of dough. We must not bake bread with pancakes or pies in one oven, as the butter or the fat may flow under the bread; and if it is so baked, it may not be used even by itself, as though it were kneaded with it.

26. If bread has been baked and meat has been roasted in the same oven and the oven was closed while the meat was uncovered, it is forbidden to eat that bread with dairy foods. It is permitted, however, to eat the bread with milk if the roasted meat was covered, or if the oven is as large as our modern ovens and has been open. Care should, however, be taken not to roast meat in an oven in which bread is being baked, as the grease may flow under the bread, and this may happen even if the roast is in a frying pan.

27. If milk or grease overflows on the bottom of an oven, the oven must be cleansed by means of glowing heat in accordance with the law, that is to say, glowing coal should be spread upon the entire surface so that it is heated white.

28. Castrated cocks may be eaten, because we rely on the presumption that the non-Jewish castrator is an expert, and would not cause any defect in the entrails of the cock by sewing it up. But if any defect is found, be it only a dislocation of the entrails, thay may not be eaten.

29. In some communities, non-Jews raise geese for the purpose of selling them to Jews, and they generally stab them with a needle or the like under their wings, so that the flesh becomes swollen and the geese may look fat. A rabbi should be consulted as to whether or not such geese are fit to eat. It happens also that when the life of an animal is endangered by being overfed, it is stuck with an awl beneath its belly as a cure, and a rabbi should be consulted whether or not such an animal is fit for use.

30. In preserving fruit, it is customary to place them in a jar which is covered and tied with a bladder skin over the opening, and it is thus placed into a hot oven so that the fruit may be preserved. The bladder skin must be from an animal that is ritually fit for food, and it must also be salted and properly rinsed to make it fit for use.

31. It is forbidden to drink the water from wells or rivers known to be infested with worms before it has been filtered; and if one has inadvertently used such unfiltered water in cooking, the food should be forbidden. It is forbidden to soak meat in such water, or to wash with it articles of food, because the worms cling to the food.

32. The water should be filtered through a closely woven cloth capable of excluding even the smallest insect.

33. Vinegar containing worms, is unfit for use even if it has been filtered, because the smallest worm in vinegar will pass through any cloth, and the straining makes it even worse, for worms contained in beverages when in vessels, are not forbidden as long as they do not become separated; and because of the straining it is possible that the worms will remain on the strainer and later penetrate into the vinegar. It is best to boil the vinegar first and then strain it, for since they are killed by boiling, they will not pass through when the vinegar is strained.

34. Worms that grow in fruit while yet attached to the tree are forbidden even if they have not moved from place to place (in the fruit). Black spots are at times found in fruit and in such vegetables as beans and lentils. This is the first stage of their breeding, and they must be removed from the fruit, as these are forbidden even as the worms themselves.

35. Fruits that usually have worms when they are attached to the tree, may be eaten without examination, if twelve months have passed from the time they have been picked off the tree, as no boneless creature can exist longer than twelve months, and they have therefore, become as dust. However, as it is possible that the fruit has become wormy after being picked, it should be examined and cleansed from all worms and animalcula found upon the surface. Afterward they should be placed in cold water and thoroughly stirred. As the worms and worm-eaten particles will rise to the surface, they should be thrown away. The rest should be placed in boiling water, so that if any worms remain they will perish immediately before becoming separated from their places. This procedure may be relied upon only in the cases of pods, lentils, and the like, and only after the expiration of twelve months.

36. All fruits having worms and requiring examination, should be opened one by one and the stones removed, in order that the examination may be thorough. Great care should be taken when preserving fruit in honey or sugar, and also when making jam, to examine the fruit thoroughly. We must

not rely upon the examination of only a portion of the fruit, be it even the greater portion of them, but each fruit must be examined separately.

37. Flour and cereals containing large worms, may be rendered fit for use by being sifted through a sieve through which the worms cannot pass. But flour containing mites must be discarded. One possessing wormy wheat should consult a rabbi as to how it should be ground into flour.

38. It is forbidden to sell any foods containing worms to a non-Jew, if it is the kind of food which is not usually examined for worms, for there is a likelihood that the non-Jew may, in turn, sell it to a Jew. But we are permitted to sell it for the distilation of brandy, and we need not fear that he might eat some of it in its present state, providing he does not keep it for a long time.

39. There are many kinds of vegetables that are known to be infested with worms, and some that are infested with mites. Some housewives say that if they singe the vegetables, the insects will be destroyed; however, such a method is of no avail. There are certain kinds of fruits and vegetables so infested with worms that it is well-nigh impossible to examine them; therefore, a God-fearing person must not eat any of these. There are certain kinds of fruit whose kernels are infested with worms, and it is forbidden to eat them.

40. Nuts are often infested with mites. The proof of their existence is, that when the kernel is taken out, we place the shell on a warm place and tap it, then the mites that remain in the shell will come out. Great care should be taken concerning this.

41. Sometimes mites are found at the edge of a vessel containing fruits preserved in honey and sugar. This part must be thoroughly cleansed and some of the surface preserves removed until it is quite certain that no mites were left in the rest of it.

42. If in cutting fruit or a radish, we happen to cut up a worm, we must wipe the knife well, and scoop out that part where the worm was cut.

43. Worms are often found in the interior of fish, especially in the brain, liver, intestines, mouths and ears. Especially is this the case with pike, which contains long and thin worms. The places where worms are likely to be found, must be thoroughly examined. Thin worms are also found in the milt of herring and it therefore, requires examination. In some regions, fish are infested

with very small insects, round as a lentil which are upon their bodies, by and upon their fins, in their mouths, and behind their ears; they should be examined in such places and well scraped off.

44. The worms found in cheese, may be eaten with the cheese if they are not loathsome to him, as long as they are not separated from it.

45. Many Divine Commands are contained in the Torah, forbidding the eating of creeping things. Many Divine Commands are violated upon eating them and they also defile the body, as it is written (Leviticus 11:43): "That ye should be defiled thereby." Therefore, one must be very careful not to become a victim of that sin.

46. If we have consulted a rabbi and he has forbidden the use of a subject in question, we must not consult another rabbi about the same matter, unless we notify him of the decision of the first rabbi.

CHAPTER 47

Non-Jewish Wine and Making the Vessels Fit for Use

1. Nowadays the ordinary wine of a non-Jew, or Jewish wine that has been touched by a non-Jew, is, according to the opinion of some authorities, forbidden only for drinking purposes, but not forbidden to derive any benefit from it. Therefore, we are permitted to take non-Jewish wine in payment of a debt due us, for it is equivalent to saving it from a loss. The same law applies to a case, when we have violated the law and have purchased wine from them. But it is forbidden in the first instance to buy wine from them in order to make a profit by it. Other authorities are lenient even as regards the latter case, but it is best to follow the stricter opinion.

2. It is permissible to make a bath out of non-Jewish wine for a sick person although he is not critically ill.

3. If *kosher* wine that has been boiled until its quantity was reduced by evaporation, is touched by a non-Jew, it may be used even for the purpose of drinking it. Wine, into which spices have been put, as long as it still retains the name wine and has not been boiled, becomes forbidden when touched by a non-Jew.

4. Victuals mixed with wine, the presence of which is not discernable, even if the victuals have not yet been brought to a boiling point, do not become unfit for use if they have been touched by a non-Jew.

5. If wine is adulterated with six parts of water, the wine becomes nullified and does not become forbidden by the touch of a non-Jew. However, raisin wine, that is, when water is poured upon the raisins, is considered as true wine.

6. If water is poured upon the kernels of pressed grapes, or upon the lees of wine, as long as it is improved for the purpose of drinking by doing so, it becomes forbidden when touched by a non-Jew.

7. If some wine has been extracted from the grapes pressed in a tank, be it even only a small quantity, or if some wine has been taken out of it into a vessel, the entire contents of the tank is legally called wine, and it becomes forbidden by the touch of a non-Jew even if only the kernels or the husks have been touched. It is, therefore, forbidden to make use of the tanks of grapes found in the house of a non-Jew, for it is likely that the non-Jew has already extracted some wine from it. It is forbidden to let a non-Jew press grapes in a tank, even if such a tank is provided with a stopper.

8. We must also be careful not to let a non-Jew remove the kernels and the husks from the wine-press, even after we have already extracted the first and second wine from it, as they might still be moist with wine.

9. If a non-Jew has poured water into wine with the intention of diluting it, we are not allowed to drink from it. But if he had not intended to dilute it, or even if it is only doubtful whether he has intended to do so, its use is permissible.

10. If vinegar is made out of *kosher* wine, and it is so strong that it seethes when poured upon the ground, it no longer becomes forbidden by the touch of a non-Jew. But if vinegar is made out of non-Jewish wine, it always remains forbidden.

11. Brandy that is made out of non-Jewish wine, or of kernels and husks or of lees, is considered like the wine itself. But brandy made out of *kosher* wine, is no longer rendered unfit for use by the touch of a non-Jew.

12. It has become a prevailing custom to permit the use of Tartaric acid, since it is not tasteful.

13. If a non-Jew touches wine by means of something else (not a part of his body), or if it is touched through his power, a rabbi should be consulted as to the fitness of the wine.

14. When we send wine through a non-Jew, we must take the precaution of doubly sealing the mouth or the faucet of the vessel.

15. There are many diverse laws regarding the wine that a Jew makes for a non-Jew, for the purpose of selling it to Jewish consumers. In certain instances, even double seals and a lock are of no avail. It is necessary to consult an ordained rabbi as to what procedure to follow in such a case. The scrupulous should avoid the use of such wine.

16. Regarding the vessels that have contained non-Jewish wine, if they are of the kind that one ordinarily used for keeping wine, but temporarily, nor have they contained the wine for twenty-four hours, whether the vessels are of leather skins, wood, glass, stone, or metal, as long as they are not lined with pitch, they should be rinsed well with water three times, and then they may be used. If they are lined with pitch, or if they are earthen vessels, they are governed by different laws.

17. Vessels that are made for keeping wine for a long time, that is, they are designed to hold wine for at least three days, although the vessels belong to an Israelite, and the non-Jew kept wine in them only for a short time, they must, nevertheless, be made fit for use by *emptying;* they should be filled with water to the very brim and be thus allowed to stay no less than twenty-four hours. After that, they should be emptied of that water and refilled with fresh water, and again be allowed to stand for at least twenty-four hours; this procedure should be repeated a third time. And in this regard, it is not essential that the three days should be successive. If the water has remained in the vessels for many days without being spilled out, it is counted as but one time. Some authorities are of the opinion, that if the wine has remained in the vessel for twenty-four hours, it cannot be made fit for use by the process of emptying, because things pressed (preserved) are considered as if it were boiled, and they require cleansing by means of boiling water. And in case of no emergency, it is best to follow the more rigid practice.

18. Glass vessels, although they are made to hold wine a long time, since they are hard and smooth, they could be made fit for use by rinsing them three times.

19. If a vessel that has contained Jewish wine is emptied of its wine, but it is still so moist as to moisten other objects with it, and has come in contact with a non-Jew, rinsing it three times will suffice to make it fit for use, although the vessel was made to hold wine in it for a long time.

20. Rinsing, as well as the process of *emptying* are available to make vessels fit for use, only when cold wine has been kept in them, but if hot wine has been kept in them, they can be made fit only by *cleansing by boiling water*, the same as if they contained other forbidden matter.

21. Vessels of the wine-press, although no wine is kept in them for a long time, but since wine is very often placed in them, are to be dealt with strictly. A rabbi should be consulted as to how to make them fit for use.

22. Any vessel that has not been used for a period of twelve months or more, may be used without preparing them ritually, as it is assumed that no moisture of any wine was left in them. Even if water has been put in them during the twelve months, it does not matter.

VOLUME 2

CHAPTER 48

Benedictions Over The Five Species of Grain

1. When we eat pastry made of any of the five species of grain, less than the quantity sufficient for a regular meal, we neither have to wash the hands before eating, nor say the benediction *Hamotzi.* The benedictions are *Bore mine mezonot* (who created various kinds of food), before eating it, and *Al hamiḥeyah* (for the sustenance) afterward. If, however, we eat a quantity sufficient for a meal, then it is governed by the same rules of law as apply to regular bread; we must wash the hands and say *Hamotzi* before eating, and afterwards, say the Grace.

2. What is the meaning of *Pat habaah bekisnin*? Some authorities construe it to mean, bread which is filled with fruit, meat, cheese, and the like, or which is prepared like coffee cake. Other authorities explain the term as referring to bread kneaded with oil, fat, honey, milk, eggs, or fruit juice, even if some water has been added, as long as it is less in quantity than the other liquids. We hold both definitions as valid.

3. The quantity of food constituting a meal, is not measured by one's own appetite, but by what the majority of people usually consume for the midday meal or for supper to satisfy their appetite. If one has eaten such a quantity of pastry, even if he is not satisfied, it is, nevertheless, governed by the same law as applies to bread. If one eats such bread with a condiment, we also estimate the amount according to what would satisfy other people if they ate the same with relish. If one eats a small quantity without a relish and he feels satisfied, whereas other people would not be satisfied with it unless they ate it with a relish, then too, it is judged as bread.

4. If one intends to eat only a little (of the pastry) and says the benediction *Bore mine mezonot,* and then one decides to eat a quantity sufficient for a meal, if the additional food in itself is insufficient for a meal, unless it is combined with the part already eaten, one continues to eat and recites Grace after meals. But if the quantity of the additional food is enough for a meal, one must first wash the hands and recite the benediction *Hamotzi* over what one desires to eat, but one need not say the concluding benediction *Al hamiḥyah* for what one had already eaten, because the Grace subsequently recited exempts it from the concluding benediction.

5. If dough is of a very soft texture and is baked either in an oven or in a stew-pot without any liquid, even if the stew-pot is smeared with oil to keep the dough from burning, it is considered as real bread. Even though we eat only the size of an olive, we must wash the hands, say the benediction *Hamotzi* before eating, and Grace afterward. However, if it is fried in any liquid, it is not considered as real bread even if we eat our fill of it. Wafers which are very thin and which are baked in a mold on a gridiron, are also exempt from the law that applies to real bread, and even if we eat enough to satisfy our appetite, we need only recite the benediction *Bore mine mezonot* before eating, and *Al hamiḥyah* thereafter. If dough is made very thin, and it is poured over vegetables and baked in an oven, this dough is governed by the law which applies to *Pat habbaah bekisnin.* (See section 2, above).

6. Dough which is first boiled and afterwards baked, such as "Bagles" or "Pretzels," is considered to be real bread, provided it is well baked.

7. If real bread is either cooked or fried in butter or the like, even though it has no longer the appearance of bread, when for instance it was smeared with eggs, the law applying to real bread applies to this as well, if the piece is no less than the size of an olive. But if every piece is less than the size of an olive, even though through the cooking the dough expanded, so that each portion is now as large as an olive, or if the cooking has made the pieces cling together and it has become a large mass, even though it has the appearance of bread, it is not considered real bread, and we recite the benediction *Bore mine mezonot* before, and *Al hamiḥeyah* after eating it, even if we eat enough to satisfy us. However, if we have not boiled it but merely poured hot broth over it, then the benediction that should be said over it is doubtful, because it is questionable whether the pouring of hot broth is considered as boiling in this case. It is, therefore, best to eat it in the course of a meal only. If it has not been cooked but soaked in some liquid, or soup, and its portions are less than the size of an olive, then it all depends upon whether it still has the appearance of bread. If it has, then the laws relating to real bread are to be applied, if it has not, the laws relating to bread do not apply, and we say the benediction *Bore mine mezonot* before eating, and *Al hamiḥeyah* thereafter, even if we eat of it until we are satisfied. If the color of the liquid has been changed by the portions of the food soaked in it, it is obvious that it has lost the appearance of bread. If it has been soaked in red wine, it has likewise lost the appearance of bread.

8. Cooked dough is considered as pastry, even if it had been kneaded with water only, and the benedictions are: *Bore mine mezonot* before eating it, and *Al hamiḥeyah* afterward. Likewise, over cooked cereal made of the five species of grain, we say the benediction *Bore mine mezonot*, and after eating it we say the benediction *Al hamiḥeyah*, even if we have had our fill.

If we eat this with soup, or we eat any farinaceous food with the soup, or milk in which it has been cooked, we need not say a benediction over the soup or the milk, for they are secondary to the food, and have lost their essential value. However, if we cook but little of the farinaceous food or cereal, and the broth or the milk, is our main object, then the soup or broth does not lose its essential value, and we recite the benediction *Shehakol* over it. And even though we have eaten the cereal, the broth or the milk must be considered as the staple element of the dish. Nevertheless, it is best to say the benediction *Shehakol* first over the broth or the milk alone, drink some of it, and then say the benediction *Bore mine mezonot* over the cereal. Although the preparation of the dish has not been on their account, since they belong to the five Biblical species of grain, they cannot be considered of secondary importance as is the case of a condiment that is being used to give flavor to a dish.

9. Over food made of *matzah* meal or crumbs of bread mixed with fat, eggs, or milk, and then cooked or fried, we say the benediction *Bore mine mezonot* before eating, and *Al hamiḥeyah* thereafter.

10. If certain kinds of grain flour have been cooked with flour of different species, as is customary to cook drops of dough with beans or peas, even if the bulk belongs to one kind, since each kind is distinct, we must say two benedictions; first we say *Bore mine mezonot* over the dough and eat some of it, and then we say *Bore peri haadamah* (who createth the fruit of the ground) over the beans. The broth is of secondary importance and no benediction need be said over it. (Also for the further reason that it has been exempted by the benediction *Bore peri haadamah*). If, however, they were dissolved and merged into one mass, as in the case of a dish consisting of flour, eggs, and cheese which is cooked or fried, even if the flour be but little, nevertheless, since it belongs to the five species of grain, it is an important ingredient, and the benediction *Bore mine mezonot* must be said before eating it and *Al hamiḥeyah* thereafter. This rule applies only when the flour is required in order to flavor the dish, but if it was used merely for thickening to keep the ingredients together, as in the case when different kinds of vegetable stews are prepared with a little flour, or when almonds, sugar and eggs are used for making pastries, then the flour loses its identity, and we say only the benediction over the principal components of the dish. Over broth which is cooked or prepared with a little flour which has been first roasted or fried in butter, we likewise say only the benediction *Shehakol*. But if we pick out the pieces that have been fried, we must say *Bore mine mezonot* before eating them, and

if we have eaten no less than the size of an olive, we must say *Al hamiḥeyah* afterward.

CHAPTER 49

Benedictions Over Wine And Hatov Vehametiv

1. Before drinking wine, we say the benediction *Bore peri haggafen* (who createst the fruit of the vine), and after drinking it, we say *Al haggefen* (for the vine) etc. If the wine is still bubbling, or fermenting, or if it is flavored with honey and spices, or absinthe which is bitter, or it has the odor of vinegar, as long as it tastes like wine, it is considered wine for the purpose of the benediction. But if it turned sour to such a degree that some people would avoid drinking it on account of its acidity, the benediction for it is a matter of doubt. We should, therefore, not drink it until we have pronounced a benediction over good wine.

2. If we pour water upon kernels out of which wine has been extracted by pressure and not in a wine-press, although the wine does not exceed the quantity of water which we have poured upon them, or even if the wine is less than the quantity of the water, nevertheless, if it tastes like wine, we must say the benediction *Bore peri haggafen* before drinking it. However, if the kernels had been squeezed in a wine-press, or if we pour water upon wine lees, it is considered as mere water.

3. If wine is mixed with water, and the wine is only a sixth part, the wine loses its identity and the drink is considered as water. If, however, the wine is more than a sixth part of the total, and it is customary in that region to drink such a beverage as wine, then before drinking it, one must say the benediction *Bore peri haggafen*, and after drinking, one says *Al haggefen;* otherwise his own opinion does not count, and he should pronounce the benediction for water.

4. Just as bread, when he eats it at a meal, exempts all other food eaten during the meal, so does wine exempt other beverages. If we sit down to drink wine, the benediction uttered over it exempts all other beverages from their first and concluding benedictions, provided they have been set before us when we said the benediction over the wine, or if we have intended to drink these beverages at the time when we said the benediction. But if they have not been before us, nor have we intended to drink them when we said the benediction over the wine, it is doubtful whether a benediction should be said over them. We should, therefore, avoid drinking other beverages until we have said the benediction *Shehakol* over some kind of food, and had in mind to include those beverages.

5. If we drink wine only casually, and we have no intention of drinking other beverages, we certainly must say the first benediction over the other beverages. And it is doubtful whether the benediction *Al haggefen* recited

afterward, exempts all the other beverages. Therefore, we should thereafter partake of some fruit after which we say *Bore nefashot rabbot* (who createst many living beings), and thereby exempt the beverages from the concluding benediction.

6. If we recite the *Kiddush* over a cup of wine and intend to drink some brandy or coffee thereafter, it is doubtful whether the latter is exempted from a separate benediction by the one recited over the wine. We should, therefore, mean not to exempt them, and even then we should say the benediction *Shehakol* over some sugar and thereby exempt the beverages from a separate benediction.

7. Before saying the benediction over wine during a meal, if other people are present, we say *Saveri rabbotai* (gentlemen, give heed), so that they might stop eating and hear the benediction.

8. If we drink one kind of wine, whether in the course of a meal or otherwise, and then another kind of wine is brought, we need not say the benediction *Bore peri haggafen* over the latter, since we have neither changed our mind about drinking wine, nor has our attention been diverted from our wine-drinking; but we should say the benediction *Hatov vehametiv*. Likewise, if a third kind of wine has been brought, we say over this also *Hatov vehametiv*, and so on. (And this we learn from the fact that "Rabbi" uttered the benediction *Hatov vehametiv* over every new jug of wine that had been opened.)

9. If one later decides to drink more wine, necessitating the repetition of the benediction *Bore peri haggafen*, one must first say *Hatov vehametiv* and then *Bore peri haggafen*, for the additional wine.

10. The benediction *Hatov vehametiv* is to be said only when we do not know whether the second wine is inferior or superior to the first. But if we do know that the second is inferior to the wine already used, then no benediction is to be said. If, however, the second is more wholesome than the first, although its taste is inferior, we should say over it the benediction *Hatov vehametiv*.

11. Even if we had two kinds of wine at the beginning of the meal, but both were not on the table when the benediction *Bore peri haggafen* was uttered, then if the second wine happens to be superior, we must say *Hatov vehametiv*. If the two kinds of wine were on the table, the benediction *Hatov vehametiv* is not to be said, but *Bore peri haggafen* must be uttered over the wine of superior quality to exempt the inferior kind from any benediction.

12. The benediction *Hatov vehametiv* is not said unless some of the first kind of wine is still left, and the second kind is partaken of merely for the sake of variety. But if the second kind is provided because the first is exhausted, the benediction *Hatov vehametiv* is not said over it.

13. The benediction *Hatov vehametiv* is not said unless there is another person who drinks of the two kinds of wine, thus implying that God is good to him and to his companion. The benediction is also uttered when one's wife and children are at the table. But if one eats all alone, he need not say that benediction.

14. If the host places a decanter of wine on the table, so that all guests may drink of it, as is the custom at banquets, then the wine is considered as everybody's property, and all the guests should say *Hatov vehametiv*. But if the host has given a glass of wine to each guest individually, they should not say *Hatov vehametiv*. Even the host himself should not say the benediction.

15. One person may utter the benediction and exempt the rest of the company from saying it. He should first say *Savri* (gentlemen, give heed), to direct their attention to the benediction, and they should respond *Amen*. This rule holds good only when each one has his glass of wine before him, so that he may immediately drink without any pause between the benediction and the drinking.

16. If we recite the Grace after meals over a cup of wine other than the one which we have drunk before, we need not recite the benediction *Hatov vehametiv* over it, as it has been included in the *Hatov vehametiv* contained in the Grace.

CHAPTER 50

Benedictions Said Before Enjoying Food and Drink

1. It is written (Psalms 24:1): "The earth is the Lord's and the fullness thereof," which implies that everything is like consecrated matter. And just as it is forbidden to derive any benefit from sacred things before they are redeemed, and he who derives any benefit from them without redemption, is guilty of a trespass, even so it is forbidden to derive any pleasure in this world without first thanking the Almighty by pronouncing a benediction. He who enjoys things without uttering a benediction, is like one who had committed a trespass against the Sanctuary of God, blessed be His name. There is no set quantity of food or drink over which a benediction must be uttered. No matter how little we either eat or drink, we must first pronounce the appropriate benediction.

2. Although if we inadvertently say the benediction *Shehakol* over any article of food or any kind of drink, be it even bread or wine, we have discharged our duty, it must not be done intentionally. It is, therefore, our duty to learn the various benedictions and say the one that is appropriate to the kind of food. If we are in doubt as to which class a certain food belongs, because the authorities differ and no definite decision is available, we should then say the benediction *Shehakol;* but it is preferable to exempt it from any benediction by partaking of it during the course of a meal.

3. We should take the article over which we are about to utter the benediction in the right hand before eating, drinking, scenting, or performing a precept thereby, and ascertain which benediction we must say, so that when

we mention the Divine Name, which is the most important part of the benediction, we may know how to conclude it. If we utter the benediction over the article without taking it in our hand, but so long as it has been before us at that time, our duty is done. However, if the article is not before us when reciting the benediction, but has been brought later, even if we had it in mind while saying the benediction, the benediction must be repeated.

4. If we have taken some fruit to eat, and after uttering the benediction it fell out of our hand and was lost, or it became too loathsome to be eaten; or if we have said the benediction over a glass of liquor and spilt it, if at that time there was no more of the same kind of food or liquor before us, and it was our intention to consume more than that which was in our hand, the benediction which we said referred also to whatever remained before us, and we need not repeat the benediction; otherwise, the benediction applied only to that which was in our hand, and we must repeat the benediction over what is brought to us. If we have intended to eat some more of the same article, but it was not before us at the time the benediction was uttered, we must repeat the benediction even if it were exempted if it had been before us when we ate or drank of the first.

5. The pause between the saying of the benediction and the consumption of the food should not be longer than it takes to say *Shalom aleḥa, rabbi umori* (peace be unto thee, my Master and teacher). Even when masticating the first mouthful of food, we must not pause until we have swallowed it (because chewing alone requires no benediction). If after uttering the benediction, we make an interruption before eating, by speaking of something which does not concern the meal, we must repeat the benediction; but if we pause silently, we need not repeat the benediction. Any delay necessary for the purpose of the meal, is not considered an interruption. Therefore, if we desire to partake of a large sized fruit which must be cut before eating it, we should say the benediction over the whole fruit (because it is best to say a benediction over an entire article of food), and the delay caused by cutting it, is not considered an interruption. However, if we desire to eat a single fruit that might be wormy and improper to partake of it, we must open it and examine it before saying the benediction.

6. If we are about to drink water and we desire to spill some of it, fearing that the surface water might be tainted, we must do this before uttering the benediction and not thereafter, so as to avoid any seeming disrespect for the benediction.

7. If we taste food to ascertain if it needs any salt, or for any other similar purpose, and we eject it, we need not say a benediction over it. However, if we swallow it, it is doubtful whether or not we need say a benediction. For, although we have swallowed it, it has not been our intention to use it

as food, and therefore, no benediction is necessary. We should, therefore, take it as food, utter the benediction over it, and then swallow it.

8. If we eat or drink something for medicinal purposes, if it is something tasteful, even though it is forbidden food, we should utter the appropriate preceding and concluding benedictions, since the law permits us now to partake of it. If, however, the article is of bitter taste and unpalatable, we should not say a benediction over it. If we drink a raw egg as an aid to our voice, we must pronounce a benediction over it; for although we do not enjoy its taste, we benefit by the nourishment it affords us.

9. If we drink some beverage or eat some bread or any other kind of food, for the purpose of dislodging something that has stuck in the throat, we must utter its preceding and concluding benedictions. But if we drink water, for that purpose, we need not say any benediction, for we do not enjoy the drinking of water unless it is to quench our thirst.

10. If a person inadvertently puts food in his mouth without saying the appropriate benediction, and it is an article that can be removed from the mouth without becoming loathsome, we should eject it into our hand and say the benediction over it; we must not utter the benediction while the food is in the mouth, for it is written (Psalms 71:8): "My mouth shall be filled with Thy praise." If, however, it is an article which would become loathsome after being ejected, inasmuch as wasting food is forbidden, we should move it to one side of the mouth, and say the benediction over it. In the case of a beverage, if we have some more of it, we should eject it and let it be wasted. But if we have no more of it, and we are in urgent need of the little we have in the mouth, we may swallow it and say the preceding benediction later (for since we have thought of the error while the drink was still in the mouth, it has some semblance of uttering it before the performance of the deed), but we must omit the concluding benediction. However, if it is wine and we drink of it one-fourth of a *lug*, we must also say the concluding benediction.

11. If there are two kinds of food which require the same benediction, such as a nut and an apple, we are to recite a benediction over one of them and intend to include the other. We are not allowed to say a benediction over one and intend to exclude the other, in order to be able to say an extra benediction; for it is forbidden to augment benedictions unnecessarily. The benediction is to be pronounced over the superior kind and the other is exempted, even though it has not been our intention to do so. But if we say the

benediction over the inferior kind, the other kind is not exempted, unless we have intended to do so; otherwise, we must repeat the benediction over the superior kind, for it is improper that the benediction uttered over the inferior kind should without intention exempt the superior kind from its benediction.

12. However, if we have two different kinds of food, for instance, fruit of the tree and fruit of the ground, or food over which the benediction *Shehakol* is to be said, we must say the benediction appropriate to each kind, in spite of the fact that if we inadvertently say *Shehakol* over all of them, or if we say the benediction *Bore peri haadamah* over fruit, our duty is done. The benediction *Bore peri haetz* takes precedence over *Shehakol.* If we have wine and grapes, and we desire to drink the wine first, we say the benediction *Bore peri haggafen,* although we may exempt the grapes by this benediction, we must not do so intentionally; but rather say the proper benediction over them, which is *Bore peri haetz.*

13. If we change our place while eating any kind of food, except bread, although our thoughts have not been diverted from the food we are eating, nevertheless, the change of place is in itself a diversion. Consequently, if we eat or drink in one room and we go into another room to conclude the eating or the drinking, even if the food or beverage is of the same kind, or even if we hold that food or beverage in our hand and carry it over to the other room, nevertheless, we are obliged to repeat the benediction. But we need not recite the concluding benediction over what we have already eaten in the first room; the one concluding benediction suffices for both.

14. If we go outside the house and then return to our former place to finish the meal, we must likewise repeat the benediction. The foregoing rule applies only to a case when one has eaten all alone, or when one has eaten in the company of others, and all of them had left their places. But, if one of the company remained in his place, while the others who have left, intended to return to their companion to finish their meal, then when they return to resume eating, the benediction need not be repeated, for inasmuch as one of the company has remained there, the status of the appointed place did not cease, and it is all considered as one meal.

15. When one goes from one corner of a room to another, it is not considered a change of place, no matter how large the room may be.

16. If one eats fruit in an orchard which is fenced in, and one said a benediction over the fruit of one tree, with the intention of eating also of the fruit of other trees, even if they are not within his view, so long as one's thoughts have not been diverted, one need not repeat the benediction. But if the orchard is not fenced in, and especially if one goes from one orchard into another, the fact that there was no diversion of thought is of no avail, and the benediction must be repeated.

Chapter 51

The Concluding Benediction

1. After eating the fruit of any tree not of the seven species mentioned in the Scriptures (Deuteronomy 8:8), or any fruit of the ground, or any vegetable, or any food that is not the direct product of the soil, one should say the benediction *Bore nefashot rabbot* (who createst many living things). If one ate and drank, one concluding benediction will suffice for both.

2. The concluding benediction, like Grace after meals, must not be said unless one has eaten a quantity of food no less than the size of an olive. For less than that quantity, we need not say the concluding benediction. According to some authorities, we need not say the concluding benediction after drinking liquor if it was less than a quarter of a *lug*. Other authorities hold that we must say the concluding benediction even after drinking a quantity the size of an olive. Therefore, in order to avoid any doubt, we must take care to drink either less than the quantity the size of an olive, or a quarter of a *lug*. It makes no difference in this regard whether the beverage is brandy or any other kind of liquid.

3. According to the opinion of some authorities, after eating a whole thing as it is produced by nature, such as a nut, or one single bean, even if its quantity is less than the size of an olive, we must recite the concluding benediction. Other authorities, however, differ on this point. Therefore, to avoid any doubt, we should not eat of it less than the quantity the size of an olive. If the article has been divided before it was eaten, it loses its special importance and all agree that we do not say the concluding benediction if it was less than the quantity the size of an olive.

4. All articles of food combine to make up the quantity the size of an olive; thus, if one has eaten about half the quantity of food, after which the concluding benediction *Bore nefashot rabbot* is to be said; and another half of food after which the benediction embodying the three blessings is said, even if it was bread, then the concluding benediction *Bore nefashot rabbot* should be said. And it seems to me that if one has eaten about half an olive of fruit after which the benediction *Al haetz* is said, and another half an olive of food after which the benediction *Al hamiḥeyah* is said, or he has eaten about half the size of an olive of bread (although in this instance he ate no kind of food after which the benediction *Bore nefashot rabbot* is to be said), nevertheless, the concluding benediction *Bore nefashot rabbot* is to be recited. If one has eaten the quantity of half the size of an olive of food after which the benediction

Al hamiḥeyah is to be said and half the size of an olive of bread, the concluding benediction *Al hamiḥeyah* should be recited. Food and drink do not combine to make up the necessary quantity.

5. If one has eaten the quantity the size of half an olive and waited, and then ate the second half the size of an olive, if the interval between the beginning and the end of the eating does not exceed the time taken to eat a piece of bread, the two acts are combined and the concluding benediction should be recited thereafter. If, however, the interval exceeded this limit, the two acts are not combined. With regard to drinking, the separate acts of drinking are not combined, even if one has made a pause of less time than the limit just mentioned.

6. If one drinks a hot beverage slowly, since one does not drink at one time the minimum quantity required for the benediction, although this is the usual way of drinking it, nevertheless, the different quantities consumed are not combined, and no concluding benediction need be recited.

7. The land of Israel is famous for the seven species of food which it produces, as it is written (Deuteronomy 8:2-10): "A land of wheat and barley, and vines and fig-trees and pomegranates; a land of olive trees and honey;" and thereafter, it is written: "A land wherein thou shalt eat bread without scarceness . . . And thou shalt eat and be satisfied, and bless the Lord thy God," etc. Since concerning bread, the Scripture is explicit in its precept: "And when thou hast eaten and art satisfied, then thou shalt bless," therefore, if one eats bread made of one of the five species of grain, namely, wheat and barley (expressly mentioned in the Scripture text loco citato 8), and also spelt, or oats, or rye, which belong to the family of wheat and barley, one must say Grace afterward, which consists of three complete benedictions, including also the benediction *Hatov vehametiv* (which was later on added by the Yavneh School). However, after eating food, which is not really bread, but which is farinaceous, prepared from the five species of grain mentioned above, also after drinking wine or eating grapes, either fresh or dried, large or small, or figs, pomegranates, olives, or dates, being the "honey" of which the Scripture speaks, inasmuch as honey exudes from them, we must say the concluding benediction, embodying in brief form the three benedictions of Grace, as well as the benediction *Hatov vehametiv* of the Grace after meals.

8. The concluding benediction embodying the three blessings which is recited after eating food over which the benediction *Bore mine mezonot* is said, begins thus: "Blessed art Thou, O Lord our God, King of the universe, for the sustenance and for the nourishment," and concludes thus: "And we will give Thee thanks for the land and for the sustenance, blessed art Thou, O Lord, for the land and for the sustenance." The benediction recited after drinking wine begins: "For the vine and for the fruit of the vine," and concludes: "For the land and for the fruit of the vine." The benediction after eating fruit begins: "For the trees and for the fruit of the trees," and concludes: "For the land and for the fruit. Blessed art Thou . . . for the land and for the fruit." In Israel and elsewhere when we eat fruit that comes from Israel, we conclude the benediction thus: "For the land and for its fruit." If we have eaten various kinds of farinaceous food and drank some wine, we combine the two benedictions into one benediction. The same rule applies to

fruit and wine. Even if we have partaken of grapes, wine, fruit, and farinaceous food, or even of farinaceous food, wine and fruit, we combine the three benedictions into one, first mentioning "For the sustenance" and then "For the wine" and finally "For the tree." When we combine "For the sustenance" with the other formulae, we do not say at the conclusion "And for the nourishment," but "Blessed . . . for the land and for the sustenance and for the fruit of the vine," or "For the sustenance and for the fruits" or "For the sustenance and for the fruit of the vine and for the fruits." The text has already been published in our prayer books, and it is the duty of every Israelite to commit this benediction to memory.

9. On the Sabbath, or festivals, or New Moon, we include in the concluding benediction whatever relates to these days, but if we have forgotten to include it, we need not repeat the benediction.

10. We must be as careful with this benediction as we are with Grace after meals (as provided for in chapter 44:6, above).

11. Some authorities hold that we should read *Shebarata* (which Thou hast created), in the concluding benediction *Bore nefashot rabbot* (who createst many souls); while others hold that we should read *Shebara* (which He hath created). The latter version is the correct one, for the meaning of this benediction is: "Who has created many living beings with their wants;" that is, He has created the living beings and also their wants, namely, the things that are absolutely necessary to sustain life, such as bread and water, and also all the other things that He has created, which are not so essential, but are rather for the purposes of gratifying the senses, such as fruit and the like—for all these we thank Thee. In the Hebrew phrase חי העולמים (He who is the life of all worlds) we must read the letter *ḥeth* with a *pattaḥ* (*hai*). (The Gaon Elijah of Vilna, of blessed memory, agrees with those authorities who hold that we should include the Divine Name in the end of this benediction, concluding thus: *Baruḥ attah adonai ḥai haolamim* (Blessed art Thou, O Lord, who art the life of all worlds).

12. If we have eaten fruit, after which the benediction embodying the three blessings should be recited, and we have also eaten some fruit, after which the benediction *Bore nefashot rabbot* is to be said, we should only recite the benediction embodying the three blessings, for since we mention in it "The fruit of the tree," we include thereby, all the other kinds of fruit. But if we have eaten another kind of food (not fruit of the tree) after which the benediction *Bore nefashot rabbot* is to be said, it is not exempted by the benediction embodying the three blessings. We should first say the benediction embodying the three blessings, and afterward the benediction *Bore nefashot rabbot.*

13. It is forbidden to leave the place of eating or to engage in any occupation before saying the concluding benediction, lest we forget to say it. If, nevertheless, we have left the place, and the concluding benediction we have omitted is *Bore nefashot rabbot,* we may say it where we are. But if we

have omitted the benediction embodying the three blessings, we must return to the place where we have eaten, just as we would do if it were Grace after meals. (See chapter 44:9, above).

14. If we have neglected to recite the concluding benediction immediately after eating or drinking, we may recite it before the food is digested, which is as long as we have no desire to eat or drink again. After this time limit, we can no longer say it. If we are unable to estimate the time properly, we should eat some more of the same kind of food, and then say the concluding benediction, thus including what we have eaten previously.

15. If one ate or drank, and then vomitted, one should not say the concluding benediction, as it is the same as though the food had already been digested.

Chapter 52

The Benediction Bore Peri Haetz, Bore Peri Haadamah and Shehakol

1. Over fruit that grows on trees, one says the benediction *Bore peri haetz* (who created the fruit of the tree). On partaking of the produce which grow in or close to the ground, such as turnips, vegetables, beans, and herbs, one says the benediction *Bore peri haadamah* (who created the fruit of the ground). A tree, to be designated by this name, must have branches that do not perish in the winter, and which produce leaves in the spring, even though the leaves be as thin as the stalks of flax. But a plant whose branches perish in the winter although its root remains, is not called a "tree," and over its fruit we say the benediction *Bore peri haadamah.*

2. Before partaking of food which is not the product of the soil, such as meat, fish, milk and cheese, and before drinking any beverage other than wine and olive oil, we say the benediction *Shehakol.* The Hebrew word נהיה is to be read with the vowel *Kometz* under the letter *Yod.*

3. Although mushrooms and truffles receive their nutrition from the moisture of the earth, since their growth depends, not upon the soil but upon the atmosphere, they cannot be called "fruit of the ground." The benediction *Shehakol* should, therefore, be pronounced over them.

4. The benedictions *Bore peri haetz* and *Bore peri haadamah* should be said only over articles of food which can be eaten raw, and it is customary to eat them in this state. But if it is customary to eat them only when cooked,

although it is also fit to eat them raw, nevertheless, when eaten raw, the benediction *Shehakol* should be said over it. Pickled food is considered the same as cooked food; therefore, before eating sauerkraut, the benediction *Bore peri haadamah* should be said. Salted food is also governed by the same law as cooked food.

5. Before eating radishes, one should say the benediction *Bore peri haadamah.* Likewise, over garlic and onions that are soft and can be eaten raw, although they are generally eaten with bread, the benediction *Bore peri haadamah* is said over them. If, however, the garlic or onion has become very pungent and is not usually eaten raw, yet it is nevertheless so eaten the benediction *Shehakol* should be said.

6. If one eats cooked articles of food that taste better when raw, one says the benediction *Shehakol.* Even if they are cooked with meat, and their taste improved because of that, nevertheless, inasmuch as the meat is the principal dish, only the benediction *Shehakol* should be said over them. However, if they improved and have also become the principal dish, as for instance, when they were fried in fat or in honey, their proper benediction should be pronounced over them.

7. Inferior kinds of fruit that grow on thorn-bushes and briars, or on other shrubs which are the spontaneous growth of the soil, such as wild apples, which are not fit to eat when raw, require the benediction of *Shehakol,* even if they are cooked or preserved in honey or sugar and made fit for food. But hazel nuts, although they grow in the woods, are considered important articles of food, and the benediction *Bore peri haetz* should be said over them.

8. Herbs which grow spontaneously without cultivation, and are fit to eat raw, although one has cooked them so that they are a proper dish, they are not considered as fruit of the ground, and the benediction *Shehakol* should be said over them. Over lettuce, however, and similar vegetables that have been planted, one should say the benediction *Bore peri haadamah.* Over fruit of a superior kind which grows on bushes, such as gooseberries and raspberries, the benediction *Bore peri haadamah* is said.

9. That portion of the fruit which is not its principal part is not considered as the fruit itself, but is one degree inferior; if it is the fruit of a tree, one says over it the benediction *Bore peri haadamah;* and if it is the fruit of

the ground, one says the benediction *Shehakol.* The caper tree has leaves that are fit for food, for they have a fruit-like growth, and caper-berries, which form the chief part of the fruit, while the caper-flowers are but husks around the fruit, like the shells of nuts, but are also eatable. Therefore, over the berries, which are the essential part of the fruit, we say *Bore peri haetz,* and over the leaves, the food-like excrescence and the flowers, we say *Bore peri haadamah.* Likewise, over preserves made from rose leaves with honey and sugar, we say the benediction *Bore peri haadamah,* for although they grow on trees, they are not fruit. Over preserves made of orange peel, we say the benediction *Bore peri haadamah.* Over preserved melon rinds the benediction *Shehakol* is said. Over the pods of peas that are cultivated in the field, although they are sweet in taste, still if we eat them without the peas, we say the benediction *Shehakol.* If, however, they have been cultivated in the garden for the purpose of eating them raw while in their pods, we say over them the benediction *Bore peri haadamah,* even if we eat the pods alone.

10. Over the seeds of fruit, we say the benediction *Bore peri haadamah,* if they are sweet. If they are bitter, they require no benediction. But if we make them palatable by roasting over fire or in any other way, the benediction *Shehakol* is to be said over them.

11. Over small almonds which are bitter, and are planted for the purpose of using their shells which are not bitter, the benediction *Bore peri haetz* should be said. But when the almonds are large, the kernels are the principal part thereof, but since they are bitter, no benediction need be said on eating them. However, if they are made palatable by being roasted over, or in any other way, inasmuch as they are fruit and are planted for that purpose, the benediction to be said over them is *Bore peri haetz.* Over sugared almonds, even if the sugar exceeds the bulk of the almonds, the benediction *Bore peri haetz* should be said. Over sugared calamus, we say the benediction *Shehakol* because the calamus is not a fruit.

12. Over fruits that were not ripened on the tree, but have been cooked or preserved in honey, we say the benediction *Shehakol.* Over citrons preserved in honey or in sugar, the benediction is *Bore peri haetz.*

13. Over spoiled fruit, such as have become withered through the heat and have fallen off the tree before becoming ripe, since they have deteriorated, the benediction *Shehakol* should be said. Likewise over moldy bread, or over a slightly spoiled dish, the benediction is *Shehakol*. But if they have been spoiled to such an extent that they are unfit for food, no benediction is required over them. Nor should a benediction be uttered over strong vinegar which bubbles when poured on the ground. However, if it has been mixed with water and it became fit to drink, the benediction for it is *Shehakol*.

14. Some fruits never ripen on the tree, but after being plucked off the tree, they ripen by being placed in stubble, or the like, like for instance, certain kinds of small pears, inasmuch as that is their natural way of ripening, the benediction *Bore peri haetz* should be said over them.

15. There are certain types of fruit which contain juice in their kernels, and while the kernels are not fit to eat, the juice extracted from them is palatable. Over such juice the benediction *Shehakol* should be said.

16. We say neither the benediction *Bore peri haetz* nor *Bore peri haadamah* unless we can at least slightly recognize the fruit. But if they are so crushed that they are unrecognizable, as is the case with plum jam, or crushed peas, the benediction to be said over them is *Shehakol*. Yet, if we have inadvertently said the benediction appropriate for their kind, our duty has been fulfilled. If, however, the fruit is mostly eaten in a crushed form, the benediction originally appropriate to them should be recited.

17. Over millet and rice that have been cooked without being dissolved, we say the benediction *Bore peri haadamah*. But if they were dissolved, or we ground them and made bread out of them; there is a difference between rice and millet. According to the strict letter of the law, the benediction *Bore mine mezonot* should be recited over rice, and *Shehakol* over millet. But we are not certain whether the Hebrew word *Orez* connotes "rice" and *Doḥan* denotes "millet," or vice versa. Therefore, a God-fearing person should eat dissolved rice and millet only in the course of a meal. However, in an emergency, when we have no bread, we should say the benediction *Shehakol* over both the rice and the millet, and later say the concluding benediction *Bore*

nefashot rabbot. Over bread made out of pulse, even where such bread is the staple food, we say the benediction *Shehakol.*

18. We say the benediction *Shehakol* over sugar. Also, when one chews sugar cane, or cinnamon, or licorice, and only the taste of it is enjoyed, while the bulk is thrown away, the benediction *Shehakol* is said.

CHAPTER 53

Benedictions Over Soup, Fruit, and Vegetable Extracts

1. Over liquids extracted from fruits and vegetables, we say the benediction *Shehakol.* This also applies to the honey extracted from dates, because no liquid is termed "fruit," except wine and olive oil. For wine, which is highly regarded, a special benediction has been set, *Bore peri haggafen* (who hath created the fruit of the vine). If one enjoys olive oil, which is also highly regarded, in such quantity that a benediction is required, one says the benediction *Bore peri haetz.*

2. If we cook fruits which are usually eaten raw, we say the benediction *Shehakol* over their juice. However, if it is a kind of fruit which is customarily dried first and then cooked, and which are plentiful and are also grown for that purpose, we say the benediction *Bore peri haetz* over the juice, even if we do not eat the fruit. Likewise, if we cook peas or vegetables, where it is customary to soak them, we say the benediction *Bore peri haadamah* over the juice, even if we do not partake of the solid dish. However, if we cook them only for the sake of the fruit or the vegetables, then we say the benediction *Shehakol* over the juice, if we do not partake of the fruit or the vegetables. If we cook them with meat, although the cooking was done also for the sake of the juice, we say *Shehakol* over the juice, because the meat is the principal part of the dish.

3. If we soak or cook fruits exclusively for the sake of their juice, the juice is subject to the benediction *Shehakol;* hence, over tea, coffee, or beer, whether made from dates or barley, the benediction *Shehakol* should be recited.

4. If fruits or vegetables such as cucumbers, beets, leeks, and cabbage, are preserved in water until they are pickled, although such vegetables are usually processed that way, nevertheless, we say the benediction *Shehakol* over their juice. Although the juice has the same taste as the vegetables or the fruit, since they were preserved not to flavor the juice, but for their own sake, the benediction *Shehakol* is to be said over the juice. But if we first eat the vegetables and pronounce the benediction *Bore peri haadamah,* and then we wish to drink the juice, it is doubtful whether or not we have to say a benediction over it, for it might have been exempted by reciting the benediction *Bore peri haadamah.* It is best, therefore, not to act in the aforesaid manner.

5. The same is the case with fruits, vegetables, peas, and the like, which are cooked in a liquid that has its own taste, as for instance when cooked in vinegar, in beetroot, or in milk, that the benediction *Shehakol* should be said over the liquid. However, if we first ate the fruit and recited the appropriate benediction over it, it is doubtful whether or not the juice is exempted by the recitation of this benediction.

6. Raisins, which have enough juice when they are pressed, if they are soaked in water for three days for the purpose of making a beverage out of them and not for eating the raisins, then, if they have begun to ferment, and after the three days the liquid is poured into another vessel, such liquid is to be considered as wine, and the benediction *Bore peri haggafen* should be recited before drinking it, and the benediction embodying the three blessings thereafter. On all occasions where the use of a cup of wine is required, we may fulfill our duty by using this type of beverage. It is necessary, however, to see that the raisins form more than a sixth part of the water used; and in so estimating, we consider the raisins as though they were fresh, before they were dried. All of the foregoing applies only to wine made by soaking raisins, but if the raisins have been boiled in water, the boiling does not cause it to become wine. If the raisins have been soaked or boiled for the purpose of eating them as well, there are diverse opinions as to the proper benediction to be pronounced over the liquid.

Chapter 54

Principal and Accessory Foods

1. If one eats two articles of food, or drinks two kinds of beverages, one of which is the principal to him, while the other is merely an accessory to it, so that if he had not partaken of the principal food, he would not eat its accessory; as for example, one feels faint and to refresh himself, he eats some salt herring or radishes, but since they are pungent, he also eats with it a small piece of bread; or if one drinks some brandy and then eats a small piece of bread or some fruit, one says a benediction only over the principal

food and not over the accessory—the latter requiring neither a preceding nor a concluding benediction—because it is exempt by the benediction pronounced over the principal article of food. Nor does it require the washing of the hands.

2. This rule concerning accessory foods, applies only to a case where we eat the principal article first and its accessory later, and when saying the benediction, we intend to eat also its accessory, or if we are always accustomed to eat them in such a manner, which is then considered as though we had consciously included the latter in the benediction over the former. Also, the accessory must be eaten in the same place; if we go into another room before eating the accessory, we must say a separate benediction over it.

3. If we eat the accessory before eating the principal article of food; as when we desire to drink some wine or brandy, and in order not to drink it on an empty stomach, we first eat a small piece of some food, we must say the benediction over the accessory as well. But since the food is only an accessory, some authorities hold that we need recite only the benediction *Shehakol* over it. In order to remove any doubt, we should first say a benediction over the wine or over the brandy and drink some of it. This benediction will thus exempt the accessory.

4. If we desire to partake of two aliments, for example, we wish to drink some brandy, and to eat some honey cake, preserves, or the like, we must recite a separate benediction over each, first over the cake or the preserves, because these are considered the more important, and then the benediction over the brandy. Especially, if we desire to eat some pastry and also drink some coffee, we must say a separate benediction over both, first over the pastry and then over the coffee.

5. If we eat two different kinds of food that were cooked together, if each kind is distinguishable, we must recite over each kind the benediction appropriate to it, but if they were dissolved, we say the benediction over the kind which predominates, and it exempts the minor ingredient from a separate benediction. However, if one kind is of the five species, even if it is least in quantity, it is considered the more important.

6. If we put milk or soup over food intending to eat the two together, if our primary object is to eat the food, we say the benediction over that only, for the milk and the soup are only accessories; but if the milk or the soup is what we principally desire, we do say a benediction over that, for then the food is the accessory. If our mind is equally set upon both, and each is subject to a different benediction, we first say the benediction over the food, and after eating some of it, say the benediction *Shehakol* over the soup or over the milk. The law that the food greater in quantity is to be considered first, does not apply to this case.

7. Over ground spices mixed with sugar, we say a benediction only over the spices, which are considered the essential elements. Over a nutmeg, we say the benediction *Bore peri haetz;* over cinnamon and over ginger, we say *Bore peri haadamah.*

8. If we drink olive oil in its natural state, inasmuch as it is injurious, we need not say any benediction over it. But if we mix it with other ingredients, it becomes a mere accessory, and we say a benediction over that which is paramount. However, if we have some ailment and we drink the oil medicinally, even if we mix it with other ingredients, inasmuch as the oil is the primary object, even if it is less in quantity than the ingredients, we say the benediction *Bore peri haetz* over it and thereby exempt all the other ingredients. If we drink a beverage to quench our thirst, and mix with it some olive oil as an aid to health, we say the benediction only over the beverage. This law applies also when we put muscatels, or cinnamon, or ginger in a beverage; in all such cases we always consider what our primary object is.

9. In all kinds of preserves, the honey and the sugar are mere accessories, and the benediction should be said only over the fruit which is the essential element.

CHAPTER 55

Order of Precedence Relating to Benedictions

1. If we have before us, several varieties of fruit and we desire to partake of all of them, we are guided by the following: If they are all subject to the same benediction, we say it over the kind which we like best. If we are equally fond of all, and there is among them one of the seven species with which the land of Israel was blessed (see chapter 51:7, above), we say the benediction over this one, even if there should be only half of that fruit, while the others are whole ones. But if there is none of the seven species among them, and only one of them is whole, the benediction should be said over the whole fruit. The same applies when we desire to eat two kinds of fruit that are subject to different benedictions, when one, for instance, is subject to the benediction *Bore peri haetz,* and the other to *Bore peri haadamah,* thus requiring the recital of both benedictions; if we like one kind best, we give that one the preference. If we are equally fond of both, then any one of the seven species has precedence, even if it is not whole. If there is none of the seven species among them, precedence should be given to the whole fruit. But if they are both the same, either whole or not, the benediction *Bore peri haetz* takes precedence over the benediction *Bore peri haadamah.*

2. If all the fruit are of the seven species, and we are equally fond of them, we should give precedence in pronouncing the benediction to that kind which is mentioned first in the Scripture (Deuteronomy 8:8). The second time the word *eretz* (land) is mentioned in the verse enumerating the seven species,

interrupts the order; consequently, dates take precedence over grapes, because dates are mentioned second after the second *eretz* in that verse, while grapes are mentioned third after the first *eretz*. That is true only in as far as grapes are concerned, but wine, being so important that a special benediction has been assigned to it, it takes precedence over all kinds of fruit.

3. The precedence given to the "seven species" applies only to ripe fruit, but if the fruit is unripe, it has no precedence, because the Scripture does not extol anything which is incomplete. Likewise, if we eat of the "seven species" in a manner that we cannot enjoy it, as when we chew wheat, the law of precedence does not apply to it.

4. If we have before us one kind of food over which either the benediction *Bore peri haetz* or *Bore peri haadamah* is said, and another kind over which the benediction *Shehakol* is recited, and we wish to partake of both kinds, we give precedence either to the benediction *Bore peri haetz* or to *Bore peri haadamah*, because these benedictions are more specific in that they are recited over certain specific foods, whereas *Shehakol* is a comprehensive benediction, being recited over many kinds of food. Even if we are more fond of the food over which the benediction *Shehakol* is to be said, still preference must be given to the benedictions *Bore peri haetz* and *Bore peri haadamah*.

5. The benediction *Bore mine mezonot* takes precedence even over the benediction recited over wine; needless to state that the benediction *Hamotzi* takes precedence over the benediction recited over wine, for the *Hamotzi* takes precedence even over the benediction *Bore mine mezonot*. Therefore, on Sabbath and festivals, when reciting the *kiddush* over wine, the *ḥallot* should be covered, so that they may not be ashamed by our giving precedence to the wine. Also, in the morning when we partake of farinaceous food after the *kiddush*, the food should be covered when the *kiddush* is recited over wine.

CHAPTER 56

Benedictions Pronounced Erroneously

1. If by error one says the benediction *Bore mine mezonot* over bread, or the *Hamotzi* over cake, he has fulfilled his duty. If, however, he has said the *Hamotzi* over cooked food, even if it has been prepared from one of the five species of grain, his obligation is not fulfilled. If by error he says the benediction *Bore peri haggafen* over grapes, or if he says after eating grapes, the benediction *Al haggefen*, his obligation is fulfilled, because grapes are fruit of the vine.

2. If by error he says the benediction *Bore peri haadamah* over fruit of the tree, or if by error, when fruit of the tree and fruit of the ground were before him, he has given precedence to the benediction *Bore peri haadamah*, with the intention of exempting thereby the fruit of the tree, his obligation is fulfilled, because the fruit of the tree also gets its sustenance from the ground. But if he says the benediction *Bore peri haetz* over the fruit of the ground, his obligation is not fulfilled. Consequently when one is uncertain whether a certain fruit is a fruit of the ground or a fruit of the tree, and it is impossible for one to ascertain the fact, one should recite the benediction *Bore peri haadamah*.

3. If one says over wine the benediction *Bore peri haetz*, and he immediately becomes aware of the error, he should at once add the words *Bore peri haggafen*. If, however, he does not become aware of the error immediately, his obligation is fulfilled.

4. If by error one says the benediction *Shehakol* over any article of food, even if it be over bread or wine, one's obligation is nevertheless fulfilled.

5. Although one must ascertain prior to the blessing, what kind of food one will consume, nevertheless, if one errs in intention, thinking, for instance that one is about to drink wine, and begins the benediction with the intention of concluding it with *Bore peri haggafen*, but before concluding it one discovers that it is water or beer and one concludes it with *Shehakol niheyah bidevaro*, one need not repeat the benediction, because no benediction must be repeated just because there was an erroneous intention on our part. It is especially so if one mistakes wine for water or beer, and one begins reciting the benediction with the intention of concluding it with *Shehakol;* but becomes aware of the error, and says *Bore peri haggafen*, that one's duty is fulfilled, for had one concluded the benediction *Shehakol* as originally intended, one would have also fulfilled one's obligation.

6. Even if one concludes the entire benediction erroneously, but instantly becomes aware of the error and rectifies it; when one takes for instance a glass of water or beer, thinking that it is wine, and one says the benediction *Bore peri haggafen*, and then one finds out immediately that it is water or beer, and concludes by reciting *Shehakol*, saying thus: *Bore peri haggafen—shehakol niheya bidevaro* (who createst the fruit of the vine—by whose word all things exist), one's duty is fulfilled.

7. If in the foregoing instance, one does not instantly become aware of the error, one must repeat the entire benediction *Shehakol*, if one desires to drink of the contents of this glass. If one has intended to drink also wine, one may take some wine and drink it without saying a second benediction, provided one had not intervened in the meantime by speaking. Even though one tastes the contents of the glass and discovers that it contains water or beer, nevertheless, this is not considered an interruption.

CHAPTER 57

Benediction Over Food Served More Than Originally Intended

1. If a person has recited a benediction over bread, having no intention to eat more than what he had; when he has purchased for instance a loaf of bread or a roll, thinking that this would suffice; but then he desired to eat more, and he sends someone to bring more of the same, even if there is still some left of what he had originally purchased, he must repeat the *Hamotzi* over the additional bread, because he had changed his mind. However, if he has bread in the house and he cuts off one slice, thinking it would be sufficient,

and then he desires to eat more and cuts off another slice, he need not repeat the *Hamotzi*, even if he has nothing left of the original piece; that is not considered a change of mind, for people usually do so.

2. If a person says a benediction over fruit, and then some more fruit is brought to him, if at the time he said the benediction he intended to include all that would be set before him, he need not repeat the benediction over the additional fruit, even if he has nothing left of the original fruit, and even if the additional fruit is not of the same kind as the first, as long as they require the same benediction. If, however, he has changed his mind, that is, if his original intention was to eat only what was before him, even if the additional fruit is of the same kind as the first and he also has some of the first still left, he must, nevertheless, repeat the benediction over the additional fruit.

3. However, if he has given no thought whatsoever concerning any additional fruit that might be set before him, then the following rules obtain; if none of the first fruit was left when the additional fruit was brought to him, he must repeat the benediction; but if there is still some of it left, there is a diversity of opinion as to whether or not the benediction must be repeated over the additional fruit. It is best, therefore, to have it in mind, when saying the benediction, to exempt thereby whatever may be set before him. If he had no such intention, he must abstain from the additional fruit, since it is doubtful whether or not the benediction should be repeated.

4. If the additional fruit is of a superior kind than the first, and the person is more fond of the second than of the first, or if the additional fruit belongs to the seven species, the benediction must be repeated, even if some of the first fruit is still left, for the benediction uttered over an inferior article of food cannot of itself exempt a superior one, unless one has intended to do so.

5. If one says the benediction *Shehakol* over beer, with the intention of exempting all other articles of food requiring the same benediction, if fish is then brought to the table, one need not repeat the benediction over the fish. If, however, when saying the benediction, one does not think of any other food that may be set before one, the benediction *Shehakol* must be repeated over the fish, even if some of the beer is still left at that time. The law that the benediction uttered over one kind of fruit, say apples, exempts another kind of fruit, like pears, does not apply to this case. For, apples and pears belong to the same class of food, whereas beer and fish are entirely two different kinds, because the latter is an edible, while the former is a beverage. The one cannot exempt the other unless they are both on the table when the benediction is uttered, or when there is an intention to exempt it.

6. The above rules apply only to one who eats his own food, but if one dines at someone else's house, the benediction he says over one kind of food, covers all that is brought subsequently, even if there is no more left of the first kind, since a guest defers to the host's will. But if there was actually a

change of mind with regard to the additional food, he must repeat the benediction. If the host has had no intention of serving his guests with more of the same food, but has served them solely at their own request, then the latter likewise need not repeat the benediction, inasmuch as they could assume that the host would supply them with all the food they desire.

7. If one comes to a feast and utters a benediction over a cup of beverage, one need not repeat the benediction over the cups that are offered later, if it is the general custom to serve more than one cup to a guest. It is assumed that when saying the benediction over the first cup, one has intended to include all the others.

Chapter 58

Benediction Over Fragrance

1. Just as we are forbidden to enjoy food or drink without a benediction, so are we forbidden to enjoy any fragrant odor without saying a benediction, as it is written (Psalms 150:6): "Let everything that hath breath praise the Lord." And what is it that only the soul and not the body derives pleasure thereof? It is the fragrant odor. However, after having enjoyed the fragrance, we are not required to say a concluding benediction, for as soon as we have ceased to inhale it, our pleasure has ceased, and it is akin to food which has already been digested.

2. What benediction do we say over a pleasant odor? If it comes from fruit or a vegetable that is fit for food, even if it can be eaten only when mixed with other ingredients, such as the nutmeg, or the lemon, or the citron (*etrog*, all year round, except during the festival of *Sukkot*), inasmuch as that fruit is used principally as food, we say the benediction "Who hath given" (*asher natan*). Some versions read "Who giveth (*hannoten*) fragrance into fruit." This benediction is said, however, only when we intentionally inhale the fragrance. If when partaking of the fruit, its fragrance has reached us unintentionally, we are not obliged to say a benediction. If we scent roasted coffee which has a pleasant odor, we say the benediction: "Who hath given fragrance into fruit."

3. If the thing out of which the fragrance arises is a tree or a plant, we say the benediction: "Who hath created fragrant woods." Therefore, over the myrtle, the rose, frankincense, or the like, we say the benediction: "Who hath created fragrant woods," since they are valued chiefly for their fragrance and not as a food. One should not scent pepper or ginger, because authorities disagree as to whether or not a benediction should be recited over their odor.

4. If the fragrance arises from grass or herbs, we say the benediction: "Who hath created fragrant herbs." A herb is distinguished from a

tree in the following manner; if it possesses a stem as hard as the stalk of flax, and is perennial and produces leaves, it is a tree. But if the stalk is always soft, it is merely a herb.

5. If, like the musk, it is neither a tree nor a herb, on inhaling its fragrance we say the benediction: "Who hath created various kinds of spices." It seems to me that the same benediction is to be said on smelling dried mushrooms, if we find their odor pleasant.

6. Over balsam oil which grows in the land of Israel, the special benediction: "Who hath created sweet-scented oil," has been instituted, on account of its special association with the land of Israel.

7. If by error we confuse the benedictions: "Who hath created fragrant herbs," and "Who hath created fragrant woods," and substitute one for the other, we cannot consider our obligation fulfilled. If, however, we say the benediction: "Who hath created various kinds of spices," over any of the odorous objects, our obligation is fulfilled. Therefore, if we are in doubt as to what benediction to say because we are unable to distinguish the species, we should say the benediction: "Who hath created various kinds of spices." It seems to me that if we say the benediction: "Who hath created fragrant woods," over the fruit of a tree, we have done our duty. Therefore, it seems to me that over cloves and over the rind of oranges and lemons we should say the benediction: "Who hath created fragrant woods."

8. Oil or wine that has been spiced with fragrant wood, is subject to the benediction: "Who hath created fragrant woods," and if spiced with fragrant plants, it is subject to the benediction. "Who hath created fragrant herbs." If spiced with both, it is subject to the benediction: "Who hath created various kinds of spices." In all cases where the fragrance is due to several ingredients, the benediction: "Who hath created various kinds of spices" is said. If the substance producing the fragrance has been extracted from oil or water, leaving none of that ingredient except its perfume, it is questionable whether a benediction is required on smelling it. One should, therefore, abstain from smelling this kind of odor.

9. If fragrant fruit, odorous wood, plants, and spices are set before us, we should say the benediction appropriate to each in the following order: first over the fruit, then over the wood, the plants, and the spices.

10. If we inhale incense: spices burnt on coals, we must say the benediction as soon as the fumes ascend, before we inhale it, as obtains in all cases where a benediction must be said over articles for human enjoyment. The benediction, however, should not be said before the fumes ascend, for a benediction must be uttered immediately before the enjoyment. If we burn fragrant wood, we say the benediction: "Who hath created fragrant wood." If we burn fragrant plants, we say the benediction: "Who hath created fragrant herbs;" and if we burn other kinds of spices, we say: "Who hath created various kinds of spices." In each case, a benediction should be said only when we

burn the spices specially to inhale their perfume, but if we burn them for the purpose of fumigating the room, as in the case of disinfectants used near a corpse, no benediction should be said.

11. Wherever the spices are not meant for the special purpose of smelling them, such as spices stored in a room as merchandise, and perfume used only to scent garments and not meant to be inhaled for its fragrance, these spices and perfumes require no benediction, even when we smell them intentionally.

12. If, however, we enter a store where various spices are sold, or a chemist's shop, and we intend to smell them, we should previously say the benediction: "Who hath created various kinds of spices," as the spices are placed there for this purpose as a means of attracting customers. If we enter and leave the place several times in succession, we need not repeat the benediction, if when we first said the benediction, we had in mind to include subsequent visits. But if our attention has been diverted from it, or if we have remained a long time outside the shop, we must repeat the benediction when we return there.

13. When the scent arises from an object other than the original source, as from fumigated garments, or from a vessel that had contained spices, or from hands, after handling citrons or other fragrant fruit, no benediction is required.

14. See chapter 152:10, and 167:7, below.

CHAPTER 59

Benedictions Over Joy and Grief

1. If one hears good tidings from a reliable eye-witness, or if one witnesses it in person, one must say the benediction *Sheheḥeyanu* (who kept us in life), if only he alone is benefited by the tidings. If, however, it benefits others as well, one says the benediction *Hatov vehametiv* (who is good and dispenseth good), which reads: "Blessed art Thou, O Lord our God, King of the universe, who is good and dispenseth good to others." If at the time, one sees the good event or hears the good tidings, one is unable to utter the benediction, either on account of one's physical condition, or owing to the locality where one happens to be, one may say the benediction later. This rule applies also to the benediction *Dayan haemet* (the just Judge), said over bad tidings.

2. It is our duty to express our blessing to the Almighty, blessed be His name, even when evil comes upon us; for it is written (Deuteronomy 6:5): "And thou shalt love the Lord thy God with all thy heart, and with all thy soul, and with all thy might." "With all thy heart," means with your

two inclinations, that is, even when we are engaged in worldly pursuits, we must fulfill the command (Proverbs 3:6): "In all thy ways acknowledge Him." "And with all thy soul," means even if He takes away your life. "And with all thy might," means with all your possessions. Another meaning of the Hebrew word *meodeḥa* (thy might) is, "For any measure meted out to you, whether it be a measure of kindness or a measure of punishment, express your gratitude to Him." How should we express our blessing? On hearing bad tidings, we say: "Blessed art Thou, O Lord our God, King of the universe, the just Judge." If many reports reach us at one time, whether they be good or evil, one benediction suffices for all. It is our duty to bless the Almighty for any misfortune wholeheartedly, just as we bless Him for the good things. For it is written (Psalms 101:1): "Of kindness and judgment will I sing; unto Thee, O Lord, will I sing." If it be kindness I will sing, and if it be judgment, I will likewise sing. For to the true worshipers of the Almighty, evil occurences, too, are a joy and a favor, believing it to be an atonement for their sins. It follows, that in accepting the misfortune, they serve the Lord thereby, and serving the Lord is a source of happiness to them.

3. If we acquire a profitable thing or hear good tidings, although evil is likely to result therefrom, as when we find a precious article, and if the matter is discovered, the king will confiscate all our property, we must, nevertheless, say the benediction *Hatov vehametiv*. If evil befalls us, or if we hear bad reports, although these misfortunes will likely have good results, as when a flood has inundated our field and has injured the crops, but it will eventually be beneficial because it watered the soil, nevertheless, we must say the benediction *Dayyan haemet* (the just Judge), since the blessing refers to the present, and not to the future.

4. A man should accustom himself to say always: "Whatever the All-merciful does is for our good."

5. Upon the birth of a son, both father and mother say the benediction *Hatov vehametiv*. If the mother dies in childbirth, the father says the benediction *Sheheḥeyanu*, not *Hatov vehametiv*, because the good has come only to one. Likewise if the father dies before she gives birth, she says the benediction *Sheheḥeyanu* (for the birth of the child), but not *Hatov vehametiv*.

6. Upon the death of a relative, or even a stranger who was a pious man, or a scholar whose death grieves us, we say the benediction: "Blessed art Thou, O Lord our God, King of the universe, the just Judge." On the demise of one whose death does not cause us so much grief, we say the benediction: "Blessed be the just Judge," omitting the Divine name and Kingdom (O Lord our God, King of the universe). If a father leaves property to

his son as an inheritance, the son also says the benediction *Sheheḥeyanu.* If there are other children to share in the inheritance, he says instead *Hatov vehametiv.*

7. If we build or buy a house, or if we purchase vessels or valuable garments, although we had previously acquired similar possessions, but had never owned these articles previously, and we rejoice in their acquisition, we say the benediction *Sheheḥeyanu.* The benediction should be recited at the time the purchase is made or upon the completion of the building, although we have not yet made use of same, as the benediction is said over the joy of acquisition.

8. Upon putting on a new garment for the first time, we say the benediction *Malbish arumim* (who clothest the naked), even if we have already said this benediction in our morning prayers. If, however, we have had the new garment on when praying in the morning, the benediction in the morning prayer exempts us from saying it again. Some authorities hold that on putting on a new hat, the benediction is: "Who crownest Israel with glory;" and on putting on a new girdle, we say: "Who girdest Israel with strength;" while other authorities disagree with this view. Therefore, it is best to put them on for the first time before the morning prayer and have them in mind when saying the benedictions in the regular prayers. If we purchase a new *tallit,* we say the benediction *Sheheḥeyanu* after inserting in it the fringes. If we omit to say it at that time, we may say it when we cover ourselves with it for the first time following the benediction *Lehitatef batzitzit* (to wrap ourselves in a fringed garment).

9. On purchasing articles for household use, we say the benediction *Hatov vehametiv.*

10. On receiving a gift, we say the benediction *Hatov vehametiv,* as both the recipient and the donor are benefited by it. If the recipient is poor, then the donor derives pleasure in that the Almighty has granted him the means of giving charity, and if the recipient is rich, the donor is gratified by the former's acceptance of the gift.

11. On purchasing new sacred books, we do not say the benediction *Sheheḥeyanu,* as the things with which sacred duties are performed are not for sensual enjoyment.

12. On purchasing an article of slight value, such as a shirt, shoes, or socks, we do not say a benediction, even if we are poor and its acquisition gives us joy. If a rich man purchases new utensils, the acquisition of which would gladden the heart of an average man, but which the rich man esteems lightly and finds no joy in it, he should not say a benediction.

13. It is customary to say to one who puts on a new garment: "Mayest thou wear it out and acquire a new one." But we do not express this wish to one who puts on new shoes or a new garment made of fur or leather, even if the fur or leather be sewn beneath cloth, and even if they come of an unclean animal because a garment like this requires the killing of a living creature, and it is written (Psalms 145:9): "And His mercy is upon all His works."

14. On partaking for the first time of a new fruit which is reproduced annually, we first say the benediction *Sheheḥeyanu* and then the benediction pertaining to that fruit. If we have forgotten and first said the benediction for fruit, we may say *Sheheḥeyanu* afterward, and it is not considered an interruption. If we have neglected to say *Sheheḥeyanu* when we first partook of the new fruit, we should not say it when we eat the same fruit later. If we have before us several kinds of new fruit, one *Sheheḥeyanu* will suffice for all. If we have before us two species of fruit, although they slightly resemble each other, such as cherries and damsons, or even if they bear the same name but differ in taste, such as white figs and black figs, and we say the benediction *Sheheḥeyanu* over one of them, we must repeat it when we partake of the other, as the eating of each of these fruits constitutes a separate pleasure.

15. Some authorities hold that if we say the benediction *Sheheḥeyanu* over grapes, we need not repeat it when drinking new wine, since wine is made out of grapes; while others hold that the benediction should be said over the new wine, because there is a greater pleasure in the latter. Therefore, it is proper that if we have said the benediction *Sheheḥeyanu* over grapes and then want to drink new wine, we should first say the benediction *Sheheḥeyanu* over some new fruit and intend to include the wine. If we have said the benediction *Sheheḥeyanu* over new wine, all agree that we are no longer required to repeat it over the grapes. This rule applies only to new wine that is not fully fermented, and can easily be recognized as new, but if we drink new wine that is fully fermented, we need not say the benediction *Sheheḥeyanu* over it, even if we have not said it over the grapes, because we cannot distinguish between new and old wine.

16. We do not say the benediction *Sheheḥeyanu* over unripe grapes; they must be fully ripe, and so must any fruit be fully ripe for the benediction of *Sheheḥeyanu.*

17. It is customary not to say *Sheheḥeyanu* over new vegetables or turnips, because they can last a long time by being kept in the ground or in sand; and also as they are plentiful, we do not take great pleasure when eating them new.

18. We do not say *Sheheḥeyanu* upon smelling a fragrant odor, for only the soul is gratified by the odor, and the soul is eternal.

19. A man will be called to account in the world-to-come for abstaining from whatever his eye beheld. Rabbi Eleazar was wont to save small coins and buy everything at least once a year. (Talmud Yerushalmi, Kiddushin, end).

20. Upon seeing a friend to whom one is greatly attached, after a separation of thirty days, one says the benediction *Sheheḥeyanu*. Especially when one sees his superior, like his father, or teacher, and he rejoices in seeing him, that one should say *Sheheḥeyanu*, even if one had received a letter from him in the interval. If the time of separation has been twelve months, one says the benediction: "Blessed art Thou, O Lord our God, King of the universe, who reviveth the dead," because he had been forgotten just as the departed ones are forgotten after twelve months, for it is written (Psalms 31:13): "I am forgotten as a dead man out of the heart; I am become like a useless vessel." Just as when a man loses a vessel and fails to recover it within twelve months he despairs of it, so are the departed ones forgotten after twelve months. But no *Sheheḥeyanu* is to be said after twelve months. If during the twelve months one had received a letter or had news of the loved one's welfare, one does not say "Who reviveth the dead," but *Sheheḥeyanu*. This law applies to both male and female; if a man sees his wife, or his mother, or his sister, or his daughter, or if a woman sees her husband, or her father, or her brother, or her son, after a lapse of time, the benediction should be said.

21. Upon meeting a friend whom one had never met, but with whom one had corresponded, one need not say the benediction, for since they had never seen each other before, the love they mutually bear cannot be so great, and the meeting is not likely to cause genuine joy.

Chapter 60

Benedictions Over Sights in Nature

1. On seeing fruit trees in blossom, one must say the benediction: "Blessed art Thou, O Lord our God, King of the universe, who hath made the world wanting in nought, but hath produced therein goodly creatures and goodly trees wherewith to give delight to the children of men." This benediction should be said only once a year. If one delayed saying the bene-

diction until the fruit grew, one should no longer say it. Some authorities hold that if one had neglected to say the benediction upon seeing the blossom for the first time, one should no longer say it.

2. On seeing shooting stars which dart across the sky with a transient light, or a comet, or a meteor, or on witnessing an earthquake, or a hurricane, or lightning, we say the benediction: "Blessed art Thou, O Lord our God, King of the universe, who hath made the work of creation." (This benediction should be said over a shooting star but once during the night, even if we see more than one. Over a comet we say a benediction but once in thirty days). On hearing thunder after the lightning has flashed, we say the benediction: "Blessed art Thou, O Lord our God, King of the universe, whose strength and might fill the world." If we see lightning and hear thunder simultaneously, we say only the benediction: "Who hath made the creation." If upon seeing lightning, we have said the benediction: "Who hath made the work of creation" and hear thunder at that instant or immediately after that, it is not necessary to say a benediction over the thunder, for the one said over the lightning covers that. The benedictions over lightning and thunder should be said directly when they happen, and if an interruption occurs, the benediction should not be said.

3. So long as the clouds have not scattered, one benediction exempts all the lightning and thunder that may be seen or heard. But if the clouds disappeared between one peal of thunder and another, we must repeat the benediction. A flash of lightning due to the heat and unaccompanied by thunder, does not require the saying of a benediction.

4. On seeing the rainbow, we say the benediction: "Blessed art Thou, O Lord our God, King of the universe, who remembereth His covenant, is faithful to His covenant, and keepeth His promise." We must not gaze too much at the rainbow.

5. At the sight of seas, or mountains famous for their great height, we say the benediction: "Who hath made the work of creation."

6. On seeing the sun at the end of its cycle, that is, after a period of twenty-eight years, when the vernal equinox of the month of *Nisan* begins, at the approach of nightfall on the eve of the fourth day, we say on the morning of the fourth day after sunrise, the benediction "Who hath made the work of creation." Before pronouncing the benediction, we are to recite Psalm 148: "Hallelujah. Praise ye the Lord from the heavens," etc. Afterward we recite the prayer *El adon* (God the Lord) up to *Veḥayyot hakkodesh* (and the holy *Ḥayot*); then Psalm 19: "The heavens declare the glory of God," etc. We conclude by saying *Alenu leshabeaḥ* (it is our duty to praise); and the recitation of the *kaddish*.

7. The above benediction should be said, if possible, immediately after sunrise, because the zealous perform precepts promptly. It is well to say it in an assembly of people, for it is written (Proverbs 14:28): "In the multitude of people is the king's glory." (It is, therefore, best to let the public know by announcing it on the day before). If it is impossible for all to assemble early in the morning, the benediction should not be postponed, but each one should recite it immediately upon seeing the rising of the sun. The rule that the "zealous fulfill precepts promptly," takes precedence over the rule that "in the multitude," etc. If we have not said the benediction in the morning, we may say it up to the third hour of the day (about nine o'clock in the forenoon), and in case of emergency, it may be said until noon. Consequently, if the morning is cloudy and the sun is obscured, we should wait until it is near noon; perhaps the sun will by then appear, and we will be able to say the benediction mentioning the Divine Name and His Kingship; but if the sun does not appear by then, we say the benediction, omitting the Divine Name and the attribute of His Kingship.

8. If the Holy One, blessed be He, has wrought a miracle for someone, having saved him in a supernatural way, then on seeing the place where the miracle occurred, he says the benediction: "Blessed art Thou, O Lord our God, King of the universe, who hath wrought a miracle for me in this place." His son, his grandson, and even those who were born before the miracle occurred, should also say a benediction. How is the blessing worded? The son says: "Who hath wrought a miracle for my father in this place," and if there is more than one son, they say: "For our father." The grandchild says: "For my ancestor," and if there is more than one grandchild, they say: "For our ancestor." One for whom many miracles have been wrought, on arriving at one of the places, should include them all in one benediction, as follows: "Who has wrought a miracle for me in this place and in that place," mentioning the other places. His sons and grandsons also should mention all the places.

9. On seeing a great Jewish scholar, distinguished for his knowledge of the Torah, one says the benediction: "Blessed art Thou, O Lord our God, King of the universe, who hath imparted of His wisdom to them that fear Him." On seeing a man, distinguished in secular knowledge, one says: "Blessed art Thou, O Lord our God, King of the universe, who hath given of His wisdom to flesh and blood."

10. On seeing a king of any of the nations of the world, we say the benediction: "Blessed art Thou, O Lord our God, King of the universe, who hath given of His glory to flesh and blood." Even if we do not see the king in person, but witness the pomp and ceremony and we are certain of the king's presence, we may say this benediction. It is desirable to make an effort to behold the glory of kings. Having seen the king once, we should not interrupt the study of the Torah to see him once more, unless he appears this time with a greater army and with more pomp than before.

11. On seeing graves of Israelites, we say: "Blessed art Thou, O Lord, our God, King of the universe, who hath formed you in judgment," etc. On

seeing graves of heathens, we say the Biblical verse (Jeremiah 50:12): "Your mother shall be sore ashamed, she that bore you shall be confounded; behold the hindermost of the nations shall be a wilderness, a dry land, and a desert."

12. The above benedictions should not be repeated on seeing the same person or object within thirty days, that is exclusive of the day on which we saw it and of the present day. But on seeing another sage, king, or other graves, even within thirty days, the benedictions should be repeated.

13. On seeing an Ethiopian, or a red Indian, or an Albino, or a freak, as a giant, or a dwarf, or one who is wholly ulcerous, or one whose entire hair is matted, or an elephant, or an ape, we say: "Blessed art Thou, O Lord our God, King of the universe, who varies the forms of His creatures." This benediction is to be pronounced only on seeing the above for the first time, for the first impression is very striking.

14. On seeing for the first time a lame person, or one without hands or, feet, or a blind person, or one who is afflicted with leprosy, or with scurfs, if they have been thus afflicted from birth, we say the benediction: "Blessed art Thou, O Lord our God, King of the universe, who varies the forms of His creatures." But if they were afflicted after birth, and the sight of them causes us grief, we should say the benediction *Dayyan haemet* (the true Judge).

15. On seeing goodly trees or beautiful creatures, whether human or animal, we say the benediction: "Blessed art Thou, O Lord our God, King of the universe, who hath such as this in His world." This benediction is to be said only upon seeing them the first time, and need not be repeated on seeing them again or even others of the same kind, unless the latter are more beautiful than the former.

CHAPTER 61

The Benediction Hagomel

1. On four occasions a man must thank God for special mercy (that is, he must say the benediction *Hagomel*): (a) On crossing the ocean and reaching the desired destination; (b) On crossing safely the desert or any dangerous road, or on being saved from any peril, as when a wall collapsed upon him, or an ox attempted to gore him, or robbers attacked him. (c) On recovering from a serious illness, or from a serious wound, or from any illness which has

confined him to bed for at least three days, and (d) On being released from prison, even if the imprisonment was due to civil matters. All these should say the benediction: "Blessed art Thou, O Lord our God, King of the universe, who vouchsafeth benefits unto the undeserving, who hath vouchsafed all good unto me," to which the listeners respond: "He who hath vouchsafed all good unto thee, may He vouchsafe all good unto thee forever."

2. The benediction *Hagomel* should be said in the presence of no less than ten male adults, in addition to the one saying the benediction. Two of the ten should be scholars who are engaged in the study of the Torah, as it is written (Psalms 107:32): "Let them exalt Him also in the assembly of the people, and praise Him in the seat of the elders." But if no scholars are available, it should not deter him from saying the benediction. It is customary to say this benediction on being called to the reading of the Torah. One must not, however, delay saying *Hagomel* longer than three days. Consequently, if the event calling for the benediction should take place on a Monday, after the Torah had been read, *Hagomel* should be said immediately, and not wait until the reading of the Torah the following Thursday. Likewise, if one is a mourner, who may not be called up to the Torah, one should say the benediction immediately after the event had occurred. This benediction must be recited while standing, in the presence on no less than ten male adults. If by chance, one has neglected to say *Hagomel* longer than three days, one may still say it afterward.

3. A person for whom a miracle was wrought, should set aside a certain sum of money for charity as much as his means will allow. He should divide it among men who are engaged in the study of the Torah, and say: "Behold, I give this money to charity, and may it be the Divine Will to count it as if I had brought a thanksgiving offering." It is also fitting that he shall establish some community project in town, and every year on the anniversary, he shall thank God, and recount the miracle.

4. Before undergoing surgery, or before eating or drinking something as a remedy, one must offer the following brief prayer: "May it be Thy will, O Lord my God, and the God of my fathers, that this serve me as a cure, for Thou art a gratuitous Healer." If the food or beverage of which he is about to partake, requires the recital of a benediction, he should first offer this prayer and then utter the benediction (in order not to interpose between the saying of the benediction and the eating). After bloodletting, one should say the benediction: "Blessed art Thou, O Lord our God, King of the universe, who healeth the sick."

5. If one sneezes, we say to him: "To your good health," whereupon he responds: "Blessed be thou." Afterward he recites the verse (Genesis 49:18): "I wait for Thy salvation, O Lord;" for he who prays on behalf of his fellow man, has his prayer answered first.

6. Praying for something that had already taken place, is called a vain prayer. For instance, a man hears an outcry in the town and he prays: "May it be His Will that this cry should not be in my house;" or, if his wife has become pregnant, and forty days after the conception, he prays: "May it be His Will that my wife should give birth to a male child," this is a vain prayer, for what has already happened cannot be altered. Within the forty days of conception, such a prayer may be offered. After forty days, he may pray, however, that the offspring be a viable child, good in the sight of Heaven and of benefit to humanity.

7. A person who is about to measure his crops or something similar, should offer the following prayer: "May it be Thy will, O Lord my God, that Thou sendest a blessing on this my heap;" having already begun measuring, he says: "Blessed be He who sendeth a blessing on this my heap," omitting the Divine Name and Kingship (O Lord, my God, King of the universe). If he had already measured it, and then offers a prayer, it is a vain petition, for God's blessing is sent only upon that which is hidden from sight (that is, the exact quantity of which is not known (Babli, Baba Mezia 42a).

8. The father, whose son has become *Bar Mitzvah* (that is, he is thirteen years and one day old), should say: "Blessed art Thou, O Lord, our God, King of the universe, who released me from the responsibility of this child." It is said when his son has been called to the reading of the Torah, and has concluded the second benediction. It is a father's duty to prepare a feast on the day on which his son becomes *Bar Mitzvah*. If the boy delivers a discourse on that occasion, it becomes a sacramental feast, even if the dinner is given on a day other than the *Bar Mitzvah* day.

9. If there was a drought which had caused general distress—even in lands where droughts are rare—and then there is a rainfall descending with such force that it runs off in bubbling streams, we are to say certain benedictions.

10. What benedictions do we say? One who does not own a field says: "We thank Thee, O Lord our God, for every drop of rain which Thou hast caused to descend for us, and even if our mouths were full of songs as the seas," (to be continued with the *Nishemat* prayer recited on Sabbath morning) as far as, "And hallow and assign kingship to Thy name, O our King. Blessed art Thou, O Lord, God of many thanksgivings and praises." If one owns a field in partnership with another Israelite, he says the benediction *Hatov vehametiv;* but if he has no Jewish partner, but he has a wife and children, he says the benediction *Sheheḥeyanu.* One may say *Hatov vehametiv* and *Sheheḥeyanu,* even if he does not see the rain, but hears it coming down. The benediction *Modim anaḥnu* (we thank Thee), however, should be recited only if one actually sees the rain.

CHAPTER 62

Concerning Commerce

1. We must take extreme care not to deceive one another. If anyone deceives his neighbor, whether a seller deceives the buyer, or a buyer deceives the seller, he transgresses a prohibitory law. For it is written (Leviticus 25:14): "And if thou sell ought to thy neighbor, or buy of thy neighbor's hand, ye shall not wrong one another." According to our Sages (Shabbat 31a), this is the first question that a man is asked when brought before the Heavenly Court: "Hast thou been dealing honestly?"

2. Just as deception is forbidden in buying and selling, so is it forbidden in hiring, in working on contract, and in money changing.

3. If a person acts in good faith, he is not guilty of deception. Thus, if one says to his neighbor: "I have bought this article at such and such a price, and this is the profit I wish to make from it," although he had overpaid for the article (which does not entitle him to deceive others), yet he is permitted to dispose of it at a profit. For he had warned the purchaser that the price he asks is not based on the value of the article, but on what he, the seller had paid for it.

4. If a person has any commodity to sell, he is forbidden to simulate its appearance to make it seem better than it really is, like giving an animal bran-water to make its belly swell up and its hair to stand erect, thus looking fat and healthy. It is also forbidden to put a coat of paint over old utensils, so that they may seem new. All similar devices are forbidden.

5. It is likewise forbidden to mix a little bad fruit with a lot of good fruit, and to sell the whole as of superior quality, or to mix poor liquor with a superior grade. However, if the taste of the liquor thus mixed can easily be recognized, the mixing is permissible, because the purchaser will detect it and not be deceived by it.

6. A shopkeeper is permitted to distribute parched grain and nuts to children, in order to win their trade. He may also sell below the market price, to attract customers; and the other merchants cannot prevent him from doing so.

7. He who gives a short measure or weight, even to a non-Jew, transgresses a prohibitory command, for it is written (Leviticus 19:35): "Ye shall do no unrighteousness in judgment, in meteyard, in weight, or in measure." The punishment for giving false measure or weight is very great, for the transgressor cannot repent properly, as he does not know how much and to whom to make restitution. Even the establishment of a public charity fund by such a sinner, is not considered adequate penance.

8. It is written (Deuteronomy 25:13-15): "Thou shalt not have in thy bag diverse weights, a great and a small. Thou shalt not have in thy house diverse measures, a great and a small. A perfect and just weight shalt thou have; a perfect and just measure shalt thou have." The words "thy bag" and "thy house" seem to be superfluous in the text; and our Sages, of blessed memory, explained (Baba Batra 89a): "Thou shalt have no money in your bag, on account of having diverse weights; thou shalt want the necessities of life in thy house, on account of having diverse measures. But if thou wilt have a perfect and just weight in thy house, thou wilt have money; and if thou wilt have a just and perfect measure in thy house, thou wilt have all thy necessities." And our Sages, of blessed memory, said again (Niddah 70b): "What should a man do in order to become rich? He should transact his business honestly, and beg for mercy of the One to whom riches belong; for it is written (Ḥaggai 2:8): "Mine is the silver, and mine is the gold."

9. It is well to give an ample weight and measure. That is, one should give somewhat more than the exact quantity required, as it is written (Deuteronomy 25:15): "A perfect and just measure shalt thou have;" by "just" is meant; "give him a little of your own."

10. One must measure according to the custom of the community, and not deviate from it. Where it is the custom to give a "heaped" measure, one must not give a "level" measure, even if it is done with the consent of the buyer who pays less than the full price; and where it is the custom to give a "level" measure, one must not give a "heaped" measure, even if the seller gets more money for it. The Torah has laid down rigid rules regarding measures, lest a stumbling block for others arise from it, for a stranger might get the impression that such is the custom of the community, and he, too, will give such a measure to a person who is also ignorant of the custom of the place, and thus unwittingly deceive him.

11. The communal leaders are in duty bound to appoint supervisors, whose duty it shall be to inspect the shops, and to punish and fine as they see fit, those who have deficient measures and weights or faulty scales.

12. A person who keeps in his house or in his shop, short measures, even if he does not use them, is guilty of transgressing a prohibitory law, for it is written (Deuteronomy 25:13-14): "Thou shalt not have in thy bag diverse weights, a great and a small. Thou shalt not have in thy house measures, a great and a small." It is forbidden to use such measures even for chamber pots, lest someone else use them unknowingly for measuring purposes. If, however, it is the rule of the community that only measures stamped with a certain well-known mark may be used, and that measure is not marked, and cannot, therefore, be used even by mistake, then it may be kept.

13. If one seeks to buy or rent property, real or personal, from a Jew or

from a non-Jew, if the price was already agreed upon, although the sale was not completed, and another one outbids him, the latter is called a *rasha*, a wicked person. If, however, the prospective buyer and seller have not yet agreed upon the price, someone else may buy or rent it. We are forbidden to encroach upon our neighbor's rights in the matter of hiring houses, Jew or non-Jew alike.

14. If a person delegates another as his agent to purchase real property or chattels, and the latter purchases the desired object for himself with his own money, he may keep the property, though he is a cheat. But if the agent has made the purchase with the principal's money, he may not keep the property even if he returns the money.

15. If one has given a deposit on a purchase and has marked the article for identification in the seller's presence, or if the seller has said to the prospective buyer, "Mark your purchase," even though the buyer does not acquire title to the commodity thereby, nevertheless, if one of the parties backs out, be it the buyer or the seller, he does not act as behooves an Israelite, and he incurs the curse of the Sages of old (Mishnah Baba Metzia 4:2): "He who dealt out retribution to the generation of the Flood, and to the generation of the Tower of Babel, and to the men of Sodom and Gomorrah, and to the Egyptians who drowned in the Red Sea, may He deal out retribution to the one who does not abide by his word."

16. It is imperative for a man to abide by his word, if the price has been agreed upon, even though no deposit or any mark has been placed on the article involved. If either the buyer or the seller retracts, he is guilty of dishonesty, and the spirit of the Sages finds no delight in him. For an Israelite must abide by his word, as it is written (Zephaniah 3:13): The remnant of Israel shall not do iniquity, nor speak lies." Furthermore, it is the duty of the truly God-fearing to carry out even his mental determination; thus, if he has decided to sell a certain article to a prospective buyer at a certain price, and the purchaser offers to pay him more, he must accept from him only that amount at which he has determined to sell it to him, so that he may fulfill the Biblical text (Psalms 15:2): "And speaketh truth in his heart." The same rule applies to the buyer; if he has resolved to buy the article at a certain price, he must not retract. This rule applies to all matters appertaining to dealings between man and man. Thus, if we have decided to do a certain favor to our fellow man, we should not change our mind, if we are able to fulfill it. But whatever relates to our own needs, we are not bound to fulfill even what we expressly utter with our lips, as long as it does not involve the performance of a precept.

17. Likewise, if a person promises a small gift to another who depends on it, being sure that he would receive it, if he retracts his promise and fails to give it to him, he is considered lacking in honesty. If, however, he promises a large gift and then retracts, he is not considered lacking in honesty, as the one to whom the promise was made did not depend upon it. Nevertheless,

even in the latter case, the promise must be made in good faith, and not with the intention of retracting it. For to speak words that are at variance with one's thoughts, is forbidden by the Torah, as it is written (Leviticus 19:36): "A just *ephah,* and a just *hin,* shall ye have." Why does the Scripture mention *hin?* Is not *hin* included in the term *ephah* (both meaning measure?) Our Sages hence inferred (Baba Metziah 49a): "That your *hen* ("yes;" note the play on words *hin* and *hen*) shall be just, and your *no* shall be just." The above rule refers only to a promise made to a rich man, but if a promise is made to a poor man, whether the promised gift is large or small, the promise is considered as a vow, and it must be fulfilled. Even an unspoken promise to a poor person, the mere determination to give him a gift, must be fulfilled.

18. If a person offers some land or a house for sale, and two prospective buyers come, each willing to pay the price, and neither owns realty adjoining the land or the house offered for sale, but one is a fellow townsman and the other comes from another community, the fellow townsman has the preference. If they are both fellow townsmen, and one of them is his neighbor, then the latter has the preference. If the other person is the seller's friend who visits him often, whereas his neighbor does not, then the friend has the preference. If one of them is his friend and the other is his relative, the friend still has the preference, for it is written (Proverbs 27:10): "Better is a neighbor that is near than a brother far off." With reference to all other people, a relative has the preference. But a scholar has preference, even over one's neighbor, and over a friend who is on visiting terms. If one of the two prospective buyers owns property adjoining the property offered for sale, he takes precedence before all others. Even after the property has already been sold to someone else, the adjacent owner has the right to return the purchase price to the buyer and make him relinquish the property. Even if this buyer is a scholar, or he is the seller's next of kin, whereas the adjacent owner is an unlearned person and is not related to the seller, nevertheless, the latter enjoys the preference and can force the purchaser to relinquish the property. All of the aforesaid rules of preference have been laid down by the Sages, so as to comply with the injunction (Deuteronomy 6:18): "And thou shalt do that which is right and good in the sight of the Lord."

Chapter 63

Wronging by Means of Words

1. Just as it is forbidden to wrong a person by dishonest buying or selling, even so it is forbidden to wrong a person by means of words, as it is written (Leviticus 25:17): "And ye shall not wrong one another; but thou shalt fear thy God," this prohibition refers to the "wrong done by means of words." This sin is even more serious than the sin of pecuniary cheating, because amends can be made for the latter, but not for the former. Again the latter wrong is directed against one's possessions, but the former against one's person. He who cries to God on account of wrong done to him by means of words, is answered immediately. A person must be especially careful not to hurt his wife's feelings. For a woman is naturally sensitive and is easily moved to tears, and the Almighty, blessed be He, heeds tears, as the Sages say (Beraḥot 32b): "The gates of tears are never closed."

2. What constitutes wronging by means of words? A person should not say to his fellow man: "At what price will you sell me this article?" when he has no intention to buy it. If a man seeks to buy certain merchandise, one must not direct him to a person if he knows that the person has no merchandise to sell. If one's neighbor is a penitent person, one should not say to him: "Remember thy former deeds!" If, God forbid, affliction befalls one's neighbor, one should not speak to him like the friends of Job, who said (Job 4:6-7): "Is not thy fear of God thy confidence? . . . I pray thee, whoever perished being innocent?" If one is asked a scholarly question, one should not say to an unlearned person: "What is your opinion?" The same applies to all forms of speech, which tend to hurt the feelings of a fellow man.

3. If he has an opprobrious nickname, although he is accustomed to it and does not seem to mind it, nevertheless, it is forbidden to call him by that nickname with the intention of insulting him. It is a wronging by means of words.

4. It is forbidden to create a false impression, that is to deceive any human being, Jew or non-Jew, even by mere words, without causing any loss. It is forbidden for example, to sell *unkosher* meat to a non-Jew, who seeks to buy meat of a ritually slaughtered animal. If one sells an article having some imperfection, although it is worth the price, one is, nevertheless, obliged to inform the purchaser of the imperfection. In the case of a gift, however, no question of deception can arise.

5. We must not invite anyone to dine, if we know that the invitation will not be accepted. Nor should we offer someone a gift, when we are certain that the gift will be refused. In all cases where one expresses something with his tongue and does not really mean it, as when one compliments his neighbor, when it does not express his true opinion, it is forbidden. One should always harmonize the tongue, with the heart, thereby cultivating the qualities of being truthful, upright, and of a pure heart.

CHAPTER 64

Dealing In Forbidden Objects

1. Any article of food, the consumption of which is forbidden, although we are allowed to make use of it, cannot be used as merchandise for sale or as security on a loan. We must not even buy it to feed non-Jewish laborers. If it is something not used for food, such as horses and asses, we may deal in it. We may also deal in the forbidden fat of a beast, for it is written concerning it (Leviticus 7:24): "It may be used for any other service."

2. If we happen to acquire a forbidden thing, as while fishing, we catch in the net a ritually unclean fish, or find on our premises an animal that has died of itself or has been killed by a wild beast, we are allowed to sell it, sinc

it has not been our intention to acquire it. But we must sell a living animal immediately and not keep it until it grows fat. We may also sell it through an agent, although the latter will make a profit by it; but the agent may not buy it outright, for this would be considered trading in forbidden animals.

3. It is also permissible to levy on unclean things for the collection of a debt, but they must be sold at once and not wait until a profit could be made on them. They may, however, be kept long enough so as not to suffer any loss on the capital.

4. We may trade in an article the consumption of which has been forbidden only by a rabbinical enactment, for instance, the cheese of non-Jews.

Chapter 65

Interest on Loans

1. It is in the nature of man to long for the acquisition of wealth. But of all the illegal commercial transactions, usury is the most common. In robbery or fraud, the victim usually tries to defend himself, and the perpetrator is often inhibited by shame or fear. When a person takes interest on a loan, however, the borrower gives it voluntarily; and he is happy that he could find a person from whom he could borrow even at a high rate of interest. The lender is also under the impression that he is doing a great favor to the borrower, who can, by means of the loan, profit many times the amount of the interest. Therefore, it is very easy for a man to be caught in the snare of usury, God forbid. And it is precisely for this reason that our Holy Torah is very strict about this law, and enjoins many specific regulations regarding it. He who lends on interest, transgresses six prohibitory laws and will not be included in the resurrection of the dead; as it is written (Ezekiel 18:13): "He hath given forth upon interest, and hath taken increase; shall he then live? He shall not live." The borrower transgresses three prohibitory laws; the scribe, the witnesses, and the broker who negotiated the loan, as well as anyone who was instrumental in bringing about the loan—even if only by pointing out a person from whom one could borrow, or by telling the lender to whom he could lend—all these transgress one prohibitory law.

2. He who erred and has taken interest, is duty bound to return it.

3. Even if no interest is fixed at the time of the loan, as when the loan has been made free of charge until a certain fixed time, or when merchandise is sold on credit for a certain length of time, and when the time of payment arrives

the debtor offers to pay the lender or seller for postponing the time of payment, this also is considered usury.

4. Even if the borrower voluntarily returns to the lender, more than he has borrowed, and even if he does not call the excess payment interest, it is forbidden.

5. Even if the borrower, when paying the interest, declares it to be a gift, the lender must not accept it. If, nevertheless, the lender has accepted the interest but later repents and wishes to make restitution, and the borrower refuses to accept it, he is then permitted to retain it.

6. It is forbidden to give interest either in advance of the loan or subsequent to it. As for instance, if Reuben desires to borrow money from Simeon, and while negotiating the loan, he sends a present to Simeon with the explanation, that he does that in order to obtain a loan; or if he makes a substantial present without any explanation, and it is obvious that he does it in order to obtain a loan; this is "advance interest." If Reuben has borrowed money from Simeon, and when he repays the loan, he makes him a present in consideration of the fact that during the period of the loan, the money yielded no profit to Simeon, this is "subsequent interest."

7. If one lends money to another for a certain length of time, with the understanding that the latter would afterwards reciprocate by lending him a larger amount for the same length of time, or the same amount but for a longer period of time, this is forbidden as unqualified interest. If one lends money to another, with the understanding that the borrower would afterwards lend him a like amount for the same length of time, some authorities forbid such a transaction, while others permit it; but it is best to heed the more rigid opinion. If no stipulation, however, has been made to that effect, and the borrower later lends money to the former lender, even though he does that because he had gotten a loan from him previously, it is permissible.

8. The lender must be careful not to derive any benefit from the borrower without his knowledge, while the loan remains unpaid, even if it be something that the borrower would have granted him even if the loan had not been made. For since he takes it without the sanction of the borrower, he presumes to rely upon the fact that the borrower would not mind it because of the loan. However, even with the borrower's knowledge, the lender may enjoy only that which the borrower would have granted, even if the loan had not been made, provided it is not done in public.

9. If the borrower had not been accustomed to greet the lender before the loan was made, he must not do so afterwards. He must not show him any special respect in the synagogue or elsewhere, if he had not been accustomed to do so in the past. All kinds of attention by the borrower on account of the loan, even by word of mouth, are forbidden, for it is written (Deuteronomy 23:20): "Interest of any *davar* (*thing;* the Hebrew word *davar* also means *word*) that is lent upon interest;" even interest in the nature of words is forbidden. The lender, too, must avoid even interest of words, like saying to

the borrower: "Let me know when so-and-so comes from such-and-such a place. Even though he does not trouble him more than to speak a few words, but since he had not been accustomed to ask such a favor from him previously, and now he bids him to do this because the borrower is obligated to him, such conduct constitutes a form of interest and is forbidden. One may argue and say: "Lo, it is written (Proverbs 22:7): 'The borrower is servant to the lender.'" But this verse applies only to a case where a controversy arises between the lender and the borrower, when the lender says: "Let us go to the High Court for trial there (naming a certain community)," and the borrower says: "Let us try our case in the local court," then the borrower must yield to the lender, as it is written: "The borrower is servant to the lender."

10. The lender is forbidden to derive any advantage from the borrower, even though no money is received directly for the loan. For instance, if the lender is a workman and the borrower had never before been accustomed to give him any work, he is forbidden to accept work from him now.

11. It is forbidden to lend a measure of grain to another to be repaid in kind, even though both grains be of the same sort, for it is possible that the price of grain will advance in the meantime, and consequently he will receive more than he had lent. To make a loan like this legal, a money valuation should be placed on the grain, so that if the price advances, the borrower will repay him only the amount of money at which the grain was originally valued. If, however, the borrower has some grain in his possession, he may borrow many *khors* (a certain measure) of the same kind. If a certain kind of produce has a fixed market price, one may borrow such produce even though he has none of it in his possession. All of the above relates only to lending and returning produce of the same kind, but it is forbidden under all circumstances to lend a measure of wheat and be repaid with a millet, although both are sold at the same price and the borrower has some millet in his possession. It is permissible under all circumstances, to lend a small article about the price of which people are usually not concerned whether it advances or decreases in value; a woman is, therefore, allowed to lend a loaf of bread to her neighbor.

12. If a person lends money, getting a lien on a house, a field, or a pew in the synagogue, and he has the usufruct of that security, this gain should be applied towards reducing the debt; that is, a fixed sum should be deducted annually from the debt. This is considered as the rental paid by the lender. They are permitted to make such an arrangement even when the sum agreed upon is smaller than the actual rental value. The lender, however, must not turn around and rent the property to the borrower. Concerning the law of pledges, there are many diverse opinions, and therefore, one contemplating to make such an arrangement, should consult an expert.

13. It is not permissible to sell an article which has a fixed market price above its value for the reason that credit is extended. But if it has no fixed price, although if he would buy it for cash he would get it for less, it is per-

missible to charge more, provided the price is not raised to such an extent (that is, one-sixth of the value or more), that it is obvious that the increase is on account of extended credit. Even if the seller does not advance the price very much, but he expressly says to the buyer: "If you pay ready cash you can have it for ten coins, but if on credit you will have to pay eleven," it is forbidden. The purchaser is also forbidden to buy merchandise above the market price, with the intention of reselling it immediately at a loss, so that he may have ready cash at his disposal.

14. If one has a note against his neighbor, he may sell it to another at less than its face value even before it is due, and the seller must give a written statement to the buyer, reading: "I hereby sell and transfer to you this note and all that it implies." The note must be accepted by the buyer at his own risk, excepting when the seller had already received payment for the note. Just as one may sell a note at less than its face value to a third party, so may he sell it to the borrower.

15. The stigma of taking interest may be avoided in the following manner: Reuben who requires a loan in the month of *Nisan*, asks Simeon to give him a note whereby Simeon obligates himself to pay Reuben, one hundred gold coins in the month of *Tishre;* and to cover Simeon against any loss, Reuben gives him a note for the same amount also due in the month of *Tishre*. Reuben may now sell the note given him by Simeon to Levi for ninety gold coins. (Much more so may this course be pursued, if Simeon has a note given him by Judah, whereby the latter obligates himself to pay a certain sum at some future date. This note, Simeon may sell to Reuben for a certain sum and receive from him a note for the amount stipulated. Then Reuben may sell this note for as much as he can get.) Reuben is not allowed, however, to make a note payable to himself, and sell it to Simeon, even through an agent.

16. It is forbidden to pay for produce or any other commodity to be delivered at some future date, because the price of the produce may advance before the delivery is made, and when the seller delivers the merchandise, the buyer will have received more than the value of his money. If, however, the seller has in his possession all the produce when the transaction is made, although he will not deliver it to the buyer until after some time has elapsed, such a transaction is permissible, for whatever a man has in his possession, he may sell even at a very reduced price, if he sees so fit. Even if the produce in the seller's possession was not yet in perfect condition, requiring one or two processes to make it perfect, nevertheless, it is considered as being ready

for delivery, and its sale is permissible. But if it still required three or more processes, the transaction is forbidden.

17. When the market price for produce is fixed, one may buy according to this rate for future deliveries by paying in advance, although the seller has none of the produce in stock. For even if the price of the produce advances thereafter, the buyer derives no benefit by his advance payment, since he could have bought the produce then for this price. And since he has made the transaction according to law, if the produce has advanced in price and the seller does not wish to deliver it to him at the original price, he may take instead some other merchandise which the seller may offer him, or the seller must give him the cash value at the present price of the produce.

18. If a person has merchandise which is sold at a low price at one place and at a higher price in another place, and his neighbor says to him: "Give me the merchandise, I will take it to that place, and I will sell it there and use the money for my own purpose until such-and-such date, when I will refund the entire sum which I got for your merchandise, after deducting the expenses incurred in selling it;" then if the risk in transit was taken by the neighbor, the transaction is forbidden, but if the seller took the risk, it is permissible, but he must, in such event reward the neighbor for his trouble.

19. A person, while at the market, may lend his fellow man one hundred *denars*, with which to buy merchandise, and after returning home, the borrower may give the lender one hundred and twenty *denars* for his loan, provided the lender carries the goods to his house, and assumes their risk in transit, for then it is considered as though he was a partner sharing in the profits of the transaction.

20. Simeon may say to Reuben who is going to a certain place where goods are sold cheaply: "Bring me goods from that place, and I will give you so much profit," provided Reuben assumes the risk of the goods in transit until it is delivered to Simeon.

21. It is permissible to increase the rent of realty in this manner: If one leases a yard to another, he may say to him before taking possession: "If you pay the rent in advance, you can have it for ten gold coins per annum, but if you pay monthly, I will charge you one gold coin per month." Such a transaction is permissible, because the rental becomes due only at the conclusion of the period of tenancy. Hence, the extra two gold coins are not given to him on account of his waiting for the money. And as regards the proposal:

"If you pay me the rent immediately, you can have it for ten gold coins per annum," he simply charges him a lower rent in consideration of his early payment.

22. Only in case of leasing realty is it allowed to increase the rent in the aforesaid manner, because the tenant acquires immediate use of the premises. But it is forbidden to decrease the wages of a workman in such manner. For instance, if one engages a workman to do some work at some future time, and he gives him his wages in advance before he begins to work, and because of this the worker agrees to do the work at a lower compensation, he is violating the law, since the workman is not employed at that time, the money he receives is in the nature of a loan. However, if the workman begins his work immediately, although he will not complete it until after some time, it is permissible to give him his wages in advance, in order that he may do the work at a lower rate, for since he has commenced the work immediately, it is considered as wages and not as a loan.

23. The dowry of a bridegroom may be increased in consideration of deferred payment. Thus, if the bride's father had pledged a certain sum of money for his daughter's dowry, he may arrange with his prospective son-in-law to pay it in yearly installments, which will total more than the promised dowry. Such an arrangement is allowed, because it is merely an increase in the dowry, and it is as if he had said: "I will give you a gift of so much and so much at a certain time, and if I fail to do so, I will add to the dowry so much and so much." The above agreement is allowed only when the terms are agreed upon when the pre-marriage settlement is put in writing, for until that time, there is no obligation on the father's part to pay anything, and therefore, this agreement is considered as a condition of this obligation. However, if they make such an arrangement later, it is forbidden.

24. When a Jew borrows money from a non-Jew on interest and another Jew becomes surety, if the terms of the loan are that the non-Jew cannot collect the debt from the surety unless the borrower refuses to pay, the payment of interest is permitted. If, however, the non-Jew can in the first instance collect it from the surety, it appears as if the surety had borrowed the money and then lent it to the Jew on interest; such a loan is forbidden. When a non-Jew borrows money from a Jew on interest and another Jew is surety for it, if the terms of the loan are that the lender cannot demand the debt from the surety unless the borrower, the non-Jew, refuses to pay, such interest is permissible. If, however, it is agreed that the lender could in the first instance claim the debt from the surety, then it is considered as though the surety were the borrower, and the interest is, therefore, forbidden. If the Jew is surety only as regards the principal but not the interest, the transaction is permitted.

25. If a non-Jew says to a Jew: "Borrow some money on interest for me from a Jew on this pawn," or even if he gives him only a promissory note, and the lender relies solely either on the pawn or on the note, while the intermediary assumes no risk whatsoever, such a transaction is allowed. Even if the Jew who is the intermediary brings the interest in person to the lender, the latter may accept it from him, provided that the lender definitely understands that all the risk connected with the loan and the security, whether in transmitting it to the borrower or to the lender, is assumed by him and that the intermediary assumes no risk of any kind in the transaction.

26. The same law applies to a case where a Jew has given a pawn or a note to another Jew, on which to borrow money on interest from a non-Jew; if the non-Jew relies solely on the security or on the note, without holding the intermediary responsible in any way, the loan is permissible. If a Jew at first lends some money to another Jew upon the security of a pledge, and thereafter the borrower says to the lender: "Borrow some money on interest from a non-Jew on this pawn, and I will be responsible for the payment of the principal and the interest," if the non-Jew relies solely on the pawn, the loan is permissible.

27. If a Jew lends money on interest to a non-Jew on a pawn at so much and so much per month, and then he asks another Jew to lend him money on this pawn and receive from the non-Jew the interest which will accrue from that day on until repayment, this transaction is permissible. But if the first-mentioned Jew has compounded the interest for the whole period and applied it to the note (that is, the note is for the full amount of the principal and interest for the whole period of the loan), it is forbidden to borrow on this note the full sum from a fellow Jew, for it is as though he had given the interest from his own pocket.

28. If a Jew deposits money with a non-Jew, and the latter lends the same to another Jew on interest, if the non-Jew assumes the responsibility, that in the event of loss, he would make restitution, the transaction is permitted; but if he accepts no such responsibility, it is forbidden. Therefore, in communities where there are savings banks, or similar institutions, in which Jews hold shares of stock, although the managers are non-Jews, nevertheless, it seems to me that it is an absolute violation of the law for Jews to borrow money from them on interest. It is, therefore, forbidden either to deposit money in such banks (lest an unscrupulous Jew may borrow money from them), or to borrow money from them, lest an unscrupulous Jew has perchance deposited his money there.

29. Partners who are in need of borrowing money on interest from a non-Jew, should consult rabbinical authorities how to go about it.

30. It is forbidden to borrow money on interest from an apostate, and lending him money on interest also should be avoided.

CHAPTER 66

Agreements to Trade in Business

1. Advancing money to another to do business with it, stipulating that the profits and losses be shared equally by both of them, is termed in Jewish law *iska*, and it is forbidden; because half of the money is considered as a loan for which the trader is responsible and out of which he receives the profits. The other half of the money is considered as a deposit in his hands, because the investor takes the profit accruing from this half and also bears the losses sustained from it. The reason the trader does business with the half, which is merely a deposit and which really belongs to the investor, is in consideration of the loan the investor had extended to him. This service is, therefore, like giving interest and it is forbidden. This transaction can be made legal by the investor giving the trader some remuneration for his work in connection with the investor's half. This remuneration should be either stipulated for or paid at the time he gives him the money. Even a nominal remuneration suffices.

2. The parties to the above mentioned agreement may stipulate that the trader's claim that he has lost a part of the capital should not be accepted as true, unless it is proven by the testimony of trustworthy witnesses, nor is he to be trusted as regards the amount of the profit, unless he takes an oath.

3. They may also stipulate, that it shall be optional with the trader, to give the investor a fixed sum of money for his share of profit, and that anything left over and above such sum should belong to the trader. This stipulation is proper, for it is assumed that a trader, reluctant to take an oath to verify the amount of profit, will rather pay the investor the amount stipulated by them. This stipulation is the "agreement to trade on shares" in vogue among us. Even if the trader knows that there has been no profit, or even if there has actually been a loss, he may still give the investor his principal, together with the profit that has been agreed upon. No violation of law whatever can arise in this case, because owing to the fact that he is liable to take an oath to verify the amount of profit made, he is permitted to redeem himself from such an obligation by paying the stipulated sum.

4. The trader is forbidden to purchase unconditionally the share of the investor's profit at a fixed sum, which he would be obligated to give him in all circumstances. The trader must have the option.

5. If one gives money to another with which to do business for a certain length of time and the money has not been returned after the expiration of that time, the trader must give the investor a profit for the extra period, because it is presumed that the money remained in the trader's possession on the same terms originally agreed upon. However, it is best to write in the "agreement to trade on shares" that if the money remains with the trader

after the time limit, the conditions set forth in the agreement should cover that period, too.

6. The text of the "agreement to trade on shares" reads as follows: "I, the undersigned, acknowledge that I have received the amount of one hundred gold coins from so-and-so, with which to do business for one-half year from the date recorded below, and I obligate myself to purchase with the sum mentioned above such merchandise as may seem to me likely that a profit can be made on it. This money shall take precedence over my own money. As regards all the profit which Providence may grant me in connection with that merchandise, half thereof shall belong to me and the other half to so-and-so. Both of us shall also equally share the losses, God forbid. At the expiration of one-half year from the date recorded below, I obligate myself to return promptly to so-and-so the principal and one-half of the profit. My statement that I have suffered a loss shall not be accepted as true unless it is substantiated by two trustworthy witnesses, and as regards the profit, I shall be trusted only by taking an oath. It is moreover agreed that if I desire to give so-and-so, ten gold coins for his share of the profits, he shall have no further claim against me, and the balance of the profit, if any, shall belong to me alone, even if it is proved that his share of profit far exceeded the ten gold coins. All the stipulations relating to credibility of my statements shall also be valid after the expiration of the term of this agreement, and as long as I do not return the sum of money mentioned above, it remains with me on the terms mentioned above. I acknowledge having received remuneration for my labor."

.... (Signature)

Place and date

Signed in our presence
.... (Signature of witnesses)

7. If there is not sufficient time to write the "agreement to trade on shares," it is permissible to agree verbally to all the conditions mentioned before.

8. If one advances money on merchandise, the instrument to be written is as follows: "I, the undersigned, acknowledge that I have received from so-and-so of .... the sum of one hundred gold coins with which to trade with the goods which I keep in .... until the first day of the month of *Nisan* (may it come to us for happiness) and the accrued profits, after deducting all the expenses, shall belong, half of it to me and the other half to so-and-so mentioned before. Likewise, if there is a loss, God forbid, the same shall be shared equally. On the first day of *Nisan* (may it come to us for happiness) I obligate myself promptly to repay to so-and-so, mentioned above, the aforementioned principal together with

the profit belonging to him. My statement that I have suffered a loss shall not be accepted as true unless it be verified by two trustworthy witnesses, and as regards the profit, my statement shall be accepted only by taking an oath. It is further agreed that if, on the first day of *Nisan* (may it come to us for happiness) I desire to give to so-and-so mentioned above, in repayment of his principal and his share of profit, five measures of spirit, he shall have no further claim against me. All the terms relating to the credibility of my statements, shall also be valid after the expiration of the period of this agreement. I acknowledge having received remuneration for my labor."

....................(Signature)

Place and date

Signed in our presence:

....................(Signature of witnesses)

9. If the investor desires a regular note showing his indebtedness, and binding according to the law of the land, so that in the event the trader refuses to pay when the term expires, or if he should die, it would be easy for him to collect his money in civil courts, but they agree verbally that this money is subject to the "agreement to trade on shares," such a transaction is invalid. Even if the note is given for the principal only, since the investor can collect the entire sum, even if there is a definite loss, such a transaction is forbidden. Even if the trader trusts the investor who is an honorable person, nevertheless, it is forbidden. Furthermore, even if the trader gives the investor an "agreement to trade on shares," wherein it is written that the note is subject to the partnership agreement, this likewise is of no avail, for there is a possibility that the investor or his heirs might conceal the "agreement to trade on shares," and collect on the strength of the note. The only permissible course of action is to deposit the "agreement to trade on shares," with a trustee, or the investor should sign the agreement and the trader should keep it, or they should write on the face of the note that it is subject to the conditions set forth in the "agreement to trade on shares," or they should at least have witnesses present, that the note is subject to the "agreement to trade on shares." In all these cases the transaction is permissible even if the principal, together with the profit is included in the note.

10. An "agreement to trade on shares," is of no avail unless the trader actually receives the money to transact business, but if he takes the money merely to pay off a debt or for any other purpose, then the partnership agreement is worthless since it is untrue. The transaction can, however, be carried through in this manner: If Reuben, who is in need of money, has certain merchandise, be it even in another locality, he can sell the same to Simeon even at a very low price, on the condition that Reuben shall have the option, that in the event the merchandise is not delivered by him to Simeon by such-and-such a date, he can pay him for it so-much-and-so-much in lieu thereof (so that Simeon will have the usual profit). Then Simeon can give the money to Reuben, and they should make a symbolical agreement to make the transaction binding, that is, Simeon the buyer should let Reuben take hold of part of his garment, and by this act he purchases Reuben's merchandise.

Even with no witnesses present, the merchandise is now held there at the risk of Simeon who is the buyer.

11. If Reuben owes money to Simeon, and when the time of repayment arrives, Reuben has no funds, and he settles with Simeon to wait a little longer, by making an "agreement to trade on shares," it is a violation of the law. But Reuben may sell to Simeon some merchandise, as provided for in the preceding section, Simeon may then return to him the note which he formerly held, and Reuben may transfer to him in writing the merchandise which Simeon has bought of him, in the manner aforementioned.

12. If an Israelite gives to another Israelite a beast to be reared, on the condition of subsequently sharing the profit, they must go through the same procedure as in the case of lending money to trade on sharing the profits.

CHAPTER 67

Vows and Oaths

1. One should avoid making vows. He who makes a vow is considered as though he had built an altar when and where it was forbidden to do so; and the one who fulfills such a vow, is considered as though he had offered a sacrfice upon the altar, incurring thereby the guilt of offering a sacrifice outside the Temple of Jerusalem. It is best to consult the proper authorities who should annul the vow. This applies only to ordinary vows, but vows made to consecrate certain objects to the Lord must be fulfilled, for it is written (Psalms 116:18): "I will pay my vows to the Lord." One must not attempt to annul these vows, except in cases of emergency.

2. One should also avoid taking an oath. If, however, one transgresses and does take an oath concerning any matter, one should not consult the authorities in an effort to annul it. One must abide by it even if it causes one distress, for it is written (Psalms 15:4): "He that sweareth to his own hurt and changeth not," and thereafter it is written (loco citato 5): "He that doeth these things shall never be moved." One should not try to annul an oath except in a case of emergency.

3. One should avoid making a vow, even to give charity. If one desires to donate something which he has in his possession, he shall give it without a vow. If not, one should wait until one has it and then give it. If a general appeal is made for charity, and one has to make a contribution in common with others, one must expressly state that he is making no vow but simply a promise. Also at *yizkor* (memorial service), when it is usual to donate charity, one must clearly say: "I am making no vow." If one is in distress, however, one is allowed to make a vow.

4. If a person resolves to set a certain time for the daily study of the Torah, or to perform a certain precept, and he fears that he might be dilatory in fulfilling it, or if he fears that he might be induced to do something which

is forbidden or to neglect the observance of a certain commandment, he is permitted to fortify his resolution by making a vow or by taking an oath. For, Rav said (Nedarim 7b-8a): "Whence do we infer that it is proper to take an oath for the sake of zealously fulfilling a Divine Command, although every Jew is already under oath to do so from the time of the Revealation? We infer it from the Biblical verse (Psalms 119:106): 'I have sworn, and I have confirmed it, to observe Thy righteous ordinances.'" Even when one makes a simple declaration, not in the form of a vow or an oath, he is, nevertheless obligated to keep it. One should therefore, take care when resolving to do a good deed or to adopt a certain good practice, to say clearly that one does so without making a vow. It is good to make such a qualification when stating that one would do something that is optional. For such a practice will prevent one from falling into the snare of violating a vow, God forbid.

5. He who makes a vow in order to improve his conduct, is a vigilant and praiseworthy man. For instance, if a man is a glutton, and he vows to abstain from eating meat for a certain time, or if he is intemperate and he vows to abstain from drinking wine or any other intoxicating liquor; or if he has become conscious and proud of his good looks, and he vows to become a Nazarite—all such vows are for the service of God, blessed be His name, and concerning these, our Rabbis, of blessed memory, said (Abot 3:17): "Vows are a help to self-control." Nevertheless, a person should not accustom himself to make vows even of this nature, but should strive to conquer his vices without making any vows.

6. A vow is not valid unless it is made with intention and uttered with the lips. If a vow is made in error, that is, he uttered it thoughtlessly, or if he merely thought of making a vow, but he did not utter it with his lips, it is not considered a vow.

7. If a person has accustomed himself to abstain from certain legitimate things in order to inculcate moderation and self-restraint, such as, fasting during the days when the *seliḥot* (special prayers for forgiveness; see chapter 127, Section 4, below) are recited, or abstaining from eating meat and drinking wine from the seventeenth day of *Tammuz* to the ninth day of *Ab*, or practices similar to these, even if he has done so only once, but had in mind to make it a permanent practice, or if he has thus conducted himself three times without making such a resolution, but he did not expressly state that he meant to make no vow, if he desires to change his custom owing to ill-health, he must have his vow absolved legally. He makes the opening remark (to those who absolve him) by declaring that he regrets that he had acted as though he had made a vow. Therefore, if a person decides to practice austerity as a help to self-restraint, he should first state clearly that he does not adopt it as a vow. He should furthermore declare that he adopts it only temporarily, or for any other time he might wish to act thus, but that he has no intention of making it a regular practice.

8. How can a vow or an oath be annulled? One goes before three men learned in the Torah, one of whom at least being well versed in the laws governing vows, to know which vow may or may not be annulled, and in what manner it may be annulled, and these men can absolve one from the vow. One who makes a vow in a dream, must be absolved from it, preferably by ten men learned in the Torah.

9. Although as regards all the precepts of the Torah, a male-child is not considered of age until he is thirteen years old and has developed signs of puberty, and a female-child is not of age until she is twelve years old and has signs of puberty, yet as regards a vow or an oath, they become responsible when they are one year younger than that. Thus a male-child who is twelve years and one day old and a female-child of eleven years and one day, even if they lack the signs of puberty, as long as they understood in whose Name the vow or the oath has been made, their vows and their oaths are binding. But vows or oaths made by ones below that age, even if they have understanding, the vows or oaths are not valid. They should, nevertheless, be reprimanded or physically punished, and warned not to get into the habit of making vows or swearing oaths. However, if the vows of such minors concern a matter of a trivial nature, not entailing any physical suffering, they should be ordered to fulfill them.

10. The father may annul the vows of his daughter until she reaches the age of twelve years and six months, if she is unmarried. Also a husband may annul the vows of his wife. How does one annul a daughter's or a wife's vow? He says three times: "It is invalid," or "it is null and void," or any other expression which indicates that he abrogates the vow; and it is immaterial whether he says so in her presence or in her absence. However, the expression: "That which was forbidden thee be permitted," is not a formula to be used by a father or a husband. Moreover, the annulment must be made within the day they have heard of the vow. Thus, if they have heard of the vow at the beginning of the night, they can declare it void during that night and the following day. If they heard of it during the day, just before sunset, they can void it only until the stars become visible, but not thereafter. If the vow is annulled on the Sabbath, one must not say: "It is null and void," as on weekdays, but he should annul it in his mind, and say; "take and eat," or use similar expressions. If the father or the husband at first says that he is satisfied with the vow, or has used such language which indicated his approval, or even if he has only thought that he approves of her vow, he can no longer annul it.

11. What kind of vows can a father or a husband annul? Only ones that involve physical privations, like abstaining from bathing, or ornaments or cosmetics. The husband can annul even such vows which do not involve physical privations, if they are matters between husband and wife and which

might engender hatred between them. These last mentioned vows, however, remain annulled only as long as she lives with him, but if she becomes a widow or is divorced, she is bound to observe the vows she had made before.

CHAPTER 68

Concerning Prayers When Traveling

1. Before setting out on a journey, whether from our own home or from a place where we have lodged overnight, as well as on returning from a journey, as soon as we have gone beyond the outskirts of the city, that is, seventy and two-third cubits (106 feet) beyond the last house, we say the traveler's prayer, reading: " May it be Thy will, O Lord our God, and God of our fathers, to cause us to walk in peace," etc. The prayer is phrased in the plural, except the clause: "And let me obtain favor." It is best to say it after having traveled one mile beyond the outskirts of the city. When we are already on the road and we have lodged overnight in some town, we may also say it in the morning before resuming our journey.

2. This prayer is to be recited only when we travel no less than a Persian mile (a parasang, equal to four miles). It is preferable to say it before passing the first parasang. If, however, we neglect to do so, we may say it as long as we are still on the road, provided we have not yet reached the last parasang before the town where we intend to spend the night.

3. This prayer is to be recited after uttering another benediction. Therefore, if we set forth on a journey in the morning, and we recite the morning prayers, or if we have lodged overnight in a certain place during a journey (when we can say this prayer before resuming our journey), and recite it before the morning prayers, we should do so after the benediction *Gomel ḥasadim tovim leamo yisrael* (who bestoweth lovingkindness to His people Israel). If we set forth from the house after saying the morning prayers, we should eat or drink something on the road, and say the concluding benediction of Grace after meals, and then recite the traveler's prayer. We may also respond to nature's call, say the benediction *Asher yatzar* (who hath formed), etc., and recite the traveler's prayer immediately thereafter.

4. This prayer should be recited while standing. If we are riding on horseback or traveling in a conveyance, we should, if possible, stop while reciting the prayer, because riding is considered as walking. But if it is impossible to stop, we may recite it while riding.

5. This prayer should be said only once a day while traveling. However, if we stop at a certain place, intending to stay there overnight, and then we change our mind and leave that place to reach some other destination or to return home, we must repeat the prayer. If we travel by day and by night and spend the night in an uninhabited place, we recite on the first day the prayer up to the end, but on the following days we omit the concluding bene-

diction, for as long as we do not spend the night in an inhabited place, it is considered as one continuous hourney.

6. Before going on a journey, one should give charity, for it is said (Psalms 85:14): "Righteousness (Hebrew *tzedek*, also means *charity*) shall go before him, and shall make level the way for his footsteps." He should take leave from the leading men of the community so that they might wish him godspeed. If possible, some men should accompany him a little way. Those who accompany him, must remain standing, watching him out of sight. People who bid goodby to a person going on a journey, should not say *Leḥ beshalom* (go in peace), but *Leḥ leshalom* (go towards peace). For when David said to Absalom, *Leḥ beshaolm*, the latter hanged himself; but when Jethro said to Moses, *Leḥ leshalom*, the latter met with success. When traveling, we should meditate on the Torah, as it is written (Deuteronomy 6:7): "And when thou walkest by the way." We should recite devoutly and humbly a few Psalms every day. We must take along some bread, even when we go to an adjacent place. We should also take extra *tzitzit* (fringes) with us, lest one of the fringes becomes unfit and not being able to obtain another, we would be prevented from performing a precept. A person should always arrive in a place while it is still day, and leave when it is day; that is, when we wish to come to an inn to stop for the night, we should go in while the sun is still shining, and on the morrow we should wait for sunrise to set out on our journey, and then it will be well with us, as it is written (Genesis 1:4): "And God saw the light, that it was good." One should not eat much while traveling.

7. A person should make inquiries concerning his lodging to ascertain if the owner and his household are honest and trustworthy. If he desires to eat meat in a strange place, he should carefully investigate who the *shoḥet* (ritual slaughterer) is, and inquire concerning the rabbi who has supervision over him. For, owing to our regrettable lack of vigilance, this violation is common, and the wise will beware. The more so is this true of wine, concerning which the number of violators has greatly increased, and, therefore, a thorough investigation is needed.

8. When saying the morning prayers while on a journey, we must enfold ourselves in a large *tallit*, even as we do when praying at the synagogue, for a small *tallit* lacks the required size. If we travel on foot, when we say the verse, *Shema yisrael* (hear, O Israel), etc., and the words *Baruḥ shem kevod malḥuto leolam vaed* (Blessed be His name whose glorious kingdom is forever and ever), we must stand still in order to be able to concentrate. If we ride or sit in a vehicle, we may recite this prayer while we move. We must stand still however, for the recitation of the *Shemoneh esreh* (silent prayer). If we are pressed for time, we should stand still at least for the recital of the first three benedictions of the *Shemoneh esreh* and for its last three benedictions, if possible. If not, we may pray while sitting in the conveyance, and perform the customary genuflections in this posture. It is better, however, to say the *Shemoneh esreh* immediately after dawn, and the *Minḥah* (afternoon) prayer even half an hour after midday, in order to be able to pray while standing.

(The distance one must walk to look for water, or for a *minyan*, a quorum of ten male adults, is stated in chapter 12, sections 5 and 8, above).

9. Concerning one who walks on the road and finds no water, when the time to eat arrives, has been explained in chapter 40:14; and the law has been laid down in chapter 42:19, that the one who eats is not allowed to leave his place before saying Grace; and in chapter 44:6, it was explained that Grace must be recited while sitting. Nevertheless, if a person eats while walking on the road, he may also say Grace after meals while walking, because he would feel uneasy were he compelled to halt to say Grace. However, if he has eaten while sitting, he must also recite the Grace in like manner.

10. It is the custom of some people, when they are on the road and eat together in the house of a non-Jew, not to unite to recite the exhortatory passages before Grace after a meal, for the reason that they have not planned to meet here for this purpose. However, if they did plan to dine together there, it is improper to neglect saying the formal Grace. They should then say: "May the All-merciful forever send His blessing wherever we are walking and wherever we are sitting." If they all eat the food belonging to one of them, they may say: "May the All-merciful bless the master of this house," referring to the owner of the food. Otherwise they say: "May the All-merciful bless us."

11. According to the strict letter of the law, a person is not allowed to walk on Friday more than three parasangs (12 miles), either on his way home or to any other place, so that the people with whom he is to stay may have time to prepare the Sabbath-meals. In this land, however, we are not meticulous about this matter, because most people prepare sufficient food. Nevertheless, we must enter an inn while it is still daytime, for too frequently the Sabbath is desecrated by people who are dilatory. Let no one be misled by natural indolence, thinking; "the day is yet long and the road is good."

12. If, while on a journey a person stops at an inn for the Sabbath, and he has money in his possession, he must not keep it on his person if he can deposit it with somebody or hide it, because money is *muktzeh* (untouchable on the Sabbath or on festivals). If he fears that the money will be stolen from him, he should sew it into his garment on Friday, and remain indoors. He shall not go out on the Sabbath wearing that garment in a place where there is no *eruv* (the symbolical act whereby a legal community is established; see chapter 81, confer, below). However, if he has cause to fear that by his remaining indoors all day, people will surmise that he has money and they might rob him, he may go out with the money sewed in his garment. But he may not go out under any circumstances if the money is loose in his pocket.

CHAPTER 69

The Minḥah (Afternoon) Service

1. "Said Rav Ḥelbo in the name of Rav Huna (Beraḥot 6b): 'A person should ever be careful to pray the *Minḥah* service, for Elijah's prayer was answered only when the afternoon sacrifice was to be offered, as it is written (I Kings 18:36): "And it came to pass at the time of the evening offering, that Elijah the prophet came near."' The reason the *Minḥah* service is so important is that the time to pray the *Shaḥarit* (morning) service is fixed and known: Immediately upon rising, we pray before we become absorbed in our every-day affairs; likewise, the time to pray the *Maariv* service is set and known, when we come home and we are already free from our daily tasks. But the *Minḥah* is to be prayed while the day is yet long and we are absorbed in our affairs; we must, therefore, think of it, stop our business deals, and pray. The reward for it accordingly is very great.

2. The proper time for the *Minḥah* prayer is at nine and one-half hours of the day (3:30 p. m.), and that is called *Minḥah ketannah* (the small *Minḥah:* short period for praying the *Minḥah*). In cases of emergency, as when we need to go on a journey, or to have a meal, it may be recited immediately after six and one-half hours of the day (12:30 p. m.), and this is called *Minḥah gedolah* (great *Minḥah*). Actually, its limit is extended to one and a quarter hours before nightfall. This is called *Pelag haminḥah* (half of the small *Minḥah*), because two and one-half hours intervene between the beginning of the *Minḥah ketannah* and nightfall, and half of this period is one hour and a quarter. However, in case of emergency, we may recite the *Minḥah* until the stars become visible. The custom now prevails in some communities to recite the *Minḥah* prayer shortly before nightfall. The hours referred to above are proportionate to the length of the day from sunrise to sunset, divided by twelve equal parts, and if the day is eighteen hours long then the "hours" have the length of one hour and a half.

3. It is forbidden to begin even a small meal, shortly before the *Minḥah ketannah*. By "shortly" is meant one-half hour. If we do not eat a regular meal, but we partake of some refreshments, like fruit or even something prepared of one of the "five species of grain," it is allowed according to some authorities. However, it is best to abstain even from refreshments. It is likewise forbidden to take a bath or to take a haircut shortly before the *Minḥah ketannah*. It is forbidden to begin an elaborate meal, such as a wedding feast, or a circumcision feast, even shortly before the *Minḥah gedolah*, that is, at noon. The meal should be postponed until after the *Minḥah*. In a community where people are summoned to attend services at the synagogue, and one is accustomed to go there to pray with the congregation, one is allowed to begin a small meal before the *Minḥah ketannah*, and even later, provided one will

respond immediately upon being called. But it is forbidden to begin an elaborate meal shortly before the *Minḥah ketannah,* even in a community where people are summoned to the synagogue.

4. Before reciting the *Minḥah* prayer, the hands must be washed up to the wrist, the same as before the *Shaḥarit* (morning) prayers, (as has been explained in chapter 12, sections 5, 6). If an interruption occurs between the *Minḥah* and the *Maariv* (evening) prayers, or between the *Shaḥarit* and the *Musaph* (additional) prayer, the handwashing must be repeated.

5. The prayer *Ashre* (Psalm 145) with which the *Minḥah* service commences, should be recited only after ten male adults have assembled, so that the *ḥazan* may recite the *kaddish* after *Ashre* has been said by a *minyan.* If *Ashre* has been said without the presence of a quorum, and afterward, ten male adults have assembled, another Psalm should be said and then the *ḥazan* says the *kaddish.* The *ḥazan* should wrap himself in a *tallit* before reciting *Ashre,* in order to avoid delay between the recital of *Ashre* and the *kaddish.* However, if he had no *tallit* until he had already said *Ashre,* he shall wrap himself in it, recite some verses of the Psalms, and then he shall recite the *kaddish.*

6. If the prescribed time for the *Minḥah* prayer is limited because nightfall is approaching, then the *ḥazan,* after saying the half-*kaddish,* should immediately begin reading the *Shemoneh esreh* aloud. The congregation should only listen and make the necessary responses until he says *Hael hakadosh* (the holy God), to which all respond *Amen.* Then they silently recite the *Shemoneh esreh.* If, however, they are very much pressed for time, and it is feared that by waiting for the *ḥazan* until he concludes *Hael hakadosh,* they would be unable to complete the *Shemoneh esreh* while it is still daylight, they may pray silently together with the *ḥazan,* word by word until *Hael hakadosh.* It is, nevertheless, proper to have at least one worshiper to respond *Amen* to the *ḥazan's* benedictions.

7. If a worshiper arrives at the synagogue while the congregation is saying the *Shemoneh esreh,* he should say it with them, and recite *Ashre* afterward. If, however, he will be unable to conclude the *Shemoneh esreh* in time to say the *kedushah* during the *ḥazan's* repetition, and if he waits until the *ḥazan* concludes the entire *Shemoneh esreh* with the following *kaddish,* the time for praying the *Minḥah* will have passed, he should wait for the *ḥazan's* repetition, and say with him silently, word by word. He even says the *ḥazan's* version of the *kedushah,* including *Ledor vador* (unto all generations), and terminates with him the benedictions *Hael hakadosh* and *Shomea tefillah* (who hearkeneth unto prayer). He should also say *Modim* (we give thanks) together with the *ḥazan,* so that he can bow together with the congregation. On a fast day, he should not say *Anenu* (answer us) together with the *ḥazan,*

but he should include this prayer in the benediction *Shomea tefillah* as it is done in private worship. If he desires to pray the *Maariv* together with the congregation, and if he should wait until the *ḥazan* concludes the repeated *Shemoneh esreh,* he would be compelled to pray the *Maariv* privately, he should then say the *Shemoneh esreh* of the *Minḥah* together with the *ḥazan.* If he has arrived at the synagogue just before the *kedushah,* he should wait until the *ḥazan* concludes the benediction *Hael hakadosh,* and after responding *Amen,* he should say the *Shemoneh esreh.* Although he will thus miss the responses of *Amen* after the benedictions *Shomea tefillah* and *Modim.* Although these responses are obligatory, it is preferable to miss these responses than to miss the opportunity of praying *Maariv* with the congregation. Especially is this rule to be followed, if the time for praying *Minḥah* is on the point of passing by.

8. If the *Minḥah* service is delayed until nightfall, *Taḥanun* (supplication for Grace) should be omitted, because this prayer may not be said at night. The utmost care should be taken not to delay the *Minḥah* service until it is actually night, for the *kaddish* including *Titkabel* (may the prayers) cannot be recited after prayers belonging to the previous day, since the night belongs to the following day.

9. If a worshiper arrives at the synagogue to pray *Minḥah* on a Friday, and finds that the congregation has already ushered in the Sabbath or the festival, that is, on the Sabbath they have already said *Mizemor shir leyom hashabbat.* (A Psalm, a song for the Sabbath), and on a festival, they have already said *Barḥu* (bless ye), he should not pray *Minḥah* in that synagogue, but go elsewhere to pray. If he hears the *ḥazan* say *Barḥu,* he should not respond with the congregation, for after responding to *Barḥu* he may no longer say a weekday *Minḥah.* If he has erred and responded, then he must recite the *Maariv Shemoneh esreh* twice (as has been provided for in chapter 21, above). If, however, he arrives at the synagogue shortly before the Sabbath or the festival has been ushered in, although he is unable to complete the *Minḥah* before the ushering in of the Sabbath or the festival, he may, nevertheless, complete his *Minḥah* in the synagogue, since he has begun it there when he was allowed to do so.

CHAPTER 70

The Maariv (Evening) Service

1. The time for reciting the *Shema* of the *Maariv* service, is when three small stars become visible. On a cloudy day, one should not commence praying the *Maariv* until one knows beyond any doubt that it is already night. Nowadays, it is the custom to pray *Maariv* with the congregation immediately after praying *Minḥah,* although it is not yet night, because of the difficulty in getting together the people again. However, the *Maariv* should not be prayed before *Pelag haminḥah* (half of the small *Minḥah*). If prayed before then, the duty of praying has not been fulfilled. Happy is the man who prays *Maariv* in a congregation at nightfall, and studies the Torah between the *Minḥah* and *Maariv* services, thus joining the night and the day with the study of the Torah, which is a matter of great merit. In any event, the God-fearing person who has prayed *Maariv* in a congregation before nightfall, should not eat any food before the night has set in. Immediately

after the stars become visible, he should read the three sections of the *Shema*. One who does not pray with a congregation, is not allowed to pray *Maariv* before the stars become visible.

2. *Maariv* should be prayed immediately after the stars become visible. It is forbidden to begin a meal, or to engage in any work, or even to study the Torah, one-half hour before the stars become visible; the same as it is forbidden to eat before the *Minḥah ketannah* (the small *Minḥah*). If, however, one has no spare time, as when one is engaged in public instruction, one should at least, not delay praying *Maariv* longer than midnight. But post facto (if one has neglected to pray before midnight), one may pray *Maariv* any time before dawn.

3. If one came to the synagogue to pray *Maariv*, and found the congregation reciting *Shemoneh esreh*, he should recite it with them, even if it is not yet night, as long as it is within one hour and a quarter before nightfall. Later when night had set in, he is to read the *Shema* with its benedictions. If the congregation is then reading the *Shema* with its benedictions, and he has sufficient time to read the *Shema* with its benedictions as far as *Shomer ammo yisrael laad* (who guardeth the people of Israel forever) before the congregation reaches the *Shemoneh esreh*, he should do so, and omit the prayer *Baruḥ adonai leolam* (blessed be the Lord forever), etc., and he need not say it even after finishing the *Shemoneh esreh*. If, however, (when he finds the congregation saying the *Shema*,) he has not yet prayed the *Minḥah*, he should recite the *Shemoneh esreh* of the *Minḥah* while the congregation is reading the *Shema* with its benedictions, wait a while, at least as long as it takes to walk four cubits (six feet), and then recite the *Shemoneh esreh* of the *Maariv* with the congregation, and after nightfall he may read the *Shema* with its benedictions.

4. The prayer *Baruḥ adonai leolam* should be recited while sitting, up to *Yireu enenu* (may our eyes behold). No pause should be made in this prayer from *Vehu raḥum* (and He being merciful) until after the *Shemoneh esreh;* but the announcement by the *shamesh* of *Yaaleh veyavo* and *Tal umatar* is not considered an interruption, inasmuch as it appertains to the requirements of the service.

5. If one lone worshiper remains, saying the evening prayer in the synagogue at night, his companion must wait for him until he completes his prayer, so that his mind may not be disturbed by fear. If, however, the worshiper has begun his prayers at such a time when he could not finish it with the congregation, his companion need not wait for him, for it is assumed that he was prepared to remain alone, and that he is not a timid person.

Chapter 71

The Order of the Night

1. A Jew should set aside some time for the study of the Torah, right after *Maariv* in order to fulfill the Biblical verse (Joshua 1:8): "And thou shalt meditate therein day and night." If he should eat first, he might become drowsy and slothful and too tired to study. Therefore, it is best to

study the Torah before having the meal. However, if he is very hungry and he would not be able to concentrate, he may taste some food in order to set his mind at ease, study a little, finish his meal, and then resume his studies, every one to the best of his ability. Said our Rabbis, of blessed memory (Eruvin 65a): "The nights were created only for the study of the Torah." This refers to the winter time when the nights are long; nevertheless, even during the short nights, a person should study, be it ever so little, in order to comply with the verse: "And thou shalt meditate therein day and night." From the fifteenth day of the month of *Av* and henceforth, he shall add to his study period gradually. The Talmud states (Ḥagigah 12b): "Said Resh Lakish: 'He who studies the Torah at night, a chord of Divine Grace is strung around him; for it is written (Psalms 42:9): "By day the Lord will command His lovingkindness, and in the night His song shall be with me." Why will the Lord command His lovingkindness by day? Because at night the song of the Torah is with him.' Others say in the name of Resh Lakish: (loco citato) 'He who studies the Torah in this world, which is compared to the night, the Holy One, blessed be He, will string a chord of Divine Grace around him in the world to come, which is compared to the day; for it is written: "By day the Lord will command His lovingkindness, and in the night His song shall be with me."'" Especially, if a person neglected the study of the Torah during the day, he must complete his assignment during the night.

2. The evening meal of a normal person should be lighter than the meal he eats during the day. The benefit of such a course is fourfold: (1) He will preserve his health; (2) He will avoid pollution during the night, which is caused by heavy eating. (3) He will have pleasant dreams, whereas excessive eating and drinking cause nightmares. (4) His sleep will not be heavy, and he will be able to rise at the proper time. For a healthy person, six hours of sleep are sufficient. One should be careful not to sleep alone in a room, and not to sleep in a place which is either too hot or too cold.

3. It is proper for every God-fearing man to examine his deeds of the past day, before going to sleep. If he finds that he has transgressed in any way, he should repent, confess and wholeheartedly resolve not to repeat the transgression. Special scrutiny is required with regard to common sins, such as flattery, lies, mockery, and slander. He should also resolve to forgive anyone who has wronged him, so that no man may be punished because of him; for the Talmud says (Shabbat 149a): "He on whose account a fellow man suffers punishment, is not admitted into the presence of the Holy One, blessed be He." He should say three times: "I forgive anyone who has annoyed me," and then say: "Creator of the universe, I forgive," etc.

4. If one had not read the three chapters of the *Shema* at the ***Maariv*** service, one should read them with the *Shema* before going to bed. If one had already said the three chapters at *Maariv*, one need not repeat all of them before retiring; the first section of the *Shema* is sufficient. Nevertheless, it is best to recite all of them. After that, one recites the Psalms and the verses referring to God's mercy, such as we find in the regular prayer books. In most prayer books, the benediction *Hammappil* (who maketh to fall) is printed before the *Shema*. But it is better to say it at the end of the prayers, so that it may immediately be followed by sleep. One should, therefore, recite the *Shema* and the Psalms before getting into bed, and when in bed, say *Hammappil*. Before going to bed one should walk over to the *mezuzah*, place the fingers on it, and say: "The Lord is my keeper," etc., and then repeat seven times the verse: "In all Thy ways," etc. After saying the benediction *Hammappil*, one should neither eat, nor drink, nor speak until one falls asleep. If one is unable to sleep, one should read again the *Shema*, the Psalms, and the verses referring to God's mercy, and if necessary read it over and over until one falls asleep. One may also repeat many times the following verses: "The Torah he commanded us," etc. "A continuous fire, etc. "I hate them that are of a double mind," etc. "Light is sown for the righteous," etc., until one falls asleep. This reading is also a preventive against pollution, God forbid. One must purpose sleep as a means of regaining strength for the worship of the Almighty, and then it will be considered as a part of God's worship. If one is to have intercourse, one should not recite *Hammappil* before the act. Afterwards, we should at least read the first section of the *Shema*, and then say *Hammappil*.

5. One should undress before going to bed. When taking off the shoes and the garments, one is to remove those on the left first. One should not place his clothes under the head, because it causes one to forget his studies. It is strictly forbidden to lie in a supine or prone position; one must always lie on his side. It is best to start sleeping on the left side, and finish on the right. This is good for one's health, because the liver lies at the right side of the body and the stomach on the left, and when we recline on the left, the liver rests on the top of the stomach and warms it, thereby aiding the speedy digestion of the food. After the food has been digested, and we recline on the right side, the waste comes down. One should not turn from one side to the other too often during the night.

Code of Jewish Law

Chapter 72

The Holiness of the Sabbath

1. The holy Sabbath is the great sign and covenant which the Holy One, blessed be He, has given us to bear witness that "In six days God made the heavens and the earth and all that is in them, and He rested on the seventh day." This belief, that God is the Creator of the universe, is the foundation of our faith. Our Rabbis, of blessed memory said: "The Sabbath is equal in importance to all the other commandments" (Yerushalmi, Nedarim 3, end). "Observing the Sabbath properly is equivalent to observing the whole Torah" (Zohar, Beshalaḥ 47). And "The desecration of the Sabbath, is like denying the whole Torah" (Ḥulin 5a). And thus it is written in Ezra: "Thou camest down also on Mount Sinai . . . and gavest them right ordinances . . . and madest known unto them Thy holy Sabbath."

2. He who violates the Sabbath publicly is regarded as an idolater in every respect; if he touches wine, it becomes unfit for use; the bread he bakes is like the bread of an idolater, so is his cooked food. "Publicly" in this regard is when ten Jews know of the desecration, even if they don't actually see it. This is the law as deduced from the Talmud and the commentaries.

3. Hence, the praise of the prophet (Isaiah 56:2): "Happy is the man that holdeth fast by it; that keepeth the Sabbath from profaning it," etc. He who observes the Sabbath according to all its laws, honoring it to his utmost ability, is rewarded in this world, besides the great reward in store for him in the world to come. This too, is set forth by the prophet (Isaiah 58:13-14): "If thou turn away thy foot because of the Sabbath, from pursuing thy business on My holy day; and call the Sabbath a delight, and the holy of the Lord honorable; and shalt honor it, not doing thy wonted ways, nor pursuing thy business, nor speaking thereof; then shalt thou delight thyself in the Lord, and I will make thee to ride upon the high places of the earth, and I will feed thee with the heritage of Jacob thy father; for the mouth of the Lord hath spoken it."

4. It is written (Exodus 20:8): "Remember the Sabbath day, to keep it holy," which means; remember the Sabbath day every day in the week to keep it holy. Thus, on coming across a delicious and rare article of food, which will not be spoiled by keeping, it should be purchased in honor of the Sabbath. We should rise early on Friday to purchase the necessities for the Sabbath. We are even permitted to make the purchases before saying the morning

prayers, provided we do not lose thereby the opportunity of joining in public prayer with the congregation. It is preferrable to make the purchases for the Sabbath on Friday rather than on Thursday. However, articles of food requiring preparation, should be procured on Thursday. While making the purchases, we should say: "It is in honor of the Sabbath." In accordance with the ordinances of Ezra, the clothes for the Sabbath should be washed on Thursday, not on Friday, as on that day all attention is needed for the preparation of the Sabbath needs.

5. Every man, even one who has many servants, must do something himself in honor of the Sabbath, thereby doing homage unto it, as it was the habit of the *Amoraim* (authors of the Talmud, or the Gemara). Rab Ḥisda, for instance, used to cut the vegetables very thin. Rabbah and Rab Joseph used to chop wood for cooking. Rab Zera was in the habit of lighting the fire over which the Sabbath food was cooked. Rab Naḥman put the house in order, bringing in all the utensils needed for the Sabbath and putting away the things used during the weekdays. We should emulate their example and not regard it as undignified, for by honoring the Sabbath, we honor ourselves.

6. It is a prevailing custom among all Jews to bake some loaves of bread in their homes in honor of the Sabbath. If a person eats non-Jewish bread on weekdays, he shall make it a point to eat Jewish bread on the holy Sabbath. Even if he eats Jewish bread during the week, he should have bread baked in the house for the Sabbath, so that the mistress of the house be given the opportunity to perform the precept requiring her to separate the *Ḥallah* (the first of the dough). For Adam was created on Friday, and he was destined to be the *Ḥallah,* the choice of the world, but this excellence was lost by the woman's sin, therefore, she has to make amends (by separating the first of the dough). Three loaves should be baked, a large one, a medium one, and a small one; the medium one for the Friday evening meal, the large one for the daytime meal, to indicate that the day is of greater importance, and the small loaf for the third meal.

7. We should procure meat, fish, dainties, and good wine for the Sabbath, in accordance with our means. It is proper to eat fish at every Sabbath meal. But if it does not agree with us, we should not eat it, because the Sabbath is given us for pleasure and not for suffering. The cutlery should be sharpened and polished, and fresh coverings should be put on the beds. We should also have the household furniture nicely arranged, and the table covered with a fresh cloth, which is to remain on the table the entire Sabbath day. Some people place two cloths on the table. We should rejoice with the coming of the Sabbath. The expectation of a dear and distinguished guest would cause us to hustle and bustle. How much more so should we act when the guest is Queen Sabbath! There is a custom in some places to make pies for the Friday evening meal, in commemoration of the manna, which lay as

if in a box, with dew on the top and dew at the bottom. It is well to taste the Sabbath food on Friday.

8. Even the poorest man in Israel should endeavor with all his might to luxuriate in the Sabbath. He should economize the whole week to save enough money for the Sabbath meals. If necessary, one should even borrow money on a pledge in order to provide for the Sabbath. Of such a person, our Rabbis, of blessed memory, say (Betzah 15a): "Said the Holy One, blessed be He, to His people Israel: 'My children, borrow for My sake and I will repay you.'" A man's needs for the year are apportioned on *Rosh Hashanah*, with the exception of his expenses for Sabbath and festivals, for which—if he spends more he is given more. If, however, one is in dire straits, one should be guided by the maxim of the Sages (Shabbot 118a): "Make thy Sabbath as a weekday, rather than depend on men." Nevertheless, if at all possible, one should do at least some minor thing in honor of the Sabbath, like procuring small fishes, or something similar. If something edible is sent to someone for the Sabbath, he should eat it on the Sabbath and not leave it for a weekday.

9. No regular work should be done on Friday from the *Minḥah ketannah* (small *minḥah;* 3:30 p.m.) on. But casual work is permissible. It is forbidden to make clothes for someone else. But when a person is poor and he desires to earn enough for the Sabbath meals, he may work all day Friday, just the same as on *Ḥol Ḥammoed* (Intermediate Days of the festivals). Giving a haircut to a Jew is permissible all day on Friday, even if one is a professional barber and he does it for pay, inasmuch as it is obvious that the hair cutting is for the sake of the Sabbath. It is customary to close shops an hour before the Sabbath sets in.

10. From the ninth hour (3:30 p.m.) on, we should abstain from having a regular meal, even the kind we are accustomed to have on weekdays. A feast, which we do not generally have on weekdays, even if it is on the occasion of performing a religious act, is forbidden even on Friday morning, if it can be postponed for another day. However, if it must be given on that day, like one on the occasion of a circumcision, or the redemption of a first-born, may be held. Nevertheless, it is proper to have it in the morning and not eat too much, certainly not to eat to excess, so that we may eat the Sabbath meal with relish.

11. A Jew must read every week the entire weekly portion of the Torah; that is, he must read the Scriptural text twice, and the *Targum* once. The reading may begin on Sunday. However, it is best to do so Friday afternoon. One should read twice each *Parshah* (subdivision), whether it ends a chapter or not, or even when it ends in the middle of a verse, and then read the *Targum* once. After finishing the *Targum*, one must read one verse of the

Torah, so as to conclude the *Parshah* with a Biblical verse. It is improper to interrupt the reading with conversation. It is also customary to read the *Haftorah* (the portion from the Prophets for the week). Some make it a practice to read *Shir Hashirim* (Song of Songs) thereafter. If a person is on the road and has in his possession only the Pentateuch, without the *Targum*, he shall read the Scripture twice, and the *Targum* whenever he arrives at a place where one is available. Devout men should also peruse Rashi's commentary upon the weekly portion. But if one is not sufficiently learned, one should study the meaning of the portion by means of a translation in the vernacular.

12. On Friday, one must wash the face, hands, and feet in warm water, and if possible, one should bathe the whole body in warm water and then immerse in a ritual pool.

13. One must not bathe together with his father, father-in-law, mother's husband, or sister's husband. Where it is customary to cover the genital organs, it is permissible. A student should not bathe together with his teacher, unless the latter needs his services.

14. On Friday one must wash his head, pare his nails, and cut his hair, if too long. Finger and toe nails should not be cut on the same day, nor should the nails and the hair be cut on *Rosh Ḥodesh* (New Moon) even when it occurs on a Friday. Some are careful not to cut the nails in consecutive order, but alternately, starting with the finger next to the thumb of the right hand. To remember the proper order, think of the word בדאגה, the numerical value of the letters from right to left being 2, 4, 1, 3, 5. On the left hand one starts with the fourth finger; and the proper order can be remembered by thinking of דבהגא, the letters from right to left, having the numerical value of 4, 2, 5, 3, 1. Some are also careful not to cut the nails on Thursday. For they begin to grow on the third day, which is the Sabbath. One must burn the nails after they are cut.

15. On Friday, one should review his deeds of the past week, repent and make amends for all misdeeds, because the Sabbath eve embodies all the weekdays, just as the eve of *Rosh Ḥodesh* embodies the whole month.

16. One should try to wear fine clothes as well as a nice *tallit* on the Sabbath; for it is written (Isaiah 58:13): "And thou shalt honor it," which is explained by the Rabbis to mean that the garments worn on the Sabbath shall not be the same as those worn on weekdays. And even when one is on a journey, among non-Jews, one shall put on the Sabbath clothes, for the attire is not in honor of men but in deference to the Sabbath.

17. Cooked food must be removed from the burning coals before the Sabbath begins. In the event one forgot to do so, one may not remove the

pot, for it might touch the coal and increase the fire. It may, however, be removed by a non-Jew.

18. It is permissible to place victuals in the oven on Friday for consumption on the Sabbath, even if the door of the oven is not sealed with mortar. However, the door of the oven is not to be opened during Friday night, for some of the food may not yet be properly cooked, and by closing the oven, the cooking will be accelerated.

19. The law permitting us to place victuals in an oven on Friday, even when its door is not sealed with mortar, applies only to meat, or peas, or any kind of dough, which is placed there a considerable time before the Sabbath begins, so that the food could be cooked before the Sabbath, until it reaches a stage when it can be eaten on occasion. If, however, the peas and dough are placed in the oven, close to nightfall, then the door must be sealed with mortar. Otherwise, it is forbidden to partake of the food before the expiration of the Sabbath.

20. The sealed door of the oven should be opened on the Sabbath by a non-Jew. If a non-Jew is not available, a minor should do it. But in the absence of either, it may be done by anyone, but in a manner which is not ordinarily done on weekdays.

21. If one puts a pot of coffee into a hole in the ground on Friday to be used on the Sabbath, and covers it with pillows or something similar so that it keep warm; if he hides it in sand, he is not permitted to cover the whole vessel with the sand. Even if only a part of the vessel is covered with the sand and the rest of it is covered with garments, so that the vessel is covered on all sides, it is likewise forbidden. To make it legal, one must cover only one-half or one-third of the pot with the sand, the rest of it should remain uncovered, and then he may put a board or an inverted vessel on the top of the hole, so that there is a vacant space between the top cover and the pot containing the coffee, then he may put pillows or garments on the top.

22. On Friday before dark, one should gently ask his household whether the *Ḥallah* (first of the dough) has been separated, and remind them that the candles should be lit.

23. Everyone must examine his clothes on Friday before dark to ascer-

tain whether a needle is stuck in them, or if there is anything in the pockets. This must be done even in places where there is an *eruv* (see chapter 94, below), because the pockets might contain something *muktzeh* (an article untouchable on the Sabbath).

CHAPTER 73

Work Done by a Non-Jew on the Sabbath

1. A Jew is forbidden to allow a non-Jew to do work for him on the Sabbath. This law is based upon the Biblical verse (Exodus 12:16): "No manner of work shall be done," which implies even by a non-Jew. However, if the work is delivered to the non-Jew on Friday, it is permissible even if he does it on the Sabbath, but only on the following conditions: (a) The non-Jew should take the work before the Sabbath, but not on the Sabbath day.

2. (b) The amount of compensation should be stipulated in advance, then the non-Jew does the work for his own sake, in order to get paid. Therefore, one who employs a non-Jewish servant, is forbidden to allow the latter to do any work on the Sabbath, as the work is done solely for the benefit of the Jew. If a non-Jew travels to a certain place (before the Sabbath), and a Jew asks him to deliver a letter, which will have to be carried on the Sabbath, he should be given some reward. Then he does it for compensation and not gratis.

3. (c) The non-Jew should be paid a stipulated amount for the entire work and not hired by the day.

4. (d) A Jew is forbidden to engage a non-Jew to complete some work before a certain time if it is clear that the non-Jew cannot complete it unless he worked on the Sabbath. If a Jew sends a written message through a non-Jew and tells him: "See to it that you deliver it on such and such a day," and it is obvious that he cannot reach there on that day unless he travels on the Sabbath, this is likewise forbidden. If a fair is to be held on the Sabbath, a Jew is not allowed to give money to a non-Jew on Friday to buy things for him, if he knows that the non-Jew cannot obtain it on any other day except on the Sabbath. Likewise, he is forbidden to give him anything to sell. However, if he does not explicitly tell the non-Jew to do the work on the Sabbath, it is forbidden only when he delivers the work to him on Friday, but before that day he is permitted to give him some work, or some money to make a pur-

chase. It is best not to live in a community where the fair takes place on a Sabbath, for it is impossible to avoid violations. But if it is held in a non-Jewish quarter, it does not matter.

5. (e) The work should not be connected with the soil, such as building, or farm work. We are not allowed to have a non-Jew work on a building on the Sabbath, even if we have agreed to pay him a certain amount for the entire work. In case of urgent necessity, we should consult a rabbi. On the Sabbath, it is forbidden even to let a non-Jew quarry stones or prepare lumber for building purposes, if it is known that they belong to a Jew, and if the non-Jew works on it publicly in the street. This rule applies also to farming, such as ploughing or reaping, even if the non-Jew is hired at a stipulated price for the whole task. If, however, the non-Jew has a share in the crops, and it is customary in that region for a farm worker to receive a share in the crops, it is permissible. If the farm is far away, where there is no Jew in the vicinity within two thousand cubits (three thousand feet), it is permissible, if the non-Jew performs the work at a stipulated sum, so long as he is not hired by the day.

6. If a non-Jew has illegally built a house for a Jew on the Sabbath, it is well to be scrupulous and not move into it. (There are many divergent opinions about this).

7. The owner of a farm or a mill may rent it to a non-Jew, although he will work there on the Sabbath. But it is forbidden to rent a bathing establishment to a non-Jew. If the Jew does not own the bathing establisnment, but only rented it from a non-Jew, he should consult a rabbi on how to act. The owner of a hotel, a glass factory, a brick factory, and the like, should also consult a rabbi how to act.

8. A Jew is forbidden, under any circumstances, to allow a non-Jew to do work at his house on the Sabbath. Even if a non-Jewish servant desires to do some work for himself on the Sabbath, he should be forbidden by the Jewish employer.

9. If a non-Jewish tailor made a garment for a Jew and brought it to him on the Sabbath, he is permitted to put it on. If, however, it is known that the tailor has completed it on the Sabbath, it should not be worn, unless in a case of extreme necessity. It is forbidden to take utensils or garments from the house of a artisan, even a Jewish artisan, on a Sabbath or on a festival. From a non-Jew who is not a manufacturer, but owns a shop where

he sells shoes, or garments, a Jew who is acquainted with him, is permitted to take a pair of shoes and put them on. There should, however, be no mention of the price, nor should it be merchandise that was brought in from outside the Sabbath boundary.

10. On Friday, it is forbidden to hire workman's tools to a non-Jew, such as a plough, or the like. For, although we are not bound to let utensils rest on the Sabbath, nevertheless, inasmuch as the owner gets paid for it, it appears as though the non-Jew is his agent, but they may be hired to a non-Jew on Thursday. One may, however, lend workman's tools to a non-Jew even on Friday, provided that he takes them from the Jew's house before the Sabbath sets in. This is permissible even if the non-Jew agrees to reciprocate by a loan of his utensils at some future date. This is not considered as being equivalent to hiring them. It is also permissible to hire to a non-Jew, even on Friday, utensils with which no work is done, provided that the non-Jew removes them before the Sabbath.

11. Hiring utensils to a non-Jew on the aforesaid conditions, is permissible only if the Jew is not paid for the Sabbath days separately, but for an entire period, as when he says: "I will charge you so much per week, (or per month)," or even if he says, "for every two or three days." But it is forbidden to be paid for the Sabbath, even if he hires it by the year, as long as the pay is based on the number of days the utensil is used, like when he says: "I hire you this by the year (or by the month) and will charge you so much per day" Even if the non-Jew pays him thereafter for the entire time in one lump sum, he is forbidden to take hire for the Sabbath. It is also forbidden to take compensation for the Sabbath, even for utensils with which no work is done, and even for the rental of a room, unless the compensation covers a whole period. The law forbidding to take compensation for the Sabbath is the same whether one takes it from a non-Jew or from a Jew.

CHAPTER 74

Embarking on a Vessel on the Sabbath

1. We must not board a sea-going vessel the three days preceding the Sabbath, that is, from Wednesday on. But if we are bound on a sacred mission, we may embark even on a Friday.

2. It is permissible to board a river boat, even on a Friday, even if the boat is pulled by animals.

3. Boarding a ship on Friday is permissible only when one goes on board and remains there until nightfall. Even if one goes home and remains there overnight, one is still permitted to embark on the Sabbath, so long as the ship does not make the trip for Jews only. But since he was home on the Sabbath, he had established a residence for the Sabbath at the house. Therefore, if the ship has made a longer journey than two thousand cubits, and has reached land on the Sabbath, he is not permitted to walk there more than four cubits from the landing. (See chapter 95, below).

4. It is permissible to board a vessel on the Sabbath for the sake of praying with an assembly of ten, or for the sake of performing another religious duty, provided the vessel makes the trip also for others. It is, nevertheless, preferable that the Jew should go on board on Friday while it is yet daytime, and remain there till after nightfall, after which he may return home and come back again on the Sabbath, but it is not permitted if the vessel makes the trip for Jews only.

CHAPTER 75

The Sabbath Candles

1. Every one must put all work aside and light the Sabbath candles at least one-half hour before the stars emerge. If *Mizemor shir leyom hashabbat* (A Psalm, a song for the Sabbath) has already been recited at the synagogue, even if it is two hours before nightfall, the Sabbath laws become binding upon the minority from that time on, and any manner of work is forbidden. Even an arrival from another town is obliged to observe the Sabbath as soon as the congregation has said *Mizemor shir leyom hashabbat.* However, in a city where there are two synagogues, one is not bound by the other.

2. It is meritorious to light as many candles as possible in honor of the Sabbath. Some light ten candles, others seven. In no event should less than two candles be lit, symbolizing the two verses: "Remember (*zaḥor*) the Sabbath day" (Exodus 20:8), and, "observe (*shamor*) the Sabbath day" (Deuteronomy 5:12). But in an emergency, also one candle is sufficient. The candles should be big enough to burn at least till after the meal, and one should endeavor to procure nice candles. The Talmud states (Shabbat 23b): "Rab Huna said: 'The one who is accustomed to buy nice candles for the Sabbath, will have children versed in the Torah, for it is written (Proverbs 6:23): "For the commandment is a lamp, and the teaching (Torah) is light," meaning: Because of the "lamp" (the candles) will come the light of the Torah.'" It is, therefore, proper for the woman when lighting the candles, to pray that the Almighty grant her male children bright in the study of the Torah. It is also well that she should give some charity before lighting the candles. A woman who has trouble in raising children, or has no children at all, should read, after lighting the candles, the *haftorah* of the first day of

Rosh Hashanah (I Samuel 1:2-10). It is best that she should understand the meaning of the words so that she may say it with feeling.

3. The precept is best performed by using olive oil or almond oil which is generally used for this purpose. But there are certain oils which are ritually unfit. The wick too, should be of good quality, such as vine-fiber flax, or hemp, for some other materials are unfit for the purpose. The Sabbath candles may also be made of tallow, as is generally done in our regions. But it is forbidden to put some tallow in a vessel and place a wick in it. The one who lights the candles should see to it that he ignites most of the wick protruding from the candles. The same applies to tallow candles.

4. It is a well-established rule that the benediction for a precept must be said prior to its performance. This, however, cannot be practiced in the case of lighting the Sabbath candles, for by pronouncing the benediction the woman usheres in the Sabbath, after which no labor is to be performed. Therefore, the woman first lights the candles, shuts out the light by covering her face with her hands while pronouncing the benediction, then she removes her hands and looks at the light, which act makes it akin to saying the benediction before kindling the candles. (In order not to differentiate, this procedure is also followed on festivals). Since the candles that are on the table where the meal is served, are the most important, she should light them last. In case of emergency, as when she has to take the ritual bath, or she has to get married, or some other important matter, she may light them with a spoken or mental reservation that she does not thereby assume the holiness of the Sabbath, pronounce the benediction and proceed with her tasks, before the Sabbath actually begins.

5. Men as well as women are obliged to light Sabbath candles. However, the fulfillment of this duty was left primarily to the woman, because she is always at home and attends to household duties. Another reason is that because the woman caused the fall of Adam and thereby extinguished the light of the world and darkened his soul which is called *light*, as it is written (Proverbs 20:27): "The soul of man is the light of God;" therefore, it is her duty to make amends by lighting the candles in honor of the Sabbath. If she is at home, she takes precedence in performing this precept. Nevertheless, the man should assist to prepare the candles and to singe them, thus making

it easy to kindle them. When a woman is in confinement, her husband should light the candles the first Sabbath, but after that, and also during menstruation, she herself should light them, and pronounce the benediction.

6. Happy are the women who make it a custom to wash themselves and to put on the Sabbath apparel before lighting the candles. However, they should first say the *Minḥah* (afternoon) prayer, as by lighting the candles, they usher in the Sabbath, and they would be unable to pray the weekday *Minḥah* afterward. If a woman is delayed by her occupation, and reaches home about one-half hour before the Sabbath sets in, and if she should wash and change, she would run the risk of profaning the Sabbath, it is better that she should light the candles as she is, rather than risk a probable profanation of the Sabbath. If the husband sees that she is tardy in coming, it is mandatory for him to light the candles, and disregard her resentment.

7. When a man lights the Sabbath candles, knowing that he will afterwards have to do some work, it is advisable that he make a spoken or mental reservation that he does not thereby assume the Sabbath. If he inadvertently omits to make such a reservation, he is nevertheless, permitted to do work thereafter, as a husband's lighting of the candles is not ordinarily an act of ushering in the Sabbath.

8. The candles should be lit in the room where the meals are served, in order to indicate that they are lit in honor of the Sabbath. They should not be lit in one place and then transferred to another, except in an emergency, as for instance, when the woman is ill and unable to go to the table, then she may light them at her bed, and then they may be placed upon the table in the dining room. It is improper for a woman to light the candles in the *sukkah* and then carry them into the house. If one wishes to use for the Sabbath a candle that has been burning, it should be extinguished and then relit, in order to make it clear that it is dedicated to the Sabbath.

9. It is necessary to light candles in every room that is being used. If one is at home with his wife, who lights candles in one room and pronounces a benediction, it is not required to pronounce a benediction over the candles lit in other rooms. If, however, he lives elsewhere, where he has a room for himself, he must light candles and say the benediction over them. If several men live in one room, they should all contribute towards the purchase of the candles. One lights them, says the benediction, and exempts the others. Both he and his roommates must have in mind that the benediction is for all. But if he has no room of his own, but is in one room with the host who is a Jew, he need not light Sabbath candles, since his wife lights for him at

home. Students who are away from home, are required to light candles and pronounce the benediction, if they have a room for themselves. They should all contribute towards buying the candles. One of them pronounces the benediction and exempts the others. It is necessary that the candles should burn long enough until the students return to the room. If they have no room for themselves, inasmuch as they have no wives to light the candles for them, they must give a coin to the host, and thus acquire a share in the candles. One who eats at a host's table is included with the household and need not contribute towards buying the candles.

10. It is the custom, that if many women light candles in the same house, each woman lights candles and pronounces a benediction, because the more light the more joy. However, two women should not put their candles in one candlestick; it may, however, be done in an emergency.

11. No water should be put into the sconce of the candlestick, so that the candle may be extinguished on reaching it. In case of necessity, this rule may be waived, provided the water is put therein when it is still daylight. It is, however, strictly forbidden, even when it is still daylight, to place a vessel filled with water near the candles, so that falling sparks might be extinguished. But it is permissible even at nightfall, to put an empty vessel near the candles to intercept the sparks, because sparks are not tangible. However, it is forbidden after nightfall to place a vessel near the candles for the reception of the dripping oil or the tallow of a guttering candle. For, should any oil or tallow drip into the vessel, the vessel may not be removed from the spot for the duration of the Sabbath. Consequently, it is considered as though we fasten it there. But it is permissible to put a vessel for that purpose before sundown. If some of the oil has dripped into the vessel, we are not allowed to make use of it on the Sabbath, and the vessel must not be removed. But if nothing has dripped therein, the vessel may be removed.

12. It is well to place the *ḥallot* (white loaves of bread) on the table before the candles are lit. (See chapter 89:2, below).

13. If a blind woman has a husband, he lights the Sabbath candles, and pronounces the benediction. But if she has no husband and she lives by herself, she lights the candles and pronounces the benediction. If, however, she resides with others who light candles, she should light her candles without saying the benediction. If she is the mistress of the house, she lights her candles first, pronouncing the benediction, and then the others light their candles, and pronounce the benediction.

14. If a woman has once neglected to light the Sabbath candles, she must light an extra candle every Friday as long as she lives. If she has neglected to light candles several times, she must add an extra candle for each time. This is done to impress upon her to be careful in the future; therefore, if she was prevented from lighting the candles by an accident, she need not light additional candles.

Chapter 76

Prayers on Sabbath and Festivals

1. On Friday evening, it is customary to hold the *Maariv* service earlier than on weekdays. This is proper in order to usher in the Sabbath as early as possible, but it should be done from *Pelag haminḥah* (one hour and a quarter before sunset) on. Even those who are accustomed to pray the *Maariv* during weekdays at the proper time, which is after the appearance of the stars, may pray earlier on Friday. Although on a weekday, the *Minḥah* (afternoon) prayer is sometimes said at the time the *Maariv* is now said, it matters not with regard to the *Maariv* on Friday, inasmuch as it is meritorious to take some of the profane and add it to the holy.

2. On concluding the benediction *Hashkivenu* (cause us, O Lord, to lie down), we do not say as we do on weekdays, *Shomer ammo yisrael laad* (who guardeth His people Israel forever), because this benediction refers to the protection of Israel. Since the Sabbath itself is a protector, the benediction is unnecessary. But we say instead, *Uferos alenu* (yea, spread over us), and conclude with, *Baruḥ attah adonai, hapores sukkat shalom* (blessed art Thou, O Lord, who spreadeth the tabernacle of peace), etc. If, however, we have ended it as on a weekday, and have become aware of the error, immediately after saying *Leolam vaed* (forever), we should instantly say, *Hapores sukkat shalom.* But if we have become aware of the error after the lapse of time that it would take us to say the benediction, we are no longer required to say it.

3. According to custom, in the *Shemoneh esreh* of the *Maariv* service, we say *Veyanuḥu bah (rest thereon;* in the feminine gender); in the *Shaḥarit* (morning) and the *Musaph* (additional) services, we say, *Veyanuḥu bo (rest trereon;* in the masculine gender), and in the *Minḥah* (afternoon) service, we say, *Veyanuḥu bam (rest thereon;* in the plural).

4. On concluding the *Shemoneh esreh* on Friday evening, the congregation says, *Vayeḥulu hashamayim vehaaretz* (and the heavens and the earth were finished), etc. This prayer must be recited while standing, in order to signify that we are witnesses to God's creation of the world and witnesses must give their testimony while standing.

5. After this, the *ḥazan* says the one benediction which embodies the substance of seven: *Baruḥ attah adonai elohenu velohe avotenu* (Blessed art Thou, O Lord, our God, and the God of our fathers), etc., then *Magen avot* (He was a shield), and concludes with, *Mekaddesh hashabbat* (who hallowed the Sabbath). The congregation must stand and listen attentively while the *ḥazan* is saying this benediction. It is customary to say with him *Magen avot* until *Zeḥer lemaaseh bereshit* (in remembrance of the creation). Even one praying privately may recite *Magen avot* until *Zeḥer lemaaseh bereshit* but no further.

6. The aforementioned benediction is recited every Sabbath during the whole year, even on a Sabbath which falls on a festival or at the close of a festival, but it is omitted on the Sabbath which occurs on either of the first two days of Passover.

7. This benediction should be said only in a place where ten male adults, regularly assembled for worship, but not where they assemble only casually, as in the house of a bridegroom, or at the house of a mourner. However, if ten male adults assemble at one place for services for several weeks, *Magen avot* should be recited there.

8. In our regions, it is customary for the *ḥazan* to recite the *kiddush* (see chapter that follows) on Sabbath and festival evenings. But inasmuch as, by saying the *kiddush* at the synagogue, the *ḥazan* is not exempt from saying it at home, and, as he is forbidden to partake of anything before saying the *kiddush* at home, the wine is given to a child who has reached the age when he is being trained in the observance of precepts. The child should hear the recitation of the benediction, thus being exempt from saying a benediction himself; and in this wise the *ḥazan's* benediction is not said in vain. If there is no minor in the synagogue, the one who recites the *kiddush*, or some other worshiper, should have it in mind to be exempted by this *kiddush*, and drink of the wine as much as a quarter of a *lug*, in order that he may recite the concluding benediction thereafter. Nevertheless, he may say the *kiddush* again at his home for the benefit of his wife and his children, if they themselves are unable to say it. The general rule is that the *kiddush* is valid only when it is followed by a meal. Yet the *kiddush* recited at the synagogue is valid, although it is not followed by a meal, because in a case of emergency, we rely upon the opinion of the authorities who hold that it is valid if we drink one-quarter of a *lug* of the wine. It is well that he should drink a quarter of a *lug* besides the mouthful that he swallows, so that the mouthful is for the *kiddush*, and the additional quarter of a *lug* in place of the meal.

9. It is customary to recite the chapter of the *Mishnah* (Shabbat 2), *Bammeh madlikin* (with what material may the Sabbath lamps be lighted?) But it is not recited on the Sabbath on which a festival occurs, nor when a festival occurs on a Friday, nor on a Sabbath of *Ḥol Hammoed* (Intermediate days of a festival).

10. It is customary to come to the synagogue on Sabbath morning, a little later than on weekdays, for sleep is one of the Sabbath joys. This is inferred from a Biblical verse, concerning the daily offering on the weekdays, it is written (Numbers 28:4): "In the *morning;*" but concerning that of the Sabbath, it is written (loco citato 9): "On the Sabbath-*day,*" thus indicating leisurely performance. However, we must not postpone the reading of *Shema* and the *Shemoneh esreh* beyond the prescribed time.

11. The time for reciting the *Musaph* (additional) service is immediately after the *Shaḥarit* (morning) service, and it must not be delayed later than the end of the seventh hour of the day (one o'clock p.m.). The person who recites it after that time is called a transgressor. Nevertheless, his obligation is fulfilled, as its time is the whole day.

12. If one must pray two silent prayers, one of the *Minḥah* and the other of the *Musaph*, as when one has delayed praying the *Musaph* until six and one-half hours of the day (12:30 p.m), he should recite first the one of the *Minḥah* and then the one of the *Musaph*, because the former is a regular duty, and it is a well-established rule that the regular takes precedence over the occasional. However, in a congregation, this rule must not be followed.

13. It is improper for the congregants to say in the *Kedushah* of the *Musaph, Eḥad hu elohenu* (One, He is our God) immediately after saying, *Shema yisrael, Adonai elohenu, adonai eḥad* (Hear, O Israel, the Lord is our God, the Lord is One), for we are not allowed to utter twice the word *eḥad* (one) consecutively; but we should say: *Adonai eḥad; hu elohenu* (the Lord is One; He is our God), etc. Only the *ḥazan* who pauses while waiting for the congregation, may begin with the word *eḥad.*

14. At the *Minḥah* (afternoon) service on the Sabbath, before reading the Torah, we say the verse (Psalms 69:14): *Vaani tefilati* (but as for me, may my prayer), etc. This is in accordance with what our Sages, of blessed memory, say (*Midrash,* quoted in the *Tur,* section 292): "It is written (Psalms 69:13): 'They that sit in the gate, talk of me; and I am the song of the drunkards.' And immediately thereafter, it is written (loco citato 14): *Vaanai tefilati* (But as for me), etc. David said before the Holy One, blessed be He: 'Master of the world, this nation is not like the other nations of the world. Other nations drink, get drunk and become boisterous, but we are not so. Although we drink, yet, my prayer, etc.''' This verse is, therefore, recited before reading the Torah to give thanks to our Creator, who has not allotted to us a portion like theirs. For even the ignorant among us come to hear the reading of the Torah. *Vaani tefilati* is not recited on a festival which occurs on a weekday when the Torah is not read, but it is recited on the Sabbath even when there is no Scroll on hand. In such an event, it is recited before the half-*kaddish,* in order that there be no interruption between the *kaddish* and the *Shemoneh esreh.*

15. After the repetition of the *Shemoneh esreh* by the *ḥazan,* we recite, *Tzidkateḥa tzedek* (Thy righteousness). These three verses serve as an acceptance of the Divine Judgment in bringing about the death of the pious three: Joseph, Moses, and David who died on the afternoons of a Sabbath. These verses are omitted, if the Sabbath occurs in a period when the *Taḥanun* (petition for Grace) is not said on weekdays. When praying with an assembly of ten, at the house of a mourner, the three verses should not be omitted, for its omission would make it a public demonstration of mourning, which is not permitted on the Sabbath.

16. If, by error we begin to recite on a Sabbath or on a festival an intermediate benediction of the weekday *Shemoneh esreh,* and we become aware of the error in the middle of the benediction, we must conclude it, and then say the proper benediction for the Sabbath or the festival service. For, in reality, the intermediate benediction of the weekday prayers, should have been incorporated in the Sabbath and festival service, and make mention of the holiness of the particular day in the benediction *Retzeh,* as it is done on *Rosh Ḥodesh* and on *Ḥol Hammoed*; but in honor of the Sabbath and festivals, in order not to burden the public, the Sages have instituted but one intermediate benediction for the occasion. Hence, since we have already begun reciting a weekday benediction, we must complete it.

17. Even if we have said only one word of the wrong benediction, and become aware of the error, we must conclude it, except when we start to say *Attah ḥonen* (Thou favorest). If we have only said the word *attah* (Thou), we need not finish it, since the *Maariv* and *Minḥah* services of the Sabbath likewise begin with the word *attah*. Hence, if we erroneously say *Attah* while praying *Maariv* or *Minḥah* on Saturday, even if we have forgotten that it was a Saturday, we need not conclude the benediction *Attah ḥonen*, but we should say *Attah kiddashta* at the *Maariv* service or *Eḥad* (one) at the *Minḥah*. If, however, during the *shaḥarit* (morning) prayer, we have made the same error, thinking that it was a weekday, we must conclude the benediction *Attah ḥonen*. If, however, we were aware that it was the Sabbath and we knew that *Yismaḥ moshe* (Moses rejoiced) was to be said, but only through a slip of the tongue, due to habit, we have said the word *attah*, we need not conclude the benediction, *Attah ḥonen*, but should say *Yismaḥ moshe*, for inasmuch as there are other prayers in the Sabbath *Shemoneh esreh* that begin with *attah*, it may look as though we are substituting one Sabbath prayer for another.

18. If we have not become aware of the error until we have begun saying the last three benedictions, that is, from *Retzeh* (accept, O Lord our God), and further, we should stop there, begin anew the Sabbath or festival prayers from the place where the error was made and conclude them in the proper order. If we have become aware of the error after we began reading *Yiheyu leratzon* (let the words of my mouth), etc., we must start from the beginning of the *Shemoneh esreh*.

19. If we have substituted a weekday benediction in the middle of the *Musaph* service, we must stop as soon as we become aware of the error, and begin the proper benediction of the *Musaph*, because for the *Musaph*, it was never thought that it ought to include all the weekday benedictions (like in *Shaḥarit*). Therefore, we need not finish it.

20. If one erred and began saying the weekday *Shemoneh esreh* on the Sabbath, it is a bad omen for him, and he should examine his deeds during the coming week and do penance.

21. If one has erroneously substituted one intermediate benediction of the Sabbath for another and he has become aware of the error before pronouncing the Divine Name, he must repeat the appropriate benediction. But if he has become aware of it after pronouncing the Divine Name, he must conclude with *Mekaddesh hashabbat* (who halloweth the Sabbath) and he need not say the appropriate benediction, inasmuch as the principal part of the intermediate prayer is the benediction *Retzeh na bimenuḥatenu* (accept our rest) which is uniform in all the Sabbath silent prayers.

22. The aforesaid rule applies only to the evening, morning and afternoon services. If, however, we substitute any other prayer for the *Musaph*, our obligation is not fulfilled, inasmuch as we have made no mention of the additional sacrifice. If we substitute the *Musaph Shemoneh esreh* for the evening, morning, or afternoon prayers, our obligation is likewise not fulfilled,

for we have made an untrue statement before the Omnipresent, blessed be He, by making mention of the additional sacrifice.

23. If we erred in the festival prayer by concluding with "Who halloweth the *shabbat,*" instead of "Who halloweth Israel and the seasons," if we instantly added, "Who halloweth Israel and the seasons," our obligation is fulfilled; but if not, we must repeat the prayer from *Attah beḥartanu* (Thou hast chosen us), etc.

Chapter 77

The Kiddush and the Sabbath Meals

1. It is a Biblical precept that the Sabbath be hallowed by means of words, for it is written (Exodus 20:8): "Remember the Sabbath day to keep it holy," implying that it must be ushered in with the recital of the *kiddush* (the sanctification of the day), and at its parting to be solemnized by reciting the *havdalah.* (See chapter 96, below). Hence, our Sages instituted the ceremony of the *kiddush* and the *havdalah,* to be recited over a cup of wine.

2. The *kiddush* may be recited and the evening meal eaten before it is night. Those who are accustomed to pray the *Maariv* on weekdays at the proper time, although they pray earlier on Friday, are forbidden to eat, one-half hour before the stars appear. If, therefore, it is only one-half hour before nightfall, they should wait till nightfall, when they shall read the *Shema* with its benedictions and then say the *kiddush.* It is forbidden to partake of anything, even water, before the *kiddush.*

3. It is meritorious to say the *kiddush* over old and good wine. An effort should be made to procure wine that is red. Where suitable *kosher* wine cannot be obtained, the *kiddush* may be said over raisin wine. While saying, *Vayeḥulu hashamayim vehaaretz* (and the heavens and the earth were finished), one should be standing while looking at the candles, afterward one may sit down, fix the eyes on the goblet of wine, and say the benedictions, *Bore peri haggafen* (who created the fruit of the vine), and *Asher kideshanu* (who hath hallowed us). If wine cannot be obtained, one may say the *kiddush* over bread, but not on any other beverage.

4. Women, too, are obliged to say the *kiddush.* They should, therefore, listen attentively when the *kiddush* is recited and respond *Amen,* but they should not say, *Baruḥ hu ubaruḥ shemo* (blessed be He, and blessed be His name). A minor, even if he has reached the age of thirteen, but it is not known whether he has symptoms of puberty cannot, by reciting the *kiddush,* exempt the woman. Therefore, she must recite the *kiddush* herself, but if she does not know how to say it, she should repeat it after the minor, word for word. Even if the *kiddush* is said by her husband, or by some other man, it is better

if she repeats each word. (For the law concerning several people residing in the same house, see chapter 135, section 6, below).

5. The *kiddush* may not be recited over wine which has turned sour. Nor should it be recited over wine which has a disagreeable odor, even if it has not turned sour and its taste and odor is that of wine over which the benediction *Bore peri haggafen* may be said, but it has a slight disagreeable scent because it has been kept in a filthy vessel, or it has the same odor as that of the barrel. If wine has remained uncovered for a couple of hours (although nowadays we do not mind leaving things uncovered), no *kiddush* should be said over it, for as the prophet says (Malaḥi 1:8): "If you bring it as a present to your governor, will he accept it favorably, or will he show you favor?" Foamy wine should be strained, but if it cannot be strained, the *kiddush* may be said over it. If, however, it is covered with a film, we may not recite the *kiddush* over it, for it has presumably lost its flavor.

6. The *kiddush* may be recited over wine that has been boiled, or which has been spiced with honey. Others, however, hold that the *kiddush* should not be said over such wine, since such wine was unfit for the altar. One should, therefore, try to obtain different wine.

7. The cup used for the *kiddush* should be in perfect condition and thoroughly clean. All the laws pertaining to the cup used at Grace after meals apply also to the cup used for the *kiddush,* both of the evening, and of the daytime, as well as to the cup used for the *havdalah.* It is well to say the Friday night *kiddush* over a large cup of wine, and leave some of the wine for the *kiddush* of the day and for the *havdalah.*

8. The *ḥallot* should be covered while the *kiddush* is recited. Even if the *kiddush* is recited over the *ḥallot,* they should be covered. This is commemorative of the *manna* which was enveloped in dew.

9. The one who recites the *kiddush,* should drink at least a mouthful of wine from the cup without interruption. All present should sip from the cup. One who drinks no wine, either because he has pledged himself to abstention, or because it is injurious to him, should not recite the *kiddush* over wine, relying upon those present to drink it.

10. The wine of the *kiddush,* being part of the meal, does not require the usual concluding benediction, for it is exempted by the Grace said after the meal. Some authorities, however, hold that it is not exempted by the Grace. If possible, therefore, one should say a benediction over a cup of wine

after Grace, recite the concluding benediction for it, and have in mind to include the wine of the *kiddush.*

11. No benediction need be said over the wine drunk during the meal, as it was exempted by the benediction, over the *kiddush* wine.

12. If one recites the *kiddush* over a cup, which he thinks contains wine, and then discovers that it contains water or some other beverage, he must repeat the *kiddush* over wine. If there was wine on the table which he intended to drink during the meal, he need not repeat the *kiddush,* as it is considered as though he had said the *kiddush* over that wine. However, if there was no wine on the table, but there was some wine in the house which he intended to drink during the meal, he need not repeat the benediction *Bore peri haggafen,* only *Asher kideshanu* (who hath hallowed us), etc. If the cup contains beer or mead, in a place where they are accepted beverages, he need not repeat the *kiddush* under any circumstances, but he should pronounce the benediction *Shehakol* (at whose words all things), and drink it. Nor is it necessary to repeat the *kiddush* where the custom prevails to recite it after the hands are washed; he says the benediction *Hamotzi,* and it is considered as though the *kiddush* had been said over the bread.

13. The *kiddush* should be recited over a cup of wine also at the morning meal. This *kiddush* consists merely of the benediction *Bore peri haggafen.* This *kiddush,* too, is obligatory upon women. Before this *kiddush* is said, it is forbidden to partake of any food, or even water, just as before the *kiddush* of the evening. It is best to recite also this *kiddush* over wine. However, if one prefers brandy and recites the *kiddush* over it, one's duty has been fulfilled. But one must see to it that the cup contains one-quarter of a *lug* (one and one-half eggshells), and one should swallow a mouthful of it without interruption. (See chapter 49, paragraph 6, relating to drinking brandy or coffee after reciting the *kiddush* over wine.)

14. Both the evening and the daytime *kiddush* must be recited in the room where the meal is served, for it is written (Isaiah 58:13): "And thou shalt call the Sabbath a delight," and our Rabbis, of blessed memory said: "Where you call the Sabbath (the *kiddush*) there you shall have the delight (the meal)." If, therefore, we recite the *kiddush* in one house and eat in another, although that has been our intention when saying the *kiddush,* we have not fulfilled our obligation. We are also required to start the meal immediately after the *kiddush,* and if we do not eat immediately thereafter, our obligation has not been fulfilled. If we do not care to have a regular meal immediately after the day *kiddush,* we may recite the *kiddush* and partake of some pastry, but we must drink a quarter of a *lug* of wine, so that we may say the concluding benediction *Al hamiḥeyah* and *Veal peri haggafen.* A *mohel* who must pronounce a benediction over the cup of wine drunk at the circumcision, but

has not as yet recited the *kiddush*, should first drink a mouthful from the cup, and then an additional quarter of a *lug*. This may be done also before praying the *Musaph* service, if one's heart is faint.

15. After praying the *Shaḥarit* (morning) service, a person who feels faint, may partake of some food before praying the *Musaph*, that is, he may eat bread no more than the size of an egg, but he may eat plenty of fruit to refresh himself. He must, however, first recite the *kiddush*, and drink a mouthful of wine, and then an additional quarter of a *lug*—for in an emergency, the drinking of that much wine may be considered as having a meal—or he may drink that quantity of wine, and then eat the size of an olive of food made of one of the five species of grain.

16. Every Jew, man or woman, is duty bound to eat three meals on the Sabbath, one on Sabbath-eve and two during the day. At each of the three meals, one must eat bread (and since the hands are washed and the benediction *Al netilat yadayim* is pronounced, one must eat of the bread no less than the size of an egg.) Therefore, one should not eat to excess at the morning meal. If, however, one finds it impossible to eat bread at the third meal, he should, at least, eat pastry or any food made of one of the five species of grain over which the benediction *Bore mine mezonot* is pronounced. If this, too, is impossible, one should at least eat something that is eaten with bread, such as meat or fish. And if this too is impossible, one should, at any rate, partake of cooked fruit. The time for eating the third meal begins at one and one-half hours past noon.

17. On the Sabbath we must say the benediction *Hamotzi* over two loaves of bread at every meal. While saying the *Hamotzi*, we hold both loaves in our hands, and we cut one of them. Before saying the *Hamotzi*, it is customary to make a mark with the knife upon that part of the loaf we desire to cut, the reason for it being, as stated in chapter 41, paragraph 3, above, that on weekdays we are required to cut a little around the bread before saying the benediction, but on the Sabbath it cannot be done, because the loaves must be whole when the *Hamotzi* is said. Therefore, we should at least mark the place to be cut, in order that we may know the exact spot where it is to be cut and not pause too long before deciding where to cut. We should place the loaves in such a way that the one we desire to cut should be closer to us, so that we would not (by passing one loaf) act as if we are ignoring a potential object of a *mitzvah*. We must have two whole loaves at every meal, even if we eat many meals during the day. In the morning when saying the *kiddush*, and we partake of pastry, we should also have two whole cakes.

18. If only one of those seated at the table is provided with double loaves, he should say the *Hamotzi* and exempt the others, who need not say the *Hamotzi* themselves. Before reciting the *Hamotzi*, he should say, *Bireshut morai verabbotai* (with the permission of my teachers and masters), and after eating some of the bread, he gives each one a slice.

19. If we have neglected to read the weekly portion of the Pentateuch on Friday, we must read it in the morning before the meal. If we forget to read it before the morning meal, we should read it at least before the *Minḥah* service, and post facto it may be read at any time before Tuesday evening.

20. On the Sabbath, it is forbidden to abstain from food, even for a short time for the purpose of fasting. And it is forbidden to abstain from eating until noontime, even if it is not intended as a fast.

21. It is forbidden to grieve over any distress, God forbid, but one should pray for mercy to the Master of Mercy.

22. On the Sabbath one should partake generously of fruits and delicacies, and inhale sweet odors, in order to complete the total of one hundred benedictions. Indeed, it is meritorious to partake of everything that provides one with pleasure, as it is written (Isaiah 58:13): "And thou shalt call the Sabbath a delight."

23. If one is accustomed to take a nap after the meal, he shall do so. But one shall not say: "I will sleep so that I may do some work or start on a journey at the conclusion of the Sabbath."

24. After such sleep, a time should be set aside for the study of the Torah. For, relating to the Sabbath, it is written (Exodus 35:1): "And Moses assembled." And our Rabbis, of blessed memory, asked (Tanḥuma, Vayakhel): "Why is in this portion written, 'And he assembled,' and not elsewhere in the Torah? God said to Moses: 'Go down, make assemblies on the Sabbath, so that the generations to come will also convoke assemblies for the study of the Torah.'" They further said (Yerushalmi, Shabbat 15:13): "Sabbaths and festivals were given to Israel for the studying of the Torah. For many are too occupied with their daily tasks during the week to study the Torah regularly, but on Sabbaths and festivals, being relieved from their work, they can study the Torah properly." Hence, those who are unable to study the Torah during the week, are especially obliged to study on the holy Sabbath, each man according to his knowledge and ability.

CHAPTER 78

The Torah Reading on Sabbath and Festivals

1. If more than seven persons had been called up to the Torah on the Sabbath, a *Kohen* or a *Levi* may be called up to the reading of the last portion, inasmuch as the requisite number of seven had already been called up, and he is last (except for the *maftir*). A *Kohen* or a *Levi* may also be called to the reading of the *maftir*. It is even permissible to call one *Kohen* to the last portion and another *Kohen* to the reading of the *maftir*, inasmuch as the *kaddish* intervenes between them. On *Simḥat torah* (Rejoicing with the Law), when three Scrolls are taken out, one *Kohen* may be called up as *Ḥatan torah* (the groom of the Torah), who ends the reading of the Torah, and another as *Ḥatan bereshit* (the groom of Genesis) who begins the reading of the Torah all over again, and a third as *maftir*, since a different Scroll is used for each. However, if *Rosh Ḥodesh* (New Moon) of the month of *Tevet* occurs on the Sabbath, when three Scrolls are taken out (one for the Sabbath, one for *Ḥanukkah*, and the third for *Rosh Ḥodesh*), even if eight persons are called up for the reading in the first Scroll, a *Kohen* may not be called as the eighth one, because the reading is not completed in this Scroll, but in the second Scroll wherein the portion for *Rosh Ḥodesh* is read, and to this one, a *Kohen* may be called. The same law applies to *Shabbat shekalim* and *Parshat haḥodesh* (see chapter 140, below) when they occur on *Rosh Ḥodesh*.

2. If a *Kohen* or a *Levi* is erroneously called up to a portion properly allotted to a *Yisrael*, some one else should be called up in his place, while he remains at the reading desk; and he is called again, either as *maftir* or to the last portion after the requisite number of seven had been called up.

3. On a Sabbath when two sections of the Scriptures are read, they merge into one with the reading of the fourth portion.

4. No interruption should be made in the curses contained in the sections *Beḥukotai* (Leviticus 26:14-43) and *Ki-tavo* (Deuteronomy 28:15-68). The reading of these curses is preceded by adding one verse of the previous chapter. But in order not to begin a portion when there are less than three verses left, it is best to begin reading the three preceding verses. At the conclusion, we should read at least one verse after the curses, but care should be taken not to end at less than three verses from the beginning of a portion. In the section *Ki-tissa* (Exodus 30:11), the entire portion which tells of the golden calf, until the words: *Umesharto yehoshua* (and his minister Joshua) (33:11) should be read for the *Levi*, for the reason that the sons of Levi did not participate in the making of the golden calf. It is customary to read in a low voice the portion beginning with: *Vayitten el moshe keḥaloto* (and he gave unto Moses as He had finished) (Exodus 31:18), until *Vayeḥal moshe* (and Moses entreated) (loco citato 32:11). From *Vayeḥal moshe* the reading may be resumed in a loud voice, until: *Vayifen moshe vayered* (and Moses turned and went down) (loco citato 15). From *Vayifen* it should again be read in a low voice until: *Umoshe yikkaḥ et haohel* (and Moses took the tent) (loco citato 33:7), then the reading is resumed in a loud voice to the end of the portion. The curses contained in *Beḥukotai* and *Ki-tavo* should likewise be read in a low voice; the verse: *Vezaḥarti et beriti yaakov* (and I will remember My covenant with Jacob) (Leviticus 26:42) should be read in a loud voice; then the following verse: *Vehaaretz teazev mehem* (and the land shall become desolate) should be read in a low voice, but from the verse: *Veaff gam zot*

(and with all this) (verse 44), until the end, the reading should be resumed in a loud voice. In section *Ki-tavo* the verse *Leyira et hashem haniḥbad* (to fear the honored Name) (Deuteronomy 28:59) should be read in a loud voice, and thereafter in a low voice until: *Veen koneh* (and there is no one to buy) (loco citato 68). It is also customary to read in a low voice in *Behaalotḥa* from: *Vayehi haam kemitonenim* (and the people were as murmurers) (Numbers 11:1), until *Vehamman kizera gad hu* (and the manna was like coriander seed) (loco citato 7). Whatever is read in a low voice, should be read loud enough for the congregation to hear, as otherwise they have not fulfilled their obligation of reading the Torah. No interruption should be made in the reading of the forty-two journeys in the section *Veeleh massei* (Numbers 33:6-49), for it is symbolic of the Divine Name consisting of forty-two letters.

5. Between the reading for one person and another, the Scroll should be rolled up, but it need not be covered. However, before *maftir*, when there is a long interval during which the *kaddish* is recited, the Scroll should be covered with its mantle. Similarly, on any other occasion where there is a long interval between the readings—for instance, when they call up a bridegroom, in a certain chant, the Scroll should be covered. It would seem that this should also be the practice when some time is spent in saying *Mi sheberaḥ* (He who blessed), etc.

6. If by error they read for the sixth person, up to the end of the *Sidra*, the *kaddish* is not recited after this reading, but the *maftir* is immediately called up with whom the required number of seven persons is completed; and after he has said the *haftorah* with its benedictions, the *kaddish* is recited. On a festival also, if they read for the fourth person until the end, the *kaddish* is not to be said then, but the *maftir* is called up immediately for the reading in the second Scroll, and after the *haftorah* and its benedictions, the *kaddish* is recited.

7. When three Scrolls are required for the reading, and only two are available, the second Scroll should not be rolled to the portion that is to be read in the third Scroll, but the first Scroll should be taken for the reading of that portion.

8. The laws concerning defects discovered in a Scroll, were discussed in chapter 24 above. If the defect is discovered during the reading for the *maftir*, then if there is a special *maftir* for that day, such as one read on a festival, or on a Sabbath on which *Rosh Ḥodesh* occurs, or on which *Shekalim* (see chapter 140, below) is read, when an extra Scroll is taken out for the *maftir*, it is governed by the same law that applies to any other portion of the Torah. But on an ordinary Sabbath, when the reading of the seventh portion is repeated for the *maftir*, which is done only in deference to the Torah (for it may look as though the Torah and the Prophets are equal, inasmuch as the reading of the Torah is preceded and followed by a benediction, and the reading of the Prophets is also preceded and followed by a benediction; therefore the one called for *maftir* also reads a portion of the Torah, to indicate by reading the Torah first, that the Torah is more important) in this case another Scroll should be taken out. The reading is to be concluded in the same Scroll, but the concluding benediction should not be said. However, the *haftorah* and its benedictions should be said. If the defect has been discovered before one said the first benediction, another Scroll should be taken out. If no other Scroll is available, then the one who was called up last,

should say the *haftorah* with its benedictions; and if the *kaddish* has not yet been recited, it should be recited after the *haftorah*.

9. It has already been explained in chapter 24, above, that if an error is discovered in a word, either having a missing or a superfluous letter, no other Scroll is to be taken out as long as it does not alter either the pronunciation or the meaning of the word. Yet, if such an error is discovered on the Sabbath, although another Scroll need not be taken out, no more than seven persons should be called up to that Scroll. The seventh person called up should read the *haftorah* with its benedictions, and the *kaddish* should be recited thereafter. (This rule applies only to an ordinary Sabbath, but when the *maftir* treats of the special day, one must be called up to *maftir*). This Scroll should not be taken for use at the *Minḥah* service.

10. On a day when two Scrolls are taken out, if a defect is discovered in the first Scroll, and there is another Scroll available, the reading shall not be resumed in the second Scroll and the portion of the second Scroll shall not be read out of the third Scroll. This law applies also to a day on which three Scrolls are taken out. If the Scrolls were changed around by taking out first the one that was intended for the second reading, the Scroll taken out by error shall be rolled up, and the other Scroll taken from the Ark, in order that each Scroll shall be used for the reading originally intended.

11. The following is the order of precedence for those who are obligated to have a reading of the Torah: (a) A bridegroom on his wedding day, and a prospective bridegroom who had never been married; they sing when called up to the Torah on the Sabbath before his wedding. (b) A lad who has become *Bar Mitzvah* during that week—all these have equal claims. (c) A *sandek* (one who holds the baby during the circumcision) on the day of circumcision. (d) A *sandek* on the day of the circumcision who carries the baby to the synagogue to be circumcised. (e) The husband of a woman who has given birth to a daughter, and the mother comes to the synagogue. (f) The husband of a woman who has given birth to a son, and the mother comes to the synagogue. But if the women do not come to the synagogue, their husbands are not obliged to go up to the Torah, except if it is the forty-first day of a son, or the eighty-first day of a daughter, as it was on these days that an offering was brought in the Temple. (g) A bridegroom whose wedding took place on Wednesday or later in the week—on the Sabbath after the wedding, but only if it is the first marriage of either one of the married couple. (h) One who has *Jahrzeit* on that day. (i) The father of a child on the day of circumcision. (j) The *mohel* (circumcisor) on the day of circumcision. (k) One who will have *Jahrzeit* during the week following the Sabbath. (l) The *sandek*, then the father, then the *mohel*—on the Sabbath before the circumcision. Two persons who have equal claims for the reading of the Torah, should abide by the decision of the president of the congregation, or else, decide by lots. A non-resident cannot take precedence over a resident who is obliged to go up to the Torah. It is customary to call up to the Torah, one who is about to start on a journey after the Sabbath, or one who has returned

from a journey. It is likewise the custom to honor an important visitor by calling him up to the Torah. All these, however, do not take precedence over anyone who is duty bound to have a reading of the Torah.

CHAPTER 79

Laws Concerning Maftir

1. Before calling up the *maftir*, the half-*kaddish* should be said. During the recitation of the *kaddish*, if two Scrolls have been used, both of them should be on the desk. When three Scrolls are used, it is not necessary to place the first one on the desk.

2. The *maftir* should not begin saying the benediction for the *haftorah* until the Scroll is rolled up.

3. After the words *Haneemarim beemet* (that were said in truth) in the first benediction over the *haftorah*, no *Amen* should be responded, because the benediction does not end until the word *Vatzedek* (and righteousness). Nor should *Amen* be responded after the words *Emet vatzedek* (truth and righteousness), in the second benediction after the *haftorah*, because the paragraph beginning with the words *Neeman attah* (faithful art Thou) is also a part of that benediction. As there are some people who erroneously respond *Amen* at these points, it is well for the *maftir* not to pause there, so as to indicate that the benedictions did not end there.

4. It is forbidden to speak when the *haftorah* is read.

5. According to law, only the *maftir* should audibly read the *haftorah*, while the congregants are to repeat after him quietly. The custom in some congregations to read aloud together with the *maftir*, stems from ignorance, and it should be abolished. There are also some slow people who still read the *haftorah*, after the *maftir* had completed it and has begun the benedictions. These are acting improperly; for if they say it aloud, they themselves do not hear the benedictions, and occasionally they also prevent their neighbors from hearing them. And even if they somewhat subdue their voices and do not disturb their neighbors, still they themselves do not hear the benedictions. Therefore, it is best, that as soon as the reading of the *haftorah* is concluded and the benedictions are begun, the listener should remain silent until the benedictions are concluded, and then he may finish reading the *haftorah*.

The *maftir* too, should be careful not to begin the benedictions until the noise in the congregation has entirely subsided.

6. On a Sabbath when two *Sidras* of the Torah are joined, the *haftorah* of the second *Sidra* is read, except when the two *Sidras Aḥare* and *Kedoshim* (Leviticus 16:20) are joined, then the *haftorah Halo kibene kushiim* (are ye not as the children of the Ethiopians?) (Amos 9) is read. In some of the books it is noted that the *haftorah Vayivraḥ yaacov* (and Jacob fled) (Hosea 12:13, 14:10) should be read in conjunction with the weekly portion of *Vayishlaḥ* (Genesis 32:4), but this is an error, because this *haftorah* belongs to the portion of *Vayetze* (Genesis 28:10), and the *haftorah* for *Vayishlaḥ* is *Ḥazon obadiah*.

7. On *Rosh Ḥodesh* which occurs on a Sabbath, the *haftorah Hashamayim kisei* (the heavens are My throne) (Isaiah 66) is read. If by error, one read the *haftorah* belonging to the portion of the week, and he becomes aware of it before saying the concluding benedictions, he should read the *haftorah Hashamayim kisei*, and then say the benedictions. If he became aware of the error after saying the benedictions, he should read *Hashamayim kisei* without the concluding benedictions. If *Rosh Ḥodesh* occurs on a Sunday, the *haftorah Maḥar Ḥodesh* (tomorrow is the new moon) (I Samuel 20:18-42) is read. If the reader erred, he is governed by the same law which applies to *Rosh Ḥodesh* occuring on a Sabbath. If *Rosh Ḥodesh* is two days and it occurs on the Sabbath and on Sunday the *haftorah* to be read is *Hashamyim kisei*.

8. On the Sabbath of *Ḥol Hammoed Pesaḥ* (the Intermediate Days of the Passover), no mention should be made of the Passover, either in the middle or at the end of the concluding benedictions of the *haftorah;* but should be concluded with *Mekaddesh hashabbat* (who halloweth the Sabbath). However, during the Intermediate Days of Sukkot, the festival should be mentioned just as it is done on the first two days of Sukkot, which occurs on the Sabbath (since the complete *Hallel* is then read, and there is also a distinction in the sacrifices).

9. A minor who has reached the age of training, who knows to whom the benedictions are addressed and who can pronounce the words distinctly, may be called up to *maftir* on the Sabbath or on festivals, excepting on the Sabbath of *Zaḥor* and *Parah* (see chapter 140, below), and on the Sabbath during the ten days of penitence. It is likewise customary not to call a minor on the seventh day of Passover when the *Shirah* (song), *Az yashir* (then sang) (Exodus 15) is read. It is customary to call up a scholarly adult to the *maftir* on the first day of *Shavuot* (Feast of Weeks), when the *Merkavah* (Chariot) (Ezekiel 1) is read for the *haftorah*. It is also customary to call up the Rabbi to *maftir* on *Shabbat Ḥazon* (during the first nine days of the month of *Ab*, when the *haftorah Ḥazon yeshayahu*, (the vision of Isaiah, chapter 1, is read).

10. The *haftorah* was instituted to be read with the benedictions only after the requisite number of persons were called up to the Torah. But, if on an ordinary Sabbath, the Scroll has been discovered to be defective, even at the reading of the seventh portion, when there was no other Scroll available, and the concluding benediction was omitted, the benedictions for the *haftorah* should not be said. Likewise, if an invalidity is discovered in the portion read for the *maftir* relating to the duties of the day, the *haftorah* should be read without its benedictions. On an ordinary Sabbath, if an error is discovered after seven persons were called, whether while reading for an extra person or while reading for *maftir*, the *haftorah* should be read with its benedictions.

CHAPTER 80

Some Labors Forbidden on the Sabbath

(The principal works we are forbidden to perform on the Sabbath, are already known to most of the children of Israel. The list given herein comprises works that are not generally known to be forbidden; they are common things performed in the course of our daily lives).

1. It is forbidden to do work that requires concentration before a lamp. The Rabbis have forbidden this, lest one forgets and tilts the lamp in order to bring the oil closer to the wick, and then one will be guilty of "igniting." Two persons, however, may read one subject out of one book, because if one will attempt to tilt it, the other one will remind him. It is, however, the prevailing custom to permit studying before the light of our modern candles, in which the tallow or the wax firmly sticks to the wick. But one must make a certain mark, so as to remember not to snuff off the wick. According to the view of Maimonides, the last named act is a violation of a Mosaic Law. It is impermissible to snuff off the wick, even through a non-Jew.

2. It is forbidden to open a door or a window opposite a burning candle, lest the flame be extinguished; but one may close the window or the door. It is forbidden to open or to close the door of an oven in which a fire is burning, for by so doing, one either increases or decreases the fire.

3. Pouring boiling gravy on pieces of bread or *matzah* is forbidden. One should first pour the gravy into a dish, let it cool off until it is fit to eat, and then put the bread or the *matzah* in it; but as long as the gravy is hot, even if it is already in the dish, it is forbidden to put either bread or *matzah* in it. It is likewise forbidden to put salt or spices into the gravy, even if it is already in the dish, and certainly not into the pot, as long as it is boiling hot, but we must wait until it cools off a little so that it is fit to eat. Some are more lenient with salt which has already been dissolved. However, a blessing upon the one who adheres to the stricter opinion regarding this. It is likewise forbidden to pour hot coffee or tea into a cup containing sugar. But we must pour the coffee or the tea into the cup and then put the sugar in it. In cases of necessity, one may be lenient about this.

4. It is forbidden to place fruit or water upon a hot stove, because the water might boil and the fruit might bake. Even if we intend only to warm it, nevertheless, since it is possible that on this spot it may boil or bake, it is forbidden to warm it there. Pudding, which has fat in it, should likewise not be placed opposite a fire or on a stove where it may boil, although it is our

intention only to warm it. However, we may put it in a place where it cannot boil, but it will merely warm it up, even if the fat is congealed or the water frozen. One is not allowed to put anything that is cold into an oven, in which things have been stored away for the Sabbath, even if it cannot boil there. If it is for a person who is slightly ill, the proper authorities should be consulted. On the Sabbath, some people are accustomed to replace into the oven, food which they had stored away there on Friday, if such food is still warm, but not if the food has entirely cooled off. A person with the proper spirit should avoid it.

5. On the Sabbath, it is forbidden to store away victuals in any wrapping, even if it would not increase its warmth. Therefore, if we remove a pot containing victuals which have been cooked or heated in it, we are forbidden to wrap it or cover it with pillows, bolsters, or the like, in order to preserve its warmth.

6. Any article of food which cannot be eaten at all without being rinsed with water, must not be rinsed on the Sabbath, even with cold water. It is allowed, however, to soak herring in cold water, since it is fit for food even before soaking.

7. Mustard, horseradish, or any kind of relish, in which no vinegar was put while it was still daylight, may not be prepared on the Sabbath, unless we do it in an irregular manner, that is, we first pour the vinegar into the dish, and then the mustard or the horseradish into it. We must put enough vinegar into it, so that the mixture be soft. Neither should we mix it with a spoon, but with a finger, or shake the vessel until it is well mixed.

8. We are not permitted to handle fruit found under a tree, for it might have fallen off that very day. The fruit of a non-Jew, which might have been plucked that very day, is likewise forbidden even to be handled.

9. On the Sabbath, it is forbidden to take honey out of a beehive. It is likewise forbidden to crush honeycombs, even if they have been removed from the hive on Friday. Thus, if the honeycombs have not been crushed before the Sabbath, it is forbidden to use the honey that oozes from them on the Sabbath; but it is permissible to take the honey that flows from the hive.

10. If fruit spilled from a vessel, either in the house or in the courtyard, they may be gathered together on the Sabbath, if they are in one spot, but if they are scattered, when it requires physical exertion to do so, they may not be gathered into a basket, but they may be picked up and eaten one by one.

11. It is permissible to remove peas or the like from their pods, if the pods are still green and can also be eaten, because this is like separating one

piece of food from another; but if the pods have become dry and no longer suitable for eating, it is forbidden to remove the peas from them. One should likewise be careful not to remove the nut kernels from their green shells, nor remove poppy seeds from their shells.

12. It is forbidden to squeeze fruit to make a beverage, like squeezing lemons into water to make lemonade. Some authorities even prohibit to suck juice out of fruit with the mouth. At any rate, in eating grapes, one should not suck out the juice and throw away the skins. However, if one has no need for the juice to make a drink one is allowed to squeeze it out; therefore, it is permissible to press lettuce or cucumbers since the water goes to waste.

13. A woman is not allowed to squeeze milk from her breasts into a vessel and feed the child with it; but she is allowed to squeeze out a little milk, in order to induce the child to take hold of the breast and suck it. It is forbidden to sprinkle some of her milk for the sake of a remedy, in a case where there is no danger or where the pain is not intense.

14. It is permissible to put congealed fat upon hot food, although it melts. It is forbidden to crush snow or hail with the hands, in order to obtain water; but it is permissible to put it into a cup of wine or water to cool the liquid, letting it melt of itself. In the winter time, we should be careful not to wash the hands with water in which there is snow or hail; if we do wash with such water, we must be careful not to crush the snow or hail with the hands. It is permissible to break ice in order to take water from underneath. If possible, it is best not to urinate in snow; it is likewise prudent not to do it on clay or pulverized earth.

15. It is permissible to separate food from offal, but not the offal from the food. The food may not be separated with a utensil only by hand, and only for the purpose of eating it immediately. When we separate food, we must take only what we need for immediate consumption, but not a quantity that will be enough also for later use, because the part to be consumed now is considered as food, whereas, whatever is to be used later is considered as

offal. We may not peel garlic or onions and put them away, because it constitutes the violations known as "separation." We are allowed to peel only what we need immediately. The upper shell which surrounds the whole garlic may not be removed even when needed for immediate consumption, because this constitutes a secondary act of "threshing."

16. The law forbidding "separation" applies also to non-edibles, such as utensils; whatever one desires for immediate use is considered as food, and the rest is considered waste.

17. It is forbidden to strain any kind of beverage, for concerning this, there are many conflicting opinions. One is, however, permitted to drink through a cloth, as the law forbidding "separation" applies only where the food or drink is prepared prior to eating or drinking it, but in this case, one is simply holding back the waste from entering into the mouth. Nevertheless, some authorities disapprove of drinking water through a cloth, because it constitutes "washing." The last law may be relaxed in cases of emergency where there is no pure water available. One, however, should not drink through the sleeve of one's shirt, because in this case it is feared that one will wring it.

18. Coffee beverage, which has grounds at the bottom, or any other beverage which has at the bottom lees or any other sediment, when we pour it into another vessel, we must be careful to leave a little over the dregs. We may remove the cream from the top of milk that has been soured, but only as much as needed for immediate use; and even in this case, we must not remove the whole of the cream, but leave some of it on top of the milk.

19. If a fly has fallen into beverage or food, we must not remove the fly only, but should take some of the food or the beverage with it.

20. Pepper or salt, needed for seasoning food, may be crushed with the handle of a knife, or in any other convenient way, but may not be crushed in a mortar.

21. It is forbidden to cut onions or any other vegetables, except immediately before a meal, and even then they should not be cut into very thin slices.

22. It is forbidden to salt any substance which will be affected by the salt in such a way as to become soft or less pungent, because it constitutes the violation known as "tanning." Therefore, it is forbidden to salt raw cucumbers, radishes, or onions, even if the quantity is limited to that which is needed for an immediate meal. But one may dip each piece in salt before eating it. Boiled eggs, meat, and other foods, upon which the salt has only the effect of imparting a salty flavor, may be salted, but only for the consumption of the immediate meal, but not for another meal.

23. It is forbidden to salt a large quantity of boiled beans or peas together, because it tends to make them softer. This is forbidden even if one intends to eat them immediately.

24. Salads made of lettuce, cucumbers or onions, may be salted immediately before the meal, because oil and vinegar are generally added immediately, which weaken the effect of the salt.

25. The law forbidding "construction" applies also to edibles, as for instance, making cheese, or arranging fruit in a certain orderly way. Therefore, when making a salad of sliced onions and eggs or the milt of herring, one must be careful not to arrange them symmetrically, but put them on the plate at random.

26. On washing the dishes, one should not pour hot water on them; but he should pour the water into a vessel and then put the dishes into that vessel. We must not wash the dishes with a cloth, lest we wring it afterward; but we may wash them with a cloth especially used for this purpose, which we are not careful to wring even on weekdays. We are not allowed to use a detergent of oats, or the like, in washing glasses. Only dishes needed for the Sabbath may be washed on the Sabbath.

27. Whatever a Jew is forbidden to do on the Sabbath, is forbidden also to have it done through a non-Jew. Nevertheless, in the winter time, since it is permissible to make a fire in the stove through a non-Jew for the purpose of heating the house, the custom prevails that the non-Jew places the cold victuals on the stove before he makes the fire; since the intention in making the fire is not to warm the victuals but to heat the house. But the victuals should not be placed on the stove after it was heated. It is certain, however, that if the intention in making the fire is not for the sake of heating the house, but for heating the victuals, it is forbidden. Some authorities forbid it even when the intention is to heat the house. Although the custom is to depend on the authorities who allow it, a scrupulous person should refrain from such a practice when it is not too urgent. Much more is this the case with ranges which

are made exclusively for cooking purposes. Although the fire is made for the purpose of heating the house, and a non-Jew places the victuals thereon before the fire is made, God-fearing avoid it.

28. One who spills liquid on the soil where anything is apt to grow, is guilty of violating the law against "sowing," because the liquid accelerates the growth. Therefore, one should be careful not to eat in a garden on the Sabbath, because it is impossible to be so careful as not to spill some liquid upon the soil; and, besides, in a garden there is a law forbidding the moving of articles.

29. It is forbidden to wipe anything with a sponge that has no handle.

30. It is forbidden to spit in a place where the wind will scatter the saliva.

31. A maiden is forbidden either to make braids or to take them apart on the Sabbath. But she is allowed to fix her hair with her hands. The hair must not be combed with a brush made of bristle if it is very hard, because it is impossible not to pluck out some hair with it; but if it is not hard, the hair may be set with it, and especially so if it is made for that particular purpose.

32. One may wipe off dirt from a garment with a rag, but no water may be spilled on it, because it would be equivalent to washing. Therefore, if a child urinates on a garment, it is forbidden to spill water on it (but if he urinates on the ground or in a vessel made of wood or of leather, it is permissible to spill water on it). When one washes the hands, one should rub them briskly, one against the other to leave as little water on them as possible before using the towel (for when there is only moisture on them, the wiping does not constitute "washing.") When a colored cloth is used for drying, no scruples should be felt (for such a cloth is not likely to be washed).

33. A barrel containing water, or any other liquid, should not be covered with a cloth which is not specifically set aside for such purpose, lest it be wrung out. However, it may be covered with a cloth which is specifically made for such purpose, where there is no cause for apprehension that it would be wrung.

34. If water spills on the table, it is forbidden to wipe it with a cloth which one values, for since it absorbs much water, one might wring it out. Neither should one use a cloth in drying glasses or other vessels having a narrow opening, for the liquid might be squeezed out of the cloth.

35. If one is caught in the rain and his clothes get wet, he may go home and remove the clothes, but he is not allowed to spread them out so that they may dry; even if one's clothes are only moist with perspiration, he is not allowed to spread them out, certainly not in front of a fire. Even when one has the wet clothes on, he is not allowed to stand in front of a fire where it is very hot. One is likewise forbidden to shake off water from a garment. A costly garment, of which one takes special care, must not even be handled when taken off, for fear that he might wring it.

36. If one walks and reaches a brook, one may jump over it even if it is wide; jumping is better than the effort of walking round about it. One is not permitted to cross it by wading, lest he will wring his clothes after crossing. One must not walk along the sloping bank of a stream on the Sabbath, for he might slip, fall into the water, wet his clothes and then wring them.

37. If one goes to perform a religious duty, such as meeting his father, his teacher, or a person greater in wisdom than he is, he may cross the stream, providing he does it in an unusual manner, for instance, if he does not remove his hands from underneath the overcoat, so as to remember not to wring the clothes. He is not allowed to cross with his sandals on, for since he cannot tighten them well, they might fall off the feet and will then carry them across, but one may cross with his shoes on. And since one has gone across for a religious purpose, he may return the same way. If one goes to guard his fruit (for taking care of one's property is somewhat akin to a religious duty), one may cross the stream on the way there, but not when one returns.

38. Wet mud on a garment may be scraped off with a fingernail or with a knife, but not when it is dry, for it is then equivalent to the act of "grinding."

39. It is forbidden to shake off snow or dust from a black garment, but it is permissible to remove feathers from it with the hand. Some people refrain even from the latter.

40. It is allowed to remove mud from the feet or the shoes with something which may be handled on the Sabbath, or they may be wiped by rubbing them on a beam, but it is forbidden to wipe them on a wall or on the ground. In cases of emergency, as when there is excrement on the foot or on the shoe, and there is nothing available which may be handled on the Sabbath, one may wipe it on a wall, and if there is no wall, he may wipe it on the ground. If there is water available, he may even wash the shoe with it, if the shoe is made of leather (because in the case of leather, the mere flushing of it does not constitute "washing," unless he rubs one side against the other, in the manner of launderers). But one is not allowed to scrape off excrement from a leather shoe with a knife, or to scrape it off with the iron fixed at the entrance of a door for the particular purpose of cleaning shoes with it, if it is sharp, but one may use it if it is not sharp.

41. If the hands become soiled with mud, we must not wipe them with the towel generally used for wiping the hands (lest we forget and rinse it).

42. On the Sabbath, it is forbidden to paint anything even with a dye that is not permanent. Therefore, a woman is not allowed to use rouge. When our hands are colored by fruit juice, we must not touch any garment, because we thus dye it. We are likewise forbidden to wipe a bleeding nose or wound with a cloth.

43. It is forbidden to put saffron into soup, because it colors it.

44. It is forbidden to tear or to twine even two threads or two loose hair on the Sabbath.

45. It is the practice when we wind a thread or a cord around an object, that we make two knots, one on the top of the other. On the Sabbath, we are not allowed to make two knots, even on an object which we generally loosen on the same day. When putting a kerchief around the neck on the Sabbath, we must not make two knots on it, and even on Friday, we must not make two knots on it, as we will not be allowed to untie it on the Sabbath, as stated herein below. It is forbidden to hold the two ends of a thread or a cord together, and make one knot on both, for in this case, even one knot will hold it fast. It is permissible to take the two ends, make first one knot, and on the top of it make a loop, if it is a thing which is generally untied the same day. If not, it is forbidden even if in this instance we intend to untie it the same day. It is permissible to make two or more loops, one on top of the other, even if it is intended to hold for many days.

46. It is forbidden to untie any knot which may not be tied on the Sabbath. If a knot causes us pain, it may be loosened by a non-Jew.

47. It is customary with tailors, that before sewing a garment, they baste the sections together with long stitches. On the Sabbath, the threads of the basting may not be removed.

48. Garments that are made with a string or a strap in them for fastening, such as trousers, shoes, or undershirts, if the garment is new, it is not permitted to insert the string in them on the Sabbath, for it is akin to per-

fecting a garment. If the garment is old, and the aperture is not narrow, so that there is no trouble inserting it, it is permissible.

49. Sometimes when a seam becomes loose and the parts of a garment become separated, the thread is pulled and the loose parts tighten temporarily. This act constitutes "sewing," and may not be done on the Sabbath.

50. If sheets of papers were stuck together unintentionally, as the pages of a book sometimes stick together by the paint or glue used by the bookbinder, or if some of the pages were stuck together by wax, it is permissible to separate them.

51. If the opening of a vessel is covered with a cloth and tied around with a cord, it may be torn off on the Sabbath, because this is "spoiling" and it is permissible when needed for the Sabbath.

52. It is forbidden to catch any living thing on the Sabbath, even a flea, but if an insect stings a person, it may be removed and thrown off, but one is not allowed to kill it, because it is forbidden to kill on the Sabbath, anything that possesses life. It is, however, permissible to kill lice, since they are created only by perspiration (nevertheless, those found on clothes may not be killed, but should be thrown off; only those found in the head may be killed).

53. If we wish to close a chest or a vessel in which there are flies, we must let them fly out first, because by closing the chest on them we snare them. However, it is not necessary to examine the chest to see that no living thing is therein; we simply have to chase out those we see.

54. It is forbidden to draw blood on the Sabbath, even to suck the blood from the gums. It is likewise forbidden to put a plaster on a wound to draw out blood and pus. And it is certainly forbidden to squeeze blood or pus from a boil.

55. Shreds of skin which have become separated from the base of the fingernails, should not be removed either by means of an instrument, or by hand, or with the teeth. A nail, most of which has been torn off and causes pain, may be removed with the hand, but not with an instrument. But if less than half has become separated, it should not be removed even by hand.

56. It is forbidden to spill any liquid into vinegar, to increase the volume of the vinegar.

57. If meat has not been salted for three days after the slaughter, and the third day occurs on the Sabbath, a non-Jew may rinse such meat on the Sabbath, so that it should not become forbidden food, but it may not be rinsed by a Jew.

58. It is forbidden to cover anything with a plaster, or wax, or tar. Therefore, it is forbidden to put wax or congealed oil into a hole in order to close it up, or to stick it onto something as a mark. It is, however, permissible to smear food, like butter, on bread.

59. It is forbidden to cut or break any object that is not food; but food, even for beasts, may be cut and broken. It is allowed to cut up straw with which to pick the teeth. It is permitted to break and to crush balsam plants for the purpose of scenting them even if they are as hard as wood. However, it is forbidden to break them for the purpose of picking the teeth.

60. It is forbidden to make any use of a tree, whether it is green or dried up, even if we do not shake the tree thereby (as shaking the tree is in itself a violation, because it may not be moved on the Sabbath). We must not climb on it, nor suspend ourselves from it. It is also forbidden to place any article on it or remove anything from it, or to tie an animal to it. It is even forbidden to make use of the sides of the tree; hence, if a basket is suspended from the tree, it is forbidden to take anything out of the basket or to put anything in it, inasmuch as the basket is considered as the side of the tree. However, if a nail is driven into the tree, and the basket is suspended from the nail, it is permissible to take things from the basket and to put things into it, as the basket is then only a side of the side of the tree. It is, however, forbidden to remove the basket itself or to hang it on there, as we would thus make use of the nail which is akin to the side of the tree.

61. Flowers or plants which are cultivated in a vessel, whether for their beauty or their fragrance, are forbidden to be plucked, just as it is forbidden to pluck them from a tree. When the vessel is standing on the ground, it must not be removed from there to any other place, because when it stands on the ground, it is nourished from the aroma of the soil, therefore, removing it from there is like plucking something from the ground. If the vessel stands on some object, it must not be removed and placed on the ground, because it is equivalent to planting. All of the above should be strictily observed, whether the vessel is of wood of or clay, and whether it is with or without an aperture.

62. It is forbidden to write or to draw a picture, even with the finger, in liquid spilled on the table, or on the rime of window panes, or anything similar to it, no matter how impermanent such writing is. It is even forbidden to make a mark upon any object with the fingernails. Wax, or the like, found on a book, even if it is only on one letter, must not be removed.

63. Just as it is forbidden to write on the Sabbath, so is it forbidden to erase any writing. Nevertheless, it is permissible to break and to eat on the Sabbath tarts upon which letters or figures have been made; but if they have been made as a charm for children, one should avoid doing it.

64. Some authorities forbid the opening or the closing of books, when words are written on the edges of the leaves. Others permit it; and this is the prevailing practice. But since some authorities forbid it, it is best to avoid writing on the edges of pages.

65. One is permitted to say to a neighbor: "Fill up this vessel for me," even if such vessel is used as a measure, and even if it belongs to the seller, so long as the buyer takes it home. It is especially permissible if the buyer brings his own vessel, and says: "Fill up this vessel for me." However, it is forbidden to fill the seller's vessel, and empty it into the buyer's vessel. One may say to a neighbor: "Give me fifty nuts," or something similar, provided one does not mention any measure or money, or the accounts, saying: "I owe you for fifty nuts, give me fifty more, and I will owe you for a hundred." And it is certainly forbidden to speak in terms of sale, even if the price is not mentioned, and even if it is for the needs of the Sabbath. On the Sabbath, it is forbidden to purchase even through a non-Jew; the same law applies to hiring.

66. One is allowed to say to a neighbor: "Fill up this vessel for me," or: "Fill it up to this mark, and tomorrow we will measure it or weigh it."

67. Just as it is forbidden to erect even a temporary structure on the Sabbath, even so it is forbidden to make a temporary addition to a permanent structure. But a doorway which is not made for general entrance and exit, but is used as such only occasionally, and one has attached a door for that opening, which does not swing on pivots (the term *pivot* signifies a piece of wood or of iron projecting from the door, which is made to fit into an aperture in the threshold and in the upper doorpost, so that the door swings both ways; the same applies to doors with hinges), but one has tied it on thereto and hung it up to close the opening therewith, as long as there is a hinge on the door, or even if there is no hinge at present, but the place where it has been is still discernible, one may close the opening with it on the Sabbath. This is permissible even when it drags on the ground when it is opened, and when it is closed it must be raised and placed on the threshold, since it is fastened and hanging and there is also a mark of a hinge it is obvious that

it is a door, and it does not seem like construction. Especially is it so, when it still has hinges, providing one does not restore the hinge into its place, for when doing this one would perform an act of building.

68. If, however, the door bears no sign of a hinge, it is forbidden to close an opening with it on the Sabbath. For since the doorway is used only on rare occasions, and it is not obvious that the door has been intended to be used as a door, it is equivalent to the act of building. However, if it is attached and hung up well, so that when it opens it does not drag on the ground, even if it is suspended above the ground only as much as a hairbreadth, it is then obvious that it has been intended as a door, and it is permissible to close the opening with it.

69. If the door is not attached and suspended, but upon opening it, it is entirely removed, it is not permitted to close with it a doorway which is not made for constant entrance and exit. But if it is an opening which is made for constant entrance and exit, it is permitted to close the doorway with it, even if there is no mark of any hinge on it.

70. A door that is made out of one board, cannot be used to close a doorway with it, if the doorway is not made for regular entrance and exit, even if it has a hinge but it does not swing on it, for since it is made out of one board, it appears as if we were building and closing up an open space. However, it is allowed to close with it an opening which is used for regular entrance and exit, providing there is a threshold, for then it is obvious that it is a doorway.

71. It is allowed to shut the opening of a window with a shutter, such as a board, or anything with which a window is generally shut, even if it is not attached to it, provided that it has already once been used to shut the window opening with it before the Sabbath, or it has been intended to close the window with it before the Sabbath. However, if one has never shut the opening with it, and has not intended to do so, it is forbidden, if it is a thing which is customary to leave it there for a long time. But if it is a thing which is generally left there only temporarily, such as a garment, or the like, it may be used for shutting the opening under all circumstances.

72. It is forbidden to remove or to reset doors or windows on the Sabbath, even when they hang on iron hinges and are easily removed or reset; one who resets them is guilty of construction, and one who removes them is guilty of demolition.

73. It is forbidden to sweep the house, even if the floor is made of stone or of boards, but it may be done by a non-Jew. However, even a Jew is allowed to sweep, if he is doing it in an entirely unusual manner, as when he sweeps it with goose feathers, or the like.

74. One shall not rub out with his foot, the saliva on the ground, but he may step on it without rubbing it.

75. On the Sabbath, it is forbidden to respond to the call of nature in a ploughed field. (As to using a field belonging to someone else for such a purpose, it is forbidden even on weekdays, as stated in chapter 183:5, below.)

76. It is forbidden to make a partition, however temporary, on the Sabbath or on a festival, if it is for the purpose of dividing something. Hence, it is forbidden to make a partition with a curtain, to shut out the view of lights or of books, in order to have sexual intercourse or to respond to the call of nature; for, since this partition legalizes his act, it creates a separate and distinct premise, it is equivalent to making a tent. However, it is permissible to cover books with two coverings, one on the top of the other, because this does not constitute the making of a tent. If the curtain in front of the bed has been spread on Friday, no less than one hand-breadth, whether on the top or on the side, the whole of it may be spread on the Sabbath, because it is considered as making an addition to a temporary structure. But the ruffled part of the curtain on the top or the bottom, does not make up the necessary hand-breadth, since that part has not been intended as a tent. It is likewise forbidden to open a partition that is commonly known as a "Spanish wall," unless it has been slightly opened on Friday. The fact that it is folded all the time, although the board is wider than one hand-breadth, makes it invalid as a partition. It is, however, permissible to make a temporary partition when it is not for the purpose of permitting anything, but to serve as a shield from the sun, or that the wind should not blow out the candles.

77. It is forbidden to make a tent, that is, a roof that shelters, even when it only protects from the sun or from the rain; and even if it is only a temporary tent, if it is one hand-breadth square, it must not be made on the Sabbath. Therefore, on the Sabbath or on a festival, it is forbidden to spread a sheet upon a cradle with arched staves on the top, unless at least one hand-breadth of it has been spread over the cradle on Friday, for then it is only making an addition to a temporary tent, which is permissible. If the staves of the cradle are less than three hand-breadths apart, they are in themselves considered as a tent (for it is a law received by Moses on Mount Sinai, that if the gap of an object is less than three hand-breadths, it is considered as closed and solid), and it is permissible to spread a sheet over it.

78. It is forbidden to remove the lid of a trunk, which is not attached with hinges, because it is equivalent to the demolition of a tent, and it is likewise forbidden to cover the trunk with it, because it is like making a tent. When a board is placed on a barrel to make it serve as a table, it is necessary to place the open side of the barrel on the ground, for if the board is placed on the opening, a tent is made thereby.

79. It is permissible to close the opening of a chimney if it is on the side of the chimney, for it is merely adding to a partition; but if the opening is on the top of the chimney, it may not be closed on the Sabbath or on a festival, for it is like making a tent. If an iron door that swings on hinges is affixed to it, it may be closed, like any ordinary door that swings on hinges.

80. We may not cover a barrel with a cloth, if the barrel is not entirely full, and there is an empty space of a hand-breadth (four inches) between the beverage and the cover, because by covering it we are making a tent; but we may do so by leaving a little of the opening uncovered.

81. A partition or a tent which may not be made on the Sabbath, must not be removed on the Sabbath, because it is like destroying a tent.

82. It is forbidden to carry a covering as a protection from the sun or from the rain, which is commonly known as an umbrella, because it is considered as making a tent.

83. If vessels that are made of different sections and dovetailed into one another had been taken apart, if they were generally kept loose, they may be put together loosely; but if they were always joined tightly, they may not be put together on the Sabbath, even loosely. If they were held tight by means of screws, since they were generally joined tightly, then upon becoming loose they may not be put together even loosely. However, the covers of vessels may be removed and put on, since they are not meant to remain closed for any length of time, but to be opened constantly.

84. It is permissible to open and take out clothes needed for the Sabbath or a festival, from a press, that is, two boards, one on the top of the other, between which clothes are pressed, if the press belongs to a private person. But it is forbidden to close the press, for this is work done on the Sabbath for weekdays. If the press belongs to a laundry man, or to any other craftsman, it may not be opened, for since their presses are tightly clamped, the opening of it is akin to demolition. Even if the press was opened on Friday, the clothes may not be taken from it on the Sabbath or on a festival, for the reason that one might be led to open it even when it is forbidden.

85. If the leg of a bench came out, it is forbidden to replace it, and it is also forbidden to lean the bench against another bench, unless one has already sat on it in this manner before this occurred. However, one is permitted to place a board on two benches or on chumps of wood which have been prepared on Friday for this particular purpose.

86. It is forbidden to wind a clock on the Sabbath or on a festival even if it is still going. It may be wound up on the second day of a festival when it is still going, only as much as it is needed for this particular day, but not for what will be needed the following day. For the sake of a sick person, it is permissible under all circumstances, if a non-Jew cannot easily be found to do it.

87. On the Sabbath, it is forbidden to make a musical sound, either with an instrument or with the limbs of the body, (except the mouth). It is even forbidden to snap the fingers or to strike on a board to make a sound, or to rattle with nuts, or ring a bell to silence a crying child. It is forbidden to clap with the hands or to dance, but it is permissible to do so in honor of the Torah; neither should a person be prevented from doing it for the sake of a crying child, since there are some authorities who permit it.

88. Making unmusical sounds on the Sabbath is permissible. One may, therefore, knock on a door to make known his presence. Some authorities hold that it is, nevertheless, forbidden to knock on the door with anything attached to it for that purpose, or to ring a bell attached to the door. Clocks that are made to strike the hour by means of pulling a chain, may likewise not be operated on the Sabbath or on a festival.

89. One who guards fruit or grain against animals and fowl, should neither clap his hands, nor smite them on his hips, nor stamp with his feet, to scare them away in a manner he is accustomed to do on weekdays.

90. It is not permitted to play with nuts, or the like, on the ground, even if it is covered with a floor. Nevertheless, it is inadvisable to protest against women and children who do it, because they will certainly pay no attention to it, and it is better that they should be innocent than conscious violators.

91. There are many divergent views regarding the folding of garments on the Sabbath, and it is best not to fold them.

92. If a garment is caught on fire, it is permissible to spill any kind of beverage on the spot which does not yet burn, so that when the fire reaches the saturated spot, it will be quenched; but it is forbidden to spill water on the garment.

93. It is not allowed to make the bed on the Sabbath to be used at the conclusion of the Sabbath. Even though there is still some time left during which one can sleep while it is the Sabbath, since it is not one's intention to sleep there before the conclusion of the Sabbath, one is thereby preparing something on the Sabbath for weekdays, which is forbidden.

Chapter 81

The Four Premises with Regard to Sabbath Laws

1. There are four classes of premises with regard to the Sabbath law: (a) the private premise; (b) the public premise; (c) the premise which can be classed neither as private nor as public; and (d) the premise which is exempt. We shall explain them briefly.

2. What is to be denominated "private premise?" A private premise is any place which measures no less than four hand-breadths (sixteen inches) square (as such a space is sufficiently large to be of use), and is surrounded either by partitions no less than ten hand-breadths high (even though they are not closely joined), or by a trench, ten hand-breadths deep and four hand-breadths wide. A well, ten hand-breadths deep and four hand-breadths square; also a mound, ten hand-breadths high by four hand-breadths square, and even a vessel, a chest, for instance, if it is ten hand-breadths high, or a barrel, if it measures four square hand-breadths in diameter, all of the above, even if they are in a public premise, or in a premise which is neither private nor public, form a separate premise by themselves, and constitute a private premise. The open space over a private premise is considered private, even to the very sky. The tops of the partitions surrounding a private premise are also governed by the law of a private premise. If there are cavities in the inside of the partitions, even if they are hollow from side to side, inasmuch as one can make use of them in the private premise, they are subordinate to the partition, and are considered a private premise.

3. What is to be denominated a "public premise?" Streets and market places which measure sixteen cubits (twenty-four feet) square, for such was the width of the road in the Levites' camp in the wilderness, and highways by which people travel from city to city, and are sixteen cubits wide, are also public premises. Anything in the public premise, measuring less than three hand-breadths in height above the ground, even if it be covered with thorns or dung upon which not many people step, is nevertheless subordinate to the ground and is considered as a part of such premise. A ditch in a public premise, is likewise considered a part of such premise, if it is less than three hand-breadths deep. The cavities in the walls facing the public premise, the hollow of which does not extend to the private domain, are subordinate to the public premise, and are considered as a part of it, if they are lower than three hand-breadths from the ground. If, however, they are higher than three hand-breadths from the ground, then their proportions must be taken into consideration; if they measure four hand-breadths square, but are lower than ten hand-breadths from the ground, they are considered neither as a public nor as a private premise. If they are higher than ten hand-breadths, they are private premises. If they do not measure four hand-breadths square, they are exempted places, whether they are above or below ten hand-breadths from the ground. Alleys leading into a public premise, are at times regarded as a public premise, and at times as neither public nor private premises; there are many divergent views regarding them. Some authorities

are of the opinion, that any place through which less than sixty myriads of people pass daily, as the numbers of the Jews in the wilderness, is not a public premise but is regarded neither public nor private premise. Therefore, nowadays, we have no public premises. However, the God-fearing should follow the more stringent view.

4. What premise is to be regarded as a *karmelit* (neither public nor private)? Any place which is not a public thoroughfare, and is not properly surrounded by partitions, such as fields; a stream which is no less than ten hand-breadths deep and no less than four hand-breadths wide, and alleys which are partitioned off on three sides. A portico erected in front of shops, where merchants linger; shelves upon which merchandise is placed, which are erected in front of columns in the public territory and are four hand-breadths wide, and from three to ten hand-breadths high, also a place which measures four hand-breadths square, and is surrounded by partitions which are not ten hand-breadths high, and a mound which measures four hand-breadths square and is from three to ten hand-breadths high, and an excavation which measures four hand-breadths square and is from three to ten hand-breadths deep. There are, besides, many other premises which are regarded as *karmeliyot* (neither private nor public; the word *karmelit* is composed of *raḥ* and *mol*, which means neither tender nor dry, but medium, the same applying to this case, as it is neither private because it has no proper partitions, nor public premise, because not many walk there).

5. What is an exempted place? Any place in a public premise which does not measure four hand-breadths square, and is three or more hand-breadths in height, or a ditch which does not measure four hand-breadths square and is three or more hand-breadths deep, and a place which does not measure four hand-breadths square, and is surrounded by partitions of three or more hand-breadths high. These places are considered exempted only when they are in a public premise; but when they are in a *karmelit*, they are considered as part of such a premise.

Chapter 82

The Prohibition Against Removing Things From One Premise Into Another

1. In a public premise and in a *karmelit*, it is forbidden to carry, throw, or hand over anything a distance of four cubits (six feet). Even carrying an object a little at a time is forbidden if the total distance adds up to four cubits.

2. It is forbidden to carry, throw, or hand over anything from a private to a public premise or to a *karmelit;* or to carry from a public premise or from a *karmelit* into a private premise. It is likewise forbidden to carry from a public premise into a *karmelit,* or from the latter into the former. But it is permissible to carry out and bring in from a place which is exempt into a pre-

mise which is either private, public, or a *karmelit*, and from the latter into the former, providing that the article is not carried four or more cubits within the premise which is neither public, or which is a *karmelit*. Now, inasmuch as there are different views as to what constitutes a public premise, a premise which is a *karmelit*, and a private premise, therefore, in a town which is not provided with an *eruv* (a symbolical act by which a legal community is established), one who is not well versed in the law, should be very careful not to carry any article from the place where it rests into an adjoining premise of a different category unless one is certain that it is permissible.

3. The lifting of an article from the place where it lies, is called *akirah* (dislodging), and putting down the article is called *hanaḥah* (depositing). It is forbidden to dislodge even without depositing, and to deposit without dislodging. Hence, a Jew is forbidden to hand an article to a non-Jew, in order that the latter should take it from a private premise and bring it into a public premise or into a *karmelit*, as thereby the Jew does the "dislodging;" but the non-Jew himself should take the article. When a non-Jew brings an article, the Jew must not take it from his hand, as thereby he does the "depositing;" but the non-Jew should put the article down. When a non-Jewess takes an infant to the synagogue on the Sabbath to be circumcised, she herself should lift the infant from the crib, and when coming into the court of the synagogue, she should put the infant down, and then a Jewess should take it.

4. If there is a breach in the partition of a court, then if what is left of the partition on one side of the breach measures four hand-breadths (sixteen inches) wide by ten hand-breadths high above the ground, or if the partition on the two sides of the breach measure each one hand-breadth wide by ten hand-breadths high, it need not be repaired, if the breach is not wider than ten cubits, for that breach may be considered as a door. If, however, the breach measures more than ten cubits, or if there has not been left of one side of the partition the width of four hand-breadths, or of the two sides the width of one hand-breadth of each, especially if there has been a complete breach, that is, nothing has been left of the partition on one side, like this ⊐, then even if the breach measures only three hand-breadths, it is forbidden to carry anything within that court until it is repaired. And the best way to repair it is to make it in the form of a door. (If there are two or more inhabitants in such a court, then an intercommunity of courts must be established, as will be explained, God willing, in chapter 94, below).

5. We have stated above that if a breach in a court did not measure more than ten cubits, it may be regarded as a door, and it is not necessary to repair it. This rule applies only when there is but one breach. If, however, there are two or more breaches, it is essential that the area of the remaining partition be at least as large as the breach. If the breaches measure more than the parts that remain standing, then every breach measuring more than three hand-breadths must be repaired.

6. What forms a door? If one erects two posts, no less than ten hand-breadths high on either side of an opening, and puts a stick or a cord upon them, it forms a door. The stick or the cord must be attached to the top of the posts and not to their sides, but if one drives nails into the top of the posts and ties the cord to them, it is also valid. It is imperative that neither of the posts be at a greater distance from the wall than three hand-breadths, nor should they be higher than three hand-breadths from the ground. In an emergency, where it is impossible to make the form of a door otherwise than by placing the posts at a greater distance than three hand-breadths from the walls,this requirement may be disregarded.

7. If a house or a court opens on the street and its door opens inward, and the doorposts, lintel, and threshold are towards the street, the space before the door is at times considered as a private premise, and at times as a *karmelit*. Inasmuch as not everybody is well versed in these laws, therefore, the laws applying to a private premise as well as those applying to a *karmelit*, must be observed in regard to this. It is forbidden to carry anything from there into the street, which is either a public premise or a *karmelit*, or from the street into this place which may be regarded as a private premise. It is likewise forbidden to carry anything into such a place from the house or from the court, or vice versa, for it might be regarded as a *karmelit*. If, therefore, the door of such entrance is locked, care should be taken to have a non-Jew insert the key in the lock, and after the door is unlocked, the non-Jew should remove the key before the Jew opens the door; for, if the Jew should open the door while the key is in the lock, he will thereby bring the key from the *karmelit* into a private premise.

8. In many places the roofs of some houses project from the wall into the street, and it is supported by pillars. It is forbidden to carry anything from such a house into the space beneath the projection, or from there into the house. It is also forbidden to carry anything there a distance of four cubits, as it is subject to the law relating to the street which is either a public premise or a *karmelit*, and although the roof rests upon the pillars giving it the form of a door which the law regards as a partition, yet since there are no partitions on its sides, nothing may be carried there. It is, therefore, necessary to erect on each side a post near the wall, opposite the post which supports the roof, thus forming other doors. If many similar houses adjoin one another, it suffices to form such a door at each side of the outermost house, and the inhabitants should then symbolically establish an intercommunity of courts.

9. One may give food to a non-Jew in a court or in a house, although he knows that he will carry it outside, so long as he does not put the food into his hand, and thus commit the act of "dislodging." This may be done

only when the non-Jew is allowed to eat the food in the house should he desire to do so; but if he is not allowed to eat it there, or if a great quantity of food is given him, so that he could not eat it all there, or if he is given other articles, when it is obvious that he will carry it out, it is forbidden, for it appears as though it was given to him for the express purpose of carrying it out.

10. A woman may lead her child, even in a public premise. She must not, however, drag it, but the child should lift up one foot and keep the other one on the ground, supporting himself thereon, while uplifting the other foot. If, however, the woman drags both feet of the child, it is just as if she carries it, and it is forbidden even in a *karmelit.* Carrying a child is forbidden even if it is big enough to walk by itself, and even in a *karmelit.* The principle, that "a living being carries itself," applies to the law which relieves the one carrying it from bringing a sin-offering, but it is still a violation of a Rabbinical ordinance. In the case of a *karmelit,* it is a violation of a Rabbinical ordinance based on another Rabbinical ordinance, and it is necessary to warn the public who err in this regard.

11. It is forbidden to draw water from a stream that runs through a courtyard.

12. While one is standing in a private premise, one is forbidden to throw water or spit into a public premise or into a *karmelit,* or from a public premise or a *karmelit* into a private premise, or from a public premise into a *karmelit,* or from a *karmelit* into a public premise. One is likewise forbidden to walk four cubits in a public premise or in a *karmelit,* or from one premise into another, having saliva in one's mouth, if the saliva has already been moved from one corner of the mouth to another.

13. It is permissible to spill slops in a courtyard which measures four cubits square, although it will run off to public premise.

CHAPTER 83

The Enclosure of Spaces

1. The enclosure by partitions, which renders the carrying of anything within permissible, applies only when it has been fenced around for dwelling purposes. By "dwelling purposes" is meant, when one builds a house to dwell in, or when one opens a door from his house, and fences it around by partitions after the manner of courts which are built around houses, then, no matter how large the enclosure is, it is an absolutely private premise. Enclosures, however, that have been fenced around for other than dwelling purposes, such as gardens and orchards, where the fences are made only for the

purpose of guarding their contents, are judged by their size. If it is an area that would not require more than two *seahs* (certain measure) of seed, it is permitted to carry things in it; but if it would require more than two *seahs* of seed, it is regarded as a *karmelit*.

2. What is the size of an area requiring two *seahs* of seed? It is the area of the court of the Tabernacle: One hundred cubits (one hundred and fifty feet) long by fifty cubits (seventy-five feet) wide. If it is a quadrangle, it should measure seventy cubits (one hundred and five feet) and four handbreadths (sixteen inches) square. If the area is circular or in any other shape, it must measure five thousand square cubits. If, however, the length of the enclosure is more than twice its breadth, even if only by one cubit, then it is forbidden to carry anything therein, for it is then considered as an area requiring more than two *seahs* of seed, since it does not resemble the court of the Tabernacle.

3. An enclosure which has been fenced around for other than dwelling purposes, and which would not require more than two *seahs* of seed, where carrying is permissible, if there is a court adjacent to it, it is permissible to carry utensils from the enclosure into the court, and from the court into the enclosure, as the enclosure and the court are considered one premise. The enclosure, however, is not considered the same premise as the house. Hence, it is forbidden to carry vessels from the enclosure into the house, and from the house into the enclosure.

4. If an enclosure has been first fenced around for other than dwelling purposes, and the dwelling was built thereafter, or if a door was made in the house leading to it, how can it be legally converted into an enclosure for dwelling purposes? By making a breach in the partitions measuring more than ten cubits (an opening of ten cubits is regarded as a door; but if it is more than that, it is a breach); thereby nullifying the partitions as a fence, after that the partition should be repaired, and it will be considered as having been fenced around for dwelling purposes.

5. If one has planted trees in a court which has an area requiring more than two *seahs* of seed, even if they occupy the greater part of the court, the fence is still considered as made for dwelling purposes, because people usually seek the shade of trees. If, however, one has planted vegetables in the court, and they occupy the greater part of the court (even if it is not in one area, but are scattered), it then ceases to be a dwelling, and the whole court is considered as a garden. If, however, the planted area occupies less than half of the court, and the area requires less than two *seahs* of seed, it is subordinate to the court, and the whole of it is regarded as a court. But if the sown area occupies more than two *seahs* of seed (in one place), then the place which was sown is regarded as a *karmelit*, and the remainder of the court, is open completely to a place which is forbidden (to carry into or from it), it is, therefore forbidden to carry anything therein four cubits.

6. A court which has an area requiring two *seahs* of seed or less, and part of it has been planted, should also be judged by the greater part of it. If the greater part of the court has been planted, although carrying is permissible therein, inasmuch as its area does not require more than two *seahs* of seed, it is, nevertheless, forbidden to carry into it utensils which were in the house on the Sabbath. It is, therefore, necessary to make a partition in front of the garden, in order to be permitted to carry things from the house into the court.

CHAPTER 84

Carrying Garments or Ornaments on the Sabbath

1. One must not walk out in a public premise or in a *karmelit,* with any article that is neither a garment nor an ornament. Hence, one is forbidden to walk out with a needle, or a pin stuck in one's garment, even when it is needed for his clothes. However, a woman (inasmuch as it is the custom of women to fasten their bands with pins, such as veils or the like), is permitted to walk out with a pin required for her apparel, but not with a needle.

2. There are also certain ornaments which our Rabbis, of blessed memory, forbid to be carried in a public premise. Some ornaments forbidden to men, and some forbidden to women, such as they might remove in order to show them to somebody. Now the custom prevails to permit it, and the authorities have given reasons for it. But the God-fearing should be strict about it. Especially, should a man be careful not to walk out with a ring on which, there is no engraved seal. One should especially refrain from carrying his watch with him, even if it is attached to a gold chain that he wears on his neck which is an ornament. The pocket watch certainly is considered a burden, and must not be carried on the Sabbath.

3. It is customary to allow to carry out on the Sabbath a silver key, although it is made for use, since it is also made for an ornament. Eye glasses may not be carried out, although they are framed in a silver frame.

4. A woman is not allowed to put a cloth on her veil, nor a man a cloth on his hat, to protect the apparel from the rain, because this is not the way a garment is worn and it is a burden. But if their intention is merely not to be annoyed by the rain, it is permissible.

5. A person who is lame, or convalescent, or very old, and it is impossible for him to walk without a cane, is permitted to walk with a cane in his hand. However, if he can walk without a cane, in his house, and he uses

a cane only when he walks in the street, he is forbidden to do so. A blind person must not walk out with a cane in a community in which there is no *eruv* (see chapter 94, below). One who has no need at all for a cane, is not permitted to walk out with it on the Sabbath even in a community which is provided with an *eruv*, because it may look like showing contempt for the Sabbath.

6. One who is fettered with chains, may walk out with them on the Sabbath.

7. It is forbidden to walk out on stilts; long poles in which there is a place for the feet, and by means of which people walk in mud and in water.

8. One may walk out with a plaster upon one's wound (providing it is not placed on the wound on the Sabbath, as is provided for in chapter 91:10, below), for since it is a remedy, it has the same status as an ornament. One may also wrap it around with a piece of cloth that is not costly, which is merely an adjunct to the plaster. But to wrap around it an article of value, like a handkerchief, or the like, is forbidden because it is neither subordinate to the plaster nor is it a garment; it is a mere burden.

9. One may walk out with the cotton placed in one's ear to absorb the pus, providing it is tightly stuck so that it cannot fall out. One may likewise walk out with cotton or straw in one's shoe, if it is put there in such a manner that it cannot fall out.

10. A woman is not permitted to walk out with the cotton which she attaches for the period of menustration, in order not to soil her clothes, neither may she walk out with the truss which she puts on for the same purpose, unless it is in the form of a true garment. However, if she puts on the cotton or the belt to save herself from discomfort, that is, if the blood will drip on her body and dry up, she will be annoyed, she is permitted to walk out with them.

11. When walking in a place of mud and clay, one may raise one's clothes slightly so as not to soil them, but one must not raise them too high.

12. A person may walk out with two garments on the Sabbath, wearing one above the other, even if he does not need the other garment for himself, but for a neighbor who is in need of it. This is only true when he wears two such garments occasionally on weekdays, then it is his usual way of dressing (even if most of the time he does not dress himself thus). If, however, he never wears two such garments, he is forbidden to walk out with them on the Sabbath, because the second one is considered a mere burden. The same law applies to two pairs of felt shoes, and with a large hat over a small one.

13. With regard to walking out with two belts, one above the other, if it is the custom of the place to wear two, a cheap one underneath, and over it an expensive one, we may do so on the Sabbath, although we are in need of only one, and we put on the second because we need it for someone else. If, however, it is not customary to put on two belts, although we choose to dress in this manner, since one girdle suffices, the second one is considered a burden. In any event, it is permissible to walk out with two belts when there is a garment intervening between the two, as for instance, when the one underneath is on the drawers and the one above is on the trousers, for then we have the benefit and the use of both.

14. It is the practice to wrap a handkerchief under the upper garment around the trousers, but we must be careful not to make two knots in it, one above the other. The God-fearing should remove the suspenders, so that the handkerchief is used for the purpose of holding up the pants. Some people are accustomed to wrap the handkerchief around their necks. This is not permissible unless they wear no other kerchief, and they are accustomed to wear a kerchief at times in cold weather. However, it is definitely forbidden if they merely throw it around their neck and allow its corners to hang loosely. It is likewise forbidden to wrap it around one's leg or one's hand, and walk out on the street with it.

15. Some authorities permit to wear gloves on the Sabbath, while others forbid it. A muff, however, is preferable to gloves.

16. It is permissible to walk out with a *tallit*, if it is worn in the usual manner, but it is forbidden to fold it and to wrap it around the neck, for it is not customary to wear it that way.

17. If a garment has two straps or two strings with which it is tied, or if it has hooks with which it is fastened, and one of these was torn off, although the remaining one is of no value, nevertheless, if the owner of the garment intends to repair it later, by replacing its mate, the remaining one does not become subordinate to the garment; it is, therefore, like a burden, and it is forbidden to walk out with such a garment on the Sabbath. But, if the owner does not intend to repair it, the remaining one is of no value, thus it becomes subordinate to the garment, and it is permissible to walk out with it. If it is an article of value, such as a silk loop or a silver hook, even if its owner does not intend to repair it, it is not subordinate to the garment, and it is forbidden to walk out with it.

18. Baldheaded persons who put on their heads a toupee of combed

flax or wool, to look like hair, may walk out with it on the Sabbath in a public premise, because it is considered as an ornament (providing it has been prepared before the Sabbath).

19. One who wears an amulet must consult a scholar as to whether or not he may walk out with it on the Sabbath, because not all amulets are of equal value. A woman who wears a stone, commonly known as *Sternshus* (eagle stone), as a protection against abortion, is permitted to walk out with it on the Sabbath.

CHAPTER 85

If a Fire Breaks Out on the Sabbath

1. If, God forbid, a fire breaks out on the Sabbath, our Rabbis, of blessed memory, were fearful that if the owner of the house and the members of his family were to engage in saving what they can, they might forget that it is the Sabbath and extinguish the fire, due to their being excited and frightened at the prospect of losing their property. They therefore, decreed that the owner is forbidden to save even those articles which may be handled and carried out into a place where it is permissible to remove them. Only that which is required for the needs of the day may be saved. If the fire breaks out on Friday evening before the meal, we may save food for three meals, and also food for the animals; if it occurs on Sabbath morning, we may save food for two meals, and if it occurs in the afternoon, we may save food for one meal. If one vessel contains much food, like many loaves of bread, or a barrel full of wine, since it can be taken out at one time, it is permissible to do so. If we spread out a sheet, and put therein large quantities of food and drink, it is likewise permissible to take it out. We are also allowed to take out all the vessels we need for that day.

2. One may say to others: "Come and save anything you can for yourselves," and everyone may save the food that he needs, or one vessel that contains even much food. Whatever they save belongs to them, since the owner renounced his ownership, and thus they take possession of abandoned property. Nevertheless, if they are God-fearing people, they should restore to the owner, whatever they saved, since they are aware that he has not abandoned it with his good will, and they are allowed to receive compensation for saving it. This will not be considered as money earned on the Sabbath, because according to law, the property saved belongs to them. However, it is a virtuous trait, not to accept any compensation for the trouble of saving anything on the Sabbath, although it is not considered as money earned on the Sabbath, because pious men should avoid doing anything which people consider wrong.

3. All of the foregoing applies only when taken to a place to which it is permissible to carry things out on the Sabbath, but to a place where it is forbidden to carry anything out, nothing may be saved. However, we are permitted to put on as many garments as we can, or wrap ourselves with them,

and carry them out even into a public premise. We may then take them off and put on others and bring them out; and this may be repeated the whole day. We may even say to others: "Come, and save," and they, too, may act in the same manner.

4. The houses in which there is no fire, but are close to the fire, and the owners fear that the fire may spread to them, they are allowed to save anything and bring it to a place which it may be carried, since they are not so excited. Some authorities hold that money and other valuables, although they may not be handled on the Sabbath, may be saved from a great sudden loss, such as a fire, a flood, or a robbery, by placing them on some edibles and carry them out together (but in any other case, it is forbidden to save anything untouchable by this method). Other authorities are even still more lenient about this, and they hold that valuables may be carried out by themselves, because in the case of a great loss which comes suddenly, the law forbidding the handling of certain objects on the Sabbath, is lifted, providing they are not moved to a place to which they may not be carried.

5. All sacred books, whether written or printed, may be saved from a fire or from a flood on the Sabbath, and they may be carried even into a court or into a lane whereto it is forbidden to carry other objects because it is not provided with an *eruv* (intercommunity of courts), providing this court and lane are in a condition where an *eruv* or a partnership would make them legal (for things to be carried into them). It is permitted to save such books by a non-Jew, even when they need to be carried into a public premise.

6. The case of a book may be saved together with the book, and the bag of the *tefillin* together with the *tefillin*.

7. A Scroll of the Torah should be saved in preference to other sacred books.

8. If there is apprehension that there might be a possible loss of life, the fire may be extinguished. Therefore, in places where Jews live among non-Jews, it is permissible to extinguish the fire even when it is in the house of a non-Jew; it all depends upon the circumstances of the case. It is only permissible to extinguish the fire, but it is forbidden to desecrate the Sabbath in order to save some property. If a person violates the law, and does desecrate the Sabbath, he should consult a rabbi, who shall point out to him the way to repentance.

Chapter 86

Bathing on the Sabbath

1. One is forbidden to wash his whole body, or even the greater part of the body, in warm water even if the water was warmed before the Sabbath. It is forbidden even if he washes the body, a small part at a time. It is for-

bidden to enter a bathhouse for the purpose of perspiring there. It is, however, permissible to wash one's face and bathe one's feet with water made warm before the Sabbath

2. It is permissible to wash the entire body with water which flows warm from its origin, such as the hot springs of Tiberias, if the water is on the ground and the place is not covered with a roof. However, if the water is in a receptacle or if the place is covered with a roof, it is forbidden. Some authorities hold that as long as the water is on the ground, it is permissible to bathe in it, even when the place is covered with a roof.

3. It is permissible to immerse the whole body in cold water, but one must not thereafter stand in front of a hot oven to warm up, for that would make it like washing with warm water. Even if one has washed only the hands in cold water, one is not allowed to warm them by an oven while they are still wet, because it is equivalent to washing with water that has been warmed up today with which even one limb of the body should not be washed, but one must first dry them well. (See chapter 80:32 above, where it is stated that one should rub one's hands well before drying them, so that there is only little water left on them.)

4. A bather must be careful not to squeeze the water from his hair. He must likewise refrain from swimming, because swimming on the Sabbath and on festivals is forbidden. It is also forbidden to make anything float, such as chips of wood. One who bathes in a place from where it is forbidden to carry anything out on the Sabbath, must shake off all the water from his body and from his hair before leaving, so that he will carry no water out from one premise into another. In the river itself, a person should also take care not to walk four cubits, since he carries the water that is upon him, and the river is *karmelit* (a premise which is neither public nor private). In view of the fact that not everybody is competent to observe all this, it has become the prevailing custom in our regions not to bathe at all on the Sabbath even in cold water, unless it is for the sake of performing a religious duty, for instance, a woman after her menstrual period (see chapter 162:7, below), or a man after a nocturnal pollution.

5. It is permissible to stand by a river and wash the hands in the river. The transfer of water from the river to the bank constitutes no violation, because both the river and the bank are considered as *karmeliot,* and it is permissible to carry something less than four cubits, from one *karmelit* into another; but care should be taken to dry the hands well before walking four cubits.

6. It is permissible to rub the hands in bran, even when they are wet, providing that the water is not poured upon the bran itself; but it is forbidden to rub the hands with salt, and certainly not with soap, because it melts.

7. One is not allowed to bathe on the Sabbath in water which is used exclusively for medicinal purposes, for it is obvious that one is using it as a cure. This is forbidden only when one lingers in it too long, but when one stays there only a short while, it is permissible, for it is clear that one was only cooling oneself. As to the hot springs of Tiberias, if people bathe in them exclusively as a cure, then bathing in them as a cure is forbidden, even when one does not linger in them.

CHAPTER 87

The Resting of Cattle on the Sabbath

1. It is written (Exodus 23:12): "That thy ox and thy ass may rest." Thus the Torah admonishes us that the cattle of a Jew must rest on the Sabbath, and not only cattle, but all animals as well. Hence, we are forbidden to suffer our beasts to carry out a burden on the Sabbath. Even if the beast goes out of itself into a public premise, carrying a burden, its owner is thereby violating a Divine Command, even if it is on the beast as an ornament, it is, nevertheless, considered a burden. If, however, it is for the purpose of healing, such as a bandage on a wound, or if it is to safeguard it, then it is considered like a garment for a human being, and it is permissible to let it walk out with it. However, that which is on the beast as a special safeguard, is forbidden, even if another animal needs this special safeguard, as long as this particular animal does not need it, it is considered a burden and it is forbidden to let the animal walk out with it.

2. We may lead out a horse either with a halter or with a bridle, but not with both. We are allowed to tie the rope of the halter around its neck, and we may lead it out with it; but we must tie it loosely, so that we can easily slip our hand between the rope and the neck to restrain it, should it attempt to get away. We are allowed to handle the halter and put it on the animal, but we are not permitted to lean on the animal on the Sabbath. We must not, however, lead out an ass with an iron bit, as that is a superfluous safeguard for an ass. We are forbidden to lead out an ox or a cow with a rope around their neck, since it requires no safeguarding, unless it is in the habit of running away. A rope tied on the horse's mouth is considered a burden, inasmuch as it is not safeguarded by it, because it slips off its mouth, and it is not akin to the halter which is tied to its head.

3. Neither a horse nor any other animal may be allowed to go out on the Sabbath with a cushion on its back. An ass may be allowed to go out with a cushion to protect it from cold, because it is natural for an ass to catch cold easily. If the cushion was tied on the animal before the Sabbath, it may go out with it, because it is its outfit; but if it was not tied on before the Sabbath it may not go out with it, because it may fall off, and the owner will then be compelled to adjust it with his own hands, whereas he is not allowed to tie it on the animal on the Sabbath, because he will necessarily have to come near it and lean against it. When the ass is in the yard, one may put a cushion on him to protect him from the cold, provided he is not let out with the cushion on him. But a cushion may not be put on a horse, unless the cold is so intense that it may harm him. One is allowed to put a cushion on a horse in the summer, when flies torment him, provided one does not lean against the animal while putting it on. It is forbidden to remove the cushion on the Sabbath, either from an ass or from a horse, since the animal suffers no pain because of that.

4. It is forbidden to let an animal out with a bell on, even if it is muffled and it does not ring, and even in a town where an *eruv* (symbolical intercommunity) was established, but it is permissible to let him have the bell on in the court. If, however, the bell is not muffled and it rings, it is forbidden to have it on the animal even in the court.

5. We are permitted to lead a horse out by the rope attached to the bridle, but we must hold the rope and not let it project from our hand even as much as the length of a hand-breadth, nor should that part of the rope between our hand and the beast be as close to the ground as a hand-breadth. If the rope is very long, we should wind it around the horse's neck.

6. We are not allowed to lead out on the Sabbath, two or more animals tied together, leading them with one rope, even in a city where there is an *eruv*. We may, however, lead out many animals at one time, leading each by its rope, if it is done as prescribed in the preceding paragraph.

7. Cocks may not be let out on the Sabbath with a thread tied on to them either for the sake of identification or to prevent them from breaking dishes. However, if their feet are tied together so that they should not run away, or when two feet of a horse are tied together while grazing in the pasture so that it should not run away, it is permissible to let them go out with it, providing it is neither *akud* nor *ragul*. By *akud* is meant the tying of the foreleg to the hind leg, and by *ragul* is meant hamshackling, the bending of one of the legs upward and tying it to the neck so that it could walk only on three legs. This is forbidden even on a weekday, as it causes suffering to the animal.

8. A non-Jewish servant who rides upon the beast to water it, need not be prevented from doing it on the Sabbath. For, riding on the Sabbath

is forbidden, not because it is a burden upon the animal, for a living being carries itself (and it is forbidden only by a Rabbinical ordinance and it does not apply to the animal); the prohibition of riding applies to the man, the Jew, who may not ride on the Sabbath, but a non-Jew, is not bound by it. It is permissible even if the non-Jew puts a saddle or a garment upon the animal to ride on it, because they are subordinate to the rider, but he must not put anything else upon the beast.

9. It is permissible to tell a non-Jew to milk the cows on the Sabbath, in order to prevent cruelty to animals, as the pent up milk causes them pain. The milk, however, may not be handled on that day. Therefore, the non-Jew should put it away in a secure place. It is also permissible to tell a non-Jew to feed geese, once during the day to prevent cruelty to living things.

10. It is forbidden to lend or hire out a beast to a non-Jew, unless the owner stipulates that he must return it before the Sabbath. If it happens that he does not return it, the Jew must renounce his ownership of it before the Sabbath, even when he does it only unilaterally, in order to save himself from violating the law. It is, however, forbidden to lend or to hire cattle to a non-Jew depending on such a device.

11. One is not allowed to measure out feed to be given to one's beast on the Sabbath, but one should estimate the amount needed.

12. A bundle of hay which is not tied with a durable knot (that is, doubly knotted), may be untied on the Sabbath in order to feed it to the cattle. It is also permitted to cut hard pumpkins for the cattle, provided they have been plucked before the Sabbath. If the pumpkins are tender and can be eaten as they are, it is forbidden to cut them.

13. We are allowed to let our cattle graze upon growing grass, because the pulling up of the grass is no work for the cattle, but a pleasure. We are forbidden to let our cattle eat grass which a non-Jew has cut on the Sabbath, and was thus rendered *muktzeh* (forbidden to be handled on the Sabbath), unless they have nothing else to feed on, then it is permissible in order to relieve them of their suffering. If the cattle have nothing to drink, we may tell a non-Jew to bring water from a well situated in a *karmelit* (premise which is neither public nor private).

14. It is forbidden to hang a bag of feed on a beast, because this is merely for its comfort, so that it would not have to bend its neck, and one is forbidden to trouble oneself on the Sabbath for the comfort of a beast. It is, however, permissible to hang a feed bag on calves or foals when they are in a court, because they have short necks and it is troublesome for them to eat from the ground, but they must not be led out with it, as it is considered a burden.

15. One may not cast grain for poultry on moist ground, as some may possibly remain there and afterwards sprout forth.

16. When giving provender to cattle, we are not permitted to put it first in a sieve to sift out the chaff, but if we do not do it for that purpose, we may take the provender in a sieve and put it in the crib.

17. One who gives bran to cattle or poultry, is forbidden to put water in it, and if he has put water in it on Friday, he may not stir it on the Sabbath, but he is permitted to empty it from one vessel into another in order to mix it.

18. On the Sabbath, we are allowed to feed cattle, beasts and poultry, as it is our duty to provide them with food. But we are forbidden to trouble ourselves to provide with food those animals which are not raised by us and we are not obliged to feed them. Hence, we are forbidden to put food before doves, as they can fly out to the fields to get their food. We are allowed, however, to place food before a dog, even if it has no owner. It is in some degree a religious duty to give a dog some food, for verily, the Holy One, blessed be He, took compassion on it; for, on account of its lack of sufficient food, He caused its food to remain undigested in its stomach for three days. Some are accustomed to cast grain to the fowl on *Shabbath shirah*, the Sabbath on which the (*Shirah*) Song of Moses, (Exodus 15), is read. But it is improper to do so, since it is not our duty to provide them with food.

19. We are permitted to invite a non-Jew to dine with us on the Sabbath. Although it may not be done on a festival, for we might be obliged to prepare extra food on his account. On the Sabbath, however, no such apprehension is to be had. Moreover, it is even permissible to serve him alone, although it is not our duty to provide him with food, but since we must provide even a non-Jew with food for the sake of preserving peace, it is considered as though it were our duty to offer him food.

20. Animals, beasts, and fowl that are not yet trained to come into their cages in the evening; or even if they are trained to do so, but they happened to escape, it is forbidden to drive them into the cage or into the house; and even if they are already in the house or in the cage, it is forbidden to close the door on them, because by this act they are being caught, and it constitutes the violation of a prohibition known as "snaring."

21. If the above are already trained and domesticated and are accustomed to enter to their assigned places in the evening, but they happened to be out, and the owner is afraid lest they be stolen, he may drive them into a place of safety, but he is not allowed to touch them with his hands, because they are *muktzeh*.

22. One may not deliver an animal on the Sabbath, not even to assist it, that is, to hold the offspring that it should not fall to the ground.

23. A fresh wound which causes suffering to the animal, may be smeared with oil on the Sabbath, but when the wound is healing already then the smearing is only for the animal's comfort, it may not be done.

24. If one's beast is in pain from overfeeding on cresses, and the like, one may cause it to trot in the court on the Sabbath, so that the exercise may relieve it. If it suffers from bleeding, one may let it stand in cold water. If it needs bleeding and it is feared that it may die if it is not bled, it is permissible to tell a non-Jew to bleed it. Other remedies for it as well should be administered through a non-Jew.

Chapter 88

Muktzeh, Things Forbidden to be Handled on the Sabbath

1. Food that has been set aside, either because it is, in its present state unfit to eat except in an emergency, or because it is to be sold as merchandise; also, food which is considered fit for a dog today, although on Friday it was not intended to be served as such, for instance, cattle or fowl which have died on the Sabbath, may be handled on the Sabbath. Likewise, things that have assumed a different appearance from that of the previous day, but which are, nevertheless, still fit for some use, such as utensils that were broken on the Sabbath, but are yet partly fit for the purpose for which they were intended, as a receptacle for food or drink; also bones which were removed from the meat on the Sabbath, and are still fit for dogs—all these may be handled on the Sabbath, except whatever one rejects, such as dried out figs and raisins.

2. Food which in its present state is unfit for human consumption even in an emergency, because it requires cooking, although it is fit food for cattle or dogs, inasmuch as it will afterwards be suitable food for man, it cannot be considered as food for cattle or dogs and it may not be handled on the Sabbath. Likewise, it is forbidden to handle anything which is unfit for any use on the Sabbath, such as wood, feathers, skins, wool, flax, living animals, even those that are domesticated, the shells of nuts and eggs, and hard bones which are not even fit for dogs, and doors and windows (as it is forbidden to hang them up on the Sabbath); likewise, fragments of broken vessels which are not

fit for any further use, all these and similar things may not be handled. Nevertheless, it is permitted to remove fragments of broken glass from any place where they may cause injury.

3. Food which may not be eaten, but of which we may derive some benefit, and it is proper food for a non-Jew in its present state, such as cooked meat, and we are able to give it to a non-Jew because it belongs to us, may be handled on the Sabbath. If, however, in its present state it is not fit for a non-Jew, such as raw meat (nor can it be considered as food for dogs, since it is fit for human consumption); or if we are unable to give it to a non-Jew, because it belongs to someone else, is forbidden to be handled on the Sabbath.

4. A thing "newly born," that is, something which has originated on the Sabbath, such as ashes from a fire kindled on the Sabbath by a non-Jew, or an egg laid on the Sabbath, and juice dripping from some trees in the month of *Nisan*, and even that which has not originated on the Sabbath, but was the result of labor which may not be performed on the Sabbath, such as fruit which has fallen from a tree or which a non-Jew has plucked on the Sabbath, or milk that has been milked by a non-Jew on the Sabbath, may not be handled. But bread baked on the Sabbath by a non-Jew in a town inhabited mostly by non-Jews, and it may be assumed that it had been baked for non-Jews, may be eaten by a Jew on the Sabbath in an emergency, or if required for a religious feast.

5. Tools intended for work that may not be done on the Sabbath, such as a mortar, a grinder, a hammer, an axe, brooms, a shofar, a candlestick, a needle, whole candles whether of tallow or of wax, cotton wicks, a garment of *shatnez* (of wool and linen) which may not be worn, and all things similar to these may be handled if the object is needed, as for instance, a hammer to crack nuts, an axe to cleave provisions, a needle to remove a splinter (if, however, its eye or point is missing, it is forbidden to be handled). It is likewise permitted to handle the above objects, if one needs the place they occupy, and as long as one handles them, either because one is permitted to do so or through inadvertence, one may then put them away wherever one pleases. If, however, one needs neither the object itself, nor the place that it occupies, such objects may not be moved or handled in order that they may not be stolen or damaged. It is likewise forbidden to handle *tefillin* on the Sabbath. If, however, they lie in an unseemly place where they might be soiled, they may be removed to a suitable place.

6. Articles set aside and not to be used because such use would impair them, such as workman's tools which one is anxious to keep in good condition, a penknife, a slaughter-knife, writing paper, notes, accounts, and letters, all of which one is anxious to keep intact; also precious utensils which one does not use at all, or any article of which one is so careful as to put it away in a special place not to make use of it, also vessels that are in one's shop for sale, even if they are culinary vessels, those which one is not in the habit of lending (otherwise they may be handled), also a purse used for keeping money, are termed "*muktzeh*, because of loss" involved in handling them, and it is, therefore, forbidden to handle them, even when the object itself or the place they occupy is needed.

7. That which is not designated as a vessel, such as wood, stones, or pieces of metal, may not be handled in any manner whatsoever, even when the object itself or the space they occupy is needed, unless it was designed for some permanent use before the Sabbath. It is likewise forbidden to take a piece of wood to pick the teeth with it. Candles which are not whole, are not considered as vessels and may not be removed in any manner whatsoever. Also a ladder is not considered a vessel.

8. A vessel that is used for permissible work, or even for both permissible and forbidden, such as pots, and even unclean vessels (for it is permitted to handle on the Sabbath what is set aside because of its being repulsive), may be handled on the Sabbath even for the protection of the vessel, not to be stolen or broken, but it must not be handled if there is no need for its handling. One, however, is permitted to handle the Holy Scriptures and food, even for no purpose.

9. Just as it is forbidden to handle what is *muktzeh*, or that which has originated on the Sabbath, even so is it forbidden to place a vessel underneath those objects that they may drop therein, for by doing this, one renders the vessel immovable, and it is considered as though one had affixed it there with clay. However, it is permissible to bend a basket before the young fowl, in order that they may walk in and out of it, as it will be permissible to handle the basket when the fowl will not be in it. If the fowl were on the basket at twilight on Friday, it is forbidden to handle the basket the whole day.

10. It is permissible to handle the soil or the sand which one has heaped up in the corner of the court or of the house, for, the fact that it is heaped up, indicates that it has been prepared for use. If, however, the sand or the earth is scattered about, it becomes subordinate to the ground, and it may not be handled. If one has cut off the branch of a tree before the Sabbath for the

purpose of chasing flies away, or the like, one is allowed to use it on the Sabbath, since he has designed it for that purpose it became a "vessel." However, it is forbidden to take out a twig from the broom, because it may not be handled, even if it has been taken out by a non-Jew.

11. Boards belonging to a householder which are not for sale, may be handled, but if they belong to an artisan they may not be handled, unless it was one's intention on Friday to make use of them on the Sabbath.

12. All things that may not be handled on the Sabbath as being *muktzeh*, may be touched if they are not moved by the touch. Hence, it is permissible to touch candlesticks, even if the candles burn in them. It is likewise permissible to remove an object that may be handled when lying upon an object that is *muktzeh*. But it is forbidden to touch a hanging chandelier, as this may be shaken by mere touch. It is permissible to cover an article that is *muktzeh* with an article that may be handled to protect it from rain or something similar.

13. In an indirect manner, it is permissible to handle an object that is *muktzeh*. Hence, if one has inadvertently left a thing that is *muktzeh* upon a vessel, or if it happened to fall on it on the Sabbath, then if one needs the vessel or the space it occupies, one is permitted to shake it off, or one may carry it to another place and shake it off there. This also applies when one needs the garment in which one has left a purse with money, but it may not be done solely for the sake of the thing which is *muktzeh*. If before the Sabbath, one has purposely placed an object which is *muktzeh* upon a vessel, the latter becomes a base for the forbidden object (and it may not be moved on the Sabbath).

14. However, if one has no need for the vessel which may be handled, one is not allowed to remove it if anything which is *muktzeh* rests on it. Therefore, one is forbidden to carry a child in one's arms, even in a private premise, if the child has in his hand a stone or any other object that is *muktzeh*. If, however, the child is very much attached to the person, and it would get sick if the person refuses to pick it up and at the same time it is impossible to throw away the object from the child's hand as it would cry, in such an event he is permitted to take the child in his arms when in a private premise. It is forbidden to hold the child's hand even in a private premise if he holds a coin, although the child is able to walk by itself, and is much attached to the person. For it may happen that the coin will fall from the child's hand, and the person, forgetting that it is the Sabbath, will pick it up, thus handling directly a thing that is *muktzeh*. This may not be done, even in the case of possible illness of the child, as long as there is no possible loss of life.

15. It is forbidden to move a dead body on the Sabbath, but it is permissible to remove the pillow from beneath the corpse in order that it shall not become malodorous, providing no limb is moved thereby. If the mouth

of the corpse keeps opening, it is permissible to fasten the jaws that they open no further, but not in a manner as to close what is already open, as one would thereby move a limb of the dead.

16. If a fire broke out, and it is feared that the corpse will be burned, it is permissible to carry it out by means of putting an object that may be handled upon the corpse or at its side, such as an article of food, and carry them out together. If an article of food is not available, a vessel or a garment which may be handled should be laid upon the corpse. If this also is unavailable, it may be carried out by itself. In any event it is permissible to carry the corpse out only where carrying is allowed, but where carrying is forbidden, it should be carried out by a non-Jew.

17. Any repulsive object, like excrements or the vomit of human beings or fowl, if found either in the house or in the court where people live, may be removed on the Sabbath to a dunghill. When a vessel for the collection of excrement, or urine is removed, it may be put back in its original place as long as it is still in one's hand, in accordance with the rule that while anything that is *muktzeh* is in one's hand, it may be carried and placed in any place that one sees fit. However, after one puts it away, it may not be handled, because it is extremely repulsive (and it is worse than the ordinary *muktzeh* because of repulsiveness). But if it is needed in deference to some person, it may be replaced. Likewise, if it is fit to put in it water for animals, it may be replaced.

18. On the Sabbath, it is permissible to place a vessel beneath dripping water, and when the vessel is filled, it may be emptied and put back in that place, provided the drippings are suitable for washing purposes. If, however, the water is filthy, no vessel may be put there, because it is forbidden to make a receptacle for filthy matter on the Sabbath. Nevertheless, if a person transgressed and did collect it in a vessel and it is in a spot which is repulsive to him, he is permitted to remove it.

Chapter 89

Concerning a Base for Things Forbidden

1. If on Friday one has placed a thing that is *muktzeh* upon one of his vessels, intending to let it lie there at the ushering in of the Sabbath, the vessel becomes a base for the forbidden article and it is forbidden to handle it. Even if the article that is *muktzeh* is removed from there on the Sabbath, since it lay there in the twilight on Friday, the vessel became the base for the forbidden article, and it must not be handled the entire Sabbath-day, even when the vessel itself or the place it occupies is needed.

2. If on the ushering in of the Sabbath, there lay, in addition to the forbidden article, something that may be handled, and the vessel thus became the base for both, then if the permissible object is of greater value to the owner, he may handle it, but if the forbidden object is of greater value to him, he may not handle it. Therefore, it is best to place the *ḥallot* on the

table before the twilight on Friday, so that the cover and the table become a base for the *ḥallot* and the candles, and it will be permissible to handle them. If it is not done so, the cover and the table become a base for the forbidden thing only (the candles), and may not be handled. Nevertheless, in cases of extreme emergency, as when a burning candle fell on the table and must be shaken off, one may rely on the opinion of some authorities who hold that a thing becomes a base only when one intends to let the article that is *muktzeh* remain there the entire Sabbath-day, and since it is customary to have the candlesticks removed in the morning by a non-Jew, it is no longer considered a base.

3. If one has money in a pocket sewed in one's garment, one is permitted to handle the garment on the Sabbath, because only the pocket became a base for the money and the pocket is subordinate to the garment. However, one should not wear such a garment even in one's house, lest one goes out with it in a public premise. It is forbidden to move a table, in the drawer of which there is money, because the drawer is a vessel in itself and is not subordinate to the table.

4. A vessel does not become a base, unless the article that is *muktzeh* lay on it in the twilight on Friday, but if it has been put on it thereafter, it does not become a base and it is permissible to handle the vessel even when the article that is *muktzeh* still lies on it. Hence, it is permitted to shake the table or the tablecloth to remove from it the bones and shells, when the cover and the table have not become a base for the candles (as has been stated in paragraph 2, above).

5. Nor does the vessel become a base, unless one puts on it the article that is *muktzeh* intentionally to let it remain there at the twilight on Friday. If, however, one has left it there inadvertently, or if it has fallen there by itself, it does not thereby become a base.

6. Nor does it become a base, unless it is his own vessel, but if one puts an article that is *muktzeh* upon somebody else's vessel, it does not thereby become a base, for one cannot render someone else's article unfit for use without his consent.

CHAPTER 90

Doing Things That Are Not Actual Work—Work Through A Non-Jew

1. There are certain things forbidden on the Sabbath although they neither have any resemblance to work, nor do they in any way lead to the performance of work. Why, then, are they forbidden? Because it is written (Isaiah 58:13): "If thou turn away thy foot because of the Sabbath, from pursuing thy business on My holy day; and shalt honor it, not doing thy wonted ways, nor pursuing thy business, nor speaking thereof." Our Rabbis,

of blessed memory, have explained, that by "And shalt honor it, not doing thy wonted ways," is meant, that the manner of thy walking on the Sabbath should not be the same as on a weekday. Therefore, it is forbidden to run on the Sabbath. But for the sake of performing a precept, it is permissible to run (because it is written, "Thy wonted ways," which implies, *thy* ways are forbidden, but the ways of Heaven are permissible); and in such a case it is even meritorious to run.

2. From the words, "Nor pursuing thy business," our Rabbis, of blessed memory, have inferred, "Thy business is forbidden thee, even when thou doest no actual work;" thus one is forbidden to survey his property to ascertain what work there is to be done there on the morrow. It is also forbidden to walk through the town in order to find a horse, or a boat, or a wagon which he can hire after the Sabbath, if it is obvious that he went there for that purpose. But one is permitted to guard either his own property or that of his neighbor.

3. On the Sabbath, one is forbidden to walk to the end of the Sabbath boundary, or even a lesser distance, and wait there until dark, in order to complete his journey sooner at the conclusion of the Sabbath, for it is obvious that he has walked there principally for that purpose. This, however, is forbidden only if he goes there to do something which may not possibly be done on the Sabbath, as to hire workmen, or to pick fruit, or to bring in fruit which is *muktzeh*, as there is no way at all by which the performance of these things may be made legitimate on the Sabbath. One is, however, permitted to wait at the Sabbath boundary line, in order to bring in his cattle, as that would have been permissible even on the Sabbath, if there were houses built up to that spot no farther than seventy cubits (one hundred and five feet) apart from each other. It is likewise permissible to bring fruit that was plucked and which is not *muktzeh*, as this also would have been permitted even on the Sabbath in case the entire route were closed in by partitions. A person is also permitted to go to his orchard on the Sabbath, within the limit of the Sabbath boundary, in order to pluck the fruit on the close of the Sabbath, as it is not obvious that he has gone there for that particular purpose; he might have gone there for his pleasure, or to look for his beast that went astray, and after being there he bethought himself of remaining until dark in order to pluck his fruit.

4. From the phrase, "Nor speaking thereof," our Rabbis, of blessed memory, have inferred that one's speech on the Sabbath should not be the same as on weekdays. Hence, one is forbidden to say, "I will do this thing tomorrow," or "I will buy this article tomorrow," This, however, applies only to things that may not be done on the Sabbath under any circumstances; but if it may be done in a certain way, although that way does not present itself now, it is permissible. One may, therefore, say, "I will go to yonder place tomorrow," provided one does not say it in a way indicating that he will ride there, nor should he speak too much about it. It is likewise forbidden to indulge too much in idle talk. And it is forbidden to relate on the Sabbath, anything which causes grief. One is forbidden to make mental calculations on the Sabbath, whether of future or past transactions which one needs to

ascertain; to figure for instance, "So much have I spent on that building to pay the workmen," and he still has to pay so much to them, so that it is of practical benefit to him to ascertain the exact figures. One is, however, allowed to make calculations for which one has no need. But one should not overdo it, as on the Sabbath it is forbidden to indulge too much in idle pursuits.

5. Inasmuch as it is written, "Thy business," our Rabbis, of blessed memory, have inferred that only personal business is forbidden, but religious affairs are permitted. Hence, one may wait at the Sabbath boundary line until dark for the purpose of performing a religious duty. It is also permissible to attend to matters of public interest on the Sabbath, for instance, to visit a governor or a council of officials to plead for the people; for, matters pertaining to public welfare are like religious deeds. One may speak to a teacher with reference to teaching one's child the Scriptures or even a trade, as the latter also is a religious duty, because if one has no trade wherewith to earn a livelihood, he may turn to robbery. However, it is forbidden to hire the teacher on the Sabbath, for hiring is a violation of a Rabbinical ordinance, and it is not permitted even for the purpose of fulfilling a religious duty. Only that which violates the spirit of "Not pursuing thy business, nor speaking thereof," is permissible for the sake of a precept. It is permissible to make a public announcement of a loss, on the Sabbath, because restoring a lost article to its owner is a religious duty.

6. From the phrase, "Nor speaking thereof," our Rabbis, of blessed memory, have inferred that only speaking is forbidden, but thinking is permissible. Hence, one may think of one's affairs on the Sabbath. Nevertheless, for the sake of Sabbath joy, it is meritorious not to give one's business any thought, but it should seem to one as though all of one's work is done. This is the meaning of the Biblical verse (Exodus 20:9): "Six days shalt thou work and do all thy labor." Is it possible for a man to do *all* his work in six days? But it means, that on the Sabbath, a man should think that all his work has been completed; there is no greater joy than this. One should especially avoid thinking of things that may cause worry and anxiety.

7. On the Sabbath one may say to a workman: "Do you think you will be able to see me this evening?" Although the workman understands that he wants to see him in the evening in order to hire him to do some work, but only a direct proposal is forbidden. One, however, should not say: "Be ready for me this evening," as that is like saying in plain words that one desires to hire him.

8. If one hires a Jewish workman to guard anything for him, the workman is forbidden to take any pay for the Sabbath by itself. If, however, he has been hired for a week or a month, he may take pay for the entire period, including the Sabbath.

9. On the Sabbath, one is forbidden to make a gift to anyone, unless the recipient needs it on the Sabbath. It is also forbidden to give anything as a pledge, unless it is necessary for the fulfillment of a precept, or it is required for the Sabbath; but even in this event, one should not say: "Here is the pledge," but simply give it to him.

10. On the Sabbath, it is forbidden to peruse ordinary documents, such as bills, accounts, or personal letters. Even when one does not read them aloud but merely thinking of the contents, it is, nevertheless, forbidden. For, thinking of business is permissible only when it is not obvious that one is thinking of it, but in this case it is apparent that one is thinking of it, one is, therefore, violating the injunction, "Nor pursuing thy business." If a letter is received and its contents is unknown, we are permitted to look at it, because it may contain something of vital personal interest. But the words should not be read aloud. If, however, we know that the letter relates only to business matters, we are not allowed even to peruse it silently. It is also forbidden to handle it, as it is a thing which is *muktzeh*.

11. If a wall or a tablet has drawings or portraits on it, and underneath is an inscription: "This is that man's drawing," or "This is that man's portrait," one must not read this inscription on the Sabbath. It is even forbidden to look at it without reading it. Likewise, books on war, histories of various nationalities, secular poetry and fables, such as the book Emanuel, and needless to add erotic novels, must not be read on the Sabbath, and it is even forbidden to peruse them without uttering the words. These works must not be read even on weekdays, because they are in the category of, "The seat of the scornful" (Psalms 1:1). This is true even if the books are written in the sacred tongue (Hebrew). Concerning the reading of erotic novels, there is an additional prohibition in that it arouses in the reader lecherous desires. However, history books which have a moral and are conducive to the fear of the Almighty, like the book of Josephus, may be read on the Sabbath, even if they are written in a secular language. Nevertheless, it is improper to read too much of these.

12. It is forbidden to measure anything that we may need for the Sabbath, unless it is essential for the performance of a precept.

13. When we are faced with sustaining a loss, we may discuss ways and means to avert it, either with a Jew or with a non-Jew.

14. Whatever we ourselves are forbidden to do on the Sabbath, we may not tell a non-Jew to do it for us, because telling a non-Jew to perform labor is a violation of a Rabbinical ordinance (known in Jewish law as *shebut*). We are forbidden even to hint to a non-Jew that we desire the performance of such a service. It is forbidden even to tell a non-Jew before the Sabbath to do work for us on the Sabbath. It is likewise forbidden to tell a non-Jew on the Sabbath, to do some work after the Sabbath. This, however, is forbidden

not because of *shebut*, since the work is done when it is permissible; but because it violates the spirit of, "Nor pursuing thy business." Therefore, if it is necessary for the sake of a precept, it is permissible.

15. If a non-Jew, of his own accord, wishes to perform some work for us, we must prevent him from doing it. If a non-Jew for instance, wishes to snuff off the candles, so that they may burn more brightly, we must prevent him from doing it.

16. If we are threatened with a loss, for instance, a cask of wine has sprung a leak, we may call in a non-Jew even when we are certain that the non-Jew will repair the damage and even if it involves real work, provided we carefully avoid talking to him in a way that sounds like a request to repair it; but we say in his presence: "Whoever will save me from this loss, will not lose anything." This, however, should not be done, unless it may result in a great loss.

17. For the sake of performing a precept, or for the sake of a slightly ill person, a non-Jew may be told to do a thing which is not real work, and is forbidden only as a *shebut*. Relying upon this, a practice has sprung up to send a non-Jew for beer, or other things to be used on the Sabbath, even though there is no *eruv* (intercommunity) in that locality. This is permitted only in case of emergency, when one has nothing else to drink. But for the mere gratification of one's pleasure, it is not permissible. Not only is it forbidden to tell a non-Jew to bring anything from outside the Sabbath boundary, but it is even forbidden to make use on the Sabbath of whatever has been brought already. Some authorities hold, that to prevent a great loss, as to remove merchandise so that it be not damaged by rain, it is permissible to do so through a non-Jew. One may rely upon this opinion in a case of great loss.

18. When it is cold, we are allowed to tell a non-Jew to make the stove, because all are subject to catch cold; but if it is not very urgent, it should be avoided. It is forbidden to tell a non-Jew to make the stove on Sabbath afternoon, so that it may be warm at night.

19. It is forbidden to send a non-Jew outside the Sabbath boundary limit to summon the relatives of a dead man, or one to deliver a funeral oration.

20. If a non-Jew brings grain to a Jew on the Sabbath, in payment of his debt, the Jew may give him the key to the warehouse, and let the non-Jew measure and count what he puts in there, because the non-Jew is doing the work for himself, as the grain does not belong to the Jew until after it is measured. Furthermore, he may stay there and see that he is not being cheated, providing he does not speak concerning the transaction. If, however,

the non-Jew delivered the Jew's grain, the Jew must not tell him to unload it and put it in the warehouse. Even if he wishes to unload it of his own accord, he must prevent him from doing it.

21. When a non-Jew is engaged in making cheese from his own milk, a Jew may watch the process of milking and cheese making to see that it is prepared in accordance with the Jewish dietary laws, so that he could buy it after the Sabbath, although the non-Jew makes it purposely for the sake of selling it to the Jew, because the cheese still belongs to the non-Jew who makes it for his own benefit. The Jew may even tell him to make it, because a Jew is allowed to say to a non-Jew, "Do your work," although he, too, will derive some benefit from it.

22. If a non-Jew had bought some merchandise from a Jew, and he comes to take it on the Sabbath, he should be prevented from doing it, if possible.

23. If one has *Jahrzeit* on the Sabbath and forgot to light the *Jahrzeit* candle, one may tell a non-Jew to light it on Friday at twilight, but not on the Sabbath.

CHAPTER 91

One in Pain, and One not Critically Ill

1. One who is slightly ill, and is able to walk about as if he were in good health, is forbidden to take any treatment, even if there is no work involved in it. He should neither rub himself with oil, nor let another one do it, be he even a non-Jew.

2. Food and beverages which healthy people consume, may be eaten and drunk on the Sabbath as a remedy, although they are harmful in certain respects, and it is obvious that one is partaking of them as a remedy. But anything which healthy persons do not eat or drink may not be partaken of medicinally. It is permissible to eat sweets or drink a raw egg to sweeten the voice; since one has no sore throat, it cannot be considered as a cure.

3. One who has an ordinary toothache and is not in great pain, must not take vinegar or some other beverage in his mouth as a remedy, and then eject it, but he shall either swallow it, or dip some bread in it, and eat it in the usual manner. Likewise, one who has a sore throat, shall not gargle it with liquid, but he must swallow it, and if he is cured thereby, good and well.

4. One who has pains in his loins, or the like, also one who has scabs on his head, is not permitted to smear it with oil on the Sabbath, because since in our regions, massaging with oil is done only for medicinal purposes, it is obvious that one is using it as a cure.

5. One who coughs because of a weak heart, and whose remedy is to suck milk from a goat, may do so on the Sabbath (because sucking is like an act of loosening something in an unusual manner, and Rabbis have not forbidden it when a man is suffering).

6. One who has abdominal pains may apply a vessel from which hot water has been emptied, although it still retains the heat. One is also allowed to warm up some clothes and put them on the abdomen.

7. One who has injured his hand or his foot may apply wine to stop the bleeding, but not vinegar, because vinegar on account of its strength is akin to medicine. If he is a delicate person, he may not use wine either, because in this case it is a styptic like vinegar. If the injury is on the back of the hand or on the foot, or if it has been caused by a metallic object, any remedy may be applied to it (as provided for in chapter 92:5, below).

8. One who has sore eyes must not apply to them tasteless saliva (that is, before one has tasted any food), because it is evident that he is doing it as a remedy. If, however, he is unable to open his eyes, he may moisten them with tasteless saliva, because this is not applied as a remedy but simply to enable him to open his eyes.

9. One who suffers pain because of overeating, may stick his finger in his throat in order to vomit.

10. On a wound which is not serious, one is not allowed to place a plaster on the Sabbath, even if the plaster was made on Friday, nor may one apply anything medicinally, but one may put something on it to guard it against scratching. If a plaster has been on it since Friday, one may raise it slightly on each side and cleanse the wound, but one must not wipe the plaster itself, as this constitutes the act of plastering. If the plaster has fallen from the wound to the ground, one may not restore it, but if it has fallen on a vessel, one may restore it. If the wound causes great pain, one may tell a non-Jew to restore the plaster, but one may not tell him to make a plaster on the Sabbath, because plastering is a type of work forbidden by the Mosaic Law, and it is even forbidden to be done through a non-Jew, unless the entire body is in pain.

11. We are not allowed to put a cloth upon a bleeding wound, because the blood colors the cloth, and especially are we forbidden to apply a red cloth, because we improve it by this. We are also forbidden to press a wound to squeeze blood from it, but we may bathe it in water or in wine to stop the flow of blood, and then bandage it. If the blood does not stop flowing through the bathing, we may put cobwebs on it, and then bandage it. Some authorities have scruples about this, because cobwebs have curative qualities; therefore, if possible, we should have it treated by a non-Jew.

12. One who enlarges the opening of an abcess, as is generally done by physicians, is guilty of violating a Sabbath law, since this is the practice of physicians. But if he opens it only for the purpose of discharging the pus which causes him pain, and he does not mind if it closes up again, it is permissible. One is allowed to pierce it with a needle, or the like, but not with his nails, because he might thereby tear off some of the skin, which constitutes a violation. If possible, even the piercing with a needle should be done through a non-Jew, since it is likely that he would want the wound to remain open, so that the pus may come out later, too.

13. If the opening of an incision on the arm has closed up a little, we may not insert some legume in it so that it may open again, since it is our intention that it should remain open. However, we may put on it a plaster that has been prepared on Friday, because the plaster is put on only for the purpose of protection. If, however, we know that the plaster will extract pus or blood, we are not allowed to put it on. Also, if we know that by wiping the wound, some blood or pus will come out, we are not allowed to do it. (This cannot be compared to the opening of an abcess, because in an abcess the blood and the pus are confined to one spot and no wound is made when it is squeezed out, but in this case the pus and the blood are soaked into the flesh, and when it is squeezed out, it makes a bruise.)

14. On a wound that has healed, one may put a plaster that has been made on Friday, because it is put on only for the purpose of protecting it. It is permissible to remove the skin that peels off the wound.

15. On the Sabbath, we are allowed to remove a splinter with a needle, but we must be careful not to draw blood, as that would be making a bruise.

16. If a person is confined to bed owing to sickness, although it is not critical, or if he feels pain through his entire body, although he is walking about, is the same as if he were bed-ridden, and a non-Jew may be told to prepare a remedy and to cook food for him. He is allowed to eat on the Sab-

bath what the non-Jew cooks, since the cooking of a non-Jew was permissible for him.

17. He is allowed to take either solid or liquid medicines, and he may also prepare the medicine himself or through someone else providing, however, that it does not involve work that is forbidden even by Rabbinical ordinance (*shebut*). Whatever requires the violation even of a Rabbinical ordinance, should be done through a non-Jew. In the absence of a non-Jew, a Jew may do it, but only if it merely involves the violation of a Rabbinical ordinance, and it is done in a different manner than it is done on a weekday.

18. If a non-Jewish physician comes to vaccinate a child, the Jew should offer him compensation to postpone the vaccination till after the Sabbath. But if it must be done on the Sabbath, the Jew should not hold the child, but a non-Jew should hold it.

CHAPTER 92

One Who is Critically Ill—Forced to Transgress a Precept

1. Like all the Divine Commands, the Sabbath laws are suspended when a human life is in danger. Hence, it is mandatory to desecrate the Sabbath for the sake of a person who is critically ill if he is a person of good character, although he is occasionally tempted to transgress a law, and even if that person is only an infant one day old. If a sick person will not allow the desecration of the Sabbath for his sake, he should be compelled to yield. For it is a grave sin to carry piety to the point of idiocy and refuse a cure because it would violate a law. Concerning such a one, it is written (Genesis 9:5): "And surely the blood of your lives will I require." Indeed, he who readily desecrates the Sabbath for the sake of one who is critically ill, deserves praise. Even if a non-Jew happens to be present, such work should be done preferably by a Jew. He who desecrates the Sabbath for the sake of one who is critically ill, even if his efforts prove unnecessary or fruitless, is sure to receive a reward; for instance, if the physician has said that the sick person needs one fig, and nine men have plucked one fig each for the sick man, they have all earned a reward from the Almighty, blessed be His name, even if the patient has recovered from the first fig. This applies to every case of danger to human life; even when it is doubtful whether or not human life is endangered, it is mandatory to disregard the Sabbath laws and perform any forbidden work that is deemed needful. There is nothing that supersedes the saving of human life. For the Torah was given to live by it, as it is said (Leviticus 18:5): "That he may live with them," and not to die on account

of them. Except the laws prohibiting idolatry, incest, and bloodshed for which one is bound to give up one's life in order not to violate them.

2. If anyone declares that a certain person is critically ill, and no competent physician is present to contradict his statement, the statement is sufficient to violate the Sabbath; even if one does not make a positive statement, but says: "I believe that the Sabbath should be desecrated for that man's sake," he should be heeded, and the Sabbath laws should be disregarded, as any law must be suspended when even there is only a possible danger to human life. If two physicians disagree; one saying that the patient is critically ill and requires a certain medicine, and the other physician maintains that he does not require it, or if the patient himself says that he does not require it, we must consider the patient sufficiently ill to violate the Sabbath laws for his sake. If the sick person says that he requires a certain remedy, and the physician says that he does not require it, we must heed the sick person; if, however, the physician says that the remedy will harm the patient, then we must heed the physlcian.

3. If an experienced physician, or any other competent person says, that although the sick person is in no immediate danger, but the illness may become critical unless a certain remedy is administered, even if the patient himself says that he does not require it, the physician should be heeded and the Sabbath laws should be disregarded. If the physician says that if a certain remedy will not be applied he will surely die, but if it is applied there is a chance that he may survive, the Sabbath laws should be disregarded for his sake.

4. It is permitted to desecrate the Sabbath for any injury or swelling in the interior of the body, that is, from the lips inward, the teeth included, nor does it require the opinion of an expert. Thus, even if no competent persons are available, and the sufferer himself says nothing, everything generally done on weekdays must be done for him. If, however, it is known that according to the nature of the illness, it is possible to wait, then the Sabbath laws should not be disregarded. General pains are not considered as injuries, but one who has a severe toothache so that his whole body aches by it, a non-Jew may be asked to extract it.

5. A wound on the back of the hand or on the back of the foot, or any wound caused by a metal object or an ulcer at the end of the rectum, or if one has swallowed a leech, or if one has been bitten by a mad dog or a reptile, even if it is doubtful whether it is poisonous or not, or one who has a very high fever—for all these the Sabbath must be desecrated. But, for an ordinary fever, the Sabbath laws must not be disregarded, but should be attended by a non-Jew.

6. Bloodletting should be performed immediately on anyone who had an attack of high blood pressure. If one whose blood was let, has caught cold, a fire should be made for him, even if it happens in the *Tammuz* season (summer months).

7. If a person has pains in both eyes, or pus in one eye, or if his eyes are watering or bleeding, or if other matter oozes from them which may endanger his sight, the Sabbath should be disregarded for his sake.

8. If a person who is critically ill requires meat and only forbidden meat is obtainable, an animal should be slaughtered for his sake on the Sabbath, in order not to feed him with forbidden meat, for it is feared that if the patient will find out that he had eaten forbidden meat, he might be nauseated by the thought of it. But if there is no danger of causing nausea, as in the case of a child, or if one who is demented, forbidden meat should be used and no animal slaughtered on the Sabbath.

9. A healthy person is not allowed to eat the food that was cooked on the Sabbath for a sick man, but he may eat it immediately on the close of the Sabbath, if it was cooked by a Jew.

10. If one is forced temporarily to transgress a precept, be it even a severe offense, the Sabbath laws should not be violated in order to save him from committing the transgression. If, however, a person is forced to apostatize and become alienated from the people of Israel, be it even a minor, we are in duty bound to exert all our efforts to save him, even if it becomes necessary to violate Scriptural Sabbath laws, just as we are bound to do for one who is critically ill, for it is written (Exodus 31:16): "And the children of Israel shall observe the Sabbath;" said the Torah: "Desecrate one Sabbath for his sake, so that he might be enabled to observe many Sabbaths." Even if it is doubtful whether our efforts will be successful, still the Sabbath must be desecrated for his sake, as it is done in the case of doubtful life-saving. However, for a transgressor who wilfully wishes to become an apostate, the Sabbath must not be desecrated by violating a Scriptural law, for since he does it deliberately, we do not in such a case say to a man "sin, so that your neighbor might remain blameless." But when it involves only a violation of a Rabbinical ordinance, for instance, to go beyond the Sabbath boundary, or to ride on horseback, or in a wagon, or to handle money, or other such interdictions, it is permissible according to some authorities.

CHAPTER 93

Laws Concerning Childbirth

1. As soon as a woman begins to feel the pangs of childbirth, whether or not she is certain of it, an obstetrician should be brought immediately, even from a place many miles away.

2. A woman at childbirth is considered as one cirtically ill; and the Sabbath laws should be disregarded for her sake in providing all she requires. If, however, it can be done in a different manner than on a weekday or by a non-Jew, it should be done so. As soon as she is in travail, or as soon as there is a flow of blood, or as soon as she is unable to walk, she is considered as a woman at childbirth. A woman who has a miscarriage forty days after her immersion, is governed by the same laws which apply to a woman at childbirth

3. During the first three days of a woman's confinement, the Sabbath laws are waived for her sake, even though she does not consider it necessary. Thereafter until the seventh day, if she has no other pains, than the usual pains that follow childbirth, the Sabbath laws are disregarded for her sake only when she says that she requires it, but not otherwise. These days are calendar days, so that the first day of childbirth does not necessarily consist of twenty-four hours. Thus, if she has given birth on a Wednesday towards evening (before sunset), Friday will complete the three day period, and if she has given birth on the Sabbath towards evening, the coming Friday will complete the seven day period. If, however, the woman is weak and there is any possible danger, it is not considered wrong if one counts the days from the actual time of childbirth.

4. After the seven days, the Sabbath should not be violated for her, even if she says that she requires it. However, until the thirtieth day, she is considered as a person who is ill but not critically, and all necessary work should be done for her through a non-Jew. If a non-Jew is not available, a Jew may make a fire to warm the house, even in the period of *Tammuz* (summer months), because as regards to catching cold, she is on the critical list up to thirty days.

5. It is permissible to bathe a new-born infant, cut the umbilical cord, straighten out the limbs, and do everything that is required. But if it is a non-viable infant, when it was born, for instance, at eight months, it is forbidden to handle it, but the mother should bend over to suckle it, because the pent up milk would cause her pain.

CHAPTER 94

Inter-community of Courts

1. Two or more Jews who share one court, each living in an apartment by himself, may not carry anything from the house into the court, or from the court into the house, or from one house into the other. Even if they do not need to pass the court, as for instance, when there is a door or a window between the two houses they are forbidden to carry anything from one house into the other, and it is their duty to establish an *eruv* (an inter-community of courts).

2. The tenants of two courts that have a door between them, may establish, if they so desire, a separate *eruv* for each court, thus making it legal for the tenants to carry things in their own court. They are, however, forbidden to carry vessels which are in the house during the Sabbath, from one court into another. All the tenants of both courts can, if they so desire, establish one *eruv*, which will enable them to carry objects from one court into another even such vessels that were in the house during the Sabbath. If there is between the courts even a window, which measures no less than four hand-breadths (sixteen inches) wide and four hand-breadths high, and it is within ten hand-breadths above the ground and it has no lattice, the tenants of both courts may also establish an *eruv* in common, otherwise they cannot make a joint *eruv*. If there is a window between two houses, even if it is higher than ten hand-breadths above the ground, the tenants of both houses may establish an *eruv* in common (because a house is considered as filled, and the window is considered as less than ten hand-breadths from the floor.)

3. If there are two courts, one inside the other, and the tenants of the inner court have no other means of exit than through the outer court, if the tenants of both courts so choose, they may establish one *eruv* together. If they have not made a joint *eruv*, then if the tenants of the inner court alone made an *eruv*, they are allowed to carry in their own court, and the tenants of the outer court are forbidden to carry anything in theirs. If only the tenants of the outer court have made an *eruv*, then the *eruv* is of no avail to them, for since the tenants of the inner court have a right-of-way through the outer court, they curtail the use of the court by the outer tenants. The foregoing is true only when the tenants of the inner court have made no *eruv*, for since they are restricting one another in their own place, it is "a foot that is restricted in its own place" (that is, they may not carry anything where they are), and as such it has the effect of causing restrictions also in some other place. If, however, they too have made an *eruv* and they are allowed to carry in their own court, then it constitutes "a foot which may move about in its own place," and they impose no restriction on the tenants of the outer court. If only one Jewish tenant lives in the inner court, since he is not restricted in his own court, he cannot restrict the tenants of the outer court. If two tenants live in the inner court and have made no *eruv*, although only one tenant lives in the outer court, since the former are restricted in their own place, they also restrict the single tenant.

4. If a house has an upper story with a balcony through which the tenants descend into the court, and from the court into the street, it is governed by the same laws that apply to two courts, one inside the other, the balcony being considered as the inner court.

5. If two tenants occupy separate apartments in a house with a common vestibule serving as the entrance to both apartments, they are forbidden to

carry anything into the vestibule from their apartments. If one apartment is so divided that the occupant of the inner room has no other exit than the door of the outer room which leads into the court, nothing may be carried from one of these rooms into the other until an *eruv* has been established.

6. How is an *eruv* best established? On Friday, towards evening, one of the tenants takes a whole loaf of his own bread, and makes all the other tenants of the court acquire a share in it by handing it to another tenant, and saying in whatever language he understands: "Take this loaf and acquire a share in it on behalf of all the Jews dwelling in this court (*or*, in these courts)." The latter then takes the loaf and raises it a hand-breadth. Then the one who establishes the *eruv* takes it from him and says the benediction: "Blessed art Thou, O Lord our God, King of the universe, who hath sanctified us by His commandments, and hath commanded us concerning the precept of *eruv;*" adding: "By virtue of this *eruv* it shall be permissible for us to take out and in from the houses into the court and from the court into the houses and from one house into another, for us and for all the Jews who dwell in the houses of this court." Since all the tenants have acquired a share in this loaf and at the beginning of the Sabbath, the loaf is in the house of the one who has made the *eruv*, his dwelling is considered as the dwelling of all tenants, and the carrying of objects from the houses into the court and from the court into the houses and in the court itself becomes permissible.

7. It is essential that the maker of the *eruv* should grant the tenants proprietary rights through a third party. He should, therefore, not grant it through his own minor son and daughter, even if they do not eat at his table, because they are considered as his own self; but he may grant it through another minor (for with regard to Rabbinical regulations, a minor may acquire rights for another). If possible, he should not grant such rights through his own wife whom he supports, nor through his adult son and daughter who eat at his table, for according to some authorities, they too, are considered as his own self. If there is no other person present, he may grant it through them. However, all authorities agree that a father may grant proprietary rights through his son who is married, even though he eats at his father's table.

8. What is the legal size of the *eruv?* If there are eighteen tenants or less, its legal size is no less than that of a fig (about one-third of an egg) for each and every tenant, excepting the one who makes the *eruv* and puts it in his house (for, since he lives there, he needs no other token to establish his residence). If there are more than eighteen tenants, be they even one thousand, one loaf, enough for two meals, that is, the size of eighteen figs, which

is equivalent to six eggs is sufficient. Other authorities hold that it is the equivalent of eight eggs (according to their opinion, then, a fig is equivalent to one-third and one-ninth of an egg).

9. It is essential that the one who makes the *eruv* should not mind if the food used for the *eruv* is eaten by a neighbor, otherwise the *eruv* is void. One should, therefore, take care not to make the *eruv* with food that has been prepared for the Sabbath.

10. The *eruv* must be placed where everyone of the tenants on whose behalf it has been made, could enter there at the twilight on Friday. Therefore, if in the place where the *eruv* has been deposited, or in the adjoining apartment, there was a dead person, God forbid, and one of the tenants happens to be a *Kohen,* who is forbidden to enter the place where the *eruv* rests at twilight, the *eruv* is rendered void.

11. The *eruv* should be established every Friday, and the loaf of bread used for it may be cut up and eaten on the Sabbath, (as is provided for in chapter 102:2, below, for it has to be on hand only at the ushering in of the Sabbath). But if one is afraid that he might, in the future forget to make an *eruv,* one may make the *eruv* with one loaf of bread for all the Sabbaths until the Passover, and when saying: "By virtue of the *eruv,*" etc., one should conclude thus: "For every Sabbath until the Passover which comes to us for our good." In this event, it is necessary that the loaf be thin and well baked so that it will not become spoiled before Passover. For the Sabbath during the Passover, the *eruv* should be made with *matzah* prepared according to the law.

12. An *eruv* should not be made on a festival. Hence, if a festival occurs on a Friday, it should be made on the Thursday before the festival.

13. One who eats in one place and sleeps in another, his eating place is his legal residence insofar as the *eruv* is concerned, and from there, other tenants are restricted from carrying anything on the Sabbath, if he eats anything of his own in a special room, but he does not restrain others from the place where he sleeps.

14. According to some authorities, a transient in a court, even if he occupies a house for himself, as long as he does not stay there more than thirty days, does not restrict the tenants of the court, and all of them are permitted to carry out objects, either from their houses or from the house of the stranger, even when there are many transients in the court and only one tenant. However, there must be at least one permanent tenant in the court, be he even a non-Jew, then the transients become subordinate to him. If all the people living in the court are transients and each and every one of them eats in a special room for himself, they do restrict one another. If there is a non-Jew among them, they must hire his residence from him, as is provided for herein below. Some authorities hold that no distinction is to be made between a resident and a transient; as long as he has a special room where he eats, his status is the same as that of a resident. It is proper to follow the stricter opinion, and an *eruv* should be made without pronouncing the benediction. However, when it is done already, one may rely upon the first opinion.

15. If a Jew resides with a non-Jew in the same court, he is not restricted by the non-Jew, and he is allowed to carry from the house into the court and from the court into the house. Even if there are two or more Jews, but they dwell there under such conditions that no *eruv* would be required (as explained in paragraph 13, above), they are not restricted by the non-Jew. If, however, two or more Jews who are required to make an *eruv*, reside there with a non-Jew, they are restricted by him, and they are not allowed to establish an *eruv* until they rent the premises from him. If two or more non-Jews reside there, the Jews must rent the premises of all of them.

16. Even if the non-Jew resides in another court, but his only means of exit to the public premise is through the court where the Jews reside, or if he lives in a garret but the staircase leads to the court, he likewise restricts them.

17. If a court is owned by a Jew but he rented or lent a dwelling therein to a non-Jew, he is not restricted by him, because he has not rented or lent it to him with the power to restrict the Jewish residents, even if the owner of the court himself does not reside there.

18. How is the renting of the dwelling to be effected? The Jew says to the non-Jew: "Rent me your dwelling for such a price," and he need not specify that it is for the purpose of legalizing the carrying of objects. If, however, he says: "Allow me the use of your dwelling," although he adds, "in order that I may be allowed to carry in the court," it is invalid.

19. The dwelling may be rented even from the non-Jew's wife, or from his servant.

20. If the dwelling was rented without mentioning any definite period of time, it continues to be in force as long as the non-Jew does not revoke the tenancy and he still resides there. But if the non-Jew has moved from there and another non-Jew has moved in, the renting agreement must be renewed with the latter. If the dwelling has been rented for a certain length of time, and during that time the non-Jew rented his dwelling to another non-Jew, the original renting agreement remains in force. If, however, the non-Jew died or sold his dwelling to another during the term of the lease, the renting agreement must be renewed with the heir or with the purchaser. If the dwelling has been rented from the non-Jew's servant, then if the duration of the tenancy was not specified, the lease remains in force only as long as the servant remains there. If, however, the dwelling has been rented for a certain length of time, then even if the servant is no longer there, the lease is valid until the expiration of the term.

21. Whenever the lease terminates and a new one is made, a new *eruv* must be made; an *eruv* is not automatically renewed.

22. If it is impossible to rent the premises from the non-Jew, one of the Jews should borrow a special place in his dwelling for the purpose of depositing some object. He should then put the object there, and by this he acquires proprietary rights in that dwelling. Even if he has removed the ob-

ject from there before the Sabbath, it is, nevertheless, considered as if he had a share in the dwelling, since he had the right to let that object remain there on the Sabbath. The Jew may then in turn rent his share in the dwelling to all the residents of the court.

23. An apostate or one who profanes the Sabbath in public (according to some authorities, even if it is only a Rabbinical violation), are considered in this regard as non-Jews, and their dwellings must be hired from them.

24. In many communities, an *eruv* is established between all the thoroughfares and streets (by making the form of a door, or something like it), and they obtain a franchise from the non-Jews, thus enabling them to carry articles throughout the city. It is essential that all the details connected with such a procedure, should be performed by a learned rabbi, well versed in these laws. In such communities, it is customary to put away the *eruv* in the synagogue (because it bears the character of partnership property, and it is not necessary that it be deposited in a dwelling only.)

25. In communities, however, where the city is not provided with an *eruv*, then even when an *eruv* is made for the residents of the court wherein a synagogue is located, the *eruv* should not be placed in the synagogue, but in one of the dwellings.

26. If the *eruv* of a city becomes defective on the Sabbath, the tenants of every court which is properly partitioned and on which there is no breach rendering it invalid—even if that court contains many houses—are allowed to carry articles the entire Sabbath day. Even if the *eruv* lay in somebody's dwelling which is now separated from this court, it is yet permissible to carry, as it is said in connection therewith: "Once it has been allowed on that Sabbath, it continues to be allowable." However, as there is a strong suspicion that many will, through the force of habit carry objects even in places where it is forbidden to do so, therefore, if it is possible to have the *eruv* repaired by a non-Jew, it may be done so. If the cord forming the door was torn, and it is possible for a non-Jew to repair it by looping it or by making one knot and a loop above it, so much the better.

27. If a festival occurs on a Friday and the *eruv* becomes defective, although the *eruv* also serves the purpose of permitting to carry articles on the festival, not needed for the festival, yet we do not say that since it is permitted to repair the *eruv* for the festival, it should also be permitted to repair it for the Sabbath, because the holiness of the festival and of the Sabbath are distinct.

Chapter 95

Inter-community of Boundaries

1. On a Sabbath or on a festival, one is forbidden to walk from the place where one spends the Sabbath or the festival, a greater distance than two thousand cubits (three thousand feet), and a man's space which is four cubits (six feet). This is only true when on Friday at twilight, one happens

to be in an open field, but if one is in a city, the entire city is considered one's abode, also the outskirts of the city which is an area of seventy and two-thirds cubits, whether or not there are buildings in that area. This is called the city enclosure, and belongs to the city; and it is from the periphery of that area that we measure the Sabbath boundary line.

2. A walled city, no matter how large it is, may be traversed on the Sabbath, including the outskirts, and from there we begin to measure the Sabbath boundary. A city not surrounded by a wall but whose buildings are separated by less than seventy and two-thirds cubits (one hundred and six feet), is considered as one city, even if it may take many days to traverse it; and it is from the last house and the "enclosure" that the Sabbath boundary should be measured.

3. Enclosures are added only to cities but not to houses; and the Sabbath boundary begins from their walls.

4. If two cities are near each other, enclosures are added to each; hence, if the distance between the two cities is not greater than two enclosures, they are considered as one city.

5. There are many laws concerning the measuring of a Sabbath boundary, and only one well versed in these laws should be entrusted with such measurements.

6. If a person needs to walk farther than the Sabbath boundary on a Sabbath or on a festival, he should put down a boundary *eruv* before the Sabbath or the festival within the Sabbath boundary lines of the city, in a place to which he would be allowed to walk on the Sabbath. The place where he puts down the *eruv* is then considered his abode, and he thereby acquires the right to walk from there two thousand cubits in any direction. Of course, it is understood that whatever he gains on the side where he puts the *eruv*, he loses on the other side. For instance, if he puts the *eruv* at a distance of two thousand cubits on the eastern side, he is not allowed to walk from the western side, because he is already distant from his legal dwelling, two thousand cubits.

7. How is this *eruv* established? One takes bread sufficient for two meals, or a relish which is eaten with bread, like onions or radishes, enough to eat it with bread for two meals, excepting salt and water, goes to the place where the *eruv* is to be deposited, and pronounces the benediction: "Blessed art Thou, O Lord our God, King of the universe, who hath sanctified us by His commandments, and has commanded us concerning the precept of the *eruv*;" adding: "By virtue of this *eruv* it shall be permissible for me to walk from this place two thousand cubits in each direction;" after which one re-

turns home. One *eruv* may suffice for many Sabbaths, but it should be put in a safe place, where it will not be lost or spoiled.

8. One may delegate another to place an *eruv* for him and pronounce the necessary benediction, saying: "By virtue of this *eruv* it shall be permissible for (naming the principal) to walk," etc. It is essential that the one so delegated be an adult of sound mind, but not a minor. Even when he does not return to report that he has fulfilled his mission, it may be taken for granted that he has done so. For it is presumed that a messenger fulfills his mission.

9. One may make one *eruv* for many people, if it comprises a quantity of food sufficient for all. If one person makes one *eruv* for a group, he should cause the others to acquire a share in it through someone else, as is done with an *eruv* of courts (see preceding chapter). The *eruv* of boundaries should not be made for anyone without his knowledge. The one who makes an *eruv* for others, should say: "It shall be permissible for such a one, and for such a one (mentioning all names)." If he includes himself, too, he says: "For me and for so-and-so one, and so-and-so."

10. It is essential that the *eruv* should be deposited in a place where it is possible to partake thereof on Friday at twilight, without violating a law of the Torah. Hence, if it has been placed in a pit and covered with earth, the *eruv* is not valid; but if it has been covered with a stone, it is valid. If the *eruv* has been placed upon a tree, if it is a hard tree, the *eruv* is valid; if it is a soft tree or a stalk, the *eruv* is not valid.

11. If one deposits an *eruv* in the middle of a city, the entire city is considered as the depository of the *eruv*, and he may traverse the entire city, no matter how large it is, also its enclosure and the entire Sabbath boundary. For it is considered as though he were a resident of the city.

12. If within the boundary line there is a city which is either surrounded by walls or in which an inter-community has been established by means of an *eruv*, such city is not included in the measurement, and it does not count for more than four cubits. This is true only when the Sabbath boundary line extends beyond the outskirts of that city, for instance, if there are five hundred cubits from the *eruv* to the city, and the length of the city is one thousand cubits, the city is not figured at more than four cubits, and he has yet one thousand four hundred ninety-six cubits beyond the city (to the Sabbath boundary). If, however, the boundary line ends in the middle of the city, he is forbidden to walk farther than that; in this event, the city is not reckoned to him as four cubits.

13. The same law also applies to a person who deposits an *eruv* near the end of two thousand cubits outside the city. If he then returns to the city, he may not walk beyond a thousand cubits from the place where the *eruv* was deposited. He is even forbidden to return to his house. (This is the opinion of most authorities, and it is accepted as law.)

14. An *eruv* for boundaries is to be made only to perform a religious act, such as to pray in an assembly of ten, to meet one's teacher or a friend who has returned from a journey, to attend a religious feast or to attend to matters of public interest, or to complete a homeward journey.

15. The *eruv* for boundaries may not be established on the Sabbath or on a festival. If, therefore, a festival occurs on a Friday and one desires to walk beyond the boundary line on the Sabbath, one should deposit the *eruv* on the Thursday before the festival. If a festival occurs on a Sunday, and he desires to pass beyond the boundary line on that day, he should make the *eruv* on Friday.

16. A man's property and livestock are governed by the same laws which restrict his own person. Thus, it is forbidden to take them to a place where he himself is not allowed to walk. If, however, he has loaned them to someone else, or he has hired them out, or he has delivered them into another's care, they are then governed by the laws applying to the one in whose charge they are. Even if the latter is a non-Jew, the cattle and the chattels are governed by the laws applying to him. Furthermore, even the property of a non-Jew is bound by the Sabbath-rest, wherever it may be on Friday at twilight.

17. If a non-Jew has brought fruit about which one need not fear that it was plucked today, on the Sabbath (or any other article concerning which one need not fear that any labor was performed on it on the Sabbath), only it has been brought from beyond the Sabbath boundary line, then if he had brought it either for himself or for another non-Jew, a Jew is permitted to make use of it at once, even to eat it. Only it is forbidden to carry it more than four cubits, unless it was brought into the house; or, if the city is equipped with an *eruv*, it is permissible to carry it in the entire city; for the place where it is permissible to carry, is considered like a man's four cubits. If, however, it has been brought especially for the Jew, he, as well as his entire family, are forbidden to make use thereof the entire Sabbath-day, and on the close of the Sabbath, they must wait the length of time it would take to bring it from the place from which it has been brought. Nevertheless, it may be carried within a space of four cubits, or in a place where carrying is permissible. Even when there is doubt as to whether it has been brought from beyond the Sabbath boundary, it is forbidden, unless it may be reasonably assumed that it has not been brought from beyond the Sabbath boundary.

18. It is an established rule, that there are no boundaries above ten hand-breadths above the ground. Therefore, if one has boarded a vessel on Friday before the ushering in of the Sabbath and the vessel sailed away, even on a long voyage, and it reached port on the Sabbath, he is permitted to walk from that place a distance of two thousand cubits in any direction,

as it is presumed that during the entire voyage of the vessel, he has always been above ten feet from the ground, and he has not acquired a resting place until he has reached land. If, however, he has left the vessel on the Sabbath and returned to it during the Sabbath, he has then acquired a resting place while on land, and if the vessel thereafter sailed beyond the Sabbath boundary line, he has only four cubits on shore within which to walk, and he is governed by the law applying to one who went beyond the boundary line. If the vessel has reached a port on the Sabbath, where it is less than ten handbreadths above the ground, he has acquired there a resting place, even if he did not leave the vessel. If he is in doubt whether the vessel has been at such a port during the voyage, he is given latitude.

CHAPTER 96

Maariv Service and the Havdalah

1. On Saturday night, the *Maariv* service should be said at a later hour than on weekdays, and when saying: *Vehu raḥum* (and He being merciful), etc., and: *Barḥu* (bless ye), we should draw out the singing, in order to add from the profane to the sacred. In the *Shemoneh esreh* we include *Attah ḥonantanu* (Thou hast favored us), etc. If we forgot to say it and we become aware of it before pronouncing the Divine Name of the benediction *Ḥonen haddaat* (gracious Giver of knowledge), we should say *Attah ḥonatanu* and then *Ḥonenu* (O favor us). If, however, we become aware of the omission only after we have pronounced the Divine Name, we should conclude the benediction *Ḥonen haddaat* and we need not repeat the *Shemoneh esreh,* since we will afterwards recite the *havdalah* over a cup of wine. But we should not do any manner of work nor taste any food before reciting the *havdalah.* If we do some work or taste food before then, we must repeat the *Shemoneh esreh.*

2. After the *Shemoneh esreh,* half-*kaddish* is recited followed by *Vihi noam* (and let the pleasantness of the Lord), etc., because this is a Psalm, wherewith Moses blessed Israel upon the completion of the Temple. It must be recited while standing, and its last verse, *Oreḥ yamim* (with length of days) should be repeated twice. Thereafter, *Veattah kadosh* (and Thou art holy), etc., is said, also the verses of sanctification that belong to *Vihi noam* should be said, because through the work of the Temple, the Divine Presence rested in Israel, and for this reason we say: *Veattah kadosh* (and Thou art holy, O Thou who dwellest amid the praises of Israel). If a festival occurs during the following week, these prayers are omitted, because since we say in it: "The work of our hand, establish Thou it," there must be six work days; and since *Vihi noam* is not said, then *Veattah kadosh* is likewise omitted, because they belong to one another. Concluding *Vihi noam,* and *Veattah kadosh,* the whole *kaddish* is recited, followed by the recital of *Veyitten leḥa* (and may God give thee). The reason the *Maariv* prayer is thus prolonged on the conclu-

sion of the Sabbath, is to delay the return of the wicked to Gehenna, for this is delayed until the last assembly in Israel concludes the rituals of the day.

3. Just as it is mandatory to sanctify the Sabbath when ushered in so is it mandatory to sanctify the Sabbath on its departure by performing the *havdalah* ritual over a cup of wine. Benedictions are also said over spices and over a lit candle. Women, too, must observe the *havdalah*. They should, therefore, listen attentively to the recital of the benedictions. When wine cannot be procured, the *havdalah* may be recited over any other beverage, such as beer, mead, or any beverage which is a national drink, except water.

4. As soon as the sun sets on the Sabbath, it is forbidden to eat or drink anything except water before reciting the *havdalah*. If, however, we linger at the third Sabbath meal until after sunset, we are permitted to eat and drink, since we began it when it was permissible. We are also allowed to drink from the cup over which Grace has been recited, as that also forms a part of the meal. This, however, is permissible only when it is our invariable custom to recite Grace over a cup of wine, but if at times we say Grace without a cup of wine, we are not allowed to drink from the cup of Grace before having recited the *havdalah*.

5. No work may be done before the *havdalah* is recited. Women who need to light the home before the *havdalah*, should first say: "Blessed be He who makes a distinction between the holy and the profane, between light and darkness, between Israel and the other nations, between the seventh day and the six work days. Blessed be He who maketh a distinction between the holy and the profane." If a festival occurs on Saturday night, the blessing should be concluded thus: "Who maketh a distinction between holy and holy" (that is, between the degrees of holiness of the Sabbath and the festivals).

6. One who defers the *Maariv* prayer on the conclusion of the Sabbath, or one who has continued his meal into the night, is permitted to tell even a Jew who has already prayed and said *Attah ḥonantanu* in the *Shemoneh esreh*, to do some work for him. He may even benefit from such work, although he will later refer to the Sabbath in the Grace.

7. The *havdalah* cup should be filled to its very brim, letting it slightly overflow as an omen of abundance. Then we take the cup in the right hand and the spice-box in the left, and hold them thus until after the recitation of the benediction *Bore peri haggafen*. Afterward we transfer the cup to the left hand and the spice-box to the right and pronounce the benedictions *Bore mine besamim* (the Creator of divers kinds of spices) and, *Bore meore haesh* (the Creator of the light of fire). Then we take the cup in our right hand again and pronounce the benediction *Hamavdil*. On concluding the benedictions, we sit down and drink the whole contents of the cup. We spill out what is left in the cup, extinguish the *havdalah* candle in it, and daub some of the

wine on the eyes as a token of affection for the mitzvah. It is the custom that women do not drink from the *havdalah* cup.

8. It is well to put some of the spice called 'musk' among the other spices, as all authorities agree that the benediction over musk is *Bore mine besamim*. One should also take some of the myrtle branches (used as one of the four species on the Feast of Tabernacles), inasmuch as a *mitzvah* has been performed with it once, it is fitting that another *mitzvah* should be performed with it.

9. It is preferable that the *havdalah* candle should be of wax and consist of several strands twisted together which makes a torch. But if we have no such candle, we should use two candles, holding them close together so that both flames merge in one like a torch. It is customary that after saying the benediction, *Bore meore haesh*, to look at the fingernails and the palm of the right hand. One should bend the four fingers into the palm of the hand, resting them on the thumb, and look at the nails and at the palm at the same time, then stretch out the fingers, and look at the back of the nails.

10. A sightless man should not pronounce the benediction over the light, nor should one who lacks the sense of smell pronounce the benediction over the spices.

11. If after pronouncing the benediction over the wine, and while holding the spices in the hand, intending to pronounce the benediction over it, we err and say instead the benediction, *Bore meore haesh*, but we instantly become aware of the error, and say, *Bore mine besamim*, it is a valid benediction over the spices, and we should afterward pronounce the benediction over the light. If, however, it has been our original intention to pronounce that benediction over the light, it is a valid benediction over the light, and we should afterward pronounce a benediction over the spices.

12. It is meritorious to light more candles than usual upon the conclusion of the Sabbath, and to chant the appropriate hymns, thus escorting the Sabbath upon its departure even as we escort a king upon his leaving town. The name of the prophet Elijah should also be mentioned, and prayers offered that he may come to bring us the tidings of redemption. For, Elijah would not come on a Friday, in order not to disturb Israel from preparing for the Sabbath, and on the Sabbath we do not pray for his coming, because we are uncertain as to whether the Sabbath boundary limit applies to an altitude above ten hand-breadths, and therefore, he could not come on the Sabbath. But when the Sabbath has passed, we pray that he shall come and bring us good tidings. Again it is stated in the Midrash, that every Saturday night, Elijah enters Paradise, where he sits under the Tree of Life, and records the merits of the Israelites who observed the Sabbath. Therefore, we mention him gratefully.

13. If possible, one should partake of bread and warm victuals in the *Melaveh malkah* feast (held on Saturday night). One should set a good table in honor of the departure of the Sabbath. One who is unable to partake of bread, should at least eat some cake or fruit.

14. One who has already recited the *havdalah*, may repeat it for the sake of his sons who have reached the age of religious initiation, in order that they may thus fulfill their obligations. Especially should this be done for the sake of an adult. The one who recites the *havdalah* for the sake of others, should inhale the aroma of the spices when saying the benediction *Bore mine besamim*, so that it may not be a benediction in vain. One who has already said the *havdalah*, should not repeat it for the sake of women (because some authorities hold that they are exempt.)

15. If a person forgot, or was prevented by an accident, or has wilfully neglected to say the *havdalah* on Saturday night, he may say it any time before the end of the third day, but he should omit the benedictions over the spices and the light; he should only say the benediction *Bore peri haggafen*. After Tuesday, the *havdalah* may no longer be said, because the first three days of the week are called "the succeeding days of the Sabbath" and are a part of the conclusion of the Sabbath, but the last three days of the week are called "the preceding days of the Sabbath," and have no relation to the past Sabbath.

CHAPTER 97

Rosh Ḥodesh (*New Moon*)

1. Some people fast on the day preceding *Rosh Ḥodesh*, calling it *Yom kippur katan* (Minor Atonement Day), and recite special prayers, for on this day the sins of the past month are forgiven, akin to the goat that was sacrificed on *Rosh Ḥodesh* in the Temple, and as we say in the *Musaph* service, "A time of forgiveness to all their children." Each place should adhere to its own custom.

2. It is meritorious to feast sumptuously on *Rosh Ḥodesh*. If *Rosh Ḥodesh* falls on the Sabbath, an extra dish should be prepared in its honor.

3. Work is permissible on *Rosh Ḥodesh*. Women, however, customarily refrain from work on that day. It is a beautiful custom, and we should not make light of it.

4. *Hallel* should be recited while standing and without interruption. We should endeavor to say it with the congregation. Hence, if we arrive at the synagogue when the congregation is about to begin saying *hallel*, we should join them and say the other prayers later. If we are then saying *Pesuke dezimerah* (special verses of the Psalms;) that is, from *Hodu*, praise ye, to the end of *Az yashir*, then sang Moses, we should recite *hallel* with the congregation, but we do not say the benedictions before and after *hallel*, because benedictions *Baruḥ sheamar* (blessed be He who spoke), and *Yishtabaḥ* (praised be), will answer the same purpose for the *hallel*. This, however, may be done only on *Rosh Ḥodesh*, and during the Intermediate and last days of Passover, when parts of the *hallel* are omitted, but when the entire *hallel* is recited, this cannot be done. One who recites *hallel* without the congregation,

if two or more persons are present, he should say *Hodu* (O give thanks) before them, in order that they may respond, for the expression *Hodu,* implies an exhortation to others. (For the law concerning the recital of *hallel* at the house of a mourner, God forbid, see chapter 207, below).

5. After the *hallel,* the whole *kaddish* is recited and a Scroll of the Torah is taken out, at which four persons are called up. The reading is from Numbers 28:1 following. For the *Kohen,* we read the three verses: *Vayedaber* (and He spoke), *Tzav* (command), and *Veamarta* (and thou shalt say). For the *Levi,* we repeat the verse *Veamarta* and add, *Et hakkeves eḥad* (one lamb), and *Vaasirit haephah* (and one-tenth of an *ephah*). For the Israelite, we read from *Olat tamid* (continual burnt offering), up to *Uverashe ḥadsheḥem* (and at the beginning of your months). For the fourth person, we read from, *Uverashe ḥadsheḥem* etc.

6. On *Rosh Ḥodesh,* it is forbidden either to fast, to deliver a funeral eulogy, or to recite the services for the dead.

7. It is obligatory to consecrate the moon each month, and it should not be done before it is actually night, that is, when its light is visible on the ground and one can derive some use from its light. If the moon is obscured by a cloud, it should not be consecrated unless the cloud is light and flimsy. If, however, the cloud obscured the moon after we began the benediction, we should conclude it. But if we know beforehand that we shall be unable to conclude the benediction before the moon will be obscured, we must not begin it.

8. The moon should be consecrated under the open sky. If, however, there is no clean place, or if we are unable to do so through some other cause, we are permitted to consecrate it in the house at a window.

9. This duty is best fulfilled when we do it on the conclusion of the Sabbath, when we are dressed in our Sabbath attire, but if it is more than ten days from the beginning of the New Moon, or if it is feared that we will then be unable to consecrate it, we need not wait until the conclusion of the Sabbath. It is best to consecrate the moon in unison with a multitude, for "In the multitude of people is the king's glory" (Proverbs 14:28). We should not, however, postpone it on that account, for the merit of performing precepts promptly, outweighs the merit of "In the multitude of people is the king's glory."

10. The moon should not be consecrated before three days have elapsed since the New Moon; some people wait seven days; but when the conclusion of the Sabbath occurs before the seven days, we must not wait, but we should consecrate it at the conclusion of the Sabbath. The moon may be consecrated only up to the expiration of fourteen full days, eighteen hours and twenty-two minutes from the New Moon.

11. The moon should not be consecrated before *Tisheah Beav* (the ninth day of the month of *Av*), nor when one is in mourning. If, however, the days of mourning will not end within the ten days after the New Moon, one may consecrate it during that period. On a fast day, the moon should not be con-

secrated before some food has been eaten. Nevertheless, we consecrate it on the conclusion of the Day of Atonement, when we leave the synagogue, for we are in a joyous spirit, confident that our sins were forgiven.

12. The moon should not be consecrated on Friday night, nor on the night of a festival, unless in an emergency, when the time for the consecration will have passed on the conclusion of the Sabbath.

13. A blind person is permitted to consecrate the moon.

14. If the moon becomes visible at the beginning of the night, before the *Maariv* service, and there yet remain several nights within which the moon may be consecrated, we first say the *Maariv* prayer, and then we consecrate the moon, because a precept which is constant takes precedence over one that is only periodic, and for the further reason that the reading of the *Shema* is a Mosaic ordinance, while the consecration of the moon is not. If, however, there remain only two or three nights, we consecrate the moon first. For since the time is short, it may happen that the moon will be obscured by clouds the entire period. And in the rainy season the uncertain period is four days, and we should consecrate the moon before praying the *Maariv,* even if there is yet four days to the end of the period. If the moon becomes visible while we read the *Shema* and its benedictions, and the time for its consecration will have passed after the recital of the *Shemoneh esreh,* then the prayers may be interrupted even in the middle of the benedictions, or in the middle of *Shema* in order to consecrate it. But, if possible, one should finish the section which one reads and consecrate the moon between the sections of *Shema.*

15. If during the month of *Adar,* the moon was not visible until the night of the fourteenth day, which is the time for the reading of the *Megillah,* the moon should be consecrated first and the *Megillah* read afterward. If it has become visible during the reading of the *Megillah,* then if it will be time to consecrate it after the reading is concluded, the reading of the *Megillah* should not be interrupted; but if the time for the consecration will have passed by the time the reading is concluded, and the entire congregation has not as yet consecrated the moon, the reading of the *Megillah* should be interrupted for the consecration, and the reading of the *Megillah* completed thereafter. If only one individual has not yet consecrated it, and if he stops for the consecration, he will have to read the *Megillah* by himself, he must not interrupt, because the public proclamation of a miracle is of greater importance.

VOLUME 3

Chapter 98

Laws Concerning Festivals

1. Any work which is forbidden on the Sabbath, is also forbidden on a festival. And just as on the Sabbath it is forbidden to have work done by a non-Jew, even so it is on a festival. On a festival, as on a Sabbath, one's cattle must be allowed to rest. The festival differs from the Sabbath only with regard to the preparation of food. As it is written (Exodus 12:16): "Only that which is eaten by any soul, this alone may be prepared by you." Thus, kneading, baking, slaughtering, and cooking are permitted on a festival. Carrying objects from one place to another, and kindling a fire are also permitted on a festival, even when not needed for cooking but for some other purpose. Our Sages, of blessed memory, received this rule by tradition, that "If certain labors are permitted for the sake of preparing food, they are also permitted for other purposes." It is not permissible, however, to light a *Jahrzeit* lamp on a festival.

2. The making of cheese or butter, and the curdling of milk by putting it in a skin, or by putting some matter therein to cause it to coagulate, are forbidden on a festival. It is forbidden to separate the cream from the milk, unless one leaves some of it on the surface of the milk, as it must be done on the Sabbath. And it is permissible to separate only as much as is needed for that day but not for the following day, because it amounts to preparing food on one day of a festival for another day, which is forbidden. However, in the event of a possible loss, we may have a non-Jew separate it in the aforesaid manner.

3. Such spices as would lose their flavor if they were crushed before the festival, may be crushed on a festival, if done in an unaccustomed manner, for instance, by inclining the mortar on its side, or by pounding them on the table. When grating horseradish on a grater, we should not grate it into a plate, as it is usually done on a weekday, but on a cloth. Coffee, too, should not be ground in a grinder, but crushed in a mortar and done in a particular manner. It is, however, best to prepare everything on the day before the festival. Articles of food which do not lose their flavor, should surely be prepared on the day before the festival; but if we have forgotten to do it before, we may prepare it in an unaccustomed manner on the festival. All of the foregoing may be prepared only as much as is required for the use of that day. One should even be scrupulous not to prepare more than is actually

needed for the particular meal. The foregoing rules must also be observed when grinding *matzah.*

4. It is forbidden to split wood or even to break it by hand. It is also forbidden to collect wood that is scattered about.

5. It is forbidden to place wood on the top of stones in order to start a fire, because we are building a tent thereby, as it is akin to making two walls with a roof over them. But it can be done in a special manner, like holding the wood in the hand and placing the stones underneath. When putting a pot on stones in order to kindle a fire beneath, we must likewise hold the pot in our hand and place the stones underneath, but we must not arrange the stones first and then place the pot on them

6. It is forbidden to fan a fire with a bellows, for, on a festival, nothing must be done in the manner of an artisan. It is the prevailing custom to use a private bellows by working it in a special manner, holding it in an inverted position. But it is forbidden to do so with the bellows of an artisan, even when operated in a special manner.

7. We are allowed to separate all the peas we need for that day, but not with a dredge or a sieve, nor should we place it in water, so that the offal or the edible should come up on the top; but we must separate them by hand and gather up what is easier, whether it be the offal or the edibles.

8. If we wish to sift flour that has already been sifted before, we should have it done either by a non-Jew, or do it in an unusual manner, like inverting the sieve. The same should be done with ground *matzah.* It is forbidden to sift flour which has never been sifted before, excepting by a non-Jew, and in an unusual manner. It is forbidden to pick out worthless matter, like splinters of wood from flour. It is even forbidden to pick out the large pieces from the ground *matzah.*

9. Kneading is permissible on a festival. Nevertheless, we must not take the flour with a measuring vessel, but we should take what we approximately need. It is, however, permissible to take it with a measuring vessel, if we do not measure it exactly, but we take either less or more.

10. Noodles or egg-barley used in soups, should be kneaded on the day before the festival, for it tastes better than the freshly kneaded. But if it has not been made on the day before the festival, it may be done on the festival

in a special manner; thus, if it is generally kneaded on a board, it should now be kneaded on a cloth, or something similar. Victuals that do not become stale, such as dried fruits, and the like, should also be cooked on the day before the festival.

11. *Ḥallah* (the priest's portion) may be taken from the dough kneaded on a festival, but it may not be burned, because no holy things may be burned on a festival. Neither are we allowed to bake the *ḥallah* portion, because it is unfit for food, for we are classed as people who are all defiled by coming in contact with dead bodies. It is also forbidden to handle the *ḥallah*, but immediately upon separating it from the dough, it should be put in a safe place until after the conclusion of the festival and then burned. On a festival, no *ḥallah* may be separated from dough which has been kneaded before the festival. But we may bake the dough and eat it, leaving a portion of it from which the *ḥallah* may be separated on the conclusion of the festival. The portion left should be sufficient for the *ḥallah* and some left over.

12. It is forbidden to mix clay on a festival, even by a non-Jew. Therefore, if we need some clay to close the opening of an oven into which food is stored away for the Sabbath, we must prepare the clay before the festival. It is also forbidden to take mud from the street for this purpose, unless it has been prepared and placed in a corner before the festival. We must be careful not to plaster the clay or the mud, but we should close up the opening without plastering, for some authorities forbid plastering on a festival, even for the preservation of food.

13. Poultry which are kept in the house or in the yard for food, and which have been domesticated, so that when they go out of the house, they come back in the evening, may be caught to be killed for the requirements of the festival, even when they are outside the yard. But if not needed for food, they may not be caught. If the fowl are new and are unused to the house, they may not be caught for the food, even when they are in the house. But they may be taken at night when they roost. In that event, care should be taken to select before the festival, those we intend to kill on the festival, lest the one we catch proves unfit, and then we shall have carried it needlessly, which is forbidden. Poultry not kept for food but for laying eggs, may not be handled on a festival.

14. It is forbidden to catch even domesticated doves that are accustomed to come to their nests or loft, although they have been chosen the day before the festival.

15. We are allowed to burn or cut the cord from the feet of poultry after they have been killed. It is also permissible to sew up stuffed poultry, provided that the needle has been threaded on the day before the festival. After the poultry is sewn up, the remaining thread may be burned.

16. Fish may not be caught from a fishpond with a vessel, if they cannot be caught with the hands. If, however, they can be caught with the hands, one may catch them, even with a vessel. If there are many fishes in the pond, one must designate, on the day before the festival, which of the fish he desires to take on the festival, by making a mark on them; and if one needs them all, then one must designate them all, by saying on the day before the festival: "I set aside all these fishes for the festival."

17. If it is doubtful whether a certain thing has been snared on the festival, or if it has been prepared the day before the festival, we are not allowed to make use of it. But if it is very urgent, this law may be disregarded on the second day of a festival, but not on the second day of *Rosh Hashanah*.

18. On a festival it is forbidden to give drink or feed at close range to any living creature that may not be handled, but it should be done at a slight distance.

19. If poultry has been killed and was found to be unfit for use, we may not handle it, because it is like any other object that has not been counted upon for use. If, however, an animal has been slaughtered and it was found to be unfit for use, we may put it away where it will not get spoiled. But if we cannot preserve it, we may sell it to a non-Jew, providing no price is fixed and it is not weighed. This law may perhaps also apply regarding fattened geese, among whom many unfit ones are generally found.

20. An animal should not be slaughtered on a festival, except in case of absolute necessity. It is forbidden to sell meat by weight and at a fixed price. But one may give another any quantity of meat to be paid for after the festival.

21. When slaughtering an animal on a festival, it is best not to examine the lungs (to determine the fitness of the animal) until after it was skinned; for, if the animal is found unfit upon the examination of the lungs, it may no longer be skinned. We are allowed to handle the skin of an animal that has been slaughtered that day in order to put it away, but we may not spread it on hooks to dry. Any other skins may not be handled at all. It is also permissible to handle the feathers of a fowl which has been killed on that day, in order to put them away; but it is forbidden to handle any other feathers.

22. It is permissible to salt meat to draw out the blood, even if it could have been salted the day before the festival, provided that it is needed on that day. If we have more meat than we need for that day, and we fear that it might spoil, we may salt it all, no matter how large the quantity, for it entails no extra labor. It is, however, forbidden to salt meat which has already been salted and cleansed of its blood, and to salt fish which could have been salted on the day before the festival.

23. On a festival we are not allowed to make figures on pastry, by a mould or by hand, such as the figures of fowl, or the like.

24. On a festival, as on the Sabbath, plastering is forbidden; therefore, we may not warm up the wax or the tallow of a candle, in order to make it stick to the candlestick or to the wall, lest we plaster it. If the socket of a candlestick is filled with tallow, it may be cleaned with an object that may be handled on a festival.

25. It is forbidden to quench a fire on a festival, even indirectly. Consequently, it is forbidden to place a lighted candle where a wind may blow it out, even, if at the time it was placed there, no wind was blowing. It is likewise forbidden to open a door or a window opposite a lighted candle.

26. It is permissible to cover a fire with a vessel or with ashes that have been previously prepared, even though this may have somewhat of a quenching effect, nevertheless, since the purpose is not to quench it (and the work is not needed for its own sake), it is permissible for the need of the festival. However, this is permitted only when it is needed for that day, but not when it is needed for the night, because the night belongs to the following day.

27. Vessels which are ritually unfit for use, may neither be scalded with hot water or incandesced on a festival (to make fit for use). (For the law regarding the purging of vessels, on a festival, see chapter 37, end, above).

28. The law concerning the washing of dishes on the Sabbath, also applies to a festival. It is forbidden to wash dishes on the first day of the festival to be used on the second day.

29. It is forbidden to make a fire in order to heat the house, unless the cold is so intense that the food congeals, then it falls into the category of preparing food, but if the cold is not so intense, it is forbidden. However, it may be done by a non-Jew.

30. We are allowed to heat water for the purpose of washing the hands, but not for bathing the whole body. It is also forbidden to heat water, even through a non-Jew and even when it is required for an infant. However, a larger quantity may be heated for the infant's sake, even if only a little water is needed for his cooking, providing that all the water is poured in there before putting it on the fire, and nothing else is added thereafter. If the infant is somewhat indisposed, we are permitted to have the water heated for his sake by a non-Jew.

31. It is not permissible to draw fire on a festival, either from a flint, or a glass, or a match.

32. We are not allowed to scatter spices upon coals, either for the purpose of scenting the odor or for perfuming the house or vessels, for it is written (Exodus 12:16): "For every soul," which implies that it must be of such a nature that everybody requires it, but perfuming is only a necessity for the delicate and the wealthy. Concerning the smoking of tobacco on a festival, the authorities, of blessed memory, disagree. Even according to those authorities who permit it, one must be careful not to light whatever one smokes with a piece of paper or with a coal, for the reason that when these are thrown on the ground, they are quenched thereby, and such an error is likely to be made because one is accustomed to do so on a weekday. If letters are written or printed on the paper, and one burns them, there is also the further violation that forbids erasing; but it must be lit from a flame. It is forbidden to smoke a new pipe, or to cut the tobacco on a festival; and it would seem that, pursuant to the same law, it should be forbidden to cut off the tips of cigars.

33. A thing which may not be termed actual work, but it is forbidden to be performed on the Sabbath for one who is not critically ill, is likewise forbidden to be performed on the first day of a festival and on the two days of *Rosh Hashanah* (see chapter 91, above, and chapter 99:2, below,) unless it is done by a non-Jew. However, on the second day of a festival (excepting the second day of *Rosh Hashanah*), it may also be done by a Jew. Whatever may be termed actual work, must not be performed even on the second day of a festival for one who is not critically ill, unless it be done by a non-Jew.

34. It is permissible to carry from one domain into another on a festival, even things that are not required for food. There must, however, be some need for it, otherwise it may not be carried out unless it be a place where it may be carried out on the Sabbath. Even regarding things that are needed for human consumption, like pitchers of wine, we should not carry heavy burdens as on weekdays, but we should do it in a different manner. If, however, we cannot do it otherwise, as when we have many guests waiting, we may bring them into the house in the usual way.

35. All the labors that are permitted on a festival, may be performed only for the requirements of man, but not for beasts, because it is written (Exodus 12:16): "Shall be done for you," which means, "For you but not for beasts." Therefore, it is forbidden to cook and carry out anything on a festival for the need of a beast, the same as on the Sabbath.

36. On a festival, we may not cook or bake for the need of a non-Jew. But if we employ a non-Jewish domestic, we may cook in the same pot, sufficient also for the domestics. However, we are forbidden to add more food for a distinguished non-Jew. Furthermore, even if we cook or bake anything for

ourselves, we may not invite the non-Jew to eat with us. However, we may give something of what we cook or bake to an ordinary non-Jew. As far as baking bread is concerned, this must not be done even for our non-Jewish domestic.

37. It is forbidden to carry any article from one domain into another on a festival, for the need of a non-Jew, unless it is carried into a place where it may be carried out on the Sabbath.

CHAPTER 99

Things Forbidden to be Handled on Festivals

1. Anything that is forbidden to be handled on the Sabbath is also forbidden on a festival. Some authorities hold that things not counted upon for use, or things set apart because they are filthy, although they may be handled on the Sabbath, are not to be handled on a festival. Therefore, fruit that has been set apart for sale may not be handled on a festival, but they must be designated before the festival, by saying: "From this fruit I will eat tomorrow." We may be lenient regarding fruit that is to be sold a little at a time.

2. An egg which has been laid on a festival may not even be handled, but it may be covered with a vessel to protect it from breaking. If it has been laid on the first day of a festival, it may be eaten on the second day, but if the second day occurs on a Sabbath, its use is forbidden on that day. If it has been laid on the first day of a festival which occurred on the Sabbath, its use is forbidden on the following day which is the second day of the festival. Whenever the Sabbath is next to the festival, whether preceding or following it, if the egg is laid on either of these, its use is forbidden on the other. On *Rosh Hashanah*, if it is laid on the first day, its use is forbidden also on the second day. (For the two days of *Rosh Hashanah* are considered as one prolonged day only concerning restrictive measures, as in the present case; but concerning the law forbidding the preparation of food on the day of a festival for another, there is no distinction between an ordinary festival and *Rosh Hashanah*, for concerning the relaxation of a rule, we do not say that it is considered as one prolonged day). If *Rosh Hashanah* occurs on Thursday and Friday, even if the egg has been laid on Thursday, its use is forbidden on the Sabbath as well. If eggs are found in poultry killed on a festival, they may be used on the same day, even though they are fully developed.

3. Wood may be handled on a festival only when it is needed to kindle a fire with it, but it may not be handled when not required for burning. Therefore, one must not support a pot or a door with a wooden wedge.

4. On a festival, it is permissible to handle ashes of wood that has been burned on the day before the festival, because it is fit to be used for some of man's necessities, as to cover excrement with it, or saliva. If the

ashes are from a fire made on the festival, then if it is still so hot that an egg can be baked on it, it may be handled, but if it has cooled off, it may not be handled, because it is like a thing that has come into being this day, for yesterday it was wood and today it is ashes, and it is even worse than things set apart not to be used.

5. It is permissible to kindle a fire with the shells of nuts that have been consumed before the festival. If the nuts have been consumed on the festival, the shells may not be used to kindle a fire, and it is even forbidden to handle them. The same law applies to peelings, although they are fit to feed animals, for the reason that they are considered like a thing that has come into existence today, since yesterday they were fit food for human beings.

CHAPTER 100

The Benediction of the Priests (Birkat Kohanim)

1. According to the Law of Moses (Numbers 6:22-27), *kohanim* must bless the people, for it is written (loco citato 23): "Thus shall ye bless the people." If a *kohen* who is not disqualified, refuses to go up to bless the people, he is guilty of transgressing a Divine Command. However, he is not considered a violator of the law, unless he is called upon to do so. For it is written (loco citato): "Say to thee," and the *Targum* translates it: "When they are told." It is customary in our regions for the *Kohanim* to bless the people only on festivals, because the people rejoice in the holiday, and on *Yom Kippur* because there is rejoicing on account of their having obtained forgiveness and pardon of sins, for only the merry of heart should bless, which is not true of other days. Even on Sabbaths they are worried about their livelihood and their being restrained from work. And on a festival they only bless the people at the *musaph* service, because they will soon leave the synagogue and rejoice with the festival. The custom prevails in our regions that if a festival (except *Yom Kippur*) occurs on the Sabbath, the *kohanim* do not bless the people. In other communities, the custom is to bless the people even if a festival occurs on the Sabbath, and this custom is the more appropriate.

2. The priestly benediction is to be pronounced only in a congregation of at least ten male adults, themselves included, because they too, are included, for it is written (Numbers 6:27): "And I will bless them."

3. The *kohanim* should drink neither wine nor any other intoxicating beverage before their benediction. If a *kohen* feels faint and he desires to eat some pastry before the *musaph*, he should listen to someone else's *kiddush*.

4. Before pronouncing the benediction, the *kohanim* must wash their hands up to the wrist, just as the *kohanim* did before their service in the Temple, as it is written (Psalms 134:2): "Lift up your hands in holiness, and bless ye the Lord." It is doubtful whether a benediction should be pro-

nounced over this ablution, since such a benediction has already been uttered upon rising in the morning. Because of the doubt, the custom prevails not to pronounce the benediction. If the *kohen* has touched an unclean spot in the meantime, he ought to say the benediction over this ablution; but this is not the custom. Every *kohen* who is God-fearing, should, therefore, take care not to touch any unclean spot after he had washed his hands in the morning, so that he would not need repeat the benediction for the ablution before the public benediction.

5. A *Levite* pours the water upon the hands of the *kohanim,* as it is written (Numbers 18:6): "And thy brethren also, the tribe of *Levi* . . . bring thou near with thee, that they may be joined unto thee, and minister unto thee." If no *Levite* is present, a firstborn of the mother pours the water, and if there is no firstborn present, it is better that the *kohen* himself should pour the water on his hands, rather than an Israelite. If the hands of the Levite or of the firstborn who is to pour the water upon the hands of the *kohen* are unclean, he must first wash them.

6. The *kohanim* are forbidden to go up to the platform with their shoes on; they should remove them before washing their hands. Out of respect for the public, they should hide their shoes under the benches where they cannot be seen.

7. When the *ḥazan* begins the prayer *Retzeh* (accept), etc., all the *kohanim* leave their places to mount the platform. They should, therefore, wash their hands before this. If, however, they washed their hands after the *ḥazan* began saying *Retzeh* it is also acceptable.

8. After they mount the platform, they remain standing, facing the Holy Ark in the east, and after saying *Modim* (we give thanks) with the congregation, they say: "May it be Thy will, O Lord our God, that this blessing wherewith Thou hast commanded us to bless Thy people Israel, be perfect without any flaw or error from now and forever." They linger in the recital of this prayer until the *ḥazan* concludes with, *Uleḥa naeh lehodot* (unto Thee it is becoming to give thanks), so that the congregation may respond *Amen* also to this prayer. The *ḥazan* says: "Our God and God of our fathers, bless us," in an undertone, but the word *Kohanim* he says aloud, as that is a call to the *kohanim* to pronounce the benediction. Then he continues silently: "Thy people Israel, as it is said, etc." After the *ḥazan* has called *Kohanim,* they begin the benediction, all saying in unison: "Blessed art Thou, O Lord our God, King of the universe, who hath sanctified us by the holiness of Aaron;" then turning their faces toward the people, they conclude: "And He commanded us in love to bless His people Israel," to which the congregation responds *Amen.* The *ḥazan* should not respond *Amen,* as this would constitute an interruption in his prayer. From the words, "With love," it is

inferred, that if the worshipers hate the *kohen,* or if the *kohen* hates the worshipers, he should not bless them. Indeed, it is fatal for the *kohen* to bless the people in such an event. He should, therefore, leave the synagogue. If there is only one *kohen* present in the synagogue, the *ḥazan* should not call out *kohanim* in a loud voice, but the *kohen* should, of his own accord, turn his face.

9. They raise their hands to the level of their shoulders, and separate their fingers in such a way that there are five spaces between them; between the two fingers on each side there is one space, and between the fingers and the thumb there is another space, the same with the other hand, making it a total of four spaces, and between the thumbs of the two hands there is another space; thus in all there are five spaces. This must be done, because it is written (Song 2:9): "He peereth through the lattice" (*he ḥarakim,* five openings). The right hand should be raised slightly above the left, the right thumb being above the left thumb. They should, however, spread their hands in such a way that the palms be turned toward the ground and the back of their hands toward heaven.

10. When the *kohanim* bless the people, they should neither look around nor divert their thoughts, but their eyes should be directed downward as in prayer. The people should pay attention to the benediction and face the *kohanim,* but they should not gaze at them, nor should the *kohanim* gaze at their hands. It is for this reason that the *kohanim* pull the *tallit* over their faces, extending their hands outside. The worshipers, also cover their faces with the *tallit* in order not to gaze at the *kohanim.*

11. Those standing behind the *kohanim* are not included in the benediction, unless they are compelled to stand there, but those standing on the sides of the *kohanim* are included. Therefore, those standing near the eastern wall, in the area where the Holy Ark projects from the wall, should leave their places and stand where they can be at least on the sides of the *kohanim.* But if it is impossible for them to do so, they are then considered as involuntary deviators and are included in the benediction.

12. The *ḥazan* recites the priestly benediction word for word, and the *kohanim* repeat after him. The congregation responds *Amen* at the conclusion of the first, second and third verses. The *ḥazan* should not recite the priestly benediction from memory but from a prayer book, so that he may not get confused. He may also respond *Amen* after the verses, which is not considered an interruption, because it is a part of the prayer. At the following

words, the *kohanim* turn first toward the South and then toward the North: *Yevareḥeḥa* (may He bless thee), *Veyishmereḥa* (and keep thee), *Eleḥa* (to thee), *Viḥuneka* (and be gracious unto thee), *Eleḥa* (unto thee), and *Leḥa* (thee); and because these words are in the second person, therefore, they turn also to their sides, in order to bless all the worshipers. They also turn thus when saying *Shalom*, because it is at the conclusion of the blessings. While the *kohanim* linger in the chanting of the concluding words of the verses, that is, *Veyishmereḥa*, *Viḥuneka*, and *Shalom*, the congregation says, *Ribbono shel olam* (Master of the universe), etc. The one who prompts the *kohanim*, even though he is not the *ḥazan*, should not recite, *Ribbono shel olam*, so that he be not distracted. Needless to add that the *ḥazan* should not say it, because it would be considered an interruption made in the *Shemoneh esreh*. The *kohanim* should chant the benediction only in the customary melody in order to avoid confusion.

13. When the *kohanim* repeat the words of the blessings, the congregation should not recite any verse, but should listen attentively to each word pronounced by the *kohanim;* for is there a slave who upon receiving a blessing, would not listen attentively? And if the worshipers recite verses in the middle, they cannot listen attentively. The people who do recite verses, should do so only when either the *ḥazan* or the *kohanim* are chanting, and not when they say the words.

14. Thereafter, the *ḥazan* begins reciting: *Sim shalom* (grant peace), and the *kohanim* turn their faces toward the Holy Ark in the East, and say: *Ribbono shel olam* (Master of the universe), and they prolong the chanting of this prayer until the *ḥazan* concludes the blessing: *Hammevareḥ et ammo yisrael bashalom* (who blesseth His people Israel with peace), in order that the congregation should respond *Amen* to their prayer as well. If they cannot prolong the chanting until then, they should recite in addition: *Addir bamarom* (the Mighty in heaven), etc. On *Rosh Hashanah* and *Yom Kippur* when *Hayyom teamtzenu* (this day Thou shalt strengthen us) is chanted, the *kohanim* should not begin reciting, *Ribbono shel olam* until that prayer is nearly concluded, in order that they finish their prayer simultaneously with the *ḥazan*.

15. The *kohanim* are not to begin the benediction, *Asher kiddeshanu* (who hath sanctified us), etc., until the *ḥazan* completely finishes the word *kohanim*, and the *ḥazan* is not permitted to begin *Yevareḥeḥa*, until the entire congregation has finished saying *Amen*. This also applies to the *Amen* said after *Veyishmereḥa*, *Viḥuneka*, and *Shalom*. The *ḥazan* should not begin: *Yaer*, *Yissa*, and *Sim shalom*, until the entire congregation has said *Amen*. The *kohanim* must not turn their faces away from the congregation towards the Holy Ark until the *ḥazan* begins: *Sim shalom;* neither are they allowed to relax their fingers before they avert their faces from the congregation. On concluding the blessing, they are not permitted to descend before the congregation responds *Amen* to the benediction: *Et ammo yisrael bashalom* (His people Israel with peace).

16. Whenever the *kohanim* turn around, either at the beginning or at the end, they should turn toward their right. Therefore, at the beginning, when they stand with their faces towards the East, they first turn South and then West, and at the conclusion when they stand with their faces towards the West, they first turn North and then East. When they descend upon concluding the blessing, their faces should be towards the Ark; they therefore, walk backwards, like a pupil departing from his master. They should not touch their shoes when putting them on, and if they do, they are required to wash their hands.

17. An effort should be made not to have a *kohen* act as *ḥazan*. And if the *ḥazan* happens to be a *kohen*, he should not go up to bless the people, neither should he prompt the *kohanim*, but someone else should stand by him to call *kohanim*, and also read to them the words: *Yevareḥeḥa*, etc., while the *ḥazan* stands there and remains silent until *Sim shalom*. He commits no sin by not going up to bless the people, although the other one has called out *Kohanim*, because the exhortation has been only to the *kohanim* who are not engaged in praying and have moved their feet after *Retzeh*. If there is no other *kohen* present, then in order not to forego the precept of blessing the people, the *ḥazan* should go up to bless the congregation, relying upon the hand-washing in the morning. How is he to act? He moves his feet slightly while saying *Retzeh*, and reads up to: *Uleḥa naeh lehodot* (and unto Thee it is becoming to give thanks). Then someone else says: *Elohenu velohe avotenu, bareḥenu babraḥa hameshuleshet* (our God and the God of our fathers, bless us with the threefold blessing), etc., and the *kohen* goes up to bless the people, while the other man recites before him the priestly blessing. The *kohen* then resumes officiating as *ḥazan*, and says: *Sim shalom* and he does not recite: *Ribbon haolamim* (Sovereign of the universe), etc., until after reciting the *kaddish*. If the *kohen* did not move his feet while saying *Retzeh*, he may not go up to bless the people.

18. If a congregation consists of *kohanim* only, then if they are no more than ten, all go up to say the blessing. Whom do they bless? Their brethren in the countryside. And who responds *Amen?* The women and the little children. If no women and children are present, the lack of the *Amen* response does not hinder the priestly blessing. If more than ten *kohanim* are present, then as many as there are above the number of ten, go up to say the blessing, and ten should remain to respond *Amen*.

19. If a *kohen* who had already blessed the congregation visits another synagogue, he may go up to pronounce the benediction again. But if he is not so inclined, he is not obliged to go up even if he hears the call *Kohanim*, inasmuch as he has already done his duty.

20. A *kohen* who has a blemish on his face, may go up to pronounce the priestly benediction, since it is the custom in our communities that the *kohanim* pull the *tallit* over their faces. However, a *kohen* who has a defect in his hands, like a white scurf or spots, or they are crooked, or he is unable to part his fingers, he is not allowed to bless the people, because the worshipers will look at his hands and be distracted. However, if the *kohen* is known in

his town, where he has already lived thirty days, he may go up to bless the people. If a *kohen's* hands are dyed, he is not allowed to raise his hands in benediction, because the people will look at him. But if the majority of the residents of the town follow the trade of dyeing, he may go up to bless the people. A *kohen* who is unable to pronounce the letters properly, interchanging the *shin* and the *sin*, should not go up to say the priestly blessing unless the entire congregation read thus. Any *kohen* who does not go up to utter the priestly blessing, should leave the synagogue before the prayer *Retzeh* is commenced, and stay out until the end of the priestly blessing.

21. A *kohen* who has wilfully killed a human being, is not allowed to bless the people, even though he has repented. But if he had slain anyone accidentally and has repented, he may go up to utter the priestly blessing. A repentant renegade may utter the priestly blessing. A *kohen* who has married a divorcee, or one who has performed the rite of *ḥalitzah* (see Leviticus 25), or one who has become defiled by coming in contact with a dead body, for whom he is forbidden to defile himself, may not utter the priestly benediction until he repents as directed by a learned rabbi. The transgression of any other precept does not disqualify a *kohen* from blessing the people. A son, born of an illegitimate marriage is likewise disqualified from blessing the people.

22. Before the interment takes place, a mourner is not allowed to bless the people, neither should a *kohen*, mourning for one of his parents, bless the people during the twelve months of mourning, nor during the first thirty days of mourning for any other relative. He should leave the synagogue before the prayer *Retzeh* is recited, and stay out until the conclusion of the priestly benediction. If, however, there are no two other *kohanim* present in the synagogue, a mourner is allowed to bless the people during the twelve month period of mourning for one of his parents, or during the first thirty days of mourning for any other relative, but not during the first seven days of mourning. If one, for instance, buried his dead on a festival, the mourner should not bless the people, even if two other *kohanim* are not present at the synagogue.

CHAPTER 101

The Preparation of Foods on the First Day of a Festival for the Second Day

1. Work is permitted on a festival only when it is needed for that day. It is, therefore, forbidden to prepare food on the first day of a festival for the second day (even on *Rosh Hashanah.*) Especially is it forbidden to prepare food on a festival for a weekday. If, however, we cook food on a festival for use on that day, we may cook it in a large pot and fill it with meat or the like, and leave some of it for the evening or for the following day. This is permitted only in the case of food which is cooked, because the taste is improved when a larger quantity of meat is boiled in one pot, provided we do not say expressly that the remainder is for the night or the following day. Other foods must not be prepared in excess of what is required for that day, if any additional labor is entailed.

2. Even if no actual labor is involved, like bringing in water, or wine for *kiddush* and *havdalah,* the act is forbidden if it is for the following day. It is also forbidden to put the candles in candlesticks, or to fix the wick and the lamps on the first day of a festival, when they are to be lit in the night-time, unless they will also be used before the night, or to illuminate the synagogue.

3. If a non-Jew brings fish or fruit on the first day of a festival, and it is feared that the fish has been caught, or that fruit has been plucked, on that very day, or that they have been brought from beyond the Sabbath boundary, they must not be handled on that day. They may, however, be used in the evening, if the non-Jew knows the Jew and gives it to him without mentioning the price. But if it is brought on the first day of *Rosh Hashanah,* it may not be used even on the second day.

4. If the non-Jew brings it to the Jew, either as a gift or for sale, it may not be used even on the second day. When the festival occurs on Thursday and Friday, and the non-Jew brings it on Thursday, it may be handled and cooked on Friday in honor of the Sabbath, if very urgent, but on *Rosh Hashanah,* this too, is forbidden.

5. Milk which a non-Jew milks on the first day of a festival in the presence of a Jew, may be used on the second day. If the milking is done on the Sabbath, and the festival occurs on Sunday, its use is forbidden on Sunday. The milk which is milked on the first day of *Rosh Hashanah,* is also forbidden to be used on the second day, and also on the Sabbath if it follows immediately.

6. Wicks which have been lit on the first day of a festival and were quenched, may be lighted on the second day of the festival. But on the second day of *Rosh Hashanah,* it is forbidden to light the wicks that have been extinguished on the first day. It is forbidden to light them even at the other end. They may, nevertheless, be handled, removed and replaced by new ones. The same law applies to a festival that occurs the day after the Sabbath.

CHAPTER 102

Eruv Tavshilin (Combination of Dishes)

1. On a festival which occurs on a Friday, it is forbidden to bake or to cook in a separate pan or pot for the Sabbath, unless an *Eruv tavshilin* (combination of dishes) is performed on the afternoon before the festival. This rite is carried out as follows: We take some bread and some cooked or roasted food which is eaten with bread, and pronounce the benediction: "Who hath sanctified us by His commandments, and hath commanded us concerning the precept of *eruv.*" Then we say: "By virtue of this *eruv* be it permitted us to bake, cook, keep the food warm, light the candles, and do all work that is necessary on the festival for the Sabbath." If one does not understand the

Aramaic—the language in which this formula is written—one should say it in the language one understands best.

2. The food used for the *Eruv* must be such as is generally eaten with bread, like fish, meat, or eggs, otherwise it is invalid. The food should be no less than the size of an olive, and the bread no less than the size of an egg. One should take a goodly portion, in deference to the precept. The bread should be a whole loaf, and it should be laid on the table on the Sabbath, as the second loaf for the *Leḥem mishneh* (double loaves of bread), and it should be eaten at the third meal, since one precept has been performed with it, it is fitting that another one be performed with it.

3. The *Eruv tavshilin,* for the purpose of allowing the preparation of food on a festival for the Sabbath, is effective only when it is done early in the day; that is, if visitors who have eaten no food that day would chance to come to the house, they would have enough time to eat what has been prepared before twilight. But if there is no time to enjoy the fruit of the labor, the *Eruv* is of no effect. It is, therefore, the custom that when a festival occurs on a Friday, we commence the *Maariv* service of the Sabbath while it is still daytime, so that the food will have been prepared at an early hour, before the recital of *Mizmor shir leyom hashabbat* (A Psalm, a Song for the Sabbath Day). The victuals for the Sabbath, should be put in the oven while it is yet broad daylight, so that at least one-third of the cooking should be done before twilight.

4. Only on Friday, may food be baked or cooked for the Sabbath, by means of the *Eruv tavshilin.* If a festival occurs on Thursday and Friday, nothing may be cooked or baked on Thursday for the Sabbath.

5. The *Eruv* must remain intact until all the necessities for the Sabbath have been prepared. If the bread has been lost or eaten, it does not invalidate the *Eruv,* and we are allowed even to bake for the Sabbath. If the other victuals are lost or eaten, but the size of an olive is still left, it does not matter. But if less than that quantity is left, we are forbidden to cook for the Sabbath, as if no *Eruv* at all has been made. And what does a person do when he has made no *Eruv?* If he has become aware of it after the morning meal, and there is no one in that community who has made an *Eruv,* he is allowed to cook only one pot, bake one loaf of bread, and light one candle for the Sabbath. If he has become aware of it before the morning meal, he may cook of every dish in a big pot and leave thereof for the Sabbath. If there is one in the community who has made an *Eruv,* he should present his

flour, meat and their concomitants, to the latter as a gift, who acquires possession of these things by lifting them, and then he cooks and bakes for him and it may be done even in the house of the one who had forgotten to make the *Eruv*.

6. Every householder is required to make an *Eruv tavshilin* for himself. Even a woman who has no husband is required to do so, if she knows how to perform it. One must not rely on the *Eruv* made by the leader of the town. If by accident, a person failed to make an *Eruv*, or if he has made one but it was lost, then if there is one in town who makes an *Eruv* for all the town people (that is, he gives them a share in the victuals and in the bread, as is explained in *Shulḥan Aruḥ*), he may rely upon such a *Eruv*. If, however, it was due to negligence, or because he had relied upon the *Eruv* of the leader, it will not avail him, and his case is to be governed by the laws laid down in section 5, above.

7. If a festival occurs on Thursday and Friday, and on Thursday we become aware that we have neglected to make an *Eruv*, we may make it that day, say the prescribed benediction, and thereafter say: "If this day is holy, then I need not make the *Eruv*, and if this day is not holy, then, 'By this *eruv*,' etc." But this cannot be done on *Rosh Hashanah*.

CHAPTER 103

Rejoicing on a Festival

1. It is our duty to honor all the festivals and take delight in them, just as we are to honor and take delight in the Sabbath, as it is written (Isaiah 58:13): "And the holy of the Lord honorable," and concerning all the festivals, it is written: "A holy convocation."

2. What constitutes honor? As our Rabbis, of blessed memory, said: On the day before the festival we must cut our hair, in order not to usher in the festival in an untidy appearance. We should also bathe in warm water, wash the head, and pare the nails on the day before the festival, even as we do on the day before the Sabbath. We should also bake *ḥallot* (white loaves of bread) in our homes in honor of the festival, just as we do on the eve of the Sabbath. On the day before a festival, we are also forbidden to eat after the time set for the *Minḥah* service (3:30 p.m.), just as on the day before the Sabbath, so that we may eat the festival meal with a good appetite. If the day before the festival occurs on the Sabbath, the third meal should be eaten before the small *Minḥah* (see chapter 59:2, above) that is, 3:30 p.m. This law also applies to the first day of a festival, as that is the eve of the second day of the festival.

3. What is meant by delight? As our Rabbis, of blessed memory, said: On each day of a festival, we must have two meals, one at night and one during the day, but no third meal is required. We should also recite the

kiddush over a cup of wine before the meal, and utter the benediction *Hamotzi* over two *ḥallot*, as we do on the Sabbath. We should be as lavish with meat, wine, and dainties as our means permit.

4. On concluding the evening *kiddush* on every festival, we say the benediction *Sheheḥeyanu* (who hath kept us in life), except on the seventh and eighth nights of Passover when this benediction is omitted, because these two days are not a distinct festival in themselves. When lighting the candles, women should not say the benediction *Sheheḥeyanu* on any festival. Some women, however, say *Sheheḥeyanu* on all festivals (except on the seventh and eighth nights of Passover), and they should not be interfered with.

5. Every man is obliged to gladden the hearts of his wife, his children, and all his dependents, in a manner appropriate to each. Thus, we should give nuts and dainties to the little children, apparel and ornaments to the women, and meat and wine to the men. It is the custom to fare more sumptuously on a festival than on the Sabbath, because concerning the festival, the Torah mentions "rejoicing" (Deuteronomy 16:14), but it is not mentioned concerning the Sabbath. The holiday garments should also be costlier than those of the Sabbath.

6. On the second day of Passover, we should add some extra dish to the regular meal, commemorative of the feast of Esther which took place on this day, for it was on this day that Haman was hanged.

7. It is customary to eat dairy food on the first day of *Shavuot*. There are many reasons for that. A hint of this custom is found in the phrase מנחה חדשה לה' בשבועותיכם (Numbers 28:26). The initials of these words spell out מחלב ("of milk"). Also honey should be eaten on this day, because the Torah (given on this day on Sinai) is compared to honey and milk, as it is written (Song 4:11): "Honey and milk are under thy tongue." Now, inasmuch as dairy food is eaten on this holiday, while it is also necessary to partake of meat, the eating of meat being mandatory on every holiday, great care should be taken not to mix the dairy and the meat foods.

8. Although eating and drinking on a festival is a positive precept, we should not spend the entire day indulging in food and drink, because it is written (Deuteronomy 16:8): "A holy assembly to the Lord your God," and it is also written (Numbers 29:35): "A holy assembly it shall be to you." The Rabbis, of blessed memory, explained it thus (Betzah 15b): "We should divide the day into two parts, devoting one-half to the service of God, and the other half to our own pleasures." Therefore, it is our duty to engage also in the study of the Torah.

9. When a man eats and drinks on a festival, it is his duty to take care also of the orphan and the widow, as well as others who are in need. He who locks the doors of his house in order to eat and drink with his wife and children, and gives nothing to the poor and the mournful souls, is not rejoicing in a precept, but merely indulging in gluttony. Concerning such people, it is

said (Hosea 9:4): "Their sacrifices shall be unto them as the bread of mourners; all that eat thereof shall be polluted; for their bread shall be for their own appetite." Such a rejoicing is a disgrace to them, for it is written (Malaḥi 2:3): "And I will spread dung upon your faces, even the dung of your festive offering."

10. When rejoicing on a festival, one should not indulge too much in wine, in laughter and levity, thinking that the more he indulges in it the greater the merit. For drunkenness, jesting, and levity constitute not rejoicing, but madness and folly, and it is not in the spirit of the commandment. Rejoicing should accompany the worship of the Creator of the universe, for it is written (Deuteronomy 28:47): "Because thou didst not serve the Lord thy God with joyfulness and gladness of heart;" from this we infer that the worship of God must be done with joy, but one cannot serve God by jesting, and levity and drunkenness.

11. It is the way of the pious, who constantly have the Lord before them, and who are cognizant of Him in all their ways, that while rejoicing they bless and praise even more the Holy One, blessed be He, who has caused them to rejoice. While rejoicing and having pleasure, a man should say to himself: If the joy of this world is so pleasant, although it is nothing but vanity, because the end of it is sorrow and vexation, how great then will be the everlasting joy in the world to come, which is not followed by sorrow. He should then pray to the Holy One, blessed be He, that He should incline his heart to serve Him and to do His will with a perfect heart, and gladden him with everlasting joy, and to be worthy of sharing in the life of the world to come, to enjoy the light of the presence of the ever-living God.

12. A man must take care of his household; they should not associate with lightheaded people who might, God forbid, lead them to levity; they must be holy, because the day of the festival is holy.

13. At the conclusion of a festival, that is followed either by a weekday or by the Intermediate Days of the festival, we say: *Attah ḥonantanu* (Thou hast favored us) in the *Shemoneh esreh* of the *Maariv* service, and to recite the *havdalah* over a cup of wine, but we say no benediction over the light or over the spices.

14. It is customary to fare somewhat better than ordinarily on the day following the three festivals. That day is known as *issru ḥag.* It is customary not to fast on that day, not even a groom and bride on their wedding day; nor should one who observes *Jahrzeit* fast on *issru ḥag.* On *issru ḥag* following *Shavuot,* it is forbidden to fast according to law, for at the time when the Temple was in existence, if this festival occurred on the Sabbath, the sacrifices were offered the following day, but on Passover and the Feast of Tabernacles, they were sacrificed on the first day of *Ḥol Hammoed.*

CHAPTER 104

Ḥol Hammoed (Intermediate Days of a Festival)

1. On *Ḥol Hammoed,* certain labors may be performed, while others may not. For instance, we may perform all work essential to the preparation of food for those days and for the festival, as well as any work that will prevent sustaining a loss; that is, if by not doing it, a loss will be sustained, then it may be done. However, great care should be taken not to perform any work that is forbidden on *Ḥol Hammoed,* for our Rabbis, of blessed memory, said (Pesaḥim 118a): "He who profanes the festivals, is considered as though he had worshiped idols."

2. Our Rabbis, of blessed memory, said again (Avot 3:15): "He who slights the festivals, even though he has Torah and good deeds to his credit, has no share in the world to come." What is meant by *slighting?* If one does not honor it by having better food and drink and by putting on better clothes. Therefore, it is one's duty to honor it according to one's means, and to put on costly garments.

3. Any work, the non-performance of which would entail a loss, may be done for us even by a Jew, and even for pay. If, however, no loss will be sustained, only the work is needed for the festival, it may not be done for us by a Jew for pay, only by a non-Jew. But if we cannot get a non-Jew to do it, and we are unable to do it ourselves, we are permitted to have it done by a Jew for pay.

4. The law that work may be performed on *Ḥol Hammoed* in order to prevent a loss, applies only to a case where it was impossible to have it done before the festival. If, however, one was able to do it before the festival, but left it for *Ḥol Hammoed,* one is forbidden to perform it on *Ḥol Hammoed.*

5. A Jew who lacks sufficient food for *Ḥol Hammoed* and the festival, is permitted to do for us any work that is otherwise forbidden on *Ḥol Hammoed,* so that he may procure the proper foods. But he should do it privately. Work forbidden to be performed, may not be done by a non-Jew, unless it is required for the performance of a precept.

6. Even the kind of work that may be performed on *Ḥol Hammoed,* must not be done for a non-Jew.

7. It is forbidden to fertilize a field on *Ḥol Hammoed;* it is even forbidden to drive sheep into the field, so that they might furnish manure. It is also forbidden to have the manuring done by a non-Jew.

8. Sowing is forbidden on *Ḥol Hammoed.* If, however, one has seeds which will completely spoil unless they are put into water, one is allowed to soak them.

9. It is forbidden to pluck out or to cut off anything that grows, excepting what is required for food on the festival, unless the failure to do so might cause the fruit to be spoiled. And we need not skimp, but we may pluck a liberal quantity, and if some is left over, it does not matter. If we need wood for the fire, we are likewise permitted to chop it off from where it grows. It is forbidden to pick wood from a field, in order to make it fit for ploughing. However, if it is evident that we pick it to be used as firewood, as when we pick the big pieces and leave the small ones, it is permissible. We are likewise forbidden to cut the branches off a tree for the purpose of trimming it. But if it is evident that we need the branches to feed our cattle and not for the purpose of trimming the tree, as when we cut the branches from one side of the tree, it is permissible.

10. If one has an orchard adjoining that of a non-Jew, and the non-Jew gathers in his fruit, and if the Jew will not gather in his fruit, he will sustain a loss, he is allowed to pick them on *Ḥol Hammoed.* If the fruit will be spoiled unless he does some additional work for it, he is allowed to do all that is necessary, even to press grapes and make wine, or any work similar to it, providing he has not purposely left that work for *Ḥol Hammoed.*

11. One is forbidden to have one's hair cut on *Ḥol Hammoed,* even though one has had the hair cut on the day before the festival. But one who has been released from prison, even on the day before the festival, but did not have sufficient time to cut his hair, is permitted to do so on *Ḥol Hammoed.*

12. Paring the nails is also forbidden, but if one has pared them on the day before the festival, one may pare them also on *Ḥol Hammoed.* A woman is permitted to pare her nails for the ritual immersion.

13. It is forbidden to wash any clothes, even when needed for the festival, unless it was impossible to have them washed before the festival. It is permissible to wash an infant's diapers, since they are constantly needed. However, all washing on *Ḥol Hammoed* should be done privately.

14. Whatever is required medicinally, either for man or beast, may be done during *Ḥol Hammoed.*

15. It is permitted to write down accounts, or the like, which might be forgotten, for it is equivalent to preventing a loss. It is also permissible to write whatever is necessary for the festival, but it is forbidden to write anything else. It is the custom to write sociable letters on *Ḥol Hammoed,* in a

slightly different manner, like writing the first line unevenly. It is also permissible to fix a pen and ink for permissible writing.

16. A person who is in need of funds, even if it is not for the requirements of the festival, but he is afraid that he might be unable to obtain the loan after the festival, and he cannot obtain it without giving the lender a note is allowed to write such note on *Ḥol Hammoed.*

17. No marriages should take place on *Ḥol Hammoed,* because it is improper to mix one celebration with another. But one is permitted to remarry a woman one had divorced. It is permissible to make a feast on the occasion of a circumcision, the redemption of a firstborn, or a betrothal.

18. It is permitted to hire laborers, even Jews, during *Ḥol Hammoed,* to do work after the festival.

19. During *Ḥol Hammoed,* we are allowed to walk outside the Sabbath boundary line, either on foot, in a vehicle, or on horseback.

20. It is forbidden to mate animals on *Ḥol Hammoed,* as no loss will be sustained by delaying it.

21. It is not permitted to set a hen on eggs for hatching. But if the hen has been set before the festival, and she ran away, she may be put back on the eggs within three days from the time she fled, but not after the three days, even if the eggs will be spoiled. It is forbidden to place another hen in her stead, even within the three days.

Chapter 105

Things Forbidden Because They Require Exertion

1. It is forbidden to remove and carry chattels or furniture during *Ḥol Hammoed,* from a dwelling in one court into the dwelling of another court, even from an unsightly to a handsome dwelling, but it may be moved from one house into another in the same court. If the two courts adjoin each other, and there is a door between them, it is likewise permissible to carry the articles through that door. Where, however, a loss may otherwise be sustained, it is permissible to remove furniture, even from one city to another. It is likewise permissible to remove from a dwelling not owned by the tenant into a dwelling owned by him, in order that he might rejoice on the festival, as it is a joy to dwell in one's own home.

2. If one must take in fruit or other merchandise for fear either of its being stolen or lost, it should be done secretly, if possible; but if it cannot be done secretly, it is permissible to take them in openly.

Chapter 106

Buying and Selling During Ḥol Hammoed

1. During *Ḥol Hammoed,* it is forbidden either to buy or to sell any merchandise, unless there is an opportunity to make a big profit, then we may buy or sell privately, but we should in such event spend in honor of the festival, more than we had intended.

2. If one has merchandise, and he fears that if it is not sold immediately, its value will be depreciated to less than its cost, one is permitted to sell it on *Ḥol Hammoed.* If, however, there is no fear of sustaining a loss but by not selling it now we will lose profit, one is forbidden to sell it, because lack of profit is not considered a loss.

3. If a fair occurs during *Ḥol Hammoed,* or if it is the ordinary weekly market day, but it is before the non-Jewish holidays, when many buyers gather together, it is permissible to sell merchandise. For inasmuch as it is an irregular occasion, the lack of profit is also considered a loss, but it is forbidden to sell on a regular weekly market day. When merchants or ships occasionally arrive, who sell merchandise cheaply or buy at a high price, which is an extraordinary occurrence, it is likewise permissible to purchase from or sell to them.

4. If one desires to buy wine at vintage time for his needs of the entire year, for the reason that the price of wine will later advance, he may buy it during *Ḥol Hammoed;* but he is not allowed to buy it for trading purposes.

5. We are permitted to sell, even openly, whatever is required for the festival, such as food and spices. And since we are allowed to open the store to sell to Jews, we may also sell to non-Jews.

6. Collecting debts, even from Jews, is permissible, because we have to consider the possibility of sustaining a loss.

7. One is permitted, during *Ḥol Hammoed,* to lend money on interest to a non-Jew who is his regular client, as otherwise a loss might be sustained if the latter will become someone else's client. If one lends money to a non-Jew who is not his regular client, one should spend the interest of one week for the celebration of the festival. But we are forbidden to sell merchandise to one who is not our regular customer and the additional luxury for the festival rejoicing (out of the profits) is of no avail. We are permitted, however, to sell merchandise to a regular customer, as otherwise a loss might be sustained if the latter will get accustomed to purchase elsewhere.

8. During *Ḥol Hammoed,* it is not permissible to exchange money.

CHAPTER 107

The Month of Nisan

1. During the entire month of *Nisan,* we do not say the *Taḥanun* (petition for Grace); we do not hold funeral services; and we do not say *Tzidkateḥa tzedek* (Thy righteousness) at the *Minḥah* service on the Sabbath. From *Rosh Ḥodesh* on, it is customary to read each day the section treating of the offering brought by the prince of the tribe on that day (Numbers 7:12 ff.); and on the thirteenth day of the month, the section *Behaaloteḥa* (when thou lightest) should be read until, *Ken asah et hamenorah* (so he made the candlestick) (Numbers 8:1-5), which is appropriate for the Tribe of *Levi.*

2. During the month of *Nisan,* we are not allowed to fast even on the *Jahrzeit,* but we may fast when we have an evil dream. The firstborn sons should fast on the day before Passover, as will be explained, if God so please it, in chapter 113, below. A groom and a bride may fast during this month, even on *Rosh Ḥodesh* of *Nisan.*

3. On *Shabbat Haggadol* (the great Sabbath), that is, the Sabbath before *Pesaḥ,* it is customary not to read *Barḥi naphshi* (bless the Lord my soul) etc., in the afternoon, but to recite instead: *Avadim hayinu* (we were slaves), etc., because on this Sabbath the redemption from Egypt and the miracles began.

CHAPTER 108

The Wheat and Flour for the Matzah

1. It is written (Exodus 12:17): "And ye shall observe the fast of unleavened bread," it is inferred from this, that we must guard the wheat out of which we are to bake the *matzah,* to see that no moisture comes thereon. According to the opinion of some of the great authorities, this watchfulness should commence from the time the wheat is reaped. However, the custom prevails to follow the view of the authorities who hold that it suffices to watch it from the time it is brought to the mill. But the zealous observe it from the time it is reaped, and this is the proper procedure. Meticulous people do not allow the stalks of wheat to remain attached to the soil until fully ripe and white, for they might become leavened if rain falls on them, since they no longer need the soil. It is, therefore, best and most proper to reap them while they are still slightly green. It is well, if possible, to use during the entire festival, *matzah* made of wheat that has been under observation from the time of reaping. If this is impossible, one should at least honor the two *Seder* nights by using such *matzah.*

2. If some of the wheat has split open or has sprouted, the rest of it may be used for *matzah,* provided the unfit ones are separated, or we must make sure that there are at least sixty times as much of the good wheat as the cracked, or as those that have sprouted. We must also be very careful to separate the wheat that has been partly nibbled by mice, or we must make sure that there is at least sixty times as much of the good wheat. Wheat brought in by a ship, or stored in pits, is valid for *matzah* if it is dry and hard and its color has not changed, but if it has been stored in a garret and the rain dripped upon it in several places through the roof, it may not be

used. If, however, a little snow or rain has fallen upon it in one place only, then only the doubtful grains of wheat should be removed, and the rest may be used.

3. It has been a long established custom in Israel, to cleanse the mill in the most scrupulous manner, and to provide new receptacles for the flour. In a community where there are learned men, the mill should be inspected by them and the cleansing of it supervised by them to see to it that it is properly done. If there are no learned men, then the God-fearing should go themselves to supervise, for it is more meritorious to do a good thing in person than to delegate it to an agent. It is customary that the flour of the first grinding after the mill has been made fit, is not used for Passover. If moist grain has also been ground in that mill, it should be separated from the other by a partition, so that none of its powder should mingle with it.

4. If part of a bag of flour has been moistened by water, whether it is still moist or already dry, we may hold that part of the bag in our hands while emptying from it the rest of the flour, the use of which is permissible; only the moist part may not be used. If, however, the bag of flour has become wet in many places, so that it is impossible to proceed as aforementioned, then if it is still moist, we sift the flour, and the lumps alone which remain in the sieve is leaven, but the rest may be used. If mice have eaten some of the flour, it should also be sifted. If, however, the bag of flour has already become dry, sifting is of no avail, and the use of the entire flour is forbidden.

5. It is forbidden to use the flour on the same day it has been ground, as the flour is then warm and will readily turn sour when water is poured on it. Therefore, we should defer its use for at least twenty-four hours after the grinding.

6. It is best to make new bags for holding the flour, or at least to open the seams of the old bags, wash them thoroughly with warm water and ashes, and rub and beat them out.

7. A bag of flour should not be loaded upon a beast unless thick leather is placed underneath the bag, as otherwise it will get warm and moist from perspiration. And if possible, one should not place many bags, one on the top of the other, as the flour will be heated by the friction and turn sour in the kneading.

CHAPTER 109

The Water Used for Kneading Matzah

1. The flour for *matzah* should be kneaded only with water that has stayed overnight, that is, it should be drawn in the twilight and then let it stay overnight. Even if the night is longer than twelve hours, it is forbidden

to use it before daylight, and if the night is short and there are no twelve hours to daylight, we must wait until twelve hours will have passed from the time it has been drawn. The masses are accustomed to commence kneading with the water immediately at dawn, although no twelve hours have passed. Although this is sanctioned by some authorities, the majority of the authorities disapprove of it, and we must be heedful of their opinion.

2. If we are unable to ascertain the exact time of twilight, we may draw the water a little earlier, providing we do not draw it before sunset. It is the custom to filter the water and to cover it; and it must be placed in a cool place. When bringing the water into the house in the morning, we must see to it that no sunrays fall on it.

3. We may draw enough water at one time to last for several days, but it is best to draw fresh water daily for each day's use. It is customary not to place the water in an old earthen vessel, although it has been used only for Passover, unless it is glazed; for the use of an old unglazed vessel cannot be considered as reverent toward a Divine Command. It is a custom that should not be altered.

4. As rivers in the month of *Nisan* are generally cooler than the wells, we should draw the water from a river. At times, however, the streams are swollen from the melting snow and the water is not so cold; it is then preferable to draw water from a well.

5. The water for baking *matzah* should not be drawn by a non-Jew, but by a Jew.

6. The water should not be placed in a vessel which had contained honey or fruit extracts unless it has been rinsed with hot water. Placing the water in a vessel which had contained something pungent, should be especially avoided, even if it is not leaven, because on account of the pungency, it will more readily cause the dough to leaven and even rinsing it with hot water will not avail in such a case. Nor should the water be put into a copper vessel, as it does not keep it as cool as other vessels.

7. If the water that has been kept overnight does not suffice, we may add other water to it, providing the water that stayed overnight is the greater part of it, but it is best that the water which was kept overnight should constitute two-thirds of the total. If possible, the added water should be obtained from a pump or from some other sheltered place where the sun does not penetrate.

8. If the *matzah* is baked on a Sunday, the water should be drawn on Thursday evening, because it is difficult to ascertain the exact time of twilight on Friday. If by accident, the water has not been drawn on Thursday, it should be drawn on Friday after the *Minḥah* service, or on the Sabbath by a non-Jew.

9. The water that has been kept overnight should not be poured out on account of a death that has occurred, or on account of the equinox, for it is written (Ecclesiastes 8:5): "Whoso keepeth the commandment shall know no evil thing." However, if one is aware that the vernal equinox will occur

on that night, one should put a small, clean piece of metal into the water, such as a needle, and it should be attached to a thread, so that he would be able to pull it out without putting his hands into the water.

Chapter 110

The Kneading and Baking of Matzah

1. If we wish to bake *matzah* in an oven in which leaven had been baked, we must make it ritually fit by making it glow, that is, incandesce it to such a degree as to cause sparks to fly from it; for anything less than that would not constitute true incandescence. Great care should be taken to spread the coal over the entire area of the oven. After the incandescing, it is highly proper to remove the ashes and to clean it thoroughly, wait until it somewhat cools off, and then make a new fire for baking the *matzah,* but not immediately after the heating.

2. Some people plaster the oven with fresh loam, without incandescing it, for the unleavened substance contained in the roof and the walls of the oven exudes when heated. This is a good practice, providing a thick coating of plaster, no less than the thickness of a finger, is put over the entire oven.

3. The *matzah* should be kneaded and prepared only in a room that has a roof, and not before an open window, even if the sun does not shine through it. However, if the window is shut and has panes, the *matzah* may be kneaded before it, if the sun does not shine through it. But if the sun shines through, it, the glass panes are of no avail, unless a curtain is spread over it to shut out the rays of the sun. Care should also be taken that the house should not be overheated.

4. No greater quantity of dough should be kneaded at one time than what is necessary to become subject to the separation of *ḥallah* (first of the dough). And it is best to make it smaller. For our Rabbis, of blessed memory, estimated that if the dough is larger than the above mentioned limit, it cannot be worked properly at one and the same time, thus leaving some part of it unworked, and it is to be feared that it may become leavened in the meantime. If the dough is loose, no flour should be added to it to thicken it.

5. When the flour is measured, it should not be stuffed into the measure, for if there is too much flour, some of it might be left unkneaded in the *matzah,* and when it is put into the soup it will become leaven. We must be careful not to keep the flour near the water, so that the flour dust should not fall therein. The one who measures the flour should likewise not go near the dough

or the water. It is well not to handle the flour needlessly, because the hands might slightly warm it.

6. The vessel used for kneading the dough must have neither holes nor cracks, where particles of dough might remain and turn into leaven. Nor should the vessel be placed upon cushioned articles while in the act of kneading lest it becomes warm. The vessel must be thoroughly cleansed every eighteen minutes, also the hands must be thoroughly washed. The boards and rollers must also be free from holes and cracks, and should be thoroughly cleansed at least every eighteen minutes. The instruments with which the perforations are made should be kept clean without any dough on them. The peel with which the *matzah* is put into the oven should be carefully examined for cracks, where a particle of dough might lodge and become leavened.

7. If anything pungent falls into the dough, such as salt, spices, or quick-lime, and has been kneaded into it, the use of the entire dough is forbidden, inasmuch as it has become heated by it. If a grain of corn is found in the dough, a mass of dough as thick as one's finger should be removed from all around the grain and thrown away, and the rest of the dough may be used.

8. The dough must not be left, even for a moment without working on it; and as soon as the kneading is completed, it should be handed to the rollers. Care should, therefore, be taken to make the dough only as large as can be immediately taken care of by the rollers. If some of the dough is left with the kneader, he should keep kneading it, so that it should not lie idle for a moment.

9. The rollers should perform their work speedily and not linger to give the *matzah* any definite shape. They must see to it that no particles of dough are left upon the boards and that none of it clings to their hands. As soon as they find any dough sticking to their hands, they must wash them thoroughly.

10. Immediately after the *matzah* has been rolled, it should be perforated quickly, not making any designs on it, and it should be put into the oven as quickly as possible. The utmost precaution should be taken not to hold it even for a moment before the opening of the oven, as it will be leavened quickly. Hence, it is necessary that the one handing the *matzah* to the baker, should be versed in the law, be God-fearing and pay scrupulous attention to it.

11. A God-fearing person should take care, before baking his *matzah*, to

have the oven well heated anew and the coals spread upon the entire oven; for who knows whether the one who baked his *matzah* before was meticulous.

12. The baker should be very careful that none of the *matzot* be doubled up, and that one should not touch the other, for in the place where it is doubled up or joined with another, it does not bake quickly and it becomes leavened. In the event one *matzah* doubles up or becomes inflated, that portion must be broken off, and the rest may be used. If, however, the *matzot* touched each other in the oven while still moist, their use may be permitted post facto. The term *inflated* connotes that the *matzah* has been divided in its thick part, and the hollow thus formed is as wide as a thumb.

13. Care should be taken not to take the *matzah* out of the oven before it is baked to such a degree that if one breaks it, there should be no fibers of dough between the pieces. Otherwise it is only like dough which, when taken out of the oven, readily becomes leavened. The peel with which such *matzah* was removed from the oven, may no longer be used for the baking of *matzah*. If it is impossible to ascertain whether or not that *matzah*, when taken out, had fibers of dough, the law should be strictly enforced. However, if the *matzah* has formed a crust, the law may be relaxed.

14. A God-fearing man should supervise personally the preparation and the baking of his own *matzah*, and to admonish the men to work with care and despatch. Thus were the great men of Israel accustomed to do in the past, and this is what we do in our own times.

15. The *matzah* eaten on the first two nights of Passover, with which one fulfills the precept of eating *matzot*, is known as *Matzot mitzvah* (mandatory), and they should be prepared "for the sake of the precept," by an adult male Jew of intelligence, aged at least thirteen years and one day, or by a female aged at least twelve years and one day. At each stage of the process, even when the water is drawn, the worker says, *Leshem matzat mitzvah* (for the sake of the mandatory *matzah*). (The foregoing rules of law concerning the baking of *matzah*, refer to the *matzah* customarily baked before Passover. In case of emergency, when the *matzah* is baked during the Passover, there are many additional regulations. Those who bake the *matzot mitzvah* in the afternoon before Passover, also have to take extra precautions.)

CHAPTER 111

The Search for Leaven

1. On the evening before Passover, a search for leaven must be made immediately after nightfall. It is forbidden to begin a meal or any work one half hour before nightfall.

2. The search should be made with only one wax candle, not by several twisted together, for then it becomes a torch. But if we have no wax candle, we may use a tallow candle.

3. All the rooms into which leaven might have been lodged, must be searched; even the cellars, garrets, stores, and woodsheds. All those vessels in which leaven has been kept should also be searched. Before the search is made, all these places should be carefully swept and cleansed from leaven, in order to facilitate the ritual search.

4. A stall in which the cattle are fed with grain, and a coop in which the fowl are fed with grain, do not require searching. For, in the first place, it is likely that the grain did not become leavened, and if it did become leavened, it is possible that all of it has been eaten and none has been left. However, if leavened grain has been put there, and there is only a single uncertainty, whether all of it has been eaten up, we do not rely on this possibility, and a search is required.

5. Every nook and cranny of all places must be searched with the utmost care. We must also search the pockets of our garments as well as those of our children's garments, as leaven is at times placed therein; and the following morning when the leaven is burnt, they should be thoroughly shaken out.

6. The rooms which are sold to non-Jews before Passover, together with the leaven they contain must be searched in the evening, inasmuch as the sale will not be consummated before the following morning.

7. Before beginning the search, we say the benediction: "Who hath sanctified us by His commandments and hath commanded us concerning the clearing out of the leaven." Although we do not yet remove the leaven, nevertheless, since after the search we annul the leaven unknown to us, this benediction refers to such leaven. We are not allowed to make any interruption between the benediction and the beginning of the search. It is well not to make an interruption until the search is completed, excepting for that which relates to the search. One benediction is sufficient for the search of many houses.

8. Before making the search, it is customary to deposit some crumbs of bread in the places where the searcher will find them, because should no leaven be found, the benediction will have been said in vain. But certainly, if we do not make a proper search for leaven, but simply gather up these crumbs, we do not thereby fulfill the commandment of searching, and the benediction has been pronounced in vain.

9. Before making the search, we put away in a safe place all our leaven, whether it be for our use or for sale. We likewise put away in a safe place the leaven we have found in the search. First we carefully wrap it up, then we put it in a safe place where it can be easily noticed in the morning, so that we may be sure to burn it.

10. We must nullify the leaven immediately after the search. The real "nullification" is our firm resolve to consider all leaven in our domain as non-existent, entirely valueless and compared to dust, and as something for which we have absolutely no use. Our Sages have furthermore ordained that we must express these thoughts by saying the formula, *Kal ḥamira* (all leaven), etc. If we do not understand the Aramaic words in which this formula is written, we are to say it in any language we understand best.

11. Although we have already nullified the leaven at night, after the search, we must, nevertheless, nullify it again in the morning after we have burnt it, including in that nullification all the leaven, and say the formula, *Kal ḥamira* (all the leaven), etc.

12. If we wish to store fruit, wood, or other articles in a room which must be searched for leaven before Passover, but no search would then be possible on account of the stored articles, then a search should be made the night before it is turned into a storeroom, in the same manner as it is made on the night of the fourteenth day of *Nisan*, even if there is yet ample time before Passover, and even if this is immediately after the Passover that has passed. If, however, by inadvertence we have neglected to make the search before transforming it into a storeroom, then if we intend to remove the articles before the time the search will be due, we need not trouble ourselves to remove them now to search the room. But if we intend to remove the articles during the week of Passover, we must remove them and search the room now, even if it involves great trouble and entails a loss of money.

13. If we deposit the articles in the storeroom with the intention of not removing them until after Passover, then it depends on the time it takes place. If it is more than thirty days before Passover, we need not search the room (except to remove from there anything that is positively leaven), and the for-

mula of nullification recited at the proper time will also cover that room. If, however, it is within thirty days before Passover, we must search the room now (since the laws of Passover are expounded thirty days before Passover). Even if we have inadvertently neglected to make the search, we must empty the storeroom and make the search the night immediately after we have become aware of the neglect.

14. If we store unleavened wheat in a silo, but later the wheat at the bottom and at the sides of the silo became leavened because of the dampness, then even if we have stored it there within the thirty days, we need not empty the silo on the night of the fourteenth of *Nisan* in order to search it, for, inasmuch as we have stored it away in a permissible manner, the recital of the nullification will suffice. There is a divergence of opinion concerning a case where some leavened wheat is found there, and in such event we must consult a competent rabbi.

15. During the thirty days before Passover, we must not throw any grain to fowls in a moist place, lest we forget to clear them away.

16. Before starting on a journey, we should appoint an agent to search and to nullify our leaven, and we must tell him expressly that he is appointed as our agent both to make the search and the nullification. The agent must mention the name of the owner in the formula, thus: "The leaven of so-and-so (naming the person)." Nevertheless, wherever we happen to be, we ourselves must also nullify the leaven which is on our premises on the morning of the day before Passover.

17. If we find leaven in our house during *Ḥol Hammoed,* we should take it out and burn it. And if it is a quantity the size of an olive, we should first pronounce the benediction: *Al biur ḥametz* (concerning the removing of leaven). If we find the leaven during the first two days of the festival or on the Sabbath of *Ḥol Hammoed,* or on the Sabbath which occurs on the day before Passover, when the *ḥametz* may not be handled, because of its being *muktzeh* (see chapter 99, above), we should cover it with a vessel until the conclusion of the festival or of the Sabbath, and then burn it. If we find the leaven during the last two days of *Pesaḥ,* we should burn it at the conclusion of the festival without pronouncing the benediction, even though its quantity is more than the size of an olive.

CHAPTER 112

Leaven Which May and Which May Not Be Retained on Pesaḥ

1. Every article of food which contains leaven, even if the bulk was removed and only the taste of the leaven remained, must not be kept during the week of *Pesaḥ.* However, if an article of food never contained any leaven, only it was cooked in a vessel used for leaven, even if the leaven was cooked in the vessel on that very day, or if an article was pickled in a vessel used for leaven, that article of food may be kept during *Pesaḥ,* providing the cooking or

pickling was done before *Pesaḥ*. However, what has been cooked or pickled during the week of *Pesaḥ*, in a vessel used for leaven, must be burnt.

2. If grain contains some seeds that have sprouted or were cracked, even if only a few of such seeds are mingled in a large quantity, or if water has been spilled upon the grain, or it has been washed with water, that grain must not be kept during the week of *Pesaḥ*, nor anything that has been prepared from it. If we sell a neighbor grain that has become moist, we must caution him not to keep it in his domaim during *Pesaḥ*. We are forbidden to sell it to a non-Jew if he is likely to resell it to a Jew who will keep it during *Pesaḥ*.

3. During *Pesaḥ*, we are allowed to wear garments that have been washed and starched, but we are not permitted to cover a table with a cloth if there is tangible starch on it for some particles of it may fall on the food; and it is most decidely forbidden to put the *Pesaḥ* flour in such a cloth.

4. It is permissible to paste paper on the windows even during the thirty days before *Pesah*, providing the leaven is not visible; for, inasmuch as the paste is not absolute leaven and it is also covered up, the law is not strictly binding. If, however, the paste is visible, it is forbidden. But before the thirty days, it is permissible in any case.

5. On *Ḥol Hammoed Pesaḥ*, it is permissible to write with ink which has been prepared with beer before *Pesaḥ*, since it has been rendered unfit even for a dog's food before *Pesaḥ*. The same rule of law applies to all leavened food which has been entirely spoiled before *Pesaḥ*. Such food may be kept during *Pesaḥ* and also benefit may be derived from it. If, however, a non-Jew has prepared ink with beer on *Pesaḥ*, no Jew may derive any benefit from it, because on *Pesaḥ*, no Jew may derive any benefit even from the leaven belonging to a non-Jew.

6. All vessels which have not been made ritually fit for *Pesaḥ*, should be thoroughly scoured and rinsed in the forenoon before *Pesaḥ* in such a manner that no leaven be visible on them, and then concealed in a place which is not frequented. It is best, however, to lock them up in a separate room and hide the key until after *Pesaḥ*.

CHAPTER 113

The Day Before Pesaḥ and the Baking of Matzot

1. On the day before *Pesaḥ*, neither *Mizemor letodah* (A Psalm of Thanks) nor *Lamenatzeaḥ* (For the Chief Musician) should be said.

2. It is forbidden to eat *ḥametz*, past one-third of the day, that is, one-third of the time from dawn until the stars appear (about ten o'clock in the morning); but we may derive some benefit from it for another hour (that is, until eleven o'clock). Hence, we may sell it until then to a non-Jew. But

after that time, no kind of benefit may be derived from it. We must burn the leaven and nullify it while we are still permitted to derive some benefit from it; that is, before eleven o'clock.

3. In the afternoon we are not permitted to do any work, except the type of work which is permitted on *Ḥol Hammoed.* But we are allowed to let a non-Jew do work for us. In some communities, the custom is to refrain from work the entire day.

4. We should take a haircut and pare the nails in the forenoon. If, however, we have forgotten to do so, we may pare the nails in the afternoon, but we may not have our hair cut in the afternoon, unless it is done by a non-Jew.

5. We are not allowed to eat *matzah* during the day before *Pesaḥ*. We are even forbidden to give *matzah* to minors who understand the import of Passover. We are permitted, however, to eat foods of *matzah meal* until the beginning of the last quarter of the day (three o'clock in the afternoon). From that time on, we may eat, in case of necessity only, fruit, meat, or fish, but we must be careful not to eat too much of it, so that we may eat the *matzah* in the evening with relish.

6. The firstborn sons, either of the father or of the mother, must fast on the day before *Pesaḥ*, even if it occurs on a Friday. One born after a miscarriage also must fast. When the child is small, the father fasts in his stead. Whether or not the firstborn may eat at a religious feast, depends on local custom.

7. A firstborn son who fasts, should say *Anenu* (answer us) in the *Shemoneh esreh* of the *Minḥah* service. If there are many firstborn and they pray with the congregation, none of them should officiate as *ḥazan*, as *Anenu* may not be said in the loud repetition of the *Shemoneh esreh,* owing to the month of *Nisan.*

8. The very scrupulous bake the "*matzah* mandatory" (see chapter 110: 15, above) in the afternoon before *Pesaḥ*, the time when the *Paschal* lamb was offered in the Temple, and inasmuch as leaven is then forbidden, it is best to nullify the crumbs by saying in any language understood best, the following formula: "All the crumbs that will fall off during the kneading and preparing, as well as the dough which will cling to the vessels. I hereby nullify and abandon."

9. The water with which the vessels are washed should be poured out in a sloping place where there is no stone paving, so that it might be quickly absorbed in the ground; for, by emptying it where the water cannot flow down,

or where there is a stone paving, the water might gather in one place and be leavened before it is absorbed in the ground, thus there will be leaven in one's domain.

CHAPTER 114

The Selling of Ḥametz

1. A Jew having leavened food in his possession during *Pesaḥ* is continuously transgressing the precept (Exodus 13:7): "No leaven shall be seen with thee," and (Exodus 12:19): "No leaven shall be found in your houses," and out of such leaven he must never derive any benefit, even if he nullified it before *Pesaḥ*. Therefore, if we have in our possession much leavened food, which we are unable to clear out, we are required to sell it to a non-Jew before *Pesaḥ*, while we are still permitted to derive some benefit from it. The matter of selling leaven to a non-Jew shall not be a mere formality, but a real and binding sale; and we should not sell it at a higher price than it is worth. After *Pesaḥ* we demand from the non-Jew to pay the debt, and when the latter replies that he has no money, we request him to resell us the leaven (together with the room) for so-much-and-so-much. The transaction should be made in a true business manner, and not as a mere jest.

2. The leaven that is sold to the non-Jew must not remain in the house of the Jew. If the non-Jew can take it into his own house, so much the better, but if he cannot take it away, then the room where the leaven is lodged must be rented to him. In the bill of sale, he must mention the name of the buyer, the amount at which the room was rented, and that by renting him the room he conveys to him the leaven that is contained there. He must state the price at which the leaven was sold, but he need not mention the number of measures. He may stipulate to get so much for every measure. He must orally speak to the buyer about the conditions contained in the written contract. He should take a deposit from him, and the balance of the purchase price should be considered as a loan. All of the foregoing should be mentioned in the agreement. He must also deliver to the buyer the key to the room. If any leaven is contained in a vessel which requires ritual immersion (when bought from a non-Jew), he should not sell it with the vessel, because if he does sell it, then after *Pesaḥ* when he buys it back from the non-Jew, it will have to be immersed again.

3. If after the leavened food has been sold, the Jew fears that the buyer may cause some damage, he may put an additional lock on the door. Or, if the buyer is willing, he may deposit the key with the Jew. But the Jew is forbidden to put a seal on the leavened food.

4. If the Jew is unable to rent the whole room holding the leaven, because he needs some space for his own use, he should make a partition before the place occupied by the leaven, and rent to the non-Jew the place occupied by the leaven up to the partition, so stating in the agreement. He should also provide in the agreement that the buyer has a right of access, at his will, to that place, and that if he, the non-Jew, should desire to sell the leaven to another non-Jew during *Pesaḥ*, or to another Jew after *Pesaḥ*, all of these should have a right of access there. If the Jew rents or sells to the non-Jew a room to which access must be had through the premises of the seller, it must likewise be so provided in the agreement that the non-Jewish buyer, as well as all the prospective buyers that he may bring there, should have a right of way to enter there.

5. If the house is not the property of the Jew, but is rented to him by another Jew, he cannot sublet it to the non-Jew without the permission of the proprietor. Therefore, he should clearly tell the non-Jew, that he does not rent it to him as a dwelling, but only to keep his vessels and chattels there. He must not, however, state that he lets it to him to keep the leaven, but generally to keep his vessels and chattels, as he sees fit. Nevertheless, if the owner of the premises is in town, permission should be obtained from him to sublet it. One who goes on a journey, and the leaven will be sold by his wife, must give her express permission to let the room.

6. It is forbidden to stipulate with the non-Jew that he must resell him the leaven after *Pesaḥ*, or that he, the Jew, is bound to rebuy it from him. However, he may promise the non-Jew that after *Pesaḥ* he will rebuy it and give him some profit.

7. It is forbidden to sell the leaven to an apostate Jew or Jewess, or to the son of an apostate Jewess, even if she has born him from a non-Jew after she became an apostate. For, as far as this law is concerned, they are considered as Jews, and the leaven will be regarded like that which has remained in the possession of a Jew, until after *Pesaḥ*, of which no benefit may ever be derived.

8. A person possessing wheat in a place other than where he lives, laden in wagons or on ships, may likewise sell it to a non-Jew together with the place holding the wheat. Nevertheless, in such a case, he should also renounce his right of ownership to it before a Rabbinical court or before three laymen. If such leaven is delivered to him on *Pesaḥ*, the non-Jewish buyer should pay for the cost of the wagons and all other expenses connected with it. If the leaven is brought to him on *Pesaḥ* from a non-Jew, which he has neither ordered nor had any knowledge of it, the non-Jew should likewise receive it and pay whatever is due to the one who brought it. The Jew must not concern himself with it at all, on the contrary, he should likewise renounce his ownership of it before a Rabbinical court or before three laymen.

9. If one possesses a mill and the customers who grind their produce, pay him in kind by grain which is leaven, he must either sell or let the mill to a non-Jew before *Pesaḥ*.

10. Regarding the sale of cattle to a non-Jew so that he may feed them with leaven during *Pesaḥ*, there is a divergence of opinion among the Sages, of blessed memory. If possible, it is best to avoid such a transaction; but if it is impossible, one should act in accordance with the decision of a sage.

11. One Jew may lend a loaf of bread to another Jew before *Pesaḥ*, with the understanding that he should return a loaf of bread to him after *Pesaḥ*. In some communities, such a deal is not sanctioned.

12. If the leaven of a Jew is in the possession of a non-Jew, or if the leaven of a non-Jew is in the possession of a Jew, one should consult a sage as to how to act in this matter, for there are many diverse opinions regarding this.

13. Care should be taken not to benefit after *Pesaḥ* of the leaven belonging to a Jew who is suspected of not having sold it properly.

Form of Agreement for the Sale of Leaven

I, the undersigned, have hereby sold to the non-Jew (so-and-so) all the brandy that I have in the cellar of my dwelling. The cellar is situated in the courtyard on the northerly side, next to the one on the easterly side. All the brandy that I have there, whether it is contained in middle-sized barrels or in big ones, I have sold to the above mentioned party, together with the vessels, for the sum of two hundred and twenty gold coins. Also the brandy that I have there in a big bottle, about seven measures, I have sold to him for five gold coins without the vessel; also the schliwovitz that I have there in a small barrel, I have sold to him for twelve gold coins, together with the vessel, I have also sold to him six small empty barrels which once contained brandy, and two big empty casks with iron hoops that once contained brandy. I have sold them all for the sum of eight gold coins and fifty cents. Also the five bags of flour that I have in a room called 'storage room,' and is part of the premises in which I reside, I have sold to the above named, together with the bags, for the sum of thirty-nine gold coins. Also all the vessels that contained leaven that I have there, such as the kneading troughs and flour chests, I have sold to him for the sum of four gold coins and fifty cents; also the barley contained in a small bag that I have there, I have sold to him for one gold coin and fifty cents, together with the bags. I have received from him a deposit of ten gold coins; the balance I charge to him as a loan, and the time for paying the same should not be later than ten days from the date hereinafter mentioned. I have rented to the said buyer the above mentioned cellar and the above-mentioned room, from now until the expiration of ten days from the day hereinafter mentioned, for the sum of four gold coins, for which I have received a deposit of three gold coins, and the balance I have charged as a loan which must be paid to me not later than ten days from the day hereinafter mentioned; and by means of the realty rented to him, that is, the cellar and the room mentioned above, I have conveyed to him all the chattels mentioned above; and I hereby make full and unqualified declaration that I have rented to him the said cellar and room, and I have conveyed to him all the chattels mentioned above, by whichsoever means may be legally effective, according to the laws of our holy Torah, and according to the law of the land, without any claim or counterclaim. He has the right to do with all of the aforementioned as he sees fit, to sell it or to give it away as a gift, or to rent it, without any interference. He also has the right to remove all of the aforementioned immediately into his house; and even if he should leave them where they are now, the responsibility for all the above is from now on assumed by the buyer, and I assume no responsibility whatsoever, not even the responsibility of loss by accident. I have also given the buyer the right of way to go through my courtway and my house, in order to enter the said cellar and the room which are let to him. Also, if he should desire, during the period of tenure, to sell some of the chattels to someone else, all those who come with his consent, likewise have the right of way. I have also surrendered to him the keys to the cellar and to the room mentioned above. This has been executed in the most effective manner, in accordance with the law of our holy Torah, and according to the law of the land.

Hungary, 14th of *Nisan*, 5,634.

(Signed).

(Form of agreement adopted by the author of *Noda Biyehudah* in collaboration with his Great Court; with emendations in accordance with the opinion of the author of *Ḥatam Sofer:*)

I testify by my signature hereto affixed, that I have rented to the non-Jew, Mr. so-and-so the room for nine (if the day before *Pesaḥ* occurs on the Sabbath, he should write *ten*, and so all the way through) consecutive days, beginning from this day, also that I have legally sold to him all foodstuffs, whether cooked or raw, and all liquids contained in this room. I have also received from the above-named buyer, the sum of .... Dollars, as a deposit, and have agreed with him upon the receipt of this deposit, that the room is now rented to him for a period of nine consecutive days beginning from today, and is at his exclusive disposition, and in consequence, he also acquires ownership of all foodstuffs, cooked or raw, and all liquids therein contained, which I hereby transfer to him in best legal form. Further, by virtue of his taking possession of the room, all that is contained therein, foodstuffs and liquids as mentioned above, are transferred to his ownership. Also, by virtue of his acquisition of the room rented to him, I have sold to the abovementioned purchaser, all grain that I own in the field, and all the brandy that I keep in such-and-such a place, for and as his property.

In witness whereof, I give to the above-named purchaser this contract of sale, so that with the receipt of this contract, he acquires a lease of the abovementioned room, and the ownership of whatever is contained therein, and the above-mentioned articles of food and drink. Finally, although the abovementioned purchaser still owes me the balance of the purchase price, agreeing to pay same on such-and-such date, I expressly declare that all the food and liquids sold to him are not mortgaged to me, and therefore, all the risk is the buyer's, and not my concern.

To witness, I have set my seal and signature.

Done at .... on the .... day of ....

When the Jew receives the deposit from the purchaser and before he delivers the agreement to him, he should also orally say to him the following:

I rent you this room for nine (*or* ten) days, for the sum of ......Dollars, and I sell you all food, cooked or raw, and all liquid contained therein, as your absolute and uncontested property, for the sum of ...... Dollars (and if he has any grain or brandy or any other kind of leaven in other places, he should also say to him that he sells to him all the grain found in such-and-such a field, or the brandy or other kinds of leaven in such-and-such a place, for the sum of ...... Dollars), and I accept this sum of money which you have given me, on these terms, that I rent to you the aforementioned room for nine (*or* ten) days, and hereby surrender to you the room as lessee, with all rights, and by virtue of your lease you acquire also the ownership in all crops and brandy which I have sold to you, and also all raw and cooked foodstuffs and drinks as aforementioned. For the balance of the purchase money, however, you are still indebted to me in the amount of ...... Dollars, and you obligate yourself to pay the same on the .... day of .... However, this obligation rests upon you personally, and the above-mentioned foodstuffs and drinks sold to you are not hypothecated to me for such indebtedness, and you and not I, are therefore assuming all risks of ownership for the future.

Chapter 115

If the Day Before Pesaḥ Occurs on a Sabbath

1. If the day before *Pesaḥ* occurs on the Sabbath, the search for leaven must be made on Thursday night, the eve of the thirteenth day of *Nisan.* On concluding the search, we nullify the leaven by saying, *Kal ḥamira* (all leaven), and on Friday morning before eleven o'clock we burn it, but without saying *Kal ḥamira.* We nullify it and say *Kal ḥamira* on the Sabbath after the morning meal.

2. The firstborn sons fast on Thursday; and if it is difficult for them to fast until after the search for leaven, they may take some refreshments before the search, or else appoint one as their agent to make the search (and then they may eat before the search).

3. For this Sabbath, no dish consisting of flour or grits should be cooked, as some particles thereof may cling to the pots, which may not be cleansed because of the Sabbath. Therefore, only victuals that are not pastry should be cooked. After the meal, the tablecloth should be well shaken and hidden away, together with the vessels used for leaven, in a room to which one is not accustomed to go during *Pesaḥ.* If any bread is left over, it should be given to a non-Jew, but care must be taken that he does not carry it out into a public place. The house should either be swept by a non-Jew, or with an object with which it may be swept on the Sabbath.

4. On the Sabbath, the *Shaḥarit* service should be held at an early hour, so that the breakfast may be completed while it is still permissible to eat leaven. It is proper to divide the meal into two parts; eat a little, say Grace,

pause for a short time, walk or discuss some religious topic, then wash the hands again, eat and repeat the Grace, thus fulfilling the precept of eating three meals on the Sabbath.

5. It is customary to read for the *Haftorah* from Malaḥi (3:4): *Vearvah* (and it shall be pleasant), etc., because it is written there (verse 10): "Bring all the tithes into the storehouse," etc. This is a fitting subject for this day, because according to some authorities, the time for the disposal of the tithes was on the day before the *Pesaḥ* of the fourth year in *Shemitah* (Leviticus 25:1-4), and on the day before the *Pesaḥ* of the seventh year of *Shemitah* (Sabbatical year). All the grain set aside as tithes during those three years and which were still kept in the house, were to be given to the Levite at the above-mentioned time.

6. On this Friday, every man must be careful to inquire at his house, whether *ḥallah* (first of the dough) has been separated from the bread baked for the Sabbath. For, in a case when the separation of *ḥallah* was forgotten on this Friday, there is great confusion as to the procedure. Because *ḥallah* can neither be separated on the Sabbath nor can the separation be postponed (on account of the Passover). The Magen Abraham holds that all the bread should be given as an absolute gift to a non-Jew, while one may still derive benefit from leaven. Other authorities disagree with him and provide other means, but they are but provisions for emergency. It is best, therefore, to be careful about it.

CHAPTER 116

The Ceremonial Purification of Vessels

1. Earthen vessels, which have been used for leaven, cannot be made fit for Passover either by rinsing with hot water or by glowing. Ovens and ranges, made of stone and bricks can be made fit by glowing. It is customary not to make ritually fit for *Pesaḥ* any stove used in the winter, and when we wish to place on it some dish during *Pesaḥ*, we must first put on it a metal plate, and place the dish on the plate. This rule applies also to an oven made of tiles.

2. Vessels made of wood, metal, stone or bone, can be made fit by rinsing them with hot water, but a vessel that will be damaged by hot water, such as one glued together, even if only the handle is glued on, cannot be made valid for use by that process, because it is feared that one will not cleanse it thoroughly.

3. Before the vessel is purified, it must be thoroughly cleansed of rust and the like, but ordinary stains do not matter. If the vessel is indented, it should be carefully scraped. If it is made of metal, hot coals should be placed upon the dents to glow them, and the vessel should be purified thereafter. If, however, it is impossible either to cleanse the dents and cracks thoroughly, or to glow them, the vessel cannot be made valid for use. Hence, it is neces-

sary to scrutinize knives with handles, whether they can be made valid by purification. If one can afford it, it is best to procure new knives for *Pesaḥ*.

4. Utensils which are used over fire without water, require glowing. Therefore, basins and frying pans in which leaven is baked, require glowing. In the first instance, one should glow them to the extent of making them emit sparks. A wooden peel cannot be made valid for use.

5. A vessel on which there is a patch, under which there may be an accumulation of leaven, that place must first be glowed until we are certain that if any leaven was there it was consumed by the heat, and then the vessel should be purified. However, if there is no fear that it contains an accumulation of leaven, then, if the patch was put on before the vessel was used for leaven, we may purify it as it is, for the purification will discharge the leaven by the hot water even as it has absorbed it. If, however, the vessel was used for leaven before the patch was put on, purification does not suffice, but one must place hot coals on the patch to glow it before purifying the vessel with hot water. If the patch was soldered with lead, or silver, or the like, it may be purified as it is, as the leaven is consumed by the soldering.

6. A mortar which is ordinarily used for pounding pungent spices together with leaven, requires a slight glowing, that is, it should be filled with burning coals until it is hot enough for straws to be burnt on its surface. But if it is customary to pound in it only pepper, and the like, a water purging is sufficient.

7. A vessel which has been regularly used for keeping brandy does not discharge the odor and taste of the brandy through ordinary water-purification. It should first be boiled in water and ashes until its odor is entirely dissipated, and then again immersed in hot water.

8. The purification of a cask should be done as follows: we place in it glowing stones, and pour upon them boiling water out of the vessel in which the water was boiled, and then roll the cask, so that the hot water may reach every part of it. The casks commonly used by us, which are made of many staves held together by hoops, if they contained such leaven as brandy, or if flour was kept in them, cannot be made fit for use by purification with hot water.

9. A vessel that requires purification, may not be made fit for use by scraping, but it must be purified.

10. A vessel that cannot be thoroughly cleansed, such as a sieve, the receptacles of a mill, baskets used for keeping leaven, or a grater, as well as any vessel that has a narrow neck, which makes it impossible to be cleaned from within, or which has staves, cannot be made fit for use on *Pesaḥ* by purification.

11. A compartment in which food is kept the entire year and in which soup is sometimes spilled from the pots, requires a slight purification, that is, pouring boiling water upon it. But it must be poured out of the very vessel in which the water has been boiled. And one should not sprinkle the water, but pour it in a stream. It is also customary to make tables fit for use by placing glowing coals upon them and pouring boiling water upon the stones which should be moved from place to place in such a manner that the boiling water should cover the entire surface. The tables must be scoured first, then purified in the above manner after twenty-four hours. Nevertheless, there are some people who do not use on *Pesaḥ*, the tables and compartments purified this way, unless a cloth or something else is spread on them.

12. Handles of vessels also require purification; nevertheless, if they protrude from the pots, the handles may be purified by spilling hot water on them.

13. Drinking or measuring vessels also require purification. In these regions, the custom prevails not to make glass vessels fit for Passover by purification. Metallic vessels, glazed from within cannot be made fit by purification; but slight glowing will suffice, just as it is the case with a mortar (section 6, above).

14. Purification must be done by water only, and nothing should be mixed therewith, not even ashes or the like. If one has purified many vessels in one boiler, so that the water became turbid like sauce, no more vessels should be purified therein.

15. If a person purifies a vessel by means of a pair of tongs with which he holds the vessel, he must loosen his grip on the vessel and then take hold of it again, as otherwise the purifying water would not penetrate to the spot grasped by the tongs. It is best to put the vessels into a net or a basket. One should not place many vessels at one time into the kettle in which they are purified, for they might touch each other, and they would not be purified in the place where they touch one another.

16. One should not purify a vessel that has been used the same day, that is, within the twenty-four hours that leaven has been cooked therein. The kettle in which the purification is done should likewise not have been used that

same day. We should also see that whenever we put a vessel in the kettle, the water should be boiling hot. If the kettle itself must be purified, it must be full when the water is boiling, and glowing stones should be thrown into it, so that the boiling water may overflow its rims. Purification must be done only until noon of the day before *Pesaḥ*.

17. It is the practice to rinse the vessel with cold water after purifying it.

18. If possible, the cleansing should be done in the presence of a scholar who is well versed in the law of purification.

CHAPTER 117

Various Laws Concerning Pesaḥ

1. If any leaven is found in food on the day before *Pesaḥ* at any time before nightfall, it is subject to the same law that governs other forbidden food which becomes a nullity when it forms only a sixtieth part of the bulk. Hence, if a grain seed is found in poultry or in cooked food, the seed is thrown away, and the rest may be eaten during *Pesaḥ*. However, during the week of *Pesaḥ*, even the smallest particle of leaven renders the food unfit for use, and no benefit either may be derived from it. Thus, wherever a seed of the five species of grain, or any other particle of leaven, is found, one should consult a learned Rabbi.

2. If grain seeds are found in a well of water, the water may not be used during *Pesaḥ*, only in a case of urgent necessity, that is, if no other water can be obtained. But if a piece of bread is found in the well, the water may not be used even if no other water is obtainable, and even filtering is of no avail.

3. It is the prevailing practice not to singe poultry with straw bearing ears of corn, as it is to be feared that they may contain a leavened grain. Hence, singeing is done either with grass, or with straw, from which the ears have been cut off. If, however, by inadvertence, the singeing has been done with straw that had ears attached to it, the poultry may be used. One should be careful to remove the crop from the poultry before singeing it.

4. All kinds of legume and all kinds of dried fruit may not be used during *Pesaḥ*, unless it is known that they have been dried in a proper manner on staves or in a stove that was made ritually fit for *Pesaḥ*. Even dried figs and raisins, whether large or small, may not be used; also the rinds of oranges are forbidden. Nevertheless, it is the practice to drink during *Pesaḥ*, a beverage prepared from raisins. Neither cloves nor saffron should be put in food, as there is a taint of leaven in them. Even in our regions where the saffron grows in the gardens, it is forbidden, in order not to make any exception to a rule of law. Other spices in which there is no taint of leaven, salt included,

should be carefully examined before being put in food to ascertain whether there are any grain seeds in them.

5. Honey should not be partaken of, unless it has not been detached from the comb, or that which has been detached by a Jew, to be used especially for *Pesaḥ*.

6. In case of emergency, for instance, like the requirements of a sick or an aged person, it is permissible to bake *matzah* with extract of eggs, or with milk or wine, and this is known as *matzah ashirah* (rich *matzah*). Care, however, must be taken not to mix water with it, no matter how little. On the first two nights of *Pesaḥ*, only regular *matzah* should be eaten. One does not fulfill one's duty with the *Matzah ashirah*. Where there is no pressing necessity, it is forbidden to bake *Matzah ashirah* even before *Pesaḥ*, to be used on *Pesaḥ*.

7. One who feeds grain or bran to fowl, should be careful to put them in a dry place, so that they should not become moist. It is forbidden to give bran to cattle, as it becomes moist from their saliva; and when giving them grain, care must be taken to give but a little at a time, so that no moist grain is left over, and if any grain is left over, it must instantly be cleared away.

8. On the day before *Pesaḥ*, from the time when it is forbidden to derive any benefit from leaven, as well as during the entire week of *Pesaḥ*, it is forbidden to derive any benefiit from leaven belonging even to a non-Jew. Hence, a Jew is forbidden to transport or to guard the leaven of a non-Jew, and he is most assuredly forbidden to purchase leaven for a non-Jew even with the money belonging to the non-Jew.

9. During *Pesaḥ* it is forbidden to hire out a beast to a non-Jew for the purpose of carrying leaven, or to rent him a room for the purpose of storing leaven in it, because no profit may be made from that which no benefit may be derived. But it is permissible to hire out a beast to a non-Jew for the week of *Pesaḥ* (excepting for Sabbaths and festivals), when the non-Jew does not expressly state that he would transport leaven with it. Even if the Jew knows that the non-Jew will do so, it does not matter; for, even if the non-Jew does nothing with the beast, he will still have to pay the full amount agreed upon. Hence, he benefits nothing by the carrying of leaven. It is also permitted to rent him a room to live in during *Pesaḥ*, although the owner of the house knows that he will bring in leaven there, because he does not receive the money for letting him keep the leaven, but rent for his dwelling there, which he has to pay anyhow.

10. We are forbidden to commit a beast to a non-Jew, even a long time before *Pesaḥ*, if we know that he will feed it with leaven during the week of *Pesaḥ*.

11. We may say to our non-Jewish servant, during the week of *Pesaḥ*: "Here is money; go buy yourself some food and eat," although we know that he will buy leaven. In a case of emergency, we are also allowed to say: "Go eat at the non-Jew, and I will pay him for it." Or we may say to another non-Jew: "Give my servant something to eat, and I will pay you for it." But we are not allowed to pay him in advance.

12. If it is necessary to feed a child with leavened food, the child should be carried to a non-Jew, who shall feed him the leaven, and the Jew shall pay him afterwards. The Jew himself must not feed the child with the leaven. But if the child is in a critical condition, everything is permissible to be done for it.

13. Some authorities forbid, while others permit, to drink on Passover the milk of a cow belonging to a non-Jew, which is fed with leavened food. The scrupulous should follow the stricter opinion; especially in a community where the custom prevails to forbid it.

CHAPTER 118

The Seder (Program) for Pesaḥ Nights

1. It is meritorious to acquire choice wine to perform the precept of drinking the four cups. If we can procure red wine which is of the same quality as the white wine, and it is also as valid for the use on *Pesaḥ* as the white, the former is to be preferred. For it is written (Proverbs 23:31): "Look not thou upon wine when it is red;" from this it may be inferred that wine is most desirable when it is red. Another reason for the preference of red wine is that it is reminiscent of the blood which Pharaoh shed in slaughtering the children of Israel. In barbarous and benighted lands, where slanderous accusations (that the Jews use human blood on the night of *Pesaḥ*) are current, people refrain from using red wine.

2. For the first dipping, termed *karpas*, many people use parsley, but it is better to use celery, which tastes good when raw. But radishes are best of all.

3. For the bitter herbs it is customary to use horseradish, which, being very pungent, may be grated; but we must take care that its bitterness should not evaporate entirely. Therefore, it should not be grated until we return from the synagogue. (See chapter 98:3, where it is stated that it must be done in a different manner than usual). It is forbidden to be grated on the Sabbath; therefore, it should be done before night, and kept covered until nightfall. It is, however, best to use lettuce which is better to eat, and it is called "bitter herbs," because when it remains in the ground for a long time,

the stem becomes bitter. We can also discharge our duty by using a herb called "wormwood." All the valid species may combine to make up the size of an olive. Either the leaves or the stems may be used, but not the roots, that is, not the little roots which branch in all directions. The large root, however, over which leaves grow, although it is hidden in the ground, is classed as a stem. Nevertheless, it is best to use the leaves and the stem which protrudes above the ground, because some authorities hold that whatever grows in the ground is called 'root.' The leaves are not valid unless they are fresh, but the stems are valid whether they are fresh or dried up, not, however, when they are cooked or pickled.

4. The *ḥaroset* (a paste-like mixture), must be made thick to symbolize the clay, but before dipping the bitter herbs into it, we add a little wine or vinegar both to soften it and to symbolize blood, and for the further reason that it may be fit to dip something in it. It is proper to prepare the *ḥaroset* from fruits to which the people of Israel are likened; for instance: figs, because it is written (Song 2:13): "The fig-tree putteth forth her green figs;" nuts, because it is written (loco citato 6:2): "Into the garden of nuts, I went down;" dates, because it is written (loco citato 7:9): "I will climb into the palm tree;" pomegranates, because it is written (loco citato 6:7): "Like the pomegranate split open;" apples, in remembrance of what is written (loco citato). "Under the apple tree I awakened thee," where the women were accustomed to give birth to their children without pain; and almonds (Hebrew *shekedim*), because the Holy One, blessed be He, was anxious (Hebrew, *shaked*) to bring about the redemption. We should put in it spices resembling straw, that is, cinnamon and ginger which cannot be thoroughly ground and they retain shreds resembling straw in remembrance of the straw the Jews used to knead into the clay. On the Sabbath, the wine and the vinegar should not be poured into the *ḥaroset,* it must be done in a different manner, by putting the *ḥaroset* into the wine or into the vinegar. The salt water should be prepared on the day before *Pesaḥ* (even though it does not occur on the Sabbath) and if it is prepared on the festival, it must be done in a manner different from the usual, by pouring the water first and putting the salt into it later.

5. After the Temple was destroyed, the Sages have ordained that during the recital of the *Haggadah,* there be on the table, two special dishes, one in memory of the paschal lamb, and the other in memory of the *Ḥaggigah* offering. It is customary to have a piece of shoulder meat, to symbolize that the Holy One, blessed be He, redeemed Israel with an outstretched arm, and it should be roasted on coal symbolic of the paschal lamb, which was roasted on fire. The second dish should be an egg, because an egg in the Aramaic language is *beah,* that is to say, the All-merciful desired (*bae*) to redeem us

with an outstretched arm. The egg may be either roasted or boiled, but it must be prepared on the day before *Pesaḥ,* while it is still daylight. If we have forgotten to do it then, or if that day has occurred on a Sabbath, we may roast or boil it at night, in which case we must eat it on the first day of the festival. And for the second night, we prepare the egg on that night and we eat it on the second day of the festival, because we are not allowed to cook on one festival for another, nor on a festival for a weekday. Now, inasmuch as no roasted meat may be eaten on these two nights, therefore, we must eat the shoulder meat during the daytime only. Even if it has been roasted on the day before the festival, the meat should not be thrown out, but it should be placed in the victuals that are cooked on the second day, and eaten.

6. We should arrange the seats at the table while it is still daylight, using the best spreads we can afford, and placing them in such a manner that we may be able to recline on the left side. Even a left-handed person should recline on the left side. The *seder*-platter should be set while it is yet day, in order that on arrival from the synagogue, we may proceed with the ceremony of the *seder* without delay.

7. Although during the rest of the year, it is best not to display too many beautiful dishes, so that we may keep in mind the destruction of the Temple, yet on the night of *Pesaḥ* it is good to display as many of our table ware as possible. Even vessels not used for the meal should be on the table, both to decorate the table and to symbolize freedom.

8. The *seder*-platter is arranged thus: Three whole *matzot* are placed on a platter and covered with a fine cloth. The shankbone is placed on the right side and the egg on the left. The bitter herbs, over which the benediction will be pronounced, are placed in the center. The *ḥaroset* is placed below the shankbone, the *karpas* below the egg, and the bitter herbs which are to be eaten with *matzah* in the center.

9. The wine cups must be whole without a flaw, thoroughly washed, and they must hold no less than one and a half eggshells.

10. It is our custom to don the ritual garment called *kittle* (a white robe), which must also be prepared while it is yet day. A person in mourning should not don the *kittle*, but he must recline like everybody else. If, however, he has observed no mourning at all before the festival, as for instance, when the dead were interred on the festival, then, according to custom, he should not recline, but he must recite the *Ḥallel* because the recital of the *Ḥallel* is obligatory.

11. A son at his father's table is obliged to recline, but a disciple at his master's table is not required to recline.

CHAPTER 119

Pesaḥ Night (Continued)

1. Although on every other Sabbath and festival it is permissible to recite the *kiddush* and have the meal while it is yet daylight, so as to add from the profane to the holy, on Passover it is not permitted to do so, because the precept of eating *matzah* on *Pesaḥ* is to be performed only at night, as was the case with the paschal sacrifice, about which it is written (Exodus 12:8): "And they shall eat the meat on this night." The precept of drinking four cups of wine, is also to be carried out only at night. Because the cup of wine over which the *kiddush* is recited is one of the four cups, the *kiddush* should not be recited until it is unmistakably night. After the *kiddush*, the head of the family dons the *kittle* and takes his seat to conduct the *seder*. It is meritorious to distribute nuts, almonds, and the like to the children to arouse their curiousity, so that they may ask the reasons for all that they see, including the reasons for eating *matzah*, bitter herbs, and for reclining. Children who have reached the age of initiation, that is, who are able to understand the importance of the festival and understand what is told about the exodus from Egypt, should be provided with a cup of wine. It is customary to fill one extra cup of wine, and it is called "The Cup of Elijah."

2. To symbolize mastery and freedom, the cups should be filled by a servant or by one of the household. The members of the household should be instructed to drink at least the greater part of each cup, and of the fourth cup no less than a quarter of a *lug*, that is, one and a half eggshells. All should bear in mind that thus they are complying with the precepts of drinking four cups, of recounting the exodus from Egypt, and of eating *matzah* and bitter herbs, because women, too, are in duty bound to perform these precepts, except the ritual of reclining. The *kiddush* should be recited as it appears in the *Haggadah*, and one should recline while drinking the wine. If possible, one should drink the entire contents of each of the four cups, in conformity with the opinion of some authorities.

3. After that, the person conducting the ceremony should wash his hands without saying the benediction, dry them, and cut the *karpas* for himself and the members of his household, giving each a smaller quantity than the size of an olive. Each dips his portion in salt water, and says the benediction, *Bore peri haadamah* (who created the fruit of the ground), intending to cover with this benediction also the bitter herbs and eats the *karpas* while reclining on the left side. The master of ceremonies then takes the middle *matzah* and breaks it in two unequal parts, putting the larger part by his seat for the *afikoman*. It is customary to wrap the *afikoman* in a napkin, symbolic of what is written (Exodus 12:34): "Their kneading-troughs being bound up in their clothes." Some people place it upon their shoulders, commemorative of the exodus from Egypt. Due to the fact that the *afikoman* takes the place of the paschal lamb, it is endowed with importance, and therefore, the greater portion of the *matzah* is designated for it. Then the smaller portion is replaced upon the platter. The person conducting the ceremony then uncovers the *matzot* slightly, raises the platter, and all at the table then recite *Ha laḥma anya di aḥalu* (this is the bread of affliction which our fore-

fathers ate), etc., to *leshanah habaah bene ḥorin* (next year we shall be free men). Those whose *Haggadah* has the version: *Keha laḥma anya* (such as this bread of affliction), should omit the word 'di' (which).

4. The cups are then filled a second time, and a child asks: *Mah nishtanah* (wherefore is this night different). If no child is present, then an adult son or daughter, or a friend, or his wife should say: *Mah nishtanah.* After that, all begin reciting the *Haggadah*: *Avadim hayinu* (slave we were), etc. It is proper to explain the contents of the *Haggadah* to the members of the family in a language they understand. If he himself does not understand the Holy Tongue, he should recite the *Haggadah* together with the vernacular translation, paragraph by paragraph, particularly the section: *Rabban gamliel ḥayah omer* (Rabban Gamaliel said), for it is essential that one understand the reasons given there for the paschal lamb, the *matzah*, and the bitter herbs. At *Vehi sheamdah* (and it is that promise), he should cover the *matzah* (so that the *matzah* is not slighted when the cups of wine alone are being raised). All take the cups in their hands and say: *Vehi sheamdah* to *Miyadam* (out of their hands), after which he again uncovers the *matzah.* When saying: *Matzah zu* (this unleavened bread), he should take the half-*matzah* from the platter and show it to those at the table. When saying, *Maror zeh* (these bitter herbs), he should raise the bitter herbs; but when saying, *Pesaḥ shehayu avotenu oḥelim* (the paschal lamb which our forefathers ate), he should not raise the shankbone, which is commemorative of the paschal lamb, for it might appear as if he had consecrated it for that purpose. When saying *Lephiḥaḥ* (we therefore), he covers the *matzah,* and each one takes his cup and holds it aloft until *Gaal yisrael* (Thou hast redeemed Israel) is concluded. All should then say the benediction *Bore peri haggafen,* and drink the second cup while reclining on the left side.

5. Afterward, all wash their hands, saying the benediction, *Al netilat yadayim* and also the benediction *Hamotzi* over the *matzah.* Now, since on a festival we must say the *Hamotzi* over two whole loaves of bread, whereas the precept of eating *matzah* is fulfilled by eating of the broken one, for the reason that *matzah* is called 'the bread of affliction,' and a poor man generally eats of incomplete loaves, he should, therefore, take the two whole *matzot* in his hands with the broken one between them, and pronounce the benediction *Hamotzi.* Then he should lay down the lower *matzah,* retaining only the upper and the broken *matzot,* and pronounce the benediction *Al aḥilat matzah.* Then he should break off a piece no smaller than the size of an olive from the upper and the broken *matzah,* and distribute the same quantity to everybody. Then he eats both pieces while reclining on his left side. If it is difficult for him to eat both pieces of *matzah* at one time, he should first eat the size of an olive of the piece over which he had pronounced the *Hamotzi,* then eat the size of an olive from the broken *matzah,* but he should not tarry between the two eatings, and eat both while reclining. It is the custom in our parts, not to dip the *matzah* in salt after saying the *Hamotzi* and the benediction, *Al aḥilat matzah.*

6. One who is unable to masticate the *matzah,* is permitted to soak it in water to soften it, providing it does not become entirely dissolved. A sick or an old person who cannot eat the *matzah* when soaked in water, may soak it in wine or in any other beverage. When soaking the *matzah* with which one

intends to fulfill the obligation of eating *matzah*, care should be taken not to let it soak for twenty-four hours, for then it would be considered as if it were cooked and the precept could not be performed by eating it. Care should also be taken that the *matzah* should not lose its identity as bread through other means. (See chapter 48:5 above.)

7. He then distributes portions of the bitter herbs, each portion the size of an olive, and they all dip their portions in the *Ḥaroset*, shaking off the *ḥaroset*, so that the bitter herbs should not lose their taste, pronounce the benediction *Al aḥilat maror*, and eat them without reclining. After that, he takes two pieces of the lower *matzah* about the size of an olive, and places between them bitter herbs about the size of an olive, which should be dipped in the *ḥaroset* and then shaken off: *Ken asah hillel* (thus did Hillel), etc., and this too, he should eat while reclining. The size of an olive, as we have already stated, is as much as half an egg. However, some authorities hold that it is somewhat lass than one-third of an egg. Since the law of eating the bitter herbs has been enacted by the Rabbis, therefore, one for whom it is hard to eat bitter herbs, may rely on the latter opinion and eat somewhat less than one-third of an egg. A person who is indisposed and cannot eat the bitter herbs, should nevertheless, chew a little of any bitter herb until he feels a bitter taste in his mouth, simply as a token, without saying a benediction.

8. Now the feast begins; and it is proper to eat the entire meal while reclining. It is customary to eat eggs in the meal. When feasting, the foresighted person does not gorge, so that he may eat the *afikoman* as is required, with relish. No roast meat, even roast poultry should be eaten on the first two nights of *Pesaḥ*, not even if it has been boiled before roasting. Some are accustomed on the first two nights, not to dip any food in a relish, excepting the two that are mandatory, thus demonstrating that those two dippings were done as a religious act. At the conclusion of the feast, the *afikoman* (the half-*matzah* put away by the seat of the one conducting the ceremony) is eaten in remembrance of the paschal lamb that was eaten at the end of the meal. It is proper to eat thereof, the quantity of two olives, one symbolizing the paschal lamb and the other the *matzah* that was eaten with the paschal lamb. At any rate, one should eat no less than the size of an olive, and while eating it, one should be in a reclining position. After eating the *afikoman*, one is forbidden to eat any kind of food. The third cup for the Grace is then filled. One must ascertain whether the cup is absolutely clean, that is, that nothing is left of the wine in which *matzah* might have been dipped during the meal. If it is not clean, it requires washing and rinsing. An effort should be made to say Grace in a group of three, but one should not go from house to house to look for company to say Grace, because Grace must be said in the place where one has eaten. It is customary that the master of the house should lead in saying Grace, for it is said: "He of a good eye

shall bless," and he is called "of good eye," because he said: "Whoever is hungry shall come and eat." After the Grace, a benediction is said over the third cup of wine, which one drinks while reclining. It is forbidden to drink between this cup and the fourth one.

9. After Grace, the cup is filled for the fourth time. The door is opened according to custom, to signify that this is a night of vigil, and nothing is to be feared. Because of this belief, our righteous Messiah will come, and the Holy One, blessed be He, will pour out his wrath upon the heathens. Therefore, we recite, *Shephoḥ ḥamatha* (O pour out Thy wrath). After that we recite *Lo lanu* (not unto us), and continue reciting the *Hallel,* until *Hodu* (give thanks), which, if there are three, be they even his wife and children who have reached the age for training, should be recited antiphonally; one reads and the others respond, as it is done in a congregation. From the fourth cup of wine a full quarter (of a *lug,* one eggshell and a half) should be drunk, and the concluding benediction is recited thereafter. The *Haggadah* is then read to the end. After the fourth cup of wine, it is forbidden to drink any beverage except water. If one is not too sleepy, one should recite *Shir hashirim* (Song of Songs) after the *Haggadah.* On the first two nights of *Pesaḥ,* it is customary to omit the reading of the *Shema* before going to bed, excepting the section *Shema* and the benediction *Hammapil* (who caused to fall), to indicate that it is a night of vigil, and that no other protection from evil is needed.

10. A person who abstains from wine all year, because it is injurious to him should, nevertheless, make an effort to drink the four cups, as our Rabbis, of blessed memory, relate (Nedarim 49b) of Rabbi Judah ben Rabbi Illai, who used to drink the four cups of wine on *Pesaḥ,* and then he had to tie his temples till *Shavuot.* In any event, such a person may either dilute the wine with water, or drink raisin wine, or mead, if this is a regional beverage.

11. If the *afikoman* is lost and we still have some of the "Mandatory *matzah*" (see chapter 110:15, above), we should eat about the size of an olive of that *matzah.* If none of that *matzah* is left, we should eat that quantity of any other *matzah.*

12. If a person has forgotten to eat the *afikoman,* and he became aware of it before saying Grace, although he has already washed his hands at the conclusion of the meal and said, "Let us say Grace," he may now eat the *afikoman* without saying the benediction, *Hamotzi.* Even though he has abandoned the thought of eating any more, yet it does not constitute a diversion of mind, since it is a duty to eat the *afikoman,* and we eat at the table of the Almighty. He should, nevertheless, wash his hands without saying the benediction, *Al netilat yadayim.* If he has not become aware of it until after saying Grace, but before uttering the benediction *Bore peri haggafen* over the third cup, he should wash his hands, without saying, *Al netilat yadayim,* say the benediction *Hamotzi,* eat of the *afikoman* no less than the size of an olive, say Grace, and afterward say the benediction over the third cup and drink it. If, however, he has only become aware of it after he said the benediction over the third cup of wine, he should drink it; and if on other occasions he is accus-

tomed to say Grace without a cup of wine, he should now wash his hands, eat the *afikoman*, and then say Grace without a cup of wine. But if he always says Grace over a cup of wine, and now he cannot do it because he will be adding to the four cups (which is forbidden), then he should not eat the *afikoman* at all, but rely upon the *matzah* he has eaten before.

Chapter 120

Sefirah (*Counting of The Omer*)

1. The counting of the *omer* begins from the second night of *Pesaḥ*, and we must count while standing. It is mandatory to do the counting at the beginning of the night, after the stars become visible. The time limit, however, is the whole night. On the Sabbath or a festival, we count in the synagogue after the recitation of the *kiddush* in order to welcome early the holiness of the day. At the conclusion of the Sabbath or a festival, we count before the recitation of the *havdalah*, in order to prolong the departure of the sacred day. When the last day of a festival occurs on a Saturday night, when the *kiddush* and the *havdalah* are recited over one cup of wine, the *omer* is likewise counted before, in order to defer the recital of the *havdalah*.

2. If a person has forgotten to count the *omer* during the night, he should do so in the daytime, without the benediction. But on subsequent nights, he says the benediction. If he has neglected to count the *omer* for one whole day, he is to count without the benediction on all the subsequent nights. If he is in doubt whether he has counted the previous night, although he has not counted during the day, he may, nevertheless, say the benediction when counting the remaining nights.

3. If we are asked at twilight or thereafter, before we counted the *omer*, how many days are to be counted on that day, we are to tell the inquirer the number of the previous day, for if we mention the number of the current day, we are forbidden to pronounce the benediction when we count the *omer* later.

4. Before pronouncing the benediction, we should know the exact number of the days. If, however, we do not know it, and we start the benediction depending that we will learn the exact count by listening to our neighbor, our obligation is also fulfilled. If we say the benediction, intending to count four days, and upon concluding the benediction, we become aware that we must count five days, we may count five and we need not repeat the benediction. Likewise, if we have erred in counting, and instead of saying "six days" we said "five days," if we have become aware of the error immediately, we should then count properly, and we need not repeat the benediction; but if we have paused a little, we must repeat the benediction.

5. If the first night of any festival occurs on the Sabbath when *maaravit* (special festival compositions) are omitted, then the *maaravit* of the first night are to be said on the second night. However, on *Pesaḥ*, even if the first night

occurs on the Sabbath, we say on the second night the *maaravit* pertaining to that night, inasmuch as it treats of the reaping of the *omer* which took place on that night.

6. Because many of the disciples of Rabbi Akiba died during the first thirty-three days of the *omer* period, certain rules of mourning are observed during those days; no marriages are permitted, and no haircuts are to be taken. There is a divergence of customs as to which thirty-three days these restrictions are applied. In some communities, these days begin from the first day of the *omer* (the second night of *Pesaḥ*), and, therefore, they forbid the above until the thirty-second day of the *omer*. But when the New Moon of the month of Iyar occurs on the Sabbath which is of double holiness, the holiness of the Sabbath and the holiness of the New Moon, they permit marriages and hair cutting on the day before the Sabbath. On the thirty-third day of the *omer*, Rabbi Akiba's disciples ceased to die, and so, on that day, a semi-holiday is observed, and the *Taḥanun* (petition for Grace) is not said, and from this day on, the restrictions are lifted. Although some of them died even on that very day, no full day of mourning is required, for it is held that a part of a day is equivalent to a full day; therefore, it is not permissible to cut the hair or to marry a woman until after dawn of the thirty-third day, and not in the evening. But if the thirty-third day of the *omer* occurs on Sunday, the hair may be cut on the preceding Friday in honor of the Sabbath.

7. In other communities, they allow all of the above until the New Moon of *Iyar* inclusive, which make a total of sixteen days, then there are thirty-three days left during which the above-mentioned things are forbidden, that is, until *Shavuot* (and they have their hair cut on the day before the festival). Nevertheless, they allow all of the above to be done on the thirty-third day of the *omer* itself (or on the Friday before, if the thirty-third day occurs on Sunday, as stated above). In still other communities, they permit it until the New Moon of *Iyar*, exclusive of that day, and the restrictions begin to take effect on the first day of the New Moon, and the period ends on the first of the three days preceding *Shavout*, concerning which we say that a part of the day is equivalent to a full day of mourning, and, therefore, it is permissible to marry and cut the hair on that day, and they also permit it on the thirty-third day of the *omer* (as stated above). It is essential that the entire community follow the same rules, and not some, one set of customs and others another set of customs.

8. The *sandek* (the person who holds the infant during the circumcision), the *mohel* (the person who performs the circumcision), and the father of the infant are allowed to have their hair cut the day before the circumcision towards evening before going to the synagogue.

9. It is permissible to conclude and to celebrate engagements during all the *sefirah* days, but dancing is forbidden at these celebrations.

10. It is the custom that neither men nor women do any work during the *sefirah* days, from sundown until after the counting of the *omer*. There is a hint concerning this custom, for it is written (Leviticus 23:15): "Seven weeks *shabattot*," the word used for "weeks" denotes *rest;* hinting thereby that during the time that the *omer* is to be counted, after sundown, it is proper to refrain from doing work until the *omer* is counted.

11. On the first day of *Shavuot*, the *Maariv* service should be put off until the stars become visible; for, if the service should be said before this time, and the festival ushered in, a little time will be lacking from the forty-nine days, and the Commandment says (Leviticus 23:15): "Seven *full* weeks they shall be."

CHAPTER 121

Public Fast Days

1. The Prophets have enacted a law to fast on those days on which tragic events occurred. The object of the fast is to stir our hearts to repentance, and to serve as a reminder of our own evil deeds as well as those of our ancestors, which caused them as well as us, all these troubles. By remembering these events, we will improve our ways, as it is written (Leviticus 26:40): "If they shall confess their iniquity and the iniquity of their fathers." Therefore, it is our sacred duty to examine our evil deeds and to repent, for the fast itself is not the main thing, as it is written concerning the people of Nineveh (Jonah 3:10): "And God saw their works," and our Rabbis, of blessed memory, said (Taanit 16a): "It is not written, 'And God saw their sackcloth and their fast,' but, 'And God saw their works, that they had turned from their evil way.'" The fast is intended only as a preparation for repentance. Therefore, those people who fast, and spend the day in taking walks and in worthless matters are adhering to an accessory and overlook the principal thing.

2. These are the public fast days: The third day of *Tishre*, when Gedaliah, the son of Aḥikam, was slain. After the Holy Temple was destroyed, King Nevuḥadnezzar appointed Gedaliah as governor over the Land of Israel. Because Gedaliah was assassinated, all Jews were exiled, and thousands of them were killed. Thus, the last ray of hope was dimmed.

3. The tenth day of *Tevet* is observed as a fast day, because Nevuḥadnezzar, the wicked king of Babylon, laid siege to the city of Jerusalem, which marked the beginning of the end of Jerusalem and the Temple.

4. The seventeenth day of *Tammuz* is observed as a fast day, because five tragic events occurred on this day: (a) The tablets on which the Ten Commandments were inscribed, were broken by Moses when he descended from Mount Sinai, as it is told in the Holy Scriptures (Exodus 32:19). (b) The regular daily sacrifice was abolished. (c) The Romans made a breach in the walls of Jerusalem during the siege of the Second Temple. Although during the siege of the First Temple, the Babylonians breached the wall on the ninth of *Tammuz*, as it is written (Jeremiah 52:6): "In the fourth month, in the ninth day of the month, the famine was sore in the city . . . then a breach was made in the city," but during the destruction of the Second Temple, the breach in the city was made on the seventeenth, and the destruction of the Second Temple is regarded as the more serious disaster. (Furthermore, it is stated in the Jerusalem Talmud that even at the destruction of the First Temple, the breach in the wall of Jerusalem was made on the seventeenth, but that on account of the troublesome times, they mistook the

date). (d) The wicked Apostomos burned a Scroll of the Law. (e) Through the wickedness of some Jews, an idol was placed in the Temple of God, and this caused the destruction of the Temple and our exile.

5. A public fast is observed on the ninth day of *Av*, to commemorate the following tragic events: (a) The spies sent by Moses to explore Canaan returned, and all Israel, believing the evil report, wept in vain on the ninth of *Av*. God, thereupon decreed that they should not enter the Promised Land, and this day was singled out by God, as a day of weeping for many generations to come. (b) The First as well as the Second Temple were destroyed. (c) The large city of Bethar, in which myriads of Jews lived, was conquered by the Roman legions (during the Bar Koḥba revolution). (d) The site of the Temple was ploughed over by the Roman Procurator, T. Annius Rufus, and the prophecy was thus fulfilled (Jeremiah 26:18): "Zion shall be ploughed into a field." (There is another public fast day, the 'Feast of Esther;' see chapter 141:2, below.)

6. If any of these fast days occurs on the Sabbath, it is postponed until after the Sabbath. When the tenth of *Tevet* occurs on Friday, the fast is observed and completed that day.

7. If any of these four fast days occurs during the seven days of one's wedding feast, the bridegroom must fast, although these days are considered as a holiday to him, because the holiday is only his own personal celebration, and is superseded by the public mourning and fasting. Besides, it is written (Psalms 137:6): "If I set not Jerusalem above my chiefest joy."

8. There is a distinction between the first three fast days and the ninth of *Av:* On the nights preceding the first three fast days, one may have food during the night until the break of dawn, if one did not have his regular nightly sleep. If, however, one did have his regular nightly sleep, one is not allowed to eat or drink, unless one so intended before going to bed. One who is accustomed to drink something on arising from sleep, need not determine to do so before going to sleep. But on the ninth of *Av*, we must abstain from food on the day before, while it is yet day. On the first three fast days, it is permissible to wash, to anoint, to wear leather shoes, and to cohabit, but on the ninth of *Av*, all these are forbidden. One who is of strong willpower and healthy should abstain from all these on the other fast days, just as on the ninth of *Av*, except the wearing of shoes, because he would be an object of ridicule. If it is the night of a woman's ritual immersion, one must perform his marital obligation on the first three fast days.

9. There is still a milder practice during the three fast days; pregnant and nursing women, if it causes them suffering, are exempt from fasting. A sick person, even if he is not critically ill, is likewise not bound to fast. Nevertheless, even one who is allowed to eat, should not indulge his appetite, but

he should eat only as much as it is needed for the preservation of his health. Also children, although they are not bound to fast, nevertheless, if they are of sufficient intelligence to understand the significance of this mourning, should be trained and given only bread and water, so that they join in the public mourning.

10. It is forbidden to rinse the mouth on a fast day. The saliva should be ejected from the mouth, if possible; but if it is not convenient to eject it, it may be swallowed even on the Day of Atonement, since one does not do it for the pleasure of it. On a public fast day, it is forbidden to savor food and then eject it. On a fast day which one undertakes voluntarily, one is permitted to savor food and then eject it; the rinsing of the mouth is likewise permissible on a private fast day.

11. Every Jewish community, faced with disaster, God forfend, should fast and pray for salvation to the Holy One, blessed be His name. But if the time is unsuited for fasting, when they are for instance, in flight and should not fast lest their strength will be undermined, they shall resolve to fast a certain number of days after being saved. This resolution will be reckoned as if they were now fasting, as we find concerning Daniel, about whom it is written (Daniel 10:12): "And he said to me, 'Fear not, Daniel; for from the first day thou didst set thy heart to understand and to fast before thy God, thy words were heard.'"

CHAPTER 122

The Interval Between the Seventeenth of Tammuz and the Ninth of Av

1. Since the catastrophe of the destruction of the Temple began on the seventeenth of *Tammuz*, it is customary to observe some rules of mourning from that day till the ninth day of *Av*. Every God-fearing person should recite the "midnight lament" daily in the afternoon. During these days, no marriages may be performed (even for one who has not yet fulfilled his obligation of propagation), but betrothals may take place, even if accompanied by feasts, until the New Moon of *Av*. After the New Moon of *Av*, betrothals may take place, but it is forbidden to make a feast on those occasions; only preserves and the like may be served. A Jew whose vocation is that of a musician is allowed to play in the house of a non-Jew for his livelihood until the New Moon, but not from the New Moon until after the Fast of *Av*. He is likewise forbidden to play on the seventeenth day of *Tammuz* and on the tenth of *Tevet*. Some people have made it a custom not to eat any meat from the seventeenth day of *Tammuz* until after the ninth day of *Av*, except on the Sabbath and at a feast held on the occasion of performing a religious duty.

2. It is the custom not to say the benediction *Sheheḥeyanu* (who hath kept us in life) during these days. Therefore, one should neither purchase nor put on a new garment, as that would necessitate uttering the benediction *Sheheḥeyanu*. But on celebrating the redemption of a firstborn son, the benediction *Sheheḥeyanu* should be recited, in order not to defer the fulfillment of a precept. If a new fruit will not be obtainable after the ninth day of *Av*, one should eat it and say the benediction *Sheheḥeyanu* on a Sabbath or, if need be, even on a weekday. No parent should strike his children and no teacher should strike his pupils during these days.

3. It is customary not to have the hair cut during these days, neither the hair of the head, nor the beard, nor of any part of the body. Adults are also forbidden to cut the hair of their children during these days.

4. It seems to me, that until the week during which the ninth day of *Av* occurs, one should be permitted to trim his mustache, if it interferes with his eating; but that it should be forbidden during the week in which the ninth of *Av* occurs.

5. The paring of the nails is forbidden only during the week in which the ninth day of *Av* occurs. However, a woman for the requirements of ritual immersion, is permitted to pare her nails. A *mohel* is likewise allowed to fix his nails for the requirements of circumcision.

6. On the three Sabbaths, occurring between the seventeenth of *Tammuz* and the ninth of *Av*, we read for the *haftorot* the three "Prophecies of Doom:" *Divre yirmeyahu* (the words of Jeremiah) (Jeremiah 1:1); *Shimeu devar Adonai* (hear the word of the Lord) (Jeremiah 2:4); and *Ḥazon Yeshayahu* (the vision of Isaiah) (Isaiah 1:1). If by error we have read on the first Sabbath the regular *haftorah* of the weekly portion, then both *haftorot, Divre yirmeyahu* and *Shimeu devar adonai,* should be read on the second Sabbath, as they are close to one another. If the New Moon of the month of *Av* occurs on the Sabbath, the *haftorah Hashamayim kisei* (the heaven is My throne) (Isaiah 66) should be read. There are communities, however, where the *haftorah Shimeu devar adonai* is read.

7. As the month of *Av* arrives, mirth lessens. We must not build any amusement house, not even a house for our comfort. If we have made a contract with a non-Jew to decorate our house, we should endeavor to induce the contractor, by offering him a small compensation, to postpone the work until after the ninth day of *Av*. If, however, the work cannot be postponed, it may be performed. If a Jew has a lawsuit against a non-Jew, he should try to postpone it, because of the unlucky period, either to the end of the month, or at least until after the ninth day of *Av*. The moon should not be consecrated before the ninth day of *Av* has passed.

8. The prevailing custom in all Israel is to abstain from meat and wine during the nine days from the New Moon till the ninth day of *Av*. It is even forbidden to partake of food cooked with meat or with fat, even the flesh of poultry is forbidden. A person to whom dairy meals are harmful, is permitted

to eat poultry. For a person who is ill, all these prohibitions do not apply. Nevertheless, if it is not too difficult for him, he should abstain from eating any kind of meat from the seventh day of *Av*, on. Also, some women in confinement abstain from meat and wine from the seventh day of *Av* on, for on that day the heathens entered the Temple. At a religious feast, such as a circumcision, the redemption of a firstborn son, or the conclusion of a Talmudic treatise, it is permissible to serve meat and wine. Not only one's parents, brothers and children, and those directly connected with the performance of the precept may partake of the meal, but also ten other guests, provided that these guests would have come to the feast had it occurred at any other time. Such a feast is permissible even on the day before the ninth of *Av* before noon, but not later than that. The feast which is generally made on the night before the circumcision is not mandatory, and, therefore, no meat or wine should be served on this occasion, but the meal should consist of dairy foods. Concerning the goblet of wine for the *havdalah* at the conclusion of the Sabbath, if there is a minor who is able to drink the greater part of the goblet, it should be given to him; otherwise the one who recites the *havdalah* may drink it himself.

9. No clothes may be washed during the nine days, not even a shirt or a garment which one does not intend to wear until after the fast day. It is forbidden to give it to a non-Jew to be washed. A Jewess may wash the clothes of a non-Jew; nevertheless, she should refrain from this work during the week in which the ninth day of *Av* occurs. During these nine days, it is also forbidden to put on or to spread even garments that have been washed previously. In honor of the Sabbath one may put on linen garments and cover the table with white cloths and to change towels, in the same manner as on other Sabbaths. But it is forbidden to spread white sheets. A woman who is required to put on clean lingerie when she begins to count the seven clean days, is permitted to wash the lingerie and to put them on. It is also permissible to wash infant's diapers during these nine days, as they are constantly soiled.

10. During the nine days, one should not have new garments or new shoes made, or to have stockings knitted, even by a non-Jewish workman. However, if it is very urgent, like for a wedding that will take place immediately after the ninth day of *Av*, it is permissible to have clothes made by a non-Jewish tailor, but not by a Jew. Before *Rosh Ḥodesh*, it is permissible in any event to give the clothes even to a Jewish tailor, who may work on them even thereafter.

11. Women who are accustomed not to arrange the threads for weaving, during these nine days, because this act is called in Hebrew *sheti*, remindful of the *Even shetiyah* (foundation stone) which had been in the Temple, these women should not be given permission to do it.

12. During the nine days, one should not bathe even in cold water, except for medical purposes, as for instance, when a woman has given birth, or is nearing childbirth, or a person who is feeble and was ordered by a physician to bathe, in these cases it is permissible to bathe even in warm water. A woman who has been menstrually unclean, may bathe and immerse herself ritually as usual. If she is to perform the immersion on the night after the ninth day of *Av*, and it will be impossible for her to wash and cleanse on the ninth, she is permitted to wash on the day before the ninth of *Av*. When putting on clean lingerie to begin counting the seven clean days, she may bathe in her accustomed manner, inasmuch as she does not do it for the sake of pleasure.

13. If the New Moon of the month of *Av* occurs on a Friday, a person who is accustomed to bathe every Friday, is likewise permitted to bathe then even in warm water. But he is not allowed to bathe in warm water on the Friday before *Shabbat Ḥazon*, when he may wash only his hands, face and feet. Likewise, a person who is accustomed to wash his head every Friday, is permitted to do so on that Friday, but not with soap or with a solution of ashes. A person who is accustomed to immerse every Friday, is allowed to immerse in cold water; but one who at times omits immersion, may not do it on that Friday.

14. A mourner whose thirtieth day of mourning occurs on the eighteenth day of *Tammuz* or thereafter, is permitted to have his hair cut until the day before the New Moon of *Av*. But from the New Moon on, he is not allowed, either to bathe or to have the hair cut.

15. At a circumcision that occurs during the nine days, it is customary for the *mohel*, the *sandek*, and the parents of the infant, to don the Sabbath clothes, but the one who brings in the infant is forbidden to do so. However, the woman who brings in the infant, customarily wears her Sabbath apparel, as that is the only part of the rite which she can perform. The above may have their hair cut before *Shabbat Ḥazon*, but not thereafter.

16. We have already stated in paragraph 9, above, that on the Sabbath, during the nine days of *Av*, it is permissible to put on white linen, that is, undershirts and stockings which are put on only because of perspiration. As regards other Sabbath clothes, it all depends upon local custom. At the synagogue, we may change the veil of the Ark, the table covering, and the mantles, during the nine days, but not on the Sabbath which occurs on the ninth day of *Av*.

17. On the Sabbath during the nine days of *Av*, it is the custom to call up for the reading of the *maftir*, the rabbi who understands the spirit of the lament, and he should not, therefore, be called up for the reading of *shelishi* (the third portion of the *sidrah*).

CHAPTER 123

The Day Preceding the Ninth of Av

1. When a circumcision, or the redemption of a firstborn son, is celebrated on the day preceding the ninth of *Av*, the feast should be held in the forenoon.

2. One should not walk for pleasure on the day before the ninth of *Av;* and it is customary to study in the afternoon only the subjects permitted on the ninth of *Av*.

3. There are many laws regarding the last meal before the fast. The proper custom is to eat the regular meal before the *Minḥah* service. Afterward, we pray *Minḥah*, omitting the *Taḥanun* (petition for Grace), because the ninth day of *Av* is called a "holiday," as it is written (Lamentations 1:15): "He has called a holiday for me." At the approach of evening, we should sit on the ground, or a low stool, but it is not necessary to remove the shoes. Three should not sit down to eat together, in order that they should not be obliged to recite the Grace in company. Only bread and a cold hard-boiled egg should be eaten at this meal, and a morsel of bread should be dipped in ashes and eaten. One should finish this meal while it is yet day.

4. If one fasts on Mondays and Thursdays during the entire year, and the day before the Ninth day of *Av* occurs on one of those days, one should consult a learned man regarding his vow. One who observes *Jahrzeit* on the day before the ninth of *Av*, should resolve on the first occasion not to fast any longer than until noon, then he should say the *Minḥah gedolah* (the big *Minḥah*), that is at 12:30 afternoon, partake of a meal, and afterwards, at the approach of evening, eat the concluding meal.

5. All that is forbidden to be done on the ninth day of *Av*, is also forbidden in the twilight. One should, therefore, remove the shoes before twilight.

CHAPTER 124

The Ninth of Av

1. In the evening upon entering the synagogue, we remove the shoes. It is customary to remove the veil from the Holy Ark, because it is written (Lamentations 2:17): "He hath performed His word," and to have but one light in front of the *ḥazan*. We pray the *Maariv* in a slow mournful voice, like mourners. *Naḥem* (comfort) is not included in the *Shemoneh esreh* until the next day in the *Minḥah* service. After the *Shemoneh esreh*, the entire *kaddish* is said, including *Titkabbel* (may the prayers and supplications, etc). The worshipers are seated on the floor or on low stools, and only a few lights burn, sufficient only to enable the reading of *Eḥah* (Lamentations) and *Kinnot* (special lamentations). *Eḥah* and *Kinnot* are likewise read in a low mournful voice. When saying *Eḥah*, one should pause briefly between one verse and the other, and a little longer between one chapter and the other. At the beginning of each chapter, the reader raises his voice slightly, and he reads the last

verse of each chapter in a loud voice. When the verse, *Hashivenu* (restore us, O Lord) is reached, the congregation recites it aloud. Then the reader concludes the reading, and the congregation repeats, *Hashivenu* in a loud voice, and the reader following suit. After that, *Veattah kadosh* (and Thou art holy) is recited, followed by the complete *kaddish* without *Titkabbel,* as it is written in (Lamentations 3:8): "He shutteth out my prayer." On the morrow, in the morning service, *Titkabbel* is again omitted, and it is said only in the *Minḥah* service. One who prays privately, having no quorum of ten male adults, should also recite *Eḥah* and *Kinnot.*

2. A man should deprive himself of some comfort when he goes to sleep on the night of the ninth of *Av.* If he is accustomed, for instance, to sleep on two pillows, he should sleep only on one. Some people sleep on the floor during the night of the ninth of *Av,* and place a stone underneath the head, to conform to what is written about Jacob (Genesis 28:11): "And he took from the stones of the place," etc., because, the Rabbis say, he foresaw the destruction of Jerusalem and the Temple, and he said (verse 17): "How fearful," etc. All these depend on the character of the individual.

3. In the morning, the *tefillin* are not put on, because they are called an "ornament." Neither is the big *tallit* put on, because it is written (Lamentations 2:17): *Bitza imrato,* and the *Targum* translates it: "He rent His purple garment;" but the small *tallit* should be put on, without saying the benediction thereon. The worshipers arrive at the synagogue a little earlier than usual. No light at all should be lit for the prayers, which are said in a low, weeping voice. *Mizemor letodah* (a Psalm of thanksgiving) is said. The *ḥazan,* in the repetition of the *Shemoneh esreh,* says *Anenu* (answer us) between *Goal yisrael* (the Redeemer of Israel) and *Refaenu* (heal us, O Lord), as on every other public fast day, but he does not say *Birḥat kohanim* (the blessing of the priests). After the *Shemoneh esreh,* he says the half-*kaddish.* Neither *Taḥanun* nor *El ereḥ appayim* (O God who art long-suffering) is said, because it is called *Moed* (festival). A Scroll of the Law is taken out, and the section (Deuteronomy 4:25): *Ki tolid banim* (when thou wilt beget children) is read for three persons. It is proper that the one called up should say quietly: *Baruḥ dayyan haemet* (blessed be the Judge of truth). After the reading of the Torah, the half-*kaddish* is said. Then we read the *haftorah* (Jeremiah 8:13): *Asof asifem* (I will utterly consume them), in the tone of *Eḥah.* The Scroll is then replaced in the Ark. The worshipers, seated on the ground, say *Kinnot,* the reading of which should be extended until about noon. Afterward we say *Ashre* (happy are they), omitting *Lamenatzeaḥ* (For the chief musician), and we say *Uva letziyon goel* (and a redeemer shall come to Zion), omitting the verse *Vaani zot beriti* (and as for Me, this is My covenant), for it would appear that He establishes a covenant for the lamentations, and for the further reason that it is inappropriate to say, "And as for me this is my covenant . . . shall not depart out of thy mouth," etc., since it is forbidden to study the Torah on this day. But at a mourner's house during the entire year, excepting on the ninth day of *Av,* it is to be said, for although the mourner himself is exempt from studying the Torah (during the first seven days of mourning), the condolers are not. Then *Veattah kadosh* (and Thou art holy) is recited, followed by the complete *kaddish,* with the omission of *Titkabbel.* After that we say *Alenu* (it is our duty to praise), and then the mourner's *kaddish* is recited. Neither *Shir hayyiḥud* (Hymn of Monotheism),

nor the *Yom* (hymn of the day), nor *Pittum haketoret* (the compounding of the incense) is said. And it is proper for the worshipers to read *Eḥah* afterward.

4. A mourner, too, should go to the synagogue on the night of the ninth of *Av* and also during the day, and stay there until the reading of the *Kinnot* is concluded. And he is permitted to go up to the reading of the Torah and to read the *haftorah,* because all are mourners that day.

5. The words of the Torah rejoice the heart, for it is written (Psalms 19:9): "The precepts of the Lord are right, rejoicing the heart." Therefore, it is forbidden to study the Torah on the ninth day of *Av,* excepting such subjects as sadden the heart, like the prophecies of Jeremiah foreboding evil, skipping the verses of consolations and the verses speaking of the punishment that will be inflicted on the nations of the world. It is also permissible to read the Book of Job, Midrash Eḥa, the Talmudic chapter *Elu megalḥin* (Moed katan, 3), which deals with the laws of a mourner and of one who was excommunicated, also the *Haggadah* (legend) of chapter *Hanizakin* (Gittin 5), and in the Jerusalem Talmud the last chapter of the Treatise *Taanit,* which tells of the destruction of the Temple. But even the above should be read casually, not indulging in speculations and homiletic interpretations of the text, as that would be a diversion. A person may teach children any subject that he himself is permitted to study. We are allowed to read the entire order of the daily prayers, even the *halaḥic* chapter about sacrifices, *Ezehu mekoman* (which are the places). But *Maamadot* should not be read even by one who is accustomed to read it daily.

6. A pregnant or nursing woman, even if they suffer very much, are required to complete the fast, unless, God forbid, there is fear of danger. One who is ill, even though not critically, is not bound to complete the fast, but should abstain from food only for a few hours. This rule applies more especially to one who is naturally weak. A woman, from the seventh to the thirtieth day after childbirth, even if she is not ill, is subject to the same law that governs a person who is not critically ill. If, however, she feels that she has completely recuperated and that the fast will not harm her, she should complete the fast. Persons who need to eat on the ninth day of *Av,* should, however, eat no more than is necessary to preserve their health.

7. Bathing for pleasure is forbidden, whether in hot or cold water; it is even forbidden to put one's finger in water. But it is permitted when not for pleasure's sake. Hence, we may wash our hands in the morning. But we must be careful not to wash more than the fingers, for this is what constitutes the ritual morning ablution, as an evil spirit rests on the fingers in the morning. After having dried the hands slightly, and while they are still moist, we may pass them over our eyes. One whose eyes are filmy after awakening from sleep and who is accustomed to wash them every morning, is permitted to wash them as usual, and he need have no scruples about it. Likewise, if

one's hands are soiled, he may wash the soiled spots. After responding to the call of nature, we may slightly wash our hands, as we are accustomed to do. We should also wash our fingers for the *Minḥah* service.

8. Women are allowed to rinse the edibles to be used for cooking, inasmuch as the purpose is not to wash the hands. One who is on his way to perform a precept, and he is unable to proceed unless he crosses a stream, may cross it on his way there and on returning, and he need have no scruples about it. However, if he is going for his own gain, he may cross on his way there, but not on returning. One who returns from the road, and his feet are sore, may bathe them in water.

9. Although only bathing for pleasure is forbidden, nevertheless, a woman whose time for taking the ritual immersion occurs on the night of the ninth of *Av*, should not perform the immersion, since cohabitation is forbidden on the ninth of *Av*.

10. Anointing, too, is forbidden for pleasure; and if one has scabs on the head, or if it is necessary for some other remedy, it is permissible.

11. Wearing shoes is forbidden if they are made of leather; but wearing shoes made of cloth, or the like, if they are not trimmed with leather, is permissible. Those who have to walk among non-Jews may wear shoes, so as not to expose themselves to ridicule; but one should place some earth in the shoes. However, a righteous person should rigidly cling to the rule. Men who stay in stores are surely forbidden to wear shoes. One who has to walk a long distance, since walking barefoot would cause him great distress, is permitted to wear shoes, but he must remove them on approaching a city. But one who rides in a vehicle is forbidden to wear shoes.

12. Cohabitation is forbidden, and one should be careful not even to touch his wife.

13. We are forbidden to greet a neighbor on the ninth day of *Av*, even to say "good morning," or the like. If greeted by an ignorant person or by a non-Jew, we should return the greeting feebly, otherwise we might incur their anger. We are likewise forbidden to send a gift to a neighbor, because this is a form of greeting.

14. We should not walk in the market place, for there we might be prompted to indulge in laughter and merriment. Some authorities forbid the smoking of tobacco the whole day, while others permit it in the afternoon in the privacy of one's home.

15. With regard to work, our custom is to forbid even unskilled labor the night of *Tishah B'av* and up to noontime, if it takes time to do it. But

work which does not take long to do, like the lighting of candles, or tying something up, is permitted. In the afternoon, all work is permitted. It is also the custom to forbid the transaction of business in the forenoon, but to permit it in the afternoon. However, a God-fearing man should not do any work nor transact any business the whole day, so that his mind be not diverted from mourning. All manner of work may be done by a non-Jew, and if the work is of a nature which if not done at once might cause a loss, one is permitted to do it himself. The milking of cows should be done by a non-Jew, but when that is impossible, one may milk them himself.

16. It is customary not to sit on a bench or a chair, either at night or in the day until noon, sitting only on the floor. In the afternoon this is permissible. All the other things that are forbidden on the ninth day of *Av*, may not be done until the stars come out.

17. It is the custom not to start to prepare the meal before noon, but it is permissible if it is to be a religious feast.

18. If there is an infant to be circumcised, the circumcision should be performed when the recital of *Kinnot* is concluded. The father and the mother of the infant, the *sandek* and the *mohel*, are permitted to don their Sabbath attire in honor of the circumcision. After the circumcision, they should remove these garments. Candles may be lit in honor of the circumcision, and the goblet of wine should be given to a minor to drink.

19. At the *Minḥah* service, we put on the *tallit* and the *tefillin*, saying the appropriate benedictions, and we say the *Yom* (the hymn of the day) and all the other portions omitted in the morning service. We then say *Ashre* (happy are they), and the half-*kaddish*. The Torah and the *maftir* are then read as on any other public fast. The Scroll is afterwards replaced in the Ark, and the *ḥazan* says the half-*kaddish*. After this we read the *Shemoneh esreh*, and in the benediction *Velirushalayim irḥa* (and to Jerusalem Thy city), we say *Naḥem* (comfort Thou). If it was then omitted, it should be said after, *Anenu* (answer us, O Lord), but it should not be concluded with, "Blessed art Thou, O Lord, who comforteth Zion," but with, *Ki attah shomea* (for Thou hearkenest), etc. But if one has not become aware of the omission until after he said, *Baruḥ attah adonai* (blessed art Thou, O Lord), he should conclude the benediction, *Shomea tefillah* (who hearkenest unto prayer), continue to pray according to the prescribed order, and he need not repeat the *Shemoneh esreh*. In the repetition of the *Shemoneh esreh*, the *ḥazan* recites *Birḥat kohanim* (the blessing of the priests), and concluding the *Shemoneh esreh*, he recites the whole *kaddish*, including *Titkabbel*. We then remove the *tefillin*, and pray *Maariv*. It is customary to sanctify the moon, if it is visible. (See chapter 91, section 11, above, where it is stated, that it is necessary to taste some food first.)

20. We are told in a *Baraita:* "On the seventh day of *Av*, the heathens entered the Temple, where they ate and drank and polluted it on the seventh and on the eighth. On the ninth, towards evening, they set fire to the Temple,

and it continued to burn throughout the tenth day until sunset. The reason the fast was not set for the tenth day, although on that day the greater part of the Temple was burnt, is that the beginning of a calamnity is the most tragic part of it." In the Jerusalem Talmud it is stated (*Taanit* 4:6): "Rabbi Abin fasted on the ninth and on the tenth; Rabbi Levi fasted on the ninth day and on the night of the tenth day; because he lacked sufficient strength to fast all of the tenth day. But as for us, our bodies being weak, we fast only on the ninth day." Nevertheless, we should abstain from meat and wine during the night of the tenth and up to noontime of the tenth, unless it be for the performance of a precept. The benediction *Sheheḥeyanu* (who hath kept us in life) should not be said, neither should one bathe, or cut the hair, or wash anything until the noon of the tenth. If the tenth occurs on a Friday, it is permissible to bathe, cut the hair, and wash immediately in the morning in honor of the Sabbath.

21. A woman who has given birth, although she fasts after the first seven days, is, nevertheless, allowed to eat meat and drink wine on the night of the tenth day.

22. It is proper not to have sexual intercourse on the night of the tenth day, unless it is on the night of the ritual immersion, or if one is about to go on a journey, or has returned from a journey.

CHAPTER 135

When the Ninth of Av Occurs on Saturday or Sunday

1. If the ninth day of *Av* occurs on a Sunday, or if it occurs on Saturday and it is postponed to Sunday, we may eat meat and drink wine during the Sabbath. Even at the third meal after *Minḥah,* we may eat everything. But we must not feast with company. If a circumcision is to be celebrated, the feast should take place before *Minḥah.* We are permitted, however, to eat the third meal with our family, in which case we may say Grace with a quorum of three. The meal must be finished while it is still daytime, as the ban on eating, drinking and bathing begins at twilight. We must not remove our shoes until after *Barḥu* (bless ye) is said. The *ḥazan* removes his shoes before saying *Vehu raḥum* (and He being merciful), so that his mind would not be troubled, but he should first say the benediction, *Hammavdil ben kodesh leḥol* (who makes a distinction between the holy and the profane), without mentioning the Divine Name (*adonai*) and the Royal Attribute (*meleḥ haolam*).

2. Cohabitation is forbidden on Friday night if it is the ninth day of *Av,* unless it closely follows the ritual immersion of one's wife.

3. We say *Av haraḥamim* (may the Father of mercies), and recite the memorial prayer in the morning, but in the *Minḥah* service, *Tzidekatḥa tzedek* (Thy righteousness) is omitted.

4. If the ninth day of *Av* occurs on a Sabbath, one should study only those subjects which may be studied on the ninth day of *Av;* therefore, it is impermissible to read *Pirke avot* (Ethics of the Fathers), but it is permissible to read twice the *Sidrah* of the week, and the *Targum* once. It is especially permissible to do so in the forenoon. If the Sabbath occurs before the ninth day of *Av,* we are not allowed to study in the afternoon, as on the ninth day of *Av.*

5. We do not say *Lamenatzeaḥ* (to the chief musician) before *Maariv,* nor *Vihi noam* (and let the pleasantness) before saying *Veattah kadosh* (and Thou art holy), for this was said upon the setting up of the Tabernacle, while now it is the date when the Temple was destroyed; nor do we say *Veyitten leḥa* (may God give unto thee); nor do parents bless their children.

6. When we see the candlelight at dark, we should say the benediction *Bore meore haesh* (who createth the light of the fire), and in the *Shemoneh esreh* we say *Attah ḥonantanu* (Thou hast favored us). The *havdalah* over a cup of wine should not be recited until the conclusion of the ninth day of *Av,* and we do not say the benedictions over the spices and over the light, even if we have neglected to say the latter benediction on Saturday night. We should warn our family not to do any work before they say, *Hammavdil ben kodesh leḥol,* without mentioning the Divine Name and the Royal Attribute. If we have forgotten to say *Attah ḥonantanu,* we need not repeat the *Shemoneh esreh,* because the *havdalah* will be recited over a cup of wine when the fast is over. We are not allowed to taste any food before the *havdalah,* and if we find it necessary to do some work, we should recite *Hamavdil ben kodesh leḥol,* without mentioning the Divine Name and the Royal Attribute.

7. When the ninth day of *Av* occurs on the Sabbath and it is postponed to Sunday, it is forbidden to eat meat or drink wine on the night after the fast, as is the case with any other ninth day of *Av,* when the mourning is extended to the tenth, but on the morrow, everything is permissible even early in the morning.

8. When a circumcision is celebrated on a postponed ninth of *Av,* the parents of the infant, the *mohel,* and the *sandek,* are permitted to pray the *Minḥah gedolah* (the great *Minḥah*), that is, after half past twelve in the afternoon, then they recite the *havdalah* over a cup of wine, and thereafter may eat and even bathe. But the feast should not be held before the night. Likewise, when celebrating the redemption of a firstborn son, which has not been postponed, the father and the *kohen* should not complete the fast.

CHAPTER 126

Commemorating the Destruction of the Temple

1. After the destruction of the Temple, our Sages, of blessed memory, ordained that on every joyous occasion, we must remember the destruction of the Holy Temple, as it is written (Psalms 137:5): "If I forget thee, O Jerusalem. . . If I prefer not Jerusalem above my chiefest joy." They have decreed that no Jew should build for himself a house painted and decorated in royal style; nor should he paint the entire interior of the house, but he may plaster the house, paint it, and leave unpainted the space of a square cubit

(one foot and a half) opposite the entrance, commemorative of the destruction of the Temple. We do not know of any good reason why this custom is not observed now.

2. They likewise decreed, that on giving a dinner to guests, even if it is a sacramental feast, one dish should be withheld. That a woman should not put on all her jewels, that we put ashes upon the head of a bridegroom, at the place where the *tefillin* are worn, before the nuptial ceremony; and that the veil with which the bride is covered should contain no silver or gold threads. It is likewise customary at the writing of the *tenaim* (betrothal contract) to break an earthen pot, after it has been read, commemorative of the destruction of the Temple, but it is the practice to use a damaged pot for that purpose; and that under the nuptial canopy, the bridegroom breaks a glass vessel; for this purpose a whole vessel may be used.

3. They likewise decreed not to listen to instrumental music, nor even to vocal songs. During meals, we may sing only the *zemirot*, the table hymns, like those chanted on the Sabbath; but other songs are forbidden.

4. We are forbidden to attend the shows of the heathens or their dances, or anything that is marked by merriment. When we unwittingly hear their joyous voices, we must sigh and grieve over the destruction of Jerusalem and pray for it to the Holy One, blessed be His name. We are even forbidden to visit the shows presented by Jews, because it is "the seat of scorners." All kinds of rejoicing is forbidden, except to entertain a groom and a bride, which may be done either with vocal songs or with musical instruments. Even in such an event, there should be no excess of rejoicing. In this world, no man is allowed to indulge in unrestrained laughter, even when rejoicing in the performance of a precept, for it is written (Psalms 126:2): "Then (when Zion was restored) was our mouth filled with laughter."

Chapter 127

Private Fast Days

1. Just as the public is bound to fast and pray in case of any disaster, Heaven forfend, even so, it is the duty of every individual to fast when any calamity, God forbid, befalls him, for instance, when one of his family is sick, or when he goes astray on the road, or if he is confined in prison on a false charge. On such occasions he must fast and pray to God and plead for mercy from Him, blessed be His name, that He should help him. This is one of the important principles concerning repentance; that a man should not say, God forbid, that the evil which has befallen him, was merely accidental. For it is written (Leviticus 26:23-24): "If ye will walk contrary (Hebrew, *bkeri; keri,* meaning contrariness, or chance) unto me; then I will walk contrary unto you with fury;" which verse is explained to mean: When I will bring any distress upon you to make ye repent, and ye will say that this was

a mere *keri* (a chance, an accident), then I will add to the wrath of the same *keri*. A man should know that it was God who has brought all this trouble upon him because of his sins; he shall then examine his deeds, return to the Lord, and He will have pity on him.

2. If an individual desires to fast, he should make a resolution to that effect on the preceding day during the *Shemoneh esreh* of the *Minḥah*. In the benediction of *Shema kolenu* (hear our voice), he should mentally obligate himself to fast, and before saying, *Yiheyu leratzon* (let the words of my mouth), he should say, "Master of the universe, I am to fast before Thee," etc., (as it is printed in the prayer books). If he eats and drinks thereafter during the night until the break of day, it does not matter. If he desires to fast on several consecutive days, although he will eat and drink during the intervening nights, one resolution suffices for all. But if he obligates himself to fast several alternate days, like Monday, Thursday, and Monday, he should make a separate resolution for each in the *Minḥah* of the preceeding day.

3. One who is accustomed to fast during the ten days of penitence (see chapter 130, below), or on the first day of *Seliḥot* (see chapter 128:5, below), or on the day before *Rosh Hashanah*, need not make any spoken resolution to do so, because there is a tacit resolution by virtue of his custom. A fast on account of an evil dream, requires no resolution, nor do the fasts of the Monday, Thursday, and Monday following the festivals of Passover and Tabernacles require any other resolution, if he responds *Amen* after the recital of the *Mi sheberaḥ* (He who blessed), etc., announcing these fasts and he mentally resolves to fast. Nevertheless, if he then changes his mind, and does not desire to fast, he may eat, since he has not expressly undertaken to fast.

4. Even if one did not orally undertake to fast, but merely planned to fast the following day, either before or after the *Minḥah*, while it was still daytime, it is a valid resolution, and he is obliged to fast.

5. A person who fasts, should not indulge in pleasure, neither should he behave irreverently and be merry and gay at heart, but he should be somber and mournful, as it is written (Lamentations 3:39): "Wherefore doth a living man complain, a strong man because of his sins?"

6. On a private fast day, one is allowed to rinse his mouth with water in the morning.

7. If one has undertaken to fast without any specification, he must fast until the stars come out, even if it happens to be a Friday.

8. One who fasts and is boasting about it, will be punished for it. However, if he is urged to eat, he may state that he is fasting.

9. He who observes a private fast, whether it is a voluntary one, or because of an evil dream, should include the prayer *Anenu* in the benediction *Shema kolenu* (hear our voice), in the *Shemoneh esreh* of the *Minḥah* service, the same as on a public fast day. And although he is only one, yet he should say it in the plural, in order not to deviate from the formula fixed by the scholars; and before saying this prayer, he should recite, *Ribbon haolamim* (Master of the universe), etc.

10. If a person has vowed to fast a certain number of days, but has not specified the days, even if he had resolved in the *Minḥah* prayer to fast on the morrow, and it becomes urgently necessary for him to partake of food, for instance, if he is invited to partake of a religious feast, although he is not a party to the celebration, or if a great man urges him to dine with him and it is hard for him to refuse him, or he is suffering because of the fast, he may substitute the fast day, that is, he may eat on that day even if he had already begun to fast, and in lieu thereof, fast on another day. This is permissible only when he had undertaken to fast to fulfill a vow. If, however, he had made no vow, but he merely obligated himself in the *Minḥah* prayer to fast on the morrow, then even if it causes him great distress, he is not allowed to substitute his fast day and repay it by another day.

11. Also, if when making the vow, he had specified certain days, and he had also obligated himself to do so in the *Minḥah* prayer, he may no longer substitute the fast day.

12. If a person has resolved to fast, and the fasting causes him great distress, he may redeem it with money, a sum according to his means, and he should distribute it among the poor. However, a fast to fulfill a vow may not be redeemed; nor may a fast day decreed by the community be redeemed, unless the community has made such a provision.

13. The one who has made a vow to fast on Monday, Thursday, and Monday, may change it to Thursday, Monday, and Thursday, but not to any other days of the week, for it is presumed that one's intention has been to fast on these particular days, as they are days of judgment.

14. Those who fast on the Monday, Thursday, and Monday, following the festivals of *Pesaḥ* and *Sukkot*, as well as on the ten days of penitence, upon which they did not resolve in the *Minḥah* prayer, but they fast in pursuance to custom, even if they have intended to do so when responding *Amen* to the prayer *Mi sheberaḥ* (He who blessed), etc., as long as they did not expressly resolve upon them in the *Minḥah* prayer, then if there is a circumcision, a redemption of a firstborn son, or any other sacramental feast, it is their duty to partake of the feast and they require no dispensation to do so, since those fasts are merely in compliance with prevailing custom, and that custom was not intended to apply to sacramental feasts.

15. If one ate on a fast day at a religious feast, where eating was permitted, the fast is thereby terminated, and he is permitted to eat thereafter even in his own house, but he may not eat before the religious feast. However, the father of the infant and the *sandek*, on the day of circumcision may eat even before the feast, inasmuch as to them it is like a festival.

16. If one eats illegally on a fast day, whether inadvertently or wilfully, he must fast the rest of the day, and as an atonement, he must also fast the following Monday, Thursday, and Monday; especially so where he had to fast to fulfill a vow.

17. If an individual fasts because of a distress, and the distress has passed, or if he fasts in behalf of a sick person, and that person has recovered or he died, he must, nevertheless, complete all the fast days that he has obligated himself to observe. If one had obligated himself to fast or to practice some other good deed until his son became *Bar Mitzvah*, and the son had died before that date, he must, nevertheless, fulfill his vow until the time his son would have become *Bar Mitzvah*. If, however, he becomes aware that the cause for fasting had passed before he had obligated himself to fast, he is not required to complete it, because it had been vowed in error.

18. Fasting and repentance completely nullify the boding of an evil dream, even as fire consumes flax, but only if observed on the same day. However, it is not mandatory to fast because of an evil dream, for Samuel said (Beraḥot 55b): "Dreams speak falsehoods." But we are in duty bound to repent and to spend the entire day in the study of the Torah and in prayer.

Chapter 128

The Month of Elul

1. The period from *Rosh Ḥodesh* of the month of *Elul* until after *Yom Kippur*, is a propitious time. Although the Holy One, blessed be He, accepts all year the repentance of those who turn unto Him wholeheartedly, these days are more appropriate and suited for repentance, inasmuch as they are days of mercy and good-will. For, in the month of *Elul*, Moses ascended Mount Sinai to receive the second tablets, tarried there forty days, and descended on the tenth day of the month of *Tishre*, when the atonement was completed. From that time on, these days have been set aside as days of good will, and the tenth day of *Tishre* as the Day of Atonement. In most communities, the custom prevails to fast on the day before *Rosh Ḥodesh* of the month of *Elul*, and to hold the special services of *Yom Kippur Katan* (Minor Day of Atonement), in order to be attuned to repentance. If *Rosh Ḥodesh* occurs on the Sabbath, the fast is observed on the preceding Thursday.

Rabbi Isaac Luria, of blessed memory, said: "It is written (Exodus 21:13): 'And if a man lie not in wait, but God cause it to come to hand, then I will appoint thee,' etc. The initials of the last Hebrew four words אנה לידו ושמתי לך spell out אלול, to signify that this is a propitious month to repent for the sins that one has committed the entire year. It further indicates that during this month, one should also repent for sins committed unwittingly." Those who interpret the Law metaphorically, said of the verse (Deuteronomy 30:6): "And the Lord will circumcise thy heart and the heart of thy seed," that the initials of the four words את לבבך ואת לבב spell out אלול. Also the initials of the verse (Song 6:3): "I am my beloved's and my beloved is mine," אני לדודי ודודי לי spell out אלול. Likewise the initials of the verse (Esther 9:22): "One to another and gifts to the poor" איש לרעהו ומתנות לאביונים spell out אלול. This is a reference to the three things, namely, Repentance, Prayer, and Charity, which should be assiduously practiced during this month. "God will circumcise," implies Repentance; "I am my beloved's," refers to Prayer, for prayer is a song of love; "One to another and gifts to the poor," indicates Charity.

2. It is the custom to sound the *shofar* daily during this month, beginning the second day of *Rosh Ḥodesh* and continuing daily after the morning service. We blow *Tekiah*, *Shevarim*, and *Teruah*. The day before *Rosh Hashanah*, the *shofar* is not blown, in order to make a distinction between the voluntary blowing of the *shofar* and the mandatory sounding. The reason for sounding the *shofar* during this month is to move the people to repentance. For the sound of the *shofar* has the quality to stir the hearts and to inspire love, as it is written (Amos 3:6): "Shall a *shofar* be blown in a city, and the people not tremble?" Every day, after the morning and evening prayers, beginning with the second day of *Rosh Ḥodesh* until *Shemini Atzeret* (eighth day of *Sukkot*), we recite the (Psalm 27) *Ledavid, Adonai ori* (Of David, the Lord is my light and salvation). This is in conformity with the *Midrash* (Shohar Tov): "The Lord is my light" on *Rosh Hashanah*, "and my salvation" on *Yom Kippur;* "for He will hide me in His tent" (verse 5) is a hint of the Feast of Tabernacles. It is also customary to have public recital of Psalms, all in accordance with local custom. Beginning with the month of *Elul* and until *Yom Kippur*, when one writes a letter to his fellow, one should mention either at the beginning or at the end, that he prays for him and wishes him to be inscribed and sealed in the book of good life.

3. Saintly men are accustomed to examine the *tefillin* and the *mezuzot* during this month; and to correct any defect in any other precept.

4. Beginning with the Sabbath following the ninth day of *Av* and thereafter for seven consecutive Sabbaths, seven *haftorot* of consolation are read. If the first day of the New Moon of *Elul* occurs on a Saturday, we omit the *haftorah* (Isaiah 54:2): "O thou afflicted, tossed with tempest," and we read instead (Isaiah 66:1): "Thus saith the Lord: The heaven is my throne," because this *haftorah*, too, contains comforts for Jerusalem. On the Sabbath, when the *Sidrah Ki tetze* (when thou goest forth) (Deuteronomy 21:10) is read, we read as the *haftorah* (Isaiah 54:) "Sing, O barren," then we continue with "O thou afflicted, tossed by tempest," which is next to it. If one has erred and read "O thou afflicted, toss with tempest" on the Sabbath of the New Moon of *Elul*, and he has become aware of the error before saying the concluding benedictions, he should also read "Thus saith the Lord; the heaven is my throne." But if he has become aware of the error after saying

the concluding benedictions, he should read the latter *haftorah* without saying the benedictions. If the New Moon of *Elul* occurs on a Sunday, the *haftorah* (I Samuel 20:18): "Tomorrow is new moon," is omitted, because it contains nothing about the consolation of Jerusalem, and we read: "O thou afflicted," instead.

5. Beginning with the Sunday before *Rosh Hashanah*, we rise early for the service of *Seliḥot* (supplications for forgiveness). If *Rosh Hashanah* occurs on Monday or Tuesday, we begin saying the *Seliḥot* from the Sunday of the preceding week. Upon rising, we wash the hands and say the benediction *Al netilat yadayim* (concerning the washing of the hands), and the benedictions for the Torah. After the *Seliḥot* we wash the hands again without saying the benediction.

6. The *ḥazan* intoning the *Seliḥot* should wear a *tallit;* and because it is doubtful whether a benediction is to be said when putting on a *tallit* in the night, he should, therefore, neither take his own *tallit,* nor one belonging to the congregation, but borrow one from someone, and wrap himself therein before saying *Ashre* (happy are they). And he should pronounce no benediction over the *tallit.* If no *tallit* can be obtained, the *Seliḥot* as well as the "thirteen attributes" may be recited without wearing a *tallit.* A custom prevails in some communities, that the *ḥazan* who intones the *Seliḥot* should also officiate at the morning and at the afternoon prayers, as well as at the evening prayers of the preceding night, taking precedence over a mourner, a *mohel* and one observing *Jahrzeit.* It is best to stand while saying the *Seliḥot.* One who finds it difficult, should at least stand while saying, *El meleḥ yoshev* (God, King sitting), etc., and the "thirteen attributes."

7. We must be particular to choose a *ḥazan* to recite the *Seliḥot* and to officiate at the services on the awe-inspiring days (*Rosh Hashanah* and *Yom Kippur*), a man of eminent respectability, well versed in the Torah and excelling in good deeds. He should be no less than thirty years old, for then the passion of his youth has already cooled off and his heart is humble. He should also be married and have children, so that his supplication will be from the bottom of his heart. The one who blows the *shofar* on *Rosh Hashanah* and the one who prompts him, should likewise be learned in the Torah and God-fearing, the best men obtainable. However, every Jew is eligible for any sacred office, providing he is acceptable to the congregation. If, however, a candidate sees that his choice will cause dissention, he should withdraw his candidacy, even if an improper person will be chosen.

8. During the twelve months of mourning for a father or a mother, one should not officiate as *ḥazan* on *Rosh Hashanah* and *Yom Kippur,* nor should he blow the *shofar* on *Rosh Hashanah,* unless there is no one else as qualified as he is. If he is in the first thirty days of mourning for other relatives, then if it had been his prerogative to officiate as *ḥazan* or to blow the *shofar,* he is allowed to do so, since *Rosh Hashanah* and *Yom Kippur* lift the thirty-day mourning; but if he has not been accustomed to do so, and there is another man just as suitable as he is, he should not be allowed to act as such. During

the entire period when the *Seliḥot* are said, even on the day before *Rosh Hashanah,* a mourner may act as *ḥazan,* but not when he observes the first seven days of mourning.

9. A person who recites the *Seliḥot* privately, is not allowed to say the "thirteen attributes" as a prayer and as a supplication, but as one who reads it from the Torah, in the same melody and with the same intonation. He should omit the passages wherein the thirteen attributes are mentioned, such as, "Remember for us this day the covenant of thirteen," and the like, as well as the entreaties written in the Aramaic language, such as, *Maḥe umasse* (He strikes and He cures) and, *Maran di bishemaya* (the Lord of heaven), for these are said only in an assembly of ten male adults.

10. A mourner during the first seven days, is forbidden to go from his house to the synagogue in order to say the *Seliḥot,* excepting on the day before *Rosh Hashanah,* when many *Seliḥot* are recited.

11. The one who is to officiate on the awe-inspiring days, as well as the one who blows the *shofar,* should abstain three days before *Rosh Hashanah* from anything that may cause contamination. They should familiarize themselves as much as possible with the meaning of the prayers, the liturgic poetry, and the laws concerning the blowing of the *shofar.* They should also study inspirational books, which tend to stir the heart of man, and which inculcate awe of the Lord and the glory of His greatness when He rises to judge the world. If we are unable to get a Torah scholar to blow the *shofar,* we should at least get a prompter who is a scholar and versed in the procedure of blowing the *shofar,* so that in the event of an error, he should know what to do. This man should also know how to examine the *shofar* to ascertain whether it is valid.

12. Many people are accustomed to fast the ten penitential days; but since this period includes four days on which no fasting is permissible, that is, the two days of *Rosh Hashanah,* the Sabbath, and the day before *Yom Kippur,* they substitute for them four other days during the period when the *Seliḥot* preceding *Rosh Hashanah,* are recited, that is, the first day when the saying of *Seliḥot* begins, the day before *Rosh Hashanah,* and two other intervening days, preferably Monday and Thursday. If a ritual feast occurs during these days, one may partake of the feast, and fast on some other day. If one knows in advance that such a feast will be held, he must fast in its stead, some day before the feast.

13. After the morning prayers on the day before *Rosh Hashanah,* it is customary to go to the cemetery and prostrate upon the graves of saintly men. Then charity is distributed among the poor, and supplications are made to exhort the saintly men to intercede for us on the day of judgment; also for the further reason, that the place where the saintly rest is holy and pure, and prayers are more readily acceptable when offered on holy ground. The Holy One, blessed be He, will show us mercy for the sake of the righteous, but we must not implore the dead who rest there, for this would violate the order of

(Deuteronomy 18:11): "And he inquireth of the dead;" but we should implore God, blessed be His name, to have mercy on us for the sake of the pious who rest in the dust. Upon arriving at the cemetery, if we have seen no graves within the last thirty days, we say the benediction, "Who hath formed you in judgment," etc. (See chapter 60:11, above.) Approaching the grave, we say: "May it be His will that the rest of (so and so) who is buried here, be peaceful, and may his merit defend me." We should place the left hand only, on the grave and not the right, and say: "And the Lord will guide thee continuously and will slake thy soul in drought, and make thy bones strong, and thou shalt be like a watered garden, and like a spring of water, whose waters fail not (Isaiah 58:11). Mayest thou lie in peace and sleep in peace until *Menaḥem* (Comforter) comes to announce peace." (When putting the hand on the grave, we should think of the verse, "And the Lord will guide thee," which contains fifteen words the same as the number of joints in the hand). It is improper to visit the same grave, twice on the same day. Reading epitaphs, if the letters are in relief, mars the memory. A remedy for that is to recite the prayer, *Ahavah rabbah* (with abounding love) up to, *Uleyaḥedḥa beahavah* (and to proclaim Thy unity in love).

14. On the day before *Rosh Hashanah*, it is the general custom to fast until after the afternoon service, at which time some food is tasted in order not to inaugurate the festival in anguish. The entire day should be spent in the study of the Torah, in performing precepts, and in repentance, especially of the sins committed against fellow men. We should not wait until *Yom Kippur* eve, but we should ask our neighbor's forgiveness prior to that.

15. We should bathe and have our hair cut on the day before *Rosh Hashanah* in honor of the festival. Care, however, should be taken to have the hair cut in the forenoon. Then we perform the ritual of immersion, and put on the Sabbath garments, to indicate that we trust in the mercy of the Holy One, blessed be His name, that He will make our judgment bright as the light.

16. On the day before *Rosh Hashanah*, it is customary to have our vows annulled. One who does not understand the Aramaic, should say the prescribed formula in the vernacular.

CHAPTER 129

Rosh Hashanah

1. In the *kaddish* recited from *Rosh Hashanah* through *Yom Kippur*, we repeat the word *leela* (He be high), thus, *Leela, leela* (He be very high above) (without adding the letter *vav, uleela*); but as there must be twenty-eight words in the *kaddish*, and the whole year we say, *Leela min kal birḥata* (above all blessings), now we contract the preposition *min* into a prefix, and we say, *Mikol birḥata* (thus making a total of twenty-eight words).

2. Some people make a practice of reading the *Shemoneh esreh* on *Rosh Hashanah* and *Yom Kippur*, with their heads bowed. But since we must bow at the beginning and the end of the benediction, *Magen Abraham* (the shield of Abraham) and *Modim* (we give thanks), it is necessary to straighten up when reaching these prayers, so that we may bow where the Sages, of blessed memory, ordered it. It is likewise forbidden to bow either at the beginning or at the end of any benediction where the Sages, of blessed memory, have not ordained. It is best to pray in an erect position, but with a humble spirit and in tears. The practice of praying the *Shomoneh esreh* in a loud voice should be abolished; it must be recited silently, as it is done the whole year. Some authorities permit to raise the voice somewhat, but not too much. Care should be taken to read the prayers correctly, not to change even a single vowel. One should obtain a well-edited Prayer Book, out of which to pray.

3. During the rest of the year, we say in the *Shemoneh esreh, Hael hakkadosh* (the Holy God), and *Meleḥ ohev tzedakah umishpat* (King who lovest righteousness and judgment); but from *Rosh Hashanah* until after *Yom Kippur*, we say instead, *Hammeleḥ hakkadosh* (the Holy King), and *Hammeleh hammishpat* (the King of judgment), because on these days, the Holy One, blessed be He, manifests His sovereignty through His judgment of the world. If we have erred and said, *Hael hakkadosh*, or if we are in doubt whether we have said *Hael hakkadosh*, or *Hammeleḥ hakkadosh*, then if we have become aware of the error within as much time as needed for an utterance (that is, a greeting), we say *Hammeleḥ hakkadosh*, and we are not required to repeat from the beginning. This law applies also to *Hammeleḥ hammishpat*. If, however, we have become aware of it after the time needed for an utterance, then at *Hammeleḥ hakkadosh*, we must repeat from the beginning of the *Shemoneh esreh* (even when only in doubt), because the first three benedictions are considered as one. Even the *ḥazan*, during the loud repetition of the *Shemoneh esreh*, is required to repeat from the beginning, and the *kedushah* must be said again. At *Hammeleḥ hammishpat*, however, even an individual need not repeat even that benediction, because the word "King" has been mentioned in this benediction. If during the rest of the year, we have erred and said, *Hammeleḥ hakkadosh*, or *Hammeleḥ hammishpat*, it is not necessary to repeat the *Shemoneh esreh*.

4. In the *Maariv* service on Friday night, in the benediction *Magen avot* (He was the shield, etc.), we also say *Hammeleḥ hakkadosh* instead of *Hael hakkadosh*. If the *ḥazan* has erred and said *Hael hakkadosh*, then if he has become aware of the error immediately, within as much time as is needed for an utterance, he should say *Hammeleḥ hakkadosh*, if he has become aware of it later, he need not repeat the prayer.

5. If we have forgotten to say *Zaḥerenu* (remember us), or *Mi ḥamoḥa* (who is like unto Thee), or *Uḥetov* (O inscribe), or *Besefer ḥayyim* (in the book of life), and we have not become aware of the omission until we have said, *Baruḥ attah adonai* (blessed art Thou, O Lord), since we have mentioned the Divine Name, we conclude the benediction and continue the prayers, and we

need not repeat any part of the *Shemoneh esreh.* If we have forgotten to say, *Ubeḥen ten paḥdeḥa* (now, therefore, bestow Thy awe) and concluded the blessing with *Hammeleḥ hakkadosh,* even if we have only said, *Baruḥ attah adonai* (blessed art Thou, O Lord), we conclude *Hammeleḥ hakkadosh,* and then say *Attah veḥartanu* (Thou hast shosen us), etc.

6. Some people conclude the *Shemoneh esreh,* with *Oseh hashalom* (who maketh "the" peace), while others conclude it as usual with, *Hamevareḥ et ammo yisrael bashalom* (who blesseth His people Israel with peace), and only in the *kaddish* do they say, *Oseh hashalom bimeromav* (He who maketh the peace in His high places).

7. If *Rosh Hashanah* occurs on the Sabbath, in some communities they say *Leḥu neranenah* (O come, let us sing) the same as on any other Sabbath; in other communities they begin with *Mizemor ledavid* (a Psalm of David); while in still others, they begin with *Mizemor shir leyom hashabbat* (a Psalm, a song for the Sabbath-day). Every community should abide by its own customs.

8. After the *Maariv* service, on the first night of *Rosh Hashanah,* it is customary to exchange greetings by saying *Leshanah tovah tikatev vetiḥatem* (be thou inscribed and sealed for a happy year), and to a woman it is said in the feminine form, *tikatevi vetiḥatemi;* but these greetings are not exchanged in the daytime, because the writing had been finished in the forenoon. Some are accustomed to exchange greetings on the second night, because the heavenly judgment is occasionally also passed on the second day.

9. At the evening meal, it is customary to perform symbols as omens for a good year; we dip in honey a portion of the *ḥallah* over which we have said the *Hamotzi* (who bringeth forth), and after eating a piece the size of an olive, we say: "May it be Thy will to renew for us a happy and pleasant year;" after this we dip a piece of sweet apple in honey and say the benediction *Bore peri haetz* (who createth the fruit of the tree), and after eating it, we again say: "May it be Thy will to renew for us a happy and pleasant year." It is also customary to eat the head of some animal, and say: "May it be Thy will that we be a head (master)." It is preferable to obtain the head of a sheep which will also serve as a reminder of the ram substituted for Isaac. We also eat some vegetables, the names of which have the connotation of good fortune, like carrots in our country, called *mehren* (meaning "increase") and we say: "May it be Thy will that our merits increase." It is also meritorious to procure for this occasion, fish which symbolizes fertility. But it should not be cooked in vinegar, for no sour or bitter foods are eaten on *Rosh Hashanah.* Also meat and confectioneries should be partaken of. It is also customary to refrain from eating any nuts or almonds, because the numeric value of the Hebrew word **אגוז** (nut) is 17, the same as that of the Hebrew word **חטא** (sin), not counting the **א** of **חטא**. Also, nuts increase the saliva and cause coughing which interferes with praying. It is well to study the Torah while at the table. Some make it a practice to study the *Mishnah,* tractate *Rosh Hashanah* (dealing with the New Year).

10. It is proper to abstain from cohabitation during the two nights of *Rosh Hashanah,* even if they occur on the Sabbath. But if it is the night of her ritual immersion, one should not fail to perform his marital duty, and in the morning one should cleanse himself from his defilement.

11. On *Rosh Hashanah,* when saying, *Avinu malkenu ḥatanu lefaneḥa* (our Father, our King, we have sinned before Thee), we must not beat our

breasts as on a weekdays and on *Yom Kippur*, because no confessions are to be recited on *Rosh Hashanah*, which is a festival. Hence, we interpret "Our Father, our King, we have sinned before Thee," thus: "Our fathers sinned before Thee because they worshiped idols, but as for us, we have no other king but Thee," therefore, "Our Father, our King, deal with us for the sake of Thy name."

12. When the Scrolls of the Law are taken from the Holy Ark, it is customary to recite the "thirteen attributes" (*Adonai, adonai, el raḥum veḥanun*). And it is proper to begin with *Vayaavor* (and He passed), and we say it thus: "And the Lord passed on before him, and He called," etc. In some communities, neither the "thirteen attributes" nor *Ribbono shel olam* (Master of the universe) is recited when the festival occurs on the Sabbath.

13. The *shofar* should be preferably sounded as follows: The *Teruah* consists of nine short sounds; the *Shevarim* is of three successive sounds, each being as long as three *Teruah* sounds so that the *Shevarim* is equal to nine sounds. One should be very careful not to protract the *Shevarim* until each one equals nine sounds, for in such an event the precept is not fulfilled, even post facto. The *Tekiot* are simple sounds. In the order of *Tekiah, Shevarim, Teruah, Tekiah,* the sound of each *Tekiah* should be as long as the *Shevarim* and the *Teruah,* that is, the length of eighteen sounds. In the order of *Tekiah, Shevarim, Tekiah,* each *Tekiah* should be as long as the *Shevarim,* that is, the length of nine sounds; the same in the order of *Tekiah, Teruah, Tekiah.* In the *Tekiot* preceding the *Musaph* service, the *Shevarim* and the *Teruah,* when they follow one another, should be sounded in one breath; the prompter should, therefore, announce them together: *Shevarim-teruah.* But in the *Tekiot* during the repetition of the *Shemoneh esreh,* they should be sounded in two breaths. Nevertheless, no undue pause should be made between them, but they should be sounded in immediate succession, and the prompter should likewise announce them at one time.

14. When the one sounding the *shofar* pronounces the benedictions, the congregation should not respond, *Baruḥ hu ubaruḥ shemo* (blessed be He and blessed be His name), but merely listen attentively and after each benediction respond *Amen.* (See chapter 6:9, above.) From there on it is forbidden to make any interruption till after the *Tekiot* during the *Shemoneh esreh.* Therefore, the sexton should not announce, *Shetikah yafah bisheat hateflllah* (silence is proper when praying), although he customarily does so at other times.

15. After each set of the *shofar* blasts during the repetition of the *Shemoneh esreh,* people generally recite, *Yehi ratzon* (may it be Thy will), as it is printed in the festival prayer books. Care should be taken not to pronounce the names of the angels given there. In many communities this prayer is not recited at all, and this is preferable. The principal reason for blowing the *shofar* is to exhort the people to wholehearted repentance. As Maimonides, of blessed memory, said: "Although the blowing of the *shofar* on *Rosh Ha-*

shanah is an unexplained Scriptural command, its connotation is: 'Awake ye that are sleepy, and ye that slumber awake from your slumber, and ponder your deeds, remember your Creator, and go back to Him in penitence. Ye who miss the truth in your hunt after vanities, and waste your years in seeking after vain things that can neither profit nor deliver, look after your own souls, and improve your ways and your deeds. Let everyone of you abandon his evil ways and thoughts and return to God that He may have mercy on you.'"

16. At the repetition of the *Shemoneh esreh,* when the *ḥazan* says, *Vaanaḥnu koreim* (and we bow), it is customary for the congregation to say it with him, and all bow and prostrate themselves. But they are not to fall on their faces, except on *Yom Kippur,* where the *Avodah* (the order of the Temple service) is read. The *ḥazan* kneels and prostrates himself, but he is not allowed to move from his place during the repetition of the *Shemoneh esreh;* he, therefore, stands at a slight distance from the desk, so that he may be able to bow and prostrate himself without moving from his place, and those who stand near him, assist him to rise. The *ḥazan* should not blow the *shofar* during the repetition of the *Shemoneh esreh,* unless he is confident that in so doing he will not become confused in his prayers.

17. Concerning the *Tekiot* during the repetition of the *Shemoneh esreh,* different customs prevail, and each community should abide by its customs. There are also different customs concerning the *Tekiot* at the conclusion of the prayers. After all the *Tekiot* have been sounded, in accordance with the local custom, the *shofar* should be hidden, to make certain that no more sounds are made. Even one who is to sound the *shofar* on the second day, is not allowed to blow it on the first day for the purpose of practicing.

18. If a circumcision is to take place at the synagogue, it should be performed after the reading of the *haftorah,* before the sounding of the *shofar.* If it is a Sabbath, the circumcision should take place after *Ashre* (happy are they) is said. If it is necessary to perform the circumcision at the house of the infant's mother, it should be done after leaving the synagogue.

19. One who has already fulfilled his obligation of blowing the *shofar,* may pronounce the benedictions if he has to blow it for the sake of others. Nevertheless, it is more proper that a person who had not yet fulfilled this obligation should pronounce the benedictions. One who sounds the *shofar* for the sake of women, then if he has already fulfilled his obligation, should not recite the benedictions, but a woman should recite them, for according to law, women are exempt from blowing the *shofar,* since it is a positive precept required only at a certain time. Other authorities hold that the one who has already fulfilled his obligation should not blow the *shofar* at all for the sake of women, and if one desires to do so, he must do it before hearing the *Tekiot* at the synagogue, and he should pronounce the benedictions thereon with the intention of fulfilling thereby his obligation. This, however, must not be done during the first three hours of the day, as it is not permissible to blow the

shofar privately at such time. He should either blow the *shofar* for them at the time it is blown at the synagogue, or thereafter, but he should bear in mind while in the synagogue not to be exempted by these *Tekiot*, but only by those which he will sound for the women, and he should say the benedictions thereon. Although he later goes to the synagogue to pray the *Musaph* service, and to hear the *Tekiot* sounded during the repetition of the *Shemoneh esreh*, the interruption does not oblige him to repeat the benedictions, as all the *Tekiot* constitute one precept. A weak woman who cannot abstain from food until after the *Tekiot*, may eat before the *Tekiot*.

20. Upon leaving the synagogue, we should walk leisurely, cheerful and confident that the Lord has mercifully heard our prayers and the sounds of the *shofar*. We should eat and drink to the fullest extent of the bounty which the Lord has bestowed upon us. Yet we must guard against eating to excess, and the fear of the Lord must always be upon us. It is well to study the Torah at the table. We must not sleep after saying Grace, but we should go to the synagogue and recite Psalms with the congregation until the *Minḥah* service. Only one who has a headache may take a short nap before going to the synagogue.

21. After the *Minḥah* service, on the first day of *Rosh Hashanah*, we go to a stream (to recall the merit of the *Akedah*, the binding of Isaac); for it is stated in the Midrash, *Tanḥuma, Vayera*, that when Abraham was on his way to offer Isaac as a sacrifice, Satan interfered and he transformed himself into a stream in order to obstruct him. Then our father Abraham, may he rest in peace, walked into the river, and when the water reached to his neck, he exclaimed: (Psalms 69:2) "Save me, O Lord, for the waters are come in even unto my soul." There is another reason for that; because on this day we proclaim the Holy One, blessed be He, as King, and it is the custom to anoint kings by a river (Horayot 12a) to hint thereby that his kingdom may flow smoothly and continuously as the river. It is preferable that such river be outside the city limits, and should contain fish as a reminder that we are compared to the fish who are caught in a net; we too, are caught in the net of death and judgment, and thus we will be moved to think of repentance; another reason is to symbolize that the evil eye shall have no effect on us, just as it has no effect on fishes, and that we be as fruitful and multiply as the fishes. Others give the following reason; fishes have no eyelids, their eyes being always open, and we implore the attention of the Ever-Open Eye of above. If, however, there is no stream containing fish, we may go to any river or to a well, and we say the verses: *Mi el kamoḥa* (who is a God like unto Thee), according to the formula of the *Tashliḥ* given in the prayer books. We then shake the ends of our garments, simply as a symbol that we are casting away our sins, and that we shall examine and scrutinize our ways from now on, so that we be white and pure from all sin. If the first day of *Rosh Hashanah* occurs on the Sabbath, we perform the *Tashliḥ* ceremony on the second day.

22. After returning to the synagogue, if the time to pray *Maariv* has not yet come, it is our duty to avoid the company of friends, so that we should not, God forbid, indulge in trivial conversation. We must devote our spare time to study the Torah, recite the Psalms, or read inspirational books, because this is a holy day to our Lord.

23. The two days of *Rosh Hashanah* are considered as one long day, and are of equal holiness. Therefore, the authorities differ as to whether the benediction *Sheheḥeyanu* (who kept us in life) should be said in the *kiddush* of the second night, or when lighting the candles, or when sounding the *shofar* on the second day. For since both days are like one continuous day, and we have already said *Sheheḥeyanu* on the first day, we need not say it again on the second day. It is customary, therefore, to place a new fruit on the table, or to put on a new garment, in order that the *Sheheḥeyanu* said in the *kiddush* may apply also to the fruit or the new garment. Yet even if this is not done, *Sheheḥeyanu* should still be said in the *kiddush* (because we follow the authorities who hold that we do have to say *Sheheḥeyanu* on the second night). A woman, too, when lighting the candles on the second night (if she is accustomed to say *Sheheḥeyanu*), should, if possible, put on a new garment, or put a new fruit on the table, so that the benediction *Sheheḥeyanu* may apply also to these. Yet if she has none of these, it does not bar her from saying the benediction. The one who blows the *shofar* on the second day, should, if possible, put on a new garment; if, however, the first day of *Rosh Hashanah* occurs on a Sabbath (when the *shofar* is not sounded), there is no need for it, for he has not yet said *Sheheḥeyanu* for the *shofar*.

CHAPTER 130

The Ten Days of Penitence

1. The ten days of repentance, as indicated by its name, are set aside for repentance, and everybody must, during these days, wholeheartedly repent before the Holy One, blessed be His name, before the great and awesome day of *Yom Kippur* comes as it is written (Leviticus 16:30): "Ye shall be clean before the Lord;" and it is written again (Isaiah 55:6): "Seek ye the Lord while He may be found," and the Rabbis, of blessed memory, said (Rosh Hashanah 18a) that this refers to the ten days from *Rosh Hashanah* to *Yom Kippur*. Hence, during this time everybody must examine his deeds, and turn away from all evil. For, there is greater need of repentance for sins of which one is uncertain than for sins of which one is certain, because one is more remorseful when he is aware of having committed a sin than when he is ignorant of it. For this reason, the trespass offering for doubtful sins was more costly than the sin-offering for positive sins. One should also devote more time than usual to the study of the Torah, the performance of precepts, and the distribution of charity, and pay less attention to his own affairs. Rabbi Moses Cordovero, of blessed memory, said that these days are to be treated like the Intermediate Days of festivals during which only necessary work may be performed. Above all, every man should make amends for all the wrongs he has committed against his fellow men for which there is no atonement unless he makes restitution of the thing stolen or obtained by force, and begs their forgiveness.

2. During these days of repentance, a man should be more scrupulous than on other days, just as we pray to God, blessed be His name, that He deal with us with special kindness. One, for instance, who eats non-Jewish bread during the rest of the year, should eat Jewish bread only during these days.

3. While saying Grace, it is customary to include: "May the All-Merciful renew," etc., as it is done on *Rosh Hashanah.*

4. It is customary not to contract any marriages during these days.

5. On the Sabbath (during the ten days of repentance), when *Shuvah yisrael* (return, O Israel) (Hosea 14:2) is read as the *haftorah,* an eminent person should be called up as the *maftir.*

6. Some people sanctify the moon at the conclusion of *Yom Kippur,* when people are cheerful, whereas prior to *Yom Kippur* they are worried. There are others who contend that, on the contrary, it is preferable to sanctify the moon before *Yom Kippur,* in order to augment our merits. In a place where *etrogim* (citrons), palms and myrtles are obtainable, pious men purchase them during these days, so that this precious precept may be added to their merits.

CHAPTER 131

The Day Before Yom Kippur

1. On the day before *Yom Kippur,* it is customary to perform the ceremony of *kapparot,* at dawn, for the attribute of mercy is predominant at that time. Men select roosters and women select hens, while a pregnant woman takes both a rooster and a hen; a rooster is taken because the child might be a male, and if the child is female, one hen suffices for the mother and the child. But at any rate, one *kappara* is sufficient for two persons. It is preferable to choose white fowl, with due attention to the Scriptural verse (Isaiah 1:18): "If your sins are as red as the scarlet thread, they will become white as snow." One should not, however, demonstrate that he is bent on buying a white fowl and pay a higher price for it, because this resembles the customs of the Amorites. But if by chance one has bought white fowls among others, one should choose the white. Each takes the fowl in his or her right hand, recites the verses, *Bene adam* (children of man), etc., and then swings the fowl around the head three times, each time reciting: *Zeh or zot ḥalifati* (this is in my stead). One who swings it around the head of another should say: *Zeh or zot ḥalifateḥa* (this is in stead of thee), etc., but he must first swing it around his own head, and then above the head of the other. It is also preferable that the fowl should be slaughtered at dawn. By no means should we imagine that the fowl atones for us, but we should reflect that what is done to the fowl should properly be done to us because of our sins. We should bemoan our sins, and the Holy One, blessed be He, in His mercy, will accept our repentance. It is customary to throw out the intestines of the fowl, the liver and the kidneys, on the roof or in the court, where the birds may fetch it, because

it is fitting to take pity upon living creatures on that day, so that pity may be shown to us from Heaven; and for the further reason that fowl generally feed on crops they steal, we therefore, throw away their innards to show our resolve to keep away from stolen goods. If chickens cannot be obtained for *kapparot*, a goose or some other living thing, which was not acceptable as a sacrifice in the Temple may be taken for that purpose. Some authorities are of the opinion that even fish may be used. But no turtle-doves or pigeons may be used because these were valid as sacrifices in the Temple, and it would appear as if we were sacrificing offerings outside the Temple. Some people are accustomed to give the *kappara* fowl to the poor; but it is best to redeem the fowl with money and give the money to the poor.

2. Neither *Mizemor letodah* (A Psalm of thanksgiving), nor *Taḥanun* (petition for Grace), nor *Lamenatzeaḥ* (For the chief musician), nor *Avinu malkenu* (our Father, our King) is recited on the day before *Yom Kippur*. But when *Yom Kippur* falls on the Sabbath, then *Avinu malkenu* is recited in the *Shaḥarit* service on the day before *Yom Kippur*.

3. It is mandatory to feast sumptuously on the day before *Yom Kippur*, and the person who does it for the purpose of fulfilling this precept, is credited with having fasted also on that day. It is fitting to eat fish at the first meal.

4. *Yom Kippur* does not atone for transgressions committed against a fellow man unless we conciliate him, for it is written (Leviticus 16:30): "For on this day He shall atone you of all your sins, you shall be cleaned before God," which means, that only sins against God shall be atoned on *Yom Kippur*, but not sins committed against our neighbor, unless we conciliate him. We should, therefore, be very careful to return to others what lawfully belong to them and to obtain their pardon. If we have some property of which we are not certain whether it lawfully belongs to us, we must inform our neighbor that immediately after *Yom Kippur* we desire to appear with him before a court conducted according to the laws of our holy Torah, and sincerely resolve to abide by the verdict rendered by such tribunal. If we have sinned against others, even if only by means of words, we are also obliged to conciliate them. It is our duty to go personally to them. If, however, it is difficult for us to do so, or if we understand that they will be easily reconciled even if approached by another, we may conciliate them through a mediator. The person whose forgiveness is sought should grant forgiveness willingly and wholeheartedly, and not be obstinate, for this is not a characteristic of Israel, but of Esau, concerning whom it is written (Amos 1:11): "And he kept his wrath forever." It is also said concerning the Gibeonites, because they would not forgive and would not be conciliated (II Samuel 21:2): "Now the Gibeonites were not of the children of Israel." The way of the children of Israel is slow to become angry and easy to be pacified, and when the offender asks for forgiveness, they grant it wholeheartedly and willingly. Even if one has been grievously wronged, one should not seek vengeance, nor bear a grudge against the one that had wronged him. On the contrary, if the offender does not come to him to beg forgiveness, the offended person should present himself

to the offender in order that the latter might ask his pardon. If a person harbors enmity in his heart, his prayers on *Yom Kippur* will not be accepted, God forbid, but the one who is magnanimous and forgiving, will have all his sins forgiven.

5. If the offended has since died, the offender should assemble ten men at the grave, and say: "I have sinned against the God of Israel and against this man (so and so)" and they pronounce three times: "Thou art forgiven." He should also be barefoot and recount in detail the nature of the offense, if it does not reflect on the dead. If the grave is more than three parasangs (Persian miles, each one equalling about four miles) distant from the place where the offender resides, he need not go there in person; he may delegate someone else who shall assemble ten men at the grave, and say: "I, the agent of (so and so), publicly declare that he has sent me to beg forgiveness for his sin," etc. If one has vilified a dead person, he is not required to go to his grave; he may beg his forgiveness in the place where he had vilified him. If, however, he had maliciously slandered him, he must do penance for having transgressed a ban of the ancients, forbidding to slander the dead.

6. Every man is in duty-bound to immerse on the day before *Yom Kippur*, to cleanse himself from nocturnal pollution, and also as a prerequisite to repentance, just as a convert to Judaism is required to immerse. Therefore, even young men and virgin girls are required to immerse. The most appropriate time for the bath of purification is after midday. One should make sure before the immersion, that there is no interposition on the body. A woman after intercourse, is apt to discharge the semen virile within three days. She is then considered like one who has had a nocturnal pollution, and the mere immersion would not suffice in such a case. She must, therefore, first wash herself well with warm water before making the immersion, so that she would have no further discharge. If, however, she has had intercourse immediately after her ritual bath of immersion, or immediately before her period of menstruation when she generally becomes pregnant, then she is not allowed to destroy the semen virile of conception, and therefore, she is not permitted to wash herself in warm water. She should, however, bathe in cold water. A mourner, even during the first seven days, may wash and bathe about one or two hours before dark, even if it is before the *Minḥah* service. He must, however, observe all the other laws concerning mourners, that is, he must sit on the ground, and not put on leather shoes till nighttime.

7. In accordance with custom, every householder prepares two candles, one for the house, symbolizing the Torah, which is called "light" because on *Yom Kippur,* Moses descended from Mount Sinai with the second tablets and the other candle is for the souls of his departed father and mother, to make atonement for them. In pursuance to custom, the candle lit in the

house, burns till the following night, and is used for the *havdalah* light. These candles should not be made out of the wax taken from a house of idolatry. Since there are some people who take it as a bad omen if their candle is extinguished during *Yom Kippur*, although in reality there is no foundation for this apprehension, it is best to avoid it, by giving the candle to the *Shamesh* who will put it among other candles so that the person will not know the identity of his candle. One should take the candle to the synagogue when going there for the *Minḥah* service to be put in its proper place and to be lit thereafter, because when people come to the synagogue for *Maariv* service, they are pressed for time.

8. It is our custom to put on the Sabbath garments when we go to the synagogue to pray the *Minḥah* service before *Yom Kippur*. Before reciting *Elohai netzor* (O my God, guard), at the end of *Shemoneh esreh* of *Minḥah*, we say *Yiheyu leratzon* (let the words of my mouth), and then we recite *Al ḥet* (confession), beginning with, *Elohenu velohe avotenu, tavo lefaneḥa* (our God and God of our fathers, let our prayers come before Thee), to *Veḥalayim raim* (and sore diseases), when we repeat the verse *Yiheyu leratzon*. If while we still recite *Al ḥet*, the *ḥazan* repeats the *Shemoneh esreh*, we may respond *Amen*, say the *Kedushah*, and *Modim* (we give thanks), since we have already said *Yiheyu leratzon*.

9. *Al ḥet* should be recited while standing and in a bowed posture as when reciting *Modim*. At the mention of each sin, we beat our breasts, as if to say: "You were the cause of my sins." *Al ḥet* should be recited by all alike, according to the version given in the Prayer Books. One, however, who has committed a sin which is not mentioned in the formula *Al ḥet*, inasmuch as he recites it inaudibly, he should mention that sin and acknowledge his guilt with a contrite heart, and with copious tears. If that sin is one that is mentioned in *Al ḥet*, he should, when coming to it, sob bitterly as he mentions it. Even when he is certain that the sin for which he had made confession the previous year was not repeated by him since then, he should, nevertheless, repeat his confession. This is a praiseworthy practice, for it is written (Psalms 51:5): "And my sin is ever before me."

10. *Avinu malkenu* (our Father, our King) is not recited after *Minḥah*, whether *Yom Kippur* occurs on a weekday or on the Sabbath.

11. After *Minḥah* it is customary to receive *malkot* (flagellation). Although this flagellation is merely nominal, it is conducive to make one aware of the need for repentance. It is best to take for this purpose a strap of calf's leather, even though it is not a handbreadth (four inches) wide. The one receiving the stripes should bend, leaning on his knees, with his face towards the North. It is customary to recite some confession while being struck. The

one who administers the stripes, repeats three times the verse *Vehu raḥum* (and He being merciful), etc., (which contains thirteen Hebrew words), making it a total of thirty-nine words, representing the thirty-nine stripes that used to be administered to sinners.

12. Towards evening, we eat the final meal before the fast, at which it is customary to dip in honey the piece of *ḥallah* over which the *Hamotzi* has been pronounced, as we do on *Rosh Hashanah*. Only food which is easily digestible should be eaten at this meal, such as the flesh of fowl. It is the custom not to partake of fish during this meal. One should not partake of food or drink which tend to generate heat, such as victuals seasoned with spices and saffron. We must be exceedingly careful to add from the profane to the sacred, that is, we should conclude the meal while it is yet day, a little before twilight. The zealous are prompt to end their meal about an hour before nightfall. If we finish the meal long before sunset and we intend to eat or drink after that, we must make a declaration, or at least have it in mind, before reciting Grace after meals, that we do not yet inaugurate the fast.

13. It is the custom in these parts not to put away any food in a hot oven on the day before *Yom Kippur* to be used at the conclusion of *Yom Kippur*, as it is done on Friday for the Sabbath, because it is the equivalent of preparing food on *Yom Kippur* for a weekday, and for the further reason that it has the appearance of gluttony.

14. It is written (Isaiah 58:13): "And the holy of the Lord honored," and the Rabbis (Shabbat 119) said that this refers to *Yom Kippur* on which day there is neither eating nor drinking. It is our duty to honor this day with clean apparel and with lights; hence, in the synagogue we spread beautiful covers and light many candles, which are called "honor," for it is written (Isaiah 24:15): "Therefore, *'baurim'* glorify ye the Lord," and the Targum renders it: "With *lights* glorify ye the Lord." Before twilight, the tablecloths are spread upon the tables and the candles are lit in the house, as on Friday. It is proper to light a candle in the wife's bedroom as a reminder not to cohabit. The benediction, *Lehadlik ner shel yom hakkippurim* (to kindle the light of *Yom Kippur*) is uttered over the candles. If *Yom Kippur* occurs on the Sabbath, then we say in the benediction: *Lehadlik ner shel shabbat veshel yom hakkippurim* (to kindle the light of the Sabbath and of *Yom Kippur*).

15. It is the custom to put on a *kittle* (white robe), which resembles shrouds. It is calculated to humble the arrogant heart of man. A mourner may also put it on. Since it is a garment specifically made to be worn at prayers, it must be removed before entering a lavatory. Women also wear clean white clothes in honor of the day; but they should not wear any jewelry, in view of the awe-inspiring day of judgment.

16. It is the custom of fathers and mothers to bless their children before going to the synagogue on *Yom Kippur* eve, because the holiness of the day has already begun and the gates of mercy are already open. They implore in

this blessing that the children should be granted good life and that their hearts be constant in the fear of God. In doing so they weep copiously, that their prayers be accepted, and also that their children be inclined to walk in the way of the righteous and to follow the path of the pious. Some go to their kin who are well versed in the Torah and are righteous to be blessed of them, and they also request them to pray for them on the holy and awesome day. It is proper that this should be done while the day has not yet advanced far, for towards evening all must be ready to receive the holy day in a quiet and peaceful mood. The version for the blessing is: *Yesimḥa elohim keefraim* (God make thee as Ephraim), etc., (Genesis 48:20), and each may add according to his gift of speech. It is preferable to say this prayer: "May it be the will of our Father in heaven, that He put in your heart His love and His fear, and may the fear of the Lord always be upon you so that you sin not. And may you long for the Torah and its precepts. Let your mouth speak wisdom and your heart meditate reverence. May your hands be engaged in the performance of precepts. May your feet run to execute the will of your Father in heaven. May He grant you righteous sons and daughters who shall be engaged in the study of the Torah and in performing precepts all their lives. May you be fruitful. May He grant your livelihood be legitimate, peaceful, and abundant, that it come from His bountiful hand and not from a mortal; an occupation which should allow you leisure to serve God. And may you be inscribed and sealed for a good long life among all the righteous men in Israel. Amen."

17. It is customary to put on the *tallit* for the evening service. But we must do so while it is yet day, and say the benediction thereon. If, however, we have not put it on until twilight, we should not say the benediction (because the precept of *tzitzit*, is to be performed during the daytime only).

CHAPTER 132

Yom Kippur Eve

1. It is the custom in our regions before saying *Kol Nidré*, that the most venerable man of the congregation takes out a *Sefer Torah* from the Holy Ark, and walks with it around the center platform, while the people lovingly kiss it, and plead for pardon and forgiveness for having slighted it. They should resolve to be guided by its precepts thenceforth. The verse (Psalms 97:11): "Light is sown for the righteous," is repeated many times. Then he takes his place on the right hand of the *ḥazan*, and another prominent man of the congregation, also with a Scroll, stands on the left of the *ḥazan*, and the three say together: "*Biyeshivah shell maalah* (by the authority of the Court on High), etc., after which the *ḥazan* recites *Kol Nidré*, chanting it in the traditional melody, all the worshipers repeating it silently with the *ḥazan*. It is proper to begin saying *Kol Nidré* while it is yet day, and to protract it until nighttime. After the *ḥazan* has said *Barḥu* (bless ye) and the congregation responded *Baruḥ* (blessed be), etc., the Scrolls are returned to the Holy Ark and the two men near the *ḥazan* return to their respective places. On the Sabbath, they may return to their places when the congregation begins reciting *Mizemor shir leyom hashabbat* (A Psalm, a Song for the Sabbath Day).

2. When the *ḥazan* says the benediction *Sheheḥeyanu* (who kept us in life), it should be his intention to say it in behalf of all congregants. Each worshiper, however, should intend not to be exempted by the *ḥazan's* benediction, and should repeat it silently with the *ḥazan*, but he should conclude it before the *ḥazan*, so that he may respond *Amen*. The women who had already said *Sheheḥeyanu* when lighting the candles, or likewise, if a man had lit the candles at home and said *Sheheḥeyanu*, need not say it at the synagogue.

3. On *Yom Kippur*, both in the evening and during the day, *Baruḥ shem kevod malḥuto leolam vaed* (Blessed be His name, whose glorious kingdom is forever and ever) should be said in a loud voice.

4. Some people stand on their feet during the evening service and also the whole day of *Yom Kippur*. If they feel faint, they may lean against something. The reason for standing is to simulate the angels; therefore, women need not stand up. One who has stood up once, intending to do so all his lifetime, and thereafter desires to abandon this practice, he must be absolved as from a vow.

5. Some people stay in the synagogue all night reciting hymns. When in need of sleep, they must remove far from the Holy Ark. The *ḥazan* should not stay awake, as he may weaken his voice thereby. Before going to sleep, one should recite the first four Psalms, which recital serves as a prevention against nocturnal pollution; for these four Psalms contain a total of three hundred and six words, and adding thereto the number of the Psalms, it makes a total of three hundred and ten, similiar to the numeric value of the letters which spell out the Hebrew word קרי (nocturnal pollution). The numeric value of the letters beginning and ending the four Psalms, is one hundred and twenty-six, and together with the number four of the four Psalms amount to one hundred and thirty-one, similar to the numeric value of the word סמאל (name of the prosecuting angel of death), and one should resolve to rid oneself of him. It is best not to cover oneself with pillows and blankets that heat the body, and by no means should one cover his legs.

CHAPTER 133

Yom Kippur

1. It is forbidden to eat, drink, bathe, anoint, wear shoes, or have sexual intercourse on *Yom Kippur*. It is forbidden also to do any sort of manual labor, nor should one carry anything from one place to another, even as on the Sabbath. Inasmuch as it is necessary to add from the profane to the sacred, all of the above are forbidden on the day before *Yom Kippur* while it is yet day, a short time before twilight, till the end of *Yom Kippur* until a short time after the stars become visible.

2. Some authorities forbid, while others allow, to touch either food or drink when it is necessary to feed a minor therewith. If possible, it is well to adhere to the stricter opinion.

3. For the prohibition of bathing, see chapter 124:7-9, below. Only washing for pleasure is forbidden on *Yom Kippur;* but even when permissible, one should be very careful not to wash more than it is actually necessary.

The hands need not be washed for the *Minḥah* or the *Neilah* or the *Maariv* services, for since we spend the entire day in the synagogue engaged in prayer, it is presumed that we kept our hands clean.

4. The *kohanim* who are to go up to bless the people, when they must wash their hands up to the wrists, must say the benediction *Al netilat yadayim* even though they had washed their fingers in the morning and uttered that benediction. For that washing does not suffice for the priestly blessing. It is best that the *kohanim* should wash their hands in the morning up to the wrists, so that they would not be required to repeat the benediction.

5. One who is ill, even though not critically, may wash in the usual manner. A bride, within thirty days of the wedding day, may wash her face on *Yom Kippur*, so that she may not become offensive to her husband.

6. One who has had a nocturnal pollution, God forbid, on *Yom Kippur*, should wipe it off with a cloth if it is still wet; but if it is already dry, he should wash only the soiled spots, for it is considered in law as excrement. He should not wash it, however, with a cloth, so that he would not wring it by mistake. He is not allowed to immerse himself, even though he is accustomed to do so on the other days of the year. He should confide this incident to one, well-versed in the Torah, and tell him of what has happened to him on this holy and awe-inspiring day, and he will be instructed by him what to do, so that it may be forgiven him, and his life may be prolonged.

7. Anointing even if only to remove dirt, and even only a part of the body, is forbidden on *Yom Kippur*. However, if one is ill, even not critically, one may anoint oneself in the usual manner. In our regions, where it is not customary to anoint on weekdays, a person who has scabs, is not allowed to anoint himself, for it is obvious that it is done as a cure.

8. Some authorities forbid to wear shoes on *Yom Kippur*, even if made of wood and not covered with leather, but shoes made of rubber or straw or cloth may be worn. One should wear no shoes, even if it is muddy and rainy and even if one has to walk among gentiles. If, however, walking in a muddy or wet place without shoes will cause him much pain, he may wear shoes without heels, and if the shoes have heels, he shall put the right shoe on the left foot. and the left one on the right foot. But he must remove them before the entrance of the synagogue. One should take care not to touch them with bare hands either when putting them on or when taking them off, so that one may not be required to wash the hands.

9. It is permissible to stand on cushions or spreads, even if they are

made of leather, but one may not stand on any object while reciting the *Shemoneh esreh*. One who has a cold may stand on some grass.

10. A person who is ill, even though not critically, or one who has a bruised foot, or a woman within thirty days of her confinement, may wear leather shoes on *Yom Kippur*.

11. One is forbidden to caress his wife, even in the daytime; one should consider her as though menstrually unclean the entire day of *Yom Kippur*.

12. Pregnant and nursing women should fast the whole day the same as other people. A nursing woman whose infant is critically ill, and will not suckle from anyone else but her, and if she should fast, it will jeopardize the child's life, should not fast.

13. If a pregnant woman has scented the odor of some food and was seized with a craving for it, and it is certain that if we do not give it to her, she and the child will be in danger, then, if she says: "I must eat it," even though her face has not been contorted, or if it did contort, even if she does not say anything, we whisper into her ear that it is *Yom Kippur* today, because sometimes her mind may be soothed by that. If, however, her mind is not soothed thereby, we feed her in the following manner: At first we give her merely a taste of the food; we dip a finger in the soup or the like, and put it into her mouth, for even one drop will sometimes allay her craving. If, however, this proves ineffective, she is given less than the legal quantity (see section 16, below), and if her mind is not yet calmed thereby, we give her as much as she requires. This procedure is also followed in the case of any person whose face was contorted by the scent of food. Such a person is considered as critically ill, and is treated in the manner described above. But if his face has not undergone any change, we will not give him the food even if he says: "I must eat it."

14. Regarding the profanation of *Yom Kippur*, for a person who is critically ill, or for a woman in her confinement, we are guided by the same laws that govern the Sabbath. (See chapters 92-93, above). However, as regards eating and drinking, even if a host of physicians say that the fasting will not harm him, and that, moreover, the eating or drinking will be injurious to him, as long as the sick person says that he does require food and even if he says that he is not in danger as yet, but if he does not eat, he will become worse and be in danger, the food should be given him, for in the matter of food and drink, a person is the best judge of his own condition.

15. When food is given to a woman that is pregnant or in confinement, or to a sick person, we say to them: "If you are sure that you may be in

danger if you do not eat as much as you require, then you may eat in the ordinary manner until you are satisfied. However, if it is possible for you to eat less than the required quantity at one time, then act as follows: Eat at one time no more than the quantity of two-thirds of an egg (for the quantity of food eaten on *Yom Kippur* for which one incurs the penalty of excision, being cut off from his people, is a little less than the quantity of a middle-sized egg without the shell), and rest somewhat. Then eat a similar quantity again, waiting between one eating and the other at least as long as it takes to eat a slice of bread." Thus he may eat even many times, provided the intervals between the eatings is not less than it takes to eat a slice of bread (for two eatings with less than such an interval between them, are combined and are considered one eating). When drinking, they should swallow less than a mouthful at one time and rest somewhat and then drink again. And these rests should be at least as long as it takes to eat a slice of bread, or in any event, at least as long as it takes to drink a quarter of a *lug* (that is, one and one-half eggshells). To ascertain the exact length of time it takes to eat a slice of bread or to drink a quarter of a *lug*, it should be checked by a timepiece before *Yom Kippur*.

16. One who has been overcome by a craving for food to such an extent that his eyes grew dim and he is unable to see, should be fed on *Yom Kippur* until he regains his eyesight.

17. All those who may eat on *Yom Kippur* because of possible danger, may be given forbidden food, if permitted food is not available. It would seem that in such a case, they should be given less than the size of an olive at one time, if this proves to be sufficient for them.

18. If the mind of the ill person is composed, he should say a benediction before and after eating, but he should not say the *kiddush*. In the Grace after meals, he should include *Yaaleh veyavo* (May it come up, etc.,) and if it is a Sabbath, he should say *Retzeh* (accept). If, however, he has forgotten to say it, he need not repeat the Grace, because there is no obligation to eat bread on this day.

19. Children less than nine years old should not be permitted to fast even if they want to fast only a part of the day, because it may affect their health. Children nine years old and in good health, should be trained to fast a little. They should abstain from food a few hours beyond their regular eating time. With regard to wearing shoes, washing, and anointing, children should be trained to abstain from these even before they are fully nine years old.

20. It is advisable to smell spices several times during the day and to pronounce the prescribed benediction, in order to complete the necessary count of one hundred benedictions a day; but as long as your mind has not been diverted from the previous scenting, we are not allowed to repeat the benediction, because that would be a benediction uttered in vain. It is, therefore, necessary to allow a long interval between one inhalation and the other, so that there may be a diversion of mind in the meantime. It is best to smell different spices each time, even if they are of the same kind, and so much the

better if they are three different kinds, such as, wood spices, herb spices, and mixed spices. If we are attentive to the benedictions recited by the *ḥazan* and to those who are called up to the reading of the Torah and *Maftir*, we will then be short only three benedictions to complete the count of one hundred, and the benedictions over the spices will complete the number.

21. On *Yom Kippur*, memorial services for the dead are said, because thinking of the departed saddens and humbles a man's heart; also for the further reason that the dead, too, need atonement, as it is written in the *Sifri:* "Forgive Thy people Israel" (Deuteronomy 21:8) refers to the living; "Whom Thou hast redeemed," refers to the dead; from this we infer that the dead need atonement. Offerings of charity are then made for their souls. A support for this practice is found at the end of section *Tetzaveh*, (Exodus 30:10) where we read: "Once a year he shall atone;" and immediately thereafter, it is stated (verse 12): "And each man shall give a redemption for his soul to the Lord." Charity is helpful for the departed, because the Lord discerns the heart of man and He knows that if this man were alive, he too, would have donated to charity. The living are able to alleviate the judgment of the departed, even as David prayed for his son Absalom (Sotah 10b), for the pious dead also plead for their offspring. Memorial services are also held on the last day of Passover, on the second day of *Shavuot*, and on the eighth day of *Sukkot*, because on these days, we read *Kal habeḥor* (All the firstborn, etc., (Deuteronomy 15:19), where it is stated (loco citato 16:17): "Everyone according to the gift of his hand." For this reason, pledges are then made for charitable purpose, and since pledges for alms are made, we have made it a custom also to give charity for the souls of the departed, that the Lord may remember them favorably, and through their merits also remember us with favor. It is customary for those whose father and mother are alive to leave the synagogue while the memorial service is said. Anyone whose father or mother has passed away during that year also leaves the synagogue.

22. If there is a circumcision to be performed, it should take place before *Ashre* (happy are they) is said, and the benediction of the circumcision should be said without a cup of wine. In our regions it is customary to say the benediction over a cup of wine, giving a taste of it to the circumcised infant, in addition to what is given him when saying, *Bedamayiḥ ḥayyi* (by thy blood thou shalt live), but none of it should be given to any other child (for the laws of *Yom Kippur* are more rigid than those of the ninth of *Av*). The *mohel* who is accustomed to sprinkle some wine before drawing the blood after circumcision, should not sprinkle it with his mouth but with his hand, and then suck the blood with his mouth as usual.

23. It is our custom to spread grass on the floor in the synagogue on *Yom Kippur*. The reason thereof is that we bow and prostrate ourselves when reciting the *Avodah* (order of the service in the Temple), and since we may not prostrate ourselves in a place where the ground is covered with stones, and even in a place which is not covered with stones, it is improper. Therefore, grass is spread as an interposition between us and the floor. But, if there is no grass, we may make the interposition with the *tallit* or with some other thing.

24. The time for beginning the *Neilah* (concluding) service is when the sun is over the tree tops, so that we may conclude it when the stars become visible. Even when the *Neilah* is extended into the night, we may say *Ḥatmenu* (seal

us), because the heavenly judgment is not concluded until Israel concludes the order of prayers below. If the stars have already become visible, we should not say, *Hayyom yifneh* (the day is nearly past), because that would be speaking falsehood. We should say instead: *Hayyom panah, hashemesh ba ufanah* (the day has passed, the sun has set and is gone). But the *ḥazan* recites *birḥat kohanim* (the priestly benediction), and *sim shalom* (bestow peace) even if it is already night.

25. We should abolish the custom to have a non-Jew light candles for the purpose of reciting the liturgic poetry of *Neilah*, but he should distribute the burning candles throughout the synagogue, because this is merely disregarding a Rabbinical enjoinder in a secondary and indirect manner.

26. When the *Neilah* service is concluded, we say *Avinu malkenu* (our Father, our King), even if it is a Sabbath and still day. Then we say once, *Shema yisrael* (hear, O Israel); three times, *Baruḥ shem kevod malḥuto leolam vaed* (blessed be His name whose glorious kingdom is forever and ever) and seven times, *Adonai hu haelohim* (the Lord, He is God). It is to send off the Divine Presence, to the higher spheres of the seventh heaven. The *ḥazan* then chants the whole *kaddish* in a joyous tone, after which the *shofar* is sounded once, symbolic of the ascension of the Divine Presence, as it was when the Torah was given on Sinai. For when the Divine Presence ascended, it is written (Exodus 19:13): "When the ram's horn soundeth long," etc., and it is also written (Psalms 47:6): "The Lord is gone amidst shouting, the Lord amidst the sound of the horn." It also commemorates the sounding of the *shofar* on the *Yom Kippur* of the Jubilee year. The *shofar* may be sounded even at twilight when the stars are not yet visible, even on the Sabbath, but it should not be sounded in the daytime. After the sounding of the *shofar*, all say three times, *Leshanah habaah birushalayim* (Next year in Jerusalem).

27. After the stars become visible, we pray the *Maariv* service, and it is well to delegate as *ḥazan* a reputable man. The prayers should be recited slowly and devoutly. Those who pray hurriedly should be rebuked. In the *Shemoneh esreh*, we include, *Attah ḥonantanu* (Thou hast bestowed upon us). If it is Saturday night, we recite *Veyitten leḥa* (and God give thee), but we omit *Vihi noam* (may the pleasantness), and *Veattah kadosh* (and Thou art holy). After the prayers, the sanctification of the moon is performed, and friendly greetings are exchanged with merriment and joy as on a festival.

28. In the *havdalah* of *Yom Kippur* night, the benediction for light must be said over a candle that had been kindled before *Yom Kippur*, and not over a light that is now produced by means of a match and the like. The most preferable way is to light a candle from the light of another candle that had been lit in the house the day before, and say the benediction over both. If there is no burning candle in the house, one should bring a burning candle from the synagogue, light another candle from this one, and say the benediction over both. In an emergency, we may say the benediction over a candle lit from the candle of a non-Jew, or by a match, and the like. We do not begin the *havdalah* with *Hinneh el yeshuati* (behold the God of my salvation), but we say the benedictions over a goblet of wine, over the light, and *Hammavdil* (who hath made a distinction); no benediction is pronounced over spices. If it is Saturday night, we also say the benediction over spices, and we begin with *Hinneh el yeshuati*, as we do on the conclusion of an ordinary Sabbath.

29. On the conclusion of *Yom Kippur*, we eat and drink and rejoice; for it is stated in the *Midrash Rabbah* (Kohelet 9): "On the conclusion of *Yom Kippur* a heavenly voice goes forth and says: 'Go, eat thy bread with joy, and drink with a merry heart thy wine, for God has already accepted thy deeds favorably.'"

30. The meticulously devout begin the construction of the *Sukkah* immediately after *Yom Kippur*, in the spirit of the verse (Psalms 84:8): "They go from strength to strength."

31. On the day after *Yom Kippur*, it is customary to rise early and go to the synagogue to pray. We do not fast, between *Yom Kippur* and *Sukkot;* even on the occasion of a *Jahrzeit*. We also omit the *Taḥanun* (petition for Grace) on these days, because they are days of rejoicing, during which the altar was dedicated in the days of Solomon. In this interval we are to engage in the building of the *sukkah*, preparing the *etrog* (citron) and the other accessory species, in honor of the Lord of Lords, who hath sanctified Israel and the seasons.

CHAPTER 134

The Sukkah (*Tabernacle*)

1. It is a meritorious act to start building the *sukkah* immediately after *Yom Kippur*, even if it is a Friday, because a chance to perform a precept should not be put off. One should choose for it a clean site. Every one should personally build the *sukkah*, even if one is an eminent person. For it is an honor to perform a precept in person. By right, the benediction *Sheheḥeyanu* (who hat kept us in life) should be said upon erecting the *sukkah*, but the *sheheḥeyanu* benediction said in the *kiddush* also includes the construction. One should embellish the *sukkah* and adorn it by placing in it fine furniture and beautiful spreads to the full extent of one's means.

2. There are many different opinions regarding the walls of the *sukkah*, in which not everybody is well versed. It is essential, therefore, to make the walls of the *sukkah* compact and strong, so that the wind could not shake them or blow out the candles. If one has not enough material with which to make four walls, one should rather erect three complete walls than four incomplete ones. A person who can afford it, should build a *sukkah* with a roof that can open and close on hinges, so that he can close it in case of rain and reopen it when the rain is over. Thus the covering of the *sukkah* can be kept dry, and the precept properly observed.

3. There are also many different opinions regarding the roofing of the *sukkah*. However, since we generally cover it with the branches of trees, or with reeds, which are detached products of the soil, and not subject to defilement, and are not tied together, there is no cause for scruples.

4. It is most desirable to avoid laying upon the roof of the *sukkah* as a prop for the branch covering, anything that is subject to defilement, such as ladders, and especially utensils, like a spade, or a shovel. One should even avoid putting them on the top to secure the covering. If, however, they have already been put on, or if one has nothing else to put on, all of the above are permissible; for we have a tradition, that it is permissible to secure the covering with something that is subject to defilement.

5. Enough boughs should be placed upon the *sukkah* so as to have more shade than sun; if it has more sun than shade, it is invalid. It is, therefore, necessary to put on enough branches, that even if they should dry up, there would still be more shade than sun. It is also essential not to leave an open space, measuring three hand-breadths (twelve inches). In the first instance, there should be space between the branches, so that the stars can be seen. Nevertheless, if the covering is so thick that the stars are not visible, it is valid. If, however, it has been so thickly covered that even a heavy rain would not penetrate it, it is then considered like a house, and it is invalid for a *sukkah*.

6. Sometimes in a permanently built *sukkah,* boards project from the upper part of the walls, and upon them are laid rafters on which the branches rest. If the board is less than four cubits (six feet) wide, it does not invalidate the *sukkah;* for it is a Sinaitic law, that whatever is less than four cubits wide is considered as a part of the wall which is simply curved at the top. However, it is impermissible either to sit or to sleep underneath that board, as the law does not recognize that space as a *sukkah,* even if the board is only four hand-breadths (sixteen inches) wide; but the rest of the *sukkah* is valid. If, however, the boards that extend from the wall are four or more cubits wide, they invalidate the entire *sukkah*. But, if the boards jutted out from one side of the *sukkah* only, as it is done in some of the built *sukkot* where a small shelf is made on one side (where the dishes are put away), then it does not matter, since there yet remain three walls upon which there is a valid covering; for a *sukkah* made of only three walls is also valid, providing it has the requisite space, which is no less than seven hand-breadths (twenty-eight inches) square. Anyway, it is not permissible to sit underneath the boards.

7. A *sukkah* that is erected underneath the branches of a tree is invalid; even if the branches by themselves would provide more sun than shade, and the *sukkah* has been adjusted by means of putting thereon extra branches, it is, nevertheless, invalid. Even if the branches of the tree are thereafter cut off, the *sukkah* is still invalid; for it is written (Deuteronomy 16:13): "The Feast of Tabernacles thou shalt make (*taaseh*) for thyself," and it is explained (Sukkah 11b): "You must *make* the *sukkah,* but not when it is already made." Therefore, after the branches are cut off, it is necessary to

remove the branches of the covering that had been laid thereon, and then put them down again expressly for the sake of the *sukkah*. It is likewise forbidden to lay the covering on before the walls are made, as it is required that the laying of the covering should make the *sukkah* valid for use.

8. When a *sukkah* is made by raising the roof, the roof should be raised before the covering of the branches is made, and if thereafter the roof is closed and then opened again, it does not matter, for it is the same as if a sheet had been spread upon it and then removed. But it is best to have it open at the ushering in of the festival. Care should be taken that the roof be wide open and standing erect in line with the wall of the *sukkah*, for if it is not vertical, but inclines slightly on the covering, even in such a degree as not to invalidate the *sukkah*, it is, nevertheless, necessary to be careful not to sit in that place where the roof slopes. Although a *sukkah* is exempt from a *mezuzah* during the festival (see chapter 11:14, above), a permanently built *sukkah* that people use during the entire year and consequently is required to have a *mezuzah*, is not exempted therefrom during the days of the festival, and it is not necessary to affix the *mezuzah* anew after the festival.

9. The obligation may be fulfilled with a borrowed *sukkah*, but not with one that is stolen; hence, a *sukkah* may not be erected on a public place. In an emergency, however, when one has no other *sukkah* available, one may sit in such a *sukkah* and say the prescribed benediction.

10. A Jew should not cut the boughs for the covering of his *sukkah* himself, but he should purchase it from someone else. In an emergency, he may cut the boughs himself, but he must obtain permission from the owner of the soil

11. It is permissible to build a *sukkah* during *Ḥol Hammoed.*

12. Utilizing the wood of the *sukkah*, either of the walls or of branches, is forbidden until after *Simḥat Torah* (Day of Rejoicing with the Law), inasmuch as they were set apart for the performance of a precept. It is even forbidden to take a splinter from it to pick the teeth, even if it was detached of itself, and even if one had made a provision before the holiday to use some of the material. If *Simḥat Torah* occurs on a Friday, the above is forbidden even during the Sabbath. It is also forbidden to make use of the ornaments of the *sukkah*, even if they fell off by themselves. And inasmuch as it is forbidden to derive any benefit from them, it is likewise forbidden to handle them on a Sabbath or on a festival, because they are *muktzeh* (set apart not to be used). It is, however, permissible to inhale the fragrance of a citron, hung up in a *sukkah* as an ornament, as it was not set apart as far as the smelling is concerned. Even if one had made an express avowal that he would make some use of the ornaments suspended from the roof of the *sukkah*, it is of no avail. However, the ornaments that decorate the walls may be used when a declaration to that effect had been made. It is the practice to remove tapestries that are hung in the *sukkah* as ornaments, when it is feared that they might be spoiled by rain, even if one had not made an express provision therefor, for it is presumed that they have been hung upon that condition. Nevertheless, it is best to make an express declaration to that effect, that is, before the twilight on the eve of *Sukkot*, he should stand there and say: "I make it a provision that I should be allowed to eat and to use the orna-

ments of the *sukkah* whenever I so desire." One must be careful not to tie with a knot, but merely with a loop, those ornaments which one intends to remove during the festival.

13. When dismantling the *sukkah* after the festival, one should not step upon the boards, nor make any degrading use of them, because they have been used for a religious precept, the same as *tzitzit.*

14. It is forbidden to engrave or to write any verse of the Torah upon an ornament of the *sukkah,* because it may subsequently be degraded, and besides, it is forbidden to write verses of the Torah needlessly.

15. On the afternoon of the day before *Sukkot,* we should not eat any bread, so that we may eat with relish the meal served in the *sukkah* at night. It is proper to dispense charity liberally on the day before *Sukkot.*

CHAPTER 135

Dwelling In The Sukkah

1. It is written (Leviticus 23:42): *Basukkot teshvu shiveat yamim* (in booths ye shall dwell seven days), which means that we should dwell in the *sukkah* seven days even as we dwell in our house during the whole year. We should make the *sukkah* our principal abode; there we should bring our fine furniture and household linens; there we should eat, drink, study, amuse ourselves, and sleep; even our friends should be entertained in the *sukkah,* and if we pray privately, we should likewise pray in the *sukkah.* It is written (loco citato): "So that your generations may know that I have made the children of Israel dwell in booths, when I brought them forth from the land of Egypt;" therefore, we must bear it in mind that we are dwelling in the *sukkah,* because the Holy One, blessed be He, commanded us to dwell in a *sukkah* to commemorate the exodus from Egypt. Concerning the connotation of the word *sukkot* mentioned in the Torah, there is a controversy among *Tannaim* (Sukkah 11b). Rabbi Eliezer says that it refers to the clouds of glory wherewith the Holy One, blessed be He, had encompassed the children of Israel, so as to protect them from the heat and the sun. Rabbi Akiba holds that it means real booths which the Israelites had made for themselves during their wandering in the wilderness as a protection from the sun. Now, although we departed from Egypt in the month of *Nisan,* He did not command us to make the *sukkah* during that month, because it is the beginning of the summer season, when it is customary for people to build booths as a shelter from the sun, and it would not be apparent that it is made in order to fulfill a precept of the Holy One, blessed be His name. Therefore, He commanded us to make it in the seventh month, the rainy season, when people usually move out of their booths into their houses. Then it is evident that we dwell in *sukkot* because the King ordered us to do so.

2. The *sukkah* should be kept trim and clean, so that precepts should not be looked upon with disdain. Hence, we must not bring in there, vessels used for menial tasks, such as pots, pitchers with which we draw water, vessels

in which we keep flour, kneading troughs, kettles, frying pans, mortars, or the like. After the meals, the dishes should be removed from the *sukkah*, but the drinking glasses may remain there. The rule is also not to bring in there earthen candlesticks because they are repulsive. We must not perform in there menial work, like washing the pots or dishes, but we wash glasses there. Needless to say that we must not urinate there even in a vessel, even if we are accustomed to do so in our house. Cohabitation may be had in the *sukkah*. The *sukkah* does not become invalidated if we bring foul vessels in it, but the benediction *Leshev basukkah* (to dwell in the *sukkah*) must not be said while they are there.

3. On the first night of *Sukkot*, we must eat in the *sukkah* a quantity of bread no less than the size of an olive (two-thirds of an egg), even if we are made uncomfortable by cold or by rain. If it rains, and we think that the rain will stop in an hour or two, we must wait, and then recite the *kiddush* and eat in the *sukkah* in the proper manner. But if it seems that the rain will not stop so soon, or if we have waited and it has not stopped, we should recite the *kiddush* in the *sukkah*, say the benediction *Sheheḥeyanu* (who kept us in life) and bear in mind that this benediction also applies to the *sukkah*, but we do not say the benediction *Leshev basukkah*. We then wash our hands, say the benediction *Hamotzi* (who bringeth forth), eat a quantity of bread of no less than the size of an olive without interruption, and then we proceed to the house to complete the meal. When washing the hands and saying the benediction *Hamotzi*, we should bear in mind that we also intend to eat in the house. If the rain has ceased before reciting the Grace after meals, we should return to the *sukkah*, say the benediction *Leshev basukkah*, and eat bread, slightly more than the size of an egg, after which we recite the Grace. If the rain has ceased after we said Grace, we should also return to the *sukkah*, wash the hands again, eat a little more than the size of an egg, saying the benediction *Leshev basukkah*, and then say Grace. If after the rain has stopped, the water still drips from the covering of the *sukkah*, and in our neighborhood there is a *sukkah* which had been closed with a roof and then opened after the rain, we should go there and eat with a merry heart.

4. On the second night of *Sukkot*, we should also eat in the *sukkah*, even if we suffer discomfort, and it is governed by the same law that applies to the first night, as stated above, with the difference that if it appears that the rain will not stop so soon, or if we have waited and it has not stopped, the *kiddush* should be recited in the house and the meal eaten there, but before saying Grace, we should go to the *sukkah* and eat there a quantity of bread of no less than an olive without saying the benediction *Leshev basukkah*, and we then return to the house and recite the Grace after meals.

5. In the evening, on returning from the synagogue, we enter the *sukkah* and immediately recite the *kiddush*, but we must first be sure that it is night. When saying the benediction *Leshev basukkah* in the *kiddush*, we must bear in mind that this benediction applies also to the meal we are about to have, as well as to our sleeping and all other needs that we will attend to in the *sukkah*, until we will recite the *kiddush* again the following morning. When saying the benediction *Sheheḥeyanu*, we should bear in mind that it applies also to the festival and to the *sukkah*. Therefore, on the first night, we first say the benediction *Leshev pasukkah*, and then *Sheheḥeyanu*, so that the latter benediction may also apply to the *sukkah;* but on the second night, we first say the benediction *Sheheḥeyanu*, and then the benediction *Leshev basukkah.*

6. When several heads of families eat in one *sukkah*, and there are also women and other members of the families who are required to listen attentively to the *kiddush* in order to fulfill their obligations, it is best that they should recite the *kiddush* one at a time, because if they all read it simultaneously, their voices would become jumbled, and consequently they will not hear the *kiddush* well. If they recite the *kiddush* simultaneously, as when there are no others who are obligated to hear it, then if one of them has finished the benediction *Bore peri haggafen* (who hath created the fruit of the vine), or some other benediction, before the others, the others should not respond *Amen*, because the saying of *Amen* constitutes an interruption between the benediction *Bore peri haggafen* and the drinking of the wine. People who recite the *kiddush* consecutively and respond *Amen*, are not acting according to the law; but they should recite it in unison (if no others are to be exempted).

7. On the remaining nights and days of *Sukkot*, we are not bound to have meals in the *sukkah*. But if we desire to have a regular meal or to sleep, we must do it in the *sukkah*. By a "regular meal" is meant, the eating of a quantity of bread more than the size of an egg, even though we have not set a time for eating it and even if it is pastry. Likewise, any dish made of one of the five species of grain (see chapter 48, above), if it is more than the size of an egg and we have appointed a time for eating it, it must be eaten in the *sukkah*, and we are to recite the benediction *Leshev basukkah*. But we are allowed to eat fruit outside the *sukkah*, even if we eat a large quantity and have appointed a time for eating it. We are likewise permitted to drink wine or other beverages, and to eat meat and cheese outside the *sukkah*, providing it has not been prearranged. If, however, we desire to set a time for drinking wine or other beverages, or for eating meat or cheese, we must eat or drink it in the *sukkah*, but without saying the benediction *Leshev basukkah*. In such a case, it is best to eat some bread first, so that the benediction may be uttered. All this complies with the law, but the more scrupulous who do not even drink water outside the *sukkah* are praiseworthy.

8. For sleeping, even for a mere nap, a *sukkah* is required; such is the practice of those who are meticulous in the observance of precepts. Nowadays, however, many people are lax as regards sleeping in the *sukkah*, and the latter authorities, of blessed memory, have advanced some reasons in

justification of this latitude. However, every God-fearing person should make a *sukkah*, fit for the habitation of himself and his wife, like his quarters where he lives the entire year, if this is possible. At any rate, the *sukkah* should be fit for himself to sleep in; for, if it is not made in such a manner, it is invalid even post facto.

9. If it rains, one is exempt from staying in the *sukkah*. To release one from staying in the *sukkah*, it must rain so hard that the food might be spoiled by the rain, or if he estimates that if it had rained that way in his room in the house he would leave it and go into another room, then he may leave the *sukkah* and go into the house. If after one began eating in the *sukkah*, the rain started to come down and he went into the house and started to eat there; or if one has begun to eat in the house on account of the rain, and the rain ceased, the meal may be completed in the house. If the weather is so cold that the food congeals, one is exempt from staying in the *sukkah*, and he may eat the meals in the house.

10. With regard to sleep, even a slight rain causes discomfort, and one is permitted to leave the *sukkah* because of that. If one has left the *sukkah* because of rain and went to sleep in the house, and then the rain ceased, one is not put to the trouble of going back to the *sukkah*, but one may sleep in the house the rest of the night.

11. One who is exempt from remaining in the *sukkah* and does not leave, is called an ignoramus, and he will obtain no reward for remaining there. Moreover, he is not permitted to say the benediction over the *sukkah*, for that would be classed as a benediction uttered in vain. When he leaves the *sukkah* on account of rain, he should not go out grumbling, but feeling humbled, like a servant who has poured a cup of wine for his master, and the latter spilled a jug of water in his face.

12. It is the prevailing custom to say the benediction *Leshev basukkah* only when we eat in the *sukkah* a regular meal. It is also the custom to say first the benediction *Hamotzi* (who bringeth forth), and then the benediction *Leshev basukkah*, before we begin to eat. Afterward, everything that we eat in the *sukkah* the entire day, and whatever we do while staying there, including sleep, is covered by this benediction until we eat another regular meal. If we do not leave the *sukkah* between the meals, either to go to business or to the synagogue, inasmuch as we have once said the benediction *Leshev basukkah*, we need not repeat it at the following meal. Even if we stay in the *sukkah* the entire week, eating, studying, praying and sleeping there, we need not say the benediction more than once, since our mind has not been diverted from the *sukkah*. And if we leave the *sukkah* temporarily with the intention of returning immediately, it is not considered a diversion of the mind, and we are not required to say the benediction at the next meal. However, if we have gone out to transact business, or to the synagogue, or the

like, or even if we have gone to our house to study, or to do something which takes some length of time, it constitutes a distraction and we must say the benediction again.

13. If one goes to a friend's *sukkah*, even in the middle of his meal, and he eats there a quantity of food which has to be eaten in a *sukkah*, he must say the benediction *Leshev basukkah* also there.

14. If one has forgotten to say the benediction *Leshev basukkah* and became aware of the omission in the middle of the meal, or even after he had finished the meal, he must still say the benediction, for the mere staying in the *sukkah* is also considered a precept.

15. Women are exempt from the precept of dwelling in a *sukkah*, yet they are permitted to say the benediction when they stay there. Children, too, are exempt from dwelling in a *sukkah*, nevertheless, if a boy is five years or over, his father should train him to eat in the *sukkah*. Even when the father is away from home, it is not proper to let the boy eat outside the *sukkah*.

16. A sick person and his attendants are exempt from dwelling in the *sukkah*. However, if the invalid is not critically ill, the attendants are exempt only when he needs them. If, however, the invalid is critically ill, they are exempt even when he does not need them so urgently.

17. After the first night, if the *sukkah* causes one distress because of its cold or windy condition, or because of a bad odor, one is exempt from dwelling in the *sukkah*. Likewise, if on the Sabbath the lights in the *sukkah* were extinguished and it is difficult for one to go to a friend's *sukkah*, one may likewise go to his house where the candles are burning. This is only true when he has originally erected the *sukkah* in a proper manner, and it is only an accident that causes him discomfort when sitting or sleeping there. But if he has originally erected it in a place where there is an obnoxious odor, or the like, or in a place where he is afraid to sleep, then he does not fulfill his obligation even when he eats there in the daytime. If the wind penetrates the walls and threatens to blow out the candles, it is permissible to hang on the wall a sheet or a garment.

18. Wayfarers are exempt from eating in a *sukkah* during the day, since they have no time to look for one, as they have to proceed on their journey. But if they are able to procure a *sukkah* without much trouble, they are bound to do so. When staying at an inn overnight, they should make an effort to dwell in a *sukkah*. Even if there is no *sukkah* in that place, if they can make one at a small cost, they should make an effort to have one made for sleeping. Those who travel during the night, are subject to the same law as those who travel in the daytime. Men who go to villages during the Intermediate Days of the festival to collect debts, should make an effort to return home every night, in order to fulfill the precept of *sukkah*.

19. Travelers who are on a religious mission, even at night when they are free, if they have trouble to look for a *sukkah,* or if it is not pleasant for them to sleep there, and if they will sleep there, they will be tired the following day and will be hindered in the performance of their duty, are exempt from this precept; otherwise, they are obliged to fulfill it.

20. Men who watch gardens, orchards, or other produce, must make a *sukkah* wherein to stay, if they can guard the property from there.

21. Those who make wine in the house of a non-Jew, are exempt from fulfilling the precept of the *sukkah* whether by day or by night, because they must constantly watch that the non-Jew should not touch it; but in the event no such precaution is necessary, they are bound to observe the precept of *sukkah.*

22. People who stay in a store, even if they reside out of town, and are accustomed to eat their meals in the store during the day, must, nevertheless, eat in a *sukkah* during the week of *Sukkot.*

CHAPTER 136

The Lulav and the Other Species

1. It is an established custom in Israel, that if one buys an *etrog* and a *lulav,* and is not sure whether or not they are valid, one should show them to a Rabbi to ascertain their validity, for there are conflicting opinions regarding the same. An effort should be made to purchase a fresh *lulav,* because a dry *lulav* is acceptable only in an emergency. Some authorities hold that if a *lulav* has no more green in it, it is considered as dry. The required length of a *lulav* is that its stock, besides its fronds, should measure four hand-breadths (sixteen inches). In an emergency, the length of thirteen and one-third thumbs (inches) is sufficient.

2. The *hadas* (myrtle bough) should be three-leaved, that is, there should be three leaves around the twig, neither one higher or lower than the others. Also, the leaves should cover the wood, that is, the top of the lower group of leaves should cover over the stems of the upper leaves. Among the *hadasim* that are brought from distant places, rarely valid ones can be found; and, therefore, they must be carefully examined. He who fears the word of God, should endeavor to purchase fresh and green *hadasim* which are three-leaved and beautiful. If raised locally, he should investigate whether or not they have been grafted, and whether they grew in a pot having no aperture at the bottom. The same investigation should be made about the *lulavim* that grow in our regions. If one cannot obtain three-leaved *hadasim,* one may take ones that are not three-leaved, but no benediction may be uttered upon them.

3. The requisite length of a *hadas* is three hand-breadths. In an emergency, the length of ten thumbs is sufficient. The entire *hadas,* from the bottom to the top, should be three-leaved; in an emergency, however, if the lesser part of the bottom is not three-leaved, but the greater part at the top is three-leaved, it is also valid. We must likewise take great care that the leaves of the *hadas* should not fall off, for even if only some of the leaves have fallen off, there is doubt about its validity and a scholar should be consulted.

4. One must also make sure that the tops of the *hadasim* are not broken off. But if one has only *hadasim* with clipped tops, one should consult a scholar. However, the small twigs that grow between the stems should be pulled off, so that they do not separate the stems.

5. The *aravah* (willow branch) is recognizable by its leaves, which are lengthy, with a smooth edge, and by its red stem. Even while the *aravah* is still green it is valid, inasmuch as it turns red when on the tree. Most of this kind grow by brooks, and, therefore, they are called *Arve naḥal* (willows of the brook). They are valid even if they grow elsewhere; nevertheless, if obtainable, those that grow by a brook are preferable. The requisite size of the *aravah* is the same as that of the *hadas.*

6. An *aravah* which is dried up, or from which most of the leaves have fallen off, or from which the top of the stem is broken off, is invalid. Some authorities hold that if the leaves have been partly detached and are dangling, the *aravah* is invalid. Special care should be taken of the *aravah,* for at times the leaves fall off, either because of its friction with the *lulav,* or because of the waving, and then it is rendered invalid.

7. A Jew should not personally cut from the tree any of the four species for his own use, even if the owner of the ground grants him permission; but a non-Jew or another Jew should cut them and then he should purchase it from him.

8. We take three *hadas* twigs and two *aravah* twigs (no more), and bind them together with the *lulav,* so that they form a single fascicle. We must take care to bind them together in the way they grow, with the cut edges downward; for if only one branch of either species is reversed, it is invalid even post facto. The *hadas* should be bound on the right side of the stem of the *lulav,* and the *aravah* on the left, that is, when taking the *lulav* with its back towards us, the *hadas* should be towards our right hand, and the *aravah* towards our left. At the bottom they should all be even, so that by taking the *lulav* we could grasp all the species. Nevertheless, we should see that the *hadas* is somewhat higher than the *aravah* and be careful that the stock of the *lulav* is at least one hand-breadth higher than the *hadas.* They should be all bound together with a perfect knot, that is, two knots, one on top of the

other. Besides binding these species together, three more bands should be placed on the *lulav,* but the space on one hand-breadth at the top of the *lulav* should be left without a band, so that it might rustle when it is waved. If a cord is twined around the *hadas,* it should be removed before binding it with the *lulav,* so that there be no intervention between the two. If one band becomes loose during the festival, it is forbidden to bind it again by making a knot, but only by making a loop; or as the practice is, to wind them around and to insert the edge of the binder into its folds.

9. If an *aravah* is plucked on the festival, either on the first or on the second day, it may not be even handled on that day, as it is absolutely *muktzeh.* If, however, it is plucked on the first day of the festival, it may be used on the second day. But if the first day occurs on the Sabbath and it is plucked then, its use is forbidden even on the second day. If an *etrog* or any one of the other species has been brought in from beyond the Sabbath boundary, it may be handled and we may fulfill our obligation with it. But if the city is not provided with an *eruv,* it is forbidden to carry them outside the house where they are, and all must repair to that house to fulfill their obligation.

10. One who does not possess a choice set of the four species, should rather fulfill the precept with a set belonging to his friend (see chapter that follows, section 8). Nevertheless, it is mandatory that everyone should have his own four species, the best he can afford to buy, with which to wave while saying the *hallel* (loco citato section 4) and for the *hakkafot* (loco citato 11).

CHAPTER 137

The Taking of the Lulav and the Hakkafot (Procession)

1. We take the *lulav,* together with what is attached, in the right hand, and the *etrog* in the left. Since the benediction must always precede the performance of the precept, and since the law requires that the *etrog* be held in the position in which it grows—that is, with the stem downward and the apex upward—therefore, when we first take the *etrog,* we must hold it in the reverse position, with the stem upward and the apex downward. Then we say the benediction *Al netilat lulav* (concerning the taking of the *lulav*) while standing, (because the *lulav* is taller than the other species, it is considered paramount, and the entire combination is designated by its name). On the first day of *Sukkot,* we also say the benediction *Sheheḥeyanu* (who kept us in life). If the first day of *Sukkot* occurs on the Sabbath when no *lulav* is taken, the benediction *Sheheḥeyanu* should be said on the second day. After the

benediction *Al netilat lulav,* we turn the *etrog* over, and holding it close to the *lulav,* with no separation between them, we wave them towards the four points (of the earth), in this order: East, South, West, North, upwards and downwards. When waving them during *hallel* and in the *hakkafot* (see 4 and 11, below), we should likewise be careful to bring the *etrog* close to the *lulav,* so that there be no separation between them. If we have done the opposite, and took the *etrog* in the right hand and the *lulav* in the left, we must take them again in the proper manner but without saying the benediction.

2. A left-handed person should take the *lulav* in the left hand, and the *etrog* in the right hand. If he has done the opposite, he should take them again without saying a benediction. A person who is ambidextrous, is considered as any other ordinary person.

3. Before taking the *lulav* on *Ḥol Hammoed,* it is proper to remove the *tefillin,* or at least remove the strap from the hand, so that nothing may intervene between the hand and the *etrog.* It is also proper to remove the rings from the fingers.

4. The order of "waving" in *hallel* is as follows: There are six words in *Hodu* (O give thanks) besides the Divine Name, and the waving should be done at every word in a different direction, but at the mention of the Divine Name, one should not wave. At *Hodu* we wave towards the East; at *Ki* towards the South; at *Tov* towards the West, and at *Ki* towards the North; at *Leolam* we wave upwards, and at *Ḥasdo* downwards. The *ḥazan* waves only in *Hodu* and in *Yomar na yisreal* (O let Israel say), but the congregation waves each time *Hodu* is said. When saying *Ana,* the *ḥazan,* as well as the congregation, waves only at *Ana adonai hoshiah na* (save we beseech Thee, O Lord); but as that phrase has only three words besides the Divine Name, the waving is done in two directions at each word. At *Hodu* at the end of *hallel,* the *ḥazan* and the congregation wave again. When waving downwards, only the hands should be lowered, and the *lulav* and the other species should remain in the position in which they grow. The people whose custom it is to turn the *lulav* downwards, should not change their custom. We should not turn our faces in the direction in which we wave, only the top of the *lulav* is waved in that direction; nor are we required to wave it with force. We shake it gently so as to make the fronds rustle.

5. It is forbidden to partake of any food before saying the benediction over the *lulav.* One who travels and hopes to arrive at a place where there is an *etrog* and a *lulav,* also those who live in country places where an *etrog* and *lulav* are sent to them, are required to wait until noon, but no longer, for it is forbidden to abstain from food longer than that on a festival and on *Ḥol Hammoed.* One who feels faint and cannot wait until noon, may partake of some refreshments before; but the one who does not feel faint should scrupulously abstain even from tasting any refreshments.

6. It is permissible to put the *lulav* back in water during the festival and add water to it, but one must not change the water. However, during *Ḥol Hammoed,* it is imperative to change the water, so that the *lulav* remain fresh and bright. During *Ḥol Hammoed,* it is also customary to make a fresh *aravah* for the *lulav* each day, and this is called "the ornamentation of a precept."

7. During the seven days of *Sukkot,* even on the Sabbath, it is forbidden to sniff the aroma of the *hadas;* but the aroma of the *etrog* may be sniffed on the Sabbath, saying the benediction, "Who put a good odor in fruit." During the other days of the festival, the aroma of the *etrog* should not be scented, even when it is not taken to fulfill the precept with it, because it is doubtful whether a benediction should be pronounced over it. The *lulav* may not be handled on the Sabbath, even when the *lulav* itself is needed or its place, because it is *muktzeh.* However, the *etrog,* the fragrance of which may be scented on the Sabbath, is not *muktzeh,* and may be handled. It is permissible also to put it in the cotton in which it had been kept before the festival, because it had already become imbued with its fragrance; but it may not be placed in new cotton or in new cloth, because that is creating an odor in a thing on the Sabbath.

8. On the first day of *Sukkot,* the obligation is not fulfilled if the *lulav* or the other species are borrowed; they must actually be one's own; for it is written (Leviticus 23:40): "And ye shall take unto yourselves (*laḥem*) on the first day," and it is explained to mean *mishelaḥem,* of your own, excluding one that is borrowed. We who live outside of Israel and observe a second day of the festival, because of a doubt in the date, should say no benediction over a borrowed *lulav* on the second day, either. If we are given a *lulav,* on condition that we return it, it is considered a gift, and we may fulfill our obligation with it. Even if it is given us merely to fulfill the obligation, it is considered as if we had been told expressly that it is presented to us as a gift on condition that it be returned. If the husband is not at home and the wife desires to give them to someone to perform the precept, the validity depends upon the disposition of the husband, whether or not he would mind it.

9. If two persons buy an *etrog* and the other species in partnership. it is presumed that they are buying it with the intention of mutually transferring their share in it to each other when each performs the precept with it. Hence, it is customary for a congregation to buy an *etrog* for all the congregants, and whoever can afford it, should pay something for it. Yet, it is best to perform the precept with an *etrog* belonging to an individual if it and the other species are of standard quality, for whatever an individual transfers to his neighbor is more preferable.

10. On the first day of *Sukkot,* minors should not be given the *etrog* and *lulav* before the adults have said the benediction over them, for according to the Mosaic Law, a minor can acquire possession of an object but cannot transfer any possession.

11. During the first six days of *Sukkot,* after the *Musaph* service, it is customary to take a *sefer torah* onto the *bimah,* and all who own a *lulav* and

an *etrog* march in a procession once around the *bimah,* while the Holy Ark remains open until after the *Hoshanot* are read. Then the *sefer torah* is returned to the Ark. On the seventh day, which is *Hoshanah Rabbah* (see chapter that follows), every *sefer torah* is taken from the Holy Ark and brought up to the *bimah,* and the procession around it is repeated seven times, commemorative of the ceremonial observed in the Temple at Jerusalem, where the altar was encircled once daily and seven times on the seventh day. The *hakkafot* should be made towards the right, and since the *sefer torah* is on the reading desk and the whole congregation faces the *sefer torah,* then the procession proceeds toward the North. A person who owns an *etrog* and a *lulav* and does not take part in the procession, is acting wrongly. In some communities it is the custom on *Hoshana Rabbah* and *Simḥat Torah,* to remove all the Scrolls from the Holy Ark and to place there a lit candle (to indicate that the Torah is light, and when the Torah is not there, another light is needed). This is not a good custom, and it should be abolished, because no profane use may be made of the Holy Ark, even temporarily.

12. No procession takes place on the Sabbath, therefore, no *sefer torah* is brought up to the *bimah*; but the Holy Ark is left open until after the *Hoshanot* have been said.

13. One who becomes a mourner on *Sukkot,* or during the twelvc months of mourning for the loss of one's father or mother, does not, in pursuance to custom, participate in the *hakkafot;* but he should give his *etrog* and *lulav* to one who has no *lulav* of his own, to take part in the procession.

CHAPTER 138

Hoshana Rabbah; Shemini Atzeret; Simḥat Torah

1. The fifth day of *Ḥol Hammoed* is *Hoshana Rabbah.* It is customary to stay awake the whole of the preceding night and to study the Torah, according to the order given in the manual (*Tikkun Lel Hoshana Rabbah*), because during the festival of *Sukkot,* we face judgment concerning water, which is the mainstay of human existence, and all depends upon the final outcome of the judgment. In the *Shaḥarit* service we slightly increase the number of candles in the synagogue, as on *Yom Kippur,* and the *ḥazan* wears a *kittle.* We say *Lamnatzeaḥ* (For the Chief Musician), as on a festival, and *Mizemor letodah* (A Psalm of Thanksgiving); but no *Nishemat* (The breath of every living) is said. We say *En kamoḥa* (There is none like unto Thee), and *Shema Yisrael* (Hear, O Israel), as on a festival. In the *kedushah* of the *Musaph* service, *Naaritzeḥa* (We will revere) is said.

2. The Prophets instituted a custom that each person take on that day a special *aravah,* besides the one which is on the *lulav.* Whatever disqualifies the *aravah* on the *lulav* also disqualifies this *aravah.* Therefore, a Jew should not cut it himself for his own use, and the only difference between these two *aravot* is, that in this one, even if most of its leaves have fallen off, and even if there is only one leaf left on the stem, it is valid. Nevertheless, to show regard for the precept, it is best that the *aravah* should have many leaves and a long stem. It is a fine custom to take for this occasion five twigs and tie them together with the frond of a *lulav* (not the one used for the precept).

3. The *aravah* should not be taken together with the *lulav.* When reciting, *Taaneh emunim* (mayest Thou answer the faithful), the *lulav* and the *etrog* are put down, and the *aravah* is taken, for then we pray for water. Concluding the *Hoshanot,* we wave the *aravah* and then beat it on the ground five times, which number is sufficient even if its leaves are not shed thereby. After the beating, the *aravah* should not be cast away, because it would show contempt for a precept. It is best to save it and cast it into the furnace where the *matzot* are baked for the following Passover, for, since one precept has been performed with it, it is fitting that another precept be performed with it.

4. On the night of *Shemini Atzeret* (Eighth Day of Solemn Assembly), the *kiddush* should not be recited before nightfall. The benediction *Sheheḥeyanu* (Who kept us in life) is included in the *kiddush,* inasmuch as it is a festival in itself; but we do not say the benediction *Leshev basukkah,* because in the prayers and in the *kiddush* we say: "This Eighth Day of Solemn Assembly," and if we said the benediction *Leshev Basukkah,* it would be self-contradictory.

5. We eat in the *sukkah* on the night of *Shemini Atzeret* and during the whole day, but we do not say the benediction *Leshev basukkah.* Before leaving the *sukkah,* we say, *Yehi ratzon* (May it be Thy will). Some permit themselves not to sleep in the *sukkah* on *Shemini Atzeret,* while others observe it, and it is best to follow the latter practice.

6. At the approach of darkness on the eighth day of *Sukkot,* the furniture may be removed from the *sukkah* into the house, but it should not be put in order while it is yet day, as it is like preparing on one festival for another.

7. The last day of the festival, which is also *Shemini Atzeret,* is called *Simḥat Torah* (Rejoicing with the Law), because on this day we conclude the reading of the Torah, and we rejoice with it. In the evening after the *Maariv* service, the ceremony of *Hakkafot* is observed, after which the Scrolls of the Law are replaced in the Holy Ark, leaving one Scroll from which the Law is read for three people, from the portion *Vezot haberaḥah* (And this is the blessing) (Deuteronomy 33). In some communities, the portion dealing with vows is read (Numbers 30:2). After the reading of the Torah, the half-*kaddish* is recited; the last Scroll is now replaced in the Ark, and *Alenu* (It is our duty) is said.

8. On *Simḥat Torah,* it is customary in many communities for the *kohanim* to bless the people at the *Shaḥarit* service and not at the *Musaph*

service, because there is a possibility that the *kohanim* might be intoxicated. The prayer *Veteerav* (And may our prayers be pleasant) is not said in the morning service.

9. In the morning, after the *hakkafot*, three Scrolls are left on the *bimah*, and many male adults are called up for the reading of the section *vezot haberaḥah* up to *Meonah* (Thy refuge) (Deuteronomy 33:27), which is repeated many times. After this, all minors are called up. It is proper for the oldest among them to say the benedictions, and for the rest to listen. Then the section *Hamalaḥ haggoel* (The angel who redeemed) is read for them. After that the *Ḥatan Torah* (The groom of the Torah) is called up, for whom the portion from *Meonah* to the end of the Torah is read. Afterward the *Ḥatan Bereshit* (The groom of Genesis) is called up, and a portion of *Bereshit* in the second Scroll is read for him. After the recitation of the half-*kaddish*, the *maftir* is called up, and a portion is read for him in the third Scroll. It is proper to call up an eminent person for *Ḥatan Torah*, as is the custom in many communities. Even one who has already been called up to the reading of *Vezot haberaḥah*, may be called up either as *Ḥatan Torah* or *Ḥatan Bereshit*. Where there are only two Scrolls of the Law, *Vezot haberaḥah* is read in one, and *Bereshit* in the other, then the first is taken again, and the portion for the *maftir* is read in it.

10. It is customary for the *Ḥatan Torah* and the *Ḥatan Bereshit* to donate to charity, and invite their friends to a joyous banquet on the occasion of the completion of the Torah and its commencement. For, it is stated in the *Midrash* (Kohelet, beginning): "It is written (I Kings 3:15): 'And he came to Jerusalem and he stood before the Ark of the Lord . . . and he made a feast for all his servants.' Said Rabbi Isaac: From this may be inferred that a feast should be made at the completion of the Torah."

CHAPTER 139

Ḥanukkah

1. During the existence of the Second Temple, the Greeks issued drastic decrees against Israel in order to destroy their religion, forbidding them to engage in the study of the Torah or in the practice of its precepts. They robbed them of their property, violated their daughters, and entered the Temple, desecrating and polluting its sanctity. Israel was in great distress because of their cruel oppression, until the God of our fathers took pity on them and saved them from their hands. The sons of the Hasmonean High Priest defeated them, and saved Israel from their power. The kingdom of Israel was reëstablished under the rule of one of the High Priests and lasted for more than two hundred years, until the destruction of the Second Temple. When the Jews prevailed over their enemies, they entered the Temple on the twenty-fifth day of the month of *Kislev*, and found only a small cruse of pure oil, bearing the seal of the High Priest. This oil was sufficient for only one day, but when they lit the *menorah* (candelabrum) with it, it lasted for eight days, until they pounded olives and extracted pure oil. For this reason, the Sages of that generation decreed the eight days, which begin on the twenty-fifth of Kislev, be set aside as days of rejoicing and thanksgiving. Every night, during these eight days, lights are lit towards evening in a conspicuous

place to proclaim the miracle. These days are called *Ḥanukkah*, a hyphenated word meaning: they rested on the twenty-fifth (*Ḥanu* they rested, *ḥaf-he*, the numerical value of these letters being twenty-five) from their enemies. Another reason for the celebration is to commemorate the dedication of the Temple, won back from the enemies who had polluted it; therefore, some authorities hold that it is imperative to feast a little more lavishly during these days. Another reason for the celebration is, that the work of the Tabernacle in the wilderness was completed during these days. On *Ḥanukkah*, every Jew should recount to his household the miracles that were wrought for our fathers in those days. However, feasting alone cannot be considered as a religious act, unless it is accompanied by songs and hymns. Charity, too, should be liberally dispensed on *Ḥanukkah*, for this is conducive to correct the flaws of our souls, especially when given to maintain poor scholars who are engaged in the study of the Torah.

2. No fasting is permitted on *Ḥanukkah*, but it is permitted to fast and to deliver a funeral oration on the day preceding *Ḥanukkah* and the day after *Ḥanukkah*.

3. It is permissible to do all kinds of work during the eight days of *Ḥanukkah*. But women customarily refrain from work while the *Ḥanukkah* lights are burning, and we should not permit them to disregard this custom. The reason the women have assumed this restraint is that the evil decrees effected them most. For the oppressor had decreed that a maiden before her marriage must first cohabit with the governor. Another reason for this, is that the miracle of deliverance was wrought through a woman. The daughter of Joḥanan the High Priest was a very beautiful woman, and the cruel king requested her to be with him. She acceded to his request, and she prepared for him dishes of cheese, which made him thirsty. He then drank wine; became intoxicated and fell asleep, whereupon she cut off his head and brought it to Jerusalem. Finding that the king was dead, they became panicky and fled. Therefore, it is customary to eat dairy dishes on *Ḥanukkah*, commemorative of the miracle wrought by means of a milk product.

4. While all kinds of oil are valid for the *Ḥanukkah* lights, olive oil is the most preferred, for the miracle in the Temple was also wrought with olive oil. If this cannot be obtained, one may choose any other oil which gives a clear and bright flame, or wax candles may be used, as their light also is clear. One should not intertwine two candles, for that would be akin to a torch. The candles should not be made of wax that has been used in a place of worship for heathens, for that makes it odious. All kinds of wicks are valid for the use of *Ḥanukkah* lights, but the most preferred are ones made of cotton. It is not necessary to take new wicks every night; one may light the same wicks until they are used up.

5. If one lights the *Ḥanukkah* candles in a candlestick made of clay, it is already considered as old, and it may not be used again, because it has become repulsive. Therefore, one should endeavor to procure a fine metal candlestick, and if one can afford it, a silver candlestick, in order that the precept may be performed in a grand manner.

6. It is a prevailing custom among the scrupulously devout in our land, for each member of the family to light *Ḥanukkah* candles, one candle on the first evening; two candles on the second, adding one candle each evening until the eighth day, when all eight candles are lit. Care should be taken that each places his candles in a separate place, so that one can tell how many candles are to be lit that evening. The candles should not be lit in a place where candles are usually lit the rest of the year, in order that it be discernible that they are *Ḥanukkah* lights.

7. The *Ḥanukkah* lights should be lit in the doorway that leads to a public thoroughfare, in order to proclaim the miracle; thus it was done in Mishnaic and Talmudic days. Nowadays, since we live among other nations, the candles are lit in the house, and if there is a window facing the public place, they should be lit there; if not, they should be lit near the door. They must be placed within a hand-breadth, near the left side of the door, so that the *mezuzah* be on the right and the *Ḥanukkah* lights on the left, and thus we find ourselves flanked by religious objects. It is preferable to place the lights within the door-space.

8. The *Ḥanukkah* candles must be placed higher than three hand-breadths (twelve inches) above the ground and lower than ten hand-breadths (forty inches). If, however, they are placed higher than ten hand-breadths above the ground, the obligation is, nevertheless, fulfilled. But if they are placed higher than twenty cubits (thirty feet) from the ground, the obligation is not fulfilled, for the eye cannot well perceive things placed higher than twenty cubits above the ground. One who dwells in an upper story, may place the lights in the window, even if it is higher than ten hand-breadths from the floor. If the window is higher than twenty cubits from the ground, so that the passersby are unable to see the lights, then it is best to place them near the door.

9. The lights should be placed in an even row; one should not be higher than the other; and there should be sufficient space between them, so that the flames may not merge and resemble a torch. Wax candles have to be spaced for the additional reason that they might melt one another by the heat and get spoiled. If we fill a dish with oil and put wicks around it, then if we put a perforated cover on it, each wick is considered as a separate candle, but without a cover, it does not even qualify as one single candle, because it is like a torch. A candlestick having two or more branches, should not be lit by two persons even on the first evening, as it would not be discernible how many candles it represents.

10. The time to light the *Ḥanukkah* lamp is immediately after the stars come out, and one should not put it off. It is forbidden to do anything, even to study the Torah, before lighting the *Ḥanukkah* lamp, but the *Maariv* prayer should be said before lighting it. One should assemble the entire household for the lighting of the candles, in order to give it an air of solemnity. Candles for the *Ḥanukkah* lamp must be large enough to burn at least half an hour. If one has failed to light the lamp immediately upon the appearance of the stars, one may do so afterwards and say the benedictions as long as the members of his family are awake, but if they are already asleep and the rite can no longer be performed in a demonstrative manner, one should light the *Ḥanukkah* lamp without saying the benedictions. If one will have no time to light the *Ḥanukkah* lamp in the evening, one may light it after "half of the small *Minḥah*" (see chapter 69:2, above), that is, one and a quarter hours before the stars become visible (that is, according to the proportions of the day, consisting of twelve hours from sunrise to sunset; and during the days of *Ḥanukkah*, if the day is only ten hours long, then "half of the small *Minḥah*" is only one hour and two and one-half minutes before the stars become visible), providing the candles are large enough to burn one-half hour after the stars come out. If they do not burn that long, the obligation has not been fulfilled.

11. The order of lighting the candles is as follows: On the first evening, the candle to be lit is placed at the end of the *Ḥanukkah* lamp, facing our right hand; on the second evening, we add one towards the left; likewise on every succeeding evening, we add one towards the left. The added candle is lit first, then the lighting of the other candles proceeds towards the right.

12. On the first evening, the one who lights the *Ḥanukkah* lamp, recites three benedictions: *Lehadlik* (To light the *Ḥanukkah* lamp); *Sheasah nissim* (Who hath wrought miracles); and *Sheheḥeyanu* (Who kept us in life). On the other evenings, the benediction *Sheheḥeyanu* is not recited. After the benedictions are pronounced, the candle that has been added that evening is lit, and while lighting the rest of the candles, we recite *Hanerot halolu* (These candles). A convert to Judaism says: "Who hath wrought miracles for Israel" in the second benediction. If, however, he has said, "For our fathers," his obligation is fulfilled. An *onan* (a mourner before the interment; see chapter 196, below), Heaven forbid, should not light the *Ḥanukkah* lamp. Someone else should do it, and he should only respond *Amen*. But if there is no one else, then he should light the lamp without saying the benedictions.

13. It is an established rule that the act of lighting the *Ḥanukkah* lamp is what constitutes the precept. It is, therefore, necessary that when lighting the candles, they should be in their proper position and of the required size. Hence, if the candles are lower than three hand-breadths above the ground when they are lit, or higher than twenty cubits, and they are properly placed later, they are of no avail. Likewise, if when lighting them they lack the required quantity of oil, and thereafter more oil is added, they are of no avail. Also, if the candles were placed where a wind is blowing and were likely to be extinguished, the precept is not properly performed, and we must light them again, but without saying the benediction. If, however, they are put in the proper place and are accidently extinguished, the precept is considered as having been properly performed; nevertheless, it is customary to relight them. It is our custom to avoid lighting one candle with another, but they should be lit by the *shamesh* (servile candle) or by some other candle.

14. It is forbidden to make any use of the *Ḥanukkah* candles during the half hour that the lights must burn. Hence, we place the *shamesh* near the *Ḥanukkah* candles, so that in the event we do something near the candles, we do same by the light of the *shamesh*. The *shamesh* should be placed a little higher than the other lights, in order that it may be obvious that it is not one of the required number of candles.

15. The *Ḥanukkah* lamp is lit in the synagogue as a public proclamation of the miracle, and the benedictions are uttered over them. The candles are placed near the southern wall, and are lit between the *Minḥah* and *Maariv* services. No one is, however, exempted from lighting the *Ḥanukkah* lamp by the one lit in the synagogue; but every one must light them in his own house. A mourner (Heaven forbid) should not light the *Ḥanukkah* lamp at the synagogue the first evening when the benediction *Sheheḥeyanu* must be said, for a mourner is not allowed to utter this benediction in public; but he may say this benediction in his house.

16. Women, too, are obligated to light *Ḥanukkah* candles, because they, also, were benefitted by the miracle of *Ḥanukkah*. A woman may light the *Ḥanukkah* lamp and exempt the entire household. Even children, who are old enough to be trained in the observance of precepts, must light the *Ḥanukkah* candles. For a blind person it is best, if he can, to contribute something towards the purchase of candles with another. If he has a wife, she lights the candles for him; but if he has no wife and he lives by himself where he has none with whom to join in purchasing the candles, he should light them with the aid of another.

17. On Friday, the *Ḥanukkah* lamp must be lit before the Sabbath candles, but it should be after *Pelag haminḥah* (half of the small *Minḥah;* see chapter 69:2, above), and the *Minḥah* prayer should be said before this. The *Ḥanukkah* candles should be large enough to keep burning for no less than half an hour after the appearance of the stars, otherwise the benedictions pronounced over them are in vain. If the candles are placed near the door, something should be put between them and the door, to prevent their being extinguished when the door is being opened.

18. On Saturday night, the *Ḥanukkah* lamp should be lit after the *Havdalah* is recited. At the synagogue, it is lit before *Veyitten leḥa* (And may God give thee) is said.

19. One who is out of town and knows that his wife lights the *Ḥanukkah* lamp at his house, should light candles wherever he is without saying the benedictions. If possible, he should hear someone else say the benedictions over candles, intend to be represented by the other, and respond *Amen,* after which he should light his own candles without saying the benedictions. But if his wife does not light the *Ḥanukkah* lamp at his house, likewise, guests in hotels, are required to light the candles and say the benedictions; or else they should give the hotelkeeper a coin and acquire a share in the oil and the wick.

The owner should add a little more oil than the required quantity for the share of the partners. They should, however, make every effort to light their own candles. One who is in the city but in somebody else's house, should return to his home when the time comes for lighting the *Ḥanukkah* lamp, and light it there.

20. The oil and the wicks that are left in the lamps after *Ḥanukkah*, should be burnt, for since they had been set apart for the purpose of a precept, we are not allowed to derive any benefit from them, unless we have specifically declared that we do not set apart what will be left after *Ḥanukkah*.

21. During the eight days of *Ḥanukkah*, we include *Al hannissim* (For the miracles) in the *Shemoneh esreh*. If we have inadvertently omitted it and have become aware of the omission before pronouncing the Divine Name (*Adonai*) in the benediction *Hatov shimeḥa* (Whose name is good), we should then start with *Al hanissim*, but if we have not become aware of the error until we have uttered the Divine Name, we conclude the benediction, and we need not repeat the *Shemoneh esreh*.

22. During the eight days of *Ḥanukkah*, we recite the entire *hallel*. We do not say *Taḥanun* (petition for Grace), nor *El ereḥ appayim* (O God who art long-suffering); nor *Lamenatzeaḥ* (For the chief musician), nor *Tzidekatteḥa tzedek* (Thy righteousness).

23. Each day of *Ḥanukkah*, we call up three male adults for the reading of the Torah, wherein is recorded the sacrifices brought by the *nesiim* (princes) contained in the *sidrah Naso* (Numbers 6). On the first day, we read for the *Kohen* from, *Vayehi beyom kalot moshe* (And it came to pass when Moses had finally set up) until *Laḥanukkat hamizbeah* (For the dedication of the altar). For the *Levi* from *Vayehi hammakrib bayyom harishon* (And he that offered his offering on the first day), until *Meleah ketoret* (Full of incense). For the Israelite from *Par eḥad* (One young bullock), until *Ben aminadab* (The son of Aminadab). On the second day, for the *Kohen* and the *Levi*, *Bayyom hasheni* (On the second day). For the Israelite, *Bayyom hashelishi* (On the third day). Thus on each succeeding day, for the *Kohen* and the *Levi* we read of the present day, and for the Israelite of the day that follows. On the eighth day, we read for the *Kohen* and the *Levi*, *Bayyom hashemini* (On the eighth day), and for the Israelite, we begin with, *Bayyom hateshii* (The ninth day), completing the entire *sidrah*, and also a part of the *sidrah Behaalotḥa* (When thou lightest), until *Ken asah et hamenorah* (So he made the candlestick).

24. On the Sabbath that occurs during *Ḥanukkah*, two Scrolls are taken from the Ark. In one we read the *Sidrah* of the week, and in the other we read the *maftir*, "The day of the *nesiim*" (see section above), corresponding to the day of *Ḥanukkah*, and for the *haftorah*, we read (Zeḥariah 2:14): *Rani vesimeḥi* (Sing and rejoice). If the New Moon of the month of Tebet occurs on a weekday, two Scrolls are taken out; in one we read for three persons the usual portion for *Rosh Ḥodesh*, and in the other Scroll we read for a fourth person "The day of the *nesiim*," corresponding to the day of *Ḥanukkah*. For, *Rosh Ḥodesh* is more frequent than *Ḥanukkah*, and it is an established principle of law, that between the more frequent and the less frequent, the more frequent has priority. If by error, the portion for *Ḥanukkah* is read first, then even if the reading has not yet begun, but the one who was called up has already said the benediction, the reading of his portion may be concluded, and for the rest who are called up, the portion of *Rosh Ḥodesh* is read. If the portion

for *Rosh Ḥodesh* has been read as need be, but by error, also a fourth person has been called up to it, even if we become aware of the error immediately after the benediction, then if only one Scroll has been taken out, no more should be read out of it. If, however, two Scrolls have been taken out, and there is apprehension that the Torah will be slighted by the worshipers, thinking that a defect has been discovered in it, a fifth person is called, for whom we read the portion of *Ḥanukkah* in the second Scroll. After this, the half-*kaddish* is recited.

25. If the New Moon of *Tevet* occurs on a Sabbath, we take out three Scrolls. In the first we read the *Sidrah* of the week for six persons; in the second we read the portion of *Rosh Ḥodesh* for the seventh person, beginning from, *Ubeyom hashabbat* (And on the day of Sabbath); after this half-*kaddish* is recited. In the third Scroll we read for the *maftir* "The day of the *nesiim*," corresponding to the day of *Ḥanukkah;* and for the *haftorah* we read *Roni vesimeḥi* (Sing and rejoice). The rule that the more frequent has precedence relates only where both are read, but in the case of the *haftorah* where only one is read, that of *Rosh Ḥodesh* is superseded by the one for *Ḥanukkah* to proclaim the miracle.

26. The fifteenth day of *Shevat,* is the "New Year" for Trees. The *Taḥanun* (petition for Grace) is not recited, and it is the custom to eat thereon many kinds of fruit.

CHAPTER 140

The Four Parshiyot

1. The Sabbath before the New Moon of *Adar* (the month close to the month of *Nisan*), is called *Shabbat Parshat Shekalim* (The Sabbath of the Section of *Shekels*). If the New Moon occurs on this Sabbath, three Scrolls are taken from the Ark. In the first one we read the *sidrah* of the week for six persons; in the second we read for the seventh person the portion for *Rosh Ḥodesh,* beginning with, *Ubeyom hashabbat* (And on the day of Sabbath), and we recite the half-*kaddish.* In the third Scroll we read for the *maftir* the portion dealing with the precept of giving half a shekel for the Temple (Exodus 30:11-16), and the *haftorah* of *Shekalim* is read. If by error we begin reading first the section for *Shekalim,* the reading should be concluded, and the portion for the New Moon is read for the *maftir,* and the *haftorah* too, is of "Sabbath *Rosh Ḥodesh.*"

2 The Sabbath before *Purim* is *Parshat Zaḥor* (The section "Remember"), because we read for the *maftir* (Deuteronomy 25:17-19): *Zaḥor et asher asah leḥa Amalek,* (Remember that Amalek hath done to thee). The Sabbath before the New Moon of *Nisan* is *Parshat Haḥodesh* (The portion of *Rosh Ḥodesh*). If the New Moon of *Nisan* occurs on a Sabbath, then that Sabbath is *Parshat Haḥodesh,* and is governed by the same law which applies to the New Moon of *Adar* which occurs on a Sabbath. The Sabbath before *Parshat Haḥodesh* is *Parshat Parah* (The portion of the *parah adumah,* the red cow.

3. Some authorities are of the opinion that the reading of *Parshat Zaḥor* and *Parshat Parah* is a Biblical ordinance, and a minor should not be called to the *maftir.* Country people who have no quorum for praying, should go to a place where there is a quorum; and if that is impossible, they should at least read the portions of these special Sabbaths with the proper intonations.

Chapter 141

The Reading of The Megillah

1. As soon as the month of *Adar* arrives, our joys increase. If a Jew has a lawsuit with a non-Jew, he should go to court during this month.

2. In the days of Mordecai and Esther, the Jews gathered on the thirteenth day of *Adar* to defend themselves against, and seek retribution of, their enemies. They had to ask for mercy from the Holy One, blessed be His name, that He might help them; and we find that when the Jews were at war, they fasted, so that the Lord might help them. Also, our teacher Moses, peace unto him, fasted when he waged war against the Amalekites. It is, therefore, presumed that also in the days of Mordecai and Esther they fasted on the thirteenth day of *Adar*. Therefore, all the Israelites have taken upon themselves to fast on the thirteenth day of *Adar*. This is known as the "Fast of Esther." This fast is to remind us that the Holy One, blessed be His name, hears the prayer of every man in time of distress when he fasts and returns to Him with all his heart, as He heard the prayers of our forefathers in those days. However, this fast is not as imperative as the four fasting days that are mentioned in the Scriptures. (See chapter 121, above). Hence, we may be lenient about this fast on occasion. Thus pregnant and nursing women, or even one suffering slightly with his eyes, if the fast would cause them discomfort, need not fast. A woman within thirty days of childbirth, and a bridegroom during his seven days of celebration, need not fast on this day, but they should make up for this fast later. However, people who are well, should not exclude themselves from the public, and even a wayfarer, for whom fasting is difficult, should also fast.

3. *Purim* is the fourteenth day of *Adar*. If *Purim* occurs on a Sunday, the fast is advanced to Thursday. If a circumcision takes place on Thursday, the feast should be held at night, but the *sandek* and the father of the infant are permitted to eat in the daytime, and they are not required to make up for the fast on Friday. But if any other person forgets and eats on Thursday, he must fast on Friday.

4. To show reverence for the *Megillah*, we should put on our Sabbath clothes in the evening, and on returning home from the synagogue, we should find the lights lit, the table set and the beds made. In the evening, after the *Shemoneh esreh*, the whole *kaddish* is said, including *Titkabbel* (May the prayers and supplications). Then the *Megillah* is read, after which *Veattah kadosh* (And Thou art Holy) is said (which is contained in Psalm 22: "For the Leader; upon *Aijeleth ha-Shaḥar*. A Psalm of David," referring to Esther. And there it is said (verse 3): "O my God, I call by day," etc., which refers to the reading of the *Megillah*. For Rabbi Joshua ben Levi said (Megillah 4a): 'Every man must read the *Megillah* in the night and repeat it in the day, for it is written: O my God, I call by day, but Thou answerest not; and at night, and there is no surcease for me.' And after that it is written: 'Yet,

Thou art holy.") Afterward the whole *kaddish* is said, omitting *Titkabbel.* If it is Saturday night, we say *Vihi noam* (Let the pleasantness) and *Veattah kadosh,* after which we recite the whole *kaddish,* omitting *Titkabbel,* and *Veyitten leḥa* (May God give thee). The *havdalah* is then recited over a goblet of wine, and thereafter we say *Alenu* (It is our duty).

5. Before *Purim* commences, it is customary to donate half the unit coin current in the country, to commemorate the half-*shekel* the Jews used to give in the month of *Adar* for the buying of the public sacrifices. The general practice is for every person to give three half-*shekels,* because in the *Sidrah Ki Tissa* (Exodus 30:11-16), the word *Terumah* (offering) is mentioned three times. It is given in the evening before the *Megillah* is read, and the money is distributed among the poor. A minor is exempt from contributing the half-*shekel;* but if his father has once contributed for him, he must continue to do so. Some authorities hold that a lad of thirteen must donate it, while others hold that he is exempt up to the age of twenty.

6. In the *Shemoneh esreh* of the evening, morning, and after noon services, we include *Al hanissim* (For the miracles), and if it has been omitted, it is governed by the same law that applies to *Ḥanukkah* (chapter 139:21, above).

7. Everyone, man and woman, is obliged to hear the *Megillah* both in the evening and in the morning. Hence, maidens, too, should go to the synagogue. Those unable to go to the synagogue, should hear the reading of the *Megillah* at home. Children, too, should be trained to hear the *Megillah.* Nevertheless, very young children should not be taken to the synagogue lest they disrupt the service.

8. At night it is forbidden to read the *Megillah* before the stars appear, even if one is in great distress on account of the fast. But one may have some light refreshments before the *Megillah* is read, such as coffee, and the like, in order to alleviate somewhat the weakening effect of the fast.

9. The precept is best observed if one hears the *Megillah* in the synagogue where there is a multitude of people, for, "In the multitude of people is the king's glory" (Proverbs 14:28). One should at least endeavor to hear it read at a quorum of ten. But if it is impossible to obtain a quorum of ten, each individual should read it out of a valid *Megillah,* and say the benedictions that precede it. If one of them knows how to read it and the others do not, that one should read it and the rest should listen, and their obligation is thus fulfilled. However, the concluding benediction of the *Megillah* is to be recited only when the *Megillah* was read at a quorum. But even an individual may recite it without mentioning the Name and Sovereignty (*Adonai elokenu meleḥ haolam*).

10. It is an established custom that the reader spreads out the *Megillah*

and folds it, folio upon folio, like a letter, because the *Megillah* is designated as *iggeret* (a letter of *Purim*) (Esther 9:29); but the listeners are not required to spread their *Megillot.*

11. The one who reads the *Megillah,* whether in the daytime or at night, pronounce three benedictions before the reading: *Al mikra megillah* (Concerning the reading of the *Megillah*); *Sheasah nissim* (Who hath performed miracles), and *Sheheḥeyanu* (Who hath kept us in life). And after reading it, he rolls it completely up, places it before him, and recites the benediction *Harav et ribenu* (Who pleads our cause). If a mourner reads the *Megillah,* someone else should say the benedictions, on account of his being unable to say *Sheheḥeyanu.*

12. When saying the benediction *Sheheḥeyanu* in the daytime, one should intend to include the precepts of sending portions to friends, making gifts to the needy, and also to apply it to the *Purim* feast. The reader, too, should say it with the intention of exempting the congregation from the *Sheheḥeyanu* benediction over these precepts.

13. The reader of the *Megillah,* should intend to exempt all the listeners from reading it, and the listeners should intend to fulfill their obligation. Therefore, they must listen to every word, for should they fail to hear even one word, their obligation would not be fulfilled. The reader is, therefore, required to cease reading while there is noise and confusion at the mention of *Haman,* and wait until the commotion is entirely over. Nevertheless, it is fitting and proper for each worshiper to own a valid *Megillah,* so that he himself may say, word for word quietly, as perchance he might fail to hear one word from the reader. Also, every literate woman in the women's section of the synagogue, should, if possible, have a valid *Megillah* out of which to read, because it is hard to hear it from that place, for a woman as already stated, is obliged to read the *Megillah* the same as a man. (If the moon had not yet been sanctified and it becomes visible during the reading of the *Megillah,* see above chapter 97:15, as to what is to be done.)

14. The reader should recite the names of the ten sons of Haman, including the word *Aseret* (ten), all in one breath, to indicate that they were all hanged at one time. It is the custom to begin with *Ḥamesh meot ish* (Five hundred men), and say it all in one breath. If, however, he has inadvertently paused between the ten sons of Haman, his obligation is fulfilled. The custom that prevails in some communities that all the worshipers read the names of Haman's sons is not proper. Only the reader should recite them and the congregation should merely listen, the same as the rest of the *Megillah.* In the evening, when the reader says (Esther 6:1): "In that night could not the king sleep," he should raise his voice, for at that verse the story of the miracle begins. When the reader says (9:29), "*Iggeret happurim* (The letter of *Purim*), he should wave the *Megillah.*

15. One who has a *Megillah* that is not valid, or a Bible, should not recite the words together with the reader, because he could not listen well to the reader, and even if he himself could pay attention, someone else might listen to him and not to the reader. Nor should anyone vocally assist the reader;

therefore, the reader must repeat the four terms of redemption, "light, gladness, joy and honor" (8:16) which the congregation reads aloud.

16. If one who has already fulfilled the obligation of reading the *Megillah*, is reading it for the benefit of others, then the listener himself should say the benedictions if he is able to do so. If it is read for the sake of a woman, it is best that the leader should say the following benediction: "Who hath sanctified us by His commandments and hath commanded us concerning the *listening* of the *Megillah*."

17. It is permissible to handle a *Megillah* on the Sabbath (on which *Purim* does not occur). Nevertheless, if *Purim* occurs on a Sunday, the *Megillah* should not be brought to the synagogue on Saturday, even in a city which is provided with an *eruv* (inter-community of domains), inasmuch as it is preparing something on the Sabbath for a weekday.

18. If there is no one in the congregation who is able to read the *Megillah* with the proper intonations, one may read it without the intonations, providing he reads the words properly, so that the subject matter is not changed. For, if he reads: *Mordecai yashav* (sat), instead of *yoshev* (is sitting); or if he reads: *Vehaman nafal* (fell), instead of *nofel* (is falling), or the like, the obligation has not been fulfilled. It is even permissible to make in the *Megillah*, vowels and notes, in an emergency, so that it may be read correctly. And this is better than each one reading silently out of a Bible (while one reads the *Megillah*), for he is unable to hear what the reader is saying, and by reading it out of the Bible, his obligation is not fulfilled. If it so happened, he must hear it again, read out of a valid *Megillah*.

19. If a congregation has no *Megillah* that is valid, nevertheless, if it is written according to the law, only some words are missing, but no entire subject is omitted, it may be read therefrom, and the benedictions may be pronounced. Wherever there is an error, the reader should repeat the part from memory, or one should prompt him silently out of a Bible. But if they have no *Megillah* at all, or if an entire subject is missing from the one they have, or if either the beginning or the end is missing, then each one should read for himself out of a Bible, without pronouncing the benedictions.

20. A mourner during the first seven days of mourning, must observe all the laws of mourning (on *Purim*), and he is forbidden to witness any kind of festivity; but he is allowed to put on his shoes and to sit on a chair, for this abnegation would be a public demonstration of mourning. If he can gather together a quorum of ten male adults at his house to read the *Megillah*, it is well; if not, he should pray at home and go to the synagogue to hear the *Megillah*. If *Purim* occurs on Saturday night, he should go to the synagogue

after the third meal on the Sabbath while it is yet day; and on the morrow, he may go to the synagogue to pray and to hear the *Megillah*.

21. One who has lost a member of his family on the Fast of Esther and he is an *onan* at night, the interment not having taken place, should hear the *Megillah* read by someone else, but he should neither eat meat nor drink wine, because feasting at night is not obligatory. In the daytime, after leaving the synagogue, the dead is buried and thereafter he prays and either reads the *Megillah* himself or hears someone else read it. If he has heard the *Megillah* read before the interment, his obligation is fulfilled. Yet it is best that he read it again, without saying the benediction. He should not put on the *tefillin* even after the interment, since it is his first day of mourning. An *onan* is permitted to eat and drink wine on *Purim*.

22. In the morning it is customary to arrive early at the synagogue. After the *Shemoneh esreh*, the half-*kaddish* is said, and three persons are called up for the reading of (Exodus 17:8): *Vayavo amalek* (And Amalek came), after which the half-*kaddish* is recited. After the *Sefer Torah* is replaced in the Holy Ark, the *Megillah* is read. *Asher heni* (Who brought the counsel of the heathen to nought) is not said after the concluding benediction of the *Megillah*. After concluding *Hael hammoshia* (O God, the Saviour), we say *Shoshanat yaacob* (The lily of Jacob), then *Ashre* (Happy are they), then *Uva letziyon* (A redeemer shall come), and then the entire *kaddish*, including *Titkabbel* (May the prayers and supplications) is recited. The *tefillin* should not be taken off before the *Megillah* is read, because in the *Megillah* is written (Esther 8:16) *Vikar* (And honor), and it has been explained that this refers to the *tefillin*. If there is a circumcision to be performed, it should take place before the *Megillah* is read.

23. In a city which has been surrounded by a wall since the days of Joshua the son of Nun, the *Megillah* is read on the fifteenth of the month of *Adar*. But such a city is not known in our regions.

CHAPTER 142

The Sending of Portions—Gifts to the Needy—Purim Seudah (Feast)

1. On *Purim* it is the duty of everybody to send no less than two gifts to one of his friends, for it is written (Esther 9:22): "And of sending *portions* one to another," which means two gifts to one. The more gifts one sends to his friends, the more praiseworthy one is. Nevertheless, it is better to give charity to the needy than to make a great feast and to send gifts to one's friends. There is no greater joy and no more glorious deed before the Holy One, blessed be He, than the gladdening of the hearts of those in need, the orphans and the widows. And he who gladdens the hearts of these unfortunates, is likened to the Divine Presence, of whom it is written (Isaiah 57:15): "To revive the spirit of the humble, and to revive the heart of the contrite."

2. "Portions" to friends, must be gifts of food which can be eaten with-

out further preparations, such as boiled meat, fish, confectionery, fruits, wine, mead, or something similiar.

3. Everybody, even the poorest in Israel who is himself dependent on charity, is to give at least one gift each to two poor persons, for it is written (Esther 9:22): "And gifts to the poor," which means, two gifts to two poor persons. One should not make any inquiries in giving to the poor. Whoever puts out his hand and begs, should be given alms. If one lives in a community where there are no poor people, one must either keep the *Purim* money until one meets poor persons, or send it to some needy persons that he knows.

4. Women, too, must send gifts to their friends and contribute to charity on this day. Women should send gifts to women, and men to men, but as regards charity to the needy, women may help men, and men may help women. Some women depend on their husbands that they give for them as well; but this is improper; they should be more exacting about it.

5. *Purim* must be celebrated by eating, drinking, and making merry. Also on the night of the fourteenth of *Adar*, one must be joyful and eat somewhat more abundantly. If *Purim* occurs on Saturday night, although one must have a third meal on the Sabbath, one should eat a little less during the day in order to be able to enjoy the *Purim* repast. Nevertheless, the obligation of feasting on *Purim* is not fulfilled by the feast that we make at night; the principal *Purim* feast is to be held in the daytime. For it is written (Esther 9:22): "Days of feasting." It is appropriate to light candles as becomes a festival occasion, even though the meal is had in the daytime. On the night of the fifteenth, there should also be some rejoicing. The giving of charity and the sending of gifts to friends also should be performed during the daytime. And because people are concerned with sending out portions, a part of the repast is had in the night time. The *Minḥah* prayer is, therefore, said while it is yet broad day, and the feast is held after *Minḥah*. But at least the greater part of the feast should be had while it is yet day. When *Purim* occurs on a Friday, the feast is held in the morning, in deference to the Sabbath. It is well to engage in the study of the Torah for a short time before beginning the feast. A support for this view is found in the verse (Esther 8:16): "The Jews had light," and "light" is defined as having reference to the Torah. Some authorities say that it is appropriate to eat some seeds on *Purim*, to recall the seeds which Daniel and his comrades ate in Babylon, and also to recall the seeds that Esther had eaten. For the *Talmud* says (Megillah 16b): "The verse (Esther 2:9): 'And he advanced her and the maidens to the best,' means that he permitted her to have seeds for her food."

6. Since the whole miracle of *Purim* was occasioned through wine: Vashti met her fate at the wine feast and Esther took the crown in her stead; the downfall of Haman was due to wine, therefore, the Sages, of blessed memory, made it obligatory on every one to become drunk, and ordained: "One is obliged to regale himself on *Purim*, until one is unable to differentiate between 'Cursed be Haman,' and 'Blessed be Mordecai.'" At least to commemorate the great miracle, one should drink more than he is accustomed, until he falls asleep, and while asleep, he will be unable to differentiate between "Cursed be Haman" and "Blessed be Mordecai." However, if one has a delicate constitution, likewise if one knows that drunkenness may cause him, God forbid, to slight some precept, a benediction or a prayer, or that it will lead him, God forbid, to levity, it is best for him not to become intoxicated; for all our deeds must be for the sake of Heaven.

7. A mourner, even during the first seven days of mourning, is obliged to send gifts to the needy and portions to his friends; he should not, however, send them anything that will cause joy. But we do not send anything to a mourner the entire twelve months, even a thing that is not of a joy-provoking nature. If the mourner is a poor man, it is permissible to send him money or any article that is not calculated to cause joy. If only the mourner and one other person dwell in that place, a gift must be sent to him, in order to observe the precept of sending portions. (For the law regarding an *onan*, see chapter 141:21, above).

8. No labor may be performed on *Purim*, and whoever performs any labor on that day, will never derive any benefit from it. But it is permissible to have work done for us by a non-Jew. It is also permissible to attend to business, to write even a social letter, to make a note of debts due, and to do anything that does not require much concentration. Especially is it permissible to write something of a religious nature or do some work for the performance of a precept. For the requirements of *Purim* it is permissible to perform any labor.

9. The fifteenth day of *Adar* is known as *Shushan Purim*. On this day we do not say *Taḥanun* (petition for Grace), nor *El ereḥ appayim* (O God, Thou art long-suffering), nor *Lamenatzeaḥ* (To the chief musician). On this day it is also forbidden to deliver funeral orations or to fast. It is customary to make rather festive meals and to be merry on *Shushan Purim*, but no *Al hannissim* (We thank Thee for the miracles) is said. Marriages are permitted on this day, but not on the fourteenth of *Adar*, when the *Megillah* is read, for it is a joyous event, and we do not join one festive event with another.

10. On the fourteenth and fifteenth days of the first *Adar* (in a leap-year), neither *Taḥanun*, nor *El ereḥ appayim*, nor *Lamenatzeaḥ* is said, and it is also forbidden to deliver funeral orations or to fast on those days. On the fourteenth, our meals are more or less of a festive nature.

VOLUME 4

Chapter 143

Honoring Father and Mother

1. One must be extremely careful to fear and revere one's father and mother, for the Scriptures compare it to the honor and fear of the Holy One, blessed be He. The Sages (Kiddushin 30b) tell us: "It is written (Exodus 20:12): 'Honor thy father and thy mother.' It is also written (Proverbs 3:9): 'Honor the Lord with thy substance.' Also, (Leviticus 19:3): 'Ye shall fear, every man, his mother and his father;' and (Deuteronomy 6:13): 'Thou shalt fear the Lord thy God.' Thus we see that we must honor father and mother in the same manner that we honor and fear His great name. Three partners share in the creation of man: The Holy One, blessed be He, the father, and the mother. (The man provides it with the white substance, the woman with the red substance, and the Holy One, blessed be He, breathes a soul into him and endows him with the faculty of sight, hearing, and speech, Niddah 31a). When we honor our father and mother, the Holy One, blessed be He, says: 'I account it to them as though I dwelt among them, and they honored Me.'"

2. What constitutes "fear?" One must not occupy the place appointed for one's father, in a council of elders or the place reserved for him to pray. One should not occupy the seat generally occupied by his father at the dinner table. One must neither contradict one's father nor even corroborate his words in his presence, like saying: "Father is right." To what degree shall parents be feared? If a son, attired in costly garments, were to preside over a meeting, and his father or his mother came and rent his garments, and struck him on the head, and spat in his face, he should neither insult them nor show distress in their presence, or display anger towards them; but he should remain silent and fear the King who is the King of kings, the Holy One, blessed be He, who thus decreed. He may, however, seek legal redress for the damage they have caused him.

3. What constitutes "honor?" One must provide them with food and drink and clothing. One should bring them home and take them out, and provide them with all their needs cheerfully. Children who provide their parents with fattened poultry, but do so with ill grace, incur Divine punishment.

4. If the father or mother is asleep, and the key to one's store lies under their pillow, one must not waken them, even if one should lose much profit thereby. However, if the father would benefit by being awakened, and if the son should fail to awake him, he will grieve over the loss of the profit, it is his duty to arouse him, since that will make him happy. It is also the duty of children to arouse their father to go to the synagogue, or for the performance of any other religious duty, as all are equally bound to honor the Almighty, blessed be He.

5. If a son desires a favor from his townsmen, and he knows that it will be granted to him for his father's sake, even though he knows that he could also get it on his own account, nevertheless, he should not say: "Do it for me," but rather: "Do it for my father's sake," in order to attribute the favor to the regard people have for his father.

6. If one is told by his mother to do a certain thing, and subsequently his father asks him: "Who told you to do this?" If he feels that by telling that his mother had told him to do it, his father would be angry at his mother, one should rather incur his father's anger than implicate the mother.

7. Children must rise and remain standing in the presence of their father and their mother.

8. One must honor his parents even after their death. Thus, if he mentions their names within twelve months after their departure, he should say: "I am an atonement in his (or her) place" (that is, all evil that is to come on his or her soul, shall befall me instead). After the expiration of twelve months (when no more punishment is meted out, for even the wicked are not judged after the period of twelve months), one should add: "May his (or her) memory be a blessing in the life of the world to come."

9. Even if his father is wicked and a sinner, he must fear and revere him. Even an illegitimate child is bound to honor and fear his father. Some authorities hold that a child is not bound to honor a wicked father as long as he does not repent, and is forbidden only to cause him grief. It is best, however, to follow the former opinion.

10. When a child sees his father transgress a Divine Law, he must not say to him: "You have violated a command of the Torah," but he should rather put it in the form of a question: "Father, is it not written in the Torah thus and thus?" As though asking for information and not admonishing him; so that the father may correct himself without being put to shame.

11. A child should not hearken to his father when he tells him to transgress a precept of the Torah, whether it be a positive or a negative command, or even a Rabbinical injunction. For, it is written (Leviticus 19:3): "Ye shall fear every man his mother and his father, and ye shall keep My Sabbaths: I am the Lord your God." The keeping of the Sabbath is mentioned in juxtaposition with the fear of father and mother, to mean: "Although I commanded you to fear your father and mother, yet if they tell you to violate the Sabbath, you must not listen to them, and so it is true concerning other precepts, for I am the Lord your God, and both you and your parents are equally bound to honor Me, therefore, you must not hearken to them to disregard My word." Also, Rabbinical injunctions are the commands of the Almighty, blessed be His name, for it is written (Deuteronomy 17:11): "Thou shalt not turn aside," etc. Thus, if a child is told by his father, not to speak to or forgive a certain person with whom the child wishes to be reconciled, he should disregard his father's behest, for it is forbidden to hate any Jew, un-

less he sees him commit a sin. Thus, the father tells the child to transgress a command of the Torah.

12. If the son desires to go to some place to study the Torah, because there he will accomplish more than in his own town, but the father does not consent to it for some reason, he is not bound to listen to him, for the study of the Torah is greater than the precept of honoring father and mother. (As we find it in the case of our ancestor Jacob, peace be unto him, that when he went away from Isaac, he retreated into the school of Eber for fourteen years, where he had engaged himself in the study of the Torah. Thereafter, he went to the house of Laban and, including the time it took him to cover the journey, he stayed away for twenty-two years. For these twenty-two years, during which he did not fulfill the precept of honoring his father, he was punished, and Joseph was concealed from him for twenty-two years; but for the fourteen years that he had spent in studying the Torah, he was not punished). If the son desires to marry, and the father does not consent to it, the son is likewise not bound to obey him.

13. It is the duty of both men and women to honor their parents. However, a married woman, who owes devotion to her husband, is exempt from the precept of honoring her parents. Yet, she is obliged to do for the parents, all she can, if her husband does not object.

14. Whoever puts his father or mother to shame, even by mere words or by a gesture, is included among those whom the Almighty has cursed, as it is written (Deuteronomy 27:16): "Cursed be he that dishonoreth his father or his mother."

15. If the father or the mother has a splinter, the son is not allowed to remove it, lest he cause a wound thereby (which act is subject to the capital punishment of strangulation). If the son is a physician, he is not allowed to bleed his parents or perform an operation on them, although he intends to cure them therewith. The above is true only when there is another physician to do it; but if no other one is available, he may bleed them and cut as much as is necessary for purposes of healing.

16. If one's father or mother becomes demented, the son should endeavor to act with them in accordance with their mental condition, until the Lord will have mercy on them. However, if the son can no longer bear it because of their aggravated condition, he may leave them and delegate others to take care of them.

17. A man is forbidden to place a burdensome yoke upon his children; he must not be too exacting in demanding honor from them, so that he may not cause them to stumble into sin. He should rather overlook their shortcomings and forgive them; for if a father allows his son to disregard an act of reverence, the son may avail himself of the permission.

18. One is forbidden to beat his grownup son. The word "grownup" in this regard, refers not to age but to his maturity. If there is reason to believe that the son will rebel, and express that resentment by word or deed,

even though he has not yet reached the age of *Bar Mitzvah,* it is forbidden to beat him. Instead, he should reason with him. Anyone who beats his grownup children is to be excommunicated, because he transgresses the Divine Command (Leviticus 19:14): "Thou shalt not put a stumbling block before the blind" (for they are apt to bring sin and punishment upon their children).

19. A man must respect his step-mother during his father's lifetime, and his step-father during his mother's lifetime. And it is proper that one should honor his step-mother or his step-father, even after the death of one's own parents.

20. A person must honor his elder brother, whether of only the same father or the same mother. He must also honor his father-in-law and his mother-in-law (as we find it about King David, peace be unto him, who honored King Saul, who was his father-in-law, by calling him "my father," as it is written (I Samuel 24:12): "My father, see, yea, see" etc). He must also honor his grandparents. But the honor due parents is greater than that due grandparents.

21. He who truly wishes to honor his father and his mother, should devote himself to the study of the Torah and to the performance of good deeds, for this is the greatest honor to his parents, because people will say: "Happy are the parents who brought up such a child." But a son who does not walk in the right path, brings reproach to his parents and disgraces them in the most ignominious manner. Likewise, a father who is concerned about the welfare of his children, should engage in the study of the Torah and the practice of good deeds, so that he may please God and men and thus cause his children to be proud of him. But he who does not walk in the straight path disgraces his children. Also, children die for the sins of their fathers, as it is written (Exodus 20:5): "Visiting the iniquity of the fathers upon the children." There is no greater cruelty than causing the death of one's own children on account of one's sins. And none is more compassionate to his children than the righteous man, for his merit holds good for a thousand generations.

22. A convert to Judaism must not curse or despise his non-Jewish father; they should not say: "We came from a holiness (religion) that is grave to a holiness which is trifling." But he should treat him with some degree of respect.

CHAPTER 144

Honor Due the Teacher, the Scholar, the Aged, and the Priest

1. A person must fear and revere his teacher more than his father, because his father has given life in this world, while his teacher prepares him for life in the world to come.

2. It is written (Leviticus 19:32): "Thou shalt rise up before the hoary head, and honor the face of the old man." By the expression 'Old man,' is meant a man versed in the Law of God, as it is written (Numbers 11:16): "Gather unto Me seventy of the elders of Israel," and there, surely, the choice was made on the basis of wisdom, not upon age, as it is written: "Whom thou knowest to be the elders of the people and its officers." Therefore, it is mandatory to reverence and honor a man learned in the Torah even if he is not advanced in years and even if he is not our teacher. It is also mandatory to respect and honor a person of seventy years or over, even if he is unlearned, provided he is not an evildoer. Even an old heathen should be shown respect by kind words and by being given a helping hand.

3. When three walk together and one of them is a rabbi, the latter is to walk in the center, while the other two should fall back and walk on his side, the older one on his right, and the younger one on his left.

4. It is a grave sin to disrespect or to hate men learned in the Torah. Jerusalem was destroyed only after they began to despise the scholars, as it is written (II Chronicles 36:16): "But they mocked the messengers of God, and despised His words, and scoffed at His prophets," that is, they despised those who teach His word. This is also what the Torah said (Leviticus 26:15): "And if ye will despise My statutes," that is, "if you despise those who teach My statutes." Whoever despises the Sages, has no share in the world to come, and he is in the category of (Numbers 15:31): "Because he hath despised the word of the Lord." It is forbidden to make servile use of a student of the Rabbinical Law.

5. If a scholar has merchandise to sell, we do not allow anyone to sell the same kind of merchandise until the scholar has sold his. This is only true where there are no gentile merchants who sell this kind of merchandise. But if there are gentile merchants who sell the same kind of merchandise, then the scholar has no benefit by restraining the Jews from selling it and thereby cause people to sustain a loss in vain.

6. One who is known to be a scholar in his generation, that is, he is competent to discuss topics of the Torah, and comprehends most of the places in the Talmud and the codes of law, and study is his main occupation, even if he has some profession or business from which he earns just enough to support his family but not to amass wealth from it, and whenever he is at leisure, he studies the Torah, such a man is, according to law, exempt from all kinds of taxations and assessments, even though he is rich. Even the personal tax which every individual is bound to pay, should be paid for him by his townsmen. And it is up to the discretion of the leaders of the town.

7. A scholar who slights the Divine Commands and is not God-fearing, is to be treated like the most worthless man in the community.

8. If a Kohen and an Israelite are equally learned, it is a Biblical or-

dinance to give precedence to the *Kohen*, for it is written (Leviticus 21-8): "And thou shalt sanctify him," and our Rabbis, of blessed memory, explained it to mean that in every matter of sanctity or importance, he shall be treated with honor, that is, he shall be called first to the reading of the Torah; he shall be the first speaker at every public gathering; at the house of learning, too, he shall be the first speaker; at a meal he shall be the first to say the the benediction *Hamotzi*, and lead in the saying of Grace after meals. Likewise, he shall be given the first choice portion, unless there is an Israelite more learned than he, then the latter is served first. However, if the *Kohen* has some partnership with an Israelite, the latter need not give him the choice portion, as it is not honorable for him to take such a portion, for he who covets a choice portion, will never see even a sign of blessing. In a place where there is no *Kohen* present, it is well to give precedence to a *Levi* over an Israelite, if they are of equal learning.

9. Even nowadays, it is forbidden to make servile use of a *Kohen*, as it is like committing sacrilege against a sacred object, for it is written (Leviticus 21:8): "And thou shalt sanctify him; for the bread of thy God doth he offer." Even nowadays that we have no sacrifices, the *Kohen* still retains the same sanctity. If the *Kohen* wishes to forego the honor due him, he may do so, for the Priesthood is his privilege and he has a right to relinquish its prerogatives and permit an Israelite to have them. Especially may the *Kohen* bestow honor upon an Israelite, by giving him precedence in all matters mentioned above.

CHAPTER 145

Laws Concerning Marriage

1. It is the duty of every man to take a wife to himself, in order to fulfill the precept of propagation. This precept becomes obligatory on a man as soon as he reaches the age of eighteen. At any rate, no man should pass his twentieth year without taking a wife. Only in the event when one is deeply engrossed in the study of the Torah, and he is afraid that marriage might interfere with his studies, may he delay marrying, providing he is not lustful.

2. As soon as a man has begotten a son and a daughter, he has fulfilled the precept of propagation, provided the son is not ungenerative and the daughter is not sterile. If a son and a daughter have been born to a man, and they died, then if they left children surviving them, his duty of propagation is fulfilled. This, however, is true only when the grandchildren are male and female and were born to both the deceased son and daughter, even if a daughter was born to the deceased son, and a son to the deceased daughter, as long as they have descended from both his son and daughter, his obligation has been fulfilled. If, however, one of the children has left no offspring, although the other child left many sons and daughters, his obligation of complying with the precept of propagation has not yet been fulfilled.

3. Even if a person has fulfilled the precept of propagation, he should not remain without a wife, and if possible, he should take one, capable of conception. However, if he is aware that he is ungenerative, it is best for

him to take a wife who is incapable of conception. If a person has many children, and he is afraid to marry a fertile woman, lest quarrels and dissentions may arise between his children and the woman, he is allowed to marry a sterile woman. But he must not stay without a wife because of such apprehension.

4. If one is married to a woman ten years, and she has given no birth to a child, he must divorce her. Concerning this practice, there are many divergent laws.

5. A woman is not enjoined to fulfill the precept of propagation; nevertheless, she should not remain unmarried, lest she become subject to suspicion.

6. Every man should endeavor to marry a respectable woman from a respectable family. "By three traits is Israel distinguished; by modesty, compassion and benevolence" (Yebamot 79a), and one should not marry a person who lacks these traits.

7. If a woman is respectable, it is permissible to marry her even if the choice is decided by a monetary consideration. This is permissible only when the money is given to the groom voluntarily, but if the man defers marriage in the expectation of obtaining a wife who will bring him the money he desires, or if one has plighted his troth in consideration of a promise to receive money, and because that promise was subsequently retracted, he causes his bride to languish, or he quarrels on account of that money—all who act thus, are designated by the Sages as (Kiddushin 70a): "He who weds for money will have delinquent children, and will be unsuccessful;" nor will such an alliance be a happy one. For the money a man takes upon marrying is not money properly earned; but whatever his father-in-law or his mother-in-law gives him he shall accept gracefully, and then he will prosper.

8. An unlearned man should not wed the daughter of a *Kohen*, because such a union will be unsuccessful. A scrupulous person should not wed a woman whose name is the same as that of his mother.

9. It is a meritorious act for one to marry the daughter of one's sister or one's brother; but one should not marry without consulting an authority, any other relative, whether she is related to himself or to his deceased or divorced wife, or if she is related to the woman to whom he has given *ḥalitzah* (Deuteronomy 25:5-10).

10. A man should ever be careful to treat his wife with respect, for it is only for the wife's sake that a man's house is blessed; and thus did our Sages say to the men of their time (Baba Metzia 59a): "Treat your wives with honor, in order that you may be blessed with wealth."

11. One is forbidden to dwell with one's wife, even a short time, without having a *ketubah* (nuptial agreement). If the *ketubah* has been lost, the husband should go immediately to the Rabbinate and have another *ketubah* written for her.

12. A *Kohen* is forbidden to wed a divorcée, a harlot, a *ḥalalah,* and the one to whom *ḥalitzah* has been given. Even a woman who has been forced to have illicit intercourse is termed a *harlot* in this regard, and a *Kohen* may not marry her. A *ḥalalah* is a woman who has been born to a *Kohen* by a woman whom he was forbidden to marry.

13. A woman who has been either widowed or divorced should not remarry before the expiration of ninety days, exclusive of the day of the divorce or of the death of her husband, and exclusive of the day of her contemplated marriage. Even if she is a woman incapable of conception, or even if her first husband was overseas or he was incarcerated in prison, it is all immaterial; even if she suffered a miscarriage in the meantime, it is of no avail. She is forbidden even to enter into marriage negotiations, unless the intended husband takes a solemn oath that he will not enter her home during the forbidden time. But he who remarries his divorced wife, need not wait such a period of time.

14. If the above-mentioned woman is pregnant or she is nursing an infant, she must not marry before the infant reaches the age of twenty-four months. Even if she has given birth after she was divorced or after she became a widow and she has not commenced to nurse the infant, she, must nevertheless wait. If there is a very important matter involved in it, she should consult a rabbi.

15. A woman whose two former husbands have died, should not marry a third one without consulting a rabbi.

16. If a woman heard that her husband died somewhere, even if she heard it from many trustworthy men, she should not remarry without consulting a rabbi.

17. If a man is suspected of committing adultery with a married woman and her husband either divorced her or he died, he is not allowed to marry her, for just as she is forbidden to her husband, even so is she forbidden to her paramour. Even if her husband has divorced her because he had heard of her improper conduct with that man, such suspected person is forbidden to marry her.

18. One who is suspected of having intercourse with a non-Jewess and thereafter she was converted to Judaism, he is not permitted to marry her.

19. A non-Jew who has intercourse with a Jewess, and thereafter he was converted to Judaism, is not allowed to marry her.

20. If one divorces his wife so that she could marry someone else, although he has not expressly made such a condition with her, but it is obvious that he had divorced her for that reason, that other man is forbidden to marry her.

21. One must not even live in the same alley with any of those women, whom the Rabbis, of blessed memory, have forbidden one to marry.

22. If a man hears a rumor that his wife has committed adultery, although he is not certain about it, he must consult an authority, whether or not he may live with her.

23. A respectable man should not marry a woman who has been divorced because of immodesty.

24. It is mandatory to divorce a bad woman who is of a quarrelsome disposition and is not as modest as a respectable woman in Israel should be, even if it is the first marriage.

25. The Sages have ordained, that a man should give his sons and daughters in marriage, immediately upon their reaching maturity, for, if he neglects them, they are apt to commit adultery, or entertain prurient thoughts. Concerning this, it is written (Job 5:24): "And thou shalt visit thy habitation and shalt not sin." The Sages have likewise commanded the children of Israel, that whoever sees his wife conduct herself in an improper manner and that she is consorting with other men, he should admonish her privately and gently to prevent her from stumbling into sin and cause her to walk in the right path. He should not tell her expressly, even privately: "Do not make secret appointments with this or that man" (for since nowadays we have no "water test" for suspected women (Numbers 5:12-31), such matters cause great confusion). He who is not strict about his wife and his children to admonish them and supervise their conduct to be sure that they are perfect and free of sin and iniquity, is called a sinner. For it is written (Job 5:24): "And thou shalt know that peace be in thy tent, and thou shalt visit thy habitation and not sin."

26. It is forbidden to perform the marriage ceremony for two brothers or two sisters on one and the same day, because one festive event should not be joined with another. Some authorities hold that it is even forbidden to do so in one week, and they infer it from Jacob our ancestor, for it is written (Genesis 29:27): "Fulfill the week of this one."

Chapter 146

The Fast of the Bridegroom and Bride

1. It is customary for the groom and bride to fast on their wedding day, because their sins are atoned on that day, and in the *Shemoneh esreh* of the *Minḥah* service, they include *Anenu* (answer us), as on any other fast day. The prevailing custom in our regions is for the bride and the groom to fast only until after the nuptial ceremony. If the ceremony is delayed until nighttime, they may have some food immediately upon the appearance of the stars, providing they do not drink any intoxicating beverages.

2. They do not fast on the following days: On *Rosh Ḥodesh,* on the day following *Shavuot,* on the fifteenth day of the month of *Av,* on the fifteenth day of the month of *Shevat,* on *Ḥanukkah,* and on *Shushan Purim* (chapter 142:9, above). They fast during the month of *Nisan,* even on the New Moon of this month, on the thirty-third day of counting the *Omer* (chapter 120:6, above), on the days that intervene between the New Moon of the month of *Sivan* and *Shavuot,* and between *Yom Kippur* and *Sukkot.*

3. On the days the groom and the bride do not fast, they must be careful not to indulge too freely in eating and drinking, and needless to say that they must abstain from intoxicating beverages (for, according to some authorities, the real reason for their fasting on this particular day, is because of the possibility that they might become intoxicated and their minds would not be lucid).

4. Before the *ḥupah* ceremony (see chapter that follows), the groom and the bride shall sanctify themselves, by repenting of their sins, by searching into all their deeds from the day of their birth until this very day, by making confession of their sins, and by beseeching the Almighty, blessed be He, that He grant them pardon, forgiveness, and atonement. They should forsake their evil deeds with a contrite heart. They should firmly resolve to devote themselves thenceforth to worship God truly and sincerely, and to be pure and holy. And when they are under the nuptial canopy they shall pray that the Holy One, blessed be He, may cause His Divine Presence to rest between them, as our Rabbis, of blessed memory, said (Sotah 17a): "If deserving, the Divine Presence rests between husband and wife." It is customary for the groom and the bride to say *Al ḥet* (confession) at the *Minḥah* service, as it is done on the day before *Yom Kippur*.

Chapter 147

The Nuptial Ceremony

1. It is customary to make the *ḥupah* under the open sky as an augury of bliss, for it is written (Exodus 15:5): "Thus (like the stars) shall your children be." It is likewise customary to make the wedding at full moon, as an auspicious augury.

2. It is proper not to make the wedding before the bride purifies herself; but now the prevailing custom is to disregard it. Nevertheless, it is well to inform the groom before the ceremony that she is menstrually unclean.

3. It is the custom in our regions, that at the marriage of a virgin, the important personages of the community place a veil on the head of the bride, saying (Genesis 24:60): "Our sister, be thou a mother of tens of thousands." The term *Ḥupah*, is generally understood to connote the spreading of a cloth upon poles under which the groom and the bride enter, and where he consecrates her to himself, and where the betrothal and marriage benedictions are uttered. In reality, however, the most essential part of the *Ḥupah* is the *privacy*, as will be explained, the Almighty willing, in the chapter that follows.

4. The groomsmen put on a *Kittle* on the groom, so that he may think of the day of death and bestir himself to repentance. It is also customary to place some ashes on the head of the groom, at the place where the *tefillin* are placed. It is likewise customary for the parents and prominent relatives to bless the groom and the bride, and pray that their union may be successful.

5. Thereafter, the groom is led to the canopy, and is placed under it with his face toward the East, while the *ḥazan* chants whatever is customary in that community. Then the bridesmaids lead the bride, while the groomsmen, together with the prominent men, walk toward the bride, and as they approach her, they turn around and proceed toward the *ḥupah*. The bridesmaids bring the bride under the *ḥupah*, and together with her, they walk around the groom seven times, the *ḥazan* intoning the customary chants. Thereafter, the bride is placed to the right of the groom, and the one who pronounces the benedictions, stands on the side, facing East.

CHAPTER 148

The Privacy Following the Nuptial Ceremony

1. The most essential part of the *Ḥupah*, is what follows the rite of consecration, when the groom and the bride are led into a private room, where they eat together in privacy. It should be scrupulously obesrved that no one enters the room, in order that there may be absolute privacy. This consummates the rite which validates the marriage.

2. In the case of a virgin, this privacy completes the marriage, even if it cannot be supplemented by cohabitation, that is, if she is menstrually unclean, or if there are people walking in and out of the room. When she is menstrually unclean, it is imperative to have people walk in and out of the room, for otherwise they are not allowed to have privacy before the first cohabitation.

3. In the case of a widow, the only privacy that validates the marriage is one that is suitable for consummation, that is, when she is clean, and no one enters the room.

4. Since no contract may be made on the Sabbath, therefore, if the wedding ceremony takes place on a Friday, care should be taken to have the ritual seclusion before the Sabbath sets in, and they may have the first intercourse on the Sabbath, whether the bride is a virgin or a widow. But if the ritual seclusion does not take place before sunset, they are forbidden to have the first intercourse on the Sabbath, for this constitutes the consummation of a contract, and no contract can be concluded on the Sabbath. (For the law regarding the cohabitation of a virgin, see chapter 157, below).

CHAPTER 149

Grace at Weddings and Entertaining the Groom and the Bride

1. Before saying Grace after meals in the company of ten male adults, the one leading in reciting the Grace should say: *Dvai ḥoser* (banish, O Lord, grief), etc., also *Shehasimeḥah bimeono* (in whose abode is joy) is said. It is proper to say, *Sheaḥalnu mishelo* (of whose bounty we have partaken), without a *vav* (a conjunction, meaning *and*); not, *Vesheaḥalnu mishelo* (and of, etc.). Concluding the Grace, the leader takes a second glass (of wine, or some other beverage), over which he pronounces six benedictions; thereafter, over the

glass with which he has said Grace, he says the benediction, *Bore peri haggafen* (who hath created the fruit of the vine). It is best not to fill the glass for the six benedictions before the Grace is concluded. Care must be taken that no men and women should eat in the same room, because if men and women eat in the same room, *Shehasimeḥah bimeono* cannot be said, because there is no joy where the Evil Impulse reigns.

2. If a young man (who has never been married before) weds a virgin, or a widow, or if a widower weds a virgin, the Grace should be recited, as mentioned in the preceding section, after partaking of the first meal following the wedding, even if it is not eaten on the day of the wedding, but at the night following the day of the wedding, or even on the following day (for the first meal is considered in law as if new guests have come to participate). But after the first meal, and also during the entire wedding week, only if new guests come to participate, the Grace should be thus recited.

3. If there are no new guests, then, if the men who dine with the groom are not members of his family but strangers, who came to celebrate as friends, we do not recite *Dvai ḥoser*, but we do say *Nodeh leshimeḥa* (we shall give thanks to Thy name) and *Shehasimeḥa bimeono* (in whose abode is joy). After Grace, he takes a second glass, and pronounces the benediction *Asher bara* (who has created). Then he takes the glass used for Grace and recites *Bore peri haggafen*. For this, the presence of ten male adults is not required; three being sufficient. But if the groom dines only with his own family, none of the above should be said.

4. In the case of a widower marrying a widow, if the first meal is eaten on the wedding day, even if it lasted till night, Grace should be said as provided for in section 1, above; but if the meal has not been eaten before the night, then if there are some men present who partake as friends, Grace should be said as is provided for in section 3, above (even if there are new guests); this likewise is true of all meals partaken of during the first three days.

5. By "new guests" is meant, when a person has just arrived to participate in the celebration, even if he does not eat with them, but they wish to prepare extra victuals for his sake. Sabbaths and the first days of festivals are regarded as new guests. This applies only to the first and second meals (to be eaten on the Sabbath), but not to the third meal, unless the groom delivers a discourse (on some learned topic of the Law).

6. If one invites the groom and the bride to feast at one's house, then, if a private room is assigned for them, where they can enjoy each other's company undisturbed, it is considered as a part of their wedding celebration, and the seven benedictions should be pronounced; otherwise, not even the benedictions *Asher bara* (who hath created) and *Shehasimeḥah bimeono* (in whose abode is joy) should be said.

7. If the wedding guests have separated into several groups after the wedding ceremony, even if they feast in houses the doors of which are not open toward the place where the groom is, nevertheless, each group must pronounce these benedictions, inasmuch as they have partaken of the feast prepared for the wedding. But the waiters who eat after the feast is over, need not pronounce these benedictions.

8. At the wedding of one who remarries his divorced wife, *Shehasimeḥah bimeono* should be omitted, and the seven benedictions should be said only at the first meal that takes place on the wedding day, but henceforth, none of the benedictions should be said.

9. It is a meritorious act to amuse the groom and bride, to dance before the bride and say that she is: *Kallah naeh vaḥasudah* (a beautiful and gracious bride); and we find in the Talmud that Rabbi Judah bar Illai used to dance before brides (Ketuvot 17a).

10. It is forbidden to look at a bride's face, but it is permissible to look at her ornaments and her uncovered head.

11. If the bride is menstrually unclean at her wedding, it is customary among some people, on the night of her ritual immersion, to make a feast to which guests are invited. This is an improper custom and should be abolished, because it is a breach of modesty. However, a small feast for the household should not be frowned at, and *Shehasimeḥah bimeono* (in whose abode is joy) is said in the Grace after meals. But it is forbidden to say the seven benedictions, except in the manner heretofore provided.

12. One who weds a virgin must rejoice with her seven days, which are called "The seven days of the feast." During these days, the groom should do no work or engage in buying and selling in the market place; but he should eat and drink and rejoice with her, whether he was a bachelor or a widower. Even if she waives her right, he is forbidden to do work. The groom, during the seven days, should not walk out alone in the street. However, if a widower marries a woman that has been married before, all authorities agree that only three days of rejoicing is sufficient. But if the groom had never been married before, some authorities hold that he must rejoice with the bride seven days, since the seven benedictions are pronounced for his sake only. Nevertheless, in this particular instance, the woman may waive her right to being rejoiced.

13. One who takes a wife to himself, must remain in town a full year, in order that he may rejoice with her; for it is written (Deuteronomy 24:5): "He should not go out with the army; he shall be free for his house one year, and shall cheer his wife whom he had taken." The woman may, however, waive this right.

CHAPTER 150

Laws of Chastity

1. A man should accustom himself to be in a mood of supreme holiness and to have pure thoughts, when having intercourse. He should not indulge in levity with his wife, nor defile his mouth with indecent jests, even in private

conversation with her. For the Scriptures say (Amos 3:13): "And declare unto man what is his conversation," and our Rabbis, of blessed memory, said (Ḥagigah 5b): "On the day of judgment, man is reminded even of the light conversations he had with his wife in privacy." He should not converse with her either at copulation or immediately before it, excepting about matter directly needed for the act. However, if he is angry with her, when it is improper for a man to have intercourse with his wife, he may speak kind words to her, in order to appease her. The intercourse should be in the most possible modest manner. He underneath and she above him, is considered an impudent act; both at the same level, is considered a pervert act. It is told of Rabbi Eliezer (Nedarim 20b), that he used to have cohabitation with such awe and terror that it appeared as if a demon was forcing him to do it.

2. When having intercourse, one should think of some subjects of the Torah, or of some other sacred subjects; and although it is forbidden during this act to utter holy words, yet thinking is permissible, even meritorious. Although in filthy alleys it is even forbidden to think of holy subjects, this is because we must abide by the Divine Command (Deuteronomy 23:15): "Therefore, shall thy camp be holy;" but where the prohibition is based on *Ervah* (unseemliness; nakedness of body), concerning which it is written (loco citato) *Ervat davar* (unseemly thing), our Rabbis, inferred from this that only speech is forbidden (because *davar* in Hebrew means also "word"), but thinking is permissible.

3. It is forbidden to have intercourse by a light, even if the light is shut out by means of a garment; but it is permissible if one makes a partition, ten hand-breadths (forty inches) high in front of the light. It is also forbidden to have intercourse during the day, unless the room is darkened. At night, if the moon shines directly upon them, it is forbidden, but if it does not shine directly upon them it is permissible if that light is shut out by a garment. If there is a lamp in another room and it throws light into this room, this light, too, must be shut out by means of a garment.

4. It is forbidden to have intercourse in the presence of any person who is awake, even if there is a partition ten hand-breadths high between them. It is permitted, however, in the presence of a child who is unable to talk.

5. One is forbidden to look at the genital organ of his wife. Whoever looks at it is devoid of shame, and violates (Micah 6:8): "And walk humbly," (which also means "in modesty"). For the one who is prudent is not apt to sin, as it is written (Exodus 20:17): "And for the sake that His fear may be before you (and this means, being bashful), so that you sin not." Also, by this he stimulates lewd thoughts within himself. Certainly, one who kisses that place violates all this, and in addition he violates (Leviticus 11:43): "Ye shall not make yourselves detestable."

6. It is forbidden to have intercourse in a room where a *sefer torah* is found, but it must be removed into a different room. If there is no other room, he must make a partition, ten hand-breadths high in front of it; this

partition must be opaque, so that the *sefer torah* should not be seen through it; the curtain around the bed is not considered a partition, since it is loose, unless it is tied at the bottom. *Tefillin*, Bibles, or other sacred writings, such as the Talmud, Midrash and their commentaries, whether they are written or printed, must be placed in a vessel within a vessel. The second vessel is valid only when it is not especially designed for such holy works; but if the vessels are especially designed for such a purpose, be they even ten in number, they are considered as only one. If a cover is spread on a chest where these books are kept, it is considered like a vessel within a vessel. If a *mezuzah* is affixed on the inside of the room, it must be covered with two coverings, in order that it may be considered as a vessel within a vessel. The Name (*Shaddai*) should also be covered; the glass covering is of no avail, since the covering must not be transparent.

7. A person must not be unduly familiar with his wife, excepting at the regular time appointed for the performance of his marital duty, as it is written (Exodus 21:10): "And her conjugal rights, shall he not diminish." Men of a strong constitution who enjoy the pleasures of life, having profitable pursuits at home and are tax exempt, should perform their marital duty nightly. Laborers who work in the town where they reside, should perform their marital duty twice weekly; but if they are employed in another town, only once a week. Merchants who travel into villages with their mules, to buy grain to be sold in town, and others like them, should perform their marital duty once a week. Men who convey freight on camels from distant places, should attend to their marital duty once in thirty days. The time appointed for learned men is from Sabbath-eve to Sabbath-eve. One must fulfill his marital duty even when his wife is pregnant or nursing. One must not deprive his wife of her conjugal rights, unless she consents to it, and when he has already fulfilled the obligation of propagation. If he deprives his wife thereof, in order to afflict her, he violates the Divine Command: "And her conjugal rights shall he not diminish."

8. It is the duty of every husband to visit his wife on the night she has performed the ritual of immersion, also on the night before he is to set out on a journey, unless he goes out on a sacred mission. When a man sees that his wife is coquetting and primping and trying to please him, he is bound to visit her even if it is not the appointed time, and from such a union will come worthy children. However, if she demands it openly, she is a brazen woman, and is considered like a harlot, with whom he must not live together.

9. When having intercourse, his intention should be not to satisfy his personal desire, but to fulfill his obligation to perform his marital duty, like one paying a debt, and to comply with the command of his Creator and that he may have children engaged in the study of the Torah and the practice of its precepts. It is also proper to think of improving the embryo; for our Rabbis, of blessed memory, said (Niddah 31a): "The first three months (of pregnancy), cohabitation is hard on the woman and hard on the child; during the three middle months, it is hard on the woman and good for the child, and during the last three months, it is good for the woman and good for the child,

for it will cause the child at his birth to be born clean and agile." If he is overwhelmed by a craving for it and he cohabits with his wife to avert sinful lust, he is likewise destined to receive reward for it. But it is better to conquer his passion. For, as the Sages say (Sukkot 52b): "A man has a small organ, if he starves it, it is contented, and if he pampers it, it is hungry." But one who has no need for it, and he deliberately arouses his lust, is following the counsel of the Evil Impulse.

10. If possible, a man should be careful not to have cohabitation either at the beginning or at the end of the night, but in the middle. One should not touch his membrum even for the sake of cohabitation, before washing his hands properly, that is, three times alternately, as provided in chapter 2, above.

11. It is forbidden to have cohabitation in market places, in streets, in gardens, or in orchards; it is permitted in dwellings only, so that it may not resemble fornication.

12. If there is a famine in the land, God forbid, that is, grain has advanced to double its price, although one has plenty of grain in his house, or if there is, God forbid, some other calamity in the land, one is forbidden to have intercourse, unless it be on the night of his wife's immersion. But those who are childless, may cohabit at any time.

13. One should not have intercourse with his wife unless she has a desire for it, but not otherwise, and certainly one is forbidden to force her. Nor should one have intercourse with his wife if he hates her, or if she hates him, and she tells him that she does not want his attention, although she does consent to having cohabitation. If he has determined to divorce her, and she is not aware of it, he is not allowed to cohabit with her even though he does not hate her. Nor should one be with his wife when she is actually asleep, nor while he or she is intoxicated.

14. Guests are forbidden to have intercourse, unless a separate apartment was assigned for them. They must not, however, sleep on the sheets belonging to the host.

15. According to the rules of hygiene, one should not have intercourse while being satiated or while hungry, but when his food has been digested. One should not have intercourse while standing, or in a sitting posture, or on the day he had a bath, or had cupping, or on the day he is going on a journey or coming from a journey if he travels on foot; it is forbidden either before the above or thereafter.

16. One should not cohabit in a bed where an infant less than one year old lies at their feet; nor should one have intercourse within one hour after leaving the privy. A nursing woman should not cohabit, except when the

infant is asleep, and she should not nurse the infant after having intercourse before the lapse of two-thirds of an hour, unless the infant is crying.

17. Semen is the vitality of man's body and the light of his eyes, and when it issues in abundance, the body weakens and life is shortened. He who indulges in having intercourse, ages quickly, his strength ebbs, his eyes grow dim, his breath becomes foul, the hair of his head, eyelashes and brows fall out, the hair of his beard, armpits and feet increase, his teeth fall out, and many other aches besides these befall him. Great physicians said that one out of a thousand dies from other diseases, while nine hundred and ninety-nine die from sexual indulgence. Therefore, a man should exercise self-restraint.

CHAPTER 151

The Sin of Discharging Semen in Vain

1. It is forbidden to discharge semen in vain. This is a graver sin than any other mentioned in the Torah. Those who practice masturbation and cause the issue of semen in vain, not only do they commit a grave sin, but they are under a ban, concerning whom it is said (Isaiah 1:15): "Your hands are full of blood;" and it is equivalent to killing a person. See what Rashi wrote concerning Er and Onan in the *Sidrah* of *Vayeshev* (Genesis 37), that both Er and Onan died for the commission of this sin. Occasionally, as a punishment for this sin, children die when young, God forbid, or grow up to be delinquent, while the sinner himself is reduced to poverty.

2. One is forbidden to bring on erection or to think about women. If a lascivious thought comes to one spontaneously, he should divert his attention to a subject of the Torah, which is "A lovely hind and a graceful doe." Lewd thoughts prevail only in a mind devoid of wisdom. A man should be extremely careful to avoid an erection. Therefore, he should not sleep on his back with his face upward, or on his belly with his face downward, but sleep on his side, in order to avoid it. Two bachelors should not sleep together. One should not watch when animals, beasts or fowl copulate. It is also forbidden to ride on an animal without a saddle.

3. It is forbidden to hold the membrum while urinating. If one is married and his wife is in town and she is clean, it does not matter, for since he has the possibility, he will not indulge in lustful thoughts or become stimu-

lated; but it is, nevertheless, a matter of piety to avoid it. When not for the purpose of urinating, the above is forbidden by law.

4. At supper, one should neither eat nor drink excessively, nor eat any food that tends to heat the body, such as fat meats, cheese, eggs, or garlic. Neither should one drink a beverage that tends to heat the body, for all these things cause the commission of this sin.

5. Whoever has had a pollution at night, God forbid, shall, upon waking up in the morning, wash his hands, and say with a contrite heart: "Master of the universe: I have done this unwittingly, but it has been caused due to evil musings and reflections. May it be, therefore, Thy will, O my God, and the God of my fathers, that Thou, in Thy great mercy, erase this iniquity of mine, and save me from sinful thoughts, forever and ever. *Amen!* So may it be Thy will."

6. One who desires to avoid this sin, should guard his mouth against obscene talk, lies, talebearing, slander, and mockery. He should likewise guard his ears against listening to such talks. One should also be careful to fulfill his vows, not worry too much, and guard himself against lewd thoughts. Before retiring, he should engage in the study of the Torah, or he should recite the first four chapters of the Psalms, and he should not sleep alone in a room.

7. Means of salvation for one who has succumbed to this sin, are recorded in the book *Yesod Yoseph,* which the author culled from holy and ancient books. I will only cite some of them briefly: He should make an endeavor to be *Sandek,* that is, to have infants circumcised on his lap; especially should he try to be *Sandek* at poor families. He should increase his donations to charity, observe the Sabbath properly, honor it, and light many candles. He should honor and love students of the Torah, pray with fervor and tears, cultivate humility, and when insulted, he should be quiet and forgiving. When performing a precept, he should do it energetically and speedily, until it warms him, particularly when preparing the *matzot* for Passover. He should raise his children in the study of the Torah and train them to be God-fearing; raise an orphan in his house and treat him as he treats his own children, and engage himself in the noble act of dowering poor brides. He should be called up to the reading of the Torah at least once a month, pronounce the benedictions in an audible voice, look into the Torah and read silently with the reader. He should be one of the first ten men who come to the synagogue, and awake in the middle of the night to perform the midnight lament for the destruction of the Temple; and if he is unable to rise at midnight, he should perform this ritual thereafter, and he should love peace and pursue peace.

Chapter 152

Prohibition Againt Being Alone With Women

1. One must not be alone with any woman, whether she is young or old, a Jewess or a non-Jewess, or whether she is related to him or not, with the exception of a father, who is permitted to be alone with his daughter, a mother with her son, and a husband with his wife, even if she is menstrually unclean. (Concerning a bride who is menstrually unclean, see chapter 157, below).

2. If one is accompanied by his wife, he may also be alone with another woman, because his wife watches him. However, a Jewess must not be alone with a non-Jew, even if his wife is present; even if there are many non-Jews with their wives, she must not be alone with them.

3. One woman may be alone with two virtuous men, but only in a town and in the daytime; but in the field or at night even in a town, there must be at least three virtuous men. A woman should never be alone with immoral men, even if they are many, unless their wives are with them. One man should not be alone with two women. Some authorities permit one man to be alone with three or more women, providing his vocation or trade is not designed to deal with women; while other authorities forbid it in any event.

4. One need have no scruples to be alone with a woman whose husband is in town, because she is in fear of her husband.

5. One is allowed to be alone with a woman in a room the door of which opens into a public thoroughfare, during the day or in the early part of the evening, as long as there are people passing by. However, a woman should not be alone with an intimate friend, like one with whom she has been raised together, or a relative, or with one concerning whom her husband warned her against being alone in his company; with any of these she may not be alone, even if her husband is in town, and even in a room the door of which opens into a public thoroughfare.

6. A man is allowed to be alone with a female child less than three years old. A woman may be alone with a lad less than nine years old.

7. One who has no wife must not teach children, because their mothers generally visit the school, and thus he will sometimes be alone with them. If he is married, his wife need not live together with him at school; as long as she is in town, it matters not even though she lives in her house and he is at school. However, a woman must not teach children even when her husband is in town, unless he lives with her in the same house, because of the fathers who bring their children to school.

8. A man should ever avoid women; thus, he should not make gestures at them, either with his hands or with his feet, nor wink at them, nor jest with them, nor act with levity in their presence, nor gaze at their beauty. It is forbidden to scent the perfume designed for women, especially when a woman holds it in her hand or when it hangs on her. One is forbidden to look at the colored clothes of a woman with whom he is acquainted, although the clothes are not upon her, lest he come to think of her. If one encounters a woman in the street, he should not walk behind her, but he should hasten his steps, so that she is either alongside of him or behind him. One should not pass by the door of a harlot, even at a distance of four cubits. He who gazes even at the small finger of a woman in order to enjoy its sight, commits a grave sin. It is forbidden to hear the voice of a woman singer, or to gaze at a woman's hair.

9. A man must not greet a woman under any circumstances, and he is forbidden to send his regards to her even through her husband. Therefore, when one writes a letter to his friend, he must not write: "Peace to your wife." But he may inquire of her husband or of someone else about her welfare. He may also write to his friend: "Let me know how your wife is."

10. One who embraces or kisses one of his female relatives, even though he derives no pleasure from it, is violating a prohibition, with the exception of a father and his daughter, also a mother and her son, who may embrace and kiss.

11. Husband and wife are not allowed to flaunt their love for each other, like a wife patting her husband's head in the presence of others, so that the lookers-on might not come to sinful thoughts.

12. A person must not dwell in his father-in-law's house, unless he has a private sleeping room.

13. The great men of Israel, of blessed memory, have already dealt at length in their holy works, concerning the custom prevailing in some communities, where there is a lack of scholarship and piety, that they hug and kiss the groom and the bride, and the young men and women dance together. Besides the grave sin of coming in contact with a woman in her menstrual period, (because all virgins are presumed to be menstrually unclean, and it matters not in this regard whether she be a married woman or single, and whoever touches her by way of endearment is amenable to the punishment of stripes), he also stimulates lewd thoughts within himself, causing erection and the vain discharge of semen, God forbid. Surely he who is able to prevent it should make every endeavor to do so. At least it is the duty of every man who is God-fearing, to have control over his household and take care that they should not do this extremely abominable thing.

Whoever is able to prevent it and fails to do so, will himself, God forbid, be accountable for this very iniquity; and by saving others from this sin, he saves himself also, and it shall be well with him.

14. It is permissible, and even desirable, to look at the woman that one wishes to marry, to see if she pleases him, but he should not regard her with lascivious eyes. Concerning this, it is written (Job 31:1): "I made a covenant with mine eyes; how then should I look upon a maid?"

15. A divorced woman is not allowed to reside in the same courtyard where her former husband resides. If her former husband is a *Kohen*, or even if he is an Israelite, but she has married another man, from whom also she has been divorced, or if she has been divorced because she was forbidden to him—all of these are required to keep at a great distance from each other. She is not allowed to live with him in the same alley if it has a dead end, but if it is an open alley through which there is traffic, they are permitted to live there. A divorced woman who remarried and lives with her second husband, should keep at a still greater distance from her first husband, and she should not reside in the entire vicinity where he resides. In all these cases, she must move away, but if the courtyard belongs to her, he must move.

16. A person is permitted to support the woman he divorced, and it is even meritorious to support her in preference to any other poor person, for it is written (Isaiah 58:7): "And that thou hide not from thine own flesh." But he may not have any personal contact with her, but he should send her support through an agent.

17. "Said Rabbi Beruna in the name of Rav (Eruvin 63b): 'He who sleeps in a compartment in which husband and wife are, the Scripture says concerning him (Micah 2:9): "The women of My people you cast out of their pleasant houses"' (because they are ashamed to be intimate because of him). And Rabbi Joseph added: 'This applies also to a case where the woman is menstrually unclean.'"

CHAPTER 153

A Woman Who is Menstrually Unclean

1. A woman from whose womb issued a drop of blood, be it ever so small, and whether or not it is her regular period of menstruation, and even if it is the result of an accident, is considered menstrually unclean until she counts seven clean days and takes the ritual bath of immersion. Both man and woman who have sexual intercourse after the menstrual flow has begun, incur the penalty of *Karet*, excision (being cut off from their people); and the temporal punishment for caressing one another is flagellation.

2. Even if she did not feel the issue of blood from her womb, but found a stain of blood upon her body, her undergarments, her sheet, or any other place, and she cannot attribute it to any other cause than to an issue

from her womb, she is menstrually unclean. A woman who finds a stain which is neither exactly red nor exactly white, should consult a competent rabbi for an opinion, for there are many divergent laws bearing on such a case, depending on the size of the stain, also on the causes to which it may be attributed. There is also a distinction as to the time she found it, whether it was on the days she was clean or on the first days of her seven-day period (after menstruation).

3. If a woman feels that she has begun to menstruate, even if she examines herself immediately and discovers no visible proof, she is, nevertheless, considered unclean; (it is necessary to call women's attention to this, because many women are ignorant of this law). But if she discovers a white secretion from her body without an admixture of red, she is considered clean.

4. It is written (Leviticus 18:19): "And thou shalt not approach unto a woman in her menstrual uncleanliness;" because it is written "Thou shalt not *approach*," it is explained that any kind of approach is forbidden; he should not play with her or indulge in foolery, or even speak words that may lead to sin. But he may be in privacy with her, for since he had already had cohabitation with her and she is also available to him after her immersion, his lust will not gain the upper hand, and there is no fear that he would cohabit with her when forbidden.

5. The husband in that period should not touch her even with his little finger. He is not allowed to hand anything to her, be it even a long object, nor to receive anything from her. Throwing anything from his hand into her hand, or vice versa, is forbidden.

6. He is not allowed to eat with her at the same table, unless something separates between his dish and hers, some object that generally does not lie there on the table, or she should change her place. If they are always accustomed to eat out of the same plate, and now each one eats out of a separate plate, this change suffices.

7. He is not allowed to drink what she left over in her cup. But if a third person drank from the cup after her, or it has been emptied into another cup, it is permissible. If she drank out of a cup, and he, unaware of it, desires to drink out of it, she need not tell him that she had drunk out of it. (If, however, he was aware that she had drunk out of it, but he did not know that she was unclean, it would seem that she has to inform him, as I have stated in my book *Leḥem Vesimelah*). She, however, is allowed to drink of whatever he had left over in his cup. Some authorities hold, that just as he is forbidden to drink of what she leaves over in her cup, so is he forbidden to eat of the food she leaves over.

8. They are not allowed to sleep in the same bed, even if the bed is not reserved for her, and even if both have their clothes on and do not touch one another, and even if each of them has a separate mattress. It is forbidden even when they lie in separate beds, if the beds touch one another. If they lie on the ground, they may not sleep facing one another, unless there is a big distance between them. The same applies to a case where they sleep in two separate beds placed parallel to one another, from which at times they face one another; unless there is a big space between the beds. The husband is forbidden to sleep in the bed especially reserved for her, even when she is not present, and she is forbidden to sleep in his bed. But they are not forbidden to sit on each other's bed.

9. They are not allowed to sit on the same swing board, unless there is someone sitting between them. They should not ride in the same wagon or take a voyage in the same ship, if the trip is made for pleasure, like riding through parks, orchards, or the like. But if they travel from one city to another in the course of business, it is permissible even though they are by themselves, provided they do not touch one another.

10. He must not look at any part of her body which she generally keeps covered, but he may look at those parts of the body that are always uncovered, even though he derives pleasure from it. He is not permitted to scent her perfume, and to hear her sing.

11. It is proper for her to wear special clothes during the days of her impurity, so that both of them may remember that she is menstrually unclean. After many scruples and objections, permission has been granted her to powder, paint, and adorn herself with colored clothes, during her menstrual period, so that she may not become repulsive to her husband.

12. She is not permitted to pour a cup of wine for her husband in his presence, nor to bring it and set it before him upon the table, nor make his bed in his presence. All these things, however, are permissible in his abscence, even if he knows that she had done it. She is forbidden to pour water for him to wash his face and hands, and bathe his feet, even if the water is cold.

13. Just as she is forbidden to fill the cup for him, so is he forbidden to fill the cup for her. Furthermore, he is even forbidden to send her a cup of wine, if the cup was especially reserved for her, be it even a cup over which a benediction has been pronounced.

14. If her husband is sick and there is none beside her to attend to him, she may do so. However, she must be careful not to come in direct contact with his body, only by means of some object. She may even raise him up, lay him down, and support him. But she should be very careful not to wash his face and hands, or bathe his feet, or make his bed in his presence. If the

woman is sick, the husband is forbidden to attend to her even without touching her, except in a case of extreme emergency, when it is impossible to obtain someone else to attend to her. If the husband is a physician and there is no other physician as competent as he is, he may feel her pulse, inasmuch as he does not do it out of lust or love.

15. All of the foregoing laws pertaining to abstinence from acts of intimacy, also apply to the seven "white days," that is, the seven days of purification after the flow has ceased, and even thereafter if she delays her immersion.

16. It is customary for a woman during her menstruation period before the white days, not to enter the synagogue and not to pray. But on the days of awe, that is, from the first day the *Seliḥot* are said (see chapter 127:5 above), and henceforth, when great multitudes assemble at the synagogue, and she will be greatly worried if not permitted to join them, she is allowed to go there and pray. When her son or daughter gets married, or when she has given birth and she has to go to the synagogue, she is permitted to go there.

Chapter 154

Regulations Concerning the Menses

1. The date of the menses is established by three consecutive times, that is, if menstruation occurs on the same date for three consecutive times, then that date is to be considered as the regular time of the menses. There are women who establish their periodic menses at certain days of the month, for instance, when a woman perceives the flow three consecutive times, on the New Moon, then her established menses is on the New Moon; or if she perceived it three consecutive times on the fifth day of the month, then the fifth day of the month is the established day of her menses. This way of reckoning is termed "the mensal, or monthly, menstruation." Although the number of days between one perception and the other is not always alike, for some months consist of twenty-nine days, while others consist of thirty days, nevertheless, since she is accustomed to perceive it on a certain day of the month, this day is her established day of the menses.

2. Most women, however, reckon their regular time of the menses by equal intervening days, that is, an equal number of days elapsing between periods; for instance, if a woman perceives a flow, then twenty-five, thirty, or thirty-two days later she again perceives a flow. If three consecutive number

of days elapse between one flow and another, this is her established date of the menses. This is termed, "diurnal menses." And after that number of days have elapsed, the following day is her established day of the menses. Since the menses must be established by no less than three times, and no interval can be established by less than two perceptions, therefore, to establish menses by equal intervening days, it is necessary to have four perceptions; that is, if she has perceived a flow today, and after twenty-five days she again perceived a flow; and after another twenty-five days, another flow; and still another after another lapse of twenty-five days, making a total of four flows, between which there were three equal periods, she thereby established her menses.

3. There are some women who are unable to reckon the time, either by the date of the month, or by equal intervening days, and they must depend upon some physical symptoms. Some women before menstruation, stretch their arms from weariness, or yawn from drowsiness, or belch after meals. If a woman sneezes, eructs, or feels a pain in the region of the navel or of the womb, or has an attack of chills and fever, or the hair of her body or of her head bristle, or her head or her limbs grow heavy, if any of these symptoms occurs immediately before the menses for three periods in succession, it may serve to establish the date of her menses. This is termed, "Menses regulated by physical symptoms." Yawning and sneezing can be regarded as symptoms only if repeated many times consecutively, but not if she yawned or sneezed but once, for this is a natural and normal thing. It is also essential for regulating the menses that the same symptoms occur three times in succession under the same conditions, but not otherwise.

4. Some women establish their menstrual periods by monthly, or by equal intervening days, combined with physical symptoms. For instance, every fifth day of the month they yawn or sneeze and thereafter, they perceive the flow, or twenty-five days from perception elapse and then they yawn or sneeze and thereafter they perceive again, this is termed, "menses regulated by combined factors," if it so occurs three times in succession. Those women should take no heed of one factor alone, since they regulated their terms by both together.

5. A woman whose periods are regular, is presumed to be clean at all times, except during her menstrual period. Her husband may cohabit with her even if she is partly asleep, and he need not inquire regarding that matter.

Nor does she have to examine herself either before or after having sexual intercourse. On the contrary, she should not examine herself in the presence of her husband, because he will have cause to suspect that she had evidently felt something, as otherwise she would not examine herself. Therefore, if she examines herself before cohabitation, her husband might keep away from her because of his scruples; and if she examines herself after having cohabitation, he may think that she felt something during the cohabitation, and he will, therefore, keep away from her the next time. For these reasons, she must not examine herself in the presence of her husband. But when not in his presence, the more a woman examines herself, the more praiseworthy she is.

6. A woman whose periods are irregular, must examine herself before and after intercourse to ascertain whether she is clean. The husband, too, must wipe himself after intercourse to ascertain whether there is a drop of blood anywhere. A woman whose flow of blood has presumably stopped, for instance, a pregnant woman after the first three months of her conception, or one who nurses, or a woman who is old, all these need not examine themselves.

7. There are women who have no regularly established menstrual periods, but have, nevertheless, a certain number of days during which they do not perceive any flow. For instance, a woman has ascertained that within twenty-five days after her perception, she never has a flow of blood, but after that, she has no definite date, sometimes it is one day, two days or three days later. Then, if it has been established by three consecutive times that during these twenty-five days she perceives no flow, she is regarded during these days like a woman that has a regular menstrual periods. But on the days that follow, when she is uncertain, she is forbidden to her husband.

CHAPTER 155

Separation Before the Menstrual Term

1. The Rabbis expounded in a Baraita (Shevuot 18b): "It is written (Leviticus 15:31): 'Thus shall ye separate the children of Israel from their uncleanliness.' Said Rabbi Josiah: From this verse an admonition to the children of Israel may be inferred, that they must separate from their wives prior to their menstrual periods. How long before? Said Rabbah (Avodah Zarah 75a): 'An *onah*.'" An *onah* is, "Either a day or a night." Thus, if her regular periods occur during the day, she is forbidden to her husband from the beginning of the day, even though she is accustomed to perceive the flow at the end of the day. Likewise, if she is accustomed to perceive the flow in

the morning and she has not perceived it, she is, nevertheless, forbidden to her husband the whole day until the night. If her regular periods occur during the night, she is forbidden to her husband the whole of that night, whether she generally perceives the flow at the beginning of the night or at the end. According to many authorities, not only cohabitation is forbidden at the time mentioned, but also all kinds of intimacies; and it is well to heed this opinion.

2. Some authorities are of the opinion that an *onah* is twenty-four hours; that is, if her periods occur at night, she is also forbidden to her husband the whole of the preceding day; and if they occur during the day, she is forbidden to her husband also the whole of the preceding night. And this is the proper course to follow. If, however, the husband is about to set out on a journey or if he has returned from one, or if the wife has performed the ritual of immersion on the night before the day on which her menstrual periods occur, they need not heed the stricter opinion.

3. A woman who has no regular menstrual periods, then thirty days after her perception of a flow is regarded as her fixed period; this is termed "an average period;" for instance, if she perceived blood on Monday of the week when the *Sidrah Noah* is read, then the Wednesday when the *Sidrah Toldot* is read (thirty days thereafter) is to be regarded by her as the fixed day of menses. In addition, she must pay attention to the other times of perception when she occasionally has a flow, whether based on equal intervening days, or on certain days of the month, as will be explained hereafter, by the grace of the Almighty. Whenever she has reason to expect a flow, her husband must separate from her on the *onah* before, as has been explained.

4. Whenever a woman perceives blood, she must suspect that perhaps she may perceive it again on the same date and at the same time. Particularly, if she has no regular menstrual period, she certainly must suspect that it may occur again at a similar time and thus establish her period of menses. But even a woman who has a set period, if she perceived a flow not at her regular period, she must take due notice of this perception, lest her regular period will henceforth be changed to some other time. If her regular period has changed, but it happened that she perceived blood, one additional time besides her regular period, then she need not be concerned about this extra perception, for since she has her regular period, she need not fear that she also has an irregular one.

5. Let us give an illustration of a woman who has no regular period: If she perceived blood on the second day of *Rosh Ḥodesh* of the month of *Iyar*, when the New Moon consists of two days, and again on the twenty-fifth of the same month, then she must be mindful of the New Moon of the month of *Sivan*, for it is likely that she will establish her menses at New Moon (and she must likewise be heedful of the second day of *Sivan*, because she may establish an average period). If she perceived no blood either on the New Moon of *Sivan* or on the second day of *Sivan*, then she must apprehend that she may establish her menses by equal intervening days. Now, since there was an interval of twenty-three days between one perception and the other (exclusive of the days of the first and of the second perceptions), she must now also count twenty-three days and then expect another flow. To the four days of the month of *Iyar*, she is to add nineteen days from the month of *Sivan*, and

expect a flow on the twentieth day of *Sivan*. If she did not perceive anything on the twentieth day of *Sivan*, she must take notice of the twenty-fifth day, as she may establish her menses on the twenty-fifth day of the month (and she must likewise, take notice of the twenty-sixth day, because of the possibility of having established an average period). However, she need not take into consideration the New Moon of the month of *Tammuz*, for the New Moon of *Iyar* has already been eliminated as a period with her failure to perceive blood on the New Moon of *Sivan* (for whatever is not established by three consecutive occurences is nullified by one time it fails to occur, as explained hereafter).

6. A case of a woman who has regular menses: She has established her menses by intervals of twenty-five days, and afterward she did not perceive any blood again until the twenty-eighth day, then she must take into consideration the twenty-fifth day after this perception, because of her regular period, and if she perceived nothing on the twenty-fifth day, she should take into consideration the twenty-eighth day because of the last perception. If she has perceived again on the twenty-eighth day, she is still forbidden to her husband on the twenty-fifth day of this perceiving, because of her established regular term. However, if she has not perceived now on the twenty-fifth day, but on the twenty-eighth day, then the twenty-eighth day is established as her regular term, and the twenty-fifth day is eliminated (for she had established the new period by three times), and she is no longer forbidden on that day. If the last perceptions were not had at equal intervals, as when they took place on the twenty-eighth, the twenty-ninth, and the thirty-first days, the former regular period has thereby been abolished, but no new term has been established, and she must, therefore, be mindful of three possible periods: The equal intervening number of days, the date of the month, and the "average period" (of the thirty days), until she establishes a new period.

7. The rule to guide every God-fearing person is this: In the event his wife has no regular period, he should write down the day and the date of the month she has perceived the flow, also the number of days that have elapsed between one perception and the other. And in the future, he must heed the intervening number of days between the last two flows, the day of the month on which the last perception occurred, and the average period, until she establishes a regular menstrual period. If after she had established a regular period, she happens to change it, then he must take into consideration the new perception with regard to the three possible new periods mentioned above. He must also be mindful of her regular period, because the regular period becomes eliminated only after three times, as stated hereafter.

8. A woman who has a regular period, even if she failed to have a perception, or any symptom on two consecutive periods, and even though she is absolutely convinced that she has not perceived anything, as when she had a meno pad during the entire period, nevertheless, her regular period is not abolished thereby, and she must be heedful also for the third time. However, if the third time has come and she perceived nothing, then she is positively

sure that she had no flow during these three times, as when she had cotton inserted evey time during the entire term of the menses, her regular period is thenceforth eliminated, and she need have no further apprehension on that date, because every regular period is nullified when it fails to happen three times, even if it had been regular for many years. But a term which is not established by three times, as when the irregular perception has occurred only once or twice, then if this day, or this sign, has come, and she failed to perceive her menstrual flux, even if she has not examined herself, as long as she did not feel anything, she need not take any notice of this period any longer, for whatever is not established by three successive occurrences is eliminated by one time, even without examination.

9. A woman who has her regular mensal period should ascertain before the time arrives, whether her menstrual flux has begun, by inserting cotton, for it is to be suspected that a drop of blood issued but was lost without her being aware of it. If she failed to do so, and the time of her regular term has passed, she is forbidden to her husband until she has examined herself thoroughly. If she bathed during that time, the examination will be of no avail, and she must consider herself as being in an unclean state, because it is presumed that the flux has come at the accustomed time. However, if she has no regular period, but she is merely apprehensive for an irregular one, then if the time has passed and she felt nothing, even though she failed to examine herself, she is thereafter presumed to be in a clean state. Nevertheless, the average period, which is the thirtieth day, is governed by the same law as that of a regular period, as has been stated before.

10. If a woman's flux continues for two or three days, coming either in a flow or in drops, the day on which she begins to perceive it, is considered the principal day. Some authorities are of the opinion, that she, nevertheless, must have apprehension for all these days, until established to the contrary.

11. Just as a woman must heed the menstrual period, indicated even once, either by a monthly perception or by an equal number of intervening days, so she must have regard for the menses, indicated by physical symptoms or by a combination of physical symptoms with diurnal perceptions, which occur even once. And just as menses regulated by monthly or by equal intervening days, if not established, are abolished by one deviating occurrence, so are the menses based on a combination of bodily symptoms with one of the above abolished by one occurrence to the contrary. Just as the menses established by month or by intervening days are abolished only by three successive occurrences to the contrary, so can the menses established by the abovementioned combination be abolished only by three successive, deviating occurrences. For instance, if she has only bodily symptoms, and she thereafter yawned on three successive periods but did not perceive any flux, then when she yawns again, she need not take notice of it. If it is by combined periods, based on days and physical symptoms, and when the established day has come three times and she yawned, but she failed to perceive anything, then the accustomed term is abolished; but a change of days alone, without yawning, and a change of the yawning alone without the days, do not abolish a term established by combined periods, because the occurrence which is to abolish it, must be exactly the same as the occurrences that establish it.

12. A woman after the first three months of her pregnancy, or while nursing a child, is presumed to have ceased her flow, and she need not be concerned about her periods even though she has an established menses. Nevertheless, she is required to apprehend any perception, just as in the case of irregular menses. When the period of nursing is over, she must resume to observe her former periods; for instance, if she reckoned her term by the New Moon, she must expect its recurrence on that date; but if her term was reckoned by equal intervening days, then she cannot predict the date of its recurrence. She must first perceive it once, and then she must expect the customary intervals between periods.

CHAPTER 156

Perception of Blood as a Result of Cohabitation

1. If a woman has an issue of blood as a result of cohabitation, even though it did not occur during cohabitation but later in the night, she may have intercourse again after purifying herself. Yet, one single occurrence like that should make husband and wife apprehensive of a repetition. Thus, if this occurred on the night of immersion, then when she takes the ritual bath again, they should be separated from each other that night, for it is possible that the immersion in conjunction with cohabitation have caused the issue of blood, and perchance on the night of the following immersion, she may perceive blood in the very act of cohabitation. However, if nothing occurred on the night of the following immersion, they need not have any apprehension on the night of the third immersion and they are not bound to separate themselves, because the main cause of concern was due to the immersion, and since nothing occurred during the night of the second immersion, they need not be concerned about it any longer. The same rule should be observed if the flow occurred on the night following the immersion; they should be separated during the night following the second immersion, and if nothing has happened then, they need have no concern about it on the night following the third immersion.

2. However, since an unfavorable tendency has been developed in that woman, therefore, even in the event she has regular periods, she must examine herself both before and after a second cohabitation, in order to ascertain whether she had a flow again by cohabitation, and she should make certain to place herself under medical care. This is all the more urgent when she perceives the flow in the very act of cohabitation, or immediately thereafter; for, should this happen to her three times, she will be placed in a most perplexing position, and it is with utmost difficulty that permission may be granted her to continue living with her husband.

3. If during the act of cohabitation, the woman feels that she has become unclean, it is her duty to tell her husband immediately: "I have become unclean." He should not separate himself from her while his organ is rigid, for this act in itself affords pleasure, but he must raise his body, supporting himself on his hands and feet and not upon her. He should be filled with fear and trembling because of this sinful occurrence, and when his organ relaxes, he should separate from her. Thereafter, he should consult a rabbi to instruct him regarding a proper penance for this sin.

CHAPTER 157

Prenuptial Laws

1. A woman who makes preparations for her wedding, must first count seven clean days. And it is immaterial whether she is a minor who has not as yet perceived any flow or whether she is an aged woman whose flow has long ceased, because it is possible that due to her longing, some drop of blood has issued from her and was lost. She is, therefore, regarded as a menstruant. After having counted the seven clean days, she must examine herself daily until she performs the ceremony of immersion and also thereafter until the mandatory consummation of the marital act.

2. If for some reason the wedding has been postponed, and thereafter they have agreed upon the original date, although she has already counted seven clean days, she is obliged to count them anew, inasmuch as a new longing was created within her, and even though she has examined herself daily during the interval, it is of no avail. If, however, the wedding has not been definitely postponed, but they were unable to agree upon the amount of dowry, or the like, and because of this the wedding was delayed until they came to terms, or if they have postponed the wedding by mutual consent to some other day, they should consult a Rabbi as to whether the first seven clean days are of any avail. If they have quarreled before the wedding and another bridegroom took the place of the first, it is self-evident that the seven clean days she counted for the first bridegroom are of no avail for the second one. But even if after giving her consent to marry the second groom, she has become reconciled with the first one, the seven clean days she originally counted for him are of no avail as her thoughts have been diverted from him. She must, therefore, count anew seven clean days.

3. A woman should be careful not to get married before she purifies herself from her unclean state. If, however, it is urgent that the wedding should take place on the day she is unclean, or if it happens that she has become menstrually unclean after the wedding ceremony and before cohabitation, the groom and the bride must not be alone in each other's company without surveillance until she will have performed the rite of immersion. It is the custom to place a male child by the groom and a female child by the bride. The bride and the groom do not remain without the children even in the daytime. The children must be old enough to understand something about matters pertaining to cohabitation, but they should not be fully mature, already having sexual desire, lest they be seduced, but they should be of average maturity. Regarding this law, no distinction is made between a groom who has never been married before and a widower, and between a virgin and a widow, for as long as the groom has never had conjugal relations with that woman, he may succumb to his passions, and therefore, they are not permitted to remain alone unobserved.

4. When one remarries a woman whom he had divorced, she must count seven clean days, even if he had divorced her while she was pregnant

and remarried her while she is still pregnant, or if he had divorced her while she was nursing a child and he remarried her while she is still nursing the child. However, if he violated this rule and remarried her before she performed the rite of immersion, they are permitted to remain alone unobserved, for inasmuch as he has already had conjugal relations with her, his longing is not overpowering.

5. Extreme care should be taken that the bridegroom should not lie next to the bride until the night he desires to perform the rite of marriage with her.

6. One who marries a virgin should perform the marital act, which is mandatory upon him; and although there is an issue of virginal blood, he may conclude the act and he need have no scruples about it. However, he must separate from her thereafter, because she becomes unclean even if no blood has been perceived, for it is possible that a drop of blood issued from her and was covered up by the semen. She is, therefore, considered as menstrually unclean.

7. If a virgin has taken the bath of immersion after the first cohabitation, and thereafter she perceived a flow of blood after the second cohabitation and also after the third and the fourth, it is questionable whether she may remain with her husband.

8. It is permissible to have conjugal relations with a virgin on the Sabbath, although the act causes a bruise.

CHAPTER 158

Childbirth and Miscarriage

1. A woman who has given birth to a child, is unclean, whether the child was born alive or dead, or even if it was a miscarriage, and even if there was no flow of blood. A woman who has borne a son is unclean for seven days, after which she must count seven clean days and then perform the rite of immersion. And if she has borne a daughter, she is unclean for fourteen days, after which she must count seven clean days and undergo immersion. In some communities, the custom prevails that women do not perform the immersion until forty days after the birth of a son and eighty days after the birth of a daughter. Wherever this is an accepted custom, it must not be disregarded, for there is some reason for this. Concerning such cases, it is written (Proverbs 1:8): "Hear, my son, the instructions of thy father, and forsake not the teaching of thy mother." In our regions there is no established custom. The custom prevailing in some communities that after the birth of a male, the immersion is not performed until after the expiration of six weeks, and in the case of a female after nine weeks, and customs of similiar nature, have no valid reason whatsoever, and they have already been abolished by the *Geonim*, of blessed memory.

2. Some authorities are of the opinion that the husband must separate from his wife on the forty-first night after the birth of a male and on the eighty-first night after the birth of a female, as on those nights she may perceive the flow the same as during her menses. Other authorities differ, but a

scrupulous man should be strict about it. In the case of an abortion, where it is doubtful whether it was a male or a female, the husband must separate from his wife on both the forty-first and the eighty-first nights.

3. If a woman has suffered a miscarriage of something, even if it had no shape of a child but looked like a lump of flesh or a piece of skin, or the like, she must consider herself unclean as after the birth of a female. She should, however, consult a competent Rabbi, for in some instances, leniency is sanctioned. If a woman first miscarries a child and thereafter she drops the afterbirth, although the child is a male, since it is likely that the afterbirth is also that of a female child, she is unclean as after the birth of a female. In this case, too, it is best to seek the opinion of a competent Rabbi.

4. If a woman is certain that she has not conceived, and she performed the ceremony of immersion, and within forty days she had an abortion, she need not deem it a birth, because the embryo is not formed in less than forty days. She is, however, menstrually unclean, even if she had not perceived any blood; for it is presumed that there was some blood but was not noticed, because it is impossible that the womb should be opened without blood.

CHAPTER 159

Putting on White Linen and Counting the Clean Days

1. A woman who has perceived blood during her period of purity, is bound to count five pure days, including the day on which she perceived the flow. Even if she noticed it at the end of the day, after the congregation, including herself, already prayed the *Maariv* service, or after they have already ushered in the Sabbath, yet if it is still daytime, this day is counted as one of the five. On the fifth day, towards evening before twilight, she should carefully examine herself, wash at least the lower limbs, and put on clean white undergarments. Her other garments also should be clean; and this is called "the end of her menstrual period." At night, she should spread clean white sheets on her bed. Also, the pillows and the bedcovering should be clean, and on the following morning she begins to count the seven clean days. It is immaterial whether she has noticed much blood or little, for even if she has found only one drop of blood or even if only a stain, she must wait thereafter five days. On the other hand, if she continues to bleed the entire five days, so long as the flow has ceased before sunset on the fifth day, her period of menses is over and she may begin the seven days of purification as prescribed.

2. In case of emergency, as for instance, when she is traveling and cannot obtain enough water even to wash the lower limbs, it does not retard the "end of her menstrual period," but she should carefully wipe herself with whatever she can. If she has no fresh chemise, she may put on an old one, provided that it is first examined to ascertain that it is free from bloodstains.

3. Some authorities hold that if on the fifth day the congregation has already prayed *Maariv*, although it is still daytime, she can no longer make it the "end of her menstrual period" on this day, and begin to count the seven clean days from the following day, since the congregations has already accepted it as night. Other authorities hold that she may take this day into account even when the congregation had already ushered in the Sabbath. In the first instance, it is advisable to be scrupulous about it, but if it is done already, she need not be concerned about it. She may then end her menstrual period as long as it is before twilight. However, if she, too, had already prayed *Maariv*, especially when she had already lit the Sabbath candles, she can no longer end her menstrual period later on that day. During the summer, when in many communities the *Maariv* is prayed while the day is long, her menstrual period ends before that time, as has already been stated. Thereafter, near twilight, she should examine herself again, for the principal time for ending her menstrual period is as close to twilight as possible. However, if she has neglected to examine herself again, until the following morning when she found herself to be clean, it is sufficient.

4. A man should ever instruct his household that the examination before ending the menstrual period should be done by inserting a cotton cloth, which should remain there during the entire twilight. Such an examination will avoid all possible doubt.

5. There is a custom prevailing in some communities, that if the time for putting on the white linen is on a Sabbath or a festival, to postpone it till after that, for the reason that not every woman knows how to observe carefully the laws prohibiting washing and wringing. However, in communities where it is the custom to be lenient about it, she may even wash her entire body with cold water. But when using warm water, she must be careful to wash only the lower limbs and between her thighs; and such water must be warmed the day before the Sabbath or the festival. In order not to transgress the law prohibiting wringing on the Sabbath and on festivals, she must be careful not to wash herself with any cloth, but with her bare hands. On *Yom Kippur*, she must not wash herself at all, but merely wipe herself thoroughly (for since she is forbidden to wash herself, it is considered an emergency, as stated in section 2, above), and put on a clean gown. On *Tisheah Beav*, and during the first seven days of mourning, she should likewise neither wash herself nor even put on a freshly washed gown, but an old one which has been previously examined and found to be free of bloodstains. However, after the first seven days of mourning, although washing is forbidden during the entire first thirty days, she is permitted to wash herself lightly, as much as is necessary for her purification, and she is also allowed to put on a fresh gown.

6. During the entire seven clean days, she must preferably examine herself twice daily, once in the morning and once near twilight. However, if she only examined herself once on the first day and once on the seventh day,

we may be lenient about it. This is only true when she has examined herself on the first and on the seventh days, but if she has examined herself on the first and on the eighth days, then the eighth day only is counted, and she is required to add six more days.

7. All these examinations, whether at the end of her menstruation period or during the seven clean days, must be made with an old white linen cloth or with a soft white woolen cloth, which she should insert to a depth that the male organ penetrates, and she should then see if there is any reddish spot on it. If it is impossible for her to insert it to such a depth, she should at least try to the best of her ability to examine herself as closely as possible; and it is urgent that at least one examination should be made to a depth that the male organ reaches. (It is the duty of every husband to instruct his wife in the laws pertaining to examination, for there are many women who are not acquainted with them). Virgins who examine themselves before the wedding, should likewise do so to the best of their ability.

8. The examination must be made by the light of day, not by artificial light. Some authorities void the purification if she has not made at least one examination on the first day and one on the seventh day by the light of day.

9. If she finds a stain or even perceives a flow of blood during the seven clean days, she may consider her menstruation as just ended. She may put on clean linen on the same day as long as it ceased before twilight, and on the following day she may start to count the seven clean days anew.

10. If a bride has perceived blood before her wedding, and if by waiting five days, the wedding will take place before the time of the ritual immersion, and it is difficult to postpone the wedding, she is allowed to consider the end of her menstrual period immediately at twilight. She may then begin to count the seven clean days from the day that follows, in order that she may be able to perform the immersion before the wedding, which is preferable to having the marriage ceremony performed while she is still menstrually unclean.

CHAPTER 160

How to Shampoo the Hair

1. On the seventh day of purification, before sunset, she should thoroughly wash her entire body with warm water, especially where there are wrinkles, and also her secret parts. She should examine her entire body, wherever she can see or feel with her hands, lest there remain on it any particle or stain, which would be an interposition between the water and her body. She should also thoroughly cleanse and comb her hair, and disentangle it, so that it would neither be matted nor knotted. All of the foregoing is called *Ḥafifah* (shampooing). It is necessary that she protract her cleansing

until nightfall, so that she may perform the immersion immediately after the cleansing. Preferably, the combing should take place close to the immersion and during the daytime. Therefore, the proper procedure is to start the cleansing while it is yet day and continue it till nightfall.

2. The hair cleansing should not be done with any ingredients that tend to tangle the hair. It is the custom to permit the use of soap, since it possesses cleansing properties and does not tangle the hair.

3. If there is no bath adjoining the ritual pool and she does the combing in the house and then goes to perform the immersion, she should take a comb with her, and there comb her hair again.

4. In an emergency, when it is impossible for her to wash her hair in the daytime, she may wash it in the night, but she should not do it hurriedly, and take pains to wash it properly. If it is impossible for her to continue the cleansing into the night, she may do the entire cleansing in the daytime.

5. If the time for the ritual immersion falls on Sabbath-eve, the shampooing should be done in the daytime, and she should be very careful to conclude it before sunset, so that she may not violate the Sabbath, God forbid. With regard to lighting the Sabbath candles, it is best, if possible, to go home after the hair washing, or she should do the hair washing in her home, light the candles before sunset, and thereafter take the bath of immersion. If this is impossible, then her husband should light the candles; and if this, too, is impossible, then she should light the candles while it is still daytime, and say the benediction over them, but she should declare before lighting them that she does not, by that act, usher in the Sabbath; for in case of emergency, a declaration in this regard is valid. But the practice of some women to say the benediction after the immersion over the burning candles, should be voided, because they are pronouncing a benediction in vain.

6. In communities where it is customary to take the ritual bath of immersion on the close of the Sabbath or a festival, a competent Rabbi should be consulted as to when and how the preparation for the immersion should take place.

CHAPTER 161

What Constitutes Interposition

1. She is required to immerse her entire body, together with all her hair at one time. She should, therefore, be very careful that there should not be upon her body while immersing, anything that interposes between the water and the body. For at times, even the slightest particle is considered an interposition and renders the immersion invalid. And not only on the external part of the body which the water must reach, must there be no interposition, but even the internal parts of the body into which the water cannot penetrate, should, nevertheless, be in condition fit for the penetration of water. For in-

stance, although the water need not enter her mouth, nevertheless, if there be an intervening particle between her teeth, the immersion is invalid, as will be explained, the Almighty willing. Every woman should be acquainted with this rule: All parts of her body must be clean and in a condition for the water to penetrate unto them during immersion.

2. The mucus of the eye is considered an interposition if it is on the outside, even when it is moist. If it is inside the eye, it is not an interposition if moist, but the dry matter which has begun to come out of the eye, is an interposition.

3. Dried blood upon a wound is considered an interposition. But the matter inside the wound is not an interposition. Discharged matter is not an interposition when wet, but when dry it is an interposition. Therefore, a woman who has scabs, must wash them until they are softened. Also the crust of a wound or blister, must be either removed or well softened with water, although it causes her pain.

4. The plaster upon a wound is considered an interposition. Also a plaster put on to stay for three or four months, and thereafter it falls off by itself, but while it is on, it cannot be removed without tearing the skin with it, and the woman says that she is accustomed to it and does not mind it, is nevertheless, considered an interposition. If a woman has a boil which has been opened and a piece of gauze has been put in the opening underneath the bandage, and even when the bandage is removed the gauze is invisible because it is deep inside, it is, nevertheless, considered an interposition.

5. Fecal matter on the body as a result of perspiration is considered an interposition when dry. Crumb-like particles found on the body, such as formed on rubbing the hands when they are soiled with clay, dough or perspiration, are considered an interposition.

6. Ink, milk, honey, juice of figs, mulberries, carobs, and the fruit of the sycamore, are considered an interposition when dry, but not when they are moist. All other juices are considered an interposition even when they are moist. Also, blood is considered an interposition even when moist.

7. The coloring used by women on their faces, hands and hair is not considered an interposition. A woman who is engaged in dyeing clothes, and because of this her hands are colored, it is not considered an interposition, since women thus engaged do not mind it.

8. Concerning the dirt underneath the nails, there are many diverse opinions, and it has long been an established custom to pare the nails of the hands and toes before taking the bath of immersion. The woman should be careful to burn her nails thus cut off, for it is dangerous for her husband or

any other man to step on them. If she has neglected to cut off her hails before the nightfall of a Sabbath or a festival, she may have them pared by a non-Jewess, according to some authorities. If she has a swelling over the nail, and she is unable either to cut it off or to clean it underneath, then if the growth is so large that the filth underneath is invisible, it is not an interposition. If a woman has forgotten to pare her nails and thus performed the ritual of immersion, then if she has become aware of it before the conjugal relation, she is required to have another immersion; but if she has not become aware of it until after the intercourse, she should consult a Rabbi.

9. She should be careful to remove her earrings and rings before taking the ritual immersion.

10. She is required to clean her teeth before the immersion, because particles of food are usually found between them. If after performing the immersion, she has found some particle, either between her teeth or clinging on them, the immersion is invalid. Some women have made it a practice not to eat any meat on the day of immersion, because meat clings to the teeth more than any other food, and it is to be feared that some of it will stick between the teeth even after they are cleaned; this is a fine custom. On the Sabbath or on a festival when meat is to be eaten, she should be extremely careful to clean her teeth well. Every woman should be careful not to taste any food between the shampooing and the immersion. The entire day of the immersion, she should not knead any dough or make any wax candles, so that nothing may cling to her. But on the day before the Sabbath when it is her custom to knead dough in honor of the Sabbath, she should not refrain from doing it, but she should be careful to wash her hands thoroughly.

11. A woman who has an artificial tooth, should consult a Rabbi, how to perform the immersion; the same applies to a woman who has a filling in a tooth. A woman who is ruptured and wears a ring in her womb, should also consult a Rabbi.

12. During the immersion, the woman attendant should not hold her, because the water will not penetrate to the place that she grasps. In case of emergency, however, the woman attendant should first immerse her own hand in the *mikvah* (ritual pool), then she may hold her not tightly, but loosely.

13. Whenever possible, she should not immerse herself in a place where there is clay on the bottom, as it is to be feared that it may cause an interposition. In case of emergency, it is the custom to be lenient about it, because the clay, generally found at the bottom of the water is not very thick. However, the mud at the edge of a stream which clings to the feet does constitute

an interposition. Therefore, she must be careful to wash the mud off her feet, thoroughly, prior to the immersion. Should she desire to place something at the bottom of the stream upon which to stand during the immersion, she should consult an competent rabbi, because there are many things upon which it is forbidden to stand during immersion.

14. The woman should not stand erect when immersing herself, for in that position, certain parts of her body would be concealed; nor should she stoop too low, lest certain parts of her be pressed too close together; but she should stoop slightly until the secret places of her lower limbs be exposed as they are when she kneads dough and spreads her feet slightly to stand firm and knead briskly. Also, the space under her breasts should be the same as when she suckles a baby. She need not separate her thighs or extend her arms too much, but her arms and legs should be relaxed as when walking. If she has stooped too low, or if she has stood entirely erect, the immersion is invalid, because wrinkles have thereby been formed in her body and the water has not penetrated there. Therefore, it is necessary that the water should reach three hand-breadths above her navel, as in such a manner she will be able to immerse herself properly. In an emergency, however, when the water is not so high, she should slowly sit down in the water until it reaches her neck, and then immerse herself. In such a manner, wrinkles will not be formed on that part of the body which is still out of the water, for the wrinkles that may be formed thereafter on her body when in the water, do not matter, inasmuch as the water has already penetrated there. If the water is very low, then in an emergency, she may immerse herself in a prostrate position like a fish, providing that her entire body, including the hair is submerged at the same time.

15. She need not open her mouth to let the water in, nor should she shut it too tightly. If she shuts it tightly the immersion is invalid. Her lips should be naturally closed. If strands of hair are in her mouth when immersing, her immersion is invalid, as the water did not reach her hair.

16. She should not keep her eyes tightly closed, because wrinkles will be formed under them, nor should she open them too much, because wrinkles will be formed above them, but she should keep them slightly closed.

17. She is also required to remove the phlegm from the nose, outside as well as inside, but whatever is higher up in the nose, constitutes no interposition. She is likewise required to remove the wax from the ears. Some authorities hold that she should also pass water before immersion, if she needs

it. She must also ascertain whether she needs to ease herself, so that she would not have to restrain herself and thereby render that area impenetrable to water. But if this has been neglected by her, it does not render the immersion invalid.

18. She should not perform the immersion having dust upon her feet; and if she did immerse herself without removing the dust, the immersion is valid if the dust was thin, for the water has washed it away.

19. Ordinary lice and fleas do not cling to the body and do not prevent the water from penetrating, and therefore, they do not constitute an interposition. But the kind of lice which bite and tightly cling to the skin, where there is hair, must be removed by means of hot water, or scraped off with the nails. However, if they cannot be removed, they are not considered an interposition. The small lice that cling to the hair, must be removed; they do constitute an interposition.

20. If a woman has an elf-lock, and it is dangerous to cut it, it does not constitute an interposition. Even if there are some threads entangled in the twisted hair-locks which cannot be removed, they are not considered an interposition, provided they are invisible.

CHAPTER 162

Immersion

1. It is the duty of every woman whose husband is in town, to perform the ritual bath of immersion at the proper time without delay, in order not to postpone the precept of propagation, even one night. For thus do we find in the case of Joshua who was punished because he caused Israel to delay the precept of propagation one night. A woman who defers immersion in order to torment her husband, will be severely punished, God forbid.

2. She is forbidden to perform the immersion on the seventh day before the stars appear. She is even forbidden to perform the immersion shortly before the approach of darkness, so that she will not return home before it is dark. Even if she has neglected to perform it on the night following the seventh day, and performs it thereafter, she is likewise forbidden to do so in the daytime. In the latter case, too, she must not take the bath of immersion before dark, so that she would reach home when it is dark, but she must do it in the nighttime only. Brides before their wedding, are allowed to perform the immersion during the daytime of the eighth day, or during the daytime of any other day thereafter. And in an emergency, when it is necessary for the bride to perform the immersion on the seventh day, she is likewise permitted to perform it during the daytime, even in the morning after sunrise. The wedding, however, should not take place before the stars appear. If she performs the immersion after the wedding, although it is the first immersion of her married life, she is subject to the same laws as apply to any other woman.

3. In case of emergency, as when she is afraid to immerse that night on account of the cold or for some other reason, or if the house of immersion is outside the city, and the city gates are locked at night, she is then permitted to perform the immersion on the eighth day during daytime. But she is not permitted to perform the immersion on the seventh day, no matter what the circumstances are. She is allowed to immerse in the daytime on the eighth day only when she is also able to shampoo her hair before the immersion. But if the eighth day is a Sabbath or a festival, and she would have to shampoo the hair before the immersion, and then perform the immersion in the daytime, such practice is forbidden, for we cannot make two concessions in one case (that is, to have the immersion take place in the daytime, and also allow a long interval between the preparation and the immersion).

4. She should not stand on anything else but the bottom of the pool during the immersion. If the water of the pool is deep and she must stand on the steps, she should then consult a rabbi.

5. She must not perform the immersion in a place where people may see her, as that would cause her to be hasty, and as a result, not do it properly. However, if she has already performed the immersion in such circumstances, if she is positive that she had done it properly, the immersion is valid.

6. When she immerses herself, it is necessary that a Jewish woman, over the age of twelve years and one day, should stand by and see to it that no strand of her hair remains floating above the water. If there is no woman available, her husband may supervise the immersion.

7. She is allowed to perform the immersion on Friday evening if this is the proper time and she was unable to perform it beforehand, provided her husband is in town. But if her husband is not in town, or if she was able to perform it before, she may not immerse on Friday evening. If it is after she had given birth, there are many diverse opinions as to whether she may perform the immersion on Friday evening. She should, therefore, consult a rabbi about it. If the time for her immersion was before Friday, but she has failed to perform it because her husband was out of town, and then he arrived on Friday, in some communities they forbid such immersion on Friday evening. In communities where there is no established custom, it is not necessary to be strict about it, but where they are strict about it, she may not perform it even on the conclusion of the Sabbath. A widow after her marriage, is not permitted to take the first bath of immersion on Friday evening, since she may not have the first cohabitation on the Sabbath. Some authorities permit her, however, to perform the immersion on the conclusion of the Sabbath.

8. After she has performed the immersion in the proper manner and while still standing in the water, she should pronounce the benediction: "Who hath commanded us concerning immersion." It is proper that before pronouncing the benediction she should cover her lower limbs with some ker-

chief, or at least hold her arms together on her body to cover it, and she should not look into the water while saying the benediction. If she takes the bath of immersion in a place where she can make the water turbid with her feet, it is best to do so before saying the benediction. Some women are accustomed to immerse again after pronouncing the benediction. This is a proper custom. Those who do so must take heed that the second immersion, too, be properly carried out.

9. After she had properly immersed in a pool, she may enter the bath-house to warm herself, even if it is a bath used for perspiring. But some authorities forbid her to wash herself again in a bath tub; and this is the prevailing custom. It is permissible to spill water on her to warm her body. However, in a community where this is frowned upon, it should not be done.

10. A woman must be modest and not reveal the night on which she is to perform the immersion, nor enter the house of immersion while people can observe her. Concerning a woman who does not act in that manner, it is written (Deuteronomy 27:21): "Cursed be he that lieth with any manner of beast." Upon leaving the bath of immersion, she should take precaution to have one of her friends meet her and touch her, so that no unclean thing, such as a dog, an ass, a pig, a horse, a leper, or even an ignorant person or a heathen, would meet her first. If any of these do meet her, a God-fearing woman should perform the immersion again. If one meets a woman leaving the bath of immersion, he may expect some mishap, God forbid, and he can obviate the evil by reciting the following two verses (Psalms 107:40): "He poureth contempt upon princes, and causes them to wander in a pathless wilderness;" and (Job 12:21): "He poureth contempt upon princes, and He looseneth the belt of the mighty."

11. Some authorities forbid, while others allow, to warm the water of the immersion pool. The custom of permitting it is already prevailing in many communities. But where no such custom prevails, people should not be lax about it. In a place where it is customary to allow it, care should be taken that, if the immersion is performed on Friday night, the water should not be hot but lukewarm.

12. According to many great authorities, of blessed memory, the immersion performed in a river is valid only when the water is so low that it is certain that the water was not augmented by rain or snow, because rain water and water from melted snow purify only when it is clean and contained in a pool, but not when it flows on the ground. Spring water, however, purifies even when it flows on the ground. In case of emergency, as in a place where there is no immersion pool, it is customary to be lenient, and to depend upon the authorities who permit it. For even when the river becomes swol-

len by rain, its main source is from the ground, because in time of rain, the air is full of moisture, and the sources of the springs increase. Consequently, most of the water in the river is supplied by the springs, and the rain water loses its identity. Therefore, it purifies, although it contains water that flowed on the ground. However, in a place where there is an immersion pool, far be it from anyone to be lenient about it. Even in a place where there is no immersion pool, if possible, she should wait with her immersion two or three days, until the river resumes its normal level. If possible, it is best that she should not immerse in the place where the river is wide only occasionally, but where it flows continuously; in such a case there is more ground for being lenient.

13. With regard to a river which is formed entirely by rain, and at times completely dries up, although during the rainfall, some other streams empty into it, no immersion can be permitted there while the water flowing on the ground is still pouring into it until the water becomes stagnant.

14. The laws regarding ritual pools are numerous. Wherever an immersion pool is made, it should be constructed under the supervision of a recognized rabbi, great in learning and in piety. If any change occurs therein, no matter how slight, a rabbi should be consulted. When it becomes necessary to draw the water out for the purpose of cleaning it, a rabbi should be consulted as to the proper procedure.

CHAPTER 163

The Law of Circumcision

1. It is a duty devolving upon a father to circumcise his son, or to bestow the honor upon another Jew to circumcise him. The father should put the infant on the knees of the *sandek*, hand over the knife to the *mohel*, and stand by him during the circumcision, to indicate that the *mohel* is his agent. In the interval between the circumcision of the foreskin and its laceration, the father pronounces the benediction: "Who hath sanctified us by His commandments and hath commanded us to bring him into the covenant of our father Abraham." The father should be careful to choose a *mohel* and a *sandek* who are the best and most righteous men available. It is customary for a father not to select as a *sandek*, a man who had already officiated as such at the circumcision of another of his sons. If the father has invited one *mohel*, he is not allowed to retract and invite another one, for it is written (Zephaniah 3:13): "The remnant of Israel will do no injustice and speak no lies." If the father had invited a *mohel* who had since left the city, and the father, thinking that he would not come on time for the circumcision, appointed another

one in his stead, but in the meantime the former *mohel* returned, the former should perform the circumcision.

2. It is customary for all those witnessing a circumcision to remain standing, for it is written (II Kings 23:3): "And all the people stood in the covenant," excepting the *sandek* who holds the baby while seated. When the father pronounces the benediction, those assembled say: "Just as he has been initiated into the covenant, so may he be initiated into the study of the Torah, to his nuptial canopy, and to the performance of good deeds."

3. It is essential that the *mohel* should be versed in the laws of circumcision, and he should examine the child to ascertain if he is healthy. The mother should likewise be told to notify the *mohel* in case she observes some weakness in the infant.

4. Extreme care should be taken not to circumcise an infant who is ailing, as the fulfillment of all ordinances are suspended if there is danger to human life. Moreover, the circumcision can be performed at a later date, but the life of a human being can never be restored. (See *Yoreh Deah,* chapters 262-263, as to when to circuncise an infant who had been ailing and recovered). As soon as the infant is fit for the circumcision, it is forbidden to defer the performance of this precept for any reason, like gaining time for providing the feast, or the like. If a circumcision has been postponed, it cannot then be performed on the Sabbath or on a festival.

5. If a woman has lost two sons from the effect of circumcision, her third son should not be circumcised until he gets older and stronger. If a woman has lost a child because of the circumcision and the same thing happened to her sister's son, then the children of the other sisters should not be circumcised until they grow older and stronger.

6. If an infant is born at twilight, or close to it, a rabbi should be consulted as to the proper time it should be circumcised.

7. An infant who dies before circumcision, whether within the eight days or thereafter, must be circumcised at the grave, in order to remove the foreskin which is a disgrace to him, but no benedictions should be pronounced over this circumcision. He should be given a name to perpetuate his memory, and that mercy may be shown him from Heaven to be included in the resurrection of the dead, and that he may then have sufficient understanding to recognize his father and his mother. If he was buried without circumcision, and they become aware of it immediately, when there is no likelihood that the body has already begun to decompose, the grave should be opened and the circumcision should be performed. But if they have become aware of it after some days, the grave should not be opened.

8. It is customary to make a feast on the day of circumcision; for every precept which the Jews have accepted with joy (such as the precept of circumcision) is to be performed with joy, for it is written (Psalms 119:162): "I rejoice at Thy word, as one that findeth great spoil," which the Sages explained (Shabbot 130a) that it refers to circumcision. He who can afford to make a feast, but economizes and serves only coffee and sweets, or the like, is not acting properly. If one is invited to a feast of a circumcision and he knows that worthy men will be present there, he must attend. It is customary to make a feast at which fruit and drinks are served on the Friday night preceding the circumcision; and this, too, is considered a religious feast. It is also the custom that on the evening before the circumcision, people assemble in the house of the infant and study the Torah, while some refreshments are served. But this is not considered a religious feast, being merely a custom.

CHAPTER 164

The Redemption of the Firstborn

1. It is the duty of every Jew to redeem his son, who is the mother's firstborn. He redeems him from a *Kohen,* by giving him five *selaim,* which in our currency is equal to five and one-third ounces of refined silver. He may give the *Kohen* some articles of that value, but no real property and no notes, and, therefore, it is improper to redeem with paper money. It is customary to make a feast when this precept is performed.

2. If the father has promised a *Kohen* that he would redeem the son from him, he is forbidden to retract; nevertheless, if he did retract and redeemed him from another *Kohen,* the redemption is valid.

3. The firstborn should not be redeemed before he is fully thirty days old, and on the thirty-first day he should be redeemed immediately, so as not to defer the performance of a precept. The redemption may not be made on the Sabbath or on a festival, but it may take place on *Ḥol Hammoed.* It is the custom to make the redemption in the daytime. Nevertheless, if the thirty-first day has passed and the infant has not been redeemed, or if that day falls on a Sabbath, or on a festival, or on a fast day, the redemption should take place immediately on the following night, so as not to postpone the precept any longer.

4. The father brings the firstborn before the *Kohen* and informs him that he is a firstborn to his mother who is a Jewish woman (not the daughter of a *Kohen* or a *Levi*). He brings the money or anything that is worth five *selaim,* places it before the *Kohen* and says: "This is my firstborn son," etc., and places the infant before the *Kohen.* The *Kohen* then asks him: "What wouldst thou rather," etc.; and the father responds: "I desire to redeem my son," etc. While the father still holds the coins and before he gives

them to the *Kohen,* he says the benediction: "Who hath sanctified us by His commandments and hath commanded us concerning the redemption of the son." He also says the benediction *Sheheḥeyanu.* Thereupon he puts the coins in the hands of the *Kohen,* and the latter takes the money, puts it on the head of the child and says: "This instead of that," etc. Thereafter the *Kohen* puts his hands upon the head of the child and blesses him, saying: "May God make thee like Ephraim," etc. "The Lord bless thee and keep thee," etc. "For length of days, and years of life," etc.; and "The Lord shall guard thee from all evil," etc. Thereafter he says the benediction over a goblet of wine. If no wine is obtainable, he may say the benediction over some other beverage which is used in the region. But in this event, the redemption should take place before the hands are washed for the meal, for during the meal it is not permissible to say a benediction over any beverage other than wine. However, when there is wine, the redemption is to take place after the *Hamotzi* has been pronounced over the bread.

5. If the father is not home, he may redeem his son wherever he is, by saying to the *Kohen:* "I have a firstborn son to redeem," whereupon the *Kohen* inquires: "What wouldst thou rather," etc.

6. The *Ture Zahab* has given a reason for the custom that the *Kohen* returns thereafter either the whole or part of the redemption money to the father (this requires deliberation). The father who desires to perform the precept properly, should choose a poor *Kohen* who is learned in the Law and God-fearing. Both he and the *Kohen* should understand that the redemption money is not to be returned; but the father may give the redemption money to the *Kohen* as a gift on condition that it be returned to him.

7. According to law, the mother is not bound to redeem her son; and if the father has died, the *Beth Din* redeems him.

8. If the father has violated the law and has failed to redeem his son, or if the father died and the *Beth Din* failed to redeem him, he is obliged to redeem himself when he is grown up, at which time he says the benediction: "Who hath sanctified us by His commandments, and hath commanded us concerning the redemption of the firstborn," and also the benediction *Sheheḥayuna.*

9. Priests and *Levites* are exempt from redeeming their firstborn sons. Even the daughter of a priest or a *Levite* who is married to an Israelite is exempt from redeeming her firstborn son. If the daughter of a *Kohen* has had sexual relations with a non-Jew and she has become pregnant, or even if she has thereafter become pregnant from lawful cohabitation, the son must be redeemed, because his mother has forfeited the prerogative of priesthood by having cohabitation with a non-Jew. This applies also to any illicit cohabitation by which she forfeits her priestly privilege.

10. If a woman had an abortion and thereafter gave birth to a viable child, a rabbi should be consulted regarding his redemption.

CHAPTER 165

The Training of Children

1. It is the duty of every father to train his children in the practice of all the precepts, whether Biblical or Rabbinical. Each child should be trained in accordance with his or her intelligence. It is also incumbent upon the father to guard his children against any forbidden act, as the Scriptures say (Proverbs 22:6): "Train up a child in the way he should go," etc. If words are of no avail, he should chastise him with a rod. But he should not strike him mercilessly, as some fools do. The father should take special care to train his children to tell no lies, but to speak the truth at all times, and to shun swearing. The above things are obligatory upon fathers as well as upon teachers.

2. The time for training a child in the performance of positive commandments depends upon the ability and the understanding of each child. Thus, as soon as the child understands the significance of the Sabbath, it becomes the child's duty to hear the *kiddush* and the *havdalah*, and the like. The time to train a child and to observe the negative commandments, whether Biblical or Rabbinical, is when he or she understands when told that this thing we are forbidden to do or that food we are forbidden to eat. It is well to train a child to respond *Amen* and other responses at the synagogue. From the time that an infant begins to respond *Amen*, he has a share in the world to come. It is important that children be trained to behave at the synagogue with awe and reverence. Children who run about to and fro and cause confusion should rather be kept home.

3. Even one who is not the child's father, is forbidden to give it forbidden food or to bid it do a forbidden act. According to the opinion of most authorities, it is forbidden to give him food or to tell him to perform an act, even when it is forbidden only by a Rabbinic ordinance. If the child is somewhat ill and it is necessary for him to eat forbidden food, he may be fed by a non-Jew with food which was forbidden only by Rabbinical law.

4. A thing which is not forbidden in itself, but forbidden because of the sanctity of the day, is not included in the precepts in which a child should be trained. It is, therefore, permissible to give a child food before the *kiddush* has been recited, although he must be trained to hear the *kiddush*. It is forbidden, however, to let a child eat outside the *sukkah;* for it is only in the matter of eating before the *kiddush*, which partakes of the nature of a negative command, that the law has been relaxed, but whenever the violation of a positive command is involved, it is forbidden to let the child transgress it.

5. It is forbidden to tell a child, even if he is under the age of nine, to carry anything on the Sabbath, even for the purpose of fulfilling a precept, like taking a prayer book or a Bible to the synagogue.

6. If a minor steals anything, he should be forced to return the stolen article if it is still intact; but if it is no longer intact, he is not required to make restitution even after he becomes of age. But to be justified in the sight of Heaven, he should make restitution after reaching the age of majority. Also, if he had committed any other sin in his minority, then when he reaches the age of discernment, it is well that he take upon himself to do a certain thing as penance. Concerning this it is written (Proverbs 19:2): "Also, that the soul be without knowledge is not good."

7. A parent should not threaten a child with future punishment. If he sees him misbehave, he should either punish him at once, or ignore it. It is told in the Talmud (Semaḥot 2:5-6) that a certain child ran away from school and his father threatened him with punishment. The child thereupon committed suicide. Said the Rabbis, of blessed memory, (loco citato): "In dealing with a child and a woman, the left hand should repel and the right hand should caress." A parent should not threaten a child with any unclean object (as stated above, chapter 33:14).

8. Legally, a Jewish child may be given to a non-Jewess to be nursed. Nevertheless, if possible to have it nursed by a Jewess, it should not be given to a non-Jewess, for it tends to dull the sensibilities and to create a bad temper. If a Jewish nurse must eat forbidden food as a remedy, she should not during those days nurse the child, if possible.

9. Every father is bound to teach the Torah to his son, for it is written (Deuteronomy 11:19): "And ye shall teach them to your children to speak of them." And just as he is obliged to teach his children, he is obliged to teach his grandchildren, for it is written (Deuteronomy 4:9): "And thou shalt make them known to thy children and to thy children's children."

10. As soon as a child begins to talk, his father should teach him the verse (Deuteronomy 33:4): "The Torah that Moses had commanded us," etc., and (Deuteronomy 6:4): "Hear, O Israel, the Lord is our God, the Lord is one." (However, one must be exceedingly careful to make certain that the child is clean while being taught). He should likewise teach him some other verses little by little, until he is fit to attend school. At such a time the father should engage a teacher who is God-fearing, so that he may train the child to be God-fearing from his very youth. When the child has advanced to the study of the Scriptures, it is customary to begin to teach him the *Sidrah* of *Vayikra* (Leviticus 1), containing the laws of sacrifices and purification. For the Rabbis, of blessed memory, said: "Let the pure, (the children) come and engage in the study of purity."

11. The teacher is bound to teach the children the whole day and also part of the night, so as to train them to study the Torah by day and by night. Under no circumstances should he interrupt their study, excepting at the close of the day preceding the Sabbath or a festival. Children should not be disturbed from their studies even for the purpose of building the Temple.

12. A teacher who leaves the children to themselves and goes out, or does some other work with them, or who teaches carelessly, is included in (Jeremiah 48:10): "Cursed be he who doth the work of the Lord with a slack hand." Therefore, the teacher appointed, should be a God-fearing man who can read fluently and grammatically. A teacher should not stay awake at night up to a late hour, in order that he may not be languid while teaching. He should not fast or eat too sparingly. Nor should he eat or drink to excess, for all these things render him unfit to teach efficiently. A teacher who deviates from these rules, forfeits his rights and should be dismissed.

13. A teacher should not punish the pupils like an enemy, with malice and cruelty, nor with a whip or a stick, but with a light strap.

14. On the Sabbath, a teacher should not teach the children a new lesson, because it is doing burdensome work on the Sabbath; but he may review with them a lesson they had learned previously.

15. It is forbidden to rob a minor of anything he had found, especially something that was given to him as a gift.

16. A Jewish child should not be given to a non-Jew to be instructed in reading and writing, or to be taught a trade, and needless to add that he should not be given to a Jewish heretic, who is much worse than a non-Jew, for it is to be feared that the child will follow in his footsteps.

CHAPTER 166

Enchantment and Superstition

1. It is written (Leviticus 19:26): "Neither shall ye use enchantment nor observe times." What constitutes "enchantment"? He who says: "Behold, the bread dropped from my mouth;" or, "The cane fell from my hand;" or, "My son called me from behind," or, "A raven croaked at me;" or, "A deer crossed my path;" or, "A snake passed on my right;" or, "A fox passed on my left, therefore, I will not go on this journey for I will not succeed;" or those who, on hearing the chirping of a bird, say: "May it mean this and not that;" or, "Now I know it is good to do this, but bad to do that thing;" or if he is asked to repay a loan, he says: "I pray you, leave me alone now, because it is early in the morning, and I do not wish to begin the day by

making a payment;" or, "It is the close of the Sabbath;" or, "It is New Moon;" or if one says: "This cock should be killed because he crowed in the evening;" or, "That hen should be killed because she crowed like a cock," or anything similiar to these. All of the above are forbidden, and he who divines by any of these, violates a negative Command. Some authorities say that if a person does not give the reason why he orders the cock or the hen to be killed, it is permissible to kill them. The prevailing custom is to sanction such an act.

2. A house, a child, or a woman, although no enchantment may be practiced through them, they may be regarded as omens. For instance, if one has built a new house, or has become the father of a child, or has taken a wife to himself, and thereafter he was successful on three occasions, he may regard it as a good omen and say: "This house brings me good luck" etc. It is likewise permissible to inquire of a child the verse he had studied at school and depend on it to engage in some work, for it is regarded somewhat in the nature of a prophecy. Some authorities hold that it is permissible to designate some future sign by which to ascertain the success of an enterprise, as was done by Eliezer the servant of Abraham, or Jonathan the son of Saul; while other authorities forbid it. However, he who walks in integrity, "And he that trusteth in the Lord, mercy compasseth him about" (Psalms 32:10).

3. What is meant by "observe times"? One who believes in astrology, saying this day is good and that day is bad; that day is lucky for such and such work; or that year or that month is bad for such and such work. The custom to make weddings at full moons, is not regarded as enchantment or as observing times, for this is done only as an auspicious sign, as the coronation of kings are held at springs, to symbolize the permanency of his rule. Nevertheless, no wedding should be postponed on this account. Needless to say that it should not be postponed to the full moon, when the bride will be menstrually unclean. It is likewise customary to begin to study on the New Moon. Some authorities also allow the custom of not starting anything on Mondays and Thursdays.

4. Our Rabbis, of blessed memory, further said: "What is meant by the term *meonen?* It refers to one who deceives the eyes (derived from the word *ayin,* in Hebrew, meaning *eye);* as if he had blindfolded the people, in doing things by sleight of hand, and creating the illusion that he is performing supernatural feats. The entertainers who practice this at weddings, are guilty of transgressing a Divine Prohibition, and they who engage them, are guilty of transgressing: "Before the blind thou shalt not put a stumbling block" (Leviticus 19:14). Therefore, the one who is in a position to prevent such practices should do so. And it is certainly forbidden to view these things, unless it is performed by a non-Jew.

5. It is forbidden to consult wizards, unless there is danger to human life. If any malady has come to one through witchcraft, mishap, or evil spirit, one may be cured by a non-Jewish wizard.

CHAPTER 167

Laws Concerning Idolatry

1. It is forbidden to derive any profit from idols, their appurtenances, their ornaments, and their sacrifices. If any of these things become mixed up with legitimate objects, be it even to the extent of one thousandth part thereof, it is forbidden to derive any profit from the entire lot.

2. The law of annulment applies to idols, their appurtenances, and their ornaments; that is, if the heathen destroys them so that they would no longer be used as idols or as ornaments to idols, it is permissible to derive benefit from them.

3. It is permissible to derive benefit from candles that have been lit in front of an idol, and thereafter extinguished by the heathen to be used for his own purpose and subsequently sold to a Jew. For this act constitutes their annulment. Nevertheless, such candles should not be used for the performance of a precept. This applies to everything belonging to an idol, although it has been annulled and it is permissible to make common use thereof, yet it is forbidden to be used for the performance of a precept, because they are still abominable to the Almighty.

4. Regarding the vestments which the priests wear in the house of idol worship, some authorities hold that they are the personal ornaments of the priests and not of the idols, and therefore do not require annullment, while other authorities hold that they must be annulled.

5. It is forbidden to look (in admiration) at idols and their ornaments, for it is written (Leviticus 19:4): "Ye shall not turn to idols." One must keep away from a house of idolatry, and especially from the idol itself, a distance of at least four cubits.

6. If a splinter has gotten into one's foot, or if one's coins were scattered in front of an idol, he must not bend down to remove the splinter or gather the coins, because it would appear as though he bows to the idol. It is forbidden even when there is no one present. One must first sit down, or turn his back or his side towards the idol, and thereafter do what he needs.

7. One authority maintains that it is forbidden to lend money for the purpose of building houses of idol-worship, or to buy ornaments or to hire sextons. It is especially forbidden to sell them accoutrements. He who refrains from doing these will prosper. It is not permissible to bind books

dealing with idolatry, excepting law books and literature. If a person fears that he will incur their hatred by refusing to bind them, he should at least try to evade it as much as possible.

8. It is forbidden to do business with idolaters where they assemble for worship and penance.

9. It is forbidden to mention the name of an idol whether for some purpose, like saying to a friend: "Wait for me near that idol," or needlessly, for it is written (Exodus 23:13): "And the name of other gods ye shall not mention." It is even forbidden to cause a heathen to mention the name of an idol, for it is written (loco citato): "It shall not be heard by your mouth;" that is, it shall not be caused by your mouth to have that name heard. If (in a lawsuit) the heathen is bound to take an oath, some authorities permit to let him swear. It is permissible to mention their holidays which are named after some individuals, provided one does not mention them in the same way as the heathens do, in a manner indicative of respect.

10. "All kinds of mockery is forbidden, except mockery of idols," says the Talmud (Sanhedrin 13b).

11. It is forbidden to give a gift to a heathen belonging to one of the seven peoples (who inhabitated Canaan), if he is not an acquaintance of the giver. For it is written (Deuteronomy 7:2): "And ye shall not show them mercy;" it is explained to mean: "Ye shall not give them a free gift." However, if he is an acquaintance, it is not considered as a free gift, for in time he will return his favor, or he has already compensated us for that, and it is the same as a sale.

12. It is forbidden to praise heathens, even as much as to say: "How handsome that heathen is," and surely one must not speak in praise of his deeds or to cherish any of his utterances, for this is likewise included in: "Ye shall not show mercy unto them;" that is, you shall not ascribe any grace unto them. But if one means thereby to praise the Holy One, blessed be He, for having created such a handsome being, it is permissible.

13. It is permitted to help their poor, to visit their sick, to bury their dead, to deliver a funeral oration, and to comfort their mourners, for the purpose of maintaining peaceful relations.

14. One should not be alone with a heathen belonging to one of the seven peoples, because they are apt to commit homicide.

15. A non-Jewess is not allowed to nurse a Jewish child in her own home, even in the presence of others. She may, however, nurse it in the house of a Jew when others are present, even if they go in and out, providing the child is not left with her alone in the nighttime.

CHAPTER 168

Images That Are Forbidden

1. It is written (Exodus 20:23): "Ye shall not make with Me gods of silver," etc. Our Rabbis, of blessed memory, have received it by tradition that this verse is a command not to draw pictures of objects on high or of below; that is: "Ye shall not make anything resembling My servants that minister before Me." Therefore, it is forbidden to make a picture of the four faces on the Chariot (Ezekiel 1), the images of the *seraphim*, *ophanim*, and the ministering angels. It is forbidden to make these even when they are not in relief, and even when made for a heathen. It is permissible, however, to keep them in the house, if they are not in relief. One is not allowed to tell a non-Jew to make them, because it is forbidden to tell a non-Jew to do anything prohibited by law, the same as it is prohibited to tell a non-Jew to perform labor on the Sabbath.

2. It is likewise forbidden to draw the picture of a man, even only the face of a man; and it is forbidden to keep it in the house, unless it be slightly disfigured. However, only a full face is forbidden, that is, when it has two eyes and a nose, but a profile is not forbidden.

3. It is forbidden to keep a ring which has a seal consisting of a man's image, if it is made in relief; but it is permissible to make a seal with it, since the signature becomes depressed. If, however, the figure on the ring is depressed, the ring may be kept, but it is forbidden to make a seal with it, because it comes out in relief.

4. We are not allowed to build a house modeled after the Holy Temple, having the same height, length, and width, nor a corridor modeled after the porch of the Temple, nor a court, a table, or a candelabrum modeled after those of the Temple. However, we are allowed to make a candelabrum of five, six or eight branches, but not of seven, even if it is made of metal other than gold and without cups, knops, and flowers, and even if it is not eighteen hand-breadths high, because all of the foregoing were not essential adjuncts of the candelabrum of the Sanctuary.

5. Some people make a seven-branched candelabrum by shaping six branches in a circle and one in the center; but many authorities forbid that, and where there is doubt regarding a Mosaic enjoinder, the stricter opinion should be followed.

6. He who prepares anointment oil in the same formula and in the same weight as prescribed in the Torah, is amenable to the penalty of *karet* (being cut off from his people); and if he does it unintentionally, he must bring a sin-offering, providing he has done it with the intention of anointing himself with it. He who prepares incense of the eleven ingredients prescribed in the Torah and in the same proportion, even if he prepared only one-half or one-third of that quantity, incurs the penalty of *karet*. However, if he prepared it only for the purpose of making a study of it, he is guiltless.

CHAPTER 169

Tattooing and Depilation

1. It is written in the Torah (Leviticus 19:28): "Ye shall not imprint any marks upon you." What is meant by the term "imprint marks?" A mark which is absorbed and sunk in the skin, so that it can never be erased. He who makes an incision in his skin and injects in the incision, stibium or ink, or any other coloring matter which leave a mark; likewise if he first dyes the skin and then makes the incision, is guilty of transgressing a negative precept. Nevertheless, it is permissible to put powder and other things on a wound for medicinal purposes even if a mark remains; for a mark will be left anyway as a result of the wound, and besides, it is apparent that he does not do it for the purpose of tattooing.

2. It is written (Leviticus 19:28): "Ye shall not make any cutting in your flesh for the dead;" also, (Deuteronomy 14:1): "Ye shall not cut yourselves, nor make any baldness between your eyes for the dead." *Sheritah* and *gedidah* (the Hebrew terms used in the Biblical text respectively) are one and the same, and are forbidden whether in front of the dead or not. Even to strike the flesh with the hand so that blood comes out is forbidden; and it is forbidden even when done for any other kind of grief.

3. By the term "baldness" is meant plucking out the hair of the head in mourning for the dead. Even the plucking out a single hair is forbidden. Women likewise are included in the rejoinder of: "Ye shall not make any baldness," and much more so with regard to: "Ye shall not make any cuttings."

CHAPTER 170

Shaving the Hair of the Temples and Beard

1. It is forbidden to shave off the hair of the temples on both sides of the head at their juncture with the cheeks at the ears. According to some authorities, it is forbidden to cut them even with scissors, close to the skin, as with a razor. Therefore, if it is necessary to shave off the hair from the temples for the sake of health, one must take care not to shave close to the skin. The length of the earlocks is estimated to be from the forehead as far as below the ear, where the cheeks widen.

2. The Torah has forbidden to shave the "corners" of the beard with a razor only. The beard has five "corners," and there are many opinions as to what they are. Therefore, he who fears God, should not use a razor on

any part of the beard, even on his upper lip or under the chin. There is no difference between a razor and a sharp stone which cuts the hair, such as a pumice stone; they are both forbidden. Those who remove their beard by means of a salve, should be careful not to scrape it off with a knife which might cut the hair; but they should use instead a strip of wood.

Chapter 171

A Male May Not Put On a Woman's Garment and Vice Versa

1. A man is forbidden to put on even a single garment worn by women, even though he can be recognized as a male by his other garments. A woman is likewise forbidden to put on even a single garment worn by men. Not only are feminine garments forbidden to men, but also the ornaments and the various toilet articles used by women of the region. Similarly, things specifically intended for men must not be used by a woman.

2. A male is forbidden to remove the hair from the armpits and from the genital organ, even with a pair of scissors if it looks as if it was done with a razor, that is, when it is cut close to the skin, for this is the practice of women. It is forbidden to rub with the hands, the hair of the armpits or of the genital organ so that it may fall out, but it may be done by means of his garment. One who has scabs in the armpits or in-between the lower limbs, is permitted to remove the hair if it troubles him.

3. A man is forbidden to pick even one gray hair from amidst the black ones, because this is the way of women and he thereby transgresses the spirit of (Deuteronomy 22:5): "A man shall not put on," etc. He is likewise forbidden to dye even one gray hair or to look into a mirror, unless he looks into it as a remedy, or when he cuts his hair, or wishes to remove a stain from his face, or remove feathers from his head. In a place where it is customary for men to look into mirrors, it is permissible for any reason.

Chapter 172

Laws Concerning New Crops

1. It is written (Leviticus 23:14): "And ye shall eat neither bread, nor parched corn, nor fresh ears to the selfsame day," etc. This is to say that we are forbidden to eat of the new crop belonging to any of the five species until after the offering of the *omer*, which took place on the sixteenth day of

Nisan. Nowadays when no *omer* is offered, we are forbidden to eat it the entire day (of the sixteenth). In countries outside Israel where two days of the festival are celebrated because of the existing doubt, it is also forbidden the entire day of the seventeenth. The *omer* makes valid for use, grain which has been sown and taken root before the sixteenth day of *Nisan,* and it may be eaten immediately after it is reaped. However, if it did not take root before the sixteenth of *Nisan,* the crop may not be used before the *omer* of the next year.

2. In the opinion of most of the celebrated legal authorities, the above prohibition applies also to countries outside Israel. Therefore, we must be extremely careful concerning crops sowed either after Passover or immediately before Passover but which has not taken root before the sixteenth day of *Nisan,* such as barley and oats, and in some places also wheat, that these be not used until the seventeenth day of *Nisan* of the next year. (If it had taken root on the sixteenth of *Nisan,* it may be used at the beginning of the night of the seventeenth of the next *Nisan,* in any event). The beer which is made out of this crop is likewise forbidden until after the next Passover. Also the lees is forbidden. If dough made of the old crop has been leavened with it, the dough may not be used because of the yeast. Concerning crops which are doubtful whether they are old or new, a rabbi should be consulted.

3. Some authorities hold that the prohibition against new crops, applies only to produce raised on a field of a Jew. Even if the field belongs to a non-Jew but it has been leased by a Jew, the law of new crops applies to the produce. But this prohibition does not apply to crops raised on the fieldof a non-Jew. Many people rely on this opinion in cases of emergency. Other authorities, however, hold that even when raised on the field of a non-Jew, it is subject to the law of new crops; and a blessing will come upon the one who follows the stricter opinion.

CHAPTER 173

The Law of Orlah (Fruits of the First Three Years)

1. The enjoyment of the fruit, seeds, and skins of all kinds of trees, whether they belong to a Jew or a non-Jew, even if they grow in a pot without a hole in the bottom, are entirely forbidden as *orlah* (during the first three years). These three years are calendar years and are not reckoned from the date they were planted. But if one has planted a tree before the sixteenth day of the month of *Ab,* inasmuch as there are yet forty-four days to *Rosh Hashanah* (it takes fourteen days for the plant to take root, and the thirty days that remain of that year are counted as a full year) we count only two more years from *Rosh Hashanah.* If, however, it was planted at any time, on or after the sixteenth day of *Ab,* that part of the year is not counted at all, and we must count three full years from *Rosh Hashanah.*

2. The fruits of the fourth year's growth is called *Neta rebai* (the growth of the fourth year), and it must be redeemed. How does one redeem it? He plucks the fruit after it is fully ripe, takes a silver coin, or some produce fit

for use to the value of a *perutah* (smallest coin in circulation), and says: "With this I redeem the fruit of the fourth year." Then he destroys the coin or the produce and throws it into a river. In lands outside Israel, no benediction is pronounced over the redemption.

3. Whether one has planted a seed, or a branch, or has transplanted a tree, he must consider the fruit as *orlah*. However, if one grafts a branch upon a tree, or if one bends the branch of a tree and inserts it into the ground in such a manner that the middle of the branch is buried in the ground while its end protrudes above the ground, even if it has been severed from the trunk of the tree, the law of *orlah* does not apply thereto in lands outside Israel.

4. If a tree is cut down, and there remains of its stump one hand-breadth, then whatever grows out of that stump is not considered as *orlah*. But if the stump is less than one hand-breadth high, whatever grows out of it is considered as *orlah*, and its years are counted from the time the tree was cut down. If a tree has been uprooted and some of its roots remained attached to the ground, even if they are not thicker than a needle, it is assumed that it can sustain itself without additional earth, and its fruit is not subject to the law of *orlah*, even if much extra earth has been heaped on it.

CHAPTER 174

The Grafting of Trees

1. The law prohibiting the grafting of dissimilar trees is implied in the verse (Leviticus 19:19): "Thou shalt not sow thy field with two kinds of seed." Therefore, it is forbidden to graft the branch of one variety of tree upon another, like the branch of an apple tree upon a citrous-bearing tree or vice versa. Such grafting is forbidden even between similiar species, as a branch of a cultivated apple tree upon a wild apple tree, because they are two different kinds of apples. A Jew must not allow a non-Jew to graft for him, two diverse kinds of trees.

2. It is forbidden to preserve a tree upon which the branch of a different kind had been grafted, but it is permissible to enjoy its fruit. It is permissible to transplant a branch of a grafted tree.

3. The law forbidding to sow a vineyard with two kinds of seeds (Deuteronomy 22:9), or a field with two kinds of seeds (Leviticus 19:19), has no application to countries outside Israel, unless one has sown two kinds of grain or two kinds of vegetables together with the seeds of the vineyard.

CHAPTER 175

The Interbreeding of Cattle

1. It is forbidden to cross-breed cattle, beasts or fowl with a diverse kind even to merely cause cross-breeding.

2. It is forbidden to do work with animals of diverse kinds, as to plough with them or let them draw a vehicle. It is even forbidden to drive them by the mere sound of the voice when they are harnessed together. Therefore, a

Jew is forbidden to walk alongside the cart of a non-Jew, drawn by diverse kinds of animals which are carrying the Jew's cargo, as it is likely that he will urge them on to hasten their pace, which constitutes driving diverse kinds of beasts.

3. We are forbidden to ride in a vehicle drawn by diverse kinds of animals, even when we do not drive them.

4. We are not allowed to tie a beast to a vehicle which is drawn by a beast of another kind, either at the side of the vehicle or behind it.

5. It is forbidden to tie two animals of diverse kinds, even for the purpose of guarding them, so they would not run away. We must likewise be careful not to tie together, two different kinds of fowl; some people are in error concerning this.

6. A mule is bred by a horse and an ass, and it has two species: One is bred by a stallion and a she-ass, and the other by a mare and an ass. These are considered two diverse kinds of beasts. Therefore, one who wishes to hitch two mules together, should first examine their characteristic features, such as the ears, tails, and voices. If these are similiar, it indicates that the female parent of both belongs to the same kind, and it is permissible to hitch them together. Some authorities, however, are of the opinion that even one mule is considered as two diverse kinds, and it is forbidden to do any work with it or to ride on it.

CHAPTER 176

Laws Concerning Shatnez (Wool Mixed With Linen)

1. It is forbidden to wear a garment mixed with the wool of ewes or rams with linen, because of the Command forbidding *shatnez* (the mixture of wool and linen; (Leviticus 19:19; Deuteronomy 22:11). Whether the woolen garment has been sewn to the linen garment even with silk or hemp thread, or vice versa, or whether a linen thread was tied to woolen thread or braided together, all of these are forbidden as *shatnez*. If one has fastened two pieces of material together only with one stitch and tied it, or if one has fastened the same with two stitches without tying them, both cases are considered to be *shatnez*. Therefore, it is forbidden to join a woolen garment and a linen garment even with pins.

2. It is permissible to make garments of sheepskin with linen threads, and we do not mind the woolen hairs that mingle with the linen thread, for the woolen hairs are not used as threads and may be disregarded.

3. To join wool and flax (linen) with something intervening between them, for instance, to take a piece of leather and sew a piece of wool on one side and a piece of linen on the other side, is forbidden by Biblical ordinance, according to Maimonides. But some authorities permit it. Therefore, according to the latter opinion, skins sewed together with linen threads may be

used as a lining of a woolen garment (and though it is likely that the hemp thread with which one sews on the lining will penetrate among the flax threads with which the skins are sewn together, we are not concerned about it). And such is the prevailing custom. Nevertheless, a God-fearing person should heed the opinion of Maimonides.

4. Even if ten mattresses lie one on top of the other, and the bottom one is *shatnez,* it is forbidden to sit on the top mattress.

5. If a garment contains *shatnez* at one end, it is forbidden to cover oneself with the other end, even if the forbidden part is resting on the ground.

6. One who sews a garment of *shatnez* for a non-Jew, may sew it in the regular manner, even if it rests upon his knees; provided, however, he does not intentionally derive pleasure from the garment while resting upon his knees. Clothing dealers are allowed to carry on their shoulders, clothing made of *shatnez,* in the course of selling them, provided they do not intentionally cover themselves with them as a protection from cold or rain. Nevertheless, God-fearing persons carry such clothes on a stick.

7. Handkerchiefs, bath towels, tablecloths, and the covering of the lectern, upon which the Torah is read, are subject ot the law of *shatnez.* It is also forbidden to make curtains of *shatnez,* but the curtain covering the Holy Ark in the synagogue may be made of *shatnez.*

8. Upholstered vehicles, the kind in which princes ride, some of which are covered on the inside with woolen cloth containing *shatnez,* (for it is presumed that they have been sewn together with linen thread) may be used for riding purposes, providing one is careful not to lean against the sides containing the *shatnez.* Especially should one be careful not to sit on cushions containing *shatnez.* Some authorities permit to sit on such cushions, since they do not bend over the sides of a person.

CHAPTER 177

The Firstborn of Clean Animals

1. If a clean animal belonging to a Jew has given birth, the owner must sanctify it by saying: "This is holy;" for it is written (Deuteronomy 15: 19): "Thou shalt sanctify unto the Lord thy God." If he neglected to sanctify it, it becomes holy on its own accord as soon as it is born, and it must be given to the *Kohen,* whether it is without any defect or it has received one after its birth, or even if it has been born with a defect. However, it should not be given to the *Kohen* when it is very young, because this does not do any

honor to the *Kohen*. The owner should raise it until it is somewhat grown up, that is, in the case of a small animal (sheep or goat) he must keep it thirty days, and in the case of a large animal (cow) he should keep it fifty days. If there is no *Kohen* to be found, the owner is bound to keep it until a *Kohen* happens to come along.

2. If the *Kohen* says to the owner: "Give it to me and I will raise it," he is not permitted to give it to him if it has no blemish, for it would appear as if the *Kohen* is doing a favor to the owner (in that he is tending it for him), in consideration of getting the animal. Such a transaction is equivalent to robbing other priests. If, however, the animal has received a blemish in the meantime and the *Kohen* says to the owner: "Give it to me that I may eat it," he may give it to him, since he may slaughter it immediately.

3. The *Kohen* is not allowed to refuse to take the animal from the owner on the ground that it is too much trouble for him to raise it until it receives a blemish, for he is thereby showing contempt for the priestly gifts. Nevertheless, the Jew is forbidden to give it to the *Kohen* in order to vex him or to take revenge on him; and if he is doing it with this intention, the *Kohen* may refuse to accept it. If the Jew has been guilty of negligence, in that he had an opportunity to sell the cow to a non-Jew before it has given birth, and he failed to do so, then the *Kohen* is not obliged to accept it from him, but he must raise it himself until it receives a blemish and then give it to the *Kohen*.

4. Nowadays it is necessary to keep the firstborn until it receives a blemish, and upon receiving a blemish, it should be submitted to three men versed in the Torah, one of whom should be an expert, to be able to decide whether or not it is a permanent blemish, and if it is, they declare it to be permissible for use. Thereafter it is slaughtered, and if it proves to be *kosher*, it may be eaten even by a Jew. It should not, however, be sold in the meat market, or weighed out by the pound, nor should any part of it be given to dogs, or sold or given to a non-Jew.

5. When a firstborn sustains a blemish, if there are men competent to pass upon its validity, it should be shown to them immediately. After it is declared permitted for use, it should not be kept very long. If it was permitted for use in its first year it may be kept until it is one year old, and if it was done near the end of one year or after it was one year old, it should be kept no longer than thirty days. If the owner has transgressed and kept it longer than the prescribed time, it is not disqualified thereby.

6. It is the duty of the *Kohen* to keep the firstborn until it receives a blemish. He may sell it to a Jew, whether it has a blemish or not, providing the latter treats it as behooves the holiness of a firstborn, and also providing he does not buy it for commercial purposes.

7. One must not flay the firstborn from its feet upward, as it is a disgrace that while the skin is still on the holy thing, he intends to make bellows of it.

8. If the firstborn is slaughtered and found to be ritually unfit for use, no benefit may be derived from its skin or from its meat, but it must be buried. If it dies a natural death, it must likewise be buried. It is customary to wrap it in a sheet and bury it in a cemetery deep in the ground.

9. It is forbidden to fleece the firstborn or to perform any work with it, whether it is with or without a blemish. Even if some of its wool has come off by itself, such wool may never be used. However, the wool found on its body when slaughtered upon having received a blemish, may be used, because the slaughtering renders its wool fit for use, just as it does the skin and the meat.

10. The firstborn becomes qualified for use only when it receives a blemish. But it is forbidden to close it up in a vault so that it would die, because one is thus destroying a sacred thing.

11. It is forbidden to make a blemish in a firstborn, or even to cause it indirectly, as for instance, to put some dough on its ear so that a dog would grab it and bite off its ear. It is also forbidden to tell a non-Jew to make a blemish in it, but it may be given to a non-Jew to raise it and to take care of it.

12. If one buys a cow from a non-Jew and it gives birth, but it is not known whether it has ever given birth before, the calf is considered of doubtful primogeniture. Even if the non-Jew volunteers the information that the cow has once given birth before, it is of no avail. Even the marks in its horns are of no avail, and even if she was being milked, it is no sign, unless we see it give suck to a calf. If the cow is milked, and in addition the non-Jew tells, innocently, and not for the purpose of promoting the sale, that she has once given birth before, these two things combine to establish the fact of a former birth as regards cows but not as regards goats.

13. Priests and Levites are also subject to the law regarding the firstborn of a clean animal, only the Priest sets it aside and keeps it for himself in a state of holiness that is attached to a firstborn.

14. If a non-Jew owns a cow in partnership with a Jew, or if a Jew tends a cow belonging to a non-Jew, in consideration of which he is to receive an equal share in the offspring, he is exempt from the law regarding a firstborn, for it is written (Exodus 13:2): "Whatsoever openeth the womb among the children of Israel," which means if the whole of it belongs to a Jew. If a non-Jew tends a cow belonging to a Jew, and they divide the offspring among them, it is of no avail (with regard to exempt it from the law of the firstborn), according to the opinion of many scholars, but the Jew must sell the mother to the non-Jew.

15. It is a commendable act to sell a clean animal to a non-Jew before she gives birth, or to form a partnership with a non-Jew before that, in order to exempt it from the law governing a firstborn. Although this transaction

strips the holiness from the firstborn, it is, nevertheless preferable, so that no violations might be committed with regard to its wool and its employment for work. If the owner transfers title to the unborn offspring, it is of no avail, since it is a thing that has not yet come into existence; but he must give title to the mother, as well. The transfer of title should be made in this wise: The owner should come to terms with the non-Jew about the price of the cow, and also rent him the place that the cow occupies; and the non-Jew gives a *perutah* (smallest coin in circulation) to the owner who says to him: "For this *perutah* you shall acquire possession of the place where the cow is standing, and this place will acquire title of the cow for you." Or, it can be done thus: After they have come to terms about the price of the cow, the non-Jew gives him a *perutah* and also takes the cow either into his own possession or into a public lane, and he thus acquires title to it by means of the *meshiḥa* (actual transfer of possession) and by the coin; even if he later returns the cow to the premises of the owner, it does not matter.

CHAPTER 178

The Firstborn of an Ass

1. If a Jew has a she-ass and she gives birth to a firstborn, he must redeem it. With what does he redeem it? With the young of sheep or of goats, and it matters not whether it is big or small, perfect or with a blemish, provided it has no organic defect, nor had it been slaughtered or found in an animal that has been slaughtered. This lamb must be given to the *Kohen*. And when he is obliged to redeem it? At anytime from the day of its birth until its death. It is, nevertheless, commendable to redeem it immediately, in order not to delay the performance of a precept. After it is redeemed, it ceases to be holy. Also the lamb in the possession of the *Kohen* is not holy.

2. Immediately upon setting aside the lamb in exchange of the ass, the latter becomes profane, even before the lamb is given to the Priest. Therefore, at the time he sets the lamb aside, he must pronounce the benediction: "Who hath sanctified us by His commandments and hath commanded us concerning the redemption of the firstborn ass."

3. No benefit may be derived from the firstborn ass before it is redeemed, even if it has already been given to the *Kohen*. Also, the *Kohen* himself is not allowed to derive any benefit from it until it is redeemed and he takes the lamb for himself. If it dies before it is redeemed, it must be buried.

4. If the owner does not wish to redeem it, he should strike it with a hatchet on the back of its head until it dies (Exodus 13:13), and then bury it, for no benefit may be derived from it. The precept of redeeming takes precedence over the breaking of its neck.

5. Priests and Levites need not redeem the firstborn of an ass. Their daughters, too, are exempt from performing this precept, but their husbands must redeem the firstborn of their asses. The partnership with a *Kohen* or a *Levi*, as well as the partnership with a non-Jew exempts it from redemption,

but it is forbidden to form such a partnership with the intention of doing away with the holiness of the ass, since this may be remedied by either redeeming it or by breaking its neck.

CHAPTER 179

Laws Concerning Loans

1. It is an affirmative precept to lend money to a poor Jew, as it is written (Exodus 22:24): "If thou lend money to any of My people, even to the poor with thee," etc. Although the word "if" is written in the Biblical text, our Sages, of blessed memory, have it by tradition that this "if" does not imply an optional act, but an obligation. It is thus stated in the *Meḥilta:* "If thou lend money to any of My people,' expresses a duty. How do we know that it is a duty, perhaps it is only an option? (For it says 'if'). Because it is written (Deuteronomy 15:8): 'And shalt surely lend him,' to teach us that it is an obligation and not an option. The word 'if' is to be interpreted thus: 'When thou lendest money, thou shalt lend it to one of My people and not to a heathen; and to whom of My people? To him that is *with thee.*" From this they inferred (Baba Metzia 71a), that a poor relative takes precedence over others, and the poor in one's city take precedence over the poor of another city. The precept of lending money to a poor man is greater than giving charity to a poor man, for the latter has already been accustomed to ask for alms, while the former has not yet reached that stage. The Torah has frowned on one who refuses to lend money to the poor, as it is written (Deuteronomy 15:9): "And thine eye be evil against thy needy brother." Concerning the one who lends money to the needy in time of his distress, the Scripture says (Isaiah 58:9): "Then shalt thou call, and the Lord will answer."

2. One is bound to lend money even to a rich man, if he is in need of a loan, to cheer him with kind words, and to give him proper advice.

3. It is forbidden to lend money even to a scholar without witnesses, unless it is secured by a pledge. The best course is to have a note drawn up on the loan.

4. It is forbidden to demand payment from the borrower, knowing that he is unable to pay. It is forbidden even to confront him lest he be put to shame. Concerning this, it is written (Exodus 22:24): "Thou shalt not be unto him as a creditor."

5. Just as the lender is forbidden to oppress the borrower, so is the latter forbidden to withhold his neighbor's money, telling him to come later, when he has no money, as it is written (Proverbs 3:28): "Say not to thy brother, 'go, and come again.'"

6. A borrower is forbidden to spend the borrowed money unnecessarily, lest it be lost and the lender will be unable to collect it. It is improper even if the lender be very wealthy. One who acts like that is called an evildoer,

as it is written (Psalms 37:21): "The wicked borroweth, and payeth not." The Sages have commanded (Abot 2:17): "Let thy neighbor's property be as dear unto thee as thine own." If the lender knows that the borrower is a man with no consideration for the property of others, he should not lend him the money, lest he be compelled to dun him, and thus transgress on each occasion the precept: "Thou shalt not be to him as a creditor."

7. The one who lends money on a pledge, must avoid making use of the pledge, for this is like taking interest. If one lends money on the security of a ploughshare or on an axe, which can be hired out at a good fee and will be only slightly depreciated by use, he may do so without obtaining the owner's permission, and he may deduct the proceeds from the debt, as it may be assumed that the borrower would agree to it. Some authorities hold that the lender may hire out these articles only to other people, but not to himself, lest he be suspected of using then free of charge merely because of the loan.

8. If the lender wants to take a pledge from the borrower, after the loan had been made, he must do so only with the consent of a Court of Law.

9. A person should avoid whenever possible, becoming guarantor or holding trust funds.

10. If one holds a note of indebtedness, which is worn out and the script thereof is likely to become faded, he should go to a Court of Law and have it certified.

11. It is forbidden to keep a paid note in one's possession, for it is said (Job 11:14): "And let not unrighteousness dwell in thy tents."

12. A lender must guard a pawn even more carefully than a bailee must guard a deposited article, because he is like a paid keeper of the article. And just as a bailee is not permitted to give the article to another person to take care of it (as will be explained in chapter 185, below), so is the lender not permitted either to deposit the pledge with someone else or to give it as a pledge without the consent of the owner.

13. If one lends money to a neighbor on a pledge, on condition that if he does not repay the loan at a certain time, he shall forfeit the pledge, then the lender must take care to tell the borrower when the loan is made: "If you do not redeem the pledge by such and such a time, I shall acquire title to it retroactive to the present time."

14. If a man owes money to another, and the latter says: "I am sure that you owe me nothing," he need not pay him, because he has apparently remitted the debt.

15. When a borrower repays the debt to the lender's messenger, the latter acquires title to the money on behalf of the lender as soon as it is handed to him. The borrower is then forbidden to take the money back, promising to repay it at a later time; it is the same as borrowing money without the owner's knowledge. The messenger is equally forbidden to return the money to the borrower.

CHAPTER 180

Cancellation of Debts in the Sabbatical Year

1. Most authorities agree that the cancellation of debts on the Sabbatical year, prevails today as well, even in lands outside Israel. The general public, however, ignore this law, and the great teachers in Israel, of blessed memory, have already inveighed against this laxity. A few of them have endeavored to find justification for the non-observance of this law, depending on a few authorities who are lenient in this matter. However, one who desires to observe precepts meticulously, should heed the opinion of the majority of authorities, of blessed memory. Particularly so, when one can surmount the difficulty by means of the *prosbol* (see section 15, below), and thereby escape a monetary loss. The last Sabbatical year was in 5684, and will occur again with the Grace of God, in 5691.

2. The Sabbatical (seventh) year (*shemitah*) cancels every loan, whether it is oral, or on a note, or even on a mortgage. If a person has given to his neighbor, money on a *shetar iska* (business partnership; see chapter 66, above), according to the terms of which one-half of the money is considered as a loan, and the other half as a deposit, the half which is a loan is cancelled, but not the one which is a deposit.

3. A loan made on the security of a pledge, is not released on the Sabbatical year; but regarding a loan made on the security of realty, there is a diversity of opinion as to the law in such a case.

4. If a surety paid the lender, and before the borrower had paid the surety, the Sabbatical year intervened, the debt is canceled.

5. If a person is obliged to take an oath concerning a monetary claim, and if he were to admit his liability, the Sabbatical year would cancel his debt, then the oath is likewise canceled.

6. If a man owes money to another but he denies it; the matter is brought to court and it decides against him. Then the judges write down their verdict, give it to the lender, then the Sabbatical year does not cancel this debt.

7. If one lends money to another and stipulates with him that the Sabbatical year shall not cancel this loan, the loan is, nevertheless, canceled. However, if they agreed that the *borrower* shall not cancel this debt, even if

this happens to be the Sabbatical year, the debtor is not released. Likewise, if he has written in the note of indebtedness and referred to this transaction as a 'bailment,' the Sabbatical year does not cancel this debt.

8. If one lends money to another for a certain number of years, and the debt is due after the Sabbatical year, the debt is not canceled, because the lender has not been able to demand the debt any earlier.

9. If a creditor delivers his notes of indebtedness to the Court, saying: "Collect my debts for me," the debts are not canceled by the Sabbatical year.

10. If one sells something to another on credit, the money due is considered as a loan, and the debt is canceled by the Sabbatical year. However, a shopkeeper who sells to people on credit, and it is not his custom to demand payment until a certain amount has accumulated, such debts are not canceled. If, however, he charged it as a loan, that is, he totted up all the items and entered the sum total in his ledger, then it is considered a loan, and the debt is canceled by the Sabbatical year.

11. The wages of a hired laborer are not canceled by the Sabbatical year, but if they were converted into a loan, they are canceled.

12. Claims acquired from a non-Jew are treated as though they still belonged to the non-Jew. Therefore, if one purchases a note of indebtedness from a non-Jew due him from a Jew, the Sabbatical year does not cancel the indebtedness, because the non-Jew can collect the debt under all circumstances. If one has become guarantor to a non-Jew on behalf of a Jew, and the latter failed to pay his debt, so that the guarantor had to pay the non-Jew, from whom he takes the note held against the borrower, this note is not canceled by the Sabbatical year. If there is no note but he sues the borrower because he had to pay the non-Jew for him, then the borrower is exempt from payment.

13. The Sabbatical year cancels loans only at its end; therefore, one who lends money during the Sabbatical year, may collect the debt during the entire year, but at sunset on the eve of the New Year, the debt is canceled.

14. If a borrower comes to pay his debt to the lender after the Sabbatiical year, the lender should say to him: "I have canceled your debt, and you are already released as far as I am concerned." If the borrower says: "Nevertheless, I wish you to accept the money," the lender may accept it, but the borrower must not say: "I pay you this money on account of my debt;" but rather say: "The money is mine and I give it to you as a gift." The lender may even make an effort to persuade the borrower to give him the money as a gift, but if this cannot be done, he must not accept it from him.

15. The document known as *prosbol* exempts one from releasing debts on the Sabbatical year. A *prosbol* is obtained in the following manner: The lender goes to three men, learned in the Torah, who form themselves into a Court of Law. He says to them: "Ye judges, I hand over to you all my claims against so-and-so, so that I would be able to collect them whenever

I desire." They then write for him a *prosbol*, reading: "In a session of three judges where we were together, so-and-so the lender, came and said in our presence, 'I hand over,' etc." The three of them sign at the bottom of the document, either as judges or as witnesses. This can also be done at the end of the year, that is, before sunset on the eve of the ensuing New Year. Some authorities say that it is not even necessary to write the *prosbol*, but his oral declaration made before them suffices. If there is no Court of Law in his town, he can say: "I hand over my notes to the Court of Law, which is in such-and-such a place."

16. The *prosbol* is of no avail unless the borrower possesses some realty, be it ever so small. Even if he has only a flower pot with a hole at the bottom; and even if the borrower has nothing at all, but his guarantor has some realty, or someone who is indebted to him has some realty, it suffices. But if all these persons have nothing and the lender possesses realty, be it ever so little, he may transfer it to the borrower even through a third party and even in his abscence, and this will suffice to make the *prosbol* valid.

CHAPTER 181

Litigation and Testimony

1. When a controversy arises between two persons, they should make every effort to compromise, in order to avoid the humiliation of a lawsuit.

2. If it is impossible for them to reach a compromise, and they are forced to go to court, they should have recourse to a Jewish tribunal. It is forbidden to bring a suit before heathen judges in their courts, even if their decision would be in accordance with the law of Israel. Even if the two litigants are willing to try the case before them, it is forbidden. Even if they made either an oral or a written agreement to that effect, it is of no avail. Whoever takes a case before them, is a godless person, and he is considered as if he had defiled, blasphemed, and rebelled against the Law of Moses, peace be unto him. Even in the case where a man may take the law into his own hands, as will be explained, if it please the Almighty, in paragraph 9, below, yet it is forbidden to do it through a heathen. Even if he does not bring the case before a heathen tribunal, but he forces his opponent, through a heathen, that he go with him before a Jewish court, he deserves to receive a flogging.

3. When the heathens are in power, or if the defendant is a hard man, the plaintiff should first summon him to appear before a Jewish court, and on his refusal to do so, the plaintiff should obtain the consent of the *Beth Din* (Jewish Court) and save his property by a suit in a general Court of Law.

4. He who is sued for the repayment of a debt which he justly owes, must not resort to subterfuge to force a compromise in order to pay less than he actually owes. If he does force the creditor to relinquish part of the debt, he does not discharge his obligation before the judgment of Heaven until he pays the claimant all that is rightfully due him.

5. A litigant is forbidden to present his case before the judge in the abscence of his opponent. For that reason, neither litigant should appear before the judge without the other, lest he be suspected of having presented his case in the abscence of his opponent.

6. Just as the judge who takes a bribe, even to acquit the innocent, transgresses a Divine Law, so does he who gives the bribe transgress the Law (Leviticus 19:14): "Thou shalt not put a stumbling block before the blind."

7. A litigant must not put in a false plea, even when he has a just claim but he knows that by telling the truth, judgment will be against him. Thus it is stated in the Talmud (Shebuot 31a): "Our Rabbis have taught: Whence do we know that he who has a claim of one hundred shekels against another, should not say, I will claim two hundred, so that he will be obliged to take an oath, and to avoid the oath, he will admit that he owes me one hundred, and then I will force him to take also an oath with regard to some other matter?" We learn it from the verse (Exodus 23:7): "Keep thee far from a false matter." Whence do we know that if one has a claim against another for one hundred shekels but he demands two hundred, that the borrower should not say, I will deny the whole claim in Court and outside I will admit to him that I owe him one hundred, in order to avoid taking an oath, and also to prevent him from making me swear as regards some other matter? We learn it from the verse: "Keep thee far from a false matter." Whence do we know that if three people have a claim of one hundred against one person, that one of them must not be the plaintiff and the others appear as witnesses in order to obtain the one hundred shekels and divide it among themselves? We learn it from the verse: "Keep thee far from a false matter."

8. Occasionally, litigants choose arbitrators to sit either jointly with the Court or apart from the Court. This is a proper procedure, because each arbitrator advances the cause of the one who has chosen him, and thus a just settlement will be reached. But the arbitration must be conducted in a just manner. Heaven forbid, that the compromise should be reached in a perverse way. For just as it is forbidden to pervert judgment, even so it is forbidden to pervert arbitration.

9. A man may, at times, take the law into his own hands. If he sees an article of his in the possession of someone, who had robbed him of it, he may take it away from him. If the latter resists, the former may even use force, if he is unable to get it by other means. He may do so even if the article is such that it will not depreciate by waiting until he summons him to court. If there are witnesses present when the owner seizes the article from the unlawful possessor, he cannot seize it by means of force unless he can thereafter prove that the article belonged to him. Should he be unable to prove ownership, his seizure of the article will be of no avail, since there were witnesses

that he seized it by force. But if there were no eyewitnesses, the seizure will be effective even if he will be unable to prove his ownership thereafter.

10. When the people of a community appoint judges, they must ascertain that each of them possesses the following seven qualifications: Wisdom in the Torah, humility, fear of God, hate of money, love of truth, the esteem and love of his fellow men, and a reputation for good deeds. Whosoever appoints a judge unfit for his position, trangresses the precept which says (Deuteronomy 1:17): "Ye shall not respect persons in judgment," meaning thereby: "Ye shall not favor anyone by saying, 'So-and-so is wealthy, so-and-so is my relative, I will appoint him as a judge.'" It is forbidden to rise for any judge whose appointment has been bought by means of silver and gold, and it is likewise forbidden to show him any other mark of respect. With reference to such a person, the Rabbis, of blessed memory, apply the verse (Exodus 20:20): "Ye shall not make with Me *gods* (the Hebrew word *Elohim* also means *judges*) of silver nor gods (or judges) of gold" (Sanhedrin 7b).

11. In communities where there are no men learned enough to qualify as judges, they should appoint the best and the wisest of the townsmen to act as judges, although they are not properly qualified, in order that the people should not take their cases before a heathen tribunal. As soon as they are accepted as judges by the townsmen, no one can disqualify them. The judges should do everything for the glory of Heaven.

12. If one is summoned by one's neighbor to testify in his behalf at a court of law, and he is qualified to do so, he is obliged to testify, whether or not there are other witnesses besides him. If he refuses to testify, he will be answerable to the Heavenly Court. A person is forbidden to testify in a matter of which he has no personal knowledge, even if his knowledge is based on what a reliable person had told him. If the litigant says to him: "Come to court and just stand by the one witness that I have in order to make the debtor believe that I have two witnesses and consequently he will admit his obligation to me," he must not hearken to him, as it is written (Exodus 23:7): "Keep thee far from a false matter."

13. The testimony of one witness is admissible only when a monetary transaction is involved, when his testimony may result in requiring the administration of an oath. Likewise, if a person is about to commit an illegal act, one witness may testify in order to prevent him from committing it. But if his neighbor has already violated the prohibited act, he should not testify, for since his single testimony is not believed, it will be considered as though he had spread an evil report about his neighbor.

14. The testimony of a witness who accepts a reward for testifying, is null and void. This, however, relates only to one who has already witnessed the facts and is in duty bound to testify. But if one is asked to witness a transaction in order to testify subsequently, he may take compensation to the extent that he has been inconvenienced, but no more. Also, if it is trouble-

some for him to appear before the court, he may take a proper compensation for the trouble involved, but no more.

15. A witness who derives some benefit from the matter involved, or who has any personal interest in it, no matter how remote, is unfit to testify.

16. It is written (Ezekiel 18-18): "And did that which is not good among his people;" this is explained (Shebuot 31a) that it refers to one who comes with a power of attorney and brings litigation in court for a matter that does not concern him. This is only true when both litigants are in town, but the borrower happens to be a strong man and a good pleader and the lender, fearing to appear against him, gives a power of attorney to someone else. Then the latter contends about a matter that is not of his concern. But if the defendant lives in another town, and the plaintiff is unable to go there in person and gives someone else the power of attorney, then the latter is doing a meritorious act in rescuing the wronged person from the hand of a robber. Some authorities hold that it is permissible for one to come to court with a power of attorney, if he is remunerated for it, for then he does not appear as a meddlesome person.

17. One should abstain as much as possible from taking an oath, even if it be a true one.

18. If a litigant is aware that his opponent, who is obliged to take an oath, will swear falsely, he should come to terms with him the best way possible, and not to let him swear falsely, for it is written (Exodus 22:10): "The oath of the Lord shall be between them both," and it is inferred from this verse (Shebuot 39b) that the onus of the oath rests on both.

19. If a Jew is in possession of evidence in favor of a non-Jew who has a lawsuit with another Jew in a non-Jewish court, then if by his testimony, he will cause his fellow Jew to become liable to a larger sum than he would be in a Jewish court, he is not allowed to testify. Otherwise, he may testify. If the non-Jew had arranged with the Jew that he would testify in his behalf, and if he should not do so, the name of God will be desecrated (by the Jew's breach of faith), he must give his evidence under all circumstances.

20. A witness may testify to any remembered fact, and he need hot fear that because it happened long ago, he would not remember clearly. He may testify even if he cannot recollect the facts unless he refers to the record he made in his book, but upon reading the record, his memory is refreshed. He is also permitted to be reminded of the facts by another person, be it even another witness, but not by one of the litigants. The litigant, however,

may bring the facts to the attention of a third party, who in turn may remind the witness.

21. A witness who is related to one of the litigants or to one of the judges, or to another witness in the case, even if the relationship be on the wife's side may in certain cases be disqualified to testify. Even if the witness is related only to the guarnator, and not to the borrower, he is unfit to testify on behalf of the borrower. The Torah has disqualified the testimony of a relative, not because of the love they bear to each other, for it is immaterial whether one testifies to the guilt or the innocence of his relative; it is an arbitrary decree. Even Moses and Aaron could not testify for one another. Therefore, any witness who is related to any of the litigants or to another witness, even if the relationship has been dissolved, must inform the judges so they may decide whether he may testify according to law.

22. If one witness knows that the other one is a sinful man, who is unfit to testify according to the Law of the Torah, and the judges are unaware of his wickedness, he is forbidden to testify with him, even though the testimony is true, for it is written (Exodus 23:1): "Put not thy hand with the wicked to be an unrighteous witness." It is a decree of the Torah, that the testimony of a whole set of witnesses, be they ever so many, becomes invalid if only one among them is unqualified to testify. Who is considered an evildoer who is disqualified by the decree of the Torah? Whoever transgresses in a matter which has been recognized in Israel to be a sin, and which is a Divine Prohibition, provided he transgressed intentionally and did not repent. If it can be presumed that he acted unintentionally or in ignorance, not being aware of the prohibition, he is not disqualified to bear testimony.

CHAPTER 182

Laws Concerning Theft and Robbery

1. It is forbidden to rob or to steal an article even of trivial value from a Jew or a non-Jew. We find in *Tanna Debe Eliyahu:* It happened that a certain man told him that he had wronged a non-Jew in measuring dates he had sold him. Thereafter, he had bought oil for the money he had received. The jug broke and the oil was spilled. I said: Blessed be the Omnipotent who regards not persons. The Torah says (Leviticus 19:13): "Thou shalt not oppress thy neighbor nor rob him," and the robbery of a non-Jew also constitutes robbery.

2. It is permissible to take from another, a thing of such little value, that no one would mind it, like taking a chip from a bundle of wood for a toothpick. However, the pious refrain from doing even this.

3. It is forbidden to steal even with the intention of returning the articles, doing it merely to annoy or to tease.

4. It is forbidden to oppress one's neighbor even in the slightest degree, as it is written (Leviticus 19:13): "Thou shalt not oppress thy neighbor." Who is considered an oppressor? He who has come into possession of his neighbor's money with the latter's consent, like a loan or wages and refuses to pay him, or he puts him off by saying, "Come again." If one has borrowed an article from a non-Jew which is still intact, he is forbidden to deny it for this constitutes plain robbery. Moreover, when buying anything whatever from a non-Jew, it is forbidden to fool him in counting out the money, as it is written (Leviticus 25:50): "And he shall reckon with his buyer," which refers to a non-Jew; when the article is conveyed only in consideration of the sum agreed, and if the purchaser fools him when paying for it, it is tantamount to stealing the article and not as just denying a debt. Even deception not involving any loss of money is forbidden, as stated in chapter 63, above.

5. If a person covets his neighbor's house, or vessel, or anything which the latter has no intention of selling, and he seeks to influence him either in person or through friends to sell it to him, he violates the injunction (Deuteronomy 5:18): "Neither shalt thou covet." From the very moment that he begins to devise ways and means how to procure the article, he has transgressed the aforesaid law (loco citato): "Thou shalt not desire;" for desire is only in the heart, and desire leads to covetousness. He who buys the things which he has desired, transgresses two Commands: "Thou shalt not covet," and "Thou shalt not desire."

6. The robber is enjoined by law to restore the very thing that he had stolen, if it is in its original state and has not been altered, as it is written (Leviticus 5:23): "He shall restore that which he took by robbery." The same law applies to a thief. Restitution in money is not acceptable, even if the owner has given up hope of ever regaining the article. But if the stolen article was lost or altered in such a way that it cannot be restored to its original state, or it was sunk in a building and can be retrieved only by tearing the building down, which would be a great loss to him, then he does his duty by paying a sum equivalent to the value of the article at the time it was stolen. If the victim of the robbery is in another town, he need not send the money to him, but he should notify him to call for it. If the victim died, restitution must be made to his heirs.

7. He who robs the public—like a shopkeeper who gives a short measure or a short weight, or a public official who is lenient towards his kin, and exacting towards others, or one who took usury from the public—for any of these it is difficult to repent effectively. He should, therefore, establish a

community project, so that those whom he robbed should benefit by it. If, however, the identity of some of the victims is known to him, he must return what he had taken; his duty is not done by merely supplying the public need.

8. It is forbidden to buy a stolen article from a thief or from a robber, whether he is a Jew or a non-Jew, for the non-Jew, too, is forbidden to rob or steal even from another non-Jew, as this is one of the seven precepts given to the sons of Noah. It is a serious sin to buy from a thief or a robber, for in so doing one is abetting evildoers. With reference to this, it is written (Proverbs 29:24): "Whoso is partner with a thief hateth his own soul," for if the thief finds no purchaser he will not steal. Although the thief could take the stolen article to a place where he is not known, this course is not so convenient for him. The purchase is permissible if it is for the benefit of the rightful owner in order to restore the property to him on payment of the outlay; provided, however, that the owner could not recover it himself. It is also forbidden to accept for safekeeping, anything which has apparently been stolen or robbed.

9. It is forbidden to derive even the slightest benefit from the property stolen or robbed while it is in the criminal's possession. Even if the benefit is so trivial that the owner would not mind it, as to exchange the money that has been stolen or robbed, it is forbidden. It is also forbidden to enter a house illegally occupied, to be protected from heat or rain, or to pass through a field that has been illegally acquired.

10. It is, therefore, forbidden to accept anything from a known thief or robber who has no other occupation, and whose property is presumed to have been acquired by theft or robbery. And a poor man is forbidden to accept charity from such a person.

11. It is forbidden to buy an article from anybody when it is apparent that it has been stolen by him, as when a fruit watchman offers to sell fruit in a secluded spot, or when one hides the article he offers for sale, or he says to the buyer: "Hide it"—in all such cases, one must not buy. It is even forbidden to buy of a woman an article, which may be suspected that she is selling it without her husband's knowledge. It is likewise forbidden to buy of a man, any of a woman's ornaments or apparel, as it may be suspected that he is selling it without his wife's knowledge.

12. One who takes someone else's coat or hat inadvertently in a banquet hall, or the like, is not allowed to use it, and when the rightful owner appears,

he must return it to him even if he had lost his own. If a person receives something that does not belong to him—as, for instance, a garment from a laundry, he must not use it, but should return it to the owner, even if one of his own garments had not been returned. If, however, the article remains in his possession a long time, he may assume that the rightful owner had made inquiries about it and had been reimbursed by the laundry proprietor, and he may use the garment.

13. It is forbidden to use a neighbor's article without his knowledge, even if one is sure that the owner would not object and even be pleased by such use because of his friendly feelings towards him. Therefore, if one comes into a neighbor's orchard, he is forbidden to eat the fruit, although the owner would not mind it; since at that moment the owner is not aware of it, he is enjoying it illegally. It is necessary to admonish the public regarding this matter, as most people break this rule for lack of knowledge.

14. Nevertheless, it is lawful for a member of one's household to give a morsel of bread to a poor man or to a child of the master's friend without his knowledge, because such is the general custom of people, and to do this is not regarded as an act done without the knowledge of the owner. For this reason it is permissible to accept small charitable contributions from women, even without their husband's knowledge, since this is the general custom, the husbands are aware of it. If a person generally eats fruit in another's garden with the owner's knowledge, he is permitted to do so on any occasion. This rule applies to any similar case.

15. If one finds fruit on the road which has fallen from a tree, the branches of which overhang the road, then if it is the type of fruit that usually falls off and becomes spoiled after it falls off, or if it does not become spoiled but most of the people who pass that place are non-Jews, or if cattle passing by usually eat this kind of fruit, so that the owner has already abandoned his right of ownership to it, then one may eat it. But if it is the kind of fruit that does not become spoiled by the fall, and most of the people passing by there are Jews, one is forbidden to take it, because it is considered as an act of robbery. If the fruit belongs to minor orphans, one is not allowed to take it under any circumstances, because minors cannot legally waive their rights of ownership.

16. The law of the temporal government must be recognized as the law (superseding the Jewish law in civil matters).

CHAPTER 183

Damages to Property

1. It is forbidden to damage another person's property, even with the intention of making reparation, just as it is forbidden to steal or to rob with the intention of making restitution. It is equally forbidden to cause damage, either by deed or by word. For instance, if Reuben has sold some merchandise to a non-Jew, Simeon is forbidden to come to the non-Jew and tell him that he had overpaid, even if it happens to be the truth. He who indirectly causes another to sustain a loss, although he is not punishable by a human court of law, is held answerable to the Heavenly Court until he conciliates the victim.

2. One who sustains a loss to property may not recover his loss at the expense of another, for one is not allowed to save himself by causing even indirectly, damage to another. But he may forestall damage to his own property, even if it involves a loss to others. Thus, if one's property is menaced by a flood, one is allowed to dam the water before reaching his property, although this will cause the water to overflow the field of his neighbor. But if the water had already inundated his field, he is forbidden to divert it to his neighbor's field.

3. Likewise, if an army arrived in town and the townspeople are obliged to billet the soldiers, one is not allowed to bribe the General to exempt him, because by doing this he is causing damage to another townsman. So also, in all cases of taxes, it is forbidden to influence the officer to exempt him, if by so doing, he makes the burden heavier for others. One who acts in this manner is called an *informer*.

4. It is forbidden to surrender the person or the property of another into the hands of a heathen, whether it be by deed or by word, to inform on him or to divulge his hiding place; and whoever acts as an informer, has no share in the world to come. It is forbidden to inform even on an evildoer, who has transgressed the Law, and thus cause him to suffer either in his person or in his property, and even if he constantly vexes him with words. If, however, the informer had informed on him and he cannot save himself without informing on the informer, he is permitted to do so.

5. It is forbidden to enter the ploughed field of another, because it will be spoiled by trampling upon it.

6. A man is forbidden to stand in a neighbor's field when the crops are at their best, in order not to harm them by an "evil eye." Especially is it forbidden to gaze at one's neighbor in a manner as to harm him personally by an "evil eye." Even with regard to business and occupation where there is no cause to fear an "evil eye," if a person is working in his own house and on his own property, it is forbidden to stare at him without his knowledge, for it is likely that he may not wish anybody to know his business. Upon seeing a fellow man engaged at his work, it is good manners to bless him by saying: "May you prosper in your task."

7. A person is forbidden to do anything, even on his own premises, which may cause damage to his neighbor. Thus, he must avoid placing in his court near his neighbor's wall, anything that generates heat, like manure, and thus cause damage to the wall, except at a distance of three hand-breadths. Hence the water that he pours out and the drain pipe that carries off the water from the roof, must be at least three hand-breadths away from a neighbor's wall. Under no circumstances may one pour out the contents of a chamber pot or urinate close to the wall of one's neigubor. If the wall is of stone or wood, without plaster, one may pour water by the wall at a distance of one hand-breadth. If the wall is of solid rock, one may pour water and urinate on the wall itself. If the wall is made of bricks or of wood, covered with plaster, one must remove from it a distance of three hand-breadths.

CHAPTER 184

If One Causes Physical Injury

1. A man is forbidden to strike his fellow man. One who does so is guilty of transgressing a divine injunction, as it is written (Deuteronomy 25:2-3): "If the wicked man deserve to be beaten . . . forty stripes he may give him, he shall not exceed." If the Torah is concerned about the wicked, ordaining that he is not to be beaten for his sin beyond the prescribed limit, how much more, then, does this apply to the beating of the righteous. He who raises his hand against another, even if he does not strike him, is called *rasha* (wicked), as it is written (Exodus 2:13): "And he said to the *rasha:* 'Wherefore smitest thou thy neighbor?' " The Biblical text reads not, *Lamah hikkita* (wherefore hast thou smitten), but, *Lamah takkeh* (wherefore wilt thou strike), although he has not yet smitten his fellow, he is called *rasha.* Whoever smote his fellow man was excommunicated by the ancients and could not be counted as one of a quorum of ten in the performance of sacred duties, until he was reinstated by the *Bet Din* (court) upon his promise to abide by their decisions. However, if someone strikes him or another fellow Jew, and he is unable to save himself or the fellow Jew except by striking him back, then he is permitted to do so.

2. It is forbidden to strike even a disobedient servant. But one is permitted to chastise his small children or an orphan whom he is bringing up in his house, in order that they behave properly, as that is for their own good.

3. One must not throw broken glass, or the like, in any place where it may cause harm to anybody.

4. If a neighbor suffers from a headache, which may be aggravated by the noise of the hammering, then one is forbidden to pound grits, or anything similar to this, even in his own house, if the noise of hammering can reach him.

5. There are many kinds of injuries which one is forbidden to inflict, either upon his neighbor or upon the public. But this is the general principle of law which applies to all such cases. One is not allowed to do anything on his own premises and especially on a public thoroughfare, that may cause damage to his neighbor or to wayfarers on the public highway, unless it be a thing that is generally done by everyone in town, which is equivalent to having received the sanction of all the townsmen, so that each in turn may have the same privilege whenever he or his children after him may wish to do it.

6. One who scares his fellow man, as by a sudden scream behind him, or by appearing suddenly before him in the dark, or the like, will be answerable to the Heavenly Court.

7. The person who injures his neighbor in any way, even though he has paid for the injury, also a thief or a robber, although he has made restitution of the stolen article or he has paid for it, cannot obtain forgiveness in heaven until he has begged forgiveness of the injured party, or of the one whose property he had robbed or stolen, because of the anguish he had caused him. The latter should be ready to forgive the wrong, and not be obdurate in refusing his pardon.

8. If one sees that his neighbor is in trouble, Mercy protect us, he shall do whatever he can or hire others to come to his rescue if he cannot do it himself. If the one who was assisted can afford it, he must repay the money thus expended on his account. But even if it is known that he cannot afford such repayment, one must not shirk his duty, but save him at his own expense. If one keeps away from doing so, one is guilty of transgressing the injunction (Leviticus 19:16): "Neither shalt thou stand idly by the blood of thy neighbor." Likewise, if a man hears wicked persons hatching a plot against his fellow man, or they are setting a trap for him, and he fails to reveal it to him, or if he can satisfy them with money, and he fails to appease them so that they would not carry out their evil design, or any other matter similar to this, is likewise transgressing the command: "Neither shalt thou stand idly by the blood of thy neighbor." Our Sages tell us (Mishnah, Sanhedrin 37a): "He who saves one life in Israel, is considered as if he had saved the whole world."

9. A person who is engaged in counterfeiting money, and it is feared that he will jeopardize others thereby, is considered a public menace, and should be warned to desist from his practice. If he does not heed the warning, it is permissible to denounce him to the government, and to declare that no one else is implicated in the crime. If a person is falsely accused of being an accomplice, he may likewise assert his innocence by stating: "I did not participate in this crime, but so-and-so was the sole criminal."

10. It had been the custom for the Seven Elders of the City to amerce fines, in cases of injuries, insults, and the like. They must not, however, act independently of the court, since there are many diverse laws concerning such matters, and it is not permitted to impose a fine greater than what the law requires, for the honor of a fellow man should not be treated lightly.

11. When a woman has severe pain in childbirth, the physician is permitted to destroy the child before its birth, either with medicine or with instruments, for as long as it has not yet been born, it is not considered a living soul, and it is permissible to save the mother by sacrificing the child; it is akin to a case of self-defense. However, as soon as it protrudes its head, it must not be touched, for one living soul must not be sacrificed to save another, and this is the way of nature.

CHAPTER 185
Borrowing and Hiring

1. He who borrows or hires a beast or chattels from his neighbor, is not allowed to lend them or to hire them out to someone else without the consent of the owner. Even in the case of books, the lending of which is considered a meritorious act, we do not take it for granted that the owner would approve of having a religious act done with his property, for it is likely that he would not wish his property to be in the possession of certain persons whom he considers untrustworthy. The borrower of a book, may, however, allow another person to use it for study in the former's house, provided he studies by himself and not together with someone else. If it is known that the owner of the article is accustomed to trust the third party in such matters, then the borrower may lend and the hirer may hire it out.

2. It is mandatory to pay the wages of a hired workman in time, and he who delays such payment is guilty of transgressing a divine injunction, for it is written (Deuteronomy 24:15): "In the same day shalt thou give him his hire, neither shall the sun go down on it." It is also mandatory to pay for the hire of an animal or of utensils at the proper time, and he who delays such payment is guilty of transgressing the law, for it is written (loco citato 24:14): "Thou shalt not oppress a hired servant that is poor and needy. . . In the same day thou shalt give him his hire." And what is the proper time? If the workman has finished his work during the day, he should be paid before the end of that day; and if the day has passed without being paid, the employer is guilty of transgressing the law: "In the same day thou shalt give him his hire, neither shall the sun go down on it." And if he finishes his work in the evening, he should be paid during the night; and if the night has passed without being paid, the employer is guilty of transgressing the

law: "The wages of him that is hired shall not abide with thee all night until the morning." So also is the case with a workman hired by the week, or month, or year, if he has finished his work during the day, he should be paid during that day; if he has finished his work during the night, he should be paid during that night, but not later.

3. If one gives a garment to a tailor to be repaired, and the latter returns it to him during the day, he can pay him at any time during that day, and if he returns it to him at night, he can pay him any time during that night. However, as long as the article remains with the tailor, although the work has been completed, the owner is not violating the law, even if it is in the tailor's possession a great many days, and even if the tailor has notified him to bring the money and fetch his article.

4. The employer does not transgress the law, unless the workman demands his wages and he, the employer has the money to pay. If the workman failed to demand his wages, or the employer lacks the money to pay the workman, then there is no violation of the law. Nevertheless, a scrupulous employer should if necessary, borrow the money to pay the wages at the proper time, for the workman is poor and sets his heart upon his pay. In cases where the employers pay their workmen after a certain sum is due, even if the workman demands a small sum, which he had undoubtedly already earned, nevertheless, if he refuses to give it to him, he is not guilty of transgressing the law, since the custom is known and the workman hired himself out on such condition.

5. If a hired workman spoiled the article on which he had worked, even if it was caused by his negligence, so that he is legally bound to make reparation, the employer should waive his legal rights and release the workman from liability, as it is written (Proverbs 2:20): "That thou mayest walk in the way of good men." And if the workman is poor and without food, it is the employer's duty to give him his wages, as it is written (loco citato): "And keep the paths of the righteous." And the path of the righteous is to keep the way of the Lord, to practice charity and justice to an even greater extent than is specifically required by law.

6. Just as the employer is cautioned not to rob the workman of his wages and not to delay payment, so is the workman warned not to cheat the employer by idling away his time. He must do all he is able to do, as our father Jacob, peace be unto him, said (Genesis 31:6): "And ye know that with all my power I have served your father." Therefore, a workman is not allowed to work all night, and then hire himself out by day (because he has already been weakened by the night work); neither is a person allowed to work his animal by night, and then hire it out by day. The workman is not allowed to starve himself or to afflict himself, for by weakening his body, he will not be able to do the work for his employer in a proper manner. This law applies also to a teacher; see chapter 165:12, above.

CHAPTER 186

The Muzzling of Animals

1. He who prevents an animal from eating when at work is punishable by flagellation, for it is written (Deuteronomy 25:4): "Thou shalt not muzzle the ox when he treadeth out the corn." And it is immaterial whether it be an ox or any other animal or beast, or whether it is a clean or an unclean animal, or whether it is treading out corn or doing some other work connected with the soil. The Torah mentions the ox and treading out corn, simply because it speaks of the ordinary custom. Even if he muzzles the beast with his voice, that is, he shouts at it and thus prevents it from eating, he is also punishable by flagellation.

2. A Jew who treads out the corn of a non-Jew with a beast belonging to the non-Jew, and he muzzles it, is guilty of transgressing the law: "Thou shalt not muzzle."

3. If the beast cannot eat any food because it is thirsty, he must give it drink.

4. If the beast is at work in a field, the products of which would be harmful to its intestines, it is permissible to muzzle it. For the Torah was interested in the well-being of the animal, and in this case it would be injurious to it.

CHAPTER 187

Articles Lost and Found

1. If one sees an article that has been lost by a Jew, he must take care of it and restore it to its owner, as it is written (Deuteronomy 22:1): "Thou shalt surely bring them (the animals) back unto thy brother." The same applies to any property of our neighbor that is threatened with destruction, for this is included in the precept of restoring a lost article to the owner.

2. Although legally, if one finds an article belonging to a Jew, in a place where the majority of its inhabitants are non-Jews, he need not return it even if the Jew has put a special mark of identification on it, since it is presumed that its owner has despaired of its recovery, it is good and right, nevertheless, to do more than the law requires and to restore it to the rightful owner, provided the latter can properly identify it. Moreover, he can be forced to restore it. If the finder of the article is a poor man and its owner is rich, the former need not do more than the law requires. Where the finder is required by the law of the land to restore the article to its owner, he must restore it under all circumstances.

3. Anyone who finds an article, whether or not it bears a special mark of identification, if it is apparent that it had been left there temporarily by the owner, such as a garment or an axe, by the side of a fence, and even if it is doubtful whether the owner had left it there temporarily or whether he had lost it, one is forbidden to touch it.

4. If an old and respected man finds a paltry article, of such a nature that even if it were his own he would not carry it home, because it would be below his dignity, he is not obliged to pay any heed to it. He should,

nevertheless, do more than the law requires, and concern himself with it, even if it is beneath his dignity.

5. If one finds an article and he does not know who the rightful owner is, then, whether or not it bears any mark of identification, since there are many divergent laws concerning cases of lost articles, he should consult a rabbi as to what he should do.

CHAPTER 188

Laws Concerning Bailments

1. Nowadays, when we are all engaged in business, and we constantly need money, we may take it for granted that when one places money on deposit, he tacitly agrees that the depositary may use that money if he needs it. Money so deposited, therefore, assumes the character of a loan. If, however, the money deposited is sealed in a package, or tied with a special knot, it is an indication that the depositor does not wish it to be used, and the depostary is not permitted to use it.

2. If any article is deposited with a person, he is not allowed to make use of it, even if the article is in no wise spoiled by such use. He who borrows an article without the owner's knowledge, is classed as a robber. If it is definitely known that the depositor would not object to his using it, he is allowed to use it. Some authorities forbid the use of it even in this case, on the ground that it is forbidden to make use of a trust, and it is best to follow the stricter opinion.

3. It is the duty of the bailee to guard the article in the best possible manner. Even if the bailee himself does not take pains to guard his own property so carefully, he must, nevertheless, take special care in guarding the property entrusted to him.

4. The bailee is forbidden to entrust into the care of others the articles deposited with him, even if the others are more trustworthy than himself, unless the depositor has been accustomed to deposit such articles with them.

5. The bailee must not return the article deposited with him to any member of the depositor's household without his consent. This rule of law applies also when one returns a borrowed article or pays a debt. He may, however, return it to the depositor's wife, as it may be assumed that because of her being the mistress of the house, her husband entrusts everything to her.

Chapter 189

Unloading and Loading

1. If one sees on the road his neighbor's beast of burden lying underneath its load, whether it was a proper load for that animal, or it was too heavy for it, he is commanded to assist him in unloading the burden, as it is written (Exodus 23:5): "Thou shalt surely release it with him." After he had helped unloading the burden, he must not depart, leaving his neighbor to worry, but he must help replace the load upon the animal, as it is written (Deuteronomy 22:4): "Thou shalt surely help him to lift them up again." If one leaves his neighbor without helping him to unload and reload, he has neglected to perform an affirmative precept and transgressed a negative precept, as it is written (loco citato): "Thou shalt not see the ass of thy neighbor or his ox fallen down by the way, and hide thyself from them."

2. If after one helped to unload and reload, the beast fell down again, one is obliged to assist again in the unloading and reloading, even a hundred times, as it is written: "Thou shalt surely release it with him," and: "Thou shalt surely help him to lift it up again." For this reason, one must accompany the carrier a distance of a parasang, as he might need help again, unless one is expressly told: "I no longer need you."

3. The unloading must be done gratis, but for the reloading one may demand compensation; also for accompanying him.

4. If the animal belongs to a heathen, and it is also driven by him, regardless whether the load belongs to a Jew or to a heathen, one is bound to help him unload merely because of the suffering of the animal, and he may receive compensation for it, but he is not bound to help him reload unless it may cause animosity, and if the heathen is not present and a Jew drives the animal, one must also help him reload, because of the distress of the Jew. If the animal belongs to a Jew and the load belongs to a heathen, one is likewise bound to help unload and reload in consideration of the Jew.

5. It is written (Exodus 23:5): "If thou see the ass of thy enemy lying under its burden," etc. This *enemy* does not refer to one of the seven nations (inhabiting the land of Canaan, who are not included in the command regarding loading and unloading, unless the animal suffers), but it refers to a Jew. And how can one Jew hate another, when the Torah expressly ordains (Leviticus 19:17): "Thou shalt not hate thy brother in thy heart." Said the Sages: For instance, when he alone saw him violate a law and warned him against it, but the latter refused to repent, in such a case it is a duty to hate him until he repents and abandons his wickedness. Nevertheless, although he has not repented as yet, if he is in distress on account of a load, one is bound to help him unload and reload, and not leave him without help, lest he will be forced to tarry a long time and his life may be in danger. The

Torah is very much concerned regarding the lives of human beings, no matter whether they are righteous or wicked, as long as they cleave to the Almighty and believe in the principal tenets of the religion, as it is written (Ezekiel 33:11): "Say unto them: As I live saith the Lord, I have no pleasure in the death of the wicked, but that the wicked turn from his way and live."

6. If a company travel together and one of the asses injured its legs, the rest of the company are not permitted to abandon him alone on the road. But if the ass has fallen down and it is unable to continue the journey, they need not tarry for his sake any longer than a reasonable time and they may then depart. Also, if a company travel together in vehicles, and one of the vehicles breaks down, so that it is necessary to pause a little, in order to repair it, the rest of the company are not permitted to abandon him, unless they would be detained beyond a reasonable time.

CHAPTER 190

Protection of Life and Property

1. We are commanded to make a parapet on the roofs of houses, as it is written (Deuteronomy 22:8): "And thou shalt make a parapet for thy roof." The height of the parapet must be not less than ten hand-breadths (forty inches), and it should be strongly constructed, so that it may not give way when one leans against it. The roofs of our houses are exempt from this law, if we do not make use of them. And not only roofs must be protected against danger to human life, but any place where there exists a possibility of danger to human life requires protection. Anyone who fails to provide proper protection, violates an affirmative precept, and also transgresses a negative precept, as it is written (loco citato): "Thou shalt not bring blood upon thy house." For instance, if a person has a well in his courtyard, he is obliged to put a fence, ten hand-breadths high around it, or he must cover it so that no one may fall therein.

2. It is likewise our duty to remove any cause that might prove dangerous to human life, or we must take good care of it, as it is written (Deuteronomy 4:9): "Only take heed to thyself, and keep thy soul diligently." If a person leaves dangerous objects and does not remove them, he violates an affirmative precept and also transgresses the negative command: "And thou shalt not put blood upon thy house;" as when he allows a broken ladder to remain standing in his house or in his courtyard, or if he keeps a vicious dog.

3. Just as a man must guard his body against all injury or harm, as it is written: "Take heed to thyself, and keep thy soul diligently," so must he guard his property against all loss. Therefore, anyone who breaks a vessel, or tears a garment, or destroys or fouls food or drink, or throws away money,

or spoils anything that is fit for man's enjoyment, violates a negative precept, as it is written (Deuteronomy 20:19): "Thou shalt not destroy the trees thereof," etc.

CHAPTER 191

Cruelty to Animals

1. It is forbidden, according to the law of the Torah, to inflict pain upon any living creature. On the contrary, it is our duty to relieve the pain of any creature even if it is ownerless or it belongs to a non-Jew. However, if they cause trouble, or if they are needed for medicinal purposes, or for any other human need, it is even permissible to kill them and we disregard their pain. For the Torah has permitted to slaughter them. Therefore, it is permitted to pluck feathers from a living goose with which to write, if no other pen is available. However, people abstain from doing it, because of cruelty.

2. When horses, drawing a cart, come to a rough road or to a steep hill, and it is hard for them to draw the cart without help, it is our duty to help them, even when they belong to a non-Jew, because of the precept not to be cruel to animals, lest the owner smite them to force them to draw more than their strength permits.

3. It is forbidden to tie the legs of a beast or of a bird in a manner as to cause them pain.

4. It is forbidden to set a bird on eggs that are not of her species, for this is cruelty to animals.

5. It is forbidden to castrate either man, beast, animal, or bird, clean or unclean, in Israel or elsewhere. It is forbidden to cause sterility to any male, man or any living being even by medicine. Violators are subject to the penalty of flagellation.

6. We are not allowed to tell a non-Jew to castrate our animals. Some authorities hold that we are even forbidden to sell an animal to a non-Jew, or to give it to him on the condition to share the profits, if we know that he will castrate it, because a non-Jew, too, is forbidden to castrate, therefore, in doing so, the Jew transgresses the precept: "And thou shalt put no stumbling block before the blind." If, however, the non-Jewish buyer will not castrate it himself, but will give it to another non-Jew to do it, such a transaction is permissible according to the opinion of all authorities, for then it is only an indirect violation of the law, and it is permissible.

CHAPTER 192

The Sick, the Physician, and the Remedies

1. Said Rab Isaac the son of Rab Judah: "One should always plead for mercy not to get sick. If one falls sick, he is told, produce your virtuous deeds, and you will be released." Said Mar Ukba: "From which Biblical verse can this be inferred? From (Deuteronomy 22:8): "Lest any man fall *from thence*" (Hebrew, *mimmenu,* also meaning, *of himself*), which means,

since he has fallen, he must produce evidence of himself and of his deeds that he is worthy'" (Shabbat 32a). It is also stated in the Talmud (loco citato): "If a person suffers from a headache, he should think of himself as if he were put in chains. If he becomes ill and he must be confined to his bed, he should think of himself as if he were placed onto a scaffold (a place where capital cases are tried) to be judged; if he has great advocates, he may be saved, but if he has none, he cannot escape. And these are the advocates of man: Repentance and Good Deeds. Even if nine hundred and ninety-nine accuse him and only one advocate defends him, he is saved, as it is written (Job 33:23-24): 'If there be for him an angel, an intercessor, one among a thousand, to vouch for man's uprightness, then He is gracious unto him, and saith: Deliver him from going down to the pit,' etc."

2. Rabbi Phineas, the son of Hama preached: "Whoever has a sick person in his house, should go to a sage and ask him to plead for mercy in his behalf, as it is written (Proverbs 16:14): 'The wrath of a king is as messengers of death, but a wise man will pacify it.'" It is customary to give alms to the poor in behalf of a sick person, for, Repentance, Prayer, and Charity avert an evil decree. It is also customary to bless the sick person in the synagogue, and if he is critically ill, he may be blessed even on the Sabbath and on a festival. At times, the name of the sick person is changed, also, for a change of name may nullify an evil decree.

3. The Torah has permitted a physician to heal the sick, as it is written (Exodus 21:19): "And he shall cause him to be thoroughly healed." Therefore, a sick person should not rely upon a miracle, but he must follow the prevailing custom and call in a physician. Many of the world's pious men have been cured by physicians. He who refrains from calling in a physician, commits two wrongs; one forbidding a person in danger to rely upon miracles, the other, in that he manifests presumption and pride in depending upon his righteousness that he will be cured in some miraculous manner. A sick person should call the most competent physician, but with all that, he should pray for mercy from Heaven, from the Faithful Healer, blessed be His name, trusting in Him alone.

4. It is the duty of a competent physician to cure the sick. This duty is included in the general rule that we must save a life in danger. If he evades doing so, he is guilty of shedding blood, even if the sick person has another physician, because the sick person may be lacking the merit of being cured by any other physician; perchance it is destined that he shall be cured by him. However, no person should practice medicine unless he is competent to do so, and unless there is no other one more competent than he is, otherwise he is guilty of bloodshed.

5. A person who is not critically ill, should not be permitted to use a forbidden article, if his cure might be effected by means of an article permitted to be used, even if there is some delay in obtaining it. If he requires to eat nothing but a prohibited article—even if it is prohibited only by a Rabbinical ordinance—he is forbidden to eat it the way the article is generally eaten. He is, however, permitted to eat it in such a manner as to derive no pleasure from it, as for instance, by mingling a bitter substance with it. It is also permitted to make a plaster of it, or something similar, even if it is an article the enjoyment of which is forbidden by the Torah, with the exception of *kilayim* (mixed seeds in the vineyard), and meat cooked with milk, the use of which is forbidden even in a manner where no pleasure is derived from it, as long as the illness is not critical. (See also chapter 3:8; chapter 61:4; and chapter 117, end, above).

6. Some authorities are of the opinion that a person may cure himself with an article, the enjoyment of which is forbidden by Rabbinical enactment, although he is not critically ill, even if used in a manner that affords him pleasure, providing he does not eat or drink the forbidden article.

7. A person who is critically ill, may use for his cure, any forbidden article, for no law can stand in the way of saving a man's life with the exception of idolatry, incest, and murder, which must not be transgressed even at the risk of losing one's life.

8. A physician is allowed to let blood, and to feel the pulse of a woman, even if she is married, and he may feel even the pudendum, as is customary with physicians, since he does not do it in a sensual and an immoral spirit, but merely following his profession. However, he should abstain from treating his own wife during her menstruation period, if she is not critically ill and there is another physician who is as competent as he is.

9. A male is not allowed to attend a woman who is suffering from abdominal pains, lest he will be overcome by desire since he is capable. But a woman may attend a male who is suffering, since he is sick and incapable.

10. If one possesses medicaments and his neighbor falls sick and is in need of them, he is forbidden to advance the price thereof unreasonably.

CHAPTER 193

Visiting the Sick

1. When a person gets sick, it is the duty of every man to visit him, for we find that the Holy One, blessed be He, visits the sick. As our Rabbis, of blessed memory, explained (Baba Metzia 86b) the verse (Genesis 18:1): "And the Lord appeared unto him in the plains of *Mamre,*" from this is inferred that He came to visit Abraham because he was sick. Relatives and friends who are accustomed to visit him often, should visit him as soon as they hear of his sickness. But strangers should not call immediately, but wait three days, in order not to spoil his chances of recovery by attaching to him the designation of a patient. If, however, one becomes suddenly ill, even strangers should visit him immediately. Even a great man should visit a less important person, and even many times during the day. It is meritorious to visit a sick person as frequently as possible, providing it does not weary the sick man. One should not visit a sick enemy, nor should he come to comfort him in his mourning, for he may think that he rejoices at his calamity. He may, however, attend his funeral, and he need not fear that people will think that he rejoices at his downfall, since this is the end of every mortal.

2. When the patient lies upon the ground, the visitor must not sit upon a chair, which is more elevated, because the Divine Presence is above the head of the sick, as it is said (Psalms 41:4): "The Lord support him upon the bed of illness." But when the invalid lies in a bed, the visitor may sit on a chair or on a bench.

3. The essential reason for the precept of visiting the sick, is to look into his needs, to see what is necessary to be done for him, and to pray for mercy in his behalf. If one visited a sick person and did not pray for him, he did not fulfill his duty. Therefore, one should not visit a sick person during the first three hours of the day, since the sickness then assumes a milder form, he will not be sufficiently moved to pray for him; nor should one visit him during the three closing hours of the day, as the sickness then takes a turn for the worse, and he will despair of his recovery and will not pray for him.

4. If one prays in the presence of the sick person, he may say the prayer in any language, because he is praying before the Divine Presence who is at the bedside of the sick. If, however, one prays in the abscence of the sick person, and the prayer is brought up by ministering angels who do not regard all languages, one should pray in Hebrew, and include him among all the sick of Israel, for by including him with all the others, the prayer will be more readily heard because of the collective merit of the multitude. In pray-

ing, one says: "May the Omnipresent have mercy upon him among all the sick of Israel," and on the Sabbath, one adds: "This is Sabbath, we are forbidden to complain, healing is sure to come; His mercy is great; His seat is in peace."

5. Visitors must use judgment and tact when talking to the sick person, so as not to give him false hopes, nor cause him to despair. They should encourage him to talk about his affairs, and state whether he has loaned to others, or has deposited anything with others, or others with him. The sick person should be given to understand that to impart such information will not hasten his death.

6. One should not bequeath all his property to strangers, not even to charity, and leave out his natural heirs, even if they do not conduct themselves properly. God takes no delight in a man who acts like that. However, if one also provides sufficiently for his heirs, it is permissible to give something to others. A pious man should not witness a will, or give counsel in making a will in which the natural heirs are disinherited, even when the son who is disinherited does not act properly, and the brother to whom the in heritance is left is a sage, because it is likely that the worthless son will have good and decent children. One authority holds that it is even forbidden to bequeath a larger portion to one child than to another; it is proper to heed his opinion.

7. If the patient has young children, or if he has both young and grown-up children, or if his wife is pregnant, he should appoint a guardian to act on behalf of the minor children until they come of age.

8. If the sick person desires to make a *kinyan* (symbolical form of making an agreement binding by handing over an object, from one to the other of the contracting parties), in order to confirm his will, it may be done even on the Sabbath. Also, if he desires to send for his kinsmen, a non-Jew may be hired on the Sabbath to go and fetch them.

9. The patient should not be informed of the death of a member of his family, because it may disconcert him; and even if he becomes aware of it, he should not be told to rend his garments, lest it will aggravate his anxiety. One should neither weep nor mourn in the presence of a sick person, whether the dead be a menber of his family or a stranger, lest he fear that he, too, will pass away. Those who comfort mourners in the presence of a sick person, should be silenced.

10. We must not visit a person who is afflicted with intestinal pains so as not to embarrass him, nor one who is troubled with his eyes, or one who has a headache, or any person who is gravely ill and to whom conversation is difficult; but we should call at an outer room, inquire regarding their condition, and ascertain if they are in need of anything. We should take an interest in their condition and pray for mercy on their behalf.

11. One who has two precepts to perform, namely, visiting a sick person and comforting a mourner, and he is able to attend to both, one should first visit the sick, so that he may pray for mercy on his behalf. If one is unable

to fulfill both duties, one should rather fulfill that of comforting the mourner, as this is an act of lovingkindness towards both the living and the dead.

12. A non-Jew should be visited during his illness for the sake of preserving peaceful relations.

13. It is expounded in the Sifri (Bamidbar 5-6): "Rabbi Nathan said: 'From the verse (Numbers 5:6): "And that soul be guilty, then shall they confess," a conclusion can be drawn, that all dying persons must confess.'" In the Mishnah (Sanhedrin 43a) it is stated: "Everyone who makes confession has a share in the world to come. For so we find it with Achan, to whom Joshua said (Joshua 7:19-20): 'My son, give, I pray, glory to the Lord, the God of Israel, and make confession unto Him, and tell me now what thou hast done; hide nothing from me.' And Achan answered and said: 'Of a truth, I have sinned against the Lord, the God of Israel, and thus and thus have I done.' Whence do we learn that his confession made atonement for him? From the verse (loco citato 25): 'And Joshua said: "Why hast thou troubled us? The Lord shall trouble thee this day,"' which signifies *this day* thou shalt be troubled, but in the world to come thou shalt not be troubled." Therefore, if the visitors notice that the patient is on the point of death, they should tactfully turn the conversation to the matter of confession, and say: "Fear not that evil will ensue because of your confession, for many who had confessed have become well again, and many who neglected to confess died. On the contrary, as a reward for making confession, you will be granted life. Moreover, all who make confession have a share in the world to come." If the patient is unable to confess by word of mouth, he should make a mental confession, and if he is able to speak but little, he should be told to say: "May my death be an atonement for all my sins." The patient should also be reminded to ask the pardon of all whom he had wronged either in money matters, or by words. These words should not be spoken in the presence of ignorant men, or women, or children, for it may cause them to weep and thereby break the heart of the sick man.

14. A brief form of confession is as follows: "I acknowledge unto Thee, O Lord my God and the God of my fathers, that both my cure and my death are in Thy hand. May it be Thy will to grant me a perfect healing. Yet if Thou hast decreed that I should die, may my death expiate all the sins, iniquities, and transgressions which I have committed perversely before Thee, and grant me a portion in Gan Eden and cause me to merit the life of the world to come, which is reserved for the righteous." If the invalid desires to make a lengthy confession, like the one for Yom Kippur, he may do so.

CHAPTER 194

A Dying Person and Watching the Body

1. A dying person is to be considered as a living being in all matters, and it is forbidden to touch him lest his death be hastened by it. Whoever

touches him is considered like one who sheds blood. To what can this be compared? To a flickering candle, which becomes extinguished as soon as one touches it. Even if the patient is agonizing a long time, and he and his kin are in great distress, it is, nevertheless, forbidden to hasten his death, by removing, for instance, the pillows from under his head, because some people believe that a certain kind of feathers defer death, or to place the keys of the synagogue under his head; all this is forbidden. Still, if there exists an external cause which prevents the departure of the soul, such as the noise of some pounding, that cause may be removed, since this is not a direct deed to hasten the end, but merely the removal of an obstacle without touching the dying person.

2. Although it is forbidden to touch a dying person, nevertheless, if the house caught fire, he must be removed from the house. Moreover, his removal takes precedence over the removal of sacred books.

3. Those present should see to it that no limb of his projects from the bed, as it is said concerning Jacob (Genesis 49:33): "And he gathered up his feet into the bed." They should, therefore, place chairs at the side of the bed, so that he would be unable to stretch a hand or a foot outside it. Yet, if they have not done this, and he did project one of his limbs, he must not be touched in order to put it back.

4. From the moment a person is in the throes of death, no one is allowed to leave him, in order that his soul may not depart when he is all alone, because it is bewildered when departing from the body. It is a commendable act to stand by the person when his soul is about to depart, for it is written (Psalms 49:10-11): "That he should still live always, that he should not see the pit. For he seeth that wise men die," etc. It is proper to get together, ten male adults to be present at the departure of the soul. They should not, God forbid, engage in idle talk, but they should rather discuss subjects of the Torah or read the Psalms, or prayers and supplications. The prayers are arranged in the book known as *Maabar Yabbok*. It is customary to light candles in the presence of a dying person.

5. After the departure of the soul, a light feather is placed at his nostrils. If it does not move, it clearly indicates that he is dead. The windows are then opened, and the mourners recite the prayer *Tzidduk haddin* (acknowledgment of Divine justice), and they include the Divine Name (*adonai elohenu*) and the title of King (*meleḥ haolam*) in the benediction: "Blessed be the Judge of truth." Then they rend their garments, as is provided for in the following chapter.

6. All those present when the soul departs, must rend their garments. To what is death compared? To the burning of a Scroll of the Torah. For there is none so worthless in Israel who did not possess some knowledge of the Torah and did not perform some good deeds. The garments must also be rent at the death of a child who had studied the Bible, and at the death of a woman. Even if the deceased had at times committed a sin because of lust, the garments must be rent for him, but not for an habitual sinner, even though he sinned only to gratify his lust, for he is then reckoned among those who had

departed from the ways of his people. Non-mourners who are present at the demise of a man, may rend their garments only slightly, even at the side or at the hem.

7. The eyes of the dead are to be closed. If there are sons, it is done by one of them, as it is written (Genesis 46:4): "And Joseph shall put his hand upon thine eyes;" and if there is a firstborn son, it should be done by him.

8. When lifting the deceased from the bed to be put on the floor, care should be taken to keep him covered, as the laws of decency apply to the dead as well as to the living.

9. It is customary to pour out all the water from the vessels in the vicinity of the dead, that is, the three houses, including the one in which the dead lies. This is done even for a child who died within thirty days of its birth. If death occurs on a Sabbath, the water need not be poured out.

10. The person who watches the deceased, even if there be no kinship between them, is exempt from reading the *Shema* and the *Shemoneh esreh*, and from observing any of the precepts of the Torah, for he who is engaged in the performance of one precept is exempt from performing another. If there are two watchmen, then they should alternate, one should watch and the other recite his prayers.

11. It is forbidden to partake of any food in the room where the deceased lies, unless a partition is put up. It is even forbidden to have just a bite of food, to eat fruit, or to drink water. The watchers should be instructed regarding this. It is likewise forbidden to pronounce any benediction there.

12. It is forbidden to move the corpse on the Sabbath, even for the sake of vacating the place for *Kohanim*, or for the sake of performing a precept. It may be done by a non-Jew, if the relatives consent to it.

CHAPTER 195

The Rending of the Garments

1. A rent in one's garments must be made for the loss of one's relative, for whom one is required to observe a period of mourning. This rite must be performed while standing, as it is written (II Samuel 13:31): "And the king arose and tore his garments." If the mourner tore his garments while sitting, his obligation is not fulfilled, and it must be repeated while standing. If possible, the garments should be torn when one's sorrow is still most intense, before the coffin is closed.

2. For the dead over whom one must observe a period of mourning, the rent in the garment must be made near the front of the neck. The rent must be made lengthwise and not crosswise, and in the very cloth of the garment and not at the seam.

3. The mode of rending the garments for one's father or mother differs from the mode of rending for other relatives. For the latter, only a rent the size of a hand-breadth should be made in the external garment alone, and tearing it more than that is forbidden, in order not to transgress the injunction (Deuteronomy 20:19): "Thou shalt not destroy." But for a father or a mother, all garments must be rent opposite the heart, with the exception of the undershirt and the upper garment which one wears only occasionally (the overcoat). If one has not rent all the garments as required, one's obligation has not been fulfilled. A woman should first rend her undergarment, privately in accordance with the dictates of modesty, turn the rent to one side, and then rend her external garments, so as not to expose herself, and even if she is covered by her undershirt, it would still be a breach of modesty to expose herself even thus.

4. It is customary to make the rent on the right side of the garment for all relatives, except for one's father or mother, which is made on the left side of the garment, for the mourner has to expose his heart which is on the left. Nevertheless, if an error has been made in this respect, it does not invalidate the fulfillment of the duty.

5. For all relatives, one may rend the garments either with the hands or with an instrument, but for one's father or mother it must be done by hand. It is customary for one of the burial society to make a slight cut with a knife in the mourner's garment and then the mourner tears with his hands from where the cut was made. The rent must be made lengthwise, not crosswise.

6. During the first seven days of mourning for all relatives, one need not make a rent every time he changes his garments. But for one's father or mother, one must make a rent every time he puts on a different garment on a weekday during the seven days. But in honor of the Sabbath, a mourner should change his garments, and not wear those in which the rent was made. If the mourner has no other garments, he should hide the torn part of the one he wears. Changing one's apparel for the Sabbath in this connection, means putting on other weekday clothes, and not the usual Sabbath apparel.

7. According to law, garments rent for the loss of relatives, may be basted together after the first seven days of mourning, and completely sewed up after thirty days. In the case of one's father or mother, the rent may be basted together after thirty days, and never completely sewed up. It is forbidden to cut out the torn part of the garment and mend it with another piece of cloth. The prevailing custom is that even for other relatives, the rents are not basted together within the first thirty days, and not even joined with pins. A woman, out of modesty, is allowed to baste together the rents immediately, even when mourning the loss of a father or a mother. All the rent garments which may not be sewed together, must not be mended even

by the one who buys them. It is, therefore, necessary in selling such garments to inform the buyer thereof. Such garments must not be sold to a non-Jew.

8. For all relatives, if one did not hear of their death until after thirty days, one need not rend his garments, but for a father or a mother, one must always rend the garments he is wearing at the time he hears of their death. One, however, need not rend the garments which he changed thereafter.

9. The intervention of a festival cancels all rules of mourning which are observed during the first thirty days, even as regards the rending of the garments. Therefore, one mourning the loss of a relative, may completely sew up the rent after the *Minḥah* service on the day before the festival, and baste the rent together when mourning the loss of a father or a mother.

10. If a person has rent his garments for the loss of a relative, and another death occurred during the first seven days of mourning, he should either make a new rent of one hand-breadth, three finger-breadths away from the first rent, or he should extend the original rent another hand-breadth. But if the second death occurred after the first seven days, so long as he is still wearing the rent garment, he may rend it a little more and his duty is fulfilled. However, if the first death was that of some relative, and the second that of his father or his mother, then he must make a new rent, three finger-breadths away from the original rent, because the loss of a parent is not considered merely as an additional sorrow. The same law applies to a case where a person first loses his father and then his mother, or vice versa.

11. If a person hears at one time of the death of his father and his mother, or of the death of two other relatives, he should rend his garments but once for both. But if he hears of the loss of his father or his mother and another relative, then he should first rend his garments for his father or his mother, leave a space of three finger-breadths, and make a new rent for the other relative.

12. If a sick person has lost a relative, and he is unable to rend his garments, owing to the serious nature of his sickness, but his mind is clear so as to realize his loss, he is exempt from rending his garments when he recovers, unless the recovery took place within the first seven days of mourning, when his grief is still intense. If, however, he was unable to rend his garments because his mind was not clear, then as soon as he regains his clarity of mind and realizes his loss, he must rend his garments within the first thirty days of mourning for other relatives, but for the loss of a parent there is no time limit.

13. If a minor, even one who has not yet reached the age for training, lost a relative, his garment should be slightly rent for him to manifest the grief and to mark his mourning. But if he has already reached the age for training, he is bound to rend his garments as if he were an adult.

14. In our regions, it is the prevailing custom for mourners to rend the garments on the Intermediate Days of a festival, only for a father or mother, whether it be the day of burial or the day one heard the news, even *delayed news* (see chapter 206, below). However, if one's father or mother died on a festival, since the rending of the garments had been postponed, one should

not rend them during the Intermediate Days of the festival, but wait until the festival is over, when his period of mourning begins. For the loss of other relatives, the garments should not be rent during the Intermediate Days of a festival, but should be done after the festival. However, if one has received *timely news* during the Intermediate Days of the festival, which news will become *delayed* after the festival, one must rend his garments during the Intermediate Days.

CHAPTER 196

Laws Concerning an Onan

1. Any person who lost a relative for whom he is bound to observe mourning rites (see chapter 203, below), is called an *onan* until after the interment. An *onan* must avoid all kinds of levity, lest he indicate by his conduct that the deceased was a worthless person, and, therefore, he is not concerned about the interment and his loss, which is a gross indignity to the departed. Such a person is included among those "*Who ridicule the poor.*" But he must manifest concern about the interment and his loss. He should not eat in the room where the corpse is lying, but in another room, and if he has no other room, he should eat in his neighbor's house, and if he has no neighbor, he should put up a partition, no less than ten hand-breadths (forty inches) high, and less than three hand-breadths above the ground, and it should be strong enough to resist the wind. If he has no material with which to erect a partition, he should turn his face aside and eat. At any rate, even if he happens to be in another town at that time, he must not have an elaborate meal, but only simple fare, and he should neither eat meat nor drink wine.

2. An *onan* is exempt from all the precepts of the Torah, even if he does not have to attend to the dead, having others to do it. Even if he desires to be scrupulous and practice some precepts, he is not allowed to do so, out of respect to the deceased. He should not utter any benediction, nor respond *Amen* to the benedictions of others. He cannot be included in a quorum of three, to say Grace after meals nor in a quorum of ten for public worship. However, he must observe all the prohibitory laws, even those ordained by the Rabbis. Therefore, if he desires to partake of bread, he must wash his hands, without saying the benediction *Al netilat yadayim*, just as he need not say the benediction *Hamotzi* over the bread. On arising in the morning, he should wash his hands three times, as is required by law, but not say the benediction.

3. If the *onan* has eaten before the interment, and the food was not yet digested after the interment, he should recite Grace after meals. If he has attended to the call of nature before the interment, he must thereafter say the benediction *Asher yatzar* any time during the whole day.

4. If the *onan* happens to be in another city, and there are relatives where the dead lies, who are required to observe the rules of mourning, he is exempt from observing the rules relating to an *onan*.

5. In a place where there is a burial society who do everything connected with the funeral, after the relatives have come to terms with them, and the relatives have nothing to do any more, then the relatives are not subject to the rules of an *onan;* they may eat meat and drink wine, and they are certainly allowed—even obliged, to read the *Shema* and the *Shemoneh esreh* and to observe all other precepts. Still it is customary for an *onan* not to pray until after the interment, because he, too, follows the funeral procession to the cemetery. If an *onan* desires to be strict and pray as soon as he had delivered the corpse to the society, he may do so.

6. Before the interment, the mourner does not remove his shoes, and is allowed to leave the house to make provisions for the funeral. But he is not allowed to sit on a chair, sleep in a bed, cohabit, bathe, participate in joyous celebrations, greet friends, cut the hair, or study the Torah. He is forbidden to perform any work, or allow others to do work for him, even where a loss is involved; but where the loss would be very great, he should consult a Rabbinical authority.

7. If one becomes an *onan* when it is time to recite the *Shema* and the *Shemoneh esreh,* and after the interment, one-fourth of the day, the time limit for reading the *Shema,* had passed, one should, nevertheless, read the *Shema* with its benedictions, until the third of the day, without the *tefillin.* If one-third of the day had passed, he should recite the *Shema* without its benedictions. But he may pray the *Shemoneh esreh* until midday, and the *Musaph* service of the New Moon, throughout the entire day. Of the morning benedictions, he should recite only three: "*Who did not create me a heathen;*" "*Who did not create me a slave;*" and "*Who did not create me a woman;*" also the benedictions over the Torah, as these benedictions may be recited the entire day. But he should not recite the rest of the benedictions after their time limit had passed, since he was exempt from saying them at the proper time. If the interment takes place before one-third of the day is over, and his house is far away from the cemetery, so that by the time he will reach his house, one-third of the day will have passed, it is best that he should walk into a house near the cemetery, so that he may read the *Shema* and pray at the proper time, or he may do so even in the open air in a clean place. The *onan* may begin to recite the *Shema* and the *Shemoneh esreh,* as soon as they begin to throw loose earth over the coffin, although his period for observing the rules of mourning has not yet begun.

8. If one becomes an *onan* when the time for reciting the morning, the afternoon, or the evening service has begun, and he did not read his prayers before he became an *onan*, and he continued in that state of mourning until the time limit set for the prayer had passed, he need not make amends for the omitted prayer by reciting the *Shemoneh esreh* twice in the next prayer (see chapter 21, above).

9. If death occurs on the Sabbath, since it is forbidden to perform the burial on that day, the mourner is not subject to the laws pertaining to an *onan*. He is, therefore, permitted to partake of meat and wine, and he must observe all precepts, but he is not allowed to cohabit, or to study the Torah, because these things are done privately. If he is a *ḥazan* at the synagogue, and there is someone else to read the service, he should not officiate, but if there is none else, he may do so. If the deceased is his father or his mother, he may say the *kaddish*, when there are no other mourners. But if there are other mourners, he should not say the *kaddish* before the burial. If the *onan* at that time has already been mourning for one of his parents, or he was observing *Jahrzeit*, he shall say the *kaddish* the same as any other mourner or a *Jahrzeit*.

10. Towards evening, he reads the *Shema* without its benedictions. He should not recite the *Maariv* service, nor perform the *havdalah* ceremony, and he is permitted to eat without saying the *havdalah*. After the interment, he should say the *havdalah* over a cup of wine. Even if the burial takes place on Sunday, he may say the *havdalah* over a cup of wine, without saying the benedictions over the light and the spices, since it is permissible to recite the *havdalah* until Tuesday (as stated in chapter 96, above). If he prays the morning service before the time for reciting the *havdalah* has passed, he need not say *Attah ḥonantanu* (Thou graciously bestowest).

11. If towards evening, it becomes necessary for the mourner to walk up to the Sabbath boundary line, in order to reach sooner a certain place in the evening to attend to matters concerning the departed, or if he need towards evening to get together the officers of the burial society, to negotiate with them concerning the price of the grave, he becomes an *onan* as soon as he begins to walk and to attend to the arrangements for the interment.

12. If one dies late Friday afternoon, when it is impossible to bury him before the Sabbath, the mourner must pray the *Minḥah* service on that day.

13. If death occurs on the first day of a festival, and the mourner desires to bury the deceased on that day, by a non-Jew, he immediately becomes subject to the laws of an *onan*. Especially is this true when death occurs on the second day of a festival, when the mourner himself is permitted to perform the interment, that he becomes subject to the laws of an *onan*, even if he does not wish to bury him on that day.

14. One, whose dead relative lies before him on the night of the second day of a festival, when in a community where the custom prevails to bury the dead by Jews, the mourner becomes subject to the laws of an *onan* even at night, and he is not allowed to recite the *kiddush*, to eat meat, or drink wine. However, on the night of the first day of a festival, or even on the night of the second day of a festival, in a community where the custom prevails even on the second day of a festival to bury the dead by non-Jews, the mourner is not subject to the laws of an *onan* at night.

15. If one becomes an *onan* at the termination of a festival, one may recite the *havdalah* on the day after the festival but not thereafter, as the proper time for reciting the *havdalah* after a festival is only until the end of the day following the festival.

16. If an *onan* has a son to be circumcised, and it is possible to bury the dead before the worshipers leave the synagogue in the morning, then the burial society should first pray and then attend to the burial, and the circumcision is performed thereafter. If that is impossible, the circumcision should, nevertheless, take place in the morning at the synagogue, and the *sandek* shall say the benediction *Lehaḥniso* (to enter him); for, when an interment and a circumcision are to be performed, the circumcision takes precedence.

17. On the eve of the fourteenth of *Nisan*, an *onan* should employ an agent to make the search for unleavened bread, but he himself should recite *Kal ḥamira* (all leaven), etc.

18. One who becomes an *onan* on a night when the *omer* is counted, shall not count the *omer* at night, but on the following day after the burial, without pronouncing a benediction, but the following nights he shall say the benediction on counting the *omer*. If he sees that the state of being an *onan* will continue until nightfall, he may then count the *omer* while being an *onan*, without saying the benediction, so that on the following nights he may count the *omer* and pronounce the benediction.

19. If a man dies in prison and the officer refuses to release the body unless he is given a large sum of money, the relatives are subject neither to the laws of an *onan* nor to the laws of mourners, since they have not despaired of being able to bury him, and still hope to compromise with the officer. Likewise, if the next of kin of the dead are confined in prison and are unable to attend to the matters pertaining to his burial, they do not become subject to the laws of an *onan*.

20. In regions where the law of the land forbids burial of the dead before the expiration of forty-eight hours, the mourners, nevertheless, are not exempt from observing the laws regarding an *onan*, since at the expiration of such time, the interment will definitely take place, the mourners must busy themselves in honor of the deceased; to prepare shrouds and a coffin and engage the necessary people. However, on the second day of a festival, the mourners may be exempted from observing the laws of an *onan*, since it is impossible to bury the dead then because of the law of the land.

21. In the above-mentioned places, if the relatives, fearing that they will be unable to procure people to cleanse the body after the expiration of the two days, have succeeded in having the body cleansed immediately after death and placed the body in a coffin having an aperture underneath, then as soon as the body is placed in the coffin, the law regarding an *onan* ceases, and the laws concerning the observance of mourning begin. However, the first seven days of mourning are counted from the time the lid of the coffin is shut in the grave.

22. If a person is unaware of a death that occurred in his family and there is no one else to attend to the needs of the burial, he should be informed thereof immediately. However, if there are other people to attend to the funeral arrangements, he should not be told until he has recited his prayers. If one's wife has lost a relative, and she is unaware of her loss, then he must abstain from having intercourse with her. (See chapter 206:9; and the case of being in the state of an *onan*, is ever severer).

CHAPTER 197

The Purification, Shrouds, and Utilization of Anything Belonging to the Dead

1. It is the custom to make the shrouds of fine white linen, to indicate our belief in the resurrection of the dead; for, it is stated in the Talmud (Ketubot 111b): "Said Rab Ḥiyya the son of Joseph: 'The righteous will rise with their clothes on;' " but they should not be too costly, for that is forbidden. It is forbidden to make in the shrouds, either a hem or a knot of any sort, either when sewing the shrouds, or when dressing the dead. A dead male should be wrapped in a *tallit* with fringes, one of which should be rendered unfit for religious use. The better procedure, however, is to tuck one fringe in the corner pocket of the *tallit* when the body is already in the grave. If the deceased had a costly *tallit* in which he prayed during his lifetime, it is not proper to wrap him in an inferior *tallit*, for a person is desirous of being buried in the *tallit* in which he prayed during his lifetime. When dressing the body, the people should think that just as his body is being attired, so may his soul be attired in spiritual garments in Paradise.

2. The purification of the body is done as follows: The entire body, including the head, is washed with warm water. The fingers and the toes, as well as all the other parts of the body, should be thoroughly cleansed. The hair of his head is washed, combed, and cut, and the nails of the fingers and toes should be cut. (In our regions it is not done). Care should be taken during the purification, not to place the body with its face downwards, as that is disrespectful, but it should be inclined, first on one side, then on the other. After the body is thoroughly cleansed, we pour on it, nine *kabbim* (see following section) of water. This is done as follows: The body is placed in a standing position on the bare ground or on some straw, and the water is poured over the head, so that it runs down the entire body.

3. Concerning the capacity of nine *kabbim*, there is a diversity of opinions. To comply with the law, it is best to take about twenty four quarts of water. It is not necessary that the water be poured out of one vessel; the contents of two or even three vessels may be combined to make up the required quantity. It is, however, necessary to commence pouring out the contents of the second vessel before the first is emptied, and of the third, before the second is emptied. Even when pouring the water from one vessel, the flow must not be interrupted. Four vessels, however, cannot be combined, even if the water is poured out from all four simultaneously.

4. Then an egg with its shell is beaten up with wine, to symbolize the revolving wheel of fortune in this world, (where wine is not obtainable, water may be used) and the head of the corpse washed with it. The custom in some places, that each one takes a little of that mixture and sprinkles it upon the head of the deceased is an improper custom and should be abolished, because it resembles the customs of the Gentiles; it is to be used only to wash his head.

5. Care should be taken not to allow the fingers of the dead to remain closed. The custom prevailing in some communities to shut his fingers should be abolished. The belief of some people that by this, they symbolize some Holy Names, is a mere fabrication. It is also a foolish custom to place in his hands, some twigs, generally called forks; if they insist on placing it, it should be put alongside the corpse.

6. After having been cleansed, the corpse should not be left where the purification had taken place, but it must be placed opposite the door, inside the house. The board upon which the corpse has been washed must not be turned over, for it may be dangerous to do so.

7. A parent must not kiss his dead children, as it is very dangerous. Most assuredly, one must not grasp the hand of the dead and say that the dead should take him along.

8. When the dead is being carried from the house, no one should walk out of the house ahead of the corpse. The pallbearers, however, who have to be out of the house first in carrying the coffin, need not heed this rule.

9. If a person falls and dies instantly, if his body was bruised and blood flowed from the wound, and there is apprehension that his lifeblood was absorbed in his clothes, he should not be ritually cleansed, but interred in his garments and shoes. He should be wrapped in a sheet, above his garments. That sheet is called *sobeb*. It is customary to scoop up the earth at the spot where he fell, and if blood happens to be there or near by, all that earth is buried with him. Only the garments which he wore when he fell are buried with him, but if the blood splashed on other garments, or if he was placed upon pillows and sheets while the blood was flowing, all these need not be buried with him, but they must be thoroughly washed until no trace of blood

remains, and the water is poured into the grave. If, however, the deceased did not bleed at all, his clothes should be removed, his body cleansed and wrapped in shrouds, as is done in the case of a natural death. A person who was drowned, must likewise be treated like one who died a natural death. In some communities the custom prevails to inter drowned persons in the clothes in which they were found; where such custom prevails, it should not be changed.

10. If blood has flown from the injured body, but it stopped and his clothes were removed, after which he recovered and lived for a few days and then died, he must be cleansed and dressed in shrouds. Even if his body is stained with the blood which issued forth from him, he must be cleansed, for the blood lost while being alive is not to be regarded as lifeblood; we are only concerned with the blood which one loses while dying, for it is likely that this was his lifeblood, or it is possible that lifeblood was mixed with it.

11. If a woman dies while giving birth, the laws applying to a slain person apply also to her, and if it is known that she had lost much blood, she must not be cleansed. If the blood had ceased flowing and then she died and there is no apprehension that lifeblood was found therein, she should be treated like other persons who die a natural death. In some communities it is customary to cleanse the body of any woman that dies at childbirth. There are many other customs prevailing in such cases; such customs should be observed in those places.

12. One who was assasinated by a non-Jew, although he did not bleed at all, should, nevertheless, be buried in the clothes which he wore at the time, as a demonstration of wrath.

13. It is forbidden to derive any profit from the dead body, or from the shrouds, whether they be that of a Jew or a non-Jew. Ornamental objects which are attached to the corpse, as for instance, a wig tied to, or woven into the hair, or artificial teeth, must be interred with the body. But ornaments which are not attached to the body, and which are not considered as a part of the body, such as jewelry and clothes, may be used in any event.

CHAPTER 198

The Removal of the Corpse, Funeral and Burial Service

1. If a death occurs in town, all the inhabitants are forbidden to perform any work. If, however, the town has appointed men to take care of the dead, then those whose services are not required are permitted to work.

2. If a death occurs in a small village, no greetings should be exchanged between the inhabitants; this is especially to be avoided in a cemetery when a corpse is awaiting burial, even in a large city. But when there is no corpse in the cemetery awaiting burial, greetings may be exchanged at a distance of four cubits from the graves.

3. It is not allowed to let the body of the dead remain overnight, for it is written (Deuteronomy 21:23): "His body shall not remain all night . . . but thou shalt surely bury him the same day." It is, however, permissible to procure a coffin, or shrouds, or to await the arrival of relatives or of an orator to deliver the funeral oration. For the Torah forbids to delay burial only when it leads to the disgrace of the dead, as in the case of one that was hanged, but not when the delay is for his honor. Likewise, if a dead person is found and his identity cannot be established, it is permissible to keep the body overnight until witnesses can appear, or his wife can come to identify the corpse.

4. As regards all next of kin, the sooner they are laid to rest the more praiseworthy it is; but in the case of one's parents, over whom one is bound to do much wailing and mourning, if one hastens their burial he is to be despised, unless it is the day preceding the Sabbath or a festival, or if rain is coming down upon the bier.

5. If there are two persons to be interred, the one who died first would be taken care of first, and then the second. After the interment of the first, those present at the burial should not arrange themselves into two rows, through which the mourners pass, nor should they say the mourner's benediction, or console the mourners, so as not to delay the burial of the second. If it is necessary to delay the burial of the first until the following day, in order to do him honor, the burial of the second must not be delayed.

6. If one of the two deceased persons is a scholar and the other is an ignorant man, the former should be buried first, even if the latter died first. If there is a man and a woman, the woman must be buried first, even if the man died first, for it is written (Numbers 20:1): "And Miriam died, and was buried there," which means; the burial came immediately after her death."

7. "The Holy One, blessed be He, counts the tears shed for the death of a virtuous person, and He stores them up in His treasure house" (Shabbat 105b). It also atones for the sin of pollution and prevents the death of little children, God forbid.

8. One who sees a funeral and fails to join the procession, is likened to "*one who mocks at the poor,*" and deserves to be excommunicated. He must accompany the dead at least a distance of four cubits. Even if one is exempt from accompanying the dead (see section that follows), he is, nevertheless, obliged to rise as the funeral procession passes by; he rises, not in deference to the dead but to those who are attending to the dead, because they are engaged in the performance of a precept; and the law requires that we rise before anyone who is engaged in the performance of a precept. Thus, workmen used to rise before those who were carrying the *bikkurim* (first ripe fruit) to the Temple at Jerusalem.

9. Nowadays, it is assumed that every Jew has studied at least, the Bible and some Mishnah; therefore, even the study of the Torah must be interrupted in order to participate in a funeral procession. However, for the sake of a woman or a child, the custom is not to interrupt the study of the Torah for their funeral. School children should at no time be interrupted from their studies, not even for the purpose of rebuilding the Temple.

10. On the way to the cemetery, and especially on returning therefrom, care should be taken that the men should not mingle with the women, because there is, God forbid, some danger involved in their being together at such a time.

11. The pallbearers should wear no sandals (without heels that can easily slip off their feet), but they may wear shoes.

12. When those who participate in the cortege arrive about thirty cubits (forty-five feet) from the grave, they halt with the bier every four cubits, so that they can halt seven times, indicative of the seven *maamadot* (the seven halts in the Temple; see Taanit 27b), the seven times *vanity*, which are mentioned in Ecclesiastes, the seven portals of the Gehenna, and the seven judgments that are passed upon the dead. They should halt before the cemetery a short while, for that delay serves somewhat as an atonement for the dead. The halts are not made on days when the *taḥanun* (petition for Grace) is not recited.

13. On reaching the burial grounds, those who have not seen any graves in thirty days, are required to say the benediction, *Asher yatzar etḥem baddin* (who hath created you in judgment), etc., then *Attah gibbor* (Thou art mighty), up to, *Lehaḥayot metim* (to call the dead to life).

14. Then they recite *Tzidduk haddin* (burial service), beginning with, *Hatzur tamim paalo* (the Rock is perfect in His ways), etc. This prayer is commenced by one of the mourners. But if no mourner is present, it should be started by the most important person present. On the days when the *taḥanun* is not recited, *Tzidduk haddin* is omitted. Therefore, *Tzidduk haddin* is not to be said on Friday afternoon or on the day preceding a festival. But on the day before New Moon, before *Ḥanukkah* and *Purim*, *Tzidduk haddin*, is said even in the afternoon. If the deceased is a learned man, *Tzidduk haddin* should be recited even on the thirty-third day of the *omer*, on the days between the New Moon of *Sivan* and *Shavuot*, on the Ninth Day of *Ab*, and on the day before New Year, in the forenoon.

15. Neither *Tzidduk haddin* nor the *kaddish* are recited at the cemetery at night.

16. *Tzidduk haddin* should not be recited for an infant less than thirty days old.

CHAPTER 199

The Interment and the Cemetery

1. The burial mentioned in the Torah, connotes the placing of the body in the soil itself. In many places, however, the custom is to place the deceased in a coffin made of boards and to inter him thus. As it is unlikely that there should be no aperture at all in the coffin, this method of burial is valid. In some places, the corpse is buried without a coffin; it is laid on the ground without any board underneath, only one board is placed on each side, and one on the top to prevent any earth from falling upon the body, which would be a dishonor to him. In other communities, ordinary men are buried without a coffin, but *kohanim* and the firstborn males, who are of special importance, are placed in coffins. Care should be taken not to use the remnants of the boards out of which the coffin was made, for any purpose other than to heat the water for the purification of the corpse. Benevolent people who in their lifetime fed the poor at their table, should be interred in a coffin made out of the boards of that table, as it is written (Isaiah 58:8): *"And thy righteousness* (Hebrew, *tzedakah,* also meaning *charity) shall go before thee."*

2. The body is laid in a supine position, with face upward. If there is earth from the soil of Israel, some of it is spread underneath the body, and some on the top, as it is written (Deuteronomy 32:43): *"And the land shall make expiation for His people."* It is chiefly desirable to place some of the earth upon the "holy covenant," also on his mouth, eyes and hands.

3. Two persons should not be buried close to each other; they must be separated by a partition which can stand by itself without a prop, which is a thickness of no less than six finger-breadths. And if possible, it should be six hand-breadths thick. However, a man may be buried together with his son or his grandson, and a woman, together with her daughter or granddaughter. This is the rule: A minor who slept with the deceased during his or her lifetime, may be buried together with the parent, but an adult son should not be buried together with his father, nor an adult daughter together with her mother. Even the burial of a minor with his parent is only permissible when they are both buried at the same time, but if one had already been buried before, it is forbidden to open the grave to inter the other near him.

4. As it has already been explained in chapter 163:6, before, that if an uncircumcised infant dies, he must be circumcised at his grave, and a name given to him. A female infant should also be given a name; and it is necessary to inform the undertakers concerning this law.

5. Two coffins must not be placed, one atop the other, unless there is a minimum of six hand-breadths of earth between them.

6. A wicked person should not be interred next to a righteous person, for it is written (Psalms 26:9): *"Gather not my soul with sinners."* We do not even bury an extremely wicked man next to one who was less wicked; nor should a righteous man, and more especially a man of average piety, be interred next to a man who excelled in saintliness. Enemies should not be buried next to one another, for even in their death, they will have no peace together.

7. It is the prevailing custom not to take from the hand of another, a shovel or a pickaxe, with which the burial was performed; but the one who used it lays it down and the other takes it up.

8. After the interment, the bier is turned over three times, because the numerical value of the letters spelling out the Hebrew word *mittah* (bed, bier) is the same as that of the Hebrew word *din* (judgment); as an omen that the judgment will be turned into mercy, and the mourning into joy. It is in the verse (Psalms 30:12): "Thou didst turn for me my mourning into dancing;" but this need not be done on a day the *Taḥanun* (petition for Grace) is not recited.

9. After the interment, if an orphan is present and it is still day, the people should step away no less than four cubits from the grave, and recite the Psalm 49: *"Hear ye this, all ye peoples;"* and on the days when the *Taḥanun* is not said, they recite Psalm 16: *"A Miḥtam of David."* The orphan then says the *kaddish: Dehu atid leitḥadta* (that He will renew), and those present recite with him up to *Vikareh* (and may this happen). In some communities, the *kaddish* is recited before the interment, after saying *Tzidduk haddin;* while in other communities, even *Tzidduk haddin* is recited after the interment.

10. When about to leave the burial grounds, it is the custom to pluck some grass and to throw it behind the back, saying (Psalms 103:14): *"He remembereth that we are dust."* The custom is symbolical of the resurrection of the dead, as it is written (loco citato 72:16): *"And may they blossom out of the city like grass of the earth."* This may be done even during the Intermediate Days of a festival. They should then wash their hands. There is a Biblical hint for this practice, for this uncleanliness can be purified only by means of water, the ashes of the *Red Cow,* and the hyssop. For this ablution, a river may not be used; but water poured from a vessel is required. One should not take the vessel from another who washed his hands; but the first puts it down and the other takes it. The hands should not be wiped. Some maintain that the custom to sit down seven times, stems from the belief that evil spirits follow them, and when they sit down the evil spirits run away. In some places they sit down only three times after washing the hands, saying each time: *"And let the pleasantness of the Lord,"* etc. If the burial takes place on a festival, they should likewise sit down in the same manner as on a weekday. It is the custom to be careful about such hand washing and the sitting down thereafter when returning from the funeral and entering the house. And the customs of our fathers has the validity of law.

11. The dead should not be removed from a city where there is a cemetery to another city, because it is a degradation to remove a body from one place to another, unless it be from the Diaspora into Israel, or to the burial ground of his ancestors. It is also permissible, if it was the will of the deceased.

12. It is forbidden to open a grave after it was closed, that is, after earth had been heaped upon the lid of the coffin; but as long as earth has not yet been piled thereon, the coffin may be opened for any reason. If it becomes necessary to remove a body from its grave, a sage should be consulted.

13. A freshly dug grave must not be left open overnight, because there is danger in it. If the deceased cannot be interred until the following day, the grave must be refilled with earth.

14. It is impermissible to step upon graves, because according to some authorities, no benefit may be derived from them. However, if one has to visit a certain grave, and one has no other way of reaching it except by stepping upon other graves, one is allowed to do so.

15. It is forbidden to walk in the burial grounds, or within four cubits of a dead body, or in a room where there is a dead body while wearing *tefillin* upon the head or *tzitzit* in the garment, for it would seem as if one mocks at the poor (at the dead who need not wear them). We may, however, wear the *tefillin* and the *tallit,* if they are covered. Neither are we allowed to pray there, or to recite Psalms, unless it be in honor of the dead.

16. One should not indulge in levity in the burial grounds, because of the respect due to the dead. One should not eat or drink there, or respond to nature's call, or allow cattle to graze, or gather the vegetation that grows there. It is, however, permissible to pick the fruit from trees which grow in the burial grounds, but do not grow over the graves.

17. It is the custom in some communities, not to put up a tombstone until after twelve months, because a tombstone is a mark of distinction, and within the twelve months, the deceased is in grief. Another reason is that a tombstone is put up so that the dead may not be forgotten, and as a rule, the departed are not forgotten within twelve months. And there are other communities where no heed is paid to it.

CHAPTER 200

Burial on a Festival

1. A Jew is not allowed to bury his dead on the first day of a festival, even if it is impossible to have the burial done by a non-Jew, and there is danger that decay may set in. But if a non-Jew can dig the grave, cut the boards, make the coffin, and sew the shrouds, then a Jew is permitted to heat the water for the cleansing, to dress the body, to carry it out and place it in the grave. The filling in of the grave, however, should be done by a non-Jew. If possible, care should be taken not to cleanse the body with a cloth, so that they might not wring the water out of it.

2. Some authorities hold that if it is possible to have the burial performed by a non-Jew as stated above, it is forbidden to keep the body till the second day, so that Jews may attend to it. Even if the body can be kept till the second day without becoming malodorous, it should, nevertheless, be interred on the same day by a non-Jew. In case of an infant, even if he lived more than thirty days, and it is known that it was not a child of premature birth, nevertheless, if the air is cool and it will be no dishonor to keep it because no decay will set in, it should not be buried on the first day of a festival, but it should be kept till the second day. Other authorities hold, that even if the body of an adult will not begin to decay, it should be kept for burial till the second day of the festival. In a community where there is no fixed custom, it is proper to follow the latter opinion.

3. On the second day of a festival, even the second day of *Rosh Hashanah*, if it is possible to have all the above-mentioned duties performed by a non-Jew, without causing any delay, a non-Jew should carry out the same, while Jews perform the other preparations mentioned above. It is also permissible to use cloths and sheets in performing the purification, only care should be taken not to wring the water out of them with the hands. If it is impossible to have the above-mentioned duties performed by a non-Jew, Jews are permitted to make all the necessary preparations for the burial, as though it were a weekday, because the Rabbis consider the second day of a festival as a weekday with regard to burying the dead. If, however, there is one who possesses ready made shrouds, they should buy it from him, in order to avoid the necessity of sewing new ones. The aforesaid things are permitted on the second day of a festival only when the burial is to take place that same day. If not, it is forbidden to make the slightest preparation for the burial; it is even forbidden to handle the body.

4. The Rabbis have considered the second day of a festival like a weekday in this regard, because of the honor due the dead, that he should not be lying in disgrace. It is, however, forbidden to do anything else (not directly

connected with the burial). Hence, it is forbidden to bargain with the storekeeper about the price of the linen for the shrouds, unless it is impossible to obtain it otherwise, as when it is bought from a non-Jew. Gravediggers are not allowed to accept any remuneration for their work on a festival, because it is forbidden to accept wages for work performed on the Sabbath or on a festival. If they refuse to work without pay, they may be paid, but will have to render an account of their conduct before the Heavenly Court. The *Ḥevrah Kaddisha* must not accept any money for the grave, on a festival, but they may accept pledges without stipulating the amount to be paid for the grave.

5. If there is no Jewish cemetery in town, although there is a place where the deceased may be buried, it is, nevertheless, permissible to convey a dead body on the first day of a festival by a non-Jew, and on the second day of a festival even by a Jew, to a place where it can be buried in a Jewish cemetery. But if the burial is not to take place on that day, a Jew is not allowed to convey the body on a festival in order to have it buried after the festival.

6. On the first day of a festival, it is permissible to accompany the dead only within the Sabbath-limit, but on the second day of a festival, it is permitted to go beyond the Sabbath-limit, and to return home on the same day. It is forbidden to ride on an animal on a festival, to accompany the dead, not even on the second day and not even mourners are permitted. The gravediggers, however, are allowed to ride on the second day of a festival, it it is impossible for them to walk. Nevertheless, they should not ride through the city.

7. If one dies on the second day of a festival, when Jews may attend to the burial, because there are no non-Jews to attend to it, ten men should rise at an early hour and perform the interment while the *ḥazan* is reciting the festival hymns. If the deceased is a distinguished person, so that a multitude of people are to participate in the funeral, the interment should take place after the morning service, before the meal is eaten. For the Midrash says: "It is written (Leviticus 19:26): *"Ye shall not eat with the blood,"* which signifies that it is forbidden to eat a regular meal before the interment takes place." If it is impossible to make all the preparations for the burial by that time, the interment may take place after the meal.

8. With regard to an infant over thirty days old, when it is already known that it is not an abortive child, the same law applies to him as to any adult person. If it is a male child, whose circumcision has for some reason been postponed, he should not be buried on the first day of a festival, even if decay is setting in, because it is necessary to remove his foreskin, which cannot be done by a non-Jew. The body should, therefore, be kept till the second day of the festival, when the body is interred after the foreskin is removed.

9. If an infant dies and it is doubtful whether or not it was an abortive child, it should not be buried on the first day of a festival, even by a non-Jew, if no decay is setting in, but it should be kept until the second day of the festival for burial by a non-Jew, but not by a Jew. If the body is in a state

of decay, it should be buried by a non-Jew on the first day of the festival. If an infant dies on the second day of a festival, it should be buried that same day by a non-Jew but not by a Jew. If it is an uncircumcised male child, even though he is in a state of decay, he should not be buried by a non-Jew on the second day of a festival. He should be kept until after the festival, when the foreskin is removed and then buried.

10. On the Sabbath and *Yom Kippur*, no one is allowed to attend to the dead, not even with the aid of a non-Jew.

11. On *Ḥol hammoed* (Intermediate Days of a festival), the dead body should not be conveyed to the cemetery before the grave is ready, so that it would not be necessary to let the bier remain waiting.

CHAPTER 201

The Suicide and the Wicked

1. There is none so wicked as the one who commits suicide, as it is written (Genesis 9:5): "*And surely your blood of your lives will I require.*" For the world was created for only one individual, to indicate that he who destroys one human life is considered as though he had destroyed a whole world. Therefore, one should not rend his garments or observe mourning for a suicide, nor should a eulogy be delivered for him. He should, however, be ritually cleansed, dressed in shrouds, and buried; the rule is: Whatever is done in deference to the living, should be done for him.

2. Without proof to the contrary, a man is not presumed to be wicked. Therefore, if a man is found asphyxiated or hanged, if it is a possible murder, he should not be considered a suicide.

3. A minor who committed suicide is considered like one who had taken his life accidently. If an adult committed suicide, and it is evident that the act was prompted either through madness, or through fear of torture, as was the case with King Saul, who feared the wanton treatment of the Philistines, he should likewise be treated as though he had died a natural death.

4. All those who deviate from the community by casting off the yoke of precepts, severing their bonds with the people of Israel as regards the observance of the Divine Commands, and are in a class by themselves; also

apostates, informers, and heretics—for all these the rules of an *onan* and of mourners should not be observed. Their brothers and other next of kin should dress in white, eat, drink, and rejoice that the enemies of the Almighty have perished. Concerning such people, the Scripture says (Psalms 139:21): *"Do not I hate them, O Lord, that hate Thee?"* Also, (Proverbs 11:10): *"And when the wicked perish, there is joy."*

5. Relatives must observe all rules of mourning for one who was executed, either by the government or otherwise, even if he was an apostate. For since he was killed by man, he had an atonement for sins.

6. For an inveterate sinner, even one whose transgressions stemmed from lust, if he died without making confession, no mourning should be observed; but if he had confessed, mourning should be observed for him, even if he had been a thief or a robber

7. No mourning should be observed for the death of a child one or two years old who was converted with either his father or his mother.

CHAPTER 202

The Defilement of a Kohen

1. The *Kohen* was commanded not to defile himself by coming in contact with a dead body. This includes the body of an abortive child whose limbs are still undeveloped. (If, however, the abortion has occurred within forty days from conception, it is considered as only a fluid). The contact that defiles need not necessarily be with the dead body in its entirety, for there is pollution even in the touch of anything that was separated from it, such as its blood and the like. He is likewise forbidden to defile himself by coming in contact with the severed limb of a living person, if there is enough flesh on it, that it would possibly heal if it were still connected with the body; even if that happens to be his own limb, he is forbidden to defile himself by touching it. He is forbidden to enter a house where a person is dying, even though a person in that state is considered like a living being in every respect and does not cause defilement. But by entering such a house the *Kohen* violates the Command (Leviticus 21:12): *"Neither shall he profane,"* for he is warned to guard his priesthood against possible profanations and here he exposes it to profanation, as death may occur at any moment.

2. A *Kohen* must not enter a tent where there is a dead body, no matter how large the tent is. Even if there are two rooms and the room where the the body is lying, is separated from the other with a wall in which there is an aperture measuring one square hand-breadth, he is forbidden to enter the adjoining room, for an aperture of this size passes impurity. Even if there is a third intervening room, but the walls separating it have apertures measuring a square hand-breadth, he is forbidden to enter the third room as well,

and thus, ad infinitum. If the aperture has been made to admit light, then even if it is the size of a small coin, it passes the impurity.

3. Therefore, in our regions where the roofs project towards the outside with a space of no less than one hand-breadth, since it is established that the width of one hand-breadth wide conveys impurity, this projecting roof is considered a tent which transmits impurity. Hence, houses which are close together, if there is a dead body in one of them, the impurity is conducted through the open window or door of that house, and passes by means of the projecting roofs through the open window or door of the second house, and the *Kohen* is forbidden to enter the second house. This is true even if there are many houses closely adjoining one another.

4. Even if the roofs of the adjoining houses are not of the same height, but one is higher than the other, or even if the roof of the house in which the impurity is found is much higher than the other roof, or vice versa, it is a law handed down by Moses from Sinai, that the height is considered as lowered, that is, we consider as if the height was pressed down and lowered until it reaches the lower one, and if when lowered the two roofs would touch, then the impurity is conducted from one to the other. But if there is a space between the roofs, be it ever so slight, the impurity is not transmitted.

5. If a beam, one hand-breadth wide, lies across an alley, on the style of an *eruv*, and is covered by the roofs projecting above it to the extent of one hand-breadth from each side (Figure A), then the impurity is conducted from underneath the roof of the house to underneath the beam, which is then conveyed to the roof of the house on the opposite side, and from there it spreads in every direction where three is a tent measuring no less than one hand-breadth until it is stopped by some open space or barrier. If there is a vault between two houses, on the style made for a court entrance (Figure B), the same law applies, although the vault has no projecting roof, nevertheless, the impurity is transmitted from beneath the roof of the house to beneath the vault. However, at times a vault is erected on extra posts from the ground up, and there is an enclosure between these posts and the walls of the houses.

Then if there is no projecting roof on the vault, and the enclosure on its sides extend further than the roofs of the houses above it (Figure C), in this case there is no place through which the impurity may be conducted, since there is some open space not forming a tent. At times there is a solid wall between one house and another, without an opening but there is a projecting roof over it, then the impurity is transmitted from one roof to the other. In a case of emergency, this situation can be remedied by removing some of the tiles in one place, so that there may be an open space, measuring one hand-breadth, without forming a tent, which acts as a barrier to the transmission of impurity. However, a careful examination should be made to ascertain whether there is nothing projecting from the wall itself to the size of one hand-breadth which is at times made to adorn the wall.

6. It is a tradition dating from Moses on Sinai, that the door through which a corpse is to be carried out from the house—since by removing the corpse through it, it renders the house clean again—is considered as legally open, even when it is actually closed, and, therefore, a *Kohen* is not permitted to stand under the lintel even though the door is closed. Likewise, if there is a roof projecting one hand-breadth from the house over the door, such roof conducts the impurity from the house as though the door were open. However, if another door or window, measuring four square hand-breadths is open on another side of the house, the closed door is then not considered as being open, and a *Kohen* is allowed to stand there, provided the impurity cannot reach him through the open door or window.

7. If a *Kohen* happens to be in a house or in a room, the doors and windows of which are closed in such a manner that there is no aperture in the door of one hand-breadth nor an aperture in the window the size of a coin, and he hears that there is a corpse lying in another room, so that if the door or the window sill be opened, the impurity will reach him, he is not allowed to open either, but he should remain there until the corpse is removed; for, as long as there is no opening measuring at least one hand-breadth, the impurity is not transmitted.

8. A *Kohen* is forbidden to approach a corpse or a grave within four cubits. This prohibition is true only when the body lies in its permanent place. If, however, it lies there only temporarily, as during the funeral procession or funeral service, or when they stop with the bier, then he need keep away only a distance of four hand-breadths.

9. If a *Kohen* is asleep in a house containing a corpse, where the impurity of the dead reaches him, and it is impossible to shut him in, in order to prevent the access of the impurity, he must be awakened so that he should go out of there. If he is undressed, he should not be informed of the impurity,

but merely called out, so that he may first get dressed, for a man's dignity is of great importance. However, as soon as he becomes aware of the impurity, he must leave immediately and not wait until he dresses himself.

10. Some authorities are of the opinion that even the corpse of a non-Jew in a tent causes impurity. A *Kohen* must pay heed to this opinion and not walk on the grave of a non-Jew. Especially when there is reason to believe that an apostate was buried there; for in this regard, an apostate is considered like a Jew. The child born by an apostate woman from a non-Jew, is likewise considered like a Jew in this respect.

11. It is a *Kohen's* duty to defile himself for his relatives; his wife to whom he is legally married, his father, his mother, his son or daughter, his brother and sister if they are the children of his father and have lived no less than thirty days; but he must not defile himself for a child of doubtful abortion nor for his married sister. Some authorities say that the permission of a *Kohen* to defile himself for his relatives is only for the needs of burial, or to bring a coffin, or shrouds, or the like; consequently, on the Sabbath when burial is forbidden, he must not defile himself even in order to guard the body. It is well to comply with this opinion. However, concerning all things necessary for burial, he is in duty-bound to defile himself. Even if all the burial preparations have been made by the *Ḥevra Kadisha* and he himself has nothing to do, he is permitted to remain in the house, in case his services are needed. But he may defile himself for these relatives only until the grave is closed, not thereafter

12. The *Kohen* is not allowed to defile himself for his parents if they had abandoned the practices of the people Israel, nor for one who had committed suicide, nor for anyone else for whom no rules of mourning need be observed.

13. A *Kohen* must not defile himself for a relative who had lost one of his limbs. Some authorities, therefore, hold that a *Kohen* is not permitted to defile himself for a relative who had been slain, for it is then considered as a defective body; and it is proper to heed this opinion.

14. Some ignorant *Kohanim* have made it a custom to visit the graves of the righteous, maintaining that their graves do not defile. They are in error, and they should be warned against this practice.

15. Just as an adult *Kohen* is warned against defiling himself, so is he warned concerning his minor children, for it is written (Leviticus 21:1): "Speak unto the priests . . . and say unto them," etc., and our Rabbis, of blessed memory, said (Yebamot 114a) that because it is written "Speak" and "say," it is inferred from this, that the adults are warned concerning the children. But it is forbidden only to cause them directly to defile themselves,

that is, to bring them into the house containing a corpse. If, however, a minor has defiled himself of his own accord, there is no need to take him out of there. However, if he had reached the age of indoctrination, he should be removed from there. The pregnant wife of a *Kohen* is permitted to enter the house containing a corpse.

16. The *Kohanim* cannot force the relatives of the decedent to hasten the removal of the corpse, so that they can enter their homes. If the *Kohen* is ill and he is unable to leave the house, the relatives of the decedent can be forced to remove the corpse so as not to cause the invalid to transgress a law of the Torah. If the dead is an abortive child, its relatives can be forced to remove it, in any event, even on the Sabbath, by a non-Jew.

Chapter 203

Relatives for Whom Mourning Must be Observed

1. There are seven next of kin upon whose death one must observe the rite of mourning: Father, mother, son, daughter, brother, sister, whether from father's side or mother's side, even a married sister, wife and husband.

2. It is the custom to observe partial mourning even for other relatives during the first week until after the Sabbath; not to bathe in warm water, and not to change the clothes for that Sabbath. Not all relatives are alike in this respect. For a second cousin, or a grandson, whether descended from a son or from a daughter, one is permitted to put on all the Sabbath clothes, with the exception of the outer garments. For a father-in-law, a mother-in-law and for a paternal grandfather, also a woman for her father-in-law, her mother-in-law, and her paternal or maternal grandfather, they only omit wearing a white shirt, and a woman does not put on her white veil. All who mourn for the death of the above, should also not bathe, not comb their hair, and not eat outside of their houses either at a religious feast, or at any social gatherings. But after the first Sabbath following the death, all these are permissible.

3. For a child who died within thirty days from its birth, even on the thirtieth day, and even if its hair and nails were fully grown, one need not rend one's garments, nor observe the rules of an *onan*, not observe the period of mourning, for it is a doubtful abortion. But for a child who died after the thirtieth day, be it even on the thirty-first day at an earlier hour than that on which he was born, one must rend his garments, observe the rules of an *onan* and also the period of mourning, unless it is definitely known that it was born in the eighth month of pregnancy (and it is a non-viable child). If it was definitely known that it was born in the ninth month, as when the father

had separated from his wife after cohabitation for nine full months before the child was born, then even if its death has occurred on the day it was born, one must rend one's garment, observe the rules of an *onan* and the period of mourning.

4. If one of twin children dies within thirty days or even on the thirtieth day from birth, while the other survives, we draw no conclusion, that since one lived after thirty days, the other one, too, was a viable child; and no mourning is to be observed for him.

5. Male and female proselytes who were converted to Judaism with their children, observe no mourning for one another; for every proselyte is considered like a new-born infant, and they are no longer considered as kinsmen.

CHAPTER 204

The Time When Mourning Begins

1. The period of mourning begins as soon as the decedent is buried and the grave is filled with earth. The mourner removes his shoes at the cemetery; but if he has to walk home through a non-Jewish neighborhood, he may wear his shoes, but he should place a little earth in them.

2. If the burial ground is near the city, and the mourner did not go there, but after having walked with the cortegé, he returned to his house, his period of mourning does not begin until he is told that the grave has been filled. However, if night is approaching and he desires that this day should be counted as one of the seven days of mourning, he may begin to observe mourning from the time he assumes that the grave was filled. If he is informed thereafter that the grave had been filled before nightfall, he may count that day as one of the seven-day-period of mourning. And if it was the day preceding a festival, the festival voids the observance of the seven days of mourning.

3. In places where the dead are conveyed to another city and the mourners who remain at home do not know when the burial takes place, they may begin to observe the rites of mourning immediately upon returning from the funeral, and they may begin to count from that time, both the seven-day and the thirty day periods of mourning. But those who accompanied the decedent to the place of interment, begin to count from the time the burial took place. Some authorities hold that if the head of the family accompanies the dead, then the members of the family who remain at home also begin to count from the time of the burial. They estimate the time when the burial takes place, and begin to observe the rules of mourning. And it is only for the sake of a more rigid observance that the other mourners are guided by the head of the family, and they begin to count the days of mourning from the time of the burial; but if the head of the family remains at home, those mourners who accompany the dead are not to be guided by him, but they begin to count the days from the time of the burial.

4. If a person was drowned or he was murdered by a non-Jew and his body cannot be found, as long as the search has not been abandoned, the next of kin are not subject to the laws of an *onan*, nor do they begin to observe the period of mourning, and they are even permitted to cohabit. But as soon as the search is abandoned, the next of kin begin to observe the rules of mourning, and if the body is found and buried after they have finished the mourning period, they need not observe another mourning period. However, if the deceased is one's father or mother, a rent should then be made in one's garments. If the lost person left a wife, and the proof of his death is not so definitely established as to permit her to remarry, no mourning should be observed for him, nor should the *kaddish* be recited for him. They should, nevertheless, delight his soul by occasionally officiating as *ḥazan*, by reading the *haftorah*, by joining others in saying Grace after meals, by donating to charity, and by studying or hiring someone else to study in his memory.

5. If a person learns of the death of a kinsman, he begins to count the period of mourning from the day he becomes aware of it. Even if he later comes to the place where the death occurred, and the other mourners there began to observe their mourning period before he did, he is not allowed to shorten his mourning period. If he becomes aware of it only when he comes to the mourners, but the latter are neither at the place where the death occurred nor where he was buried, he must also begin to count the days of mourning from the time he became aware of it.

6. If the mourners are at the place where the death occurred or where he was buried, then if at the time of the burial he was no farther than ten parasangs, which is a day's walk, it is considered as though he had been present at the burial and he counts the period of mourning with the other mourners. Even if he has come on the seventh day before the people leave the synagogue after praying the mourning service, since the mourners still observed some mourning on that day, his count of the seven and thirty days correspond with theirs. This is only true when the head of the family is among them whose lead they all follow, but if the head of the family is not there, the new arrival must count the period of mourning for himself. If he has come from a far off place, he must also count the mourning for himself, even though the head of the family is there.

7. One who begins to count the days of mourning, together with those that were present, continues to do so even when he returns to his house.

8. Who is to be considered as the head of the family? One who is respected to such a degree, that if a question of dividing the estate were to arise, his judgment would be accepted and his advise followed. Such a one is called the head of the family, even if he is young in years and even if he is not one of the heirs; for instance, if there is a widow who manages the house, she is the head of the family. If a person who lives together with his father-in-law lost his wife, then his father-in-law is the head of the family.

9. If one becomes aware of the death of one's kinsman after the congregation had already prayed the *Marriv* service, but it is still day and he has not yet prayed, he does not follow the congregation, and he can include that day in the period of mourning. If, however, he too, had already prayed the evening service, this day is not counted, and he has to count the seven and the thirty days from the following day. This rule is only for the more rigid observance of it, but not for making it more lenient. Thus, if he becomes aware of the death on the thirtieth day after having said the evening prayers, we do not say that it is night already, and therefore, it is *delayed news* (see chapter 206, below), thereby exempting him in some measure; but we consider it as daytime and the news is considered as *timely*. But he may include that day in the period of mourning. With regard to *tefillin*, if he heard of the death after he said the evening prayers while it was yet day, he should lay the *tefillin* on the following day without saying the benedictions. But if it happened on the thirtieth day, he has to put on the *tefillin* on the following day and say the benedictions over them. If a woman becomes aware of the death of a relative after the congregation had already said the evening prayers and it is still day, then if she is not accustomed to say the evening prayers, she must abide by the act of the congregation for the strict enforcement of the law, and that day is not to be counted as one of the days of mourning.

10. During a plague, God forbid, it is customary not to observe any mourning, because of the general panic. However, if the visitation had passed within the thirty days from the demise of one's kinsman, one must then observe mourning. If it did not pass until after the thirty days, or if a festival had intervened in the meantime, one need no longer observe any mourning.

CHAPTER 205

The Meal of Condolence

1. On the first day of mourning, the mourner is forbidden to eat his own food at his first meal. It is, therefore, the duty of his neighbors to send him food for the first meal, which is known as the *meal of condolence*. This meal should begin with eggs or lentils, which are round and have no mouth (dent), just as the mourner presumably has no mouth. But these may be followed by all manner of food, even meat. The mourner is also permitted to drink a little wine during the meal, just enough to help digest the food, but not to satiation. Some authorities hold that all of the first day, a mourner is not allowed to eat of his own food, even if he has many meals during that day.

2. If the mourner does not wish to eat until nightfall, since the first day after burial has passed, he is permitted to eat his own food. It is, therefore, proper for a mourner who lives alone in a village and he has none to send him food for the meal of condolence, to fast until nightfall. Nevertheless, if he is unable to fast, he is not obliged to afflict himself, and he may eat his own food.

3. A married woman is not allowed to take the first meal of her husband's food, for inasmuch as it is his duty to support her, it is considered as her own food. Likewise, a hired person, who has board as a part of his wages, if he becomes a mourner, should not eat his employer's food at his first meal. But an orphan who is supported by a stranger, or grownup children who are supported by their father, since they are not legally entitled to such support, if they become mourners, may have their first meal of the householders food, because it is not considered their own food.

4. To a woman in mourning, the meal of condolence should be supplied by women and not by men.

5. If the burial takes place at night and the mourner desires to eat during the night, he is forbidden to eat his own food, but he should be provided with a meal of condolence. Should he not desire to eat during the night, he is forbidden to eat his own food at the first meal of the following day, since the day is from sunset to sunset, his first day of mourning is not yet over.

6. If the burial takes place on a Friday, after the ninth hour (three o'clock in the afternoon), when no regular meal may be had, the mourner should not be served with a meal of condolence, in deference to the Sabbath. And the mourner should not eat anything until the evening.

7. The meal of condolence is served only to one who received *timely news* (see chapter that follows), but not *delayed news*. If the mourner received *timely news* on the Sabbath, the meal of condolence should not be served to him, for he may eat his own food; nor should a meal of condolence be served to him on Sunday, inasmuch as the day when he has received the news had passed.

8. If the burial takes place on a festival, no meal of condolence should be served to the mourner; neither should it be served to him after the festival, since the day on which the burial took place has already passed. But if the burial takes place on the Intermediate Days of the festival, he is served with the meal of condolence, only he must eat while sitting on a chair at the table as usual, for no mourning may be observed during the Intermediate Days of a festival.

9. It was the custom to fast on the day a man learned in the Torah passed away.

Chapter 206

"Timely" and "Delayed" News

1. If one heard of the death of a relative for whom he is required to observe the rites of mourning, within thirty days, even on the thirtieth day, the tidings are *timely*, and he must rend his garments, and observe the seven days of mourning, counting them from the day he received the news. He must also observe the thirty days of mourning, counting them from the same day. The day when the news reaches him is governed by the same rules as obtain on the day of burial. The thirty-day period which is considered as *timely* is to be counted from the day of the interment and not from the day of death.

2. If the news reached him after thirty days it is *delayed* news and he need not observe mourning for more than an hour; it makes no difference whether he received the tidings by day or by night. One hour's mourning is sufficient

in that event even for one's parents, with the exception of the limited twelve-month mourning for one's parent, which is to be observed even if the tidings of the death were *delayed*. The twelve months of mourning are to be counted from the day of death. If the news have reached him after the twelve months, he need not observe any kind of mourning for more than one hour, not even the kind observed the entire twelve months.

3. One who has received *delayed* news, need not observe any mourning ritual other than the removing of his shoes, but he is allowed to work, bathe, anoint himself, have sexual intercourse, and study the Torah. If he had no shoes on when the tidings have reached him, he must do something else which will indicate that he is in mourning, as to sit on the ground or on a low stool for one hour.

4. One who has received *timely* news on the Sabbath, the Sabbath is counted as one day, and at the termination of the Sabbath he has to rend his garments and observe six days of mourning thence.

5. If one has received *timely* news on a Sabbath or a festival, but this news will become *delayed* after the Sabbath or the festival, one must observe the rules of mourning pertaining to private matters, and at the conclusion of the Sabbath or the festival, he observes one hour's mourning as though it were *delayed tidings*.

6. If one has received *timely* news on the Sabbath which is on the eve of a festival, inasmuch as he must observe mourning in privacy, the festival suspends the seven day-mourning.

7. One who receives *delayed* news on a Sabbath or a festival should not observe any mourning even in privacy, but at the conclusion of the Sabbath or the festival, he has to observe one hour's mourning, and that is sufficient.

8. If one heard after a festival of a death that had occurred before the festival, although a festival voids the mourning for those who had already observed some mourning before the festival, nevertheless, it does not effect him, inasmuch as he had not observed any mourning at all before the festival. Therefore, if the news reached him even on the thirtieth day after the burial, it is considered *timely*, and he must observe the seven and the thirty days of mourning.

9. If anyone lost a relative and he does not know about it, he must not be informed thereof. Concerning the one who bears such news, it is said (Proverbs 10:18): "*He that uttereth a report is a fool.*" As long as a person is unaware of his relative's death, he may be invited to a betrothal or wedding feast or to any joyful gathering, like any other person. If a husband knows that his wife lost a relative, he may have intercourse with her, since she is unaware of it.

10. If one is asked concerning the welfare of a relative who had died, he should not say that he is alive, for it is written (Exodus 23:7): "*Keep thee far from a false matter,*" but he should answer ambiguously, so the inquirer will surmise that the relative had died.

11. It is customary to inform sons of the death of their father or mother in order that they may say the *kaddish.*

CHAPTER 207

Comforting the Mourners

1. It is a highly meritorious act to console mourners, for we find that the Holy One, blessed be He, consoled mourners, as it is written (Genesis 25:11): "*And it came to pass after the death of Abraham, that God blessed Isaac his son.*" This is an act of lovingkindness to the living as well as to the departed. The comforters are not allowed to say anything before the mourner commences to speak, as was the case with Job, as it is written (Job 2:13): "*And none spoke a word unto him;*" also (loco citato 3:1): "*And after this, opened Job his mouth;*" and further (loco citato 4:1): "*Then answered Eliphaz.*" If the comforters perceive that the mourner wishes them to withdraw, they are not permitted to remain any longer.

2. A mourner or a sick person is not required to rise even before a *Nasi* (Prince). If one wishes to rise for another as a token of respect, it is proper to say: "Keep your seats;" but one must not say so to a mourner or to a sick person for it sounds like saying: "Sit down and remain in your mourning;" or, "Remain in your sickness."

3. A man must not say: "I have not been punished sufficiently for my evil deeds," or expressions similiar to this, in order not to open his mouth for Satan (to invite misfortunes by ominous words).

4. The comforters must not say to the mourner: "What can you do? It is impossible to alter the decree of the Holy One, blessed be He." Such an expression is akin to blasphemy, implying that were it possible for him to change it, he would do so. A man must accept the decree of the Almighty, blessed be He, lovingly.

5. Mourners are to observe the mourning rites in the place where the deceased gave up his soul, for the soul of the departed is grieving in that place, and it behooves to comfort it there. It is desirable to pray there with a *Minyan* (quorum of ten male adults) in the morning and in the evening (see chapter 20, section 6, above), even if there is no mourner present, for it is a consolation for the soul. If there is a mourner present, he may be counted in the quorum. A *sefer torah* should be brought there, and put in a suitable place for the duration of the time they pray there. If two deaths occur in

two different homes, in one of which there is a mourner, while in the other there is none, and there are not enough worshipers in that community to have a quorum of ten in both houses, then they should hold services in the house where there is no mourner. In the house of the departed, it is customary to recite after the morning and afternoon service (Psalm 49): *"For the Leader . . . Hear this, all ye peoples,"* etc., and it is certainly well to study there some *Mishnah* for the sake of the soul (the letters *Mem, Shin, Nun, He,* spelling out the word *Mishnah* משנה also spell out the Hebrew word *Neshamah* נשמה *soul*).

6. If the mourner is present in the house where the death occurred, no *hallel* is recited during the first seven days of mourning (because it is considered like *sneering at the poor,* for in it we say: (115:17): *"The dead praise not the Lord."* If there is another room, then the mourner should go into that room, and the congregation should recite the *hallel.* If there is no other room, then on the New Moon, those who prayed there need not recite the *hallel* later in their own homes, but on *Ḥanukkah,* they must recite the *hallel* in their own homes. If the services are held in the house where the death occurred but where there is no mourner present, or if it is held in the house of the mourner, but the death did not occur there, the *hallel* should be recited even on the New Moon, but the mourner himself should not recite it (because in it is written (Psalms 118:24): *"This is the day which the Lord hath made; we will rejoice and be glad in it."* If the seventh day of mourning occurs during the days of *Ḥanukkah;* then after the comforters leave, at which time mourning ceases, the mourner must recite the *hallel.* Other authorities are of the opinion that on *Ḥanukkah, hallel* should be recited with the congregation, even in the house of a mourner. If the New Moon occurs on the Sabbath, *hallel* should be recited with the congregation even in the house of a mourner, for on the Sabbath, no public mourning is observed.

7. It is not customary nowadays to recite the special benedictions for mourners contained in the Grace after meals; we rely on the opinion of those authorities who hold that these benedictions must be said only when Grace is recited with a quorum of ten.

CHAPTER 208

The Work a Mourner is Forbidden to Perform

1. During the first seven days, a mourner is forbidden to perform any work, to bathe, to anoint himself, to wear shoes, to have sexual intercourse, to study the Torah, offer greetings, wear freshly washed garments, cut his hair, or be present at any festivity. On the first day, he is also forbidden to put on the *tefillin.*

2. What are the rules concerning work? During the first three days, a mourner must not perform any work, even if he is a poor man who relies on charity. But from the fourth day on, if the mourner is a poor man and has nothing to eat, he may work privately at home. A woman also may work privately in her own home to earn enough for her sustenance. Our Sages say: "May a curse fall on the mourner's neighbors who made it necessary for him to do work," for it is their duty to provide for the poor, especially during the days of mourning.

3. The mourner is forbidden to have his work done even by others, not even by a non-Jew. If, however, the work is very urgent, and he might sustain a great loss by not doing it, he should consult a competent Rabbi as to what may be done.

4. Just as a mourner is forbidden to perform work, so is he forbidden to transact business. If, however, he possesses some merchandise and he will sustain a heavy loss by not selling it now, he should consult a sage. If caravans or ships arrived with merchandise, which is being sold at a low price, and which he will be unable to obtain later on, or if he happens to be in at a fair when he receives *timely* news of the death of a kinsman, he may transact business through others.

5. A mourner is allowed to lend out money on interest through an agent to non-Jews who have been accustomed to borrow from him before. If he has regular customers who buy merchandise from him, and he is afraid that they will get accustomed to trade elsewhere, he may also sell to them through others.

6. He is likewise permitted to send someone to collect a debt, if he has cause to fear that he will be unable to collect it later.

7. Such writing as is allowable during *Ḥol Hammoed,* is also permissible to a mourner (see chapter 104, section 15, above), if it cannot be done by a non-Jew.

8. A tenant who holds the field of a mourner, either as a share cropper, or on a fixed amount of the produce, or on a lease for a certain sum of money, may attend to the work in the field as usual, during the owner's period of mourning, for since he derives the profit of his labor, he need not suffer any loss on account of the owner's mourning. However, if the mourner has a day laborer to do work in his field, he is forbidden to let him work, even if the field is in another city, since the work is being done for the benefit of the mourner and it is done publicly.

9. If the mourner is a share cropper in the field of another, he is not allowed to do the work himself, but he may employ others to work therein, for it is not called the work of the mourner but that of the owner of the field. However, if he has to do other kinds of work for others, he may not have it done even by employing other people. But if it is something that must be done now, otherwise he will sustain a heavy loss, he may have it done by others.

10. If a man hired some animals before their owner became a mourner, he may continue to do work with them during the owner's period of mourning, for the hirer legally acquires a proprietary right in the article hired; but after the expiration of the time for which they were hired, he is forbidden to use them.

11. A mourner is allowed to accept work to be done after his period of mourning, provided he neither weighs nor measures the same, as he would do at other times.

12. If a mourner had given out work to a contractor, before he became a mourner, since the work is done privately at the house of the workman, the latter is allowed to do it.

13. A mourner is forbidden to allow the construction of his building, even through a non-Jew who works on a contract in a distant locality where no Jews reside. If he had contracted with others to do work on his farm, paying them a stipulated amount for the entire work, such as ploughing, sowing, reaping, and the like, some authorities permit such work during the owner's period of mourning, while others forbid it.

14. Domestic chores are not forbidden to a mourner. Thus, a woman in mourning is allowed to bake, cook, and attend to all her domestic needs. She is, however, forbidden to do unnecessary work. Also, a domestic servant who is in mourning is permitted to do all the housework, although she is paid for it, but not work which she is not required to do, but she does it in order to earn money. Needless to say, that like any other mourner, she is not permitted to leave the house.

15. If two persons are partners in a store and one of them becomes a mourner, the shop must be closed so that the other partner shall not do any business publicly. He is, however, allowed to transact business privately in his own house, even such matters in which both partners are interested. This is, however, forbidden where the mourner is an eminent person, and the business bears his name. In the event a great loss would be sustained if the partner of the mourner will not open the store, a qualified Rabbi should be consulted as to whether it may be opened after three days.

Chapter 209

The Prohibition to Bathe, Anoint, Wear Shoes and Cohabit

1. The mourner is forbidden to wash his entire body, even in cold water; but he may wash his face, hands, and feet with cold water, but not with warm water. Bathing or washing the head with warm water is forbidden during the entire thirty days, and if done for pleasure, it is forbidden to bathe the entire body even in cold water. A woman who must bathe before the ritual immersion, is allowed to bathe in warm water after the seven days of mourning. (See chapter 159, section 5, above).

2. If a woman who has given birth to a child, becomes a mourner, then if it is necessary for her to bathe, she may do so even during the seven days of mourning, but she must not bathe on the first day, unless it is abso-

lutely necessary. A person of delicate constitution who would greatly suffer and his health would be effected by abstaining from bathing, is permitted to bathe. Also one who suffers disturbing head pains, is allowed to wash his head even with warm water.

3. A mourner is forbidden to anoint himself in the slightest degree for the sake of pleasure. However, for hygienic purposes and especially for medicinal purposes, as one who has scabs on the head, anointing is permissible.

4. One who starts a period of mourning immediately after concluding another period of mourning, is allowed to bathe in cold water.

5. The prohibition against wearing shoes applies only to shoes made of leather; but shoes of cloth, rubber, hair, or wood are permissible, for the term "shoes" refers only to shoes made of leather. Wooden shoes covered with leather also are forbidden. Although a mourner is forbidden to wear shoes, he should, nevertheless, say the benediction: *"Who hath supplied my every want"* in the morning service.

6. A woman within thirty days of confinement, and a person who has a swelling on his foot are allowed to wear leather shoes during the seven days of mourning, because the cold will harm them.

7. A mourner who walks on the road, is allowed to wear shoes. He should, however, put a little earth in them. This would be in every case when a mourner must put on shoes.

8. Sexual intercourse, as well as embracing and kissing, are forbidden. Other acts of intimacy, such as filling a cup, make the bed, and the like, are permissible whether the husband or the wife observe the rites of mourning.

Chapter 210

The Study of The Torah and Exchange of Greetings by Mourners

1. A mourner is forbidden to study the Torah, for it is written (Psalms 19:9): *"The precepts of the Lord are right, rejoicing the heart,"* and a mourner is not allowed to rejoice. He is not allowed to study the Scripture, the *Mishnah*, and the *Talmud*, either the *hallakot* (laws) or *haggadot* (legends). But he is permitted to read the Book of Job, Lamentations, and the mournful parts of Jeremiah; and in the Talmud, he may study the chapter *Veelu megalḥin* (Moed katan 3), dealing with the laws of the excommunicated and the mourner, also the treatise *Semaḥot*. And in the Code, he may study the laws concerning mourning. However, even the subjects he is allowed to study, he is not permitted to peruse them analytically.

2. A teacher who is in mourning is allowed to teach his pupils all that is necessary after three days of mourning, so that their studies would not be interrupted, because the study of young children whose mouths are not con-

taminated by sin, is more precious than the study of adults. Likewise, a mourner's young children should not be interrupted from their studies, because they are not obliged to observe mourning.

3. Even if the mourner is the only *Kohen* in the synagogue, he may not be called up to the reading of the Torah during the seven days of mourning.

4. During the seven days of mourning, the mourner should not recite, *Pittum haketoret* (the compound of incense), nor *maamadot,* nor *Yehi ratzon* (may it be Thy will) contained in *Ezehu mekamon* (which is their place); and when reciting the *havdalah,* he should omit the preceding verses of joy, and begin with the benedictions.

5. Within the seven days of mourning, a mourner should not officiate as *ḥazan* at the synagogue, unless there is no one else capable of acting as such. If, however, he mourns the loss of a parent, the custom prevails to permit him to act as *ḥazan,* even if there is another person who is capable to act as *ḥazan.* It is customary for a mourner not to officiate as *ḥazan* on Sabbaths and festivals during the entire year, unless there is no one else to officiate. If he was accustomed to officiate before he became a mourner, he is allowed to continue to do so, in any event. (See chapter 128, section 8, above).

6. What is the rule concerning exchange of greetings? During the first three days, the mourner must neither greet anyone, nor respond to the greetings of others, but he should inform them that he is a mourner. After the third day until the seventh day, he must not greet others, but he may respond to the greetings of others. From the seventh until the thirtieth day, he may greet others, since they have peace of mind, but others should not greet him, because he lacks peace of mind. If, however, they do greet him, he should respond to their greetings. After the thirty days, he may exchange greetings like any other person.

7. Since a mourner is forbidden to greet anybody, he is certainly not allowed to laugh or rejoice. Therefore, during the seven days of mourning, he must not take a child in his arms, in order that he may not be led to laughter. He is likewise forbidden to hold much conversation with people, unless it is to show his respect to a number of people, as when many come to console him, he may say when they leave: "Go to your homes in peace."

8. It is permissible to greet mourners on the Sabbath, where it is customary to do so. The mourner may also greet anybody on the Sabbath, since it is done publicly.

9. It is permissible to say the benediction *Sheheḥeyanu,* even during the seven days of mourning, when the occasion requires it, for instance, on *Ḥanukkah,* or on partaking of a new fruit, and the like.

CHAPTER 211

Other Things a Mourner May Not Do

1. During the seven days of mourning, one is forbidden to sit on a bench or upon pillows and cushions. He must sit only on the ground. An invalid or an old man, to whom sitting on the ground is painful, may place a small pillow underneath. The mourner is not necessarily compelled to sit; he may walk about and stand, but he must be seated in the presence of consolers. He is also forbidden to sleep in a bed or on a bench; he must sleep on the ground; but he may put on the ground, pillows and cushions, just as he generally does in his bed. Other authorities permit to sleep in a bed; and such is the prevailing custom, because men have frail constitutions, and they are considered as though they were sick in this regard.

2. On the first day, the mourner is not allowed to put on the *tefillin,* and it makes no difference whether the death and the burial both occurred on that day, or the burial only. If the burial takes place at night, he is forbidden to put on the *tefillin* the following day. He should put them on the day after, at any time after sunrise. The day on which one receives *timely* news, is equivalent to the day on which the death and burial take place. If death occurs on a festival, or *timely* news is received on a festival, he may put on the *tefillin* on the first day after the festival.

3. It is not an accepted custom in our regions for mourners to wrap their heads. Nevertheless, a token of wrapping is observed, like pulling down the cap, close to the eyes during the first seven days of mourning, except on the Sabbath, because this is a public act of mourning.

4. During the first seven days, a mourner is not allowed to wear a freshly washed garment, even a shirt, and even if it is in honor of the Sabbath. He is even forbidden to use freshly washed sheets, bedspreads, or towels. In honor of the Sabbath, however, he may cover the tables with tablecloths that were washed before the period of mourning began.

5. During the first seven days, a mourner is not allowed to wash his own garments, even with the intention of putting them on after the seven days, because it constitutes labor. However, if some other people have his garments, they may wash them, like any other work which they had contracted to do for him.

6. One who observes a period of mourning immediately following another, is permitted to wash his garments with water only (not with soap or the like), and to wear them.

7. After the first seven days until the thirtieth day, according to law, a mourner is forbidden to wear a freshly washed garment, only if it is ironed,

white and new. But it is the custom not to permit the wearing of freshly washed garments even if they are not ironed, unless another person had first worn them for a short time. If, however, they were merely washed with water, it is not necessary that another person should wear them first.

8. If he does not change his garments for pleasure, but out of necessity, as when the clothes which he wears are soiled, or if it is necessary because of a rash, he is permitted to make the change even during the first seven days and even on a weekday, if the fresh clothes have already been worn by someone else.

9. After the seven days, a mourner is permitted to wash and iron a garment to be worn after the thirty days, or even to be worn within the thirty days, after someone else will wear it.

10. During the thirty days of mourning, one is forbidden to wear his Sabbath clothes even on the Sabbath, and certainly one is forbidden to put on new clothes. One who mourns for a parent is forbidden, according to custom, to put on new garments during the entire year. If, however, he is in need of them, he should let another person wear them first for two or three days, and then put them on.

11. A woman after her confinement, who wishes to go to the synagogue on a Sabbath during the thirty days of mourning, or even during the first seven days, since women usually consider that Sabbath like a festival and put on their best clothes and wear jewels, she is permitted to put on her Sabbath clothes, but not her holiday garments, lest her mind be diverted and she forget that she is in mourning. It is not necessary for her to change her seat at the synagogue.

12. A mourner is not allowed to cut his hair during the thirty days of mourning, whether it is the hair of the head, the beard, or any other part of the body. If he mourns for the loss of a parent, he is not permitted to cut his hair until he is reproved by his friends. The time presumed to warrant a reproof is a subject of controversy between authorities. The custom in our regions is that a mourner does not cut the hair during the entire year, unless his hair is a burden to him, or if he mingles with people of different nationalities, who would look upon him with scorn. No actual reproof is necessary, but if his hair grew to an extent which alters his appearance, and he looks different from other people so as to arouse comment, in such circumstances he is allowed to cut his hair, but only after the thirty days of mourning.

13. Just as a mourner is forbidden to cut his hair within the first thirty days, so is he forbidden to pare his nails with an instrument. He is, however, allowed to do so with his hands or teeth even during the first seven days of mourning. Even a *mohel* is not allowed to trim his nails as is required for the laceration of the foreskin, unless there is no other *mohel* available to perform the circumcision, then he is permitted to do so even during the first seven days of mourning. A woman who needs to take the ritual bath of immersion

after the seven days and within the thirty days, should engage a non-Jewess to pare her nails. But if a non-Jewess is unavailable, a Jewess may do it.

14. Combing the hair is permissible even during the first seven days of mourning.

15. It is customary for a mourner to change his seat in the synagogue during the first thirty days of mourning. If he mourns for the loss of a parent, he changes his seat during the entire year. The new seat should be at least four cubits away from his accustomed seat and farther away from the Holy Ark

CHAPTER 212

Things Forbidden as "Rejoicing" After the Seven Days

1. A mourner is forbidden to join in the feast of a circumcision, of the redemption of a firstborn, or on the occasion of concluding the study of a *Talmudic* tractate, and especially of a wedding feast, during the first thirty days of mourning for any kinsman, and for one's father or mother, during the first twelve months (even in a leap-year, twelve months are sufficient). The mourner may, however, participate in a sacramental feast celebrated at his house. But he must abstain from joining in a wedding feast, even if it is held at his house, unless one of the couple is an orphan whom he has given in marriage, and his keeping aloof from the feast might cause the match to break off, he is then permitted to eat even if the feast is held in another house. He is also allowed to put on the Sabbath garments if it is after the thirty days of mourning for his father or his mother, or even within the thirty days, if he mourns for other relatives.

2. He is not permitted to invite others or to accept invitations from others. He must neither send gifts to others, nor accept gifts from others during the thirty days of mourning for his next of kin, or during the twelve months of mourning for his father or mother. (As concerns the Sabbath, see chapter 210, section 8, above).

3. After the thirty days of mourning, even for the loss of his father or his mother, the mourner who officiates either as *sandek* or as *mohel*, is allowed to wear his Sabbath clothes until after the circumcision, and he may even join in the feast.

4. During the first thirty days of mourning for one's next of kin, or during the twelve months for one's father or mother, the mourner may not enter a house where a wedding feast is being celebrated, even if it is merely for the purpose of hearing the benedictions recited on that occasion. During the ceremony of a marriage performed in the court of the synagogue, the mourner is allowed to stay there and to listen to the benedictions, if it is after the first thirty days of mourning even when observed for the loss of his father or his mother. He is even permitted to pronounce the benedictions himself, and to act as best man, escorting the bridegroom under the nuptial canopy, and he may wear his Sabbath garments, provided it is after the thirty days of mourning. But he is not allowed to enter the house to partake of the feast. Some authorities permit even that.

5. A mourner is permitted to attend a wedding feast if he serves as a waiter, and he may eat in his own house, what is sent him from the feast.

CHAPTER 213

The Marriage of a Mourner and of a Groom or a Bride who Becomes a Mourner

1. A mourner, whether man or woman, is not allowed to marry during the thirty days of mourning. Thereafter, however, it is permissible even when one mourns the loss of a parent. It is permissible to arrange a betrothal, not accompanied by a feast, even during the first seven days of mourning.

2. If one's wife died, one is not permitted to remarry until three festivals have passed, because by rejoicing on three festivals, he will have forgotten the first love when he marries the second, for a man should not drink out of one cup and have his mind on another cup. *Rosh Hashanah* and *Yom Kippur* are not considered as festivals in this respect, nor is *Shemini Atzeret* considered a separate festival in this respect. If, however, the widower has not yet fulfilled the precept (Genesis 1:28): "*Be fruitful, and multiply,*" or if he has young children, or if he has no one to look after him, he need not wait for the passage of three festivals. But at any rate, it is proper to wait until after the thirty days of mourning. A woman whose husband died, must wait ninety days before marriage.

3. If, after everything had been prepared for the wedding, a kinsman either of the bridegrrom or of the bride dies, be it even the father of the bridegroom or the mother of the bride, since it is possible nowadays to have things prepared by others, the marriage must be postponed until after the seven days of mourning.

4. Even if death occurs after the nuptial ceremony, the bridegroom is not allowed to cohabit until after the seven days of mourning. And since he is not allowed to cohabit, he must not be left alone with his bride without a chaperone. After the seven days of mourning, he may have the mandatory cohabitation, and then celebrate the wedding week.

5. If the death of a relative, either of the bridegroom or of the bride, occurs after the newlyweds have already had intercourse, they are already subject to the laws governing the wedding week which is considered to them as a festival, during which time the rites of mourning are not to be observed. They may put on ironed clothes and cut their hair, and are forbidden to do only things that are done privately. After the wedding week, the seven days of mourning begin, and even the first thirty days are to be commenced with the seven days of mourning. (Although the days of a festival are included in

the first thirty days of mourning, as stated in chapter 219, section 7, below, yet the wedding week is not to be included, since hair cutting is permissible during that week).

CHAPTER 214

When a Mourner May Leave His House

1. A mourner must not leave his house during the first seven days of mourning, unless a death occurs in his family, or if a stranger dies and there are no people to provide for his burial, he is then permitted to leave his house even on the first day of mourning. Also, if he is summoned by the governor, or if he must go to attend to an important matter, as otherwise he will sustain a heavy loss, he is permitted to leave the house, but he should put some earth in his shoes.

2. He is forbidden to leave his house even to go to the synagogue to pray during the first seven days of mourning, except on the Sabbath. But if it is impossible for him to gather ten male adults in his house to make up a *minyan*, and he would be compelled to pray privately, while there is a *minyan* in his neighborhood, he may go there to pray rather than be prevented from participating in public worship.

3. If a mourner has a son to be circumcised, he may go to the synagogue where the circumcision takes place, even during the first three days of mourning. If a mourner is *sandek* or *mohel*, he may not on that account leave his house during the first three days of mourning; but after the three days, he should first pray at home, and when the infant is brought to the synagogue, he is allowed to go there to attend to the circumcision. If, however, there is no other *mohel* in town, he may leave his house to attend to the circumcision even on the first day of mourning.

CHAPTER 215

Excessive Grief is Forbidden

1. It is forbidden to grieve excessively over the dead, as it is written (Jeremiah 22:10): "*Weep ye not for the dead, neither bemoan him,*" and our Sages, of blessed memory, said (Moed Katan 27b): "Is it possible to say thus? But, '*Weep ye not for the dead,*' means excessively, and '*Neither bemoan him,*' means inordinately. How is one to mourn Three days should be allowed for weeping, seven days for mourning, and thirty days for abstaining from wearing ironed clothes and from cutting the hair. Henceforth, the Holy One, blessed be He, says: 'You are not permitted to be more compassionate than I am.'" Our Sages, of blessed memory, said again (loco citato): "He who mourns for the dead to excess, will have cause to mourn for another death." This applies only to an ordinary person, but when a scholar passes away, his death is mourned in proportion to his wisdom. In no case, however, should the mourning period be more than thirty days, for none is greater than Moses our teacher, peace to him, of whom it is written (Deuteronomy 34:8): "And they wept for Moses thirty days."

2. Our Rabbis, of blessed memory, said: "If one of a family dies, the entire family has cause to worry." To what can this be compared? To a vault made of stones, when one stone shakes, all of them are insecure. For the judgment hovers over all of them, until it is gradually related. During the first seven days, the sword is drawn, up to thirty days it is gradually withdrawn. But it is not restored to its sheath until after twelve months. Therefore, the first three days, the mourner should consider as if the sword rests between his shoulders; from the third day to the seventh, as if it was standing upright in a corner facing him; from the seventh day to the thirtieth, as if it was passing before him in the street; and thereafter during the entire year, the judgment is still hanging over this family. If a son is born in that family, the entire family is saved by it; but only a male, for when a male comes into this world, peace comes into the world. If one of a group has passed away, judgment is likewise hanging over the entire group, and all members have cause to worry.

3. He who does not mourn in accordance with the regulations laid down by our Sages, is considered a heartless person. But it is his duty to awake from his sleep, and examine his deeds with fear and anxiety, and do penance, perchance he may escape the sword of the Angel of Death. For it is written (Jeremiah 5:3): *"Thou hast stricken them, but they were not affected;"* which indicates that it is necessary to awake, examine, and repent.

Chapter 216

Parts of the Seventh and Thirtieth Mourning Days

1. On the seventh day, after the comforters had departed from the mourner, he is permitted to do all the things that were forbidden him during the seven days. For the Rabbis say: *A part of a day is considered as the entire day,* except as regards cohabitation which is forbidden the entire day (even in a dark room). In those regions where the consolers are not wont to visit the mourner on the seventh day of mourning, the mourner should wait until the time that they are wont to come on the other days, that is, after going out from the synagogue in the morning. If the seventh day of mourning occurs on the Sabbath, he may study the Torah after going out from the synagogue.

2. As to the thirtieth day, we likewise reckon a part of the day as the entire day, and since no comforters come then, the mourner is absolved from the restrictions pertaining to the thirty days of mourning immediately after sunrise. If the thirtieth day occurs on the Sabbath, the mourner is permitted to bathe in warm water on Friday in honor of the Sabbath. He may

put on the Sabbath garments, and resume his regular seat in the synagogue; but he may not cut his hair.

3. The rule that "part of the day is like an entire day," does not apply to the twelve months of mourning for one's father or mother. On the contrary, it is customary to add the *Yahrzeit* (anniversary of death) day to the twelve months of mourning, even if it occurs on the Sabbath. During a leap year (which consists of thirteen months) mourning need not be observed for the loss of a parent, longer than twelve months, and inasmuch as the twelve-months have expired before the *Yahrzeit* day, the mourner is not required to resume mourning on the *Yahrzeit* day.

CHAPTER 217

If One Neglected to Observe Mourning

1. If one has neglected to observe mourning during the first seven days, whether it has been done inadvertently or intentionally, he may make amends for this neglect during the first thirty days. However, as regards the rending of garments, if the mourner has neglected to do so at the distressing moment, he may do it only during the first seven days of mourning. But for one's father or mother, one must rend his garments at any time.

2. A minor need not observe the rites of mourning, even if he reaches his majority during the first seven days of mourning. For since he is exempt from observing it when the death occurs, the law of mourning no longer applies to him. However, he must observe the twelve-month period of mourning for his father or his mother, to show his respect for them.

3. If an invalid lost a relative for whom he is bound to observe the rites of mourning, and he becomes aware of it and recovers during the first seven days of mourning, he must observe mourning during the rest of those days. He must also observe mourning during the rest of the thirty days, but he need not make up for the days of his illness, since he had observed some mourning also during his illness, it is like the Sabbath-day which is included in the seven days of mourning, but it does not suspend it. Also, a woman in confinement is not required to make up for the days that have passed during her confinement, but she merely observes mourning during the rest of the days.

CHAPTER 218

Testimony Relating to Mourning

1. One is obliged to observe the rites of mourning on the information of one witness, or by the hearsay of one witness, or by the disinterested statement of a non-Jew.

2. If one receives a letter notifying of the death of a relative, but it is not clear whether it is still within the first thirty days or thereafter, then if the writer of the letter is an unlearned man, it must be assumed that the relative was alive shortly before the letter was written, and he is obliged to observe mourning. If the writer is a man versed in the Torah, it may be assumed that it is after the thirty days, for if there was any possibility of the letter reaching its destination within the thirty days, he would not have written to him regarding the death of a relative without specifying the date.

If, however, he was informed of the death of father or mother, of whose death it is customary to notify the son immediately, he must observe mourning

CHAPTER 219

Mourning on a Sabbath or a Festival

1. On the Sabbath that occurs during the first seven days of mourning, all the rules regulating the mourner's private life must be observed, such as sexual intercourse and bathing. No rites of mourning, however, are to be observed in public. Therefore, before the recital of *Mizmor shir leyom hashabbat* (A Psalm, a Hymn for the Sabbath), the mourner may put on his shoes, sit on a regular chair, and put on another garment in place of the one bearing the mark of mourning (as provided for in chapter 195, section 6, above). However, he is not allowed to study the Torah, because this is a private matter, but he is permitted to read the weekly portion of the Torah twice, and the Targum once; for since it is the duty of every Jew to read the current portion of the Torah, it is akin to the reading of the *Shema*, or the like, contained in the prayers of the day.

2. If on the Sabbath, a mourner is called up to the reading of the Torah, he must go up, for his refusal would be a public display of mourning. Rabbenu Tam used to be called up to the reading of the third section every Sabbath, and when he happened to be in mourning and the Reader failed to call him, he went up by himself, and he said that since he had been accustomed to go up to the reading of the Torah every Sabbath, those present would know that he had not been called this time because he was in mourning, and it would then constitute a public observance of mourning on the Sabbath. A *Kohen* who is in mourning should be called up to the Torah if there is no other *Kohen*. But it is best that he should leave the synagogue before the Scroll is taken out of the Holy Ark. If a mourner has a son to be circumcised on the Sabbath, and it is the prevailing custom that the father of the infant must be called up to the Torah, he should be called up, otherwise, it would constitute a public observance of mourning. But it is best to absent himself from the synagogue during the reading of the Torah. (As for a woman who must go to the synagogue during mourning, see chapter 211, section 11, above).

3. If the official reader of the Torah becomes a mourner, he should not go to the synagogue on the Sabbath during the first seven days of mourning, as his presence there would raise a question of law as to whether he should read or not.

4. The Sabbath day is included in the seven days of mourning. Even if he received *timely* news of the death of a relative on the Sabbath when he had not yet begun mourning, yet this Sabbath is counted as one of the seven days, and he must rend his garments at the conclusion of the Sabbath.

5. If a burial takes place, or *timely* news is received on the festival itself or during *Ḥol Hammoed*, no rites of mourning are to be observed until after the conclusion of the festival. This rule applies only to the observance

of mourning in public; but all the rules regulating the mourner's private life must be observed; one must not change his garments on the festival, as that would constitute a public observance of mourning. (Although any other mourner is bound to change his garments even on a festival, nevertheless, in this case, since his mourning has not yet begun, he should not change his garments). One who puts on *tefillin* during *Ḥol Hammoed,* should put them on the first day after burial.

6. At the conclusion of the festival, the mourner begins to count six days of mourning, because the last day of the festival is counted as one of the seven days. Even the second day of *Rosh Hashannah* is included in the seven days of mourning.

7. Although the period of mourning does not begin on the festival itself or during *Ḥol Hammoed,* nor do the laws pertaining to the first thirty days of mourning apply to them, and it is permissible to wear ironed clothes, these days are, nevertheless, included in the total of thirty days of mourning, since the cutting of the hair is then forbidden because of the festival. One should, therefore, count the thirty days from the day on which the burial took place. Although *Shemini Atzeret* (Eighth Day of Solemn Assembly) is a festival by itself, still it does not cancel the period of mourning, since mourning has not yet begun, and it counts as but one day in the total of thirty days.

8. If a bridegroom marries before a festival and celebrates the wedding week during the festival, during which time, one of his next of kin dies he cannot include the wedding week in the total of the first thirty days of mourning.

9. Although no mourning is observed during a festival, still it is proper to console a mourner (this does not constitute mourning, since the mourner himself does nothing). After the festival, at the end of seven days from the burial, although the seven days of mourning have not yet expired, he may employ others to do his work in their homes, and his working people may do his work privately in his home. After the festival, it is not necessary to console him as many days as they comforted him during the festival, but they should, nevertheless, come to see him during those days.

CHAPTER 220

The Mourning Period is Voided by a Festival

1. A festival suspends the seven-day and the thirty-day periods of mourning. Thus, if the burial takes place before a festival, and the mourner observes some rules of mourning, his mourning ceases as soon as the festival begins. Even if the burial takes place toward the close of the day, and the

mourner has removed his shoes only for a short time before the festival begins, his mourning is suspended and it is considered as though he had observed the entire seven days of mourning. The first day of the festival is counted as the eighth day of mourning, from which time he completes the thirty-day period of mourning. Even if the day before the festival is a Sabbath, and one has received *timely* news towards the evening, although on the Sabbath, only the rules regulating the mourner's private life are observed, the festival cancels the seven days of mourning.

2. If the mourner either inadvertently or intentionally had neglected to observe some rites of mourning before the festival, or if he had been unable to observe them because the burial took place at the approach of night, the festival in this case does not cancel it, and he is subject to the same law as applies to one who buries his dead on a festival.

3. If one of the days of mourning, except the seventh, occurs on the day before a festival, according to the opinion of some authorities, the mourner is allowed to wash his garments, but he should not put them on before night, since the festival will annul the seven-day mourning period. It is best not to wash them until the afternoon, so as to make it evident that he washes them on account of the festival. But he is not allowed to bathe until shortly before nightfall. Some authorities permit bathing after the *Minḥah* service towards nightfall; where the custom so prevails, it may be followed. However, all authorities agree that he is not allowed to cut his hair.

4. If the dead was buried seven days before the festival, since the mourner had already observed the seven-day mourning period before the festival, the festival voids the thirty-day mourning period. Even if the seventh day of mourning occurs on the day before the festival, since we hold that a part of the day is considered as an entire day, the seven-day mourning period had expired as soon as the worshipers had left the synagogue in the morning, and the rest of the day is counted as belonging to the thirty-day mourning period, which is canceled by the intervention of the festival. The mourner may wash his garments, bathe himself, and cut his hair on the day before the festival towards nightfall, since he does it in honor of the festival. If the seventh day occurs on the day before Passover, the mourner may bathe himself immediately after midday, for as that was the time when the paschal lamb was offered, it is regarded as somewhat of a festival, but he should cut the hair in the forenoon (as in the afternoon, another person is not allowed to cut his hair for him).

5. If the seventh day of mourning occurs on Friday, and that Sabbath is the eve of a holiday, the mourner is allowed to wash his garments, bathe, and cut his hair on Friday.

6. If a mourner has neglected to cut his hair on the day before the Sabbath or before a festival, he is not permitted to cut it during *Ḥol Hammoed*, since he was able to cut it before that time, but he is allowed to cut it after the festival. If, however, the seventh day of mourning has occurred on a Sabbath which is the eve of a festival, since he was prevented from cutting his hair, not because of his mourning, but because of the Sabbath, he is considered like one who was prevented by an accident, and he is, therefore, allowed to cut his hair during *Ḥol Hammoed*.

7. A festival suspends the thirty-day mourning period as regards hair-cutting, only if the mourning is observed for any other relative, but not for one's father or mother, when the mourner is not allowed to cut his hair until he is reproved by his friends.

8. If one had observed the rites of mourning for an hour, or even less than an hour before the Passover, he is considered as having observed mourning for seven days, which together with the eight days of Passover makes a total of fifteen days, and he needs only fifteen more days to complete the thirty-day period. If he had observed mourning, one hour before *Shavuot*, that hour is reckoned as though he had observed mourning seven full days, and the first day of *Shavuot* is also reckoned as seven days (since for the omission of its sacrifices amends can be made during all the following seven days), while the second day of *Shavuot* is the fifteenth day, and only fifteen more days are needed to complete the thirty-day period. If one had observed one hour's mourning before *Sukkot*, it is counted as seven full days, which together with the seven days of *Sukkot*, make a total of fourteen days; the festival of *Shemini Atzeret* (the Eighth Day of Solemn Assembly) also counts as seven days (for it is a festival by itself, and amends can be made for its sacrifices), making it a total of twenty one days; *Simeḥat Torah* counts for one day, so we have twenty two days, and only eight more days are needed to complete the thirty-day period.

9. *Rosh Hashanah* and *Yom Kippur* are also considered festivals with regard to voiding the seven-day and the thirty-day periods. Thus, if a mourner has observed the rites of mourning for one hour before *Rosh Hashanah*, it voids the seven-day period, and *Yom Kippur* voids the thirty-day period. If he has observed one hour of mourning before *Yom Kippur*, *Yom Kippur* voids the seven-day period, while *Sukkot* voids the thirty-day period.

10. Although a festival voids the seven-day mourning period, the candle, generally lit and kept in the place where the death occurred in honor of the deceased, should also be lit on a festival. It is best, however, to light the candle at the synagogue.

CHAPTER 221

Fasting on The Day of Yahrzeit

1. It is a meritorious practice to fast on the anniversary of the death of one's father or mother, as an incentive to repentance, and to self-introspection. By doing this, one obtains Divine Grace for one's father and mother in heaven. In the *Shemoneh esreh* of the *Minḥah* service, he must include *Anenu* (answer us), the same as on any private fast day. If a person fasted on one *Yahrzeit*, it is presumed that it was his intention to fast on that day all his lifetime, and it is like a vow to fast, which is binding upon him by law. If he becomes ill, or if he is otherwise unable to fast, he must have his vow annulled. However, if he distinctly declared that his fasting is not a vow, annulment is unnecessary. It is customary to light a *Yahrzeit* candle.

2. The anniversary is always to be observed on the day the death occurred, even in the first year. Even if the death occurred at the close of the day, after the *Maariv* service had been said, but it is still day, then that day is fixed as the *Yahrzeit*. However, if there was an interval of a few days between the death and the burial, then the first year the *Yahrzeit* is observed on the day of the burial, but in subsequent years on the day of death.

3. If a death occurs during a leap year, either in the first or the second month of *Adar*, then in a regular year, the fast must be observed on the like date in the month of *Adar* and in a leap year it should be observed in the month when death occurred, whether in the first or in the second *Adar*. If death occurs in the month of *Adar* in an ordinary year, then in a leap year, he should fast on that particular date in the first *Adar*, and on the same date in the second *Adar*, he should also say *kaddish*, but he may not bar others from saying *kaddish*.

4. The month of *Ḥeshvan* is sometimes full, that is, it consists of thirty days, and then the New Moon of *Kislev*, which follows, is two days, the first day of which is the thirtieth of *Ḥeshvan*, and the second day is the first of *Kislev* (and this is true of every New Moon which consists of two days, that the first day belongs to the preceding month and is the thirtieth day thereof). At times the month of *Ḥeshvan* is defective, that is, it consists only of twenty nine days, and the New Moon of *Kislev* that follows it, is only one day. Also, the month of *Kislev* is at times full, and the New Moon of *Tebet* which follows, is two days, and at times it is defective and the New Moon of *Tebet* is only one day. If the death occurred on the New Moon of *Kislev*, when it was but one day, then in the year when the New Moon of *Kislev* consists of two days, the *Yahrzeit* should be observed on the second day of the New Moon which is the first day of *Kislev*. However, if the death occurred on the first day of the New Moon of *Kislev*, when it was two days, then in the year when the New Moon of *Kislev* is but one day, it is doubtful whether the *Yahrzeit* should be observed on the twenty-ninth of *Ḥeshvan*, since the death occurred on the last day of *Ḥeshvan*, or since as regards the law of vows, we are guided by colloquial language, the *Yahrzeit* should be observed on the New Moon of *Kislev*, as the first of the two days of the New Moon is generally so called. The following procedure is proper: If, in the first year after the occurrence of death, the New Moon of *Kislev* is but one day, he should observe the *Yahrzeit* on the twenty-ninth of *Ḥeshvan*, and so whenever the month of *Ḥeshvan* is defective. Nevertheless, if on the morrow of the New Moon, there is no other mourner present, he should also recite *kaddish* and officiate at the services on that day, but he may not bar others from saying *kaddish*. If, however, in the year following the death, the New Moon of *Kislev* also consists of two days, then he establishes the *Yahrzeit* to be observed on the New Moon of *Kislev*, and he should so continue to observe it on that day all his lifetime, even when the New Moon will consist of but one day. This applies also to the month of *Tebet*.

5. Since the New Moon of *Tevet* is at times one day, then that day is the sixth day of *Ḥanukkah,* the second day of *Tevet,* the seventh day of *Ḥanukkah,* and the third day of *Tevet,* the eighth day of *Ḥanukkah.* But when the New Moon of *Tevet* consists of two days, and the month begins with the second day, then the first of *Tevet* is the seventh day of *Ḥanukkah,* and the second of *Tevet* is the eighth day of *Ḥanukkah.* Therefore, one who observes *Yahrzeit* on one of these days, should not err in counting the days of *Ḥanukkah* (to ascertain the day of the *Yahrzeit*), but be guided by the days of the month.

6. On a day when the *taḥanun* (petition for Grace) is not recited, no fasting should be observed on the *Yahrzeit.* On the following occasions, one does not fast on the *Yahrzeit:* The father, the *sandek,* and the *mohel* on the day of circumcision; the father and the *Kohen* on the days of a *pideyon habben* (redemption of the firstborn), and a bridegroom during the wedding week. But it is not permissible to partake of the meal served at a *siyum* (completion of a *Talmudic* treatise) on the day of *Yahrzeit.* On the days when no fasting is observed, one should devote his time to the study of the Torah and to the practice of precepts and good deeds, thereby obtaining heavenly grace for the souls of one's father and mother.

7. On the evening when *Yahrzeit* is observed, one should not partake of a wedding meal, because there is music and merriment in honor of the groom and bride. One may, however, partake of a feast served at a circumcision, *pideyon habben,* or at a *siyum.*

8. If one is not certain of the date of his parent's death, he should select the approximate date, and observe that day as *Yahrzeit;* but he may not encroach upon the rights of others with regard to reciting the *kaddish.*

"He will swallow up death forever; and the Lord God will wipe away tears from all faces," (Isaiah 25:8).

Blessed be He "Who giveth power to the faint; and to him that hath no might He increaseth strength," (Isaiah 40:29).

NOTES

Volume I

[1] Satan (Tempter, or Evil Impulse), is personified in later Biblical writings, and in the Talmudic literature. (See note 58, below.)

[2] Midnight service, known as *ḥatzot* (*half*, shortened for *half of the night*), when in the silence of midnight, the pious Jew would sit on a low stool after the fashion of one who observes the rites of mourning, and read *tikkun ḥatzot* (special prayer arrangement for *ḥatzot*), shedding tears for the destruction of the Temple at Jerusalem, the dispersion of Israel among the nations, and the *galut* (exile), so to speak, of the Divine Presence.

[3] The term *Mishnah*, generally refers to the Mishnah *par excellence*, compiled and edited by Rabbi Judah ha-Nasi (the Prince) at the beginning of the third century C.E. (See also note 40, below.)

[4] Form of prayers, containing selections from the Scripture and the Talmud, arranged for each day of the week of Creation, generally recited by pious Jews after the morning prayers, as contained in many prayer books under the title *Maamadot.*

[5] The exact citation of this quotation could not be ascertained by the author.

[6] *Zohar* (Splendor), a prominent cabbalistic work, first published by Moses de Leon (born 1250; died 1305 C.E.), attributed to the authorship of the Tanna Simeon ben Yoḥai of the second century C.E., who had kept himself concealed in a cave with his son Eleazar for fourteen years, to escape the cruel persecution of the Roman Emperor Hadrian.

[7] *Bet Yoseph* (House of Joseph), on the *Arbaa Turim*, by Joseph Caro, upon which his famous Code, the *Shulḥan Aruḥ*, was based. (See notes 35 and 130, below.)

[8] See Chapter 9, below.

[9] It has been ordained by our Sages of old that a prayer in the form of a benediction should be pronounced on the occasion of performing a religious duty. In this benediction we bless, or rather praise, the Almighty for having made us a holy people by ordering us to fulfill His commandments. The Jew thus not only expresses his willingness to obey God, but he even expresses his gratitude to his God for having been privileged to receive His commandments.

[10] See note 52, below.

[11] See Chapter 10, below.

[12] See Chapters 16 and 17, below.

[13] See Chapter 18, below.

[14] Written by Judah ben Samuel he-Ḥasid (the pious) of Regensburg, Germany; died February 22, 1217.

[15] Originally the morning benedictions had been pronounced progressively upon awakening in the morning, each benediction had been uttered upon the happening of an event and upon performing a certain act (Beraḥot 60b). Immediately upon awakening, one said, *Elohai, neshamah* (my God, the soul), etc.; upon hearing the cock crow, one said, *Asher natan laseḥvi binah* (who gave understanding to the cock); upon dressing oneself, one said, *Malbish arumim* (who clothes the naked); upon putting one's hands upon the eyes, one said, *Pokeaḥ ivrim* (who opens the eyes of the blind); upon sitting down, one said, *Mattir asurim* (who sets the captives free), and so on. Now, this benediction has no reference to the releasing of men from being incarcerated, as is generally understood by many. It means that the Almighty loosens the joints of our bodies to give us free movement and coördination of muscles.

However, due to the ignorance of the masses, who are not familiar with the above procedure, a custom was established to recite these benedictions at the synagogue, and we are fulfilling our obligation by responding *Amen* after each benediction. (See *Shulḥan Aruḥ, Oraḥ Ḥayyim* 46:1.)

[16] See note 22, below.

[17] See Chapter 176, below.

[18] Thus the number of coils adds up to thirty-nine, equalling the numerical value of the Hebrew letters spelling out the Holy Name consisting of the four letters (Tetragrammaton): YUD (ten), HE (five), VAV (six), HE (five), and the Hebrew word EḤAD (one), the numerical value of which letters total thirteen; the *tzitzit* are thus made to proclaim the unity of God: ADONAI EḤAD, *the Lord is One.*

[19] See note 22, below.

[20] See note 30, below.

[21] The *tefillah* of the head as well as that of the hand, contains four *parshiyot* (sections from the Torah): *Kaddesh li kol beḥor* (sanctify unto Me all firstborn) (Exodus 13:1-10); *Vehayah ki yeviaḥa* (and it shall come to pass, when the Lord bring thee) (Exodus 13:11-16); *Shema* (hear, O Israel) (Deuteronomy 6:4-9); and, *Vehayah im shamoa* (and it shall come to pass, if ye shall hearken) (Deuteronomy 11:13-21). According to the views of Rashi (note 125, below) and Maimonides (note 70, below), the above is the proper arrangement of the four sections, because they appear in the Torah in the same order. However, Rabbenu Tam (note 157, below) differs, and he holds

that the section *Vehayah im shamoa* should be placed in the *tefillin* before *Shema.* We generally follow the former arrangement. However, some scrupulous Jews have two sets of *tefillin,* in order to comply with both opinions: one set is known as *Rashi's tefillin,* and the other as *Rabbenu Tam's tefillin.* (See Tosafot to Menaḥot 34b, *sub verbo, Vehaḥore;* and *Shulḥan Aruḥ, Oraḥ Ḥayyim* 34.)

[22] We, as Jews, must bear in mind, that in the Jewish religion there are no amulets. The *tefillin,* the *tzitzit,* the *mezuzah,* as well as all other ceremonials, are religious symbols which convey certain truths, facts, doctrines, or events of the past. In the Holy Scriptures they are called *otot* (signs) and *edot* (testimonies). They are symbols of, and serve to testify to, the special relations of God to His people. They are outward expressions of the Jewish inner thoughts, of purity, holiness, and righteousness. They act as reminders to the Jews that they must understand and obey the Law of God.

The Jewish religion is a way of life; it controls and regulates every phase of Jewish life. Its rules of conduct apply not only to our behavior in the synagogue, but also to our everyday dealings with our fellow men, to the conduct of our private lives, the way we conduct our homes, and even in our mode of thinking.

The Jewish home must bear a distinctive character. God is to be found everywhere, not only in temples and synagogues. Our homes, too, can be made holy by our deeds and thoughts. If our homes have a Jewish atmosphere, if peace and harmony exists between the members of our family; if in our homes, God's word is heard and discussed; if sacred books are studied there, then our homes become shrines, holy places; and our tables become altars of God.

The very entrance to our homes must be marked with holiness. The Almighty commanded us to write His laws on the doorposts of our homes. We therefore procure a *mezuzah,* a small piece of parchment upon which are inscribed by hand two sections of the Law of God which are read by us in the *Shema* every morning and evening. (See Chapter 17, below.) They are also contained in the *tefillah* of the head (see preceding note). On the reverse side of the parchment, the word *Shaddai* (Almighty) is inscribed. This parchment is encased in a metal or wooden tube and affixed to the doorpost.

The inscription in the *mezuzah* begins with the words: *Shema Yisrael, Adonai Elohenu, Adonai Eḥad* (Hear, O Israel, the Lord is our God, the Lord is One). Thus the *mezuzah* fastened to the door reminds us: a) That those who occupy these premises believe that there is only One God in heaven and on earth; and b) That God is present in our homes. And since our Father in heaven is always in our midst, our homes must always be holy, godly and peaceful, and we must always abstain from doing anything evil in His sight. There must be no quarreling, nor cursing, nor hatred, nor slanderoud talk. (From *The Jew and His Duties,* by Hyman E. Goldin.)

[23] Prayer is a very important part of Jewish spiritual life, and it is the special duty of every Jew to worship God by offering prayers to Him, thereby acknowledging His sovereignty over the universe. By praying to Him, we also recognize that He is our Master in whose hands are the destinies of all men, and that nothing can be accomplished without His will. Prayers and other forms of devotion are expressions of our religious sentiments, our longing to give expression to our feeling of awe and adoration. And although we may pray for our needs at all times and in any manner we think proper, nevertheless we must follow the formulas of prayer instituted by our Sages in olden times. We must also pray in the language chosen by them for praying, which is Hebrew, and pray at the times fixed by them for offering such prayers. For, by praying in the same language, in the same formulas, and at fixed times, the Jews in Diaspora will remain one people, though they speak the language and follow the customs peculiar to the land of their adoption.

Private devotion has its proper place in the family circle, where morning and evening and mealtime are the hours set for prayer and grace. But public service has its higher object of uniting the worshipers in prayer as brothers, children of our Father in heaven. (See also note 63, below.)

[24] As in ancient times, when daily sacrifices were offered by the priests every morning and evening and additional ones on holy days, the congregation was enjoined to erect a sanctuary to bring God to the people, so has it become the duty of Israelites living together in a township or city to provide for a place of divine worship and religious instruction and to keep it sacred.

[25] King Solomon said (Proverbs 19:28): "In the multitude of people is the king's glory." Therefore it is the duty of every Israelite to make an effort to pray with the congregation. Public service not only creates a greater religious sentiment and enthusiasm, but it has, as its higher object, the uniting of many hearts in prayer to our common Father in heaven and awakening the loftier sentiments of faith and loyalty in the individual. According to the Talmud, public service may be conducted only in the presence of ten male adults, which constitutes a *minyan,* a legal quorum for the performance of any religious function.

[26] The term *Shema* applies to the three portions of the Holy Scriptures (Deuteronomy 6:4-9): *Shema yisrael* (Hear, O Israel); (Deuteronomy 9:13-21): *Vehayah im shamoa* (And it shall come to pass if ye shall hearken); and (Numbers 15:37-41): *Vayomer adonai* (And the Lord said), as is contained in all

Prayer Books. Because the first portion of the Biblical texts begins with the word *Shema*, all the three portions are designated by *Shema*.

The founders of the synagogue, *Anshe Knesset ha-Gedolah* (the Men of the Great Assembly), in obedience to the command of God (Deuteronomy 6: 4-7): "And thou shalt speak of them . . . when thou liest down, and when thou risest up," prescribed that every faithful son of Israel should recite every morning and evening such prayers and parts of Scriptures as were best fitted to express his *acknowledgement of the sovereignty of God*, and his *willingness to serve Him and fulfill all His commandments*.

They instituted our daily prayers for morning and evening which consists chiefly of: a) *Shema*, with the benedictions that precede and follow it, having reference either to sunrise or sunset, to the love of Israel for the light of the Law and the redemption of Israel by God, both in the past and in the future; b) The *Tefillah* (prayer proper), or *Shemoneh esreh* (see Chapter 18, below); and c) Readings from the Torah (see Chapter 23, below).

In the *Shema*, we, as Jews, first proclaim the basic doctrine of the Jewish religion, the Unity of God, the belief that there is One God, and only One, in heaven and on earth. Morning and evening, twice daily, we proclaim our confession of faith which is the basic principle of the Jewish creed: *Shema yisrael, adonai elohenu, adonai eḥad* (Hear, O Israel, the Lord is our God, the Lord is One). Throughout the ages, thousands of Jewish martyrs, suffering torture and death for the sake of their God and His Law, breathed their last breath with this confession of faith on their lips.

Then we declare our highest duty towards God, which is to love God as our Father, "With all thy heart, with all thy soul, and with all thy might." Belief in God alone is not enough, but it is necessary to love God, and this love must be translated into deed and into obedience; we must manifest our gratitude and love to God by obeying His will and by avoiding sin, both in action and in thought. The love of God—and consequently, obedience to God—is the basis of Jewish life: "And these words which I command thee this day shall be upon thine heart; and thou shalt teach them diligently to your children." (From *The Jew and His Duties*, by Hyman E. Goldin.)

[27] As has been stated in the preceding note, the Men of the Great Assembly formulated prayers to be offered by every Israelite, consisting of the *Shema* and the *Tefillah* (prayer proper), or *Shemoneh esreh* (eighteen; silent prayer).

This prayer is very ancient, as is generally referred to in the Talmud as *Tefillah* (prayer *par excellence*), because it is considered as the most important prayer in the morning, afternoon, and evening services.

Notes

This prayer is also known as the *Amidah* (standing), because it is to be recited while standing up. But it is most commonly known as the *Shemoneh esreh* (eighteen), because it originally had consisted of eighteen benedictions. Later on a nineteenth benediction, *Velamalshinim* (and for slanderers), was added.

The *Shemoneh esreh* is composed of three groups of benedictions: a) Three benedictions of praise at the beginning; b) twelve (now thirteen) benedictions containing petitions in the middle part (on the Sabbath and Festivals, the middle part consists of but one petition); and c) three benedictions of thanks at the close. (See note 68, below.)

[28] It must be borne in mind that the Almighty has not the limitations of a body. He is a Spiritual Being, the Spirit of all existence, permeating all and everything

When the Holy Scriptures, and other sacred writings, speak of God's arm, or hand, or face, as though He had a human form, such anthropomorphisms are figurative. They are merely human expressions that convey ideas within human comprehension; as the Talmud frequently expresses it (Beraḥot 31b): *Diberah torah kileshon bene adam* (the Torah speaks according to the language of men). The Scriptures, as well as other sacred writings, use metaphors and phrases adapted to human understanding. God, being a Spirit, has no corporal parts.

[29] The year is divided into four equal cycles, called in Hebrew *tekufot*. Each cycle, *tekufah*, consists of ninety-one days and seven-and-a-half hours. The four cycles are: *Tekufat Nisan*, vernal equinox; *Tekufat Tammuz*, summer solstice; *Tekufat Tishri*, autumnal equinox; and *Tekufat Tevet*, winter solstice.

[30] After the *Ḥazan* completes the reading of the silent *Shemoneh esreh* with the congregation, he repeats the prayer in an audible voice, so that the congregation may respond *Baruḥ hu ubaruḥ shemo* (Blessed be He and blessed be His Name) after hearing the Name of God (*Adonai*) mentioned in the benedictions, and *Amen* at the end of each benediction.

When the *Ḥazan* finishes reading the first group of the three benedictions of praise (see note 27, above), ending with *Meḥayeh hammetim* (Who reviveth the dead), the congregation recites the *kedushah* (holiness), in which it proclaims the holiness of God by reading: *Kadosh, kadosh, kadosh* (Holy, holy, holy), even as it was proclaimed by the angels in the prophetic vision of Isaiah (6:3).

The Almighty is holy. He is free from every fault and defect. He loves only truth and righteousness. He hates falsehood and wrong. He is absolutely good. No mortal being knows what God is. He is the Absolute Being to whom all beings owe their existence. God revealed His Law to the Israelites whom He admonished to follow the commandments of morality and ethics so that they might become a holy people.

[31] See note 21, above.

[32] After reciting the *Shemoneh esreh* of the *Shaḥarit* (morning) service, we read the *taḥanun* (petition for grace), offering supplication for pardon of sin. Psalm 6 has been chosen for the offering of such supplication for pardon, preceded by the verse *Vayomer david* (and David said) (II Samuel 24:14).

It is told in the Scriptures (II Samuel 24) that when David sinned against God, by counting the Jewish people, the Prophet Gad was commissioned to rebuke him for his crime. Gad offered the king a choice: punishment by God or punishment by men. Whereupon David threw himself upon the mercy of God, uttering the immortal preference: "Let me fall, I pray thee, into the hand of the Lord, for His mercies are many; but let me not fall into the hand of man."

This *petition for grace* was known as *Nefilat appayim* (falling on the face), because it used to be recited while lying face down upon the ground. But this has been since modified into an inclination of the head on the arm.

[33] One of the main objects of public worship was instruction in the Law of God. For this reason the *Anshe Knesset ha-Gedolah* (the Men of the Great Assembly) ordained that portions of the Five Books of Moses be read on certain days of the week, on certain festive seasons and twice on the Sabbath, at the morning and afternoon services.

In ancient times, the villagers of Palestine used to come into the nearest town on Mondays and Thursdays to attend the Law Courts and the markets. Because many of these villagers might not hear the Torah read on Sabbaths, it became customary to read a portion of the Pentateuch on market days. For the same reason, Mondays and Thursdays have been chosen for offering the Special Supplications of *Vehu raḥum* (see preceding Chapter, Section 9).

On Mondays and Thursdays, after the reading of the *taḥanun*, a *sefer torah* (Scroll of the Law) is taken out of the Holy Ark; and three persons are called up to pronounce the benedictions over the Torah, while we read the first *parshah* (section) of the *sidrah* (weekly portion) which is to be read the following Sabbath.

[34] See Chapter 140, sections 2-3, below.

[35] The last great code of Rabbinical Judaism, collected and classified by Joseph Caro, born in Spain or Portugal in 1488; died at Safed, Palestine, March 24, 1575. (See note 130, below.)

[36] The mourner's *kaddish* has no special reference to the dead. But great importance has been attached to the reciting of the *kaddish* for several reasons. First, the son, by reciting the *kaddish* is instrumental in calling forth the most important congregational utterance: *Amen, yehe shemeh rabba meboraḥ lealam ulealme almaya* (Amen, let His great name be blessed for ever and to all eternity). The parent's memory is honored by this public participation of his child in honoring God through the voice of the assembled people. The Talmudic authorities speak often of the importance of this utterance.

Secondly, the *kaddish* is Messianic; it points toward the establishment of the Kingdom of God, after the Resurrection. Indirectly, then, the *kaddish* contains the assurance of immortality, and hope for the day when the reign of death shall be over, and life eternal be established. Thirdly, the *kaddish* is a touching expression of reverential submission to the Divine Will. At the very moment when death has laid its cold hand on the mourner's heart, he stands forth to pronounce before the congregation the greatness and holiness of God. "The Lord gave and the Lord hath taken, blessed be the name of the Lord" (Job 1:21).

[37] The Jewish religion has, from time immemorial, not tolerated ignorance. Great emphasis has been laid by the Jewish spiritual leaders on the importance of studying and acquiring knowledge, even the knowledge of God. The philosophy of the Jewish religion has been that man should know and understand God as He is manifested through His works. Hillel the Elder, who lived in the first century B.C.E., used to say (Mishnah, Abot 2:6): "A man void of intelligence cannot be sensitive to sin, nor can an ignorant person be pious."

The Jewish religion teaches that it is the duty of man endowed with reason to learn the ways of God, observe His works in nature and history, and study His revelations through the sacred books, in order to arrive at an ever higher conception of His greatness and of His will, and thereby grow ever better and wiser.

[38] *Ḥok Leyisrael* (Statute for Israel), containing selections from various sacred writings, such as *Mishnah, Pentateuch, Zohar,* etc., arranged for the *sidrahs* (weekly portions of the Torah), by Isaac Baruch. No information about this author is available.

[39] The Almighty commanded us (Leviticus 19:1): "Be ye holy, for holy am I, the Lord your God." This concept of holiness is the fundamental principle of all moral duty, which we owe to ourselves. This Divine Command enjoins us to strive for the utmost purity of life, and thus come nearer to our Father in heaven, the highest ideal of perfection.

The chief duties which the Jewish religion imposes upon us are Fear of God and Love of God. As has been stated in note 26, above, Love of God is love of obedience; our love for Him must be translated into action by obedience to His precepts. Fear of God will necessarily result in the prevention of moral turpitude. When we think of Him as the great Lord and Master, in whose hands are our destinies, whose will we must all obey, we stand in awe and reverence before Him. Fear of God will save us from pride. Dread of His displeasure will keep us from doing wrong and from behaving immorally even when not seen by human eyes.

We should refrain from indulgence in intemperate habits of eating and drinking or in our sensual pleasures. Only by remaining within the limits of God's Law is there blessing in our enjoyments. When overstepping these, we sink to the level of the animal. We should, therefore, observe moderation in all things and soberness on all occasions.

We should also be kind and polite in our relations with our fellow men and omit offensive words. We must keep our friends and companions in high esteem and never betray their trust. Those that are beneath us in station we must treat with fairness and friendliness, those above us with respect.

Idleness is the chief source of mischief and sin. A noble occupation dignifies man as a useful member of society.

[40] Rabbi Judah ha-Nasi (the Prince), patriarch and redactor of the Mishnah, was in a large portion of Talmudic literature simply called *Rabbi*, the master *par excellence.*

Rabbi Judah ha-Nasi is also referred to quite often as *Rabbenu ha-Kadosh* (our Holy Rabbi), a title seldom, if ever, conferred upon any Talmudic authorities. (See also note 3, above.)

[41] Man's honor is his most precious possession, and the Divine Law therefore warns us against slander which tends to deprive a man of his good name. The Talmudic authorities sought to protect this inalienable right of man, by expounding this Divine Law to the extent given in the text herein.

[42] The Jewish religion conceives of life on earth as a sacred thing, and must not be spent merely in bodily pleasures, but must be devoted chiefly to carrying out the will of the Almighty. In recognition of the sacredness of life, the Jew must perform every deed in sanctity. Every act must be done for the sake of Him who gave us life. (See note 151, below.)

According to Talmudic authorities, the Law of Moses contains six-hundred-and-thirteen commandments. Of these, two-hundred-and-forty-eight are mandatory, that is, they make the performance of certain things compulsory. The remaining three-hundred-and-sixty-five are prohibitory, that is, they prohibit the performance of certain acts. Rabbi Simlai, a Palestinian *Amora*, says (Makkot 23b) the number of mandatory laws corresponds to the number of bones in the human body, and the prohibitory laws equal in number the days of the solar year.

Rashi (note 125, below), ad locum, says in explanation that every bone in the human body is ordered to perform a religious duty, and every day in the year a human being is warned to abstain from transgression. Thus, a man's very existence, every fiber of his body, and every day in his life must be devoted to the love of God, by obeying and carrying out His will.

[42a] See note 40, above.

[43] A measure of capacity.

[44] Because we are all the children of one Father, there is imposed upon the community and upon every individual, according to his means, the duty of providing for the needy; the protection of the helpless, the widow, and the fatherless; the safety and shelter of the stranger and homeless; the care of the sick; and the burial of the dead.

Moreover, according to the religious concept of the Jew, God is the real owner of the world, and we, the inhabitants of the earth, are merely His trustees. Whatever we possess is simply entrusted to us by His graciousness with the charge of providing for the needy. If we withhold our share from them, we rob them of what by Divine Law belongs to them, and we abuse our trust.

[45] This saying is found, with slight variations, in Midrash, Bamidbar Rabbah (9:11), and Shir Hashirim Rabbah (10:17) where it is quoted by Rabbi Yehoshua ben Levi as a *matla*, a proverb; but this author has been unable to ascertain where it is contained in the Jerusalem Talmud, as stated in the text.

[46] Many of the Jewish ceremonies are connected with the cherished memories of the Jewish past. They go back to a time when the Jew practiced his impressive rites in the Temple of Jerusalem.

The following Divine Command is contained in the Holy Scriptures (Numbers 15:21): "Of the first of your dough ye shall give unto the Lord a portion for a gift throughout your generations." When the Temple was in existence, this gift, known as *ḥallah*, was given to the priest. The Jewish concept was that all our possessions belong to the Almighty and therefore must be consecrated to His service (Beraḥot 35a). Since we must make use of our possessions, the Almighty decreed that the dedication of a part of them serves to release the remainder for our own use.

Ever since the destruction of the Temple, the fulfillment of the precept to set aside the first of the dough, *ḥallah*, was practiced by the Jews, according to the rules of law laid down in this Chapter.

47 The Almighty was very emphatic in His command that we must abstain from eating the blood of animals and fowl. He repeated this command several times in His Law (Genesis 9:4; Leviticus 17:14; Deuteronomy 12:16, 23-34; 15:23). Our Talmudic Sages have accordingly laid down the law that, in order to remove the blood from the meat effectively, the meat must be first soaked in water to open the pores, and then salted to draw the blood out, in the manner laid down in the present Chapter. (See also Chapter 46, below.)

48 The wisdom and value of the practice of washing the hands before meals is too obvious to need comment. But Judaism, to make the practice more impressive, elevates it to the dignity of a religious ceremony.

49 Our tables can be turned into altars of God, if the food we eat at them is *kosher* by the Law of God, and if God's name is mentioned at meals. According to the concepts of the Jewish religion, eating is more than just a necessary process of keeping alive. It partakes of the nature of sacrifice and is invested with the nature of holiness, when we utter the necessary benedictions over our food; when we express our gratitude to the Almighty for His kindness in providing us with the necessities of life, by saying Grace after meals, and by engaging in conversation, while at the table, about serious and not frivolous things.

The Talmud (Beraḥot 35a) says: "It is written (Psalms 24:1): 'The earth is the Lord's, and the fulness thereof,' which infers that everything belongs to God and is sacred. Just as one is guilty of a trespass when one derives any benefit from sacred things before they are redeemed, so is it forbidden to derive any pleasure in this world without thanking the Almighty by pronouncing a benediction. He who does derive benefit without a benediction is considered as if he had committed a trespass against the sanctuary of God." And Rabbi Levi adds: "According to the Psalmist, everything belongs to God, but when consecrated by a benediction, it becomes man's privilege to enjoy it."

As regards the utterance of a benediction, some products of the soil are treated as a class, and an identical benediction is pronounced over all the various kinds that compose that class (see Chapters 48:1, and 52, below). Other products, because of their importance and distinguished character, such as wine and olive oil (see Chapter 49, below), require a special benediction, although they are products of the tree.

Bread, although made from the products of the soil, such as wheat, oats, rye, and the like, nevertheless requires a special benediction, known as *Hamotzi* (who bringeth forth), and not the one generally pronounced over such products of the soil. The reason advanced for the uniqueness of bread is that it is regarded as the most important of foods which is needed for the sustenance of life. (From *The Jew and His Duties*, by Hyman E. Goldin.)

[50] See Chapter 172, Section 2, below.

[51] Another law ordained by the Almighty for the purpose of distinguishing Israel as a holy people from the rest of mankind, is that regarding unclean meat. This distinction between clean and unclean meat was observed by priests of many ancient nations in Asia and Africa. But that which, among other nations, only the priests and saints observed as a means of sanctification and distinction, the whole Jewish people were ordered to observe as a "kingdom of priests and a holy nation" (Exodus 19:6).

According to the Holy Scriptures (Leviticus 11; Deuteronomy 14:3-22), the Almighty forbade the use of certain classes of animals as food. Any meat of animals that have cloven hoofs and do not chew the cud, or of those that do chew the cud but have no cloven hoofs, is unfit for use by the Jewish people. An animal to be considered *kosher* (fit for use) must have cloven hoofs and chew the cud. Concerning ham, bacon, and other hog meat, there is a specific commandment in the Law of Moses (Leviticus 11:7; Deuteronomy 14:8): "And the swine, though it has cloven hoofs, but since it cheweth not the cud, it shall be unclean to you; of their flesh ye shall not eat."

The Holy Scriptures forbids us the use of all kinds of shellfish such as lobsters, oysters, clams, and crabs, as well as all creeping things. The general rule regarding fish is (Leviticus 11:9-10; Deuteronomy 14:9-10) that "fish that do not have scales and fins" are forbidden.

The Law of Moses enumerates twenty-four kinds of fowl, the meat of which is forbidden to Jews (Leviticus 11:13-19; Deuteronomy 14:12-18). The most common among them are: The vulture, eagle, raven, ostrich, owl and bat. (See also Chapter 36, above.)

[52] The Jewish law, even from the time of Moses, was very severe with the idolater. From the very inception of Jewish legislation, idolatry was looked upon as an offense which tended to undermine the very foundation of the Jewish law, religion, and national existence. Idolatry, they argued, would tend to lead the Jewish people into the evil, immoral practices of the pagan peoples. They therefore shunned everything and anything resembling the customs of the idolaters, directly or indirectly.

For this very reason, the Jewish law forbids any Jew to derive any benefit from idols, their appurtenances, their ornaments and their sacrifices. (See Chapter 167, below.)

From the above prohibition sprang the law known in the Talmud as *yayin neseḥ*, that is, wine consecrated to use in idolatrous worship and therefore absolutely forbidden to a Jew. The term *yayin neseḥ* also applies to wine made and used by pagans as well as wine made by and for Jews but that which has been touched by an idolater, if he knows that the vessel contains wine and he intentionally touches it. For then there is a likelihood that the pagan has touched it with the intention of consecrating it to the worship of idols, and as such it becomes absolutely forbidden to a Jew.

VOLUME II

[53] Wine and oil, because of their importance and distinguishing character, require a special benediction, although they are products of the tree. (See also note 49, above.)

[54] See note 40, above.

[55] Jabneh, or Jamnia, became the center of learning immediately after the fall of Jerusalem at the hands of the Roman legions. Rabban Joḥanan ben Zakkai established there the seat of the Sanhedrin and a great Academy of learning. Many of the great Tannaim, Talmudic authorities, were raised in that great Academy which was destined to perpetuate Judaism and wisdom of the Torah for everlasting generations. This seat of learning was founded by Rabban Joḥanan ben Zakkai about the year 70 C.E.

[56] Elijah of Vilna (1720-1798), a great scholar of the purest character and highest endowments. His name is mentioned to this day with reverence and love by thousands of scholars familiar with his work, under the designation of *Gaon*.

[57] As regards the utterance of a benediction, most of the products of the soil are treated as a class, and an identical benediction is pronounced over all the various kinds that compose that class. Over all the products of the tree, for instance, the benediction *Bore peri haetz* (who created the fruit of the tree) is said, whether one partakes of apples, pears, plums, or the like. And *Bore peri haadamah* (who created the fruit of the ground) is pronounced over all products which grow in or above the ground, whether it is over turnips, vegetables, beans, or the like. (See note 49, above.)

[58] The Jewish religion ordains that just as we owe thanks to the Almighty when we are prosperous and happy, for He is the Author of life and health, the Giver of all joy and success, so also must we express our blessing when affliction and trial are upon us, for these are sent to chasten and better our souls. As God, the Creator and Ruler of the world, is both Goodness and Wisdom, so does all that occurs in the world serve a good and wise purpose. Every evil in life, whether physical or moral, must, therefore, lead to some good in the end. Death and Sin are not powers of evil, but agencies of God sent to

test man's power, trials that bring out the good in ways often mysterious to us. The Jew does not believe in a devil. Satan is represented as one of the angels of God, sent to try Job and not to act as a friend.

The duty, then, we have towards God is to have perfect faith in Him and feel confident that, whatever danger or distress may beset us, He will in the end lead us to the path of salvation.

[59] See note 29, above.

[60] As has been pointed out in note 26, above, belief in the Unity of God is the quintessence of the Jewish Creed. The primary duty of every Jew is to believe in the existence of One God, the Creator of all existing things. Yet mere belief in God and His Unity does not suffice. Love of God is the quintessence of Jewish Life. And this love must be translated into deeds, for the Jewish religion is based on action, not on mere belief. In fact, there is no express command in the Pentateuch which orders the Jews to *believe* in God. All we are told is to *know* God as He is manifested by His works, and to follow His ways and to adopt His attributes by being just, forbearing, kind, and merciful.

According to our great teacher Hillel the Elder, who lived in the first century B.C.E., this duty toward our fellow men is considered the foundation of the entire Jewish religion. He said (Shabbat 31a): "What is hateful to thee, don't do to another; this is the basis of the entire Jewish Law, while the rest is a mere commentary thereon. Go and complete its study."

It is stated in Midrash (Bereshit Rabbah 24:8): "Ben Azzai said: '"These are the generations of men; in the day God created man, in the likeness of God created He him" (Genesis 5:1)—this is the most comprehensive rule in the Torah.' Rabbi Akiba said: " 'Thou shalt love thy neighbor as thyself" (Leviticus 19:18) is the most comprehensive rule of the Torah.' "

Ben Azzai is of the opinion that reverence for the divine image in man is of wider scope than love to our fellow man.

[61] The phrases "men of Sodom and Gomorrah and the Egyptians," etc., are not found in the text of the Mishnah.

[62] The law forbidding the taking of interest on loans, is based upon the Law of God (Leviticus 25:37): "Thy money shalt thou not give him upon interest, nor lend thy victuals for increase." And again (Deuteronomy 23:20): "Thou shalt not lend upon interest to thy brother: interest of money, interest of victuals, interest of anything that is lent upon interest." The Law of God considers the taking of interest as unlawful gain.

In interpreting these commandments, the Talmud says that the taking of any kind of interest, no matter how trivial, is forbidden by the Mosaic Law.

The Talmud (Mishnah, Baba Mezia, Chapter 5) likewise draws a distinction between Biblical and Rabbinical interest.

Interest as forbidden by the Mosaic Law is *direct* or *express;* interest as forbidden by the Talmud is *indirect* or *contingent.* The Law of Moses forbids any loan when effected by the parties with the express understanding that the lender shall receive some compensation; while the Talmud forbids any transaction or negotiation which, although legitimate in its inception, may ultimately result in a usurious transaction. (For the law regarding the unlawful taking of interest on loans, see *Mishnah, Baba Mezia,* by Hyman E. Goldin, Chapter 5.)

[63] After the destruction of the Temple at Jerusalem, when sacrifices were no longer possible, the Jewish Sages adopted the method of establishing communion with God by offering prayers, public or private, at certain fixed times and seasons, and on special occasions. The founders of the synagogue instituted prayers to be offered three times each day at certain fixed times and in certain formulas in the Holy Tongue, Hebrew. The Jews have accordingly established houses of prayer, synagogues, in every Jewish community in the lands where their destiny has taken them.

The custom of praying three times each day is very ancient. The Psalmist sings (55:17): "Evening, morning and noon will I pray," and Daniel prayed three times daily (Daniel 6:10). Our Talmudists say (Beraḥot 27b) that Abraham instituted the *Shaḥarit* (morning prayer), Isaac the *Minḥah* (afternoon prayer), and Jacob the *Maariv* (evening prayer).

The second service of the day, as instituted by the *Anshe Knesset ha-Gedolah* (Men of the Great Assembly), is known as *Minḥah,* the afternoon service. *Minḥah,* in Hebrew, means *gift,* or *gift-offering,* to God. During the existence of the Temple at Jerusalem, the *korban tamid* (the regular sacrifice) was offered twice daily, in the morning and in the afternoon. With these daily sacrifices, there was offered a sacrifice of grain or cereal which was known as the *minḥah.* The term *minḥah* came to designate the afternoon and not the morning service, because it was so called im the Holy Scriptures, where, in describing the contest between the Prophet Elijah and the priests of Baal at Mount Carmel, the Biblical narrative begins with the words (II Kings 18): "And it came to pass at the time of the offering of the *minḥah,*" etc.

The third prayer of the day is the *Maariv* (evening service), at which the *Shema* must be recited. (See note 26, above.)

These public prayers are seldom offered for individuals and their needs. They are mostly national in their character, calling for the restoration of Zion and the coming of the Messiah, at whose advent all people will recognize the existence of the true God in heaven. Thus, while scattered in foreign lands, suffering untold persecution and humiliation, the Jew prays for universal peace, the cessation of hostilities, and the brotherhood of men. (See also note 23, above.)

64 The Talmudic text quotes Resh Lakish as saying: "The סיהרא (moonlight) was created," etc., not *nights*, as quoted herein.

65 The Almighty ordained that after six days of work, we should set aside the seventh day of the week as a day of rest consecrated to God and the higher purposes of life. "Remember the Sabbath day to keep it holy," is God's command (Exodus 20:8). The main object of the Sabbath, then, is to keep it holy. While abstaining from work, we should devote the Sabbath solely to those things which draw us nearer to God.

The Sabbath reminds us of the great religious truth that God is the Creator of the universe.

The Sabbath also reminds man of his higher destiny, as a child created in the image of God. He is therefore obligated to have reverence for the divine image in man. (See view of Ben Azzai, quoted in note 60, above.)

God gave us the Sabbath to permit us to enjoy the needed bodily rest and recreation after six days of toil, worry, and care. And God proclaimed it from Mount Sinai as the Fourth of the Ten Commandments, that as children created in His image, all men are equal and free before Him. This rest is to be enjoyed equally by all our fellow beings, the servant as well as the master, the hired laborer as well as the employer who lives in ease, the citizen as well as the stranger. Even the beast in our employ is to have rest:—

"Remember the Sabbath-day to keep it holy. Six days shalt thou labor and do all thy work; but the seventh day is a Sabbath to the Lord thy God; in it thou shalt not do any manner of work, thou, nor thy son, nor thy daughter, nor thy manservant, nor thy maidservant, nor thy cattle, nor the stranger that is within thy gates."

In short, every man is to enjoy the bliss of peace and rest.

66 This quotation is from Nehemiah (9:13-14), and not from Ezra, as given in the text.

67 The term *Targum* generally refers to the official Aramaic translation of the Pentateuch by the proselyte Onkelos, in the first century C.E. According to a Talmudic statement (Megillah 3a): "The Targum to the Pentateuch was composed by the proselyte Onkelos at the dictation of Rabbi Eliezer and Rabbi Joshua."

68 The thirteen benedictions of the *Shemoneh esreh*, between the first and the last three, are called "the intermediate benedictions." (See note 27, above.)

[69] These two *ḥallot* (loaves of bread) are known as *leḥem mishneh* (double bread). They recall how the Israelites, while in the wilderness on their way to the promised land, gathered on Friday a double portion of the *manna* (heavenly food) to last them for two days, because on the Sabbath none could be found. (See Exodus 16:11-36.)

[70] This refers to the famous code of law, known as *Yad ha-Ḥazakah,* by the great Maimonides, generally referred to as the RaMBaM, initials of Rabbenu Moses Ben Maimon, born at Cordova, Spain, March 30, 1135 C.E.; died at Cairo, Egypt, December 13, 1204.

[71] Books written by the satirical poet Immanuel ben Solomon; born in Rome, 1270; died at Fermo, 1330.

[72] Josephus Flavius lived in the first century C.E., during the destruction of the Second Temple by the Romans. His best known works are: *Antiquities of the Jews; Wars of the Jews;* and *Contra Apionem* (Against Apion).

[73] *Rosh Ḥodesh,* the beginning of the month, had always been considered a semi-holiday among the Hebrews. On this occasion special sacrifices were offered in the Temple at Jerusalem, and trumpets were blown by the Levites. As far back as the days of Saul, the first Jewish king, *Rosh Ḥodesh* was celebrated with a family feast.

The New Moon day had to be accurately fixed by the Jews so that the Festival days might be exactly determined. During the existence of the Second Temple, the calendar was regulated by direct observation. The *Sanhedrin,* the highest court at Jerusalem, consisting of seventy-one members, sent witnesses to observe the first appearance of the new moon. A special court, called *Bet-Yazek,* was established in Jerusalem to hear and examine the witnesses. After the testimony of at least two witnesses had been accepted by the court, the ceremony of announcing the new month was observed by that judicial body in the following manner. The president of the court said: "The new month is proclaimed (sanctified)," and all present said after him, "Proclaimed, proclaimed" (Mishnah, Rosh Hashanah 2:5-7; Rosh Hashanah 23b, 24a).

That night, torches and bonfires would be lit on the highest peak near Jerusalem, as signals to the nearby towns and villages that the new month had been officially declared. The people on other peaks, farther away, would in turn light torches and bonfires as signals to more distant settlements. Thus the signals carried the news to all the inhabitants of Israel. Even the Jews in Babylonia were informed of the New Moon by relays of torches and bonfires. The following day was celebrated as *Rosh Hodesh,* the beginning of the month. (See note 79, below.)

After the destruction of the Temple by the Romans, the offering of sacrifices ceased, and special prayers were adopted instead. On the Sabbath before *Rosh Ḥodesh,* the coming of the New Moon is announced. The congregation is informed of the exact time when the new moon is to appear, commonly known as the *molad* (birth). Then a special prayer, *birkat haḥodesh* (blessing of the month), is offered, praying to the Almighty that the new month will be a time of blessing and good for all Israel, a period characterized by reverence for God and dread of sin. (From *A Treasury of Jewish Holidays,* by Hyman E. Goldin.)

[74] *Hallel* is a term describing the Psalms from 113 to 118, read after the *Shemoneh esreh* of the morning service of *Pesaḥ, Shabuot, Sukkot, Ḥanukkah,* and *Rosh Ḥodesh.*

VOLUME III

[75] See note 67, above.

[76] By the act of combining the dishes, we are actually beginning to prepare food on Thursday which is needed for the Sabbath, then all the cooking for the Sabbath which is done on Friday, merely continues the preparation already begun on Thursday.

[77] See note 35, above.

[78] Religious sentiments can best be awakened by means of observing holy seasons, which commemorate the great events of the past and hold before us lofty visions of the future. Besides the Sabbath, which has become the cornerstone of the Jewish religion, there are three Festivals of joy: *Pesaḥ* (Passover), *Shabuot* (Feast of Weeks, or Pentecost), and *Sukkot* (Feast of Tabernacles).

These Festivals are known as *Shalosh Regalim* (Pilgrim Festivals). The Almighty commanded us (Deuteronomy 16:16): "Three times in a year shall all thy males appear before the Lord thy God in the place which He shall choose: on the feast of unleavened bread, and on the feast of weeks, and on the feast of tabernacles." Accordingly, during the existence of the Temple at Jerusalem, the Holy City, the people of the land of Israel, from far and near, travelled in gala procession to Jerusalem three times during the year.

While near the Temple of God at Jerusalem, the Jews observed certain ceremonies appropriate to the occasion of each Festival. Before *Pesaḥ* (Passover), the first pilgrim festival, the Jews made their pilgrimage to Jerusalem, so that they might eat of the paschal lamb, the Passover offering, near the Temple of God.

[79] The days intervening between the first two days and the last two days of a Festival are known as *Ḥol Hammoed* (literally, *the unholy days of the Fes-*

tival; the Intermediate Days of the Festival), which are observed as semi-holidays.

According to the Law of Moses, on Passover and Sukkot only the first and the last days are to be observed as a strict Festival on which no manual labor may be performed. Shabuot and Rosh Hashanah, according to the Biblical law, were to be observed for only one day each. However, the changing conditions of Jewish life before the fall of Jerusalem were responsible for the introduction of an extra day of the feast.

Until the middle of the fourth century C.E., no calendar had yet been established, and the dates for the observance of the Festivals were fixed by the *Sanhedrin,* the Supreme Court at Jerusalem. (See note 73, above.) Because of the persecution of the Jews by the Roman Caesars, the decision of the Sanhedrin could not readily be conveyed to the distant Jewish settlements. The communities outside the land of Israel were therefore instructed to add an extra day to each Festival, to make certain that the Festival would be observed on the proper day as required by the Law of God. *Pesaḥ* was then extended to eight days instead of seven, and *Sukkot* to nine days instead of eight, the first two days and the last two days of which were observed as a strict Festival. *Shabuot* and *Rosh Hashanah* were given one additional day each.

In 360 C.E., Hillel II framed a permanent calendar, the principles of which hold good even to this day, and fixed precisely the dates of the various holidays. The dates no longer being in doubt, the Rabbis of Babylonia wished to drop the extra day of the Festival, but they were advised by the Palestinian authorities not to break an established custom. Even today, therefore, Jews dwelling in lands outside Israel observe this long established custom. (From *The Jewish Woman and Her Home,* by Hyman E. Goldin.)

[80] The Almighty ordained (Exodus 12:2): "This month shall be unto you the beginning of months; it shall be the first month of the year to you." Hence, the month of *Nisan,* also designated as *Ḥodesh Haaviv* (month of the harvest) (Exodus 13:4), has become the first ecclesiastical month of the Jewish year, but it is the seventh civil month. It is probably for this reason that the month of *Nisan* is regarded as sacred, because due to Israel's exodus from Egypt that had occurred in it, the Almighty Himself elevated it above all other months. The *Beer Heteb* (to *Shulḥan Aruḥ, Oraḥ Ḥayyim,* 429) says that on the first day of *Nisan,* the Tabernacle was erected (Exodus 40:17), and during the first twelve days, the twelve princes of the twelve tribes each sacrificed his offering (Numbers 9:10-83), and these days were considered like Festivals to the princes. Now, together with the day before Passover which is considered as semi-festival, and the seven Festival days of Passover

and the day following the Passover which is likewise a semi-festival, we have a total of twenty-one festival days in *Nisan*. Since most of the month is hallowed by Festival days, the whole month is considered as sacred. The author further states that according to Talmudic authority (Tractate Menaḥot), the continual burnt offering (*olat tamid*) was established in it.

[81] The *matzah* which the Jews eat during the Passover week, is known as *leḥem oni* (bread of affliction), because it is reminiscent of the hardships of our forefathers in Egypt. *Matzah* has no special flavor, as it contains no salt and no yeast. The dough for baking the *matzah* must not be allowed to become leavened. For this reason, while kneading the dough, special precautions are taken against fermentation. It must be kneaded quickly, rolled into shape, and then perforated to keep the *matzah* from rising and swelling.

Matzah is also symbolic of the haste with which our forefathers departed from the land of Egypt, the land of their woe, that midnight when Pharaoh drove them without bread from the land, forcing them to carry their unbaked bread with them wrapped in bundles (Exodus 12:34).

[82] See Chapter 194, Section 9, below.

[83] See Chapter 33, Section 8, and note 29, above.

[84] See Chapter 35, Section 2, and note 46, above.

[85] While we are forbidden to eat leavened food, the eating of *matzah* is not compulsory during the entire eight days of Passover. We may eat any kind of food that we prefer, provided it is not classed as leavened. On the first two nights of Passover, however, the eating of *matzah* is compulsory. Everyone must eat some *matzah* during the evening meal (*seder*), and pronounce the proper benedictions over it (see Chapter 119, Section 5, below). For such was the command of God (Exodus 12:18): "In the first month, on the fourteenth day of the month in the evening, ye shall eat unleavened bread."

[86] This search for leaven is in compliance with the command of the Almighty that we must remove all manner of leavened food from our domain, so that during the Passover week, "No leaven should be found in your houses" (Exodus 12:19), and, "No leavened bread shall be seen with you, in all your borders" (Exodus 13:7).

[87] Because the Almighty spared the firstborn of the Jews when slaying the firstborn of the Egyptians (Exodus 11:1-8; 12:29-36), there developed a custom for the firstborn among the Jews to fast on the day before Passover.

[88] Written by Ezekiel ben Judah Landau, famous Rabbi. Born in Opatow, Poland, October 8, 1713; died at Prague, April 29, 1793.

[89] Written by Moses Sofer. Prominent Rabbi. Born at Frankfort-on-the-Main, September 14, 1763; died at Presburg, October 3, 1839.

[90] *Magen Abraham* (Shield of Abraham) on *Shulḥan Aruḥ, Oraḥ Ḥayyim* by Abraham Abele Gombiner; born about 1635, at Gomblin, Russian Poland; died at Kalisz, about 1683.

[91] On the first two nights of Passover, the *seder* is celebrated. *Seder* is a special order or program designated for these two nights. No other ceremony among the Jews is performed with such pomp and gladness of heart as the *seder*. This interesting ceremony was originally designated to stimulate the interest of the Jewish child in the glorious past of his people, and to inspire him with hope for the future. When the child asks, upon seeing the special order of things on *seder* night, "What is the meaning of this?" he is told in explanation the story of his people's deliverance from Egyptian bondage. And, by reciting the *Haggadah*, the special book adopted for the *seder* night, the entire family, man, woman, and child, are imbued with a spirit of loyalty to their God and their people. They are encouraged by an unswerving faith in their God to face the trials of life. As their fathers, they say, were helped in time of darkness and persecution, so they too will survive their tormentors, until at last the true Messiah will bring an era of freedom, justice and good-will to men. (From *A Treasury of Jewish Holidays*, by Hyman E. Goldin).

[92] The four cups of wine, which are to be drunk by every participant in the ceremony of the *seder*, are symbolic of the four Biblical expressions used by the Almignty in promising Moses the redemption of the Jews from the Egyptian bondage (Exodus 6:6-7): "*Vehotzeti*, and I will bring you out; *vehitzalti*, and I will deliver you; *vegaalti*, and I will redeem you; *velakaḥti*, and I will take you to Me for a people."

[93] The *maror*, bitter herbs, eaten at the Passover meal reminds us of the bitter lot of the Israelites in Egypt.

[94] *Ḥaroset*, a paste-like mixture of nuts, apples, cinnamon, and raisins, finely chopped and mixed with wine, which in appearance resembles mortar, is symbolic of the hard construction labor of the Jews in Egypt.

[95] On the *seder* nights it is customary to fill one cup of wine, which is known as the *Cup of Elijah*. The Prophet Elijah is invited to our homes for the following reasons: In the Biblical text there is a fifth Divine Promise which follows the four mentioned in note 92, above, and that is (Exodus 6:8): "*Veheveti* and I will bring you to the promised land." Some legal authorities would, therefore, have it that a fifth cup of wine is required in the *seder*, for there are Five Divine Promises. Talmudic authorities left the decision of all moot points of law to the Prophet Elijah, who in time to come would decide them, and the question of the fifth cup, too, was left to the same judge.

Moreover, this Prophet, who was drawn up to heaven alive in a fiery chariot drawn by fiery horses (II Kings 2:11), is believed to have become immortal and to have become the heavenly guardian of the Jewish people. Elijah is the great champion of righteousness and the pure worship of God, who will appear, in the end of days to announce the arrival of the Messiah (Malachi 3:23-24). At that time, this messenger of God will announce to the dwellers on earth the good tidings of peace and salvation, comfort for the sorrowing, the resurrection of the dead, and the establishment of the Divine Kingdom upon the earth.

On Passover night, at the celebration of the Feast of Freedom (*zeman ḥerutenu*), the Jews invite Elijah to their homes, thereby indicating their implicit faith in the belief that some day the Almighty will send this immortal Prophet to announce their deliverance from the hands of modern Pharaohs. (From *The Jew and His Duties*, by Hyman E. Goldin.)

[96] During the existence of the Temple at Jerusalem, the paschal lamb—the Passover sacrifice—was eaten at the close of the meal. After having partaken of the sacrificial meat, no other food might be eaten. When the offering of sacrifices ceased with the destruction of the Temple, a piece of *matzah* was eaten instead at the close of the meal. This piece of *matzah* was known as the *afikoman*, the Greek word for *dessert*.

[97] The festival of Passover not only commemorated the departure of the Israelites from the land of Egypt; it was celebrated also as an agricultural festival in the land of Israel during the existence of the first and second Temples.

Like all peoples who live by the soil, the Jews when in Palestine joyfully celebrated the harvest seasons. Israel, a semi-tropical country, had several harvests. The grain harvest lasted seven weeks and was observed by the Jews as a season of gladness and joy. This festive season began with the harvest of barley on the second day of Passover, the sixteenth day of the month of *Nisan*.

No one had been permitted to eat of the new crop of grain until the second day of Passover, when a thanksgiving offering was brought to the Almighty in gratitude for the products of the soil which He had caused to grow. The offering—called *omer* (sheaf) in Hebrew—was a sheaf of new barley, the first of the cereals to ripen. The grain harvest ended with the harvesting of wheat on the fiftieth day after the bringing of the *omer*, and this occasion was celebrated by the Festival of *Shabuot* (Feast of Weeks, or Pentecost). (From *A Treasury of Jewish Hoildays*, by Hyman E. Goldin. See *opus citato* page 130, for a full description of the *omer* ceremony as had been practiced by the ancient Hebrews.)

[98] Among the Jews, fasting, as an expression of grief and extreme sorrow, is very ancient. The Jewish religion adopted it as a sign of remorse and penitence by which forgiveness might be obtained from the God against whom one has sinned. The Jew on public fast days not only commemorates his great national calamity, but also seeks forgiveness for his personal sins. Implicitly he believes that had not the Jews sinned against their God in the past, they would not have been punished by losing their sanctuary and their land, as had been foretold by their Prophets. He therefore fasts in expiation of the sins of his ancient forebears and for his own sins as well; for he believes that by purging himself of sin, he will become worthy of national restoration. In other words, the Jewish fast days are national memorial days, recalling the misfortunes of the past; and at the same time they serve as a plea to God for the revival of Jewish national existence. The fast days are a means of keeping alive the hope and courage of the Jewish people. (From *A Treasury of Jewish Holidays,* by Hyman E. Goldin.)

[99] It is stated in the Talmud (Mishnah, Yoma 5:2): "Since the Holy Ark disappeared, there was a stone in its stead, since the days of the first Prophets, which was called *Even shetiyah* (foundation stone), three finger breadths above the ground."

In Talmud Yerushalmi (Yoma 5), it is stated: "Why is it called *Even shetiyah*? Because from it the world was started."

[100] *Shabbat Ḥazon* is the Sabbath on which we read for the *haftorah* the first chapter of Isaiah, beginning with the word *ḥazon* (the vision of); the Sabbath before the Ninth Day of *Av*.

[101] See note 4, above.

[102] See note 67, above.

[103] During their long history, the Jews have found need for a period of solemn contemplation, prayer, and self-examination. They have set aside a period of forty days for this purpose, beginning with the first day of the month of *Elul* and ending with the day of *Yom Kippur* (Day of Atonement).

[104] Rabbi Isaac Luria, a famous cabalist and founder of modern cabalah; born at Jerusalem in 1534; died at Safed, August 5, 1572.

[105] These *shofar* soundings serve to remind the people that the great Holy Days, at times called *Yamim Noraim* (Days of Awe), are approaching, and urge them to begin taking stock of their religious conduct and their relations with their fellow men. (See also Chapter 129, Section 15, below.)

[106] *Menaḥem* (comforter) is one of the names ascribed to the Messiah to come (Sanhedrin 98b).

[107] Unlike all other Jewish Festivals, *Rosh Hashanah* is neither connected with great historical events nor with festivities of the soil. It is purely a religious holiday devoted to prayer and serious thought, a time when Jews contemplate their ideals and their deeds of the past. It ushers in for the Jews a period of penitence.

This solemn Festival is celebrated on the first and second days of the month of *Tishri*, the seventh month, which is the first month of the Jewish civil calendar. (See note 80, above.) The Festival is called in the Holy Scriptures (Nunbers 29:1): *Yom Teruah* (Day of Blowing the Horn).

In Talmudic literature, *Rosh Hashanah* is also known as *Yom Hazzikaron* (Day of Memorial), and as *Yom Haddin* (Day of Judgment). On this day, our Sages of old tell us, the Ruler of Life sits on the world's throne and investigates the behavior of men, and allots to each one his destiny for the coming year, whether for life or for death, for happiness or for woe.

On this solemn day, therefore, every Jew must look upon his behavior during the year that has passed. He must recognize that God, the stern Judge of the World, searches our hearts and reads every thought therein, and he must resolve to begin a new life with higher ideals and purposes. The Jew must renew his trust in God, the Ruler of our destiny, and must express his gratitude to Him, as he looks back upon the past year with experiences of joy and sorrow. (From *The Jew and His Duties*, by Hynam E. Goldin.)

[108] The ten days from the first day of *Rosh Hashanah* through *Yom Kippur* (Day of Atonement) are known as *Aseret Yeme Teshubah* (Ten Days of Penitence).

[109] Moses ben Jacob Cordovero, Rabbi of Safed; born in 1522; died June 25, 1570.

[110] This very solemn and holy day, *Yom Kippur* (Day of Atonement), is observed on the tenth day of the month of *Tishri*. On this day, the Rabbis of old tell us, the destiny of all mankind, as written down on *Rosh Hashanah*, is sealed by the Heavenly Court. The deeds of every man are considered and weighed. If his good deeds outweigh the bad, the man is declared deserving. If his bad deeds outweigh the good, the man is considered undeserving. Sins, however, are forgiven by our merciful Father after sincere repentance, prayer and charity. Therefore the whole day of *Yom Kippur* is spent at the synagogue, repenting, praying, and donating to charitible institutions.

Yom Kippur is a day of self-retrospection. Every Jew must solemnly contemplate his past conduct, repent, and resolve to improve and follow the ways of God in the future.

This holy day, then, teaches us the following sublime principles of the Jewish religion:

1. No priest and no mediator is necessary to obtain forgiveness of sin; man himself can obtain such forgiveness from his Creator by solemnly repenting of his actions, and beginning a new life of virtue and goodness.

2. Sin is not an evil power ruling over man and plotting his downfall; sin is merely a weakness of man, always subject to his control, if he but makes an earnest endeavor to overcome it.

3. As a child of God, man is always certain that the Father will receive him in favor and dorgive his sins, as soon as he returns solemnly to Him. (From *A Treasury of Jewish Holidays*, by Hyman E. Goldin.)

[111] Originally, the white garments worn by pious Jews in the synagogue of old, did not serve as reminders of the grave. On the contrary, they were symbolic of the festal character of the days appointed for life's spiritual renewal. The Jerusalem Talmud (Rosh Hashanah 1:3) remarks: "When men are summoned before a mortal ruler to defend themselves against a charge lodged against them, they appear downcast and dressed like mourners, being uncertain of the verdict. The children of Isreal appear before their God, on the day of judgment, dressed in white as if going to a feast, because they are confident that their Father will pardon not condemn." White stood for purity, innocence, confidence and hope.

[112] The Jewish system of time reckoning was as follows: When the Israelites first settlled in the Promised Land, they commenced to count six years, during which period they cultivated the soil, but on the seventh year they were to let the soil lie fallow (Exodus 23:10-11; Leviticus 25:1-7). The seven years were known as the *sabbath of years,* and the seventh year was known as *shemitah* (sabbatical year).

Seven sabbaths of years formed a jubilee cycle, and at the expiration of this cycle of years, that is, on the fiftieth year, the Israelites celebrated the jubilee year (Leviticus 35:8-13), when proclamation was made with the blast of the horn on the Day of Atonement, proclaiming liberty throughout the land to all inhabitants thereof; and every man returned to his possession, and every slave returned as a free man to his family.

[113] *Sukkot,* the third pilgrim festival, begins with the fifteenth day of the month of *Tishri* and ends with the twenty-third day. The first two days of the Festival are followed by four days of *Ḥol Hammoed,* then by *Hoshanah Rabbah* on the seventh day of the feast, and the last two days bear special names: *Shemini Atzeret* (Eighth Day of Solemn Assembly), and *Simḥat Torah* (Rejoicing With the Law).

The Almighty commanded the children of Israel (Leviticus 23:43): "Ye shall dwell in booths seven days; that your generations may know that I made the children of Israel to dwell in booths, when I brought them out of the land of Egypt." Thus, the dwelling in booths is a token of gratitude for God's protection of the Israelites when He shielded them in their frail tents from the storms and dangers that beset them during their forty years journey in the wilderness.

114 Like *Pesaḥ* and *Shabuot*, *Sukkot* is also an agricultural Festival, designated as *Ḥag Haasiph* (the Harvest Festival). It was really a Festival of thanksgiving. The agricultural year was over at this time, particularly the fruit harvest. All the products of the soil had been gathered, and the Israelites, who were closely attached to the soil, celebrated the event with merriment and festivity and rendered thanks to the Lord for the prosperous season.

To show their appreciation for the Lord's bounty, the Jews were commanded to take the four species (Leviticus 23:39-40): the *etrog* (citron-like fruit), the *lulav* (palm branch); *hadasim* (myrtle boughs), and *aravot* (willow branches), and rejoice before the Lord God seven days.

There have been many reasons advanced by our Sages for the Divine Command bidding us to take the four species during the *Sukkot* Festival. The most noted of these interpretations is the one given in the Midrash (Vayikra Rabbah 30:11): "The four species represent the Jewish people: just as the *etrog* has both taste and fragrance, so do some Jews possess both a knowledge of the Torah and good deeds; just as the date-palm has taste but no fragrance, so do some Jews possess a knowledge of the Torah but no good deeds; just as the myrtle has fragrance but no taste, so do some Jews possess good deeds but no knowledge of the Torah; and just as the willows of the brook have neither taste nor fragrance, so do some Jews possess neither a knowledge of the Torah nor good deeds. And what did the Holy One, blessed be He, do? To destroy them all was impossible. So the Almighty said: 'Let them all be tied together with one band of brotherhood, and let one procure forgiveness for the other.'"

115 Many reasons have been advanced by mystics for the method of waving the four species as prescribed by law. However, it would seem that the most plausible one is that advanced by Rabbi Joḥanan, the brilliant Palestinian *amora*, who said (Sukkah 37b): "It is put forward and brought backward to the One to whom the four sides of the universe belong; it is put upward and downward to the One to whom the heaven and earth belong." In other words, the waving is done to acknowledge God's sovereignty over the universe.

116 See note 79, above.

117 See note 111, above.

[118] On the first of *Adar*, the people were called upon to donate half a *shekel* towards the purchase of necessary sacrifices for the Temple, during the year. (See also Chapter 141, Section 5.)

[119] We read the Biblical section bidding us to remember Amalek, because Haman, the arch enemy of the Jews, was of the descendants of Amalek.

[120] It is so called because on this Sabbath we read for the *maftir* (Exodus 12:2-20): *Haḥodesh hazzeh laḥem rosh ḥadashim* (this month shall be unto you the beginning of months); thus, *Nisan*, by the command of God, was designated as the first month of the religious year. (See also note 80, above.)

[121] On this Sabbath we read for the *maftir* the portion of the Torah (Numbers 19:1-22) containing the precept of the *parah adummah* (the red cow). In ancient times this reading served as a reminder to those who had become polluted by contact with a dead body, that they must purify themselves by having the ashes of the *parah adummah* sprinkled upon them, so that they might sacrifice the paschal lamb the day before Passover.

[122] On *Purim* the Jew displays the greatness of his soul, his unswerving faith in his God and his people. Haman, the hater of the Jew, and Mordecai, the Jew, who insists on worshiping his God in his own way, are not mere figures in history. Hamans are to be found in every land where there are Mordecais, Jews determined to observe their traditions of life and thought.

The Jew laughs; he does not lose courage. He resists the Hamans who seek to destroy him. He is convinced that in the end the determined Mordecais will overcome the heartless Hamans as of old. Therefore the Jew celebrates *Purim* with all his heart.

The Jew reveres the synagogue in which he worships his God, and he permits nothing to be done or said there which might imply contempt for the holy place. But on *Purim*, when he makes sport of the Hamans past and present, the Jew allows and sometimes even encourages conduct which on other days would be impermissible in the synagogue.

The Jew, as a rule celebrates his Festivals with merriment, but at the same time with a certain degree of reserve and solemnity, in accordance with his religious principles and traditions. Frivolity and intoxication he does not tolerate.

Purim, however, is a special occasion. Merrymaking and wine-drinking is not only allowable, but even encouraged by our Sages of old, as a means of expressing our faith in the Almighty. But this alone does not suffice. We must send gifts to our friends, but most important of all we must not forget the needy, on this happy day. Faith and charity are the essentials in the celebration of *Purim*.

VOLUME IV

123 See note 111, above.

124 Among all other nations of antiquity, a wife was considered chattel, the possession of her husband. The social status of the Jewish wife was one of equality with her husband. A family-loving people, the Jews maintained a reverent attitude toward womanhood. Not the husband but the law determined to the minutest detail the personal and social status as well as the dower rights of the wife. (See note 129, below.)

Even in the earliest days of Jewish history, the woman was qualified to attain the highest social position, even that of judge and prophetess of God. Miriam, the sister of Moses and Aaron, was crowned with the title Prophetess by the Almighty Himself (Exodus 15:20; Numbers 12:1-8). Deborah, Huldah, and others were worthy of receiving God's word. Women were eligible to occupy the throne of the Jewish kingdom. (See also Chapter 31, and note 42, above.)

125 RaSHI (initials of Rabbi Shelomo Itzhaki), most famous commentator of the Holy Scriptures and the Talmud. His commentaries are commonly known by his name *Rashi*. Born at Troyes, France, in1040 C.E.; died there on July 13, 1105.

126 This is a quotation from Proverbs 5:10.

127 *Yesod Yoseph* (Foundation of Joseph), by Joseph ben Yudle of Dubnow; no information could be obtained about him.

128 See note 2, above.

129 The Jewish religion governs and regulates the physical relations of man and wife. It takes precautions to safeguard the health of the Jewish woman and the health of the offspring. Chief of these precautions is the law that dictates a cessation of sexual relations for a certain number of days each month.

These periodic separations, as required by Jewish law, have the sanction of modern medical authority. Noted scientists support the Biblical law which forbids sexual intercourse during the woman's menstrual periods.

There is also a moral and spiritual significance to this law. Since, among the Jews, women enjoy equality with men, they must not be considered as having been created by the Almighty for the purpose of satisfying male lust. They were created by Him as helpers to their husbands, to raise families, and to enjoy all the freedom that the Almighty saw fit to bestow upon men.

Men, among most nations of the world, were brutal in their conduct towards their wives. Women had no say in the matter of their marital relations, but were treated like slaves. The Almighty, to put an end to this condition, endowed marriage with a touch of holiness. He decreed that the husband, under threat of the severest penalty that can meted be out to men, must abstain from his lust and control his desires during certain periods of his wlfe's life. (See note 124, above.)

130 This refers to the *Shulḥan Aruḥ, Yoreh Deah,* the two volumes which deal with the ritual law, compiled by Joseph Caro. (See note 35, above.)

131 *Ture Zahab* (Rows of Gold), commentary on the *Shulḥan Aruḥ,* by David ben Samuel ha-Levi, born in Ladmir, Poland, about 1586; died at Lemberg, January 31, 1667.

132 It is the sacred duty of every Jew to have implicit faith in the Almighty, and to look only to Him in time of trouble and distress and sickness. Salvation can come only from our Father in heaven who is the Healer of all diseases. In Him alone must we put our trust even when we consult a physician (Chapter 192:3, below), and if we look for help from any other source, or believe in superstition and enchantments, we are guilty of the very serious crime of idol worship and disbelief in the Almighty, denying His control over human destinies.

133 See note 52, above.

134 There are twenty-one offenses mentioned in the Torah for which the offender is punishable by *karet* (excision), or, as the Torah expresses it, *by being cut off from his people.* As the Mosaic Law is not very precise in its definition of that punishment, there has arisen much speculation as to its true nature, among modern scholars, and even by Talmudic authorities, as well as by later jurists. For a full discussion of this subject, see *Hebrew Criminal Law and Procedure,* by Hyman E. Goldin, pages 40-41.

135 This is one of the many laws contained in the Torah, which is forbidden by the Almighty as being idolatrous practises.

136 See note 97, above.

137 See note 79, above.

138 This refers to the Biblical injunction (Leviticus 19:23-24): "And when ye shall come into the land, and shall have planted all manner of trees for food, then ye shall count the fruit thereof as forbidden; three years shall it be as forbidden unto you; it shall not be eaten. And in the fourth year all the fruit thereof shall be holy, for giving praise unto the Lord."

Some of the Divine Laws contain certain prohibitions known as *Ḥukkim* (statutes), because the reason for their observance has not been divulged. And this injunction known as *Arlah* belongs to this class.

[139] See note 70, above.

[140] *Meḥilta,* or *Meḥilta debe Rabbi Yishmael,* a *Halaḥic* and *Midrashic* book on Exodus from Chapter 12 to 35.

[141] For a full explanation of interest on loan, see note 62, above.

[142] This refers to the Divine Law (Deuteronomy 15:1-2): "At the end of every seven years thou shalt make a release. And this is the manner of the release: every creditor shall release that which he hath lent unto his neighbor; he shall not exact it of his neighbor and his brother; because the Lord's release has beem proclained."

Similar laws, known in modern law as *The Statute of Limitation,* have been enacted in almost all civilized nations of the world.

[143] *Prosbol,* a word of Greek origin. It is stated in the Mishnah (Shebiit 10:3): "A loan secured by a *prosbol* is not cancelled by *shemitah* (the seventh year). This is one of the things that Hillel the Elder (born in Babylon about 110 B.C.E.; died at Jerusalem about 10 C.E.) ordained. When he saw that the people refrained from making loans one to another and transgressed what was written in the Torah (Deuteronomy 15:9): "Beware that there be not a base thought in your heart," etc., Hillel ordained the *prosbol.*"

[144] *Tanna debe Eliyahu,* a midrash consisting of two parts: *Seder Eliyahu Rabbah,* and *Seder Eliyahu Zuta.* The final redaction of this Midrash took place at the end of the tenth century C.E.

[145] See Chapter 191, below, and note that follows.

[146] In the concept of the Jewish religion, there is a certain sanctity attached to the life of every creature, and it must therefore be treated with regard.

While we are permitted by Divine Law to kill an animal for the nourishment of our body, we are by no means allowed to take the life of an animal for mere sport or pleasure in the sheddlng of its blood, nor to torment it. No life, not even of the lowest creature, should be wantonly desroyed and wasted, for God alone is the Author of Life.

[147] The Jew implicitly believes that life, as a precious gift given to man by the Creator, could neither be given up nor taken away, except by Him who gave it. In no event, therefore, are we permitted to accelerate the death of

any human being, no matter how much distress and trouble that life may cause us. (See note 151, below.)

[148] *Maabar Yabbok* (the Ford of Yabbok), a book containing all prayers and rituals connected with sickness and death, compiled by Aaron ben Moses of Modena, and printed at Mantua, 1624.

[149] It was an ancient custom among the Hebrews to rend their garments as a sign of grief upon receiving bad news. Jacob, for instance, tore his garments when he learned that the coat of his beloved son Joseph had been found torn and stained with blood. From this the custom has developed to make a rend in one's garment for the loss of one's next of kin for whom one is required to observe the rite of mourning.

[150] *Ḥebrah kedoshah* (the Holy Brotherhood), was a voluntary society established in every Jewish community, whose business it was to provide a grave for the dead, with or without pay, depending upon the financial condition of the deceased or his next of kin; also to take care of and attend to all the rituals in connection with the burial.

[151] According to Judaism, life is no mere empty struggle or dream that ends with death. Human beings do not exist and perish like cattle. They have a soul, a very portion of the throne of the Almighty, which was sent down from heaven to dwell in the body that it may perform the will of the Almighty, and then receive its reward in the world of everlasting life.

Death, as the Jew conceives of it, does not terminate life. Only the material body returns to dust, but the soul, which is a portion from God, returns to heaven when it rids itself of the body. For the soul, life begins anew, after the body's death, in the world to come. There people receive their reward and punishment in accordance with their merits and deeds during the body's span of life on earth.

Life is therefore a sacred thing, and must not be spent merely in bodily pleasures, but must be devoted chiefly to carrying out the will of the Almighty. Death, according to this conception, is really the ultimate goal of life, when the soul freed from its material encasement, becomes pure and holy, soaring to its origin in the high heavens. Death is therefore more sacred than life

In recognition of the sacredness of life, the Jew must perform every deed in sanctity (see Chapter 31, above). Every act must be done for the sake of Him who gave us life. To show that death is the holy goal of a sacred life, the Jew, from time immemorial, laid down many rules of law concerning the dying person, the treatment of the dead, and mourning.

[152] See preceding note concerning the sanctity of life. See also note 147, above.

[153] This is a Talmudic axiom (Beraḥot 39a).

[154] *Semaḥot* (Rejoicings). One of the minor Tractates of the Talmud. The name is euphemistically used for *Ebel Rabbati* (Great Mourning).

[155] For the definition of *Maamadot,* see note 4, above.

[156] See note 67, above for the definition of *Targum.*

[157] Rabbenu Jacob Tam, one of the famous Tosafists; grandson of Rashi; died in the year 1117 C.E. (See also note 21, above.)